COMMUNITY DEVELOPMENT
IN THE 21ˢᵀ CENTURY

Empowerment for breaking the cycle of poverty

SEVENTH EDITION

Making illegal copies of this publication, distributing them unlawfully or sharing them on social media without the written permission of the publisher may lead to civil claims or criminal complaints.

Protect the communities who are sustained by creativity.

COMMUNITY DEVELOPMENT IN THE 21ST CENTURY

Empowerment for breaking the cycle of poverty

SEVENTH EDITION

Frik de Beer
Andries de Beer

juta

Community development in the 21st century: Empowerment for breaking the cycle of poverty

First edition 1989
Second edition 1992
Third edition 1997
Fourth edition 2006
Fifth edition 2011
Sixth edition 2016
Seventh edition 2024

Juta and Company (Pty) Ltd
First Floor, Sunclare Building, 21 Dreyer Street, Claremont 7708
PO Box 14373, Lansdowne 7779, Cape Town, South Africa
www.juta.co.za

© 2024 Juta and Company (Pty) Ltd

ISBN: 978 1 48513 247 9
eISBN: 978 1 48513 238 7

All rights reserved.

Production Specialist: Mmakasa Ramoshaba
Editor: Lee-Ann Ashcroft
Proofreader: Language Mechanics
Cover designer: Genevieve Simpson
Typesetter: Henry Daniels at Elinye Ithuba DTP & Print Solutions (Pty) Ltd
Indexer: Lexinfo

Typeset in: Fairfield LT Std 11.5/14pt
Printed by:

> No part of this publication may be reproduced, stored in a retrieval system, or transmitted in any form or by any means – electronic, mechanical, photocopying, recording or otherwise – without written permission from the publisher, except in accordance with the provisions of the Copyright Act 98 of 1978.
>
> Please contact DALRO for information regarding copyright clearance for this publication. Any unauthorised copying could lead to civil liability and/or criminal sanctions.
>
> Tel: +27 (0)10 822 7469
> Fax: +27 (0)86 649 1136
> Postal address: PostNet Suite #018, Private Bag X9951, Sandton 2146
> Email: dalro@dalro.co.za
> http://www.dalro.co.za
>
> Please email permissions@juta.co.za for permission to use text excerpts from a Juta and Company publication.

The author and the publisher believe on the strength of due diligence exercised that this work does not contain any material that is the subject of copyright held by another person. In the alternative, they believe that any protected pre-existing material that may be comprised in it has been used with appropriate authority or has been used in circumstances that make such use permissible under the law.

CONTENTS

	Introduction (Fifth Edition)	xxiii
	Introduction (Sixth Edition)	xxv
	Introduction (Seventh Edition)	xxvii
	Acronyms and Abbreviations	xxix
	List of Contributors	xxxi
SECTION A	THE DEVELOPMENT CONTEXT	1
Chapter 1	Towards Understanding Poverty and Deprivation Frik de Beer	3
1.1	Introduction – Who Owns Community Development?	3
1.2	Absolute and Relative Poverty	6
1.3	Understanding the Socio-Economic Context of Development	8
1.4	Getting to Understand Poverty and Development	10
1.4.1	Maslow's hierarchy	10
1.4.2	The Human Development Index (HDI)	12
1.4.3	Global Multidimensional Poverty Index (MPI)	12
1.5	The Deprivation Trap	14
1.5.1	Shelter	16
1.5.2	Unemployment	17
1.5.3	Water, drainage and sewage	18
1.5.4	Health facilities	18
1.5.5	Food security	19
1.5.6	Education	20
1.5.7	Stagnant local economy	20
1.6	The Equilibrium of Poverty	21
1.7	Conclusion	22
	References	22

Chapter 2	The Development Environment	27
	John Ntema and Frik de Beer	
2.1	Introduction	27
2.2	The Global Context of Policy Formulation for Development	28
2.3	The Local Development Environment	30
	2.3.1 Political environment	32
	2.3.2 Social environment	33
	2.3.3 Cultural environment	34
	2.3.4 Economic environment	36
	2.3.5 Psychological environment	37
2.4	Conclusion	37
	References	39

Chapter 3	Stakeholders in Community Development	43
	Frik de Beer	
3.1	Introduction	43
3.2	Identifying Stakeholders	44
	3.2.1 Public sector stakeholders	44
	3.2.2 Private sector stakeholders	45
	3.2.3 Non-government (civil society) stakeholders	46
	3.2.4 Popular or community-based sector stakeholders	46
	3.2.5 Social enterprise sector stakeholders	47
3.3	The Organisation as an Enabler of Community Development	48
3.4	Finding Ways to Coordinate Community Development	50
	3.4.1 Understanding the environment in which coordination must take place	51
	3.4.2 Preparing the way for collaboration: establishing discussion forums	52
	3.4.3 Constraints and barriers to collaboration	53
	3.4.4 Practices of collaboration in community development	54
3.5	Conclusion	58
	References	59

SECTION B	THE PROCESS OF COMMUNITY DEVELOPMENT		61
Chapter 4	The Origins of Community Development Frik de Beer		63
4.1	Introduction		63
4.2	Early History		63
4.3	A Change of Focus: From Co-Option to Community-Initiated Action		66
4.4	Radicalised Approach		69
	4.4.1	The (social) learning process approach	70
	4.4.2	Human scale development approach	71
	4.4.3	Capability approach	72
	4.4.4	'Another Development'	73
	4.4.5	Asset-based community development	73
4.5	Conclusion		74
	References		74
Chapter 5	Features and Outcomes of Community Development Hennie Swanepoel and Frik de Beer		77
5.1	Introduction		77
5.2	The Features of Community Development		77
	5.2.1	An integrated approach	77
	5.2.2	Collective action	78
	5.2.3	Needs orientation	79
	5.2.4	Objective orientation	80
	5.2.5	Action at grassroots level	81
	5.2.6	Asset based	82
	5.2.7	Democratic	82
5.3	The Outcomes of Community Development		83
	5.3.1	Awareness creation	83
	5.3.2	Further development	84
	5.3.3	Demonstration effect	84
	5.3.4	Learning	85
	5.3.5	Community building	85

5.4		Conclusion	87
		References	87
Chapter 6		**Principles of Community Development**	89
		Hennie Swanepoel and Frik de Beer	
6.1		Introduction	89
6.2		Ethical Principles	89
	6.2.1	Human orientation	89
	6.2.2	Participation	92
	6.2.3	Empowerment	95
	6.2.4	Ownership	97
	6.2.5	Sustainability	98
	6.2.6	Release	101
	6.2.7	Conscientisation	102
6.3		Practical Principles	102
	6.3.1	Learning	102
	6.3.2	Compassion	104
	6.3.3	Adaptiveness	105
	6.3.4	Simplicity	106
6.4		Conclusion	108
		References	109
Chapter 7		**The Community as Main Actor in Community Development**	113
		Hennie Swanepoel and Frik de Beer	
7.1		Introduction	113
7.2		The Meaning of Community	113
7.3		Community as Stakeholder and Role Player	116
	7.3.1	The interest group	118
	7.3.2	The ad hoc group	119
	7.3.3	The elected committee	120
7.4		Conclusion	120
		References	121

Chapter 8	Place and Role of Community Development Practitioners	123
	Hennie Swanepoel and Frik de Beer	
8.1	Introduction	123
8.2	Contextual Aspects Guiding the CDP's Task	124
	8.2.1 The law	125
	8.2.2 Training	126
	8.2.3 Human resource practices	126
8.3	Ethical Guidelines	126
8.4	Position	128
8.5	Goals	129
8.6	Attitude	130
8.7	Role	132
	8.7.1 Guide	132
	8.7.2 Adviser	133
	8.7.3 Advocate	134
	8.7.4 Enabler	135
	8.7.5 Facilitator	137
8.8	Conclusion	137
	References	138
Chapter 9	Participatory Decision Making and Management	141
	Edith Phaswana and Frik de Beer	
9.1	Introduction	141
9.2	Participatory Management	141
	9.2.1 Participatory management – the concept	141
	9.2.2 Goals of participation	142
	9.2.3 Participation in projects	144
	9.2.4 Important aspects regarding participatory management	147
	9.2.5 The benefits and value of participation	149
	9.2.6 Constraints to meaningful participation	150
9.3	Group Decision Making	151

9.4	The Need for Information in Decision Making	153
	9.4.1 Motivational information	154
	9.4.2 Organisational information	154
	9.4.3 Management information	154
	9.4.4 Professional/technical information	154
9.5	Conclusion	155
	References	156

SECTION C	SKILLS FOR COMMUNITY DEVELOPMENT	159
Chapter 10	Communication Skills	161
	Frik de Beer	
10.1	Introduction	161
10.2	A Communication Model	161
10.3	Barriers to Communication	164
	10.3.1 Barriers to reception	164
	10.3.2 Barriers to understanding	165
	10.3.3 Barriers to acceptance	166
	10.3.4 Reasons for barriers to communication	168
10.4	Overcoming Barriers to Communication	169
	10.4.1 The psychological level	169
	10.4.2 The technical level	171
10.5	Development Communication	176
10.6	Conclusion	178
	References	179

Chapter 11	Leadership and Group Facilitation in Community Development	181
	Abel Mafukata and Frik de Beer	
11.1	Introduction	181
11.2	Defining The Concept 'Leadership'	182
11.3	Leadership for Successful Community Development	184
	11.3.1 The importance of leadership	185

	11.3.2	Improving leadership behaviour	187
	11.3.3	Leadership and communication	189
11.4	Groups		190
	11.4.1	Types of small groups	191
	11.4.2	Group dynamics	192
	11.4.3	Group psychology	193
	11.4.4	Group wellbeing	194
11.5	Support and Enablement of Leaders and Groups		197
	11.5.1	Leadership support	197
	11.5.2	Group support	198
11.6	Threats to Group and Leadership Success		198
	11.6.1	Domination	199
	11.6.2	Distraction	199
	11.6.3	Non-participation	199
	11.6.4	Irresponsibility	199
	11.6.5	Reprehensibility	200
11.7	Group Facilitation Skills		200
11.8	Conclusion		201
	References		202
Chapter 12	Development Projects, Change and Conflict Resolution		205
	Francois Lategan		
12.1	Introduction		205
12.2	Conceptual Understanding of Conflict		206
12.3	Origins of Conflict in Development Projects		209
	12.3.1	Poorly planned project schedules	209
	12.3.2	Unresolved conflicts from the past	209
	12.3.3	Poor alignment between community expectations and project priorities	210
	12.3.4	Competition for project and other resources	210
	12.3.5	Role dependency	211
	12.3.6	Cultural differences	212
	12.3.7	Technical issues	213

		12.3.8 Team or clique and the need for consensus	213
		12.3.9 Conflicting personalities	214
		12.3.10 Insufficiently recognised community structures and institutions	214
	12.4	Communication Barriers Causing Conflict in Development Projects	216
	12.5	Unintended Consequences Causing Conflict in Development Projects	217
	12.6	Prevention of Conflict	218
	12.7	Negotiation as Conflict Resolution	220
	12.8	Perceptions of Conflict in the Development Process	228
	12.9	Conclusion	234
		References	235
Chapter 13		**Mobilisation and Motivation** Marliane Owen	239
	13.1	Introduction	239
	13.2	What is behaviour?	240
	13.3.	What is motivation?	241
	13.4	Relationship between behaviour and motivation	246
		13.4.1 Why do people help?	247
		13.4.2 What will prevent people from helping?	248
	13.5	Behaviour change models	249
	13.6	Motivation and mobilisation in human development	251
	13.7	Conclusion	255
		References	255
Chapter 14		**Operational Writing** Frik de Beer and Andries de Beer	259
	14.1	Introduction	259
	14.2	Report and Proposal Writing	259

	14.2.1	Preparing to write the report	260
	14.2.2	Presentation of a report	261
14.3	Business Plan		264
	14.3.1	Proposed business plan format	265
	14.3.2	Fundraising: a special type of report and some pitfalls to avoid	268
14.4	Taking Minutes		270
14.5	Conclusion		271
	References		272

Chapter 15 Meetings … 273
Frik de Beer

15.1	Introduction		273
15.2	The Meeting Cycle		273
15.3	Types of Meetings		274
15.4	Common Problems Encountered in Meetings		274
	15.4.1	The multi-direction syndrome	274
	15.4.2	Confusion about procedure	274
	15.4.3	Personal attacks	275
	15.4.4	Traffic problems	275
	15.4.5	Unclear roles and responsibilities	275
	15.4.6	Manipulation by the chairperson	275
	15.4.7	Data overload	275
	15.4.8	Repetition and wheel spinning	276
	15.4.9	Win-lose approach	276
	15.4.10	Expectations and questions of power	276
	15.4.11	Problem avoidance	276
	15.4.12	Poor meeting environment	277
	15.4.13	Pre-set ideas and assumptions	277
15.5	Basic Criteria for a Good Meeting		277
15.6	Meeting Procedures		278

15.7	Role Players in a Meeting	280
	15.7.1 Chairperson	280
	15.7.2 Secretary	285
	15.7.3 Members	286
15.8	Conclusion	286
	References	287

Chapter 16 Public Speaking 289
Hennie Swanepoel and Frik de Beer

16.1	Introduction	289
16.2	Basic Characteristics of Effective Verbal Communication	289
	16.2.1 Clarity	290
	16.2.2 Accuracy	290
	16.2.3 Completeness	291
	16.2.4 Conviction	291
	16.2.5 Tastefulness	292
16.3	Your Presentation	292
	16.3.1 Preparation	292
	16.3.2 Delivery	297
16.4	Conclusion	302
	References	302

Chapter 17 The Community Development Practitioner and Technology 303
Andries de Beer

17.1	Introduction	303
17.2	Resources and platforms	304
	17.2.1 Availability of resources	305
	17.2.2 Applicable platforms for the community development practitioner (CDP) and the community	306
17.3	Management with technology	308
17.4	Advantages and disadvantages	309
17.5	Ethics and the POPI Act	309

| 17.6 | Conclusion | 310 |
| | References | 310 |

SECTION D	THE LIFE OF A PROJECT	313
Chapter 18	Contact Making. Andries de Beer	315
18.1	Introduction	315
18.2	Case Study	316
18.3	Preparation for Entry	322
18.4	Entry	325
18.5	Goals of Contact Making	326
	18.5.1 Getting to know the CDP	326
	18.5.2 Getting to know the people	329
	18.5.3 Analysing the needs	329
18.6	Conclusion	331
	References	331

Chapter 19	Participatory Research Methodology Frik de Beer and Andries de Beer	333
19.1	Introduction	333
19.2	Ethical Principles	334
	19.2.1 Informed and voluntary consent	334
	19.2.2 Anonymity and confidentiality	334
	19.2.3 Do no harm	335
	19.2.4 Participants' entitlement to withdraw	335
19.3	Identifying Community Needs	335
19.4	Principles and Characteristics of PRAP	337
	19.4.1 Advantages of PRAP	338
19.5	Some PRAP Techniques	339
	19.5.1 Secondary data review	340
	19.5.2 Direct observation	341

	19.5.3	Transect and group walks	341
	19.5.4	Venn diagrams	341
	19.5.5	Semi-structured interviews	342
	19.5.6	Group interviews and discussions	342
	19.5.7	Sketch mapping	342
	19.5.8	Time lines (chronologies of events)	343
	19.5.9	Stories, portraits and case studies	343
	19.5.10	Seasonal calendars	343
19.6	Application of PRAP		344
19.7	Some Problems with and Limitations of PRAP		345
19.8	Conclusion		347
	References		348

Chapter 20 — The Start of a Project — 351
Frik de Beer

20.1	Introduction		351
20.2	Resource Identification		352
20.3	Types of Resources		353
	20.3.1	Natural resources	353
	20.3.2	Manufactured resources	354
	20.3.3	Human resources	355
	20.3.4	Organisational (entrepreneurial) resources	357
20.4	Consensus on Needs		358
20.5	Formulating Needs		359
20.6	Feeling a Need		362
20.7	The First Project Meeting		363
	20.7.1	The role of the CDP during the first meeting	364
	20.7.2	Contents of the first project meeting	365
20.8	The Committee		366
20.9	Problem Solving		367
	20.9.1	Problem perception	368
	20.9.2	Problem definition	368

	20.9.3	Problem analysis	368
	20.9.4	Thinking of alternatives	369
	20.9.5	Decision making	370
	20.9.6	Planning	370
20.10		Conclusion	371
		References	371

Chapter 21	Planning and Implementation	373
	Frik de Beer	
21.1	Introduction to Planning	373
21.2	The Rationalistic, Synoptic Approach	373
21.3	The Adaptive Incrementalist Approach	376
21.4	Conclusion on the Approaches	377
21.5	The Planning Process	379
	21.5.1 A rational planning method: the logical framework as a planning method	379
	21.5.2 An adaptive incrementalist planning method: the planning cycle method	382
21.6	Recording Planning	388
21.7	Introduction to Implementation	389
21.8	Implementation with Strong Community Participation	390
	21.8.1 Implementation checklist	391
	21.8.2 The conclusion of implementation	391
21.9	The Role of the Community Development Practitioner in Planning and Implementation	392
21.10	Conclusion	394
	References	395

Chapter 22	Monitoring, Evaluation and Control	397
	Frik de Beer	
22.1	Introduction	397
22.2	The Evaluation Debate	398

22.3	Monitoring and Evaluation	401
22.3.1	Criteria for monitoring and evaluation	401
22.4	Record Keeping and Monitoring/Evaluation	406
22.4.1	Records of planning meetings	406
22.4.2	Reports	407
22.4.3	Event cards	407
22.5	Discussion and Observation as Monitoring/Evaluation Techniques	408
22.6	Dos and Don'ts Regarding Evaluation	409
22.7	Control	410
22.8	Conclusion	411
	References	412

SECTION E — TRAINING FOR COMMUNITY DEVELOPMENT ... 415

Chapter 23 The Training Dialogue ... 417
Frik de Beer and Andries de Beer

23.1	Introduction	417
23.2	Training as a Dialogue	419
23.2.1	The concept explained	419
23.2.2	The meaning of participation in training	422
23.2.3	Setting the climate for learning	422
23.2.4	Ensuring participation	424
23.3	Interactive (Workshop) Techniques	425
23.3.1	Open session discussion	425
23.3.2	Group work	426
23.3.3	Buzz groups	428
23.3.4	The nominal group technique	429
23.3.5	Brainstorming	430
23.4	Teaching Aids	431
23.4.1	The relevance of games, role play and case studies for training	431

		23.4.2	The rationale for using games, role play and case studies	432
		23.4.3	Case studies	434
		23.4.4	Facilitating role play and games	435
		23.4.5	Video and audio clips	436
		23.4.6	PRAP exercises	436
	23.5	Conclusion		437
		References		437

Chapter 24	Planning and Facilitating a Training Workshop	441

Frik de Beer and Andries de Beer

	24.1	Introduction		441
	24.2	Training as a Workshop		441
		24.2.1	Workshop setting	442
	24.3	Raising Issues		442
		24.3.1	Adult learners	442
		24.3.2	Establishing a teaching agenda	445
		24.3.3	Drawing a picture of the milieu	447
	24.4	Training as Communication		448
		24.4.1	Communication	448
		24.4.2	Motivation and group dynamics	450
		24.4.3	Discipline and coping with problem people	451
	24.5	Planning and Presentation		457
		24.5.1	Timing and time management	458
		24.5.2	The venue and seating arrangements	458
		24.5.3	Study and relaxation	463
		24.5.4	Visual aids	464
	24.6	Assessment		466
		24.6.1	The role of assessment in training	466
		24.6.2	Monitoring and assessment of progress	467
		24.6.3	Product and process assessment	468
		24.6.4	Feedback	469

24.7	Contents and Relevancy	470
24.8	Conclusion	471
	References	472

SECTION F	OVERVIEW OF THE PROFESSIONALISATION CONTEXT	473
Chapter 25	Legislation and Policy Frameworks Associated with Community Development in South Africa	475
	Cornel Hart	
25.1	Introduction	475
25.2	Policy Types and Purposes	476
25.3	Three Spheres of Government	481
25.4	Actioning and Driving Policies for and in Community Development	484
25.5	Policies Guiding Community Development Practice Quality	487
25.6	The Community Development Practitioner's Role in Policy	489
25.7	Conclusion	490
	References	491
	Appendix 25.1: Legislation and policy frameworks associated with community development	493

Chapter 26	Challenges of Community Development Practice at Government and Non-Government Levels: A Case Study from South Africa	499
	Ndwakhulu Tshishonga	
26.1	Introduction	499
26.2	Community Development Background	500
26.3	Community Development Professionals as Change Agents	503
	26.3.1 Community development practitioners as community and capacity builders	504
	26.3.2 Community development practitioners as advocates for social justice	505
	26.3.3 Community activists as development professionals	508
	26.3.4 Building social capital	511

26.4	Political challenges to the profession	514
26.5	Challenges to the profession	516
26.6	Economic challenges to the profession	518
26.7	Conclusion	519
	References	520

Chapter 27	The Professionalisation of Community Development in South Africa	531
	Cornel Hart	
27.1	Introduction	531
27.2	Professionalisation of Community Development in South Africa	532
	27.2.1 Professionalisation purpose and process	534
	27.2.2 Standardised legislated qualification frameworks	536
	27.2.3 Community development sector scoping and profiling	537
	27.2.4 Norms and standards for community development practice	537
27.3	Regulation of Professional Community Development	539
	27.3.1 Policy for Social Service Practitioners	539
	27.3.2 Social Service Practitioners Bill	541
	27.3.3 Community Development Practice Policy Framework (CDPPF)	542
27.4	Conclusion	546
	References	547

Case Studies 549

Addendum: Questions and answers for participatory self-evaluation 579

Glossary 591

Index 597

INTRODUCTION (FIFTH EDITION)

In this, the fifth revision, we strengthen some theoretical aspects, include a brief history and better explain some practical aspects.

While some may argue (correctly) that the Millennium Development Goals are past their sell-by date, they still perform an important function as an umbrella for investigating and explaining development objectives in the international global arena. These we now address. Sustainability and compassion are identified as principles for community development and are explained in Chapter 6. The progression in the debate and origins of community development is illustrated with reference to Max Neef's Human Scale Development and Sen's Capability Approach. These approaches have gained prominence internationally and community development workers should know about them.

The UK Department for International Development and other development actors from the North are increasingly supporting research into and the use of the social enterprise sector in promoting development. Although we have some reservations about the theoretical sharpness of this concept we briefly introduce this theme in the fifth edition. Finally, we revised the chapter on co-ordination in development, added a discussion on specific PRAP techniques and fine-tuned the chapter on planning and implementation.

In South Africa, community development has gained more prominence and support from government and the private and NGO sectors over the past decade. We trust that this may enhance community development as a profession. We would like, as stated in the previous edition, to see new professionals in community development backed by adaptive organisations giving their all to eradicate poverty. We hope that this revised edition will play a role in achieving this.

Hennie and Frik
2011

INTRODUCTION (SIXTH EDITION)

This edition was updated, inter alia by showing some of the criticisms of the Millennium Development Goals (MDGs). By 2016 these had been replaced with the Sustainable Development Goals (SDGs) 2030. We briefly introduce the SDGs 2030 and added new case studies. We also changed the structure of the book by including references per chapter. We trust that the glossary included in this edition will make the work more accessible to students.

With the sixth edition of *Community development: Breaking the cycle of poverty*, we were reminded of the importance of enriching work and how the questions and activities can assist students in understanding the text. Consequently we developed a *Lecturer's Guide* as an aid, but not a replacement, for the lecturer and human interaction that is so important in the learning situation.

Initially we had ambitious plans to design a lecturer's guide that could be fully published as an e-learning source, with access to students, to be supervised by lecturers. The dream was to have a fully interactive website where lecturers could provide inputs and students could access information and complete their assessment activities. However, currently all universities have their own e-learning platform (Sakae, Blackboard, Noodle, Moodle and more) and we realised it would be unwise to compete with them.

In the *Lecturer's Guide*, which will be a separate, electronic publication, we provide guidance on the use of visual material, including questions for assessing knowledge and reflection, and developing questions related to the case studies. We trust that the *Lecturer's Guide* will be of help to lecturers and students alike and look forward to constructive comments for the further improvement of this new learning tool.

Hennie and Frik
2016

INTRODUCTION (SEVENTH EDITION)

This book was conceptualised in May 2022 during an extended breakfast at Cherry Lane coffee shop in Malmesbury. The revision was guided by inputs from three reviewers and our own conclusion that the book needs to be updated and new themes developed and included. We also realised that adding the voices of colleague academics to the revision would benefit the publication and readers. The editors reviewed and revised all the chapters. However, in some instances, as are indicated in the table of contents, co-authorship of colleagues was obtained from Abel Mafukata, Edith Phaswana and Johnny Ntema. Five colleagues, Cornel Hart, Ndwa Tshishonga, Andries de Beer, Francois Lategan and Marliane Owen contributed entirely new chapters. We are grateful to the colleagues for their focussed and energetic participation and for keeping to the time schedule. We acknowledge the pioneering work that Hennie Swanepoel (24 October 1941 – 8 July 2017) contributed to earlier versions of the book.

As always, we dedicate this book to our loved ones who suffered from attention deficiency while we worked! They are indeed the bright stars in the lives of academics.

Frik de Beer and Andries de Beer
March 2023

ACRONYMS AND ABBREVIATIONS

BNA	basic needs approach
CBO	community-based organisation
CDP	community development practitioner
CDW	community development worker
GDP	gross domestic product
HIV/AIDS	Human Immunodeficiency Virus or Acquired Immune Deficiency Syndrome
HSD	Human Scale Development
IDP	Integrated Development Plan
ILO	International Labour Organization
IT	information technology
LED	local economic development
LPA	learning process approach
MDG	Millennium Development Goals
MLL	minimum level of living
NAFCOC	National African Federated Chamber of Commerce
NCR	National Credit Regulator
NGO	non-governmental organisation
NPO	non-profit organisation
PLA	participatory learning and action
PME	participatory monitoring and evaluation
PRA	participatory rural appraisal
PRAP	participatory rapid appraisal and planning
RRA	rapid rural appraisal
SDG	Sustainable Development Goal
SMME	small, medium and micro-enterprise
TAC	Treatment Action Campaign
TB	tuberculosis
WIL	work integrated learning

LIST OF CONTRIBUTORS

Andries de Beer (PhD) is a lecturer at Cape Peninsula University of Technology (CPUT) with more than 22 years of theoretical and practical experience in the tourism and event management industries. Industry experience ranges from a cultural representative at Disney World USA, to a river, field, and overland guide in the SADC countries, to specialising in logistics and organising events and music festivals. The last decade has been dedicated to being a lecturer and researcher in the higher education environment. Research focus areas include tourism (development, marketing and management), with a community development focus.

Cornel Hart (DLitt et Phil) is the programme coordinator for the community development (CD) professional degree, and evaluator for the Scholarship of Engagement Framework at the University of the Western Cape (UWC). She has been a member of the CD Professionalisation Steering Committee since 2009 and the head of research for drafting the South African policy framework for CD practice. She is a member of the International Association for Community Development (IACD) and the Community Development Society (CDS) from which she received the CDS International Community Development Best Practice Award in 2017.

Edith Dinong Phaswana (PhD) is academic director and associate professor at the Thabo Mbeki School of Public and International Affairs, University of South Africa. She holds a PhD in Development Studies from London South Bank University. She is the co-editor of the award-winning title *Black Academics voices: The South African Experience*. Her research interests are in decolonising Development Studies. She is the first woman president of the SA Development Studies Association and serves as a critical friend of the International Accreditation Council (IAC) of the European Association Development Institutes (EADI).

Francois Lategan (DTech Agriculture) is an assistant professor at Mendel University in Brno, in the Czech Republic. He has more than 30 years' experience in the practice and academic research and teaching of agricultural production systems, innovation and change, and agricultural development processes. He has published 25 articles in peer-reviewed journals and completed 14 technical scientific reports on agricultural change in different contexts. He currently teaches extensively on the role and importance of agriculture in economic growth and development. He is a past board member of the South African Society for Agricultural Extension and past director of the Southern African Institute of Agricultural Extension.

Frik de Beer (DLitt et Phil) is emeritus professor and research fellow in development studies, University of South Africa. In an academic career spanning almost 40 years, he published more than 30 articles in national and international peer-reviewed journals and co-authored several books, many on community development, but also on training for development and environmental issues. He is co-founder and was the first president of the South African Development Studies Association.

John Ntema (PhD) is professor in the Development Studies at the University of South Africa. He has authored, co-authored and compiled more than 20 research reports for commissioned studies, 15 peer-reviewed journal articles and 8 book chapters. He serves on the editorial advisory boards of *Africanus Journal of Development Studies* (University of South Africa) and *African Journal for Housing and Sustainable Development* (University of Lagos, Nigeria).

Marliane Owen (MSc, City University London) is a London-based behavioural economics consultant, advising companies and trustees on how to harness the power of human nature to achieve better outcomes for their employees and pension scheme members. In an industry career of over 20 years, she has worked in the United Kingdom and in South Africa with a focus on improving communication in financial services. She was the communications manager of the Barclays Bank UK Retirement Fund for six years and has consulted to a number of blue-chip companies, including Santander, HSBC, IBM, the Royal Mail and Centrica.

Mavhungu Abel Mafukata is professor and current Chair of the Department of Development Studies at the College of Human Sciences, University of South Africa. Professor Mafukata holds a PhD in Development Studies. His published books include *African perspectives on reshaping rural development*, *Impact of immigration and xenophobia on development in Africa* and *Impact of party politics on development in Africa*. His research interest is in the main focused on rural development in Africa.

Ndwakhulu Tshishonga (PhD) is an academic and a research fellow within the School of Built Environment and Development Studies at the University of KwaZulu-Natal. He specialises in community development, local economic development, local governance and citizenship, and over the past two decades, has contributed more than 30 scholarly papers and chapters to local and international journals and edited books. His academic citizenship includes presenting at both national and international conferences as well as engaging government departments in policy issues relating to governance, democracy and professionalising community development in South Africa.

SECTION A
The Development Context

CHAPTER 1

Towards Understanding Poverty and Deprivation

Frik de Beer

> Poverty is like heat; you cannot see it; you can only feel it; so, to know poverty you have to go through it *(words by a poor person living in Ethiopia, quoted by Narayan, Chambers, Shah & Petesch 2000:33)*.

1.1 INTRODUCTION – WHO OWNS COMMUNITY DEVELOPMENT?

Community development must be the form of development most abused over the past six decades. It was used to placate dissatisfied people; get development done in a cheap way; soften up the people before the government's bulldozers moved in; indoctrinate the people to get their blessing for programmes that had very little benefit for them; and westernise especially women to demonstrate that they too subscribe to the Western notion of the wholesome wife.

The basic points of departure of community development decades ago were crude, but not bad; even less so were they evil. Yet, in the hands of powerful people, community development became a tool of marginalisation and disempowerment. The basic tenets of community development should have been developed in an evolutionary way and should have been followed by adapted techniques and methodologies. Unfortunately, however, community development was nearly wiped off the map before it found a rebirth through the basic needs approach and other similar approaches. It must be noted that these new approaches were the result of opposition to the modernisation paradigm that became more than a paradigm by being elevated to an ideology by policy makers all over the world, and also in South Africa. This sounds a definite warning to today's policy makers: if community development is still seen within this outdated and discredited paradigm, there is no chance of success, even if the technique and methodology are perfect. The masses, especially in South Africa, have awakened and if proponents of community development do not take cognisance of this fact, community development will be spurned by those who are supposed to be the beneficiaries.

Community development must find a home within two other paradigms, namely participation and sustainable development. Very few institutions concerned with development will oppose the idea of participation, but the interpretation of participation may be questionable. A liberal viewpoint of participation will just not have the required results. The liberal viewpoint sees participation as something given to the poor by the authority or NGO working for the alleviation of poverty. It is a paternalistic view in that the local people are guided to accept more and more responsibility as and when they are judged by their 'guides' to be ready for it. It recognises the learning process, but the learning is done by the poor and the teaching is done by the development institution. People are supposed to be introduced to the techniques of planning, implementation and maintenance. Their position is seen as one of assisting the planners, as one of contributing indigenous knowledge to the planning package. The reasons given for the necessity of this participation have to do with the value it may have for the development effort and that it will ensure a continuous involvement of the people. Human beings are clearly in service of development. Their 'participation' will hopefully benefit the project. This viewpoint of participation is in line with the modernisation paradigm and is therefore equally outdated and discredited.

Following the ideas of Freire, Gran and Korten, our viewpoint is that empowerment must be a bottom-up process. In other words, the people must take empowerment. Ledwith and Springett (2022:xv) argue eloquently and convincingly that achieving community development through empowering people is 'to engage in collective action for justice and democracy …'. However, this taking of empowerment is still a process and can be carried by community development. Community development therefore becomes the vehicle, not for physical outputs, as has been the view in the past, but for the very human process of empowerment. The role of the authorities or NGOs in community development is then an enabling and supportive one. The main objective of this role must be to create space for communities and to provide the necessary information to the communities so that their empowerment will be meaningful.

With this supportive role, people's capacity will be built, not to assist planners and developers from outside, but to take full responsibility for their own development. The end result will be that people will enjoy ownership of development which they will execute in a responsible and enlightened way.

The paradigm of sustainable development also requires the empowerment of people to be responsible for their own development. By definition of 'sustainable' development, the local development effort must be in harmony with the local ecology. The local people are the experts on that local ecology. They will know and understand the subtleties of their area best. Guidelines can be drawn on a national or regional level, but they must leave scope for the uniqueness of local development to fit in with the local ecology for the sake of sustainability.

From this it is clear that we emphasise the human factor in community development. And by human factor we do not only mean the basic concrete needs of people. Community development must involve a process in which the capacity of people is built so that they can take responsibility for their own development, through which their human dignity is enhanced. The physical outputs of this process are secondary, even incidental. Primary and foremost is the freeing of people through development so that they can take responsibility for all other development concerning them.

It is also clear that this process of community development is political. The taking of power and the resulting decision making on the utilisation of scarce resources are political acts. The efforts in the past to separate development from politics as if politics would adulterate development, is a vestige from the liberal modernisation view and is simply impossible to realise in practice. Development is part of local politics, whether anyone wants it like that or not. Therefore, this political process of development should be supported rather than disclaimed, ignored or opposed.

A further consequence of our viewpoint is that the learning process through community development requires adaptive administration of development, not only on the local level, but also on all other levels. It is important that the local process will create structures for itself within which to operate. Take note that these structures must be the result of the process – they must evolve from the process. They cannot be created beforehand according to an accepted model. That will restrict the process. The structures that will evolve from the process will be unique because they will evolve from a unique process to carry that process further.

In their supportive role in this process, the authorities or NGOs must themselves follow an adaptive mode of administration. This may represent the single most serious obstacle in the way of community development. Bureaucracies, whether public or private, find it extremely difficult to change their own structures. However, they will need a change to become supportive instead of being the primary role player, to enable decision making instead of making the decisions, to enhance ownership instead of being the owner of development. This needs a reassessment of philosophies, missions, policies, strategies and structures which becomes a continuous process of adaptation.

This book has been written with this viewpoint in mind. We would like to see new professionals backed by adaptive organisations giving their all to eradicate poverty. We hope that this book will play a role in achieving this.

In this chapter, we introduce the context of poverty within which the community development practitioner (CDP) and community development professional (CDP) work. In this book, we shall use CDP to denote both.

1.2 ABSOLUTE AND RELATIVE POVERTY

Even though most people recognise poverty when they see it, it is difficult to define in universal terms and often impossible to attach figures, numbers or amounts to it. Because poverty is a relative concept, we cannot give it a precise description. Poverty is a relative term because it can either describe the situation of an individual or a family, or it can describe a whole community or society.

In cases where poverty in a community or society is the exception, we talk about individual poverty. Therefore, when an individual and his/her family experience deprivation and hardship, we say the person is an example of individual poverty, especially if they are the only family or one of only a few families that are poor.

People as poor as those discussed in the first three case studies (Case study 1: *The story of Sipho*, Case study 2: *Jacob in the poverty trap* and Case study 3: *A desperate woman*) are found in all communities. In some communities, only a few such people are found, but if there are hundreds or even thousands of other families in a similar situation, we can no longer describe it as individual poverty; then it becomes societal or community poverty. Some people also talk of mass poverty, where a whole country or large parts of society and communities suffer poverty.

Our concern is with this latter type of poverty. The few poor people in a relatively prosperous community can be looked after by the community through actions by welfare- and faith-based organisations. Community or mass poverty, however, needs more than that. This is why CDPs concern themselves with societal or community poverty and not individual poverty.

In South Africa, where some areas experience unemployment of more than 50 per cent, societal poverty or mass poverty is the order of the day.

However, not all people are equally poor. Put differently, the level of ill-being differs between individuals, communities and countries. What we are talking about here is classifying poverty as *absolute* or *relative* poverty. A person is in absolute or extreme poverty if he/she has an income of below US$2.15, in 2017 purchasing power parity. This amount is said to cover the minimum cost of food and other subsistence needs. Put differently, 'an individual who is absolutely poor is *poorer* than an individual who is only relatively poor, regardless of the income standard in their respective societies' (Decerf & Ferrando 2022:2–3, emphasis in original).

Absolute poverty is best illustrated in a situation where the next meal (or its absence) means the difference between life and death; or, as Sen (1981:12) puts it: 'Starvation, clearly, is the most telling aspect of poverty'. The Food and Agriculture Organization (FAO) estimates that nearly 690 million people (8.9% of the world population) are hungry (FAO, IFAD, UNICEF, WFP & WHO 2022). People with incomes so low that food, shelter and personal necessities cannot be maintained find themselves in a position of absolute poverty (earning less than US$2.15 per day) (Filmer, Hashan & Sanchez-Paramo 2022).

Among the absolute poor, we find the chronic poor. The World Bank (Roser & Ortiz-Ospina 2022) estimated that in 2018 the absolute or chronic poor numbered about 650 million, but expected this figure to drop to 500 million by 2030. Relative poverty is defined by the International Labour Organization (ILO) as 'circumstances in which people cannot afford actively to participate in society and benefit from the activities and experiences that most people take for granted' (ILO 2020). Relative poverty can include the ability of a person to participate in social activities, even if they are not necessary for survival; it can also refer to the overall distribution of resources within, or between, different countries. Relative poverty is therefore an expression of the poverty of one entity in relation to another entity. For example, in relation to South Africa, Lesotho is poor. In relation to the United States of America, South Africa is the poorer country. In relation to the average American family, the African-American family suffers poverty or deprivation; while in relation to an African-American family, an average Malawian family is poor.

Relative poverty is not a kind of poverty that is different from absolute poverty, but should rather be seen as supplementary to the definition of absolute poverty. The concept 'relative poverty' refers to people whose basic needs are met, but who, in terms of their social environment, still experience some disadvantages. In other words, while managing to survive, some people are materially disadvantaged compared with others living in the same community or society.

Whether people are absolutely or relatively poor, some action needs to be taken to improve their position. In practice, poverty alleviation measures often lead only to short-term relief, after which the beneficiaries return to their previous balance or equilibrium of poverty. CDPs need to be aware of this 'danger' in order to plan projects to overcome the tendency of returning to the equilibrium of poverty. A return to the equilibrium of poverty means that the chronic poor will remain chronically poor and pass the poverty on to their children.

1.3 UNDERSTANDING THE SOCIO-ECONOMIC CONTEXT OF DEVELOPMENT

> An estimated 1.2 million people died as a result of unsafe water sources in 2017. This was 2.2% of global deaths *(Ritchie & Roser 2021)*.

The world population was expected to grow to 8.0 billion in 2022, with a further rise to 8.5 billion by 2030 (UN World Population 2022:i). Schoch and Lakner (2020) reported that by 2017, about 9.2 per cent of the global population lived below the $2.15 international poverty line.

Table 1.1 Serious deprivations in many aspects of life in developing countries' health

HEALTH			
People without access to safe water (2021)	People without access to basic sanitation (2021)	People living with HIV/AIDS (end of 2020)	People suffering from air pollution using solid fuels and kerosene (2022)
2.6 billion	3.6 billion	37.7 million	2.4 billion
EDUCATION			
Illiterate adults (2022)	Illiterate women (2022)	Children and adolescents not achieving minimum proficiency levels (2017)	Girls out of school at primary and secondary school
781 million	515 million	617 million	129 million
INCOME POVERTY			
People living on less than US$2.15 a day (2018): 650 million			

Source: Adapted from UN-Water (2021); UNAIDS (2022); WHO (2021); Decerf and Ferrando (2022); UNICEF (2022)

If the world were a village of 100 people ...

At least 18 villagers would be unable to read or write but 33 would have cellular phones and 16 would be online on the internet.

27 villagers would be under 15 years of age and 7 would be over 64 years old.

There would be an equal number of males and females.

There would be 18 cars in the village.

63 villagers would have inadequate sanitation.

30 villagers would be unemployed or underemployed while of those 70 who would work, 28 would work in agriculture (primary sector), 14 would work in industry (secondary sector), and the remaining 28 would work in the service sector (tertiary sector). 53 villagers would live on less than two U.S. dollars a day.

One villager would have AIDS, 26 villagers would smoke, and 14 villagers would be obese.

By the end of a year, one villager would die and two new villagers would be born so thus the population would climb to 101.

Source: Adapted from Rosenberg (2019)

In developing countries (where 92 per cent of children live), 7 in 100 will not survive beyond age 5 (five million children below the age of 5 died in 2020); 50 in 100 will not have their birth registered, 68 will not receive early childhood education, 17 will never enrol in primary school, 30 will be stunted in growth and 25 will live in poverty. 'Every year 3,575,000 people die from water related diseases. This is equivalent to a jumbo jet crashing every hour. Most of these people are children (2.2 million)' (The World Counts 2023). The information in the box illustrates the general socio-economic condition of the 'global village'. In specific areas of the Third World, the picture is bleaker, with high rates of unemployment, poor service delivery, high infant mortality and food insecurity, among others.

1.4 GETTING TO UNDERSTAND POVERTY AND DEVELOPMENT

CDPs have some instruments at their disposal to help with understanding the context of poverty and motivation of people and communities towards development. This section briefly introduces Maslow's hierarchy of needs, the Human Development Index (HDI) and the global Multidimensional Poverty Index (MPI).

1.4.1 Maslow's hierarchy

In many disciplines in the social sciences, such as psychology and sociology, the hierarchy of needs developed by Abraham Maslow is used to understand the developmental stages of humans. The hierarchy, in the form of a pyramid of five steps (see Figure 1.1), places *physiological needs* at the bottom, as a foundation for the rest of the needs. Maslow argues that the basic needs of humans are food, water, warmth and rest, which must be fulfilled before higher needs are sought. The next level of the hierarchy is *safety needs*, also a basic need. Moving up to the next stage, we get *belongingness and love needs*, and this is followed by *esteem needs*, for prestige and a feeling of accomplishment. At the top of the pyramid is *self-actualisation*, more a result than a need. In the late 1960s, Maslow revised the hierarchy, adding aesthetic (appreciation of beauty), cognitive (realising personal potential) and transcendence (mystical, aesthetical experiences beyond the personal self) needs. The new hierarchy became known as Maslow's theory of motivation (McLeod 2018).

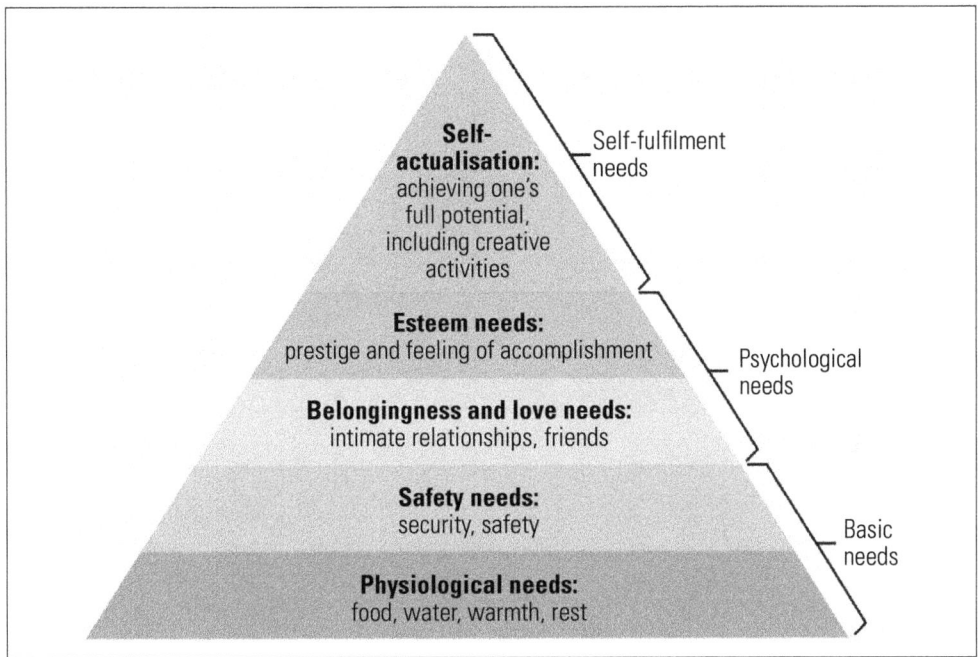

Figure 1.1   **Maslow's hierarchy of needs**

Source: Based on McLeod (2018)

Maslow developed his hierarchy of needs in the environment of his home country, the US. The hierarchy is criticised for various reasons: it may mean something different to different people; it may not apply to large sections of society; progression from one need to the next cannot be assumed; basic needs and priorities can differ. One should also consider that people need more than food and water: they need healthy food and clean water. Also: human beings can (and do) experience different needs simultaneously, even if the intensity of some needs differs from that of others. The hierarchy is therefore somewhat crude and does not fully and appropriately describe needs.

In a developmental context, Aruma and Hanachor (2017:19, 26) argue for the appropriate application of Maslow to identify needs in communities and that it '… can be used as a method of assessing needs in community development in various communities in the contemporary society'. However, Mawere, Mubaya, Van Reisen and Van Stam (2016:56 et seq) show, convincingly, that in the Third World the individual is not placed centrally. Rather – and referring to ubuntu (the African philosophy of 'I am because we are') specifically – they argue that '[i]n many parts of the world it is the group, or the community … that are central, and worthy to be pursued'.

1.4.2 The Human Development Index (HDI)

One way of measuring improvement of living circumstances is through the Human Development Index (HDI). The HDI was created in 1990 by Mahbub ul Haq, a Pakistani economist (ul Haq 1995). The HDI aims to put human development in the centre and focuses on three dimensions of poverty: health, education and standard of living (see Figure 1.2).

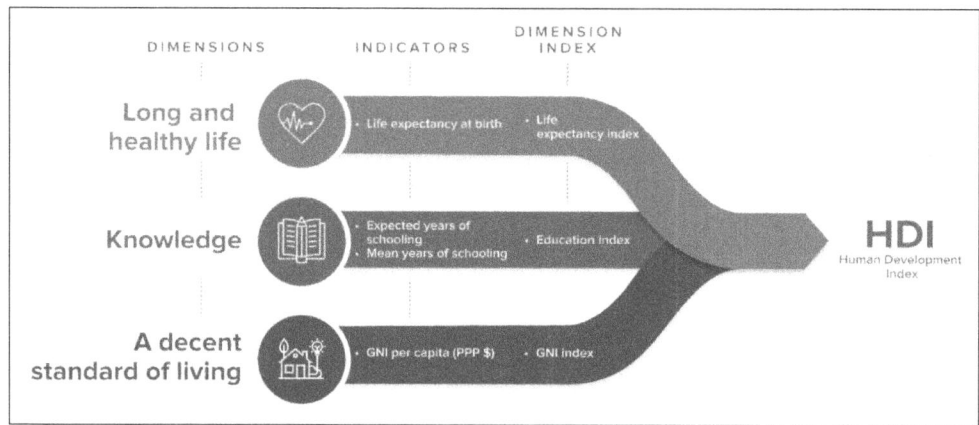

Figure 1.2 **The Human Development Index (HDI)**

Source: Adapted from https://hdr.undp.org/data-center/human-development-index#/indicies/HDI

The HDI relates to capabilities of people: it emphasises that the capabilities of people should provide the criteria for assessing development of a country (see the discussion of Amyrtya Sen's capabilities approach in Chapter 4). However, the HDI does not provide the full picture, as issues of human security, inequalities and empowerment, for instance, are not covered.

1.4.3 Global Multidimensional Poverty Index (MPI)

In 2018, the Oxford Poverty and Human Development Initiative (OPHI) collaborated with the United Nations Development Program's Human Development Report Office (HDRO) to monitor the Sustainable Development Goals (SDGs) better. The global Multidimensional Poverty Index (MPI) that resulted from this collaboration uses the three dimensions of poverty of the HDI (health, education and standard of living), and identifies and defines circumstances regarded as manifestations of deprivation. In addition, each of the indicators is linked to a specific SDG (the SDGs are discussed in more detail in Chapter 2).

Table 1.2 MPI measurement of poverty: dimensions, indicators, deprivation cut-offs and related SDGs

Dimensions of poverty	Indicator	Deprived if ..	SDG
Health	Nutrition	Any adult under 70 years of age or any child for whom there is nutritional information is undernourished	SDG 2
	Child mortality	Any child has died in the family in the five-year period preceding the survey	SDG 3
Education	Years of schooling	No household member aged 10 years or older has completed six years of schooling	SDG 4
	School attendance	Any school-aged child is not attending school up to the age at which he/she would complete high school	SDG 4
Living standards	Cooking fuel	The household cooks with dung, wood, charcoal or coal	SDG 7
	Sanitation	The household's sanitation facility is not improved (according to SDG guidelines) or it is improved but shared with other households	SDG 6
	Drinking water	The household does not have access to improved drinking water (according to SDG guidelines) or safe drinking water is at least a 30-minute walk from home, round trip	SDG 6
	Electricity	The household has no electricity	SDG 7
	Housing	At least one of the three housing materials for roof, walls and floor are inadequate: the floor is of natural materials and/or the roof and/or walls are of natural or rudimentary materials	SDG 11
	Assets	The household does not own more than one of these assets: radio, TV, telephone, computer, animal cart, bicycle, motorbike or refrigerator, and does not own a car or truck	SDG 1

Source: Based on Alkire and Jahan (2018); Alkire, Kanagaratnam and Suppa (2020)

The physiological needs of the Maslow hierarchy of needs and the poverty dimensions of the HDI and global MPI are very clear and similar. Yet, however important fulfilment of the needs is for human development, the CDP should be reminded that human beings are more than their needs: whatever the level of poverty, all human beings experience a need for safety, belonging, esteem and self-actualisation (see also discussion of the principle of human orientation in Chapter 6).

1.5 THE DEPRIVATION TRAP

The preceding discussion focused on the needs and requirements of people in the struggle for development. However, the reason for the struggle and the reality that some human beings are held captive by poverty, needs also to be explained. The deprivation trap, designed by Robert Chambers, still offers one of the most comprehensive explanations of why people are trapped, and often remain, in poverty.

Behind the cold statistics in Table 1.1 are real people fighting a daily battle to survive the deprivation trap in which they find themselves (see Chambers 1983:111 et seq). The majority of people in this trap live in rural areas and squatter settlements on the outskirts of cities and towns. Case study 3: *A desperate woman* illustrates some of the challenges faced by the poor to survive the deprivation trap.

Figure 1.3, taken from Chambers (1983:112), shows how the clusters or groups of deprivation interact to form a trap. Each arrow points in two directions, indicating that each cluster influences the other. For example, the arrow between physical weakness and powerlessness shows that not only does physical weakness lead to powerlessness, but that powerlessness can, in turn, lead to physical weakness.

> Poverty is a strong determinant of the other elements of the deprivation trap. It contributes to physical weakness through lack of food, small bodies, malnutrition leading to low immune response to infections, and inability to reach or pay for health services; poverty leads to isolation because of the inability to pay the cost of schooling, to buy a radio or a bicycle, to afford to travel to look for work, or to live near the village centre or a main road; it contributes to vulnerability through lack of assets to pay large expenses or to meet contingencies; poverty leads to powerlessness because a lack of wealth goes with low status: the poor have no voice *(Chambers 1983:111).*

Isolation, powerlessness and physical weakness render people vulnerable. In the physical sense, they are vulnerable to disease, and in the psychological sense they are vulnerable to abuse and the destruction of self-esteem. People are vulnerable to unscrupulous landlords and uncaring officials, and to the forces of nature that may bring droughts or floods.

The poor have limited access to information, services, labour organisations, opportunities and to opinion leaders and policy makers. Poverty renders them voiceless and powerless. Their powerlessness is exacerbated by physical weakness. Poor hygiene, malnutrition and undernourishment, and lack of education and life skills cause physical weakness; the consequences are, among others, poor school performance and an inability to perform manual work.

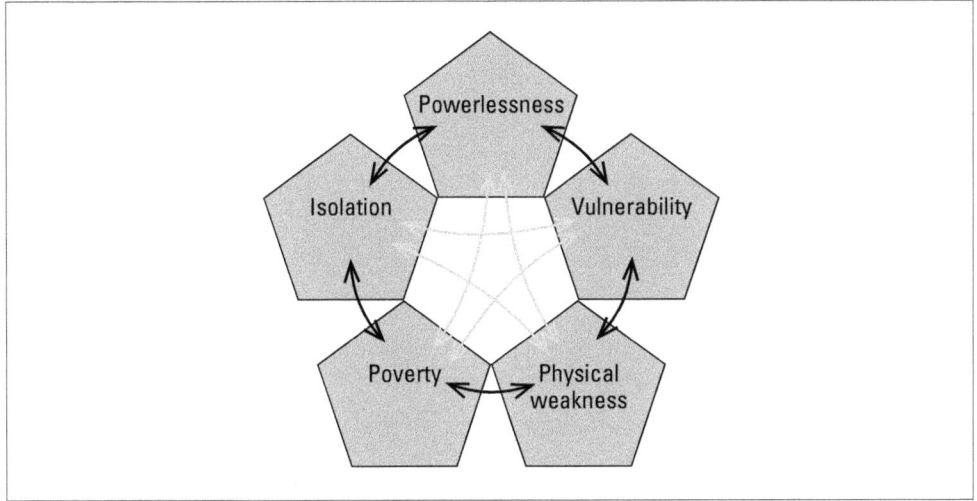

Figure 1.3 **The deprivation trap**

To break the hold of the deprivation trap (or cycle of poverty) over poor people, the links in the chain of the trap need to be broken. The CDP should consider at which point intervention can be considered (in cooperation with the community) by analysing the community in terms of the deprivation trap:

- Poverty is caused by lack of assets, be it land, money or job-related skills. A recent study by Balboni, Bandiera, Burgess, Ghatak and Heil (2021:4) confirms that poor people remain in the poverty trap because 'they cannot move into productive occupations due to an initial lack of assets'.
- Vulnerability is seen in the lack of reserves and choices, and the ease with which poor people can be coerced.
- Isolation is often in a geographical sense, but also shown by the lack of education and exclusion from systems and structures.

- The powerlessness of the poor is illustrated by lack of social and economic influence and the ease by which they can be exploited by others.
- Physical weakness is seen in the lack of physical strength and chronic illness.

A community development project cannot, nor should it, address all these issues at once. Yet, an understanding of the issues and their manifestations in a specific community can help in identifying a focus for a project. At this point, a word of caution is appropriate. While we work with and address problems, issues and shortcomings in the community, this should be done by working with the assets and building on them, to find solutions. Chapter 20 discusses the importance of assets and an asset-based approach to community development.

The plight of the poor is illustrated in Case study 1: *The story of Sipho*, where the situation of a child-headed household is explained. Case study 2: *Jacob in the poverty trap* shows how the clusters of the deprivation trap keep a family from rising from their poverty. The impact of the deprivation trap and how it keeps people from improving their lives can be illustrated with examples about shelter; employment or lack of employment opportunities; water, drainage and sewage; health facilities; food security (nutrition); education and the stagnant local economy. Combined with poverty, these factors keep households like trapped mice in the deprivation trap. One factor reinforces the other.

However, the CDP should not only identify aspects of the deprivation trap, but also look beyond and identify positive aspects – the assets in poor communities – on which development can be based. In the discussion of the deprivation trap below, some examples of community assets are briefly introduced (see Chapter 20).

1.5.1 Shelter

In urban areas, many people build shacks in squatter or informal settlements. Some shacks are quite neat and safe to live in, but many leak rain and dust, have bad or inadequate foundations, and almost all are too small for the number of people living in them. In rural areas, the shelters built with traditional building materials need a lot of maintenance. Because of a shortage of these materials (such as a shortage of thatch during droughts), it is difficult for people to maintain their dwellings properly. Also, they invariably do not have the time or physical strength to spend on repairing their homes.

Living in poor conditions affects people's health. It is difficult for an unhealthy person to find – and keep – a job. The rural poor have an added problem: because they are 'out of sight', officials do not know of their problems. The rural poor are consequently isolated. They are isolated from urban areas where social and economic infrastructure and services are available. The isolation is caused by distance, poor roads and telecommunications, and by their poverty which renders communication impossible or unaffordable. Their isolation is compounded by the tendency of government to invest in urban areas and neglect integrated urban–rural development.

Yet the housing created by the people, in spite of shortcomings, represents an asset on which further community development can be based. Small investments over many years, sometimes decades, lead to improvements of housing and represent large capital investments – assets controlled by the poor. De Soto (1998:18–19) illustrates this point in discussing housing in Lima, Peru. To obtain shelter, people occupied land, built houses, installed infrastructure and only then obtained legal ownership – quite the reverse of the traditional process. Between 1960 and 1984, the people, mostly migrants moving to the city, invested US$8 319.8 million in their own housing, compared to the US$173.6 million invested by government.

Sakaya et al (2011:476) correctly point out the value of shelter:

> Housing and its improvements has [sic] an important role in squatter settlement development because more than the building and the construction management, it aims to be the template of a sustainable model of socio-economic, political and environmental development.

1.5.2 Unemployment

The isolation of people in the deprivation trap contributes to their experience of poverty and powerlessness. Unemployment is both a cause and a result of the poverty situation. It is a cause, since without a job, people have no income and cannot pay for proper housing, food, medical care and education for themelves and their children. It is a result because poor health caused by an unbalanced diet, poor housing and lack of appropriate education (all on account of poverty) prevent people from finding and keeping gainful employment.

Unemployment is, in many instances, also the result of isolation, physical weakness and vulnerability. Because of distance and poor communication, the poor are isolated from the job market. They find it difficult to gain access to employment opportunities. An unbalanced diet and prolonged illness lead to physical weakness. Physical weakness increases vulnerability to other diseases, such as tuberculosis (TB), while diseases such as HIV/AIDS and malaria break down a person's natural immune system. On another level, the poor are also vulnerable to exploitation by employers and people in positions of power. As they have nothing to bargain with, the poor are powerless (see also 1.4.7). In the Third World, women must especially deal with '[u]nequal conditions … with less protection and resilience against unemployment, health emergencies, paid sick leave and other basic rights' (UNDP 2022b:98).

1.5.3 Water, drainage and sewage

The absence or inadequate provision of water, and poor drainage and sewage services, pose serious health problems. Lack of safe drinking water is one of the clearest signs of poverty. People, especially children, suffer poor health as a result of drinking unsafe water. With no proper sewage system (for instance, when using pit latrines), rainwater washes sewage into streams and stagnant pools. Diseases flourish and spread under such conditions. In urban squatter areas, the problem is worse because of the population density. In rural areas, however, the same problem occurs, but is perhaps also less visible to people from outside the settlements. Prolonged and repeated illness leave the victims physically weak.

Yet even infrastructure development projects to address sanitation needs are not beyond community development. In Karachi, Pakistan, the Orangi Pilot Projects made it possible, through research, organisation and commitment, for the communities to lay self-financed and self-managed underground sewage lines, involving almost 70 000 houses (Ekins 1992:190).

1.5.4 Health facilities

Because of the mushrooming of urban settlements and the long distances between scattered villages in rural areas, providing healthcare facilities lags far behind the need. Preventive primary healthcare facilities need to be expanded. Curative facilities provided by large clinics and hospitals are situated long distances from where the poor find themselves. Transport facilities, such as ambulance services, to health centres are inadequate.

On the other hand, poverty contributes to the squalor in which many people live, and this leaves them vulnerable to disease. It limits their access to proper medical care, causing prolonged illness which contributes to their physical weakness. They are vulnerable to diseases such as tuberculosis. Their vulnerability extends to employment because it is difficult for a sickly, uneducated person with little access to proper transport to find and keep a job.

1.5.5 Food security

Access to food depends on the purchasing power of the money that people earn, their access to land to grow food crops, foraging, such as occurs in rural areas, and the support in kind received from other members of the community. The coping strategies of households may include migration to places perceived to offer jobs (mainly urban areas) and obtaining various grants for the indigent and vulnerable (children, disabled and the elderly) provided by governments.

In the absence of food security, too little food and food of low nutritional value form the diet of poor people. Balanced and nutritious meals are important for the cognitive development (perception, thinking and learning) of children and adults. Even before birth, nutrition affects the development of a child. Under-nutrition of the mother negatively affects brain development and may cause permanent and irreversible damage to the baby. Breastfeeding of babies leads to higher IQ development, and fewer cases of rashes and bacterial infections. Iron deficiency during the early years of childhood can cause permanent damage to the brain. Iodine deficiency in the early years is associated with reduced cognition and achievement in school-age children. Poorly nourished children are more prone to infections and are likely to be frequently absent from school.

The lack of food security and under- and malnourishment experienced by the poor (and especially their children) contributes to *physical weakness*. Physical weakness makes people *vulnerable*; it may keep them from finding well-paid jobs and generally makes them *powerless*.

1.5.6 Education

The relationship between a child's ability to learn and the need for nutritious food is illustrated above. Weak, under- and malnourished children have a clear disadvantage at school. They may have lacked brain development at an early stage and may regularly be absent from school, making their disadvantage worse.

The lack of education and/or inability to obtain education keep people in a position of vulnerability and powerlessness. Education is viewed as one of the most effective preventive weapons against HIV/AIDS. Knowledge of this disease lowers the vulnerability and powerlessness of people. Education helps to prepare people to find or create their own jobs. In this way, it helps to combat poverty. A lack of education makes it difficult for people to escape the deprivation trap.

Education has many advantages for the individual and for society. For the individual, education can improve health and nutrition. Better education means better chances of obtaining jobs with better earnings. Inequality is reduced through education, especially where girls have equal access to opportunities. For society, education means a skilled workforce and improved productivity. Education can therefore support the eradication of poverty by increasing incomes.

In many poor areas, informal and private schools and early childhood development centres are established by people. This is a community-based asset that can, with proper support, develop into real resources in the fight against poverty.

1.5.7 Stagnant local economy

Lack of economic development at the local level contributes to high levels of unemployment and consequently, poverty. In urban squatter and informal settlements, unemployment rates of 70–80 per cent are common. These areas are home to many migrants from rural and peri-urban areas, and migrants from cities that experience economic slumps. In Africa, migration between countries in search of jobs and social services contributes to the growth of squatter and informal settlements. These settlements are mostly 'labour reservoirs' for the closest city and, because of their relative isolation and lack of proper education, the inhabitants have little access to proper jobs and remain poor, vulnerable and powerless.

In poor areas, much entrepreneurship is shown by people who run small enterprises – hairdressers, motor mechanics, spaza shops and shebeens abound. These are assets that, with proper local economic development (LED) support and infrastructure, can make a meaningful contribution to combat and eradicate poverty.

1.6 THE EQUILIBRIUM OF POVERTY

Attempts to alleviate poverty may bring some relief, but soon the balance or equilibrium returns and the poor remain as poor as before. In Chapter 6, we argue that development must bring release, not relief from poverty.

Galbraith (1979) argues that, in a poor society or community, any progress (in economic terms) is soon cancelled out due to, for example, an increased birth rate or a natural disaster. So, the fruits of successful development such as job creation are nullified by an uncontrolled increase in population numbers. These forces operate in such a way that they return the people to a situation more or less the same as before the development project. Improvements in the socio-economic position of a community or society are thus obliterated by some force or another operating in society. The poor community or society comes to accept their poverty as normal – they accommodate their poverty.

Savings that might accrue from development aid are often spent on means of survival and not invested in productive enterprises. A country may, for example, invest development aid in the building of social infrastructure such as schools or hospitals, or the paying of public service salaries, in which case no long-term interest will be earned or job opportunities created. A small-scale farmer may be granted a loan to buy farming equipment, but decides rather to spend it on school fees; no income is generated and the loan must be paid back. Once the surplus money of the household is depleted, it automatically returns to its previous level of subsistence; thus the balance (equilibrium) of poverty is restored. Accepting this position is what is called accommodation to a culture of poverty. It is a survival attitude inside the deprivation trap. It is clear that CDPs must instil in poor people an anti-equilibrium attitude, a will to fight the situation in which poverty thrives, even against all the odds.

The equilibrium of poverty points to the presence of chronic poverty. 'Some poverty passes from one generation to another as if the offspring sucks it from the mother's breast' (a group of disabled Ugandan women quoted in Chronic Poverty Research Centre 2005:vi). For the chronic poor to escape, much more is needed than equal opportunities. For them, specific and targeted programmes are required. According to the Chronic Poverty Research Centre (2005:50), such support should include policies and strategies that prioritise livelihood security, and ensure chronically poor people can take up opportunities, take empowerment seriously and recognise obligations to provide resources.

It is the task of CDPs to be well informed about government policies and strategies that will benefit the poor and the chronically poor. It is also their task to find resources and assist poor and chronically poor communities to gain access to them.

1.7 CONCLUSION

In the African context, poverty affects the masses, not just the individual. Masses of poor people are trapped in deprivation, and it is extremely difficult for them to break free of this trap. In fact, the tendency exists for poverty to constantly reintroduce itself in new guises, thus ensuring that the equilibrium of poverty continues. This is particularly so in sectors such as agriculture, construction and domestic work: 'Chronic poverty is found especially where there are intersecting inequalities and spatial poverty traps' (CPAN 2019:9).

It is developers' greatest task – no, it is their only task – to break the deprivation trap and to bring about disequilibrium in the poverty situation. In the final instance, it is human beings who must be released from the trap. They must be given the chance to look after their own wellbeing in a self-reliant way. It is the task of CDPs to guide and enable them to do so.

REFERENCES

Alkire S & Jahan S. 2018. The new global MPI 2018: Aligning with the Sustainable Development Goals. OPHI Working Paper 121, University of Oxford.

Alkire S, Kanagaratnam U & Suppa N. 2020. The global Multidimensional Poverty Index (MPI) 2020. OPHI MPI Methodological Note 49, Oxford Poverty and Human Development Initiative, University of Oxford.

Aruma EO & Hanachor ME. 2017. Abraham Maslow's hierarchy of needs and assessment of needs in community development. *International Journal of Development and Economic Sustainability*, 5(7):15–27.

Balboni C, Bandiera O, Burgess R, Ghatak M & Heil A. 2021. *Why do people stay poor?* NBER Working Paper Series. Cambridge: National Bureau of Economic Research.

Chambers R. 1983. *Rural Development: Putting the Last First*. Essex: Longman.

Chen S & Ravallion M. 2008. The developing world is poorer than we thought but no less successful in the fight against poverty. *Policy Research Working Paper No 4703*. Washington: World Bank.

Chronic Poverty Research Centre. 2005. *The Chronic Poverty Report 2004–05*. Institute for Development Policy & Management. Manchester: University of Manchester.

CPAN (Chronic Poverty Advisory Network). 2019. The fourth chronic poverty report growth. ODI. Available at: https://odi.org/en/publications/the-fourth-chronic-poverty-report-growth/ (accessed 19 August 2022).

Decerf B & Ferrando M. 2022. Unambiguous trends combining absolute and relative income poverty: New results and global application. *World Bank Economic Review*, 00(0):1–24.

De Soto H. 1998. *The Other Path: The Invisible Revolution in the Third World*. New York: Harper & Row.

Ekins P. 1992. *A New World Order: Grassroots Movements for Global Change*. London: Routledge.

FAO, IFAD, UNICEF, WFP & WHO. 2022. *The State of Food Security and Nutrition in the World 2022: Repurposing Food and Agricultural Policies to make Healthy Diets more Affordable*. Rome: FAO.

Filmer D, Haishan F & Sanchez-Paramo C. 2022. An adjustment to global poverty lines. Available at: https://blogs.worldbank.org/voices/adjustment-global-poverty-lines (accessed 24 April 2023).

Galbraith JK. 1979. *The Nature of Mass Poverty*. Cambridge: Harvard University Press.

ILO (International Labour Organization). 2020. *Beyond the Goal of Eradicating Absolute Poverty in China: Relative Poverty Indicators and Social Security Policies*. Research brief 1. Rome: ILO.

Ledwith M & Springett J. 2022. Glossary. In Ledwith M & Springett J (eds), *Participatory Practice: Community-based Action for Transformative Change*. 2nd ed. Bristol: Policy Press.

Mawere M, Mubaya TR, Van Reisen M & Van Stam G. 2016. Maslow's theory of human motivation and its deep roots in individualism: Interrogating Maslow's applicability in Africa. In Makwere M & Nchemachena A (eds), *Theory, Knowledge and Politics: What Role for the Academy in Sustainability in Africa*. Bamenda: Langaa Research and Publishing Common Initiative Group.

McLeod S. 2018. Maslow's hierarchy of needs. *Simply Psychology*. Available at: https://www.researchgate.net/figure/McLeod-2018-Maslows-Hierarchy-of-Needs-theory-1943-supports-the-conceptual_fig1_342645776 (accessed 10 January 2023).

Narayan D, Chambers R, Shah MK & Petesch P. 2000. *Voices of the Poor: Crying out for Change*. Oxford: Oxford University Press.

ODI (Overseas Development Institute). 2014. *The Chronic Poverty Report 2014–2015: The Road to Zero Extreme Poverty*. London: ODI.

PRB (Population Reference Bureau). 2014. *2014 World Population Data Sheet*. Washington DC: Population Reference Bureau.

Ritchie H & Roser M. 2021. Clean water. Available at: https://ourworldindata.org/water-access#unsafe-water-is-a-leading-risk-factor-for-death (accessed 10 March 2023).

Rosenberg M. 2019. If the world were a village ... Available at: https://www.thoughtco.com/if-the-world-were-a-village-1435271 (accessed 24 April 2023).

Roser M & Ortiz-Ospina E. 2022. Global extreme poverty. *OurWorldInData.org*. Available at: https://ourworldindata.org/extreme-poverty#citation (accessed 27 July 2022).

Sakay C, Sanoni P & Hanazato T. 2011. Rural to urban squatter settlements: The micro model of generational self-help housing in Lima-Peru. *Procedia Engineering*, 21(2011):473–480. Available at: http://www.sciencedirect.com/science/article/pii/S1877705811048740 (accessed 10 March 2016).

Schoch M & Lakner C. 2020. Global poverty reduction is slowing, regional trends help understanding why. Available at: https://blogs.worldbank.org/opendata/global-poverty-reduction-slowing-regional-trends-help-understanding-why (accessed 26 July 2022).

Sen A. 1981. *Poverty and Famines: An Essay on Entitlement and Deprivation*. Oxford: Clarendon.

The World Counts. 2023. Global challenges. Available at: https://www.theworldcounts.com/challenges/planet-earth/freshwater/deaths-from-dirty-water (accessed 20 March 2023).

ul Haq M. 1995. *Reflections on Human Development*. Oxford: Oxford University Press.

UNAIDS. 2022. Global HIV & AIDS statistics – fact sheet. Available at: https://www.unaids.org/en/resources/fact-sheet (accessed 27 July 2020).

UNDP (United Nations Development Programme). 2014a. *MDG Report 2014: Assessing Progress in Africa toward the Millennium Development Goals*. Addis Ababa: United Nations Economic Commission for Africa, African Union, African Development Bank and United Nations Development Programme.

UNDP. 2014b. *Human Development Report 2014: Sustaining Human Progress*. New York: UNDP.

UNDP. 2022a. *World Population Prospects 2022 Summary of Results*. New York: United Nations.

UNDP. 2022b. Special report. *Threats to human security in the Anthropocene Demanding greater solidarity*. New York: UNDP.

UNICEF. 2022. Girls' education: Gender equality in education benefits every child. Available at: https://www.unicef.org/education/girls-education (accessed 27 July 2022).

UN-Water. 2021. Summary progress update 2021 – SDG 6 – Water and sanitation for all. July. Geneva: United Nations. Available at: https://www.unwater.org/publications/summary-progress-update-2021-sdg-6-water-and-sanitation-all (accessed 24 April 2023).UN World Population. 2022. *World Population Prospects 2022*. New York: United Nations.

WHO. 2021. Household air pollution and health. Available at: https://www.who.int/news-room/fact-sheets/detail/household-air-pollution-and-health (accessed 24 April 2023).

CHAPTER 2

The Development Environment

John Ntema and Frik de Beer

2.1 INTRODUCTION

The ever-growing societal and individual poverty, particularly in developing countries (see Chapter 1), is in the main **perpetuated** by a widespread lack of development. With all member states made to adopt the Sustainable Development Goals (SDGs) on 25th September 2015, the ultimate aim of the United Nations is, among others, to end all forms and types of poverty while ensuring that *'no one is left behind'* (United Nations 2022).

Both poverty and underdevelopment are known to run counter to any form of development, including community development, as they affect the socio-economic and environmental wellbeing of communities. It is through community development that poor communities in particular could put into action their collective vision of how to organise things differently so that in their experience, human community could realise a genuine social justice and ecological sustainability, which for the longest time has seemed unachievable either at global or national levels (Ife 2013). Hence, it may be appropriate to argue that, on one hand, it is through community development that social ills such as societal and individual poverty could be alleviated, while on the other, realisation of community development requires local resources and strategies that, among others, could include human empowerment, community empowerment, public participation and competent community development workers (CDPs).

It is therefore important that all these local resources and strategies are not only being studied, but that efforts are made to understand their interdependence, which is crucial in knowing the environment and circumstances under which eradication of poverty and community development must be adequately addressed. The struggle against underdevelopment and societal and individual poverty has become more than just a local and national agenda and is now an integral part of global agenda as well. For the attainment of any development, including community development, all countries, particularly those in the global south (developing countries), should seek to align their national agenda on development with the United Nation's 2030 Agenda and its Sustainable Development Goals (United Nations 2019).

2.2 THE GLOBAL CONTEXT OF POLICY FORMULATION FOR DEVELOPMENT

Both the principle of '*no one must be left behind*' and 'Goal 17: Partnerships to achieve the goals' by the Sustainable Development Goals (SDGs) and its 2030 Agenda (United Nations 2022), demonstrates a need for individual countries to be able to align their national development policy and programmes with the global agenda and rules on development. It shows how the concept of development has become a universal language. Notwithstanding progress made prior to the COVID-19 pandemic and the Ukraine-Russia war, if cascading and interlinked crises and highest number of conflicts faced by the global community since the creation of the United Nations are anything to go by, it may be appropriate to argue that the developmental targets set out in the 2030 Agenda for sustainable development are in jeopardy, as most developing countries are not on track to end poverty by 2030 (United Nations 2022).

Confirming this argument could be a twofold view. First are the remarks by the UN secretary noting that: '[d]espite considerable efforts, our world as we know it and the future we want are at risk as we are not on track to achieve the SDGs by 2030' (Arora & Mishra 2019). Second is the reversal and derailing of progress in poverty reduction caused mainly by the COVID-19 pandemic and to some extent, the Ukraine-Russia war (United Nations 2022; United Nations Development Programme (UNDP) South Africa 2022). The impact of these combined crises demonstrates not only the relevance of SDGs as a framework for a global agenda on development but also how nations and their institutions, particularly governments, do not exist in isolation, unaffected by global developments outside their borders.

Attempts by a government to enforce regulation of different environments or spaces through policy frameworks are equally influenced by the global context within which we all co-exist. Consequently, it may be appropriate to argue that it is not only activities and debate within a country that influence policy formulation, including government's response to the development needs of citizens. Global activities and debates could also influence national policy and government's response and performance on national development. For example, the impact of these combined crises saw the number of people living in extreme poverty increasing for the first time, with an additional 95 million people globally in 2022 (United Nations 2022). This despite a historical decline in extreme poverty rate from 10.1 per cent to 8.6 per cent between 2015 and 2018. The war in Ukraine has in particular led to a sudden increase in prices for food, fuel and fertilisers, and caused disruptions of supply chains and global trade, fuelling the threat of a global food crisis, especially in poorer nations. For example, with Russia and Ukraine accounting for 29 per cent of global wheat exporters and 62 per cent of sunflower oil exporters, it did not come as a surprise to see the price of wheat on global markets being almost 80 per cent higher in 2022 than a year earlier (World Bank 2022) and countries suddenly battling record inflation and rising interests rates (United Nations 2022). Since Russia invaded Ukraine on 24 February 2022, South Africa has seen a more than 100 per cent hike in the prices of primary agricultural inputs compared to January 2021 (UNDP South Africa 2022). Consequently, since March 2022, the world has seen an increase in the eruption of protests over rising food prices (particularly sunflower oil and wheat/grains) in several countries (World Food Programme 2022) while continued invasion increases the risk of more social unrest in both advanced and emerging economies (UNDP South Africa 2022). Some of recent food price-related protests were seen in Tunisia, Kenya, Sri Lanka, Iran and Greece, to mention but a few.

Due to crises such as COVID-19 and the Ukraine-Russia war and their global impact, individual countries are often required to reformulate their short- and long-term policies and programmes on development agendas so that the policies not only respond to local needs but are also able to fit into the changing global context as well (Mukarram 2020). To survive the implications of the Ukraine-Russia conflict, the South African government, working in partnership with the UNDP, was left with no option but to develop a responsive and appropriate holistic financing framework that leveraged all sources of funding for the SDGs and Agenda 2063 (UNDP South Africa 2022). This to a large extent confirms not only interdependence among countries of the world but also how state policies of developing nations are unable to survive as both their formulation and implementation are tied to the dictates of global rules (Teryima 2013). It further confirms how in a globalising world, a systemic national approach to development has not only become irrelevant but impractical as well (Ferrer 1997).

Notwithstanding its significance and strides made, in critiquing this linkage between global rules and domestic policies, Teryima (2013) argues that it often enhances poverty and underdevelopment in developing countries. A typical example is how through the 'new international financial architecture', the US has unduly imposed on the rest of the world, particularly developing countries, its own rules that determine how local policies in these countries are to be formulated and implemented. This confirms a twofold criticism levelled against the SDGs. First, SDGs are labelled as goals and processes that failed to take sufficient note of local and national contexts. Second, they are criticised for, among others, being obligations for Western countries or being promoted only by multinationals (Del-Aguila-Arcentales, Alvarez-Risco, Jaramillo-Arevalo, De-la-Cruz-Diaz & Anderson-Seminario 2022).

The global context discussed in this section does have a significant influence on how individual countries conceptualise, formulate and implement their local policies and programmes on development, including community development. Next is the discussion on the significance of the local development environment.

2.3 THE LOCAL DEVELOPMENT ENVIRONMENT

Besides the global context and its influential rules and activities, the local context and environment in which development is being undertaken is, to a large degree, dependent on the amount and type of support given by aspects such as national policy discourse and regulatory framework. To be effective as instruments of development, laws are translated into development programmes and projects. In community development discourse, it is difficult for scholars and practitioners to ignore exploring related concepts such as participation, empowerment and human development (Shembe 2015), including a facilitative role by community development workers (CDPs) due to their interconnectedness. Participation is important as it may enhance a sense of community, while empowerment could enhance a collective sense of efficacy or control over public and private entities that affect one's life (Perkins, Hughey & Speer 2002). From a Sustainable Development Goals (SDGs) perspective, the United Nations emphasise the significance of a collective and inclusive approach to development by arguing as follows:

> We must adopt a resilient and inclusive development pathways [sic] that will reduce carbon emissions, conserve natural resources, transform our food systems, create better jobs and advance the transition to a greener, more inclusive and just economy *(United Nations 2022:3)*.

Despite governments' claim to follow a community-led development approach in such projects, evidence shows how most are conceptualised and implemented in a top–down instead of bottom–up manner. A top–down approach to community development does not make provision for principles of public participation and this eventually eliminates any sense of belonging and ownership among ordinary local community members (see Chapter 6 for a discussion of these principles). Programmes and projects become the vehicles of bringing development to poor local people where the people are often cast in the role of 'clients' receiving a 'service' from the government. Contrary to government's view, such a service delivery model seldom allows for the community to take initiative and make decisions concerning their own development. (See Case study 5: *A dam can bring hardship*, Case study 7: *A community hall with no purpose* and Case study 10: *The project that had its fences brought down*.) To a large extent, realities represented in these case studies show the unintended consequences of government's imposition of service delivery in the name of community development. It is thus important for the government to realise the following:

- First, 'that people cannot be developed, they can only develop themselves' and their community. While it took a community of Shallcross in Durban less than a month to mobilise all necessary fiscal and human resources and only five days to complete a community-led initiative to rebuild Pompeni Bridge, in other neighbourhoods such as iNanda and Mzinyahti (where there was overreliance on government and a lack of strong sense of community activism), communities had to wait over three months to get new bridges (Nair 2022). This delayed response of the government to emergency infrastructural development should be understood within the political context, which has South African politicians avoiding accountability by resorting to political rhetoric such as 'things are in the pipeline' (Ntema 2021).
- Second, 'community development is not about *delivering* services' (Maistry 2012:36).

- Third, community development should focus on creating the conditions for members of local communities to become active agents of change rather than being passive recipients or victims of change effected (Tjarve & Zemite 2016).
- Fourth, approaches and strategies to development, especially community development, must be adapted to local circumstances and conditions that are often shaped by different socio-economic, cultural, environmental and political realities (Mubita, Libati & Mulonda 2017).
- Fifth, it is through adoption and implementation of community-led development programmes that countries could address underdevelopment and alleviate societal and individual poverty. In a nutshell, community development represents a vision of how to organise things differently, so that in their experience (and as stated previously), human community could realise a genuine social justice and ecological sustainability, which for the longest time has seemed unachievable either at global or national levels (Ife 2013).

Other than policy discourse, it could be argued that the local context in its political, social, cultural, economic and psychological manifestations could either enhance or hinder any community development. Below is a brief reflection and contextualisation of some grassroots realities on these factors that could potentially influence formulation and implementation of policy and programmes on development.

2.3.1 Political environment

Both community empowerment and community development require not only supportive CDPs but also the creation of a conducive and stable political environment. For instance, only through active and engaged recognition of the politics of a community is one able to diagnose properly the main cause of problems related to community development (Shaw 2008). It is important for key local stakeholders such as CDPs to appreciate the fact that community development usually takes place in an environment which is highly political. Local politics and power dynamics can create a highly contested environment for community development projects (Gray & Mubangizi 2010). Without putting in place empowered and capacitated CDPs, there could never be meaningful and impactful community development in any society.

Key to the success of CDPs is their ability to understand their role as facilitators in community development and to adopt an apolitical posture. As facilitators in community development (Webber & Jones 2013), CDPs would (in our view) require both sound interpersonal skills and a neutral stance to work effectively with local role players such as political organisations, civil society movements, non-governmental organisations, the private sector, government entities and agencies, while possessing adequate skills in order to know and interpret all development guidelines and policies at local, national and global level. The significance of such a collective community approach to development should be understood in the context of a general consensus among contemporary development scholars and practitioners that the process of development through the implementation of local projects and programmes will only be meaningful if the local population collectively participate fully in their planning and implementation (Mubita et al 2017).

Acknowledging the significance of recognition of political and social environments to a certain extent, Mubita et al (2017) argue that there is a need for development project design and implementation to be informed by careful political and social analysis. Consequently, understanding these dynamics calls (particularly on the side of CDPs) for an approach that regards collective participation as an inherently political process rather than a technique. It is further important to appreciate that in order to achieve 'empowerment', which is one of the key ingredients of community development, participation should be considered as political since it is conditioned by, among others, the political background of various participating local stakeholders. It is important that in any community development, the local community is treated as heterogeneous, with different interests, power (including political power) and social relations that can either constrain or enhance the success of any development project (Mubita et al 2017). Unless properly analysed and handled, political differences in a community can render it incapable of agreeing on development projects. Case study 12: *The divided community* gives an example of how destructive politics can be. The political situation is not an excuse to withdraw from the community, but it is important that CDPs recognise and consider it.

2.3.2 Social environment

In development discourse, there are social factors such as social relations and networks, institutions and civic organisations which do not only influence but also assist in explaining dynamics in such development

(Bhandari & Yasunobu 2009). The social environment consists of the primary institution of the family as well as secondary institutions such as schools, churches, clubs and interest groups (see Chapter 3). The significance of the social environment in development discourse is supported by the SDGs and Agenda 2030, which is essentially socially driven in its social values and trajectories (Filho et al 2022). Through social relations, stakeholders and institutions need to strike a balance between individualism and a sense of community, and strive towards upholding social values that promotes inclusion, equity and social justice. Development involves improvement in quality of life, which requires equal consideration of underlying social and cultural systems (Bhandari & Yasunobu 2009; Dale & Newman 2010).

The social environment can become an 'enabling environment' for sustainable development within community-based projects, provided its social values are seen to be strengthening resilience and supporting change and transformation (Filho et al 2022). However, where misunderstood, the concept of social environment and its manifestations could cause a conflict between a need to create a healthy sense of individual self and a need to maintain a healthy and coherent community with established social mores, which are both key ingredients for successful community development. For example, evidence shows how practice of the rampant social value of individualism without a sense of community continues to make development within community-based projects very hard, if not impossible, to achieve (Filho et al 2022). In a social environment deprived of a sense of community, one is likely also to find negative factors such as delinquency, power struggles, group forming and antisocial behaviour such as prostitution, crime, drug abuse and child abuse.

2.3.3 Cultural environment

The cultural environment comprises the human values and mores of a society that are embodied in tradition (Daskon & Binns 2010). Evidence in existing literature and research shows that not only is culture an integral part of development but it also has a causal effect on development (Huggins & Thompson 2015). Even development institutions such as the United Nations and World Bank have gone beyond just recognition of cultural diversity as a key component of the development process and have since incorporated local cultural factors in their development programmes (Bhandari & Yasunobu 2009). It is through proper understanding of the concept of culture that individuals and societies would appreciate its significance in the context of community development, and incorporate cultural values into development policy and practice.

In a development context, culture should be seen as a flexible rather than rigid resource that can offer innovative solutions to challenges facing development projects (Daskon & Binns 2010). The local cultural context must be taken into consideration and used as a starting point for dialogue and possible participation by all stakeholders, including the most marginalised, in community development projects. If communication about a project seems to imply that the project is going to attempt to change tradition or it seems critical of traditional values, there will be an uphill battle to get the project accepted (see Chapter 13). Therefore, community development projects should not only legitimise and strengthen indigenous culture, but allow these indigenous people themselves to set the agenda for development and exercise complete control over process and structures (Giampiccoli & Kalis 2012). Any community development project perceived not to resonate with culture and cultural activities is likely to result in dissatisfaction among the local community. For example, the residents of Riga (capital city of Latvia) perceived a mismatch between development and culture in their neighbourhood and because of this expressed (through a survey) high dissatisfaction with their quality of life (Tjarve & Zemite 2016).

Unless properly understood and applied, culture and tradition may constrain development projects. The cultural environment is bound to affect development negatively due to a tendency by development practitioners to perceive cultural norms and traditions as being quite separate from and unaffected by development values. Furthermore, where traditional culture is rigid and constraining rather than flexible and supportive, development is likely to either stall or fail (Daskon & Binns 2010). History has shown that both traditional local relationships of power and local culture could hinder participation in community development by being oppressive to certain members of the community (Mubita et al 2017). For example, there was a community development group in the Aotearoa community (New Zealand) called the Women's Advocacy Group (WAG). Its members were Samoan and Tongan migrant women. Being raised in a traditional system driven by hierarchy and patriarchy, these women never found themselves in a position where they felt empowered enough either to express themselves in public community meetings, especially where their male counterparts were in attendance, or openly criticise a dissenting view expressed by an elderly person when matters and issues that concerned community development were under discussion (Williams 2004). In contrast to this, and contrary to a longstanding tendency for women in rural areas to be forced to engage in the informal sector as domestic servants or street sellers, in a Kandyan village in Sri Lanka, women can be a privileged group in terms of their resource ownership and possession of skills and knowledge, which are comparable to their husbands or male counterparts (Daskon & Binns 2010).

2.3.4 Economic environment

The economic context refers to rate of employment, presence and activity of commerce and industry, and the presence and scope of informal economic activity. Economic capital remains a necessary first condition to sustainable development (Dale & Newman 2010).

Every community has its own economy, manifested in both the informal and formal systems, and is also generally economically layered, consisting of very poor people (the chronic poor), poor people and those who are better off. Fortunes of community members are intimately linked to the level of local economic development, which in turn is dependent on dynamics at play in the broader community (Sharman 1981). For example, the level of activity of the economy would determine the affordability of community development through, among others, people's ability to pay for municipal services, education, food and clothing.

Although rural areas are mostly affected, there are poor people in both rural and urban areas. The poor communities are synonymous with a high rate of unemployment and a high level of informal economic activities as part of their livelihoods. Though activity in the informal economic sector mostly escapes **scrutiny** by tax collectors and population census officials, it contributes significantly to the economy and the local economic environment in poor communities.

The presence of infrastructure also gives an indication of the level of economic activity. In rural and in urban areas where the poor live, the infrastructure is most often either not developed or badly maintained. There are usually very few shops, workshops and factories present. Public transport is often inadequate and unaffordable to a significant number of the working class who (due to long commuting distances) spend no less than 30 per cent of their monthly income on transport. The economic environment poses some of the most difficult and **tangible** challenges not only to poor ordinary community members but to community leaders and CDPs as well.

2.3.5 Psychological environment

Psychological or behavioural factors operate simultaneously at individual, organisational and community level. From a psychological environment point of view, it is important to understand what motivates individuals to exhibit certain behaviours and participate in certain settings, including community development projects (Perkins, Hughey & Speer 2002). Across most big cities and towns in Africa (South Africa included), economic migrants from neighbouring states are growing in their numbers and their mere presence has huge implications for the available social and economic resources. Their presence also impacts on the psychology of the poorest, most marginalised and often unemployed local residents, and leads to xenophobic attitudes and conduct, as illustrated by the recent xenophobic attacks in Diepsloot township, Johannesburg, in April 2022 (Misago & Landau 2022). While the inhumane treatment and violence usually meted out against undocumented foreigners by 'Operation Dudula' cannot be condoned, the proliferation of community-based movements such as 'Operation Dudula' is indicative of a worrying current state of affairs in these poor communities. 'Operation Dudula' seems to have gained traction and is widely being embraced as a community structure through which the poor and unemployed community members can successfully address their current state of hopelessness, insecurity and fear, usually associated with a perceived takeover of their livelihoods and sense of belonging by illegal foreigners. Xenophobic sentiments also dominated the political speeches and campaigns of some political parties during the November 2021 local government elections (Misago & Landau 2022).

Lack of self-esteem is another psychological characteristic of people caught in a high rate of unemployment and poverty situation. They become more and more dependent on aid from the government or NGOs. Having experienced negative situations in the past, they are often distrustful of strangers and even people they know who might come up with new ideas.

2.4 CONCLUSION

Despite being contextual, the concept of development is universal. While responding to national development needs of citizens, the formulation and implementation of policies and programmes on development should be in alignment with global agendas and rules on development. World events such as the ongoing conflict in Ukraine have far-reaching implications, particularly for countries in the Third World. Besides global influences, development projects could also be impacted locally by, among others, level of involvement or participation by civil society organisations, ordinary community members and the calibre of CDPs. There could never be community development without community empowerment and participation. It is also evident that the cultural environment, political environment, economic environment, psychological environment and social environment are not only an integral part of development but also have a causal effect on the implementation of development programmes and projects.

The Millennium Development Goals (MDGs) have been replaced by the SDGs – Sustainable Development Goals 2015–2030 (United Nations 2019). In summary, the 17 SDGs are as follows:

1. End poverty.
2. End hunger.
3. Ensure health.
4. Ensure quality education.
5. Achieve gender equality.
6. Ensure water and sanitation for all.
7. Ensure energy for all.
8. Promote economic development and employment for all.
9. Build infrastructure to promote industrialisation.
10. Reduce inequality within and between cities.
11. Make human settlements inclusive and sustainable.
12. Ensure sustainable consumption.
13. Combat climate change.
14. Use the oceans sustainably.
15. Protect ecosystems and halt loss of biodiversity.
16. Promote peaceful societies by building effective institutions.
17. Revitalise the global partnership for sustainable development.

These 17 SDGs are supposed to level the playing field between countries from the south and the north (the developed world and the Third World), and are assumed to guide policy, implementation and funding up to 2030. The goal of the SDGs is to 'produce a set of universally applicable goals that balances the three dimensions of sustainable development: environmental, social, and economic' (UNDP 2022).

REFERENCES

Arora NK & Mishra I. 2019. United Nations Sustainable Development Goals 2030 and environmental sustainability: Race against time. *Environmental Sustainability*, 2:339–342.

Bhandari H & Yasunobu K. 2009. What is social capital? A comprehensive review of the concept. *Asian Journal of Social Science*, 37(3):480–510.

Dale A & Newman L. 2010. Social capital: A necessary and sufficient condition for sustainable community development. *Community Development Journal*, 45(1):5–21.

Daskon C & Binns T. 2010. Culture, tradition and sustainable rural livelihoods: Exploring the culture-development interface in Kandy, Sri Lanka. *Community Development Journal*, 45(4):494–517.

Del-Aguila-Arcentales S, Alvarez-Risco A, Jaramillo-Arevalo M, De-la-Cruz-Diaz M & Anderson-Seminario M. 2022. Influence of social, environmental and economic sustainable development goals over continuation of entrepreneurship and competitiveness. *Journal of Open Innovation*, 8(73):1–24.

Giampiccoli A & Kalis, JH. 2012. Community-based tourism and local culture: The case of amaMpondo. *Revista de Turismo y Patrimonio Cultural*, 10(1):173–188.

Gray M & Mubangizi B. 2010. Caught in the vortex: Can local government community development workers succeed in South Africa. *Community Development Journal*, 45(2):186–197.

Ferrer A. 1997. Development and underdevelopment in a globalized world: Latin American dilemmas. In Emmerij L (ed), *Economic and Social Development into the XXI Century*. Washington: Inter-American Development Bank, pp 178–188.

Filho WL, Levesque V, Sivapalan S, Salvia AL, Fritzen B, Deckert R, Kozlova V, LeVasseur TJ, Emblen-Perry K, Azeiteiro UM, Paco A, Borsari B & Shiel C. 2022. Social values and sustainable development: Community experiences. *Environmental Sciences Europe*, 34(67):1–13.

Huggins R & Thompson P. 2015. Culture and placed-based development: A socio-economic analysis. *Regional Studies*, 49(1):130–159.

Ife J. 2013. *Community Development in an Uncertain World*. New York: Cambridge University Press.

Maistry M. 2012. Towards professionalisation: Journey of community development in the African and South African context. *Africanus*, 42(2):29–41.

Misago JP & Landau LB. 2022. 'Running them out of time': Xenophobia, violence and co-authoring spatiotemporal exclusion in South Africa. *Geopolitics*. doi: 10.1080/14650045.2022.2078707

Mubita A, Libati M & Mulonda M. 2017. The importance and limitations of participation in development projects and programmes. *European Scientific Journal*, 13(5):238–251.

Mukarram M. 2020. Impact of COVID-19 on the UN Sustainable Development Goals (SDGs). *Strategic Analysis*, 44(3):253–258.

Nair N. 2022. Shallcross residents rebuild flood-ravaged bridge in five days. May, 9. *Sunday Times*, Johannesburg.

Ntema J. 2021. Relocation and informal settlement upgrading in South Africa: The case study of Mangaung township, Free State Province. In Nubi, T, Anderson, I, Oyalowo, B & Lawanson, T (eds), *Housing and SDGs in Urban Africa: Advances in 21st Century Human Settlements*. Singapore: Springer Nature, pp 177–192.

Perkins DD, Hughey J & Speer PW. 2002. Community psychology perspectives on social capital theory and community development practice. *Journal of the Community Development Society*, 33(1):33–52.

Sharman N. 1981. Community work and local economy: The Influence of the British community development projects. *Community Development Journal*, 16(2):142–147.

Shaw M. 2008. Community development and the politics of community. *Community Development Journal*, 43(1):24–36.

Shembe C. 2015. Community participation in the Zimbabwe community development association (ZCDA) ISAL project: A development communication perspective. Unpublished Masters thesis, University of KwaZulu-Natal, Durban.

Teryima AB. 2013. Poverty, inequality and underdevelopment in third world countries: Bad state policies or bad global rules? *IOSR Journal of Humanities and Social Science*, 15(6):33–38.

Tjarve B & Zemite I. 2016. The role of cultural activities in community development. *Acta Universitatis Agriculturae Et Silviculturae Mendelianae Brunensis*, 64(6):2151–2160.

UNDP (United Nations Development Programme) South Africa. 2022. Policy brief: The impact of the Ukraine war on the South African economy. Available at: https://www.undp.org/south-africa/publications/policy-brief-impact-ukraine-war-south-african-economy (accessed 25 April 2023).

United Nations. 2019. UN Sustainable Development Goals. Available at: https://sdgs.un.org/topics (accessed 25 April 2023).

United Nations. 2022. The Sustainable Development Goals report. Available at: https:// Sustainable Development (un.org) (accessed 25 April 2023).

Webber R & Jones, K. 2013. Implementing 'community development' in a post-disaster situation. *Community Development Journal*, 48(2):248–263.

Williams L. 2004. Culture and community development: Towards new conceptualizations and practice. *Community Development Journal*, 39(4):345–359.

World Bank. 2022. The impact of war in Ukraine on food security |World Bank expert answers. 5 April, YouTube. Available at: https://www.youtube.com/watch?v=GF0qRtxeR4Y (accessed 25 April 2023).

World Food Programme. 2022. War in Ukraine drives global food crisis. Available at: https://www.wfp.org/publications/war-ukraine-drives-global-food-crisis (accessed 25 April 2023).

CHAPTER 3

Stakeholders in Community Development

Frik de Beer

3.1 INTRODUCTION

A person or group's interest in achieving goals is what guides participation in action and projects. People interact in different ways with those around them and may belong to different groups or entities. Once they have an interest or stake in an activity or project, the individual or organisation becomes a stakeholder in it. According to Siswanto, Kridawati and Tomo (2017:43), the term stakeholder is used 'to describe communities or organizations that are permanently impacted by activities or policies, where they are interested in the outcome of such activities or policies'.

In community development, stakeholders can be identified at the levels of government, private sector, non-governmental organisations and community sector stakeholders. Strictly speaking, the community sector stakeholders are also in the non-governmental sector. Yet, because the community sector is so important, we classify and discuss them separately. Stakeholders can also be classified according to functional areas (or areas of analysis) such as cultural, political, economic, legal, social or psychological. We can, for example, classify the national Department of Social Development as a governmental institution working in the social functional area.

What this means is that the conduct of individuals, groups and organisations in society is regulated by socially agreed-upon rules and understandings, which may be recorded or not. Typically, then, the stakeholder organisation operates according to some laws, rules and guidelines, usually contained in constitutions, laws and operational procedures. In less formal organisations, such rules may not be in a written format, but the members would agree between themselves about the rules.

One stakeholder who deserves special attention is the community development practitioner (CDP). CDPs are 'cross-cutting' stakeholders, meaning that they are found in the public, private, non-governmental (NGO), community and social enterprise sectors. CDPs play an important part in networking and coordinating development activities in communities.

In addition to being able to identify and describe the various stakeholders, we also need to know about their interaction with one another, and the difficulties around such interaction or, as we call it here, collaboration. This chapter is consequently devoted to introducing the various types of stakeholders and providing an overview of the ways of coordinating, through collaboration, the development activities and projects of stakeholders.

3.2 IDENTIFYING STAKEHOLDERS

A stakeholder, or role-player, in poverty eradication is a person, a group or an institution that performs a certain task. A stakeholder may be actively doing something or may have an untapped potential to perform a function. An active stakeholder is, for instance, a school, a town clerk, a utility supplier (for example, electricity), a church group or a civic organisation. To outsiders, some stakeholders may not seem to be doing anything, but they have the potential for action, for example informal organisations like stokvels. A stokvel is a rotating savings and credit mutual aid group. Members make their own rules, regularly contribute and receive whole or part of the fund on a rotation basis at regular intervals (Hossein 2017:30).

In Kenya, the Chama, 'a group of people with a common interest in coming together', plays a role similar to stokvels (Kilongi 2011). In reality, these stakeholders are, or may become, active in their own way in poverty alleviation and eradication.

Stakeholders may be classified into four main groups or sectors: public sector, private sector, NGO sector, and popular or community-based sector.

3.2.1 Public sector stakeholders

The public sector consists of national, provincial and local government. The national government is organised according to broad functional areas with departments dealing with issues such as social development, land affairs, environmental affairs, water affairs, forestry and agriculture.

Provincial government has certain specified competencies at provincial level. In South Africa, provincial government has competencies over functional areas such as education, health and road-works. To perform these functions, specific departments are established.

In South Africa, local government has wide-ranging powers and responsibilities for, among others, social and people development, local economic development and also – in the metropoles – local policing.

Parastatals (for example, Eskom and water regulators such as the Rand Water Board) provide utility services. While they form part of the public sector, their services are usually commercialised; this means they aim to at least recover the cost of services provided.

3.2.2 Private sector stakeholders

The private sector consists of stakeholders or groups active in commerce, industry and mining. Here we find industries, or factories, which manufacture consumer goods. Commerce, consisting of shops, banks and services such as dry cleaning and motor repairs, also fall within the private sector. Commerce and industry associations such as the National African Federated Chamber of Commerce (NAFCOC) are important stakeholders in this sector.

Apart from big corporations, the private sector contains small, medium and micro-enterprises (SMMEs). In South Africa, it is estimated that 91 per cent of all business enterprises are SMMEs, which contribute almost 55 per cent of the gross domestic product (GDP) and employ 61 per cent of the country's labour force (Abor and Quartey, quoted in National Credit Regulator (NCR) 2011:7). SMMEs may be part of the formal economy, meeting legal registration requirements, or they may be part of the informal economic sector.

Some authors argue that the informal sector (for example, hawkers, shebeens or sex workers) also fall within the private sector. While privately owned enterprises in this sector are usually small, they are not regulated by laws and are poorly developed. In the Tshwane area, for instance, only 15 per cent of the entrepreneurs in this sector make a profit equal to, or slightly higher than, the minimum level of living (MLL) of R2 000 in 2005 (*Beeld* 2005:21).

3.2.3 Non-government (civil society) stakeholders

This sector consists of organisations that are not in any way dependent on or responsible to either the public or private sectors. Usually, NGOs come into existence to address specific problems, for example health, education or housing. More often, though, they address a number of problems in the field of development. Examples of NGO or civil society stakeholders are local government associations; development institutions; international, national and local development organisations, and advocacy organisations such as the Treatment Action Campaign (TAC) in South Africa. Mazibuko (2020:25) lobbies for cooperation between civil society and government, contending that community development would depend on 'the ideology of the state which is the vanguard in the development process'. In support of Mazibuko (2020), Maathai (2009:18) calls for 'engagement in grassroots democracy and the strengthening of civil society, so people's energies can be released to shape their own lives and development priorities, and governments can support them in realizing their vision'.

NGOs have social or economic development aims and are non-profit organisations. They depend on grants from large corporations and government aid agencies, and donations from the public.

3.2.4 Popular or community-based sector stakeholders

The popular sector, also called the community-based sector, consists of organisations founded and run by individuals or groups within communities. Examples of community-based organisations (CBOs) are:
- clubs such as women's clubs, youth clubs, ratepayers' associations, farmers' co-operatives, burial societies and sports clubs
- faith-based groupings such as choirs, prayer groups and care groups
- more formal organisations such as clinic committees and school committees
- political associations, groupings and parties, and traditional leaders and structures.

CBOs are at the grassroots level and grapple daily with issues of development. In the approach to community development used in this book, they are considered the small groups and the building blocks around which 'community' can be identified.

3.2.5 Social enterprise sector stakeholders

A more recent development is the emergence of what is called the social enterprise sector. One way of looking at social enterprise is to say that it attempts to unify business principles with social **ventures**. According to Martin and Osberg (2007), understanding the concept of 'social entrepreneur' depends on understanding what an entrepreneur is. They view an entrepreneur as a person with 'an exceptional ability to see and seize upon new opportunities, the commitment and drive required to pursue them, and an unflinching willingness to bear the inherent risks' (Martin & Osberg 2007:31). Defourney and Nyssens (2017:2472) assert that the driving force behind the social enterprise sector is not profit; the focus is primarily on social challenges, to address social aims.

To get to a definition of social enterprise, Martin and Osberg distinguish social activism (for example, the Ghandian movement) from social service provision (a school or clinic). Whereas social activism works on a grand scale, attempting to change the equilibrium of social service delivery to have it replaced by something better (but at a large scale), social service delivery works within the equilibrium and attempts to alleviate and assist with social development issues (Martin & Osberg 2007:32).

Social entrepreneurship combines the grand scale of social activism, within the social field, with the drive and risk taking of an entrepreneur. The social entrepreneur works in the social field but attempts on a grand scale (and taking the accompanying risk) to make changes that will disturb the equilibrium and create a new equilibrium at a higher level of services. Alonso, Kok and O'Brian (2020, quoting Christopoulos & Vogl 2015) say that 'social entrepreneurs are perceived as actors simultaneously playing civic, economic and political roles while aiming to increase general welfare through their services or products'.

According to their definition of the social entrepreneur, Martin and Osberg (2007:39) say that the social entrepreneur should be understood:

> ... as someone who targets an unfortunate but stable equilibrium that causes the neglect, marginalization, or suffering of a segment of humanity; who brings to bear on this situation his or her inspiration, direct action, creativity, courage, and fortitude; and who aims for and ultimately affects the establishment of a new stable equilibrium that secures permanent benefit for the targeted group and society at large.

The Grameen Bank in Bangladesh is cited as an example of a social enterprise because it has social development aims, works with and for poor people, but uses business principles to achieve its objectives. The social enterprise sector is thus a hybrid, lying somewhere between the private sector and the NGO sector.

3.3 THE ORGANISATION AS AN ENABLER OF COMMUNITY DEVELOPMENT

Stakeholders (institutions) responsible for working towards an enabling environment, including policy making, work in an uncertain and ever-changing environment. These institutions should therefore be of a special orientation to be successful in their quest. Their orientation should be one of readiness to adapt to ever-changing situations. In a community development context where sustainable livelihood is the objective, Cafer, Green and Goreham (2019:201–202) argue that for community development to succeed, an adaptive approach is required to promote community resilience to shock. 'Community resilience involves, first, having the capacity to recover from previous debilitating events, but it also requires building adaptive capacity to prevent or withstand future events' (Cafer et al 2019:206).

Adaptiveness is a concept which you will meet throughout this book. It is in direct contradiction to blueprint planning (see Chapter 21 for a detailed discussion of the different approaches to planning). An adaptive approach requires complete organisational and procedural changes. Management should be fluid, open to change and adaptable. Structures should give space for manoeuvring and should be flexible, allowing new actions where and when necessary.

An adaptive orientation will identify the following necessities in order to ensure an enabling environment for CDPs (Rondinelli 1993:158):

- *Adjusting planning procedures and methods of administration to the political dynamics of local policy making.* Circumstances differ from one area to another; stakeholders also differ. While national policies such as the Integrated Development Plan (IDP) give guidelines and steps to follow, these must be applied flexibly to suit local circumstances.
- *Increasing the responsiveness of bureaucracies engaged in development activities.* This means networking and personal contact with relevant stakeholders from all spheres: government, private sector, NGOs and

CBOs. Since CDPs do not have power to force responsiveness, other methods, such as good interpersonal skills, must be used.

- *Adopting a learning approach to planning and administration.* This will allow communities to participate and learn by doing. CDPs must be actively aware of their role and responsibility in facilitating learning by community members.
- *Developing widespread and appropriate forms of administrative capacity.* This must be done within the community and its committees.
- *Decentralising authority for development planning and administration.* CDPs are not the leaders and decision makers in the community. They must **foster** capacity and provide information for the community leadership to become masters of their own development planning and administration.
- *Relying on* **adjunctive** *and strategic rather than comprehensive and control-oriented planning.* CDPs invariably work in communities trapped in deprivation (see Chapter 1). They therefore work with people exposed to uncertainty and fear, with few resources available for 'development'. In this situation, comprehensive planning will fail as there is no guarantee that a project will be completed successfully. CDPs know where they are going (thus have a blueprint in mind) and will know how to communicate and achieve the end result through adjunctive and strategic planning. They will also be prepared to adapt the 'blueprint' as required by circumstances.
- *Encouraging error detection and correction rather than suppression and punishment.* When working with people, this is a most important guideline to which to adhere. The operational strategy must be clear on corrective measures to be taken when error is discovered. As important as detection and correction are, sometimes punishment may be called for if mistakes are made on purpose. The strategy also needs to deal with the nuts and bolts of punishment within a community group.

Sustainable and **equitable** community development requires strengthening administrative capacity of relevant institutions. It implies expanding participation, strengthening a wide variety of public and private organisations, and increasing the access of individuals to resources and opportunities. Case study 11: *The project that was taken over* illustrates the enabling organisation doing too much and going in the wrong direction.

3.4 FINDING WAYS TO COORDINATE COMMUNITY DEVELOPMENT

All or most of the stakeholders identified above will be found in any community. They all have an interest, or stake, in proposed or intended poverty alleviation and eradication projects. The government official, be it a professional or CDP or the **altruistic** NGO approaching a community to facilitate development, must be sure to establish clearly who the stakeholders are and promote their participation in identifying, planning, implementing and evaluating any development project in the area. In addition, stakeholders must be brought together, and systems designed and implemented that harness them, focus energies and make possible collaboration between them and coordination of all their efforts.

Acceptable and applicable mechanisms for the coordination of community development should be based on knowledge gained from the literature that reflects mostly on the practical situation, practical examples from research and experience, and the needs and experiences of the relevant stakeholders. To be successful, it should be appropriate to the empirical reality and be backed by policy and political support. In general, very few of these inputs exist. The literature on the co-ordination of community development mostly speaks about collaboration, but we use cooperation and collaboration interchangeably.

Government bureaucracies are legally and functionally set up in silos. They operate on the principle of competition and independence. The nature of business (private sector) also requires them to be independent and competitive. While non-governmental organisations exist for altruistic reasons (to serve some just cause), they also operate independently and in competition with other NGOs. In this context of competition and independence, communities attempt development actions and projects to meet their aspirations. The question is how to get the actors out of their silos, united in a collaborative way of doing projects.

One way of getting cooperation going and of coordinating development activities is through networks. According to Agranoff (2006:56), a collaborative network includes all structures cooperating in 'the act of working jointly with others, usually to resolve a problem or find a corner of activity'. Mandell, Keast and Chamberlain (2017:326) are of the opinion that complex social and public problems confronting society can be best addressed through collaborative networks. These networks ought to bring together people and organisations that differ, but the network should also 'mould these people and their resources into a different functioning entity underpinned by new ways of thinking, talking and behaving'.

Collaborative networks can be organised in terms of formal statutory requirements, or they can be 'informal in legal status but equally permanent, organized, and mission oriented' (Agranoff 2006:56).

A network is a set of relationships (Kadushin 2009:14) between two or more people. By extension, a social network connects people in an area or who share ideas or interests. The network we are talking about, however, is different. The development network we have in mind has very specific goals involving two or more organised groups (institutions) working toward a shared goal or goals. They must therefore work in a collaborative way to coordinate activities and projects.

3.4.1 Understanding the environment in which coordination must take place

It is clear that the environment is tremendously complicated. In fact, there are various environments with different political, social, cultural, economic and psychological realities (see Chapter 2). This complexity makes it important to know the environment in detail, to know the role players, the situations and the potential conflicts. Through coordination, a seemingly unworkable situation must be made to work, a potentially explosive situation must be defused, and the diversity of stakeholders must be utilised in a positive manner to the greatest advantage of local people.

We can say that the following principles should form a basis for identifying a coordination strategy:

- Coordination is an essential management function and tool in a varied and complex environment.
- There is a firm commitment to a transparent and effective relationship with all stakeholders and impacted audiences.
- Accountability to the people in a local government area is a key element of a coordination strategy.
- There is a commitment to empowering target audiences.
- The coordination strategy must be seen at all times as part of a wider strategy.

- An analysis of the coordination environment and the challenges that the coordination strategy must concentrate on and have certain priorities. These priorities will be determined by the stakeholders and the way in which those in power (politicians and officials) relate to local communities and civil society.

In more detail, these themes are as follows:
- All three spheres of government forge partnerships with communities to act decisively in order to improve their lives.
- Community participation is key to equity, efficiency and sustainability of local government.
- Community development is the key to socio-economic development in the municipal or local area.

These principles and themes are **cemented** by forging linkages and networks. Linkages are more than mere coordination activities. While they are forged through collaboration and quite often kept alive through coordination, they are more than just that. They are structures that must be created and formalised. A linkage can consist of a loose organisation with, say, one meeting per month, or it can be a partnership to share information on the internet. Linkages can consist of focus groups, or beehives, for relevant local government institutions that are not necessarily part of the institutions but interact with them in various ways. The important aspect in this case is that some linkage/network structure must exist and be used. This structure must also fit the situation, in other words, it must conform to the criterion of appropriateness.

With the diverse nature of the target audiences in mind, any collaboration structure or network must be innovative and include all stakeholders.

3.4.2 Preparing the way for collaboration: establishing discussion forums

The establishment and management of forums must be a participatory process through the medium of workshops followed by small task teams to each attend to a specific aspect of the brief. Guidelines must be formulated and agreed upon by all stakeholders involved.

Once forums have been established, they begin a survival struggle that can last for a long time. It is important to realise that groups such as forums are naturally frail and that they need, among others, support to continue to exist, never mind make a success of their task. It needs knowledge and understanding of the psychology and dynamics of such groups to facilitate them. (See Chapter 11 for more on group dynamics.)

3.4.3 Constraints and barriers to collaboration

Practical examples of successful collaboration are not well documented. Empirical reality in South Africa was, and still is, in flux and a policy and political support for coordinating community development is only now in the process of taking shape.

When designing mechanisms for coordinating community development, three simple but very important questions must be asked and clearly answered:

1. Who are the stakeholders that need to collaborate?
2. Who are the owners of the envisaged development?
3. What is community development?

The answer to the first question will vary from one situation to another, but generally speaking, the stakeholders will include a community group; local, regional and central government; NGOs, and the private sector.

However, only if agreement on the answers to the second and third questions is reached, can we make headway in determining appropriate mechanisms for coordinating community development. Regardless of the **rhetoric** to the contrary, politicians, officials, aid agencies and private sector stakeholders often regard development projects as 'theirs' and not belonging to the affected community. As long as this spirit prevails and as long as communities are not allowed to take ownership of community development projects, efforts at developing acceptable and applicable mechanisms of collaboration will fail.

Furthermore, in many circles, community development is still perceived as a line function, that is creating clubs and promoting sewing and knitting classes for 'idle women'. Community development as a process of empowerment (as we argue in Chapter 6) to be applied by all professionals in line functions, needs to be recognised before any attempt at coordinating community development will succeed. When ownership belongs to the people, the matter of coordination will become less of an issue. Development will not belong to a ministry or other line functionary, and therefore the duty, and power, of establishing coordination will not lie with any of them, but with the community.

3.4.4 Practices of collaboration in community development

Due to a perception that attempts at coordination have mostly failed, the concept is used less often in recent literature. Authors more frequently use the concept collaboration. In this chapter no attempt will be made to debate the philosophical and analytical differences between them; we rather use them as synonyms, with the meaning of a framework for **collective** development action (Selsky 1991).

The literature on coordination deals with principles, preconditions and stumbling blocks on a macro level. Coordination of development projects is dealt with in some detail, but inter-agency co-ordination receives scant attention (Blunt 1990; Cusworth & Franks 1993; Franks 1989; Honadle & Cooper 1989). As Selsky (1991) says, 'Development in inter-organisational settings is poorly conceptualised in the literature'. Case studies and analysis of coordination are rarely found in the literature.

The available literature shows that coordination cannot be enforced. At the same time it cannot be successful without certain structures in place (Khosa 1991). However, the mere existence of structures is not a guarantee for coordination. Mandell et al (2017:328) succinctly outline the challenge of collaboration: 'The emphasis in collaborative networks, instead of being on securing resources while protecting organizational boundaries, is on breaking down boundaries through enhancing trusting relationships and realizing that each organization is only one piece of a new entity'.

The work of Lippitt and Van Til (1981) gives a useful framework for developing mechanisms for coordination. They identify a number of constraints or barriers to coordination, or 'collaboration' as they put it. These are the following:

- Organisations and institutions are kept apart to maintain fair play.
- An ethos exists in which competition and independence is the rule (see also Agranoff 2006).

- It takes so much time and effort to establish coordination that it is regarded by many as not worth the trouble.
- Institutions survive because they maintain their turf.
- In society emphasis is put on the individual's rights and a strong ego is built.
- The idea of negotiation and compromise is seen as negative.
- The bad name of the 'committee' is a way to express distrust in coordination.

A further constraint is that of communication. The one factor that makes coordination succeed or fail is the inability of people to communicate.

These constraints are all present in any given situation. Add to that the sectorally or functionally structured (in silos) government institutions, and it becomes obvious why coordination is such a difficult goal to achieve (Swanepoel 1986:49). Holdcroft (1982:222) talks of this separateness of institutions as the 'battle of departments' which renders coordination, let alone integration, impossible.

Yet, coordination is an absolute necessity if one thinks of community development as a total transformation. If this holistic character of development is recognised and acknowledged, if it is accepted that it should touch the total **milieu** and the hearts and minds of people, 'all the participating organisations, be they governmental or private, [will] have the same goals and objectives which they strive to obtain through an interrelated and integrated programme' (Swanepoel 1985:101).

Lippitt and Van Til (1981) suggest a six-step process to achieve coordination. The six steps are as follows:

Step 1: Establish the preconditions for collaboration

Coordination begins with a vision or idea of how something will be better if two or more organisations work together. Without this vision, coordination will not materialise. The initiation of coordinative activity is both a highly personal and **idiosyncratic** event with structural determinants.

Step 2: Test the collaborative waters

The articulation of coordinative potential must be followed by a fuller exploration of the idea's viability. Four tests are suggested in this regard: assuring that the proposed coordination does not threaten organisational domain; assuring that the proposed coordination does not threaten organisational **autonomy**; sketching an image of potential domain **consensus**; and checking limits of pre-existing coordinative networks.

Step 3: Initiate the idea of collaboration

From the very first conversation that broaches the idea of collaboration, attention must be given to the mood and setting of the exploratory discussion. If parties to the proposed coordination do not see it as a necessary way of problem solving, they will not easily become part of the process.

Step 4: Define the collaborative venture

Clear definitions of member and team roles need to be developed. Coordination will work best if a clearly identifiable coordinative team can be developed. As this team comes into existence, it must be able to show that it can act independently of the several organisational loyalties its members carry. As they learn to trust and work with each other, the group begins to draw a social contract of their coordinative venture.

Step 5: Invigorate the collaborative process

Coordination has its low points and pitfalls. Surmounting them requires insight, patience, sensitivity and perspective. There are two things that are playing a role in the invigoration of collaboration. They are the following:
1. The greater the complementarity of functions between the collaborative venture and the individual members, the greater the likelihood of coordinated action.
2. The larger the collaborating group, the more likely it is that an uncooperative coalition will develop within it.

Step 6: Evaluate the collaborative experience

Collaborative ventures should be evaluated even more frequently than more established organisational ventures. The validity of the initial idea that brought the coordination into existence requires renewal and review.

This whole process is fascinating and thought provoking when we consider the South African situation. The reason why coordination is so often a failure in this country lies perhaps in the fact that the care with establishing collaboration, as suggested above, has to a large extent been absent. We could surmise from this that the ground for collaboration must be carefully prepared; that the coordination venture must be nurtured all the time; that the venture should not be a threat to any participating organisation; and that collaboration must be absolutely necessary before it is attempted.

To the above we can add a seventh step, that of *establishing a legal body such as a trust for facilitating collaboration*. To establish a legal body, the following should be considered:

- Investigate the desirability of one legal body community, district or municipality.
- Investigate the legal ramifications and requirements for establishing such a body.
- Investigate and list the functions to be performed by the legal body.
- Establish the legal body in terms of the guidelines gleaned from the previous steps.

If community development is owned by the community, it is important that supportive and enabling organisations work together as a team. It is also important to note that if the ownership of projects is in the hands of the community, the community will be the initiator of collaboration. This means that the community will have to follow the suggestions made by Lippitt and Van Til (1981). This may be a **daunting** task which will require careful thought and study. In the absence of community initiative, it may fall to the CDP to play an enabling role in promoting and establishing collaboration.

In 2018, North Carolina University published *Working Together: A Guide to Collaboration in Rural Revitalization*, which shows remarkable similarity to Selsky's model. Their model is divided into three main themes: (1) coming together, (2) staying together and (3) growing together. Coming together is based on a shared geographical location, shared connection and shared concerns and objectives. The shared location is a place: it may be a town, a school or a clinic. The connection is formed by relationships between people and may include the overarching social capital present in communities. Shared concerns and objectives is the 'oil' smoothing efforts at collaboration (Savage, Brune, Hovis et al 2018:1–2).

Collaboration is divided into three phases: (1) defining the problem, (2) analysing constraints and opportunities, and (3) agreeing on an action plan. Yet to succeed, the following preconditions should be met: (1) include all stakeholders with an interest in solving the problem or issue, (2) foster social assets, (3) build trust, and (4) identify and build leadership. The CDP should, however, heed the following:

'Successful collaboration focuses on superordinate, or long-term, goals of the engaged stakeholders while pushing aside their differences and varying backgrounds to look at what they have in common' (Savage et al 2018:3).

CDPs should guide and assist empowered communities to take ownership of their own development by also creating collaborative ventures around shared interests and objectives.

3.5 CONCLUSION

CDPs never work in isolation. There are always a number of stakeholders present in any development environment. Hopefully, most of them will be friendly, but there may be a few who are not. Much of the coordination problems of the past and also the present are the result of a misplaced view by many of the stakeholders from the government, private and non-governmental cadres that development projects belong to them. It then becomes a turf war in the development environment, with the **concomitant** lack of any collaboration, the duplication of activities and expenses, and quite often the bewilderment of those who are supposed to be the owners of projects – the community. However, even if all agree that the projects belong to the people, it will still be difficult to establish collaboration and to develop it. Wisdom and tenacity are needed to be successful.

Case study 20: *The story of KwaMpofu* gives an idea of the various stakeholders present in a specific area and the presence and lack of collaboration at the same time.

The community at large is the most important stakeholder in poverty alleviation. The community knows its own assets, needs, resources and capabilities. It is the community that will win – or lose – the most in any attempt at development or poverty eradication.

REFERENCES

Agranoff R. 2006. Inside collaborative networks: ten lessons for public managers. *Public Administration Review*, Special Issue, December:76–88.

Alonso AD, Kok SK & O'Brien S. 2020. 'Profit is not a dirty word': Social entrepreneurship and community development. *Journal of Social Entrepreneurship*, 11(1):11–23.

Beeld. 2005. Meeste informele sake oorleef nét. 26 January: 21.

Blunt P. 1990. Strategies for enhancing organisational effectiveness in the Third World. *Public Administration and Development*, 10(3):299–313.

Cafer A, Green J & Goreham G. 2019. A community resilience framework for community development practitioners building equity and adaptive capacity. *Community Development*, 50(2):201–216.

Cusworth JW & Franks TR (eds). 1993. *Managing Projects in Developing Countries*. Essex: Longman.

Defourny J & Nyssens M. 2017. Fundamentals for an international typology of social enterprise models. *Voluntas*, 28(6):2469–2497.

Franks TR. 1989. Bureaucracy, organisation culture and development. *Public Administration and Development*, 9(4):357–368.

Grassroots Collective (GC). 2022. *Using a stakeholder analysis to identify key local actors*. Available at: https://www.thegrassrootscollective.org/stakeholder-analysis-nonprofit (accessed 24 October 2022).

Holdcroft LE. 1982. The rise and fall of community development in developing countries, 1950–1965: A critical analysis and implications. In Jones G & Rolls M (eds), *Progress in Rural Extension and Community Development, Vol. 1: Extension and Relative Advantage in Rural Development*. Chichester: John Wiley, pp 207–231.

Honadle G & Cooper L. 1989. Beyond coordination and control: An interorganizational approach to structural adjustment, service delivery and natural resource management. *World Development*, 17(10):1531–1541.

Hossein CS. 2017. Fringe banking in Canada: A study of rotating savings and credit associations (ROSCAs) in Toronto's inner suburbs. *Canadian Journal of Nonprofit and Social Economy Research*, 8(1):29–43.

Kadushin C. 2009. *Understanding Social Networks: Theories, Concepts and Findings*. New York: Oxford University Press.

Khosa JHM. 1991. Coordination in social development in order to combat poverty for the reconstructed society – a rural perspective. *Maatskaplike Werk/Social Work*, 27(3/4).

Kilongi M. 2011. Chama the best choice for tjommies. *Mail & Guardian*, 18–24 March.

Lippitt R & Van Til J. 1981. Can we achieve a collaborative community? *Journal of Voluntary Action Research*, 10(3/4).

Maathai W. 2009. *The Challenge for Africa*. London: Arrow Books.

Mandell M, Keast R & Chamberlain D. 2017. Collaborative networks and the need for a new management language. *Management Review*, 19(3):326–341.

Martin RL & Osberg S. 2007. Social entrepreneurship: The case for definition. *Stanford Social Innovation Review*, Spring:29–39.

Mduduzi JK. 2018. *The Role of Stokvels in the Economic Transformation of Ethekwini Municipality*. DBA thesis, University of KwaZulu-Natal, Durban.

NCR (National Credit Regulator). 2011. *Literature Review on Small and Medium Enterprises' Access to Credit and Support in South Africa*. Pretoria: National Credit Regulator.

Rondinelli DA. 1993. *Development Projects as Policy Experiments: An Adaptive Approach to Development Administration*. 2nd ed. London: Routledge.

Savage A, Brune S, Hovis M, Spencer SE, Dinan M & Seekamp E. 2018. *Working Together: A Guide to Collaboration and Revitalization*. Chapel Hill: North Carolina University.

Selsky JW. 1991. Lessons in community development: An activist approach to stimulating interorganizational collaboration. *Journal of Applied Behavioral Science*, March 27:91–115.

Siswanto B, Kridawati S & Tomo Y. 2017. Community participation and stakeholders in village fund management. *Journal of Economics and Sustainable Development*, 8(20).

Swanepoel HJ. 1985. Some guidelines for rural development in southern Africa. *Africa Insight*, 15(2):99–102.

Swanepoel HJ. 1986. Participation as principle in rural development. Inaugural lecture. Pretoria: University of South Africa.

SECTION B

The Process of Community Development

CHAPTER 4
The Origins of Community Development

Frik de Beer

4.1 INTRODUCTION

Historically, a number of key themes stand out which can be tied to the history of community development. These are, inter alia, participation, empowerment, project management, training, community, coordination and funding. These themes formed the debating points around which the 'idea' of community development evolved and developed. Attempting to define community development, Smart (2017) says that it is 'a process where community members are supported by agencies to identify and take collective action on issues which are important to them'. We, however, do not attempt to define the concept but rather identify principles of community development, as tools for analysis (see Chapter 6).

This, then, is what the history of community development points out: in spite of attempts over the past 50 years by practitioners and academics to give meaning to the concept, no generally accepted definition of community development has evolved. What did happen, however, was that ideas about development crystallised into what were regarded as radical viewpoints some years ago, but are now the accepted approach to poverty eradication.

4.2 EARLY HISTORY

The practice of what we may loosely call community development dates back to the history of the early civilisations when mankind initiated actions from which groups or parts of groups benefited in some or other way. According to Chile (2012:43), it evolved from practice over thousands of years '… in Africa and other countries, including western European countries'. However, we are interested in the more recent origin of community development, which is attributed by some American authors to the practice of agricultural extension, instituted in 1870 in some midwestern states of the US (De Beer & Swanepoel 2013:2).

Phifer, List and Faulkner (1980:19–20) give a different explanation of the origin of community development. According to them, it originated in the US in 1908 with the Country Life Commission report and the 1914 Smith-Lever Act, in terms of which the Co-operative Extension Service came into being. With this exercise, the aim was to establish community organisation in order to promote better living, better farming, more education, more happiness and better citizenship. According to Cornwell (1986:12), the aims of the Co-operative Extension Service concur with the aims attributed in recent literature to community development, although the development of leadership did not feature.

While these community organisation efforts remind us of community development, a more realistic starting point for explaining the origin of community development is perhaps the attempts by the Institute for Rural Reconstruction, created in 1921 in India.

The aim of this institute was:

> ... to bring back life in all its completeness, making the villagers self-reliant and self-respectful, acquainted with the cultural tradition of their own country and competent to make an efficient use of modern resources for the fullest development of their physical, social, economic and intellectual conditions *(Brokensha & Hodge 1969:40–41).*

This programme emphasised the use of local resources and the need for an integrated approach toward development. The Gandhian rural reconstruction experiment, which started in 1931, was similar in approach to the Institute for Rural Reconstruction, with an emphasis on self-sufficiency and attitude change as prerequisites for community development (Brokensha & Hodge 1969:41).

The British Colonial Office incorporated the gist of the rural reconstruction programmes into subsequent colonial development approaches. It was, however, not until 1944 that this policy took shape. Community development formed an important part of British colonial policy, not only in India but also in the African colonies. By the end of the 1940s, the term community development was in use worldwide. By then it was used to denote government programmes aimed at the stimulation of local initiative for community self-development efforts (Cornwell 1986:16).

According to Monaheng (2000:126), influences on the character of community development came from the launching of India's community development programme after its independence in 1947; this occurrence also stimulated community development efforts in neighbouring Asian countries and further afield in the Third World.

To Korten (1980:481), it was a Ford Foundation funded project in the Ettawah district of Uttar Pradesh, India in 1948 that brought community development into prominence in the late and post-colonial era. This pilot project involved 64 villages and established the village-level worker as a key role player. The Ettawah project concentrated on increasing productivity in agricultural and local industry. It also addressed needs of the local population like education, health and sanitation. The spectacular success of the project (an increase of 165 per cent in production in the first four years) was attributed to the problem-oriented framework within which needs were identified, the strong personality of the project leader and the fact that carefully selected and well-trained officials were responsible for implementation.

The success of the Ettawah project contributed to the establishment of India's national development programme which, with American aid, was launched in 1952. The programme's eventual failure was measured in terms of its inability to encourage community initiative and a failure to develop local leadership. In the end, the elite benefited more than the poor villagers at whom the programme was initially aimed (Holdcroft 1987, in De Beer & Swanepoel 2013:4).

The popularity of community development reached a peak during the 1950s and 1960s. This period coincided with the time of the Cold War, a period during which the US regarded community development as a tool or method through which democracy could be established and communism kept at bay. In Greece, Korea and Burma, community development programmes were used in the reconstruction of community facilities, the creation of jobs for demobilised soldiers and to combat poverty (Cornwell 1986:17).

By the early 1960s, community development programmes were in place in more than 60 countries, and in more than half of those countries the community development programmes represented the national development efforts. This was perhaps reason for its problems later on. Community development did not work as well on the macro level as it did on the micro level.

Before 1994, the then South African government used the rhetoric of community development to disguise the paternalistic, top–down and abusive aspects of the apartheid policy as *developmental*. In the 1980s, it established a Community Development Committee to promote community development in the homelands as part of its strategy to 'win the hearts and minds' of the people, however it was nothing more but the same. During the same period, non-governmental organisations such as Grassroots Educare Trust, the Transvaal Rural Action Committee (TRAC) and the Soweto Crisis Committee emerged as community-based organisations operating in the sphere of the United Democratic Front (De Beer & Swanepoel, 2013:7–8).

Section 52 of the Constitution of South Africa 1996 states that one of the objectives of local government is 'to encourage the involvement of communities and community organisations in the matters of local government'. The current government demonstrates its rhetorical allegiance to community development simultaneously with its underperformance in practice. What now happens at local level is best described as consultation, a form of involvement that Arnstein (1969:217) typifies as tokenism rather than real participation. In an evaluation of the role of community development practitioners in municipal wards, Davids and Cloete (2012:94) asserted, for example, that community development practitioners' primary focus was supporting communities to access government services. It is clear that there is much room for improvement. Real participation leaves no room for tokenism because the participants themselves control processes, decisions and outcomes in an environment of scarce resources. See Chapter 25 for a discussion outlining the legislative framework for community development in South Africa.

4.3 A CHANGE OF FOCUS: FROM CO-OPTION TO COMMUNITY-INITIATED ACTION

Community development programmes were not nearly as successful as was envisaged and this lack of success forced academics, officials and policy makers to think again. Disappointment with the lack of success with community development led to the emergence of 'new' or 'alternative' approaches. On closer scrutiny it becomes apparent, however, that the new approaches basically represented a change in emphasis on the themes underlying community development (Swanepoel 1985, in De Beer & Swanepoel 2013:5).

The early practice of community development emphasised the means or method to bring about change. *Method* is consequently one of the themes constantly present in the earlier writings on community development. The method usually entailed the use of a change agent such as a community development practitioner (CDP) who had the aim of stimulating participation of 'the community' in development projects. Most often, such projects were decided on and planned by 'outsiders' – be it government agents or non-governmental organisations (NGOs) – who decided on the needs of the community. To these people, community development was a method and a tool to bring about 'desired change' according to their view. Put differently, it was an attempt to co-opt, in a friendly way, poor people to *participate* in projects decided on, planned and managed by outsider agencies.

In reaction to this emphasis, others saw community development as a process in which local (or community) groups took the initiative to formulate objectives involving changes in their living conditions (Roberts 1979:39). We can see that the process idea gives more initiative and freedom to the ordinary people to begin a process, while the method idea wants the change agent to apply a certain method in order to generate the necessary result (De Beer & Swanepoel 1998:4).

Roberts' idea of community development as a process stemming from community initiative was supported by others such as Brokensha and Hodge (1969:48), who argued that community development is 'the educational process by which people change themselves and their behavior and acquire new skills and confidence through working in cooperation'. Yet, even if this process approach seemed liberal, the emphasis was still wrong if judged in terms of our views today. The onus was on the poor to change, and not primarily their situation, but their behaviour. Nothing or very little was made of the approach and objective of CDPs and whoever they represented. Even when the radical approach to community development was professed, the action of external organisations and groups remained paternalistic. As Botes and Van Rensburg (2000:43) put it: 'Often, professional experts dominate decision making and manipulate, instead of facilitate, development processes'.

Over time, the method/process debate became stale and lost its vigour. In subsequent debates on community development, the focus moved more toward the question of whether the community was the master or client in development.

In the mid-1970s, a variation on the theme of community development occurred when the basic needs approach (BNA) was developed by the World

Bank and the International Labour Organization (ILO). With this change in emphasis came a broader concern to eradicate poverty and a shift from a preoccupation with means to a renewed awareness of ends. According to Cornwell (1986:23), this shift represented a radical change from emphasising the *method* to emphasising the attainment of concrete objectives identified by the poor. In other words, we were again dealing with method and process.

The BNA attached fundamental importance to poverty eradication within a short period as one of the main objectives of development. It defined poverty, not in terms of income, but as the inability to meet certain basic human needs on the part of identifiable groups of human beings. Poverty was characterised by hunger and malnutrition, by ill health, and by lack of education, safe water, sanitation and decent shelter. A vital aspect of the elimination of poverty, then, was securing access to these goods and services for the poor. In spite of its focus on grassroots level, however, the BNA was still perceived as a top–down approach of involving people, rather than allowing them decision-making powers. Reader (2006:339) correctly observed that, 'Recipients, given little opportunity to identify their own needs, felt patronised'.

While focusing on the *what* (basic needs), the BNA never really developed a methodology of how to achieve the satisfaction of basic needs. The BNA also focused on needs, an approach which was criticised for looking at the negative. As a response, the asset-based approach focused on the positive – on what communities had and could do in their own development (see discussion below). Consequently, in the early 1980s, the BNA lost its appeal as a separate approach toward the development of Third World/ poor communities. It fulfilled the role of a guiding principle and objective. It surfaced again, however, as part of the more elaborate people-centred approach, which we will discuss later on.

The BNA did, however, contribute towards the debate on the process character of community development. Wisner (1988:27), for example, distinguishes between a strong (radical) and a weak (liberal) version of BNA: '... the weak BNA either imposes a set of needs on the poor from the outside and/or limits the radical potential of participation'. By contrast, when the poor collectively reflect on their needs, a radical BNA manifests itself. 'In this process, the poor themselves define and control their own struggle. The development project becomes, in other words, radically participatory' (Wisner 1988:26). This theme was carried further in the third variant of community development, namely participatory development.

One of the biggest proponents of participatory development, Gran (1983:327) defines the concept as:

> ... the self-sustaining process to engage free men and women in activities that meet their basic needs and, beyond that, realise individually defined human potential within socially defined limits ...

4.4 RADICALISED APPROACH

The radical viewpoint of the BNA marked an early era of questioning of the commonly held truth about community development. Within the participatory development debate, we can differentiate two distinct schools of thought: on the one hand, the advocates of the liberal or humanistic views, and on the other, the advocates of a radical participatory development. The latter group argues that participation can only be effective if it is direct and allows ultimate control to communities to decide their own affairs. Scope must be allowed for the production of new knowledge, the mapping out of new directions and the design of new organisational methods; all of which are to engender an upward progression from the bottom to management level (Oakley & Marsden 1984:13). Since the middle 1980s, the radical approach has gained ground and has come to dominate the debate on community development.

The radical viewpoint takes the debate away from the mobilisation of community resources, community organisation and involvement in pre-planned projects, to issues of powerlessness, decision making and empowerment. We agree with Margaret Ledwith (2020:14) that participation 'has a transformative agenda, an intention to bring about social change that is based on a fair, just and sustainable world'. It rejects the notion of community development aimed at simply 'making life a little bit better around the edges' (Hutchings & Lewis 2020:311).

The debate on the more radical version of participation coincided with or stimulated the development of even more variants of community development: the learning process approach, human scale development, the capability approach, 'Another Development' and asset-based community development. The debate on these approaches, it must be stressed, blends to such an extent that it becomes difficult to disentangle concepts, let alone understand the meaning attached to them in different settings. For analytical purposes, and as far as it is distinguishable, the broad outlines of these variants will nevertheless be discussed here.

4.4.1 The (social) learning process approach

The (social) learning process approach (LPA) aims to meet the need for 'a flexible, sustained, experimental, action based capacity building style of assistance' (Korten 1980:484). It is a bottom–up approach, avoiding the restrictions of a blueprint (top–down) approach. Consequently, it envisages development programmes arising from a learning process in which the local people and programme staff have an equal share, and in which their knowledge and resources are shared to establish a programme.

The logical result of using the LPA should be greater emphasis on the autonomy of the poor, their right to decision making and their empowerment. According to Gran (1983:345), the success story of the LPA has proved that 'people can lead their own change processes. They can be the actors, not merely the subjects of change'.

The people-centred or empowerment strategy builds on the participatory approach and LPA; it also represents a further development of the BNA. The components integral to a people-centred approach are:

- population participation in development
- the need for sustainable development
- the support and advocacy of the people's role in development by the bureaucracy, NGOs and voluntary organisations.

The people's role becomes clear in the empowerment strategy's definition of development, formulated by Korten (1990:67) as:

> a process by which the members of a society increase their potential and institutional capacities to mobilize and manage resources to produce sustainable and justly distributed improvements in their quality of life consistent with their own aspirations.

This definition places the decision as to what development is in the hands of the community – outsiders do not prescribe to a community or a society. The emphasis is on a long-term process whereby those who are involved in it develop the ability to manage and utilise local resources to their own benefit. Moser (1983:3) sees people-centred or empowerment strategies as aiming at capacity building; in this instance, participation is not a means, but becomes an end in itself in that 'the objective is not a fixed, **quantifiable** development goal but a process whose outcome is an increasingly "meaningful" participation in the development process'.

In the people-centred or empowerment strategy, institutions, as in the past, play an important but vastly different role. What is required from the bureaucracy, for instance, is a change in its role from 'giver of good things' to that of enabler; a role that relates to the premise of adaptive administration. The bureaucracy, to succeed, needs to open itself and become, in the words of Denis Goulet (1974:37–38), 'institutionally vulnerable'.

Korten identifies four generic principles which would enable bureaucracies to promote participatory, people-centred or empowerment development (Korten 1991:17):

1. Assistance to each individual community group should be designed and managed as a discrete activity with its own specifications and timetable responsive to the particular situation of that group, based on a careful study of existing practices, technical capacities, resource availabilities and power structures.
2. The emphasis should be on community control and management of the resource, with every aspect of the intervention geared to this outcome. This should include provision for legal confirmation of the resources management group as an autonomous body with legal rights.
3. Actual design of the facilities does not take place until the beneficiaries are fully prepared to make their needs and preferences known and, once completed, is not implemented until formally accepted by an association of the beneficiaries.
4. Organising takes account of and works within existing social and organisational structures to the extent possible, while building member strength from the bottom up to ensure broadly based participation by the actual producers and avoid domination by traditional leaders.

4.4.2 Human scale development approach

The human scale development (HSD) approach (Max-Neef 1991) shows many similarities with the people-centred approach. HSD evolved mainly in Latin America under the strong inspiration of Manfred Max-Neef. In this approach, a distinction is made between needs and satisfiers. Needs are viewed to be universal and basic. Not only material needs are addressed, but individual and community needs dominate this model. Satisfiers are those aspects that are contextually defined and may differ from one place to another. Both needs and satisfiers are addressed in HSD, since the human being is viewed as a whole, responsible for his/her own development within the norms of society. The approach is about people, not objects, and goes beyond the economics of life, speaking about the totality of human beings (Cruz, Stahel & Max-Neef 2009:2023).

4.4.3 Capability approach

A related approach also acknowledging the central place of the human being is the capability approach, emphasised by the Indian development philosopher Amartya Sen. This approach was influenced by the work of Adam Smith, Karl Marx and the Greek philosopher, Aristotle (Clark 2005:2).

The capability approach provides a framework to tackle human development and addresses poverty and inequality. It consists of two core concepts: functionings and capabilities. Functionings refer to a person's state of being and doing. Capabilities refer to real or effective opportunities to achieve functionings. The capability approach sees development as a process of expanding people's human capabilities. This, then, is an approach that places human development – and not, for instance, economic development – at the centre. The development of human beings becomes an end in itself and not a means to other ends.

In the field of development, 'capabilities', according to Sen, do not refer to income, resources, goods, emotions or the satisfaction of preferences. 'Capabilites' refer to 'what people are effectively able to do and be' or the freedom 'to enjoy valuable beings and doings' (Robeyns 2005:91). Sen does not provide a list of specific capabilities; what he does is to stress the role of activity and freedom in people's ability to make their own choices.

While Sen did not identify capabilities, Martha Nussbaum (2003:42–42) provides us with a list of what she calls the central human capabilities (see also the discussion on human orientation in Chapter 6):

- Life
- Bodily health
- Bodily integrity
- Senses, imagination and thought
- Emotions
- Practical reason
- Affiliation

- Other species (being able to live with concern for and in relation to animals, plants and the world of nature)
- Play
- Control over one's environment (political and material).

4.4.4 'Another Development'

Over the years, practitioners and theorists of the international 'community development movement' have departed from a strong emphasis on centralised government decision making and a reliance on international financial power as a driving force behind people's involvement. As part of the historical development described above, what is known as 'Another Development', evolved in the late 1970s and early 1990s.

Ekins (1992:100) says the following about it:

> Another Development has emerged as a clear and coherent system of developmental analysis to contrast with the top-down, finance-oriented economism of conventional development strategies.

The five main characteristics of 'Another Development' are as follows:
1. It is need-oriented and addresses material and nonmaterial human needs.
2. It is endogenous in that every society's values and vision of the future should determine development.
3. It is self-reliant in that the power and energy in every society's natural and cultural environment are used for development.
4. It is ecologically pure because planning and action occur within the confines of the ecology.
5. It is based on structural transformation of social relationships, economic activities and power relationships (Nerfin 1977:10).

4.4.5 Asset-based community development

This approach moves away from the conventional problem-based approach toward a more positive assets viewpoint. The point of departure is what assets are available in the community which can be utilised by the people for their own development. 'In an asset-based approach the idea [of development] is built from within and focuses less on what can be added from outside' (De Beer & Swanepoel 2013:21).

Assets in this case refer not only to money and objects but also include skills, the relationships between people and networks between them (Mathie & Cunningham 2003:5).

Harrison, Blickem, Lamb, Kirk & Vassilev (2019:7) assert that:

> [a] key quality of ABCD practice is the strong emphasis on building and sustaining meaningful relationships within communities and developing networks of reciprocal exchange and acceptable support.

4.5 CONCLUSION

In the coming years, all these approaches, from BNA to 'Another Development', will probably dominate the debate on development. A confluence of these debates into yet another debate is possible. Much more debate will go into the questions of needs and poverty, relief and release from the deprivation trap, centralisation versus decentralisation, a redefinition of the role of bureaucracy, a closer scrutiny of the role of NGOs, more emphasis on the role of the social enterprise sector and the question of empowerment and ownership in terms of control over community resources and sustainable development.

REFERENCES

Arnstein SR. 1969. A ladder of citizen participation. *Journal of the American Planning Association*, 35(4):216–224.

Botes L & Van Rensburg D. 2000. Community participation in development: Nine plagues and twelve commandments. *Community Development Journal*, 35(1):41–58.

Brokensha D & Hodge P. 1969. *Community Development: An Interpretation*. San Francisco: Chandler.

Chile L. 2012. International experience of community development professionalization: Indicators for South Africa. *Africanus: Journal of Development Studies*, 42(2):42–54.

Clark DA. 2005. *The Capability Approach: Its Development, Critiques and Recent Advances*. Global Policy Research Group. Institute for Development Policy and Management. Manchester: University of Manchester.

Cornwell L. 1986. Community development: a phoenix too frequent? Working Document in Rural and Community Development. Development of Administration and Politics. Unisa.

Cruz I, Stahel A & Max-Neef M. 2009. Towards a systemic development approach: Building on the human-scale development paradigm. *Ecological Economics*, 68:2021–2030.

De Beer FC & Swanepoel HJ. 1998. *Community Development and Beyond. Issues, Structures and Procedures*. Pretoria: Van Schaik.

De Beer FC & Swanepoel HJ. 2013. *The Community Development Profession. Issues, Concepts and Approaches*. Pretoria: Van Schaik.

Ekins P. 1992. *A New World Order. Grassroots Movements for Global Change*. London: Routledge.

Goulet D. 1974. Development administration and structures of vulnerability. In Morgan EP (ed), *The Administration of Change in Africa*. New York: Dunellen.

Gran G. 1983. *Development by People: Citizen Construction of a Just World*. New York: Praeger.

Harrison R, Blickem C, Lamb J, Kirk S & Vassilev I. 2019. Asset-based community development: narratives, practice, and conditions of possibility – a qualitative study with community practitioners. *SAGE Open*, 1(11):1–11.

Hutchings S & Lewis AL. 2020. Reflections on our critical service learning provision: Is it critical or are we social justice dreamers? In Scandrett E (ed), *Public Sociology as Educational Practice: Challenges, Dialogues and Counter-Publics*. Bristol: Bristol University Press.

Korten DC. 1980. Community organization and rural development: A learning process approach. *Public Administration Review*, 40(5):480–511.

Korten DC. 1990. *Getting to the 21st Century: Voluntary Action and the Global Agenda*. West Hartford: Kumarian.

Korten DC. 1991. Participation and development projects: Fundamental dilemmas. Unpublished paper.

Ledwith M. 2020. *Community development: A critical approach*. 2nd ed. Bristol: Policy Press.

Mathie A & Cunningham G. 2003. From clients to citizens: Asset-based community development as a strategy for community-driven development. *Development in Practice*, 13(5):474–486.

Max-Neef M. 1991. *Human Scale Development: Conception, Application and Further Reflections*. New York: Apex.

Monaheng T. 2000. Community development and empowerment. In De Beer FC & Swanepoel HJ (eds), *Introduction to Development Studies*. Cape Town: Oxford University Press.

Moser CON. 1983. The problem of evaluating community participation in urban development projects. In Moser CON (ed), Evaluating community participation in urban development projects. Unpublished Working Paper 14. London: Development Planning Unit.

Nerfin M (ed). 1977. *Another Development: Approaches and Strategies*. Uppsala: Dag Hammarskjöld Foundation.

Nussbaum MC. 2003. Capabilities as fundamental entitlements: Sen and social justice. *Feminist Economics*, 9(2–3):33–59.

Oakley P & Marsden D. 1984. *Approaches to Participation in Rural Development*. Geneva: ILO.

Phifer BM, List EF & Faulkner B. 1980. History of community development in America. In Chritenson JA & Robinson JW (eds), *Community Development in America*. Armes: Iowa State University Press.

Reader S. 2006. Does a basic needs approach need capabilities? *The Journal of Political Philosophy*, 14(3):337–350.

Roberts H. 1979. *Community Development: Learning and Action*. Toronto: University of Toronto Press.

Robeyns I. 2005. The capability approach: a theoretical survey. *Journal of Human Development*, 6(1):93–114.

Smart J. 2017. *What is community development?* Expert panel resource sheet published by the Australian Institute of Family Studies, January 2017 (last updated October 2019). Available at: https://aifs.gov.au/resources/practice-guides/what-community-development (accessed 22 August 2022).

Wisner B. 1988. *Power and Need in Africa: Basic Human Needs and Development Policies*. London: Earthscan.

CHAPTER 5
Features and Outcomes of Community Development

Hennie Swanepoel and Frik de Beer

5.1 INTRODUCTION

At the beginning of this book, we had a vague idea of the meaning of community development. The first four chapters have given us context and, with it, an understanding of poverty all over the world and how community development aims to deal with it. We have also been made aware of various approaches to eradicate or at least address the poverty problem. To answer the questions of what community development is and what makes it different from other approaches and viewpoints, we must look at the features and outcomes of community development.

There are various kinds of development or betterment or change that can be undertaken. Some of the principles discussed in the next chapter (Chapter 6) will also be relevant to these different forms of change, but the combination of those principles as a unit is true only for what is known all over the world as community development. These principles inform, even sculpt, the features and outcomes of community development. In this chapter we will look at these features and the end results of community development, and will show how the principles play a role in their formulation.

5.2 THE FEATURES OF COMMUNITY DEVELOPMENT

5.2.1 An integrated approach

The most fundamental characteristic of community development is that it follows an integrated approach to the problems of poverty and development, with end goal being the eradication of poverty (Monaheng 2000:127). Integration in community development has two major implications (ibid). The first is that the problems, requiring development action, are multifaceted and that they should be tackled together in a coordinated fashion. It emphasises the fact that social, political and cultural aspects should be treated together with the economic aspects, because they are all interrelated. The second element of integration is that different role players should coordinate their efforts. Government agencies, non-governmental organisations and community-based organisations should work hand in hand in order to optimise the impact of their efforts and to avoid duplication and conflict. (See Chapter 3 for a further discussion of this.) In fact, community development cannot be sectoralised. A person who has a need for health services invariably also has a need for other basics such as clean water and a balanced diet (Swanepoel 2000:72).

5.2.2 Collective action

Community development is not the action of an individual or of a few individuals. The individual is important, and it is therefore a collective activity in that a group of people sharing a mutual problem, need, sentiment or concern, act together and in concert, and share a certain responsibility for the action. Such a collective action is a human activity, dealing with human problems and needs. It is also a voluntary action.

Not all people who stand to gain from community development will act together. There is a personal freedom for individuals to join the collective activity or not. Community development practitioners (CDPs) are sometimes disheartened by the small number of people who seem willing to participate in collective action to solve problems and address needs. However, the positive outcome of this is that the freedom of the individual is respected; no one is forced to participate in community development; further, those participating are truly committed; and, finally, a small group is, in fact, very strong when it comes to addressing abstract human needs, participating in the true sense of the word and learning from the activity.

Collective action means that a group of people that can be defined as exclusive will be involved. The exclusivity of the group enhances the learning process because the same people are involved throughout and learn to work as a team. This does not mean that individualism is banned from projects. There are examples of projects also favouring the individual. The individual inputs are also important in group action because that is how the group grows as an entity, the individual inputs being the building blocks for whatever venture. (See Case study 18: *Food garden in Mapayeni*.)

5.2.3 Needs orientation

Projects are sometimes built around interests or hobbies. The large majority of these never come to fruition. People do not have the strength, energy or the commitment for those types of actions. The better vehicle to proceed with that type of activity is the club, which has a different set-up and different procedures from a project. Without a need or the perception of a need, community development cannot take place. This need or perception of a need must be heartfelt among the people who must participate in the project. People are not going to rally together around needs that have been identified by some expert and which people find intangible. Our point of departure in this book is that needs ought to be identified by the community, through participation. People, and their participation, is more important than their needs (see also Chapter 6). Therefore, the identification of the needs (abstract and tangible) of people is a prerequisite for action – it is the first step to be taken before a project commences (see also Nel 2018). A project without a clearly defined need is a dead project. This needs identification exercise is a participatory process because it is the people who must identify the need before they will organise themselves to do something about the need (Monaheng 2000:127). A project with a need that is not perceived or understood by the people is also a dead project. A community development project is not aimed at vague, ill-defined or broad, abstract needs. People will not rally round for the eradication of vaguely felt needs and such a project will have limited hope for success.

A perception of need, crisis and urgency must underline community action for it to be purposeful. The principle of release is important here (see Chapter 6). Relief cannot engender the same commitment and enthusiasm as release. A 'total transformation' is much more of a war cry than 'some improvement'.

There are dangers attached to participatory needs identification. There is a right and a wrong way in which to go about it and, unfortunately, the wrong way may often sound the easier and more official way. The needs identification aspect will be discussed in later chapters; suffice to say here that the principle of ownership is very important in this process.

If needs identification becomes the drawing up of a shopping list for some development agency to attend to, the process is heading for disaster. People must be the owners of their situation. They must realise that they have a certain need and they must decide that they are going to do something about it. In other words, they must take ownership of the action as well as the need. Of vital importance is the fact that if they have taken ownership of the need, it is so much easier also to take ownership of the action.

Another aspect of needs identification is that it is basically a negative activity. Poor people are negative about their situation and their chances to improve it. It is interesting with how much ease a group of people from a deprived area can enumerate their needs. If they are then asked to identify their assets, they usually find it difficult. One of the psychological manifestations of poverty is a negative self-perception. Needs identification lies easily within this psychological characteristic.

If something is not done about this negative self-perception, needs identification will remain a finite, isolated process that will make participants more aware of their dire situation and will bring about a heightened sense of negative self-perception. CDPs must regard it as one of their prime tasks to change the negative self-perception to a positive one. CDPs must also realise that this change is a process and an arduous one at that.

Finally, it is important to realise that needs identification can lead to expectations. It is fine if people's expectations are raised because they have decided to do something about their situation. It is, however, sad if people's ingrained dependency on do-gooders raises their expectations that something will be done for them every time that they are facilitated to identify their needs. Recurrent disappointments every time that their expectations are not met hardens their negative self-perception and makes them suspicious of all potential development initiators and reluctant to react positively to inputs from these people such as CDPs. (See Case study 16: *The felt need and the real need*.)

5.2.4 Objective orientation

Each identified concrete need must be addressed by trying to realise a concrete objective. Because community development is born of a need, it is obvious that it must be directed at an objective addressing that specific need. Projects are by definition activities or sets of organisational measures aimed at or associated with clear objectives (Morgan 1983:330). Just as needs are not vaguely felt and broadly described, objectives are precise and concrete. Preciseness is the first requirement. A community development project cannot have a vague objective. Take the example of establishing a crèche. Where is the crèche to be situated? Whose children may attend it?

How many children will it accommodate? Answering these questions will lead a group to describe their objective precisely, or at least give them a better idea of what they need and how they are going to achieve it.

The second requirement is that an objective must be concrete. A project's objective cannot be a better life. Every participant's concept of a better life will be unique and therefore different from others' concept. Besides, how is a plan to be devised and implemented for a better life? People's norms and values influence their perceptions. If an objective is stated broadly or vaguely or in the abstract, the chances are that diverse perceptions and interpretations will make collective action very difficult.

5.2.5 Action at grassroots level

Community development is not a method whereby the elite, government officials or experts keep the people busy by involving them in worthwhile actions. Neither does it consist of huge infrastructural projects where the community is confronted with ready-made blueprints from engineers or professional planners. This is a very old, traditional and outdated view of community development. It is primarily a process in which ordinary people play the leading part, with government, experts and the elite playing a facilitating role.

Community development is really grassroots oriented in the sense that the main role players are just ordinary and, usually, poor people. Care must be taken not to put barriers in a project that successfully keep the poor out. If projects are meant for the 'enterprising members of a community', we are not really at the very grassroots and we are not touching the poor. If a local government is involved in a project as role player, the ordinary people are not necessarily present. The local government may, being the lowest sphere of government and the nearest institution to the people, look as if it is part of the grassroots, but it is rather somewhere slightly higher, such as the blades of grass.

Because they are grassroots oriented, community development efforts are small, simple and address the basic needs of those at this level. This last aspect is of great importance. The needs at grassroots level must be tackled. Community development is not meant to fulfil the needs of a community over the whole spectrum. With the principle of simplicity in mind, we can safely say that community development seeks simplicity, avoids complexity and lies at the micro level. It does not mean that the type of development is second rate. It simply acknowledges the reality.

5.2.6 Asset based

Community development is not an action whereby local people draw up shopping lists for government agencies to fulfil. Community development makes use of the assets at its disposal. That is why no community development project can operate without the identification of local assets. Those assets come from a very broad spectrum. It covers natural assets such as soil and water. However, it also includes infrastructural assets such as roads, electricity, buildings and a sanitary system. The most important of all assets, though, is human beings and their ability to organise.

This is what makes community development different and what makes development management different from any other management (Mathie & Cunningham 2003). It is not a kind of development by demand or command. It emphasises building of meaningful relationships and networks, and 'within the context of growing inequalities and politics of austerity, is likely to benefit the most vulnerable people and communities' (Harrison, Blickem, Lamb, Kirk & Vassilev 2019:7). It is a development making use of the available resources, especially human resources, in order to reach the objective (De Beer & Swanepoel 2013:21). The beauty of this is that, as the assets are used, they improve. This is especially true of the humans and their organisational skills. The whole activity is therefore geared to build the assets for better use in future. It does not mean that money is not an important asset; it simply puts it in its place. Chapter 19 deals with techniques of identifying resources and assets in a community.

5.2.7 Democratic

The concept of community development gives a special meaning to community. It first tells us that community is regarded as various kinds of vehicle to carry development forward (Sihlongonyane 2001). For some professionals, it also carries the implicit meaning that democracy and community development are the same (Rios & Lachapelle 2015:192). It also emphasises that the third sphere of government, which is tied to the community in a special way, is involved. This sphere of government, known as local government, has a special function in developmental government. Community development forms part of this democratic activity. Community development also forms part of the local government's integrated development planning and, as such, it is a democratic activity (Gray & Mubangizi 2010).

However, community development has a special democratic function in that it extends democracy beyond the ordinary three-sphere government structure (Sen 1999). It gives a lower than grassroots opportunity to the poorest of the poor, the most deprived, the isolated and vulnerable, and the politically weak to participate in a democratic action that will give true meaning to their democratic rights as citizens. It is also democratic in giving the opportunity to people with little political clout to break the deprivation trap.

5.3 THE OUTCOMES OF COMMUNITY DEVELOPMENT

Not all community development projects are a success. In fact, quite a large percentage never reach their objectives. Many reasons can be given for the failure of projects. (See Case study 7: *A community hall with no purpose*, Case study 10: *The project that had its fences brought down*, Case study 11: *The project that was taken over* and Case study 14: *The case of the community worker who met his match*.) These reasons must be sought in the running of projects, not in the characteristics of community development. It was alleged in the past that community development does not work, but it will not work if the approach is wrong and the activities flowing from that approach are therefore also wrong. To blame community development for that is to throw the baby out with the bath water, as the saying goes. Community development has all the attributes needed for positive results. The following are a few of those positive results.

5.3.1 Awareness creation

Communities gain a lot by the awareness that is being generated through community development. This does not mean that communities are ordinarily lacking in awareness. Community development, however, encourages a certain kind of awareness. People become aware of themselves in terms of their environment, their needs and their resources. They also become aware of positive objectives that will change their situation. Community development, therefore, changes people's apathy as the victims of poverty into a positive disposition as active participants in eradicating the need. (See Case study 4: *The story of Thembalihle* and Case study 17: *Mothers of the mountain community*.)

A community is normally aware of its situation of need, but if people go through a community development process, they start to see themselves as an active organism that is able to, and does, change its environment. This positive awareness ties in with the first principle that abstract human needs, such as that of self-reliance, are fulfilled at the same time as concrete needs. It also underlies the idea of asset-based development.

5.3.2 Further development

Community development projects quite often spark further activity that can lead to the setting and reaching of further goals which bring about further development. Success in attaining goals that they have set for themselves does something very positive to people. They become aware of further needs and they set new objectives to address those needs. We see clearly that this leads to the fulfilment of abstract human needs. Apart from the confidence they gain, they have an enthusiasm to tackle further problems or needs, born out of optimism. In this way, one successful project can easily lead to another project. (See Case study 17: *Mothers of the mountain community* and Case study 20: *The story of KwaMpofu*.)

However, quite often, projects that have been successfully completed are in fact not at an end. What was established through a project must be managed and maintained. It must be used or sold or adapted for changing circumstances. A project may have a continuous marketing and/or bookkeeping function. In short, a project's establishing function may end once the objective has been reached, but then its management function may still continue (Mathie & Cunningham 2003).

5.3.3 Demonstration effect

Projects have an influence that spans much wider than only the project and those participating in it. They broadcast their effect over a wide area so that people become aware of their success. Poor people are, justifiably, concerned about the risk that goes with any project. A successful project tends to allay fears, not only among the participants, but also among observers from outside.

A successful project demonstrates to all that people who stand together and work together can bring about changes that will make a difference. A successful project usually leads to similar projects being launched in the area. In a few cases of note, this has become an avalanche with projects springing up everywhere. Apart from the physical results of such a dramatic growth in projects, it also has a psychological effect on people, so that the threat and risk of poverty become less of an issue and new ideas to cope with old problems become uppermost in their minds. When this happens, a community can very quickly look after its own development efforts and will only need some expert advice from time to time. In these cases, there is genuine ownership by the people of the local development efforts. (See Case study 17: *Mothers of the mountain community*.)

5.3.4 Learning

The learning process in community development projects has a wider reach than only the project. The participants learn to be successful in many other spheres. The organisational sphere is a good example. A community's organisation becomes more efficient, more effective and develops the ability to expand – the outcome of the learning process in Korten's mind (1980).

The participatory rapid appraisal and planning (PRAP – see Chapter 19) process opens many opportunities to observe through research and to learn through observation. The participants, including the CDPs, learn not only what is – the context – but also what should be – the activity of poverty eradication. The participants in community development also learn skills. A project can be in service of skills training such as sewing, but usually the learning is not an end in itself, but is in service of the project. Then people learn to organise, to plan, to implement and to evaluate. They can also learn more specialised skills tied in with the project such as agriculture, nursing, horticulture, masonry, bookkeeping and welding.

In summary, we can say that community development will continuously improve the ability of the people to deal with the challenges confronting them (Monaheng 2000:128). One of the most important things participants learn is communication. It is the life blood of any project and if people do not learn quickly to communicate, the project is doomed. (See Case study 18: *Food garden in Mapayeni*.)

5.3.5 Community building

Community development greatly strengthens a community. This strengthening takes place at both the abstract and concrete levels. People become more self-sufficient and self-reliant, which does a lot for their dignity. However, they also learn how to organise more effectively. In other words, they learn how to run projects and their leadership structures develop accordingly (Maistry 2012:33–35). They therefore become valued participants in development planning and the structure supporting this.

Through the improvement of organisational skill, institution building also takes place. Institutions become adaptable and development oriented. Through these institutions, leadership is fostered and developed. According to Korten (1991:15), enhancing institutional capabilities is one of the most important human objectives of community development. Franco and Tracey (2019:691–692) identified with reference to Chaskin (2001) a number of broad elements contained in capacity building:

> … the existence of and access to resources, the presence of networks and collaborative action, a degree of commitment and responsibility among stakeholders and elements of leadership, collective action and problem solving.

The importance of linkages in society is often negated or simply forgotten. Community development forges new linkages between institutions, between individuals, and between institutions and individuals. Existing linkages are consequently strengthened. The isolation of poor communities is addressed by the creation of external linkages between communities or between communities and various authorities and agencies.

True leadership can gain much from community development. Existing leaders are enabled to lead more effectively and new leaders (especially on the project level) are thrust to the fore through institutions and project activities. Leadership is enhanced specifically through skills attainment. The skills we are talking about lie at two levels. First, there are organisational skills such as organising, negotiating, planning and evaluating. Second, there are also many other hard skills such as agriculture, horticulture, building, arts and crafts, healthcare, childcare and needlework. All these skills are necessary ingredients of a self-sufficient community. Added to this is the fact that the results of projects lead to improvement in health, education, childcare, sanitation and housing, to name but a few. Quite a few types of projects create jobs and/or generate incomes and this has a direct bearing on overcoming crime and antisocial behaviour.

5.4 CONCLUSION

Community development is a collective grassroots action to tackle felt concrete needs. Because it is so directed at everyday needs, it is not Utopian. Its ideals are never grand and idyllic. Yet, community development achieves much more than what it sets out to do. It may involve only a handful of people, but its effects will touch many more. It may entail a simple action not requiring much skill and insight, but people participating will find that they have gained much more than what the simple activity would initially promise.

Finally, it is important to remember that it is a human activity with the goal to transform the lives of the poor, not on a grand scale or in action leading to glory, but bit by bit through small and simple activities of human beings who learn through experience that they are assets contributing to a better life.

A community development project is not aimed at vague, ill-defined or broad, abstract needs. People must be helped to move to the point where they will see themselves as capable of doing something about their position. People's norms and values influence their perceptions. An awareness of itself in terms of objectives is one of the greatest strengths a community can enjoy.

Many of the aspects mentioned and discussed in this chapter are illustrated in the appended case studies.

REFERENCES

De Beer F & Swanepoel H. 2013. *The Community Development Profession: Issues, Concepts and Approaches*. Pretoria: Van Schaik.

Franco IB & Tracey J. 2019. Community capacity-building for sustainable development: Effectively striving towards achieving local community sustainability targets. *International Journal of Sustainability in Higher Education*, 20(4):691–725.

Gray M & Mubangizi B. 2010. Caught in the vortexes: Can local government community workers succeed in South Africa? *Community Development Journal*, 45(2):186–197.

Harrison R, Blickem C, Lamb J, Kirk S & Vassilev I. 2019. Asset-based community development: Narratives, practice, and conditions of possibility – a qualitative study with community practitioners. *SAGE Open,* 1(11).

Korten DC. 1980. Community organization and rural development: A learning process approach. *Public Administration Review*, 40(5):480–511.

Korten DC. 1991. Participation and development projects: Fundamental dilemmas. Unpublished Paper.

Maistry M. 2012. Towards professionalisation: Journey of community development in the African and South African context. *Africanus*, 42(2):29–41.

Mathie A & Cunningham G. 2003. From clients to citizens: Asset-based community development as a strategy for community-driven development. *Development in Practice*, 13(5):474–486.

Monaheng T. 2000. Community development and empowerment. In FC De Beer & HJ Swanepoel (eds), *Introduction to Development Studies*. Cape Town: Oxford University Press.

Morgan EP. 1983. The project orthodoxy in development: Re-evaluating the cutting edge. *Public Administration and Development*, 3(4):329–339.

Nel H. 2018. A comparison between the asset-oriented and needs-based

community development approaches in terms of systems changes. *Practice*, 30(1):33–52.

Rios M & Lachapelle P. 2015. Community development and democratic practice: *Pas de deux* or distinct and different? *Community Development*, 46(3):190–197.

Sen A. 1999. *Development as Freedom*. New York: Albert Knopf.

Sihlongonyane MF. 2001. The rhetoric of community in project management: The case of Mohlakeng township. *Development In Practice*, 11(1).

Swanepoel H. 2000. The dynamics of development. In De Beer FC & Swanepoel HJ (eds), *Introduction to Development Studies*. Cape Town: Oxford University Press.

CHAPTER 6
Principles of Community Development

Hennie Swanepoel and Frik de Beer

6.1 INTRODUCTION

Thousands of people calling themselves community development practitioners (CDPs), community facilitators, development officers or social ecologists are busy with 'development work' in deprived areas. Their job entails organising local people attached to projects that address real or perceived problems among the people. These workers come from different backgrounds and different training regimes and may represent as wide a spectrum as engineering, education, health, agriculture, religion, childcare and culture; they do not come into this job with the same point of departure, following the same set of rules or moving within the same parameters. The potential for chaos is obvious. It therefore becomes extremely important to bring some order to the chaos, to provide a universal set of principles, both at the ethical and practical level, to serve as guiding lights to the varied multitude. See De Beer and Swanepoel (2012), who touch on the problem of diversity in approaches toward community development and ways to address it.

This chapter endeavours to do just that by first looking at certain ethical principles which hold universal importance. All practitioners, whether they are social workers or engineers, should abide by these principles. The repercussions of standing by the ethical principles are discussed below.

6.2 ETHICAL PRINCIPLES

6.2.1 Human orientation

People in the 'deprivation trap' have basic physical needs that are not being met. (See Chapter 1 and Chambers (1983) for a discussion of the deprivation trap.) People caught in this trap, who have unfulfilled, basic physical or concrete needs such as food, clean water, clothing and shelter, also have needs that are not, strictly speaking, physical, such as happiness, self-reliance and human dignity. In fact, people's physical and abstract needs go hand in hand and are present at the same time.

The principle that must be followed here is that while people's concrete needs are addressed and, hopefully, fulfilled, their abstract human needs must also be fulfilled. The physical aspects of a project cannot be separated from the abstract human aspects. They must go hand in hand otherwise we do not have development. We cannot have an electricity project that costs the community members a lot of money, but which is also out of order regularly. Does this mean that every project must have two objectives – one lying within the concrete sphere and one found in the abstract humanities? Not necessarily, but projects should be planned and formulated in such a way that the process of abstract objective attainment flows naturally from the process to address physical and concrete needs.

Poor people are not going to participate in projects with vague abstract objectives. Their concern is with a concrete need or problem and that is what they will concentrate on. However, this action of the participants must take place in such a way that the abstract needs are also addressed. This responsibility falls squarely within the ambit of the CDP, who must ensure that every project succeeds in both these objectives, without confronting the participants with the objectives. We cannot tell participants that they must launch a project to improve their human dignity. These abstract objectives lie on a more subtle plane, but may not be neglected for that reason. For the CDP this means that, as people strive to meet their basic physical needs, they realise many of their abstract human needs. CDPs must ensure that the assessment of projects also provides answers to the attainment of these abstract goals. The efforts of CDPs to bring about both physical and abstract results from a project need to be evaluated. Later in this chapter, when we discuss the practical principles, we will take a closer look at the CDP's endeavours.

It also means that, under no circumstances, may we address the basic physical needs to the detriment of the people's human dignity and other abstract human needs, such as happiness and contentment. The human fabric of people should never suffer as a result of so-called physical development. Those who are tasked to mobilise people must make it their objective not only to mobilise people for physical development, but also to help people gain in self-reliance, happiness, fulfilment and eventually human dignity.

People may not be ignored, bypassed or be forced into, or made dependent on, development projects addressing their physical needs. Himanen (2014:298) puts it as follows:

> Dignity means the worthiness of every human being as a subject. For example, freedom then means the subject's right to freedom: to make free choices about one's life that are consensual with the free choices of the other subjects.

The most important abstract human need is dignity. This entails functioning properly as a human being or exercising fully the capabilities that are characteristically human (see Chapter 4 on the capability approach). The characterisation of a fulfilled life boils down to identifying human capabilities that make such a life possible. The core idea is that of human beings as dignified free beings who shape their own life in cooperation and reciprocity with others, rather than being passively shaped or pushed around in the manner of a 'flock' or 'herd' of animals. A life that is really human is one that is shaped throughout by these human powers of practical reason and sociability.

Nussbaum (2020:13–39) lists the following central human capabilities as an indicator of human dignity:

- *Life*: the ability to avoid premature death
- *Bodily health*: the ability to have good health with adequate nourishment and shelter
- *Bodily integrity*
- *Senses, imagination and thought*: the ability to use these to imagine, think and reason in a truly human way
- *Emotions*: the ability to have attachments to things and people outside oneself
- *Practical reason*: the ability to conceive of the good and engage in critical reflection about the formulation and implementation of one's life plan
- *Affiliation*: the ability to live with and reach out to others, and to engage in various social interactions with dignity and respect
- *Other species*: the ability to live with concern about the world of nature
- *Play*: the ability to enjoy recreational activities
- *Control over one's environment*: both political and material.

Physical improvements to an area can have negative effects on people and can harm their human dignity. Dignity is promoted by giving people recognition; by recognising them as capable of making their own decisions and accepting responsibility for their decisions. Dignity is enhanced when people become self-reliant and self-sufficient; when they become capable of organising themselves and engendering and maintaining benevolent and farsighted leadership. People must progress in realising their inner potential while working to fulfil their physical needs.

A further important aspect of this principle is that human beings do not live in a vacuum. Human beings live in an environment that is physical, but there is also an abstract environment such as a social, political, economic and cultural milieu of immense importance to human beings. Furthermore, people carry with them a oneness that influences their whole existence. Their needs are part of this oneness and can therefore not be separated. Their health needs cannot be separated from their educational and their social needs. Development agencies must be careful not to create tension within people by dividing their needs into sectors that can create a dichotomy leading, for example, to problems of existentialism.

In our efforts to address poverty and fulfil basic needs, it is appropriate to remember that the human being is more important than his/her needs. (See Chapter 4 on the basic needs approach.) CDPs should not trample on human beings or bedevil their environment in their rush to do something about their needs. A well-meaning, but misguided, stampede by government agencies, NGOs and other well-wishers will trample the views of the people. In spite of the great need among poor people, it is always wise to approach development with caution. Case study 5: *A dam can bring hardship* illustrates this principle of community development. Case study 23: *The old chief's story* shows how a well-meaning, but misguided approach can generate negative reactions because human dignity has played a minor role in the CDP's approach.

6.2.2 Participation

We are mobilising people to participate in development efforts or projects, but we must have a clear view of what participation really means; what it really is. We cannot mobilise people and then limit or prescribe their participation. That is tokenism. Participation does not mean involvement. When we involve people in projects, we allow them in, under certain conditions, to take part in certain actions in a prescribed way. This whole process is then pre-planned and prescribed by the CDPs and their organisations. When people are mobilised to participate, they do so fully – in all aspects of the project. Then they become part of the decision making and planning of the project. They are part of the implementation and evaluation of the project. And, if need be, they decide on project course adaptations to keep a project on track; in short, they then participate fully in the management of the project.

The 'buzz value' of participation is so great that debate on whether it is good or bad has ceased. The liberal view of participation sees it as good, especially if it is organised and orderly. The liberal view emphasises two points. The first point is that, through participation, a solid, local knowledge base is used for development. Local people, who have lived in deprivation for years, surviving the hardships of their poverty, have a certain ingrained knowledge that outsiders do not have. Their 'common sense' knowledge of environmental dynamics can be of immense value to development efforts. Developers who do not use this knowledge base to the full are placing limitations on projects.

The second point is that it has now been established that people who do not participate in their own development have no affinity for development efforts and their results. The huge problem of sustaining development and maintaining facilities can be solved by having the local people fully present. To illustrate the different levels of participation, Arnstein (2019) developed the ladder of participation. The bottom rungs of the ladder, which she names manipulation and therapy, are the levels of non-participation. Then follows three degrees of tokenism: informing, consultation and placation. The top three rungs represent degrees of citizen power: partnership, delegated power and at the top, citizen control. See Figure 6.1 for a graphical representation.

Community Development in the 21st Century Section B

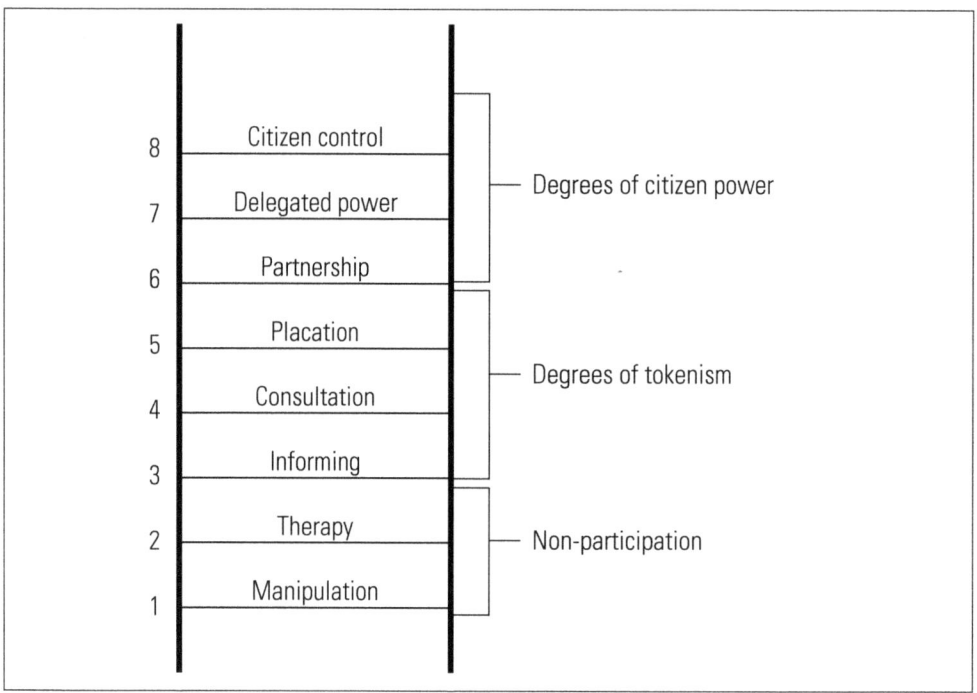

Figure 6.1 **Arnstein's ladder of participation**

Source: Arnstein (2019)

Arnstein (2019:1) says that '[t]he idea of citizen participation is a little like eating spinach: no one is against it in principle because it is good for you'. However, when participation is defined by the have-nots as redistribution of power, the agreement weakens.

We must take note of this radical view on participation (and empowerment) which is supported throughout this book. (See Chapter 4 on the radical approach to participation.) According to this view, participation becomes a way of ensuring equity. Often, the poorest of the poor do not get their fair share of the fruits of development. Further, we must realise that it is the democratic right of people to participate in matters affecting their future. Every adult, whether relatively poor, poor or the poorest of the poor, has a right to be part of the decision-making mechanism affecting his/her development (De Beer & Swanepoel 1998:20–24). When people are mobilised to participate in a project, they are not just there to make them feel part of the project; they are not present so that we can make use of their local practical knowledge; they are not there to do the physical work. They are there because it is their democratic right to be there and to make decisions regarding the project that involves their future. The guiding principle is quite clear: do not mobilise people to play a minor role in a project and to fill a subordinate position in relation to professionals, bureaucrats and donors. If the people are not the main role players, there is something wrong with their participation.

What do people of a community do when they participate? In what do they participate? Is the people's participation limited to an advisory role? If the local people act only as advisors to the planners and decision makers, we cannot talk of participation. Power must accompany participation (El Sherbini 1986:9). As far back as the 1960s, Arnstein (2019) declared that participation without power 'is an empty and frustrating process for the powerless'. People do not like advisory roles. However, worse can happen; under the banner of participation, people can be used as cheap labour.

The excuse is often made that ordinary people are not capable of anything other than physical labour, that decision making and planning are outside the ambit of ordinary people because participation is seen as interfering with the effective provision of basic needs (Spalding 1990:105). It is necessary for CDPs to facilitate the ordinary people's full participation through enabling strategies. They must also guard against the subtle undermining of the participation of the poor so that it becomes co-option (Sowman & Gawith 1994). Participation can only be meaningful if it goes with empowerment. Development decision making will be governed by perceptions of power and how these perceptions can be changed (Guaraldo Choguill 1996). De Beer and Swanepoel (2013:35) cite Tremblay and Gutberlet (2012:283), who came to the conclusion that active radical participation is crucial to achieve good governance and accountability. Ledwith and Springett (2022:xv) summarise the importance of participation as follows: 'Social change comes from bottom-up grassroots action, not top down'. (See Case study 6: *The parson who became a painter*, which illustrates what can happen if people do not really participate in a project.)

6.2.3 Empowerment

People use the term empowerment very loosely. If they teach people a skill, they say that they have empowered them. If they give them representation on a council or committee, they call it empowerment. Basically, though, empowerment refers to political power. Empowerment is both process and end goal. According to Kamin, Kubacki and Atanasova (2022:1109):

> The empowerment process is defined as a participatory-developmental process through which individuals, organisations and communities gain greater control, self-efficacy, access to and control over resources, social justice, personal, interpersonal or political power, and awareness of the socio-political environment to address issues of powerlessness and to influence decisions that affect their lives.

We must be careful that our mobilisation does not lead to tokenism. Tokenism – or window-dressing – means that people are apparently mobilised, involved or placed on committees just so that it looks good. Sometimes people are mobilised just to do some physical work and then they are taught various skills in order to do that labour and this is then called empowerment. However, empowerment does not mean having certain skills or having a certain token representation. That is an extremely thin and shallow view.

Empowerment is to have decision-making power (Taconni & Tisdell 1993:413). And, yes, they do need certain skills to make those decisions, so skills do come into it, but not as the primary ingredient of empowerment. It is only a tool of enablement.

Associated with the skills needed for decision making is the fact that people can only make enlightened decisions if they have the correct information. Therefore, empowerment also includes information or knowledge, but then in service of the people's responsibility to make wise and informed decisions.

The guiding principle is that mobilisation must aim at giving people the power or the right to make decisions and not to stop there, but continue a supportive function by providing the necessary information to make good decision making possible. This can be regarded as one of the primary roles of CDPs. They and their organisations should be reservoirs of information to provide communities and committees with relevant, unadulterated and fresh information.

Softer options for empowerment, such as skills training and co-option, abound for the simple reason that empowerment can cause vulnerability among the development agencies and loosen their grip on the process of development. To what extent should agencies 'let go'? Are there limits to the power of project steering committees? By whom and to what extent should the steering committee's work be supervised, overseen and assessed?

These are not simple issues. However, the issue of empowerment cannot be put on the back burner because of these questions. Development agencies must approach the issue with open minds and in the spirit of the new professionalism of Chambers (1983). Maistry (2012:35) makes use of Cook (nd) when she points out that a shift of power occurs when the development process enables the community to change. She also makes the interesting comment that once structural change takes place in a community, that community system cannot return to what it was previously (Maistry 2012:35). Case study 7: *A community hall with no purpose* is a case in point where the people's inputs were not heeded because they were not empowered. You will find a similar situation in Case study 20: *The story of KwaMpofu*.

6.2.4 Ownership

Too often, mobilisation is done in a spirit of inviting the people to come and join someone else's activity, to treat people as guests on someone else's property. According to Mulwa (2012:68), it is dangerous to imagine the presence of expertise as always external; community development practice is essentially a community-driven process. We agree with Mulwa that this perception is altogether wrong.

People must have the power to make decisions. It is their destiny, it is their future, and it is their development. This is clear and straightforward logic. Because the people are the owners, no one else can be the main role player. Kiefer (2014) agrees: 'The focus on ownership for sustainability puts communities in control of development interventions'. All other role players must be there to support and to assist the people in carrying out their owner's responsibility.

Development agencies who regard development projects as their property will find that they are forever going to be burdened with the responsibility of the project's smooth progress and if they are successful in doing this, they may find one day that the people have 'stolen' their project.

The principle tells us that mobilisation is not about inviting people to join some outsider's project or effort on the terms and conditions of that other someone. This is token participation, token empowerment and token ownership maintained by established interests that are threatened by the mass ownership of development (Wisner 1988:294). See Regan (2012:84–85) for a discussion of the ever more important role of the government agencies.

Mobilisation is to activate people to take up the responsibilities of ownership and manage their future through their project. This principle also warns us that development agencies should never assume ownership at first with the idea to transfer it later on 'when the people are ready'. Apart from the fact that it is paternalistic for development agencies to decide when people are ready, this approach is fraught with danger because ownership transfer does not take place easily.

A CDP who emphasises from the start that it is the people's effort to address their problems will find that people are at first reluctant to accept this ownership or are unsure of what the ownership entails, but as they go along they become more and more aware of their special position and what it means in practical terms. Then their acceptance of ownership is a natural process facilitated by the CDP. Because every owner wants to regard the ownership as long term, a project's life can be so much longer because its life is being sustained by the owners. At the same time, we should not be blind to the fact that ownership claims can cause strife and animosities. Whitehead et al (2005) found that the issue of ownership of the project arose as a point of contention throughout. Case study 19: *Stealing or taking ownership*, which is actually a combination of two true stories, clearly illustrates the wrong and the correct perception of ownership.

6.2.5 Sustainability

Human beings and their communities are an integral part of the natural environment. If the natural environment is under threat or is damaged for one or other reason, humans will also be under threat or will be harmed. This fact is the basis on which this principle of sustainability is built. The golden rule is that no community development project should harm the environment.

Sustainable development does not comprise a single universal goal. It is rather a broad direction which is context specific. What is important about this seeking of answers to issues regarding sustainability is that it is the result of a revolutionary paradigm shift in science and development practice. We call this shift the view on holism. This simply means that the human being and the rest of nature form a oneness, a whole, and from this we can argue that if this whole is not managed properly, all living things will suffer.

Popularised in the 1920s, it was claimed that the whole was more than the sum of the parts. This claim moves the emphasis away from the parts in the direction of the whole as a collective and self-regulating unit. A core component of holism is structure determinism that implies basically that the structure and patterns of the whole determine the course thereof. We should take a look at our planet as a whole and examine our existing patterns with regard to affecting the environment (Treurnicht 2000:67). However, there is a common, very simple question to be asked.

De Beer and Swanepoel (2013:31) quote De Beer (2012:11): '[C]an it be expected of poor (rural) communities, in the face of excruciating poverty, to conserve natural resources in order for governments to meet their conservation obligations?'

The accepted definition of sustainable development is that it is development that meets the needs of the present without compromising the ability of future generations to meet their own needs. If we meet the needs of the present through projects, but we compromise the ability of future generations to meet their own needs, then we have negated this principle. The big question is how to address the needs existing now without jeopardising future generations. This is a real problem that requires deep thought and wise actions. Poor people should not be expected to conserve resources for the future when they are struggling to survive.

The trend today is based on the realisation that knowledge, culture and the environment seldom operate in isolation. There should be ample opportunity for knowledge systems to share information in a reciprocal way. Because no knowledge system is complete, there should always be space to learn and adapt. The problem with this approach is that there is seldom real space for reciprocal relationships (Treurnicht 2000:86). Unfortunately, one knowledge system usually dominates the other with a resulting limiting of reciprocal learning.

Approaches to sustainability occur with varying degrees of a preferable mix. Any development process in a social and environmental system needs particular inputs and outputs to maintain equilibrium and to grow and sustain itself over time. Growth and progress is seldom an unlimited process that can be sustained indefinitely. Any environmental system can only handle so much pressure before imbalances start to occur. This is precisely the reason why sustainable development at grassroots level is so vitally important.

Those knowledge systems that have helped to sustain environmental systems over long periods of time should be revitalised for promoting sustainable development where possible. Many civilisations before ours have come and gone or perhaps have changed into something completely different. We will have to live within the limits of our natural system. People-centred development will have to take note of the limits of our natural system, otherwise it may destroy the resource base crucial for our survival. The point of departure is that the local context with its own unique needs and dynamics is a determining variable in development. The people are the professionals because they have indigenous coping strategies that help them to make the most of their local environment (enabling setting). Participation is a key in the whole issue of context. New approaches to grassroots-level development deal with local dynamics finding operationalisation in participation.

Any system, whether a social or natural one, needs a certain measure of stability in order to cope with a specific challenge. Usually, coping with a challenge means to bring about changes. We therefore have the apparent anomaly that we need stability in order to change. If stability is not present, it is unlikely that change will be accepted. A manifestation of that stability is that the people themselves should control the process of development. They should determine the tempo and direction of the change. They will give meaning to the whole process so that it becomes much more than an externally induced change. This does not mean that all local development will automatically be sustainable and in harmony with the natural system. The chances are, however, that some local role players will want to protect that which is to their own good and in their own interest. The central focus in this regard is therefore who should manage environmental problems and who should decide how to address these problems. (See Case study 24: *Water to waste*.)

A further requirement for sustainability is that all development efforts should be experimental. Through learning from reality, through obtaining wisdom through experience, CDPs and the local people can build on appropriate structures that will be sympathetic to future needs. Learning for sustainable development should be open-ended and people should realise that collectively and individually they seldom have the knowledge to approach development with confidence. They have to realise their own limitations. This goes for indigenous people and Western experts.

6.2.6 Release

The real goal of development is to eradicate poverty, not to address poverty or deal with some of the manifestations of poverty. Release from poverty is a transformative practice. As Ledwith (2022:195) puts it: 'Participatory practice becomes a transformative practice when social justice is placed at the forefront of its agenda, prioritising an intention to act together for social change'.

Put another way, development wants to free people from the deprivation trap. Development efforts are efforts to break the deprivation trap so that people can become free. We are therefore talking about a vicious attack on the current situation in order to bring radical change. Development is not an effort to bring some relief to poor people or to improve their situation somewhat. Such efforts would rather fit in with welfare and betterment programmes.

The negative spin-off of such efforts is that they make the people increasingly dependent on their benefactors because their need for relief does not stop. Relief and improvement will not free people. The objective of these efforts is not to free people, but to help them to survive in their situation. Relieving efforts therefore tend to perpetuate the poverty situation. Therefore, we should rather be critical and alert in our judgement of so-called development efforts. Development agencies and their CDPs should gain clarity on whether their efforts try to address the symptoms of the situation without doing anything about the status quo. The direct opposite of this approach focuses on the whole person (the first principle) in his/her environment and on a total transformation so that his/her situation as a whole can be drastically changed or transformed.

If the whole person is to be the target of development, and if development aims to meet his/her abstract needs of self-reliance and dignity (the first principle), then it must be more than a relief operation. Development becomes an effort at releasing the whole person from the jaws of poverty. Projects often tend to maintain the status quo and this forces them to restrict themselves to bringing short-term or repetitive relief to a situation without addressing its causes. These efforts try to bring relief to trapped people without the slightest effort to free them from the trap.

Transforming efforts, on the other hand, do not try to bring relief. They attempt to release people from the trap so that, free and self-reliant, they can gradually improve the situation themselves. It is obvious, therefore, that transforming efforts are long-term activities that bring radical change to people's lives over a period of time. Case study 17: *Mothers of the mountain community* illustrates this process of transformation and release.

6.2.7 Conscientisation

According to Springett (2022a:170): 'Conscientisation is the antidote to thoughtless practice through reclaiming spaces for dissent, but in a space of trust and through an expansive loving process'.

Conscientisation is associated with group dynamics, reflection and learning. It takes place where members of a group share, listen and comment in a non-aggressive, searching way. Sensitisation is not an easy process because participants can feel exposed and threatened if they 'speak their mind'. In a teaching context, Armitage (2013:14) concludes that:

> ... the process of conscientization as the foundation where students [and group members in community development] can challenge and re-construct their personal and professional practices, and assumptions must be embedded within a PBL [problem-based learning] pedagogy.

6.3 PRACTICAL PRINCIPLES

A transforming, releasing approach and policy must also be carried out by transforming releasing actions. Appropriate actions are just as important as appropriate policies and approaches. In other words, you need to follow and respect certain practical principles in order to carry out the ethical principles.

6.3.1 Learning

The first of these practical principles goes without saying, but in our Western culture we have become so conditioned to ideas of excellence, perfection and professionalism that we need to be reminded of this axiom, namely that by continuously striving to fulfil their needs, people learn to realise their objectives more easily. This simple truism underpins the principle of learning.

Participation in a project therefore brings about learning. This is another important reason why people should participate in projects. And it is not only the poor people who learn. All role players, whether government, NGOs or CBOs, learn as they go along. Maistry (2012:36) makes use of Taylor (1998:294) when she points out that CDPs do not deliver development, but participate in a process that is developing. The CDP is therefore not the superintendent of development projects, but a participant of a learning process with the community and any other role player.

No one role player is the teacher. All are students and the teacher's position is taken up by the prevailing circumstances. This principle tells us something of the spirit in which community development projects should be approached. (See the principle of compassion in section 6.3.2.) It is clear that there is no place for elitism; so-called professional aloofness is quite out of place. It is also clear that CDPs should approach their task with humility, aware of the fact that there is a lot for them to learn, much of which will come from ordinary, simple people.

The intention of the learning process approach is to meet the need for '... a flexible, sustained, experimental, action based capacity building style of assistance ...' (Korten 1980:484). It is a bottom–up approach, avoiding the restrictions of a blueprint (top–down) approach. You can read more about this approach in Chapter 4.

Such a project can only result when unity can be attained between the following:

- *The needs of the 'target group' and the results of a project*: The project must address their 'felt' needs.
- *The formulation of needs and the power (of participants) to make decisions*: The participants must be in a position to decide on their needs and on what to do about it.
- *The objectives of the project and the capacity of the institution (responsible for the project)*: The institution must have the capacity to reach the objective.

An organisation must meet certain requirements in order to be able to do all these things. According to Korten (1980:498), this approach requires 'organisations with a well-developed capacity for responsive anticipatory adaptation – organisations that (a) embrace error; (b) plan with the people; and (c) link knowledge building with action'.

The logical result of using this approach should be greater emphasis on the autonomy of the poor, their right to decision making and their empowerment. This principle has certain strong consequences for development. An important one is that non-negotiable or preselected frameworks cannot curtail learning. The moment that a development agency approaches this task with certain set procedures and a decision-making mechanism that is removed from the people, the process of learning is impeded; in fact, it is just about wiped out.

Development agencies must send their CDPs to communities with an empty agenda. They should come into a community with a clean slate (Korten 1980); with nothing to offer but themselves, their compassion and their willingness to become involved through a learning process in the people's efforts to break free of the deprivation trap. In later chapters, we look at practical ways to accomplish this.

The principle here is quite clear, namely that CDPs should create as many learning opportunities as possible. (See Case study 16: *The felt need and the real need*.) There may be shorter and quicker routes to objective attainment, but if we want the results of projects to be permanent and the transformation of the situation lasting, then the longer and perhaps more arduous route of learning is the only way to bring self-reliance and eventually self-sufficiency.

6.3.2 Compassion

By now it must be quite clear that CDPs must be unique people with a broad range of skills that are carried by something that is akin to sympathy or empathy. The facilitating and enabling task of the CDPs is simply not just another job. The most skilful CDPs will still find it quite impossible to fulfil all these other principles if they miss the principle of compassion. Springett (2022b:21) emphasises that compassion is fundamental to participatory practice. An easy explanation of compassion is that people with compassion stand in the shoes of the object of their compassion (De Beer & Swanepoel 2013:39). While people find themselves in the deprivation trap, the CDPs should also experience that entrapment.

It is clear that this principle demands that aloofness on the side of the CDPs should be totally absent. CDPs should embrace compassion because it releases kindness (Ledwith 2022:205). It also demands that human dignity and happiness should be uppermost in their minds. The objective of CDPs and their organisations should not be just to help poor people gain some objective they had identified themselves. Yes, they should help, but the objective must be so much broader because the CDP and enabling institutions must be driven by compassion. For this reason, we place emphasis on aspects such as human orientation, sustainability and release. For this reason, CDPs are prompted to use research methodologies where the people 'receive the stick', where they obtain the responsibility to learn through their own efforts.

Compassion also has a very practical benefit in that it wins friends and draws out a response that makes cooperation possible within a project.

6.3.3 Adaptiveness

If the principle of learning is followed, we cannot be anything but adaptive. Adaptiveness is in direct contradiction to blueprint planning. Blueprint planning is technical, clean, precise and comprehensive, but inflexible. The learning takes place before planning begins. Learning consists of community profiles and feasibility studies. The situation in which development must take place is stable. Planning and implementation are the prerogatives of the professional planner and engineer. Their success is measured through cost–benefit analysis and impact studies. In this scenario, there is no place for adaptiveness and for learning as you progress. There is also no place for ordinary community members – most definitely not to make decisions (Swanepoel 2000:91). Professional planners are removed from reality, not only in mind, but also in body (Korten 1980:499). Most important, however, is that the blueprint approach simply cannot work in a situation where the poor are present and where it is the distinct objective to help them to break from the deprivation trap (Rondinelli 1993:90 et seq). If the CDPs play this role in this fashion, adaptiveness is thrown out of the window and therefore there is no learning process either.

This does not mean that there is no place for feasibility studies, cost–benefit analyses and impact studies. However, it does mean that, first, those tools must be adapted to the poverty or learning situation. Second, they must become the property of the participating poor who must be able to use them, and third, they are not the only tools, therefore they have a specific function that will not jeopardise the participation of the poor. There are other planning and evaluation tools just as well suited or even better suited to the situation.

Adaptive administration encapsulates bottom–up decision making, participation by communities and an improved responsiveness, creativity and innovative ability of institutions. Adaptive administration is characterised by partnership action with the aims of reducing the dependence of communities, to set democratic processes in action and to enhance human potential. The partnership can be described as follows: decisions on development strategies and the availability and allocation of resources are taken at central level, while decisions on implementation are taken locally in consultation with the communities concerned. CDPs treat the population as partners in the definition and solution of problems. Evaluation is based on process and results; development personnel are considered responsible for any improvement in the local communities' capacity for participation.

The principle of adaptiveness requires a change of mindset. It demands a willingness to learn as we go along. It stands for experimentation and therefore disjointed, sometimes dirty, short-term, trial and error planning and implementation. When the mindset conducive to this is achieved, the principle also requires complete organisational and procedural changes. Management should be fluid, changeable and adaptable. Structures should give space for manoeuvring and should be flexible, allowing new actions where and when necessary (De Beer & Swanepoel 1998:103). We therefore agree with Rosen and Painter (2019:239–240) that 'planning practice needs models that create more inclusive and adaptive processes to deconstruct the power and resource inequalities that prevent planning processes from building sustained community power'.

Adaptive institutions by definition will be highly adaptable to a wide variety of problems with no universally prescribed design and will be built on culturally accepted arrangements, practices and behaviour, but at the same time will try to transfer traditional practices and behaviour into more suitable arrangements. Cafer, Green and Goreham (2019:206) discuss the relationship between adaptiveness and community resilience to shocks, and declare the following: 'Community resilience involves, first, having the capacity to recover from previous debilitating events, but it also requires building adaptive capacity to prevent or withstand future events'.

6.3.4 Simplicity

The principle of simplicity contrasts sharply with the notion that 'bigger is better'. We tend to go for the big, the complex and the sophisticated. Gellert and Lynch (2003:22) explain this as follows:

> The faith in technology and belief in domination of nature central to modernisation ideology easily lead to a specific bias toward large scale on the part of international lending institutions, construction firms, and monumentalist states.

The situation of mass poverty is such that it seems that only large projects will make a dent. Also, it is politically expedient to tackle the problems of poverty in a big and grandiose way. Finally, we can also say that our psychological make-up is such that we believe in faster, higher, further; those who do not have this notion are looked upon as uncivilised, stupid and backward.

This is all part of Chambers' (1978:211) big project trap, saying that the learning, releasing approach is not suited to complex techniques. When the opportunity for learning and participation is curtailed, the very humanistic nature of development is in jeopardy. The enhancement of self-reliance and dignity becomes more remote. At the same time, the release from poverty becomes less of an issue. Adaptiveness is much more difficult to attain with complex projects.

We can say that all the principles that we have thus far discussed are jeopardised by large, complex and sophisticated projects. Does that mean that these principles are only of relevance to small and simple projects? Not necessarily, but it means that large projects should be broken down into smaller parts where the learning process can be enhanced. It also means that technical content should be explained to lay people so that they can make sense of it and still make informed decisions.

Gunton (2003:518) says that the impact of large projects should be assessed beforehand. These projects can generate significant growth, but the growth is not necessarily beneficial to the region. Gellert and Lynch (2003:15) add to this line of thinking when they argue that displacement is intrinsic to megaproject development.

The principle is quite clear, namely that the smaller and simpler a project, the easier it is to get long-lasting results. Therefore, if we want to adhere to all the principles that we have discussed so far, it is necessary to keep projects simple, at least as simple as can be, but when a project is of necessity large and sophisticated, CDPs should be aware of the warning signs and be focused to make the best of a difficult situation. Case study 8: *Small is better* illustrates the principle of simplicity.

This principle also tells us something about our approach to development efforts. It is again a matter of mindset. Chambers (1993:27–28) phrases the necessity for a different approach as follows:

> [T]he right starting point is not the means but the end, not the library but the village, not the methodology of appraisal but the poorer rural people. Starting from them rather than from the cost-benefit paradigm, and trying to see what approaches will help them rather than consummate the training project appraisal which many economists have received, leads away from complex procedures and towards the conclusion that for these purposes true sophistication lies in simplicity: in short, that simple is optimal [emphasis added].

6.4 CONCLUSION

The principles that we have discussed in this chapter are not objectives. They are not aims to be attained somewhere in the future. They are absolutely necessary to make community development work as it should work with the result of freeing people from the deprivation trap. They are the building blocks of the characteristics of community development as we have discussed them in Chapter 5.

Projects provide a concrete structure that makes it possible to have funds allocated or donated to the project. Because projects are well structured, they provide scope for various roles to be played and they arrange these roles into a viable entity so that the roles will be mutually supportive and will serve the same purpose. However, projects can be used for all the wrong reasons and do more damage than good. So, in order to be this good foundation for development and in order to accomplish what it sets out to do, it is necessary that projects follow the guiding principles discussed in this chapter. The ethical principles must inform the approach towards development even before projects are established, but also during the life of projects. The practical principles must guide the implementation of development so that the poor will reap the benefits.

People must progress in realising their inner potential while working to fulfil their physical needs. The huge problem of sustaining development and maintaining facilities can be solved by making the local people owners. Empowerment is therefore a mixture between the right to make decisions and the ability to make decisions.

People must have ownership of their own development. They must be the owners of their own destiny. Relief and improvement will not free people. The objective of these efforts is not to free people, but to help them to survive in their situation.

To create as many learning opportunities as possible can be regarded as another of the prime tasks of the CDP.

REFERENCES

Armitage A. 2013. Conscientization, dialogue and collaborative problem based learning. *Journal of Problem-based Learning in Higher Education*, 1(1):1–18.

Arnstein SR. 2019. A ladder of citizen participation. *Journal of the American Planning Association*, 85(1).

Cafer A, Green J & Goreham G. 2019. A community resilience framework for community development practitioners building equity and adaptive capacity. *Community Development*, 50(2):201–216.

Chambers R. 1978. Project selection for poverty-focused rural development: Simple is optimal. *World Development*, 6(2):209–219.

Chambers R. 1983. *Rural Development: Putting the Last First*. Essex: Longman.

Chambers R. 1993. *Challenging the Professions: Frontiers for Rural Development*. London: IT Publications.

De Beer FC & Swanepoel HJ. 1998. *Community Development and Beyond: Issues, Structures and Procedures*. Pretoria: Van Schaik.

De Beer F & Swanepoel H. 2012. A postscript as an introduction: Do we know where to go with the professionalisation of community development in South Africa? *Africanus Journal of Development Studies*, 42(2):3–13.

De Beer F & Swanepoel H. 2013. *The Community Development Profession: Issues, Concepts and Approaches*. Pretoria: Van Schaik.

El Sherbini AA. 1986. Alleviating rural poverty in sub-Saharan Africa. *Food Policy*, 11(1):7–11.

Gellert PK & Lynch BD. 2003. Mega-projects as displacements. *International Social Science Journal*, 55(175):15–25.

Guaraldo Choguill MB. 1996. A ladder of community participation for underdeveloped countries. *Habitat International*, 20(3):431–444.

Gunton T. 2003. Megaprojects and regional development: Pathologies in project planning. *Regional Studies*, 37(5):505–519.

Himanen P. 2014. Dignity as development. In Castells M & Himanen P (eds), *Reconceptualizing Development in the Information Age*. Oxford: Oxford University Press.

Kamin T, Kubacki K & Atanasova S. 2022. Empowerment in social marketing: Systematic review and critical reflection. *Journal of Marketing Management*, 38(11–12): 1104–1136. doi: 10.1080/0267257X.2022.2078864

Kiefer L. 2014. Community ownership key to sustaining community-based interventions. Available at: https://www.comminit.com/content/community-ownership-key-sustaining-community-based-interventions (accessed 10 September 2022).

Korten DC. 1980. Community organization and rural development: A learning process approach. *Public Administration Review*, 40(5):480–511.

Ledwith M. 2022. Transformative practice. In Ledwith M & Springett J (eds), *Participatory Practice: Community-based Action for Transformative Change*. Bristol: Policy Press.

Ledwith M & Springett J. 2022. *Participatory Practice: Community-based Action for Transformative Change*. Bristol: Policy Press.

Maistry M. 2012. Towards professionalisation: Journey of community development in the African and South African context. *Africanus*, 42(2):29–41.

Mulwa FW. 2012. The practice of community development in Kenya: Challenges and issues for professionalisation. *Africanus*, 42(2):67–80.

Nussbaum M. 2020. The capabilities approach and the history of philosophy. In Chiappero-Martinetti E, Osmani S & Qizilbash M (eds), *The Cambridge Handbook of the Capability Approach*. Cambridge: Cambridge University Press.

Nussbaum MC. 2000. *Women and Human Development: The Capabilities Approach*. Cambridge: Cambridge University Press.

Regan C. 2012. Too much problem solving and not enough mischief making. Community development in Ireland: Issues and challenges. *Africanus*, 42(2):81–92.

Rondinelli DA. 1993. *Development Projects as Policy Experiments. An Adaptive Approach to Development Administration*. 2nd ed. London: Routledge.

Rosen J & Painter G. 2019. From citizen control to co-production. *Journal of the American Planning Association*, 85(3):335–347.

Sowman M & Gawith M. 1994. Participation of disadvantaged communities in project planning and decision making: A case study of Hout Bay. *Development Southern Africa*, 11(4):557–571.

Spalding NL. 1990. The relevance of basic needs for political and economic development. *Studies in Comparative International Development*, 25(3):90–115.

Springett K. 2022a. Critical reflection and reflexivity. In Ledwith M & Springett J (eds), *Participatory Practice: Community-based Action for Transformative Change*. Bristol: Policy Press.

Springett K. 2022b. Participatory practice. In Ledwith M & Springett J (eds), *Participatory Practice: Community-based Action for Transformative Change*. Bristol: Policy Press.

Swanepoel H. 2000. The state and development. In De Beer FC & Swanepoel HJ (eds), *Introduction to Development Studies*. Cape Town: Oxford University Press.

Taconni L & Tisdell C. 1993. Holistic sustainable development: Implications for planning processes, foreign aid and support for research. *Third World Planning Review*, 15(4):411–428.

Treurnicht S. 2000. Sustainable development. In De Beer FC & Swanepoel HJ (eds), *Introduction to Development Studies*. Cape Town: Oxford University Press.

Whitehead KA, Kriel AJ & Richter LM. 2005. Barriers to conducting a community mobilization intervention among youth in a rural South African community. *Journal of Community Psychology*, 33(3):253–259.

Wisner B. 1988. *Power and Need in Africa: Basic Human Needs and Development Policies*. London: Earthscan.

CHAPTER 7

The Community as Main Actor in Community Development

Hennie Swanepoel and Frik de Beer

7.1 INTRODUCTION

Community is usually defined in terms of geographic locality, of shared interests or needs, or in terms of deprivation and disadvantage. In our (African) situation, implicit in the use of the concept is either the (sometimes romantic) image of the traditional African village or, because of its prominence and visibility, the urban squatter or informal settlement (De Beer & Swanepoel 2013:49). These groupings of people, be it rural village or urban informal settlement, are always seen as poor, deprived or disadvantaged, and are described as receivers or non-receivers of services, as targets for development and as beneficiaries. Unfortunately, they are not often seen as very important role players in their own development.

This chapter will describe and discuss these groupings specifically as role players, in other words, mobilised to do rather than prompted to receive. We have already seen in chapters 5 and 6 that to do means much more than only physical labour, and this chapter will reiterate that.

7.2 THE MEANING OF COMMUNITY

A community consists of individuals, groupings and a physical environment. A community is a unique, living entity and, like its people, it undergoes continuous physical and psychological change. Parker (2018:4) has a more romantic, perhaps psychological view when he states the following: 'Community offers the promise of belonging and calls for us to acknowledge our interdependence. To belong is to act as investor, owner, and creator of this place'.

Societies consist of individuals and institutions. Institutions are groupings of people sharing common characteristics, circumstances or goals.

They are in varying degrees organised and include primary institutions or groups such as families, and secondary institutions such as schools, churches and various interest groups (eg burial societies and sport clubs); we can even count friendships under this category. Most institutions or groups have a certain hierarchical structure. These various institutions are bound together by people and by interests. They also interact with one another in ways that suit their interests.

A community, therefore, is not an easily defined, isolated or permanent entity that can be approached and organised for community development purposes. We can safely say that community development practitioners (CDPs) do not necessarily enter a community. More often than not, they enter an inhabited area, an area inhabited by communities.

Edwards and Jones (1976:12), with whom we mostly disagree, define community in terms of geography:

> ... a grouping of people who reside in a specific locality and who exercise some degree of local autonomy in organizing their social life in such a way that they can, from that locality base, satisfy the full range of their daily needs.

This definition is open to criticism. What degree or measure of local autonomy are they talking about? Many entities practising community development have very little autonomy and would be disqualified in terms of this definition (De Beer 1984:43). It would be a mistake to see community as homogeneous with shared norms and values (Sihlongonyane 2001:38). Similarly, it would be exceptional to find a community that is able to 'satisfy the full range of their daily needs' from local resources. The important thing is that this definition describes a community as 'all the people' residing in a certain locality. When we regard the community as a role player or stakeholder in development, we cannot view it as the entire populace. First, any community will be represented by a political structure such as a ward with a councillor. Second, it will never happen that the whole community will share the same concern, the same level of deprivation or the same sense of urgency because of a certain need or problem.

We prefer not to see the community as the entire populace in a certain locality for other reasons of incorrect use. The first is that there is a notion that the community is intrinsically good. This has been challenged by those who argue that it is morally and culturally narrow-minded; oppressive to women, outsiders and minorities; and not harmonious as sometimes painted

(Sihlongonyane 2001:38). The second reason is that the community is often given a false sense of identity when political parties or senior government officials claim that they have 'consulted the community'. In other words, 'it can be used as an agent of stereotyping, in order to legitimise state or sectional interests' (Sihlongonyane 2001:38). Ojha, Ford, Keenan et al (2016) view community from a natural resource management perspective. They are of the opinion that small-scale, geographically focused groups might remain functional in more secluded areas, but they deem it important to 'emphasize that a continued focus on the localized view of a community is not helpful in understanding contemporary socio-environmental challenges associated with community based resource management' (Ojha et al 2016:275).

The emphasis expressed in the quote above should be noted for different settings in which CDPs work.

CDPs sometimes fall into the trap of trying to organise the whole community for which they are responsible. This is impossible, and therefore a waste of time. The best attempts to organise a whole community will only yield small groups of willing participants.

CDPs might well spare themselves a lot of unnecessary work and frustration by starting with small groups. The rule should be to work from the inside outwards, to start with one group and one project. The learning process that takes place and its demonstration effect will allow other action groups to be established for further projects.

Therefore, only those who share a maximum of concern will come together and work together to address that need. Parker (2018:11) describes this working together, almost poetically and innocently:

> In community building we choose the people and the conversation that will produce the accountability to build relatedness, structure belonging and move the action forward ... weaving and strengthening the fabric of a community is a collective effort.

We view community as the point of departure in any discussion about community development. At its most basic, community is defined on two levels: (1) a shared space, be it geographic or virtual, and (2) shared interests, concerns and/or ideas. Now we are dealing with a group within the society and they are an entity because they share a common need or problem that they want addressed. However, not all individuals in a particular space (community) share all the ideas, interests or passions, and therefore it is not fair to assume that all individuals of a given community will as a matter fact be in close association with a project; for example, people without children of school-going age would not share the school as a concern, they may not believe that anything can (or should) be done about the concern, they might not have the time to participate, or they may simply be one of a majority of individuals with no sense of society or community.

While we have indicated in Chapter 5 that ordinary people play a primary role in community development, we can now say that those ordinary people do not represent the whole community. Our use of the term 'community' refers to that group of ordinary concerned people, despite its size. We are in agreement with the UN (2020:1), which defines community as:

> ... often a geographical subset of society at the local level, a 'community' can be defined by commonalities such as, but not limited to, norms, religion, shared interests, customs, values and needs of civilians. A community is not static or closed, but constantly evolving subject to internal and external construction and reconstruction.

It is important to emphasise that a lot of assumptions regarding community are wrong, misleading or even outright dangerous to the success of community development. Communities are not homogeneous entities where all work together in a spirit of sharing. Very few individuals will share the notion of the common good for society. Communities, for our purposes, can consist of spatially separated people who share common needs and values. Regarding this larger society, it should be remembered that the society is not asleep, waiting to be woken by the CDP. Neither is society at its last breath waiting to be redeemed by the CDP. Society is busy with a rational existence that makes sense to its citizens.

7.3 COMMUNITY AS STAKEHOLDER AND ROLE PLAYER

It is dangerous to see the community as a role player or just one of a number of stakeholders. The danger lies in the fact that if the community is not the main role player, our principles discussed in Chapter 6 fly out of the window. As we have shown in Chapter 6, participation is an elusive concept. However, it is quite often made elusive in order to weaken the meaning. The word is used by those opting for a systems-maintaining, conforming kind of participation. Community is also, in the system-maintaining context, nostalgically viewed as a thing (such as in a gone-by golden age) of a secure neighbourhood, a place of intimacy, and warmth and social cohesion (Popple 2015:12).

It is also recognised as a liberal, even conservative, approach with an absence of 'participatory experiences from self-reliant grassroots organizations' (Burbidge 1988:188). On the other hand, the word is also used by those who equate it with power. They are regarded as the radicals, or those in favour of systems transformation.

Wisner (1988:14) distinguishes between a 'strong' and a 'weak' interpretation of participation. The strong interpretation:

> ... advocated a new style of development which was radically participatory and in which land reform, asset redistribution and other necessary preconditions set the stage for the poor to take control of their own development, usually through grassroots organizations ... On the other side was the 'weak' interpretation of participatory development ... [that] saw participation as a limited, formalized process, stripped of the political volatility of direct popular involvement.
>
> This division between systems-maintaining, weak or conservative interpretations and systems-transforming, strong or radical interpretations is of pivotal importance in the debate on participatory development. The debate distinguishes between two analytical groupings, the 'participation as involvement' and the 'empowerment' schools.

To us, involvement refers to co-option, or at best the mobilisation of communities, a system-maintaining mechanism to attempt involvement of people in the execution of top–down determined development plans and projects (De Beer & Swanepoel 1998:33). This is simply not good enough. In this instance, the community is not the main role player.

When the community becomes the main role player, the other role players and their roles become clearer. Government and NGOs will still give support and material assistance to communities. Aid agencies have a role to play, as does the private sector. Finding the appropriate role for each and accommodating the various roles is part of the question addressed by empowerment. It is not a matter of the community versus the rest, but of the community and the rest.

Mulwa (2012:68) distinguishes between external expertise and community driven processes Both of these play a role, but the role of the professional

(CDP) cannot be more conspicuous than facilitating. In fact, the support and facilitation included in this radical approach are of the greatest importance, without which community development simply cannot operate. (See De Beer and Swanepoel (2013:49–50) in this regard.)

What is needed is true decentralisation of decision-making processes:

> ... decentralisation means freedom of civil society and the whole realm of associational life to organise their membership to engage in actions that are beneficial to them or to question the state *(Makara 2018:24, quoting Tostensin 2001).*

We are dealing here with the idea of citizen control of development (Reed 2008).

There are three types of grouping suited to becoming action groups for community development projects: the interest group, the ad hoc group and the elected committee.

7.3.1 The interest group

An interest group can act as an action group. The knitting club can launch a project to provide every child with a jersey for the winter. A youth club can launch a city-cleaning project, and a farmers' association can launch a woodlot project. In these three examples, it is clear that the interest group is working towards goals outside of itself. It is obvious, therefore, that those in need, those agreeing with the concern to be addressed, must form part of the project and therefore the decision making of the project.

If an interest group decides to start a community development project, it cannot do so as part of its normal functions. A community development project is too intense and requires too much attention to be treated as just one of many activities to be undertaken by that interest group. The interest group will be well advised to give a smaller group of people, perhaps those with a special interest in that type of project, responsibility for the project. Such a group can then function as a subcommittee of the interest group's executive and can report to it at regular intervals.

The advantage of an existing interest group is that it is already established, with a structure and a certain way of doing things as well as infrastructure that can be used for a project. The knitting club that wants to provide every child with a jersey will use its knitting machines for the job and will buy the wool or yarn from its regular supplier. The members of an interest group also know one another and are used to working together. It will not be necessary to go through an initial period of finding and accepting one another as will be the case with newly formed groups.

The disadvantage of existing interest groups is that they may be busy with so many things that the community development project is given little attention, or it may be so dedicated to its primary objective that the community development project's objective may be regarded as secondary. A church deciding to launch a project is a good example. The church's normal interest and occupation, that is religion, may take up so much of its time and attention that the community development project is neglected. There is another disadvantage attached to established structures and functions. While they may have tremendous advantages, they may be so entrenched in their ways that the learning process cannot proceed properly. If this happens, the principle of adaptiveness is not adhered to. A very positive grouping can therefore still be a danger for the success of the project.

7.3.2 The ad hoc group

The second type of group that can fulfil the role of an action group in a community development project is the ad hoc group of concerned individuals united by a common need or concern. When individuals start finding common ground with others around a certain issue, they are becoming a group of concerned citizens. The next step will be to talk among themselves about possible solutions to their common problem and the final step will be taken when, together, they decide to do something about it collectively. They will then have reached the stage where they can start to act as an action group for a community development project.

The fact that they share a common characteristic (eg mothers of babies) will not make them a potential action group. The necessary ingredient is not the common characteristic, but the fact that they are all concerned about the same thing. Their concern is the important criterion. Added to this is the input of a CDP. This does not mean that a project cannot be started and completed without the CDP. It simply makes the process easier and the participants aware of the situation in which they operate.

The main weakness of this type of group is the newness of association. Members may not know one another very well and a system of working together may be absent. It may take quite some time for them to gel as a group and only then can a concerted effort begin. CDPs should make it their special task to form such a group of individuals into a group that can work together in a community development project. (See Chapter 11 in this regard.)

7.3.3 The elected committee

It may happen that a relatively large group of people, present at perhaps a public meeting for a ward or constituency, will decide on a project and will then elect a development committee to address the identified problem or a project steering committee to launch and run a project.

The advantage of such a group is that it usually has a relatively clear brief. It can therefore start with its work immediately. The disadvantages are that it may have such narrow parameters that it has little freedom for learning and adaptation. Such a committee may consist of representatives of various groupings within a community; this may make it difficult to operate simply because rivalries and animosities may exist among the members. There may be experts in this group, which can be a good or a bad thing.

The other type of elected committee usually acts in a more permanent way. That is the clinic committee or school committee. These committees are not created specifically to launch projects. They are elected to look after the interests of institutions such as clinics and schools or to improve a service such as water reticulation or sewage. In this role these committees can decide to launch some project or projects or even a programme consisting of a few projects.

7.4 CONCLUSION

It is clear that the action group in a community development project cannot be an amorphous mass of individuals. It must be possible to define it in terms of certain criteria. The most important criteria will be a common, genuine concern and a committed membership.

It is also clear that in most poverty environments, the size of a group and the proximity of its members are important aspects determining the ease with which it will operate. The larger the group, the more difficult it will be to identify a common need and objective. The further they live from one another, the more difficult it will be for them to come together for collective action. Chapter 11 deals with groups in more detail.

Community development is meant for communities, according to our view of communities. The action, including planning and decision making, takes place at grassroots level with ordinary people. Just as the need is something experienced, felt and identified by the ordinary people, so is the action to address that need taken by the people. The community is therefore the main role player and all other agencies or stakeholders, be they governmental, non-governmental or private sector, play a supporting, aiding and facilitating role as is illustrated in the next chapter when the CDP is discussed.

REFERENCES

Burbidge J (ed). 1988. *Approaches that Work in Rural Development: Emerging Trends, Participatory Methods and Local Initiatives*. München: Saur.

De Beer FC. 1984. *Gemeenskapsontwikkeling, hervestiging en behuising in Steilloopdorp*. Unpublished MA thesis, University of South Africa, Pretoria.

De Beer F & Swanepoel H. 2013. *The Community Development Profession: Issues, Concepts and Approaches*. Pretoria: Van Schaik.

Edwards AD & Jones DG. 1976. *Community and Community Development*. The Hague: Mouton.

Makara S. 2018. Decentralisation and good governance in Africa: A critical review. *African Journal of Political Science and International Relations*, 12(2):22–32.

Mulwa FW. 2012. The practice of community development in Kenya: Challenges and issues for professionalisation. *Africanus*, 42(2):67–80.

Ojha HR, Ford R, Keenan RJ, Race D, Carius Vega D, Baral H & Sapkota P. 2016. Delocalizing communities: Changing forms of community engagement in natural resources governance. *World Development*, 87:274–290.

Parker P. 2018. *Community: The Structure of Belonging*. 2nd ed. Oakland: Berret-Koehler.

Popple K. 2015. *Analysing Community Work: Theory and Practice*. Berkshire: Open University Press.

Reed M. 2008. Stakeholder participation for environmental management: A literature review. *Biological Conservation*, 141(10):2417–2431.

Sihlongonyane MF. 2001. The rhetoric of the community in project management: The case of Mohlakeng township. *Development in Practice*, 11(1):34–44.

Sowman M & Gawith M. 1994. Participation of disadvantaged communities in project planning and decision making: A case study of Hout Bay. *Development Southern Africa*, 11(4):557–571.

United Nations. 2020. United Nations community engagement guidelines on peacebuilding and sustaining peace. Available at: https://www.un.org/peacebuilding/content/un-community-engagement-guidelines-peacebuilding-and-sustaining-peace-0 (accessed 6 May 2023).

Wisner B. 1988. *Power and Need in Africa: Basic Human Needs and Development Policies*. London: Earthscan.

CHAPTER 8

Place and Role of Community Development Practitioners

Hennie Swanepoel and Frik de Beer

8.1 INTRODUCTION

Community development practitioners (CDPs) need not be professionals, but quite often they are. A CDP can be a specialist professional, such as an agricultural extension officer, an engineer, a social worker, teacher, nurse or occupational therapist. These professionals will not be called CDPs, but will operate under their occupational titles.

A second category of professionals is generalist CDPs, who usually have a coordinating task and who concern themselves mostly with the mobilisation of people for development and the running of development projects. These so-called generalists comprise many people not trained for a specific task, who have been appointed to the bottom of the departmental hierarchy by government departments and provincial and local governments. These people need immediate and appropriate training so that they can get to grips with their jobs (see Chapter 26 in this regard).

In the NGO cadre, there are also professional specialists with a keen interest in community development and then there are volunteers who may have some specialist training or who may have no specific training for what they are doing.

This is quite a mixture, enhancing the possibility of misunderstanding, competition and animosity. The development of professionalisation of the CDP's task asks a lot from decision makers and policy makers. The positive aspect is that there are professionals with professional knowledge and experience for every need and concern in a community. The CDP's task is the least professionalised and this book, together with others, tries to address this shortfall.

We can conclude that CDPs are either employed by government, or they are volunteers or employees of NGOs. They are either employed or tasked to play a broad, general facilitating role in community development, or they are specialists in various fields who can play the role of CDP if a project is about their speciality. They are, in other words, executing their line functions, but through projects. When we deal with the place, attitude and role of the CDP in this chapter, we try to include all these different types of workers.

The extremely vulnerable position of the poor and the great difficulties they encounter in breaking out of the deprivation trap make it essential that CDPs act as resources to these people. The role of resource can be either overplayed or underplayed. In most instances, it is overplayed in that the CDP is more, or becomes more, than only a resource. The tendency is always to overplay the role: to be too forceful, to take leadership, to do things by oneself. In most cases overplaying the role is the result of a poor perception of the CDP's task and role or an inconsiderate attitude. Even if the attitude is right, the situation is such that it invites overplay. To compound the situation, few people will see anything wrong in playing a more forceful and primary role, especially if the action group lacks vitality.

Yet, it is of critical importance that the role should never be overplayed because then the opportunity is taken away from the people to take charge and responsibility for their own fate. It also leads to a situation where it will be very difficult for the CDP to 'get rid' of a project, so to speak. People will either be fairly satisfied with the CDP's execution of the role of owner or manager, or they will feel themselves obliged to leave things as they are because it is the 'right thing' to do. However, in the meantime, ethical principles are ignored, with very bad consequences.

The fact is that the position of the CDP is precarious and difficult at the best of times, and for that reason attention must be paid to this role. It is clear that CDPs can be resources only if they are very careful regarding their position, their goals and attitudes, and their part in the process.

8.2 CONTEXTUAL ASPECTS GUIDING THE CDP'S TASK

CDPs do not work in a vacuum. They and their organisations are part of a group of stakeholders and, as such, they need to take a certain position and represent it. We have heard many times that we must be prepared before we start doing anything. CDPs' operational strategy is their preparation for their work as CDP. (See Chapter 18 for more on the operational strategy of the CDP.) This operational strategy reflects CDPs' relationship with the organisation they work for. We can safely say that the relationship between CDPs and their organisations determines what CDPs will do and how they will do it. It is this relationship between CDPs and their organisations that we will contemplate further.

The operational strategy is guided by the relationship between CDPs and their organisation. It is also influenced by the expectations held of each other. The relationship between CDPs and their organisation is determined by, among others, the law, training and human resource practices.

8.2.1 The law

The national Constitution and the laws laid down in terms of it, provide the framework or guidelines according to which a government institution functions. The law usually spells out what policy goals need to be achieved by certain institutions. While NGOs and CBOs determine their goals somewhat differently since they are not established in terms of a statute, they too have to abide by the Constitution and work within the parameters set by laws.

In South Africa, the following are examples of laws that influence and set guidelines for the work done by CDPs:

- *The Constitution of the Republic of South Africa, 1996*: In section 152, references are made to the encouragement of community involvement as an aim of local government. In fact, the Constitution is very specific on the aims when it states that local government must aim to 'promote social and economic development' (s 152(1)(c)) and 'a municipality must ... promote the social and economic development of the community' (s 153(a)).

- *Municipal Demarcation Act 27 of 1998, Municipal Structures Act 117 of 1998 and the Municipal Systems Act 32 of 2000*: These all contribute to the development aims of the government.

- *Spatial Planning and Land Use Management Act 16 of 2013 (SPLUMA)*: This came into operation in July 2015. SPLUMA is national legislation, applicable to the whole of South Africa and intends to 'consolidate the fragmented system of planning previously in place'. It is essentially a tool for land and spatial planning in urban areas (Malehan 2018:24).

8.2.2 Training

With training, certain values, skills and attitudes can be engendered within employees. Training that is interactive will probably achieve the best results. Yet, it is not only the CDPs who need training.

Middle and top management also need training on topics similar to those to which the CDPs are exposed. The managers especially need to be trained to understand their role as facilitators and enablers of CDPs. If they do not grasp how this role should work, CDPs will have an uphill battle in achieving the goals set for community development. Training as a tool to establish and strengthen a healthy relationship between the employee CDPs and their organisation applies equally to employees in government, private and NGO institutions. Development training is dealt with in detail in chapters 22 and 23.

8.2.3 Human resource practices

Following standard human resource practices encourages an atmosphere of transparency and fairness. Employees know the rules that apply to their remuneration and benefits. They should also know what is expected of them and have the tools to perform optimally. Yet, sometimes the most important tool – a job description – is weak or non-existent and the CDP is expected to perform in a void. In all types of organisation, the setting of a clear, well-organised and negotiated job description is crucial for the achievement of optimum results. Middle and senior managers must understand the contents of the job description and also know what is required of them as managers or 'enablers' in terms of support needed for the CDPs to be effective in their jobs. In addition, the necessary hardware, logistical support and maintenance must be available for CDPs to do their work.

8.3 ETHICAL GUIDELINES

The code of ethics for CDPs is expected to become effective after inauguration of the professional board during 2023. If, however, CDPs are specialist professionals such as nurses, teachers and social workers, they will have their own code of ethics for their professions. Any set of ethical guidelines is based, roughly, on the following beliefs:

- Every human being has unique value and potential, irrespective of origin, ethnicity, sex, age, beliefs, socio-economic and legal status.
- Each individual has the right to the fulfilment of his/her innate and acquired skills.
- The professional has a responsibility to devote his/her knowledge and skills to the benefit of each individual, group, community and mankind.
- The professional has a primary obligation to render service professionally.

The following acts or omissions are usually regarded as improper:
- Negligent performance of duties
- Execution of duties in a manner which does not comply with generally accepted standards
- Behaviour which is detrimental to the occupation
- Dishonesty in the execution of duties
- Receiving or agreeing to receive direct or indirect compensation or any other form of incentive other than a normal salary
- Refusing, without sufficient cause, to render services which he/she took on or for which he/she was employed
- Failure to keep a record of acts performed, money managed and fees charged in all matters dealt with by him/her in his/her professional capacity
- The receipt of any bribe, or agreement to receive any bribe, in connection with any matter which is directly or indirectly related to his/her duties
- Direct or indirect criticism of the work of a colleague or a professional person he/she has dealt with in the execution of his/her duty
- Casting of reflections directly or indirectly upon the probity, professional reputation, skill, competence, knowledge or qualifications of a colleague or such other professional person
- Breaching his/her contract of service or behaviour that would justify his/her summary dismissal at common law
- Practising or carrying out from his/her offices any business, trade, work or occupation apart from his/her ordinary job.

In summary, a phrase used by Ledwith (2022:135) gives a suitable ethical guideline to dealing with people: 'Relate well to others and the world by living with kindness, caring, compassion and cooperation'.

8.4 POSITION

We will agree that CDPs occupy very delicate and, at the same time, difficult positions. If we remind ourselves that CDPs usually have more expertise than the people, are usually better educated than they are, are better able to organise and plan, are in a better position to anticipate the outcome of actions, and are equipped with more external links, it seems quite natural that they take up leadership positions. Yet, this is the last thing they should do. CDPs must never accept positions that lead to situations of dependency between them and the people. They may, therefore, not accept leadership positions.

Their position may never put the people's preeminence in danger by remembering the principle of human orientation (see Chapter 6): viewing human beings as more important than their needs (De Beer & Swanepoel 2013:81). The community fills the primary position and CDPs hold secondary positions. Because many of them are specialists, there are those among them who expect the people from a poor and less sophisticated community to respond to them in a sheep-like way. However, if we accept the importance of listening in contact making and learning with people, then we also agree with the Freirean understanding of the importance of dialogue in a situation where power is not equal between participants in the conversation. Professionals as CDPs must open themselves to authentic dialogue: 'Authentic dialogue overtly intends to equalise power between people, whereas in most conversations the power relations of wider society get acted out in personal encounters' (Springett 2022:149).

It is again, as we have seen in Chapter 6, a matter of ownership. As long as CDPs regard a project as their property, people will be invited on the CDPs' terms and conditions when in fact, the roles should be reversed and CDPs should respond to the invitation from the people to become involved in their effort.

It will be to the advantage of CDPs to play their role with the utmost care from the moment of entry. The people should realise from the outset that no activity and no organised effort will ever belong to the CDP. It is not a matter of gradually transferring ownership, which is, if not impossible, then at least a very difficult task. CDPs should never talk of 'my' or 'our' project. Just as the needs and problems are those of the people, to the same extent efforts to address the needs/problems should be the property and responsibility of the people.

8.5 GOALS

It may sound strange, but CDPs' goals are not to fulfil people's concrete needs. Although people address their concrete needs in projects and therefore have concrete objectives, it is dangerous for CDPs to make the concrete objectives their own, because they can then begin to pull the community along towards the concrete objectives at their own pace. It is natural for CDPs to want communities to reach their concrete objectives, but that is not paramount for them, even in the case of a specialist line functionary such as an agricultural extension officer. CDPs' goals lie on another, perhaps less concrete level. Their goals are as follows:

- *To enable the people to fulfil their abstract human needs*: In other words, the CDP is interested in an enhanced human dignity among the poor, a lasting self-reliance that softens their dependency, a positive self-perception that bodes well for efforts to break out of the deprivation trap, and a general air of happiness and contentment that tells us that people are becoming free of the deprivation trap. The CDP's goals lie on an altogether different (perhaps higher) plain. It will be a happy day for community development if more CDPs and the organisations employing them will realise and understand this aspect.

- *To enhance the learning process*: The growth in self-reliance, dignity and contentment is the result of a vigorous learning process where each and every person involved learns as much as there is to be learnt so that the next step, the next effort, the next project will be better. If CDPs share the concrete goals of the people, they may be tempted to take short cuts in order to reach the goal sooner; in fact, is that not what efficiency is all about? However, if CDPs' goals lie on a different plane, they will not mind going the longer route through learning opportunities.

- *To help the people achieve meaningful empowerment*: In the final analysis, development should be more than mere service delivery. It should follow a path and produce results that are ensured by careful decision making by those nearest to the situation. In order to make this possible, the CDP's whole effort should be aimed at providing the people with the information they need to make informed decisions.

To fulfil the first principle is, in a way, to fulfil them all because abstract human needs such as self-reliance, happiness and dignity lie at the heart of empowerment and release. To enhance the learning process is the practical way to enable people to fulfil those needs while they learn to cope with the situation. Eventually, the end result is true empowerment that transcends the scope of the liberal and often overused meaning of the word.

8.6 ATTITUDE

We are dealing with an extremely difficult and complex job. We can state without fear of opposition that this task demands from the CDP wisdom, dedication and the correct attitude. The CDP needs to be more than just a smart professional. The CDP needs a vast collection of knowledge to use personally and to share with the community. However, the CDP also needs the insight to be able to predict the reaction of people and the progress and advancement of a project. When we run through these attitudes it becomes clear that the CDP's job also requires dedication. It is not a job with large remuneration; it is not an eye-catching job; it is a backroom job by a dedicated professional.

Yes, it is clear that the attitude of the CDP is of prime importance. The correct attitude opens doors, while the wrong attitude closes them. The wrong attitude can also cause misunderstandings regarding the CDP's role and obligations. Good planning, reliable funding and prompt action are all ingredients necessary for success, but the attitude of the CDP is more important.

The following are a number of important guidelines addressed to CDPs regarding their attitude:

- Do not regard yourself as a superhuman person who will save the people. You are not superhuman and it is not your job to save the people.

- Never regard your job as mundane. What you do can decide whether people live on in abject poverty or are released from the deprivation trap.
- Have respect for the knowledge and wisdom of the people. The fact that some of them are illiterate and most of them are not well educated does not mean that any of them are stupid.
- Show respect for the people's views and feelings. These things are dear to them and disrespect will solicit the wrong reaction. If you respect their knowledge and wisdom, you will also respect their views and feelings. Their views and feelings are usually informed by their culture and world view which are valuable resources in the fight against poverty. (See Case study 9: *The daughter of hope*.)
- Respect the people as human beings. They already suffer a lack of human dignity and quite often they have a negative self-perception that should not be made worse by your attitude.
- Have and show compassion for people who are suffering in poverty. Compassion is not only to have sympathy for people. It is a willingness to share their situation and their experience of that situation. It is the willingness to stand in the shoes of other people. Aloofness never goes down well, but compassion generates a willingness to accept CDPs and work with them. It is very difficult to react negatively to compassion. On the other hand, absence of compassion will frustrate CDPs and will make of them the type of person that poor people will not trust and accept as someone to help them fight against poverty (see Chapter 6).
- Guard against paternalism (and often 'maternalism'). The people are not children awaiting your kind, benevolent, but strict leadership. (See Case study 21: *The loving teacher*.)
- Do not underestimate people and do not belittle them. CDPs come to the people with an empty slate and only themselves to offer.
- Regard yourself as the people's servant and supporter. This will take care of your position *vis-à-vis* theirs.
- Be humble. Poor people are usually very humble and you should not stand out while you are among them. See Case study 22: *Brutal force among the cabbage plants* as an illustration of the opposite attitude. Your humility will also give credence to their leadership because your position will not be a threat to them.

- Align yourself with the people's success. They are so seldom successful in a spectacular kind of way and they therefore get so little credit for anything, that you can acknowledge their accomplishments, even if they are small. In this way you can build their dignity.

We can conclude that it takes a certain type of person to be a successful CDP. In Chapter 10, we will see that people at peace with themselves and those who do not mistrust all other people are usually good communicators. We can say the same of being a successful CDP. Hopefully, the right people will fill most of the CDP positions. The case study about Ms Najafi in Chapter 18 reveals the place and attitude of the CDP and the kind of person needed for the job. Case study 22: *Brutal force among the cabbage plants* illustrates the wrong attitude. The right attitude is a dialogical approach, one acknowledging that '[o]ur challenge is to be creative, to find forms of engaging dialogue appropriate to the community' (Ledwith 2022:141).

To Ledwith (2022:141), the plight of the poor requires a radical empathy that leads to action and change.

8.7 ROLE

The CDP's role is quite difficult to describe because any word that describes a role or function can be misinterpreted or can have a broader or narrower meaning for different people. When we deal with the following five categories of role, we must be aware of the fact that all these roles can be played in different ways. We will try to show a more acceptable way of playing these roles in terms of the principles and the attitude of the CDP, and also point to the wrong way of seeing them.

8.7.1 Guide

CDPs' views and perspectives are much broader and longer term than those of the people with which they work. They usually have a better idea what the consequences of any action might be. They are also more aware of pitfalls and obstacles than are the people. It is therefore their task to guide the people through those pitfalls toward objectives that may be somewhat murky to the people. However, they do this conscious of their own limitations. CDPs do not know everything. They are also a part of the learning process. They do not have answers to all problems. All this is enough reason to play their role as guide in a specific way instead of trying to be smart all the time.

Furthermore, the people should never become dependent on them. This is another very good reason for a specific approach toward this role. It simply means that CDPs' role as guide is more contextual, that is providing understanding within a certain situation, and it therefore does not entitle them to lead from the front. They are not guiding blind or crippled people and they are themselves far from perfect. At best CDPs make discoveries with the people as they go along. Within the learning process approach (Korten 1980), guidance can only follow this route. The beauty of this is that the learning can be lasting so that the poor and those who help them can make a success of their efforts to break the deprivation trap.

8.7.2 Adviser

Because of their greater knowledge and broader view, CDPs must give advice. However, the role of adviser is also limited. Its sole purpose is to motivate and enable, therefore this advice should be in the form of information on the possible choices people can make and the probable consequences of each choice. If we keep in mind what the goals of the CDP are and when we realise that those tie in with the principles discussed in Chapter 6, it is clear that advice should never take the form of telling people what to do and what not to do. (See Case study 14: *The case of the community worker who met his match*.)

As advisers, CDPs should never take the responsibility for making decisions on behalf of the people; they should only motivate and enable them to make those decisions. In Case study 6: *The parson who became a painter*, we may grin at the parson and think, it serves you right, but ultimately an injustice has been done regarding the decision making to fulfil basic needs.

Empowerment becomes hollow rhetoric if people are starved of information so that they cannot make informed decisions. CDPs should act as conduits, passing information on to the people. However, a conduit should be connected to a reliable source. In this age of computerised information systems, it should be possible to serve even remote communities with the necessary information – but the question is, are they linked to these sources? If they are starved of information, it is impossible for CDPs to empower the people through information. CDPs and their organisations should make sure that they are linked to reliable sources of up-to-date information so that they can extend that access to the groups of people with which they work (see Chapter 13 for more detail about working with groups).

8.7.3 Advocate

CDPs have contacts with the outside world that communities usually lack. They also know which channels to follow, when the situation may look like a maze to ordinary people. CDPs know how to deal with the authorities, where to go and who to see to get approvals and obtain concessions. They may therefore be valuable to the community if they use their links and point out the correct channels. This does not mean that community facilitators should always represent the people to the outside world. They should play this role only if the situation demands it and all concerned are convinced that it is the best option. In any case, a CDP should never go it alone. One or more people should be delegated to accompany the CDP so that the learning opportunity can be utilised. They remain conduits through which information flows.

They can also play an advocacy role in helping their group to complete a business plan or project proposal. The content of these documents is so important that the CDP can play a vital role. The professional appearance of such a document is also important and this is one way to make good use of a CDP's contribution. This does not mean that CDPs should complete these documents on their own. The completion of these documents can be a good learning opportunity. Communication with the authorities or professionals outside of the community should not remain a closed book for the community. When the community learns who to see and what to do, the people become empowered in the fact that they have broken from their isolation.

Sometimes it is also necessary for CDPs to defend the people's wishes, interests and actions, and their right to autonomy against outside misunderstanding, jealousy, bureaucracy and apathy.

In Case study 7: *A community hall with no purpose*, the CDPs did not play this role well enough.

Again, this role can be misunderstood. CDPs do not act independently from their groups. They remain conduits through which messages can travel to and from communities. They are not the people's 'foreign affairs ministers'. They do not have that legal standing and therefore they may not compromise the people in any way.

8.7.4 Enabler

CDPs aim to enable the people to fulfil their abstract human needs, to enhance their learning processes and to help them gain meaningful empowerment. For this reason, they are present primarily to enable the people to do what should be done.

Through all of these activities, CDPs must foster a climate for the people to act. They must create space for the people to move forward. This provision of climate and space is not a chaotic role. In their enabling role, CDPs are catalysts – they are there to make things happen without being active themselves. CDPs will be well advised to calm their role playing down. People do not want to be pressurised into action. To them, every step forward is an accomplishment. So, the CDP's actions can never be accomplishing, but must remain enabling, establishing opportunities without enforcing them. Case study 18: *Food garden in Mapayeni* gives a good example of a CDP who enabled.

Understanding and working with group dynamics requires knowledge and experience. This should be obtained through capacity building, an important goal of CDPs and one of their enabling tasks. Capacity building means the strengthening of personal and institutional ability to undertake tasks. The Organisation for Economic Cooperation and Development (OECD) defines capacity building as actions focusing on 'enabling all members of the community, including the poorest and the most disadvantaged, to develop skills and competencies so as to take greater control of their own lives and [it] also contributes to inclusive local development' (Noya & Clarence 2009:1). In the context of community development (which is ideally a responsibility of local government), this includes the necessary functions of governance, other local government-related activities, increasing access to resources, improving power relationships between all parties involved, increasing the general awareness of local communities regarding resources management, development in general and the ability to secure an enabling environment for promoting stakeholder participation.

The capacity-building needs of the stakeholders are directly related not only to the existing skills levels of the stakeholders and the desired level of appropriate skills, but also to the relevance of their skills to the organisational requirements. Different levels of capacity building would be needed for different stakeholders and categories of stakeholders. The level and focus of the capacity building process would depend on the skills level of the participating stakeholders, their expected roles and the needs of the forum.

Capacity building must be contextually appropriate. The capacity building process should also take cognisance of and accommodate the variety of societal, economic and cultural differences found in the typical developing society. Capacity building also needs to be grounded in the contextual realities of local government within a specific municipal area.

Developing the level and focus of a capacity-building process would be dependent upon an analysis of the existing skills of the participants, compared to the functional, personal and organisational skills required. It should also recognise and accommodate the personality traits of the participants.

It is very important that any capacity-building process be developed in consultation with the participants involved in the process. This will ensure high levels of relevance and acceptance by stakeholders.

All stakeholders from communities and from relevant government institutions (local, provincial and national) should undergo some form of capacity building. It must be recognised that the level and focus of the capacity-building process will differ from group to group and even on an individual basis. The specific role, functions and responsibilities of individuals or groups combined with existing levels of skill, knowledge and awareness, will serve as a basis to determine the type of capacity building that will be required.

Capacity building must be understood as an integral part of an ongoing process that seeks to acquire, transfer and match skills and competence of people to equip and enable them to enter into a range of situations with stable abilities, independence and self-confidence, allowing them to actively engage in seeking agreements and solutions that work for them.

Within the context of local development and participation in organisational activities, this would mean that they would acquire sufficient knowledge, competencies and skills to allow an understanding of the core principles involved. They would also need an understanding of the needs, interests and concerns of other stakeholders and to actively engage in working towards shared goals.

There is only one way to ensure that capacity building takes place and that is to ensure that a structure exists for it and that able people staff the structure. One of the great dangers regarding capacity building is that it will take place haphazardly by uncommitted and ill-trained trainers, who have no one to report to and have no support system to assist them. Such training is mostly a waste of time and leads to immense frustration.

8.7.5 Facilitator

The primary concern of CDPs is to help the people make rational decisions, to enable them to participate fully, to assist them in taking the initiative, to help them to discover their resources, and to help them to plan and to implement. Put differently:

> Facilitation is the practice of providing leadership without taking the reins. As a facilitator for community engagement your role is to get others to take responsibility and to take the lead on different tasks that will result in collaborative efforts to address the issue around which the engagement is taking place *(Pennstate Department of Agricultural Economics, Sociology, and Education nd)*.

The three operative verbs used here, 'help', 'enable' and 'assist', make it clear that this role is the fulfilment of the attitude a CDP should harbour. This role differs vastly from the situation that is the rule rather than the exception where CDPs overplay their hand by making the decisions, taking the initiative, doing the planning and allowing the people to assist them. This is not a facilitator's role. Instead, it describes the role of leader or boss or manager where participation, empowerment and ownership are liberal 'concessions', the measure of which is decided upon by the initiating organisation. A facilitator cannot be but in the background, cannot play any other than a secondary role and cannot do anything else other than assisting and enabling.

8.8 CONCLUSION

The place and role of CDPs can be described as very delicate and nearly impossible to fulfil if the correct attitude, along with dedication and wisdom, is not present. CDPs will be well advised to approach these roles and their position with the attitude Korten (1980) suggests: 'All I have is myself to offer'. Case study 15: *The inspector whose help was dumped* shows what we can learn from the mistakes of a CDP as summarised here:

- Those working in NGOs often come from the affluent part of society and do not share the language and culture of the poor.
- CDPs hold behind-the-scenes positions.

- CDPs might find themselves forced to champion the causes of the people, sometimes in the face of opposition from all and sundry, including their superiors.
- In their enabling role, CDPs must remove obstacles, steer clear of trouble, and provide know-how to make it possible for people to act.
- The CDP has a very difficult role to play and it is easy to get it wrong.

REFERENCES

De Beer F & Swanepoel H. 2013. *The Community Development Profession: Issues, Concepts and Approaches.* Pretoria: Van Schaik.

Korten DC. 1980. Community organization and rural development: A learning process approach. *Public Administration Review*, 40(5):480–511.

Ledwith M. 2022. Storytelling praxis. In Ledwith M & Springett J (eds), *Participatory Practice: Community-based Action for Transformative Change.* Bristol: Policy Press.

Malehan N. 2018. Almost three years after commencement of the Spatial Planning and Land Use Management Act 16 of 2013: An analysis of challenges to its implementation with relation to planning applications and appeals. Research project submitted in partial fulfilment of the regulations for the LLM degree at University of KwaZulu-Natal, Durban.

Noya A & Clarence E. 2009. *Community capacity building: Fostering economic and social resilience. Project outline and proposed methodology.* Working document, CFE/LEED, OECD. Available at: https://www.oecd.org/dataoecd/54/10/44681969.pdf?contentId=44681 970 (accessed 15 May 2023).

Pennstate Department of Agricultural Economics, Sociology, and Education. nd. Facilitating community engagement. Available at: https://aese.psu.edu/research/centers/cecd/engagement-toolbox/facilitation (accessed 3 December 2022).

Springett J. 2022. The role of dialogue. In Ledwith M & Springett J (eds), *Participatory Practice: Community-based Action for Transformative Change.* Bristol: Policy Press.

LEGISLATION

Constitution of the Republic of South Africa, 1996

Local Government: Municipal Demarcation Act 27 of 1998

Local Government: Municipal Structures Act 117 of 1998

Municipal Demarcation Act 27 of 1998

Municipal Structures Act 117 of 1998

Municipal Systems Act 32 of 2000

Spatial Planning and Land Use Management Act 16 of 2013 (SPLUMA)

CHAPTER 9
Participatory Decision Making and Management
Edith Phaswana and Frik de Beer

9.1 INTRODUCTION

No one can deny that participation in activities that affect your and your children's future is a democratic right. This clearly means that no politician and no official has the right to decide when people should participate and to what extent they should do so. The local, provincial and national governments are there to serve the people, not the other way around; therefore, the primary role players, also in decision making, are the people, not the government. It is, however, easier to say than to facilitate these things. People, especially if they are poor, not well educated and unsophisticated, find it very difficult to make decisions that they can defend as logical and reasonable. On the other hand, there are people and parties who prefer that the poor and the ordinary remain in the background and play the docile role of beneficiaries.

Participation can happen in two ways: individually or collectively (Thomas 2006). The former entails a person's view being sought for decisions about, for example, a personal health matter (Alderson 2002). An individual is engaged throughout the process. With the latter, people may come together in a forum to make their views heard to those in authority (Matthew 2001). At every stage, their views are sought and considered when decisions are made. Within the context of this chapter, the focus is on collective participation at a community level.

9.2 PARTICIPATORY MANAGEMENT

9.2.1 Participatory management – the concept

The concept of 'participatory management' has become more widely used within the NGO sector, particularly those involved in development work.

To be understood, participatory management must be seen in its entirety. It is not meant as something whereby the government, in any of the three spheres, runs and controls the community. Participatory management is done by the community itself. It refers to the self-reliance of a community to organise itself in such a way that policies can be implemented, projects can be initiated and sustained, and the necessary cost recovery can take place. It therefore means that a community can organise itself to take responsibility for itself. If a community can begin to do this, it is on its way toward being free of the shackles of deprivation and poverty that previously bound it. (See Case study 17: *Mothers of the mountain community*.)

The application of participation management can range from the involvement of community citizens in the decision-making processes, to political activities or organisations. It is a form of management which seeks to distribute leadership or transfer decision-making power to members of the community who are at the bottom end of the hierarchical chain of command (Mitchell 2017). This is in contrast to the traditional authoritarian system or management paradigm which recognises an upward flow of power and decision making in an organisation and does not recognise inputs or efforts of those who are not in leadership positions (Bernardes 2015).

In a community context, participation management allows involvement of broader community members in consultative decision making as means of bringing about social change and promoting democracy (Kennelley 2018).

9.2.2 Goals of participation

The process of participation has the following broad goals:
- The active participation of individuals and groups in the promotion of their own wellbeing through actions that will lead to effective problem solving
- Individual and group participation in decisions about the type of projects that are required in a community. Three specific and essential aims are served by ensuring participation on this level. They are:
  1. the enhancement of the capacity of communities to make informed decisions and prioritise needs
  2. the promotion of the legitimacy of any institutional structure that is formed within a community

3. the promotion of ongoing participation of the community in the planning and monitoring of existing services, facilities and projects and the extension or alteration of such services or facilities.
- The active mobilisation of community resources and assets (human and natural) for the promotion of project objectives.

With the above in mind, we can say that centralised decision making does not work. Centralised decision making carries very little accountability and therefore decision makers are removed from the very real human situation influenced by their decisions. When development processes do not take the local structures into consideration, an institutional vacuum is created. There is no institutional support for development processes with the result that efforts collapse as soon as benefactors start to withdraw structural support. Finally, we can say that there is no holistic approach by centralised, non-participatory decision making. Development efforts are fragmentary, quite often contradictory and nearly always in competition with each other, to the detriment of those who need the help.

Having said this, we can go back to the principles of community development covered in a previous chapter. We should concentrate on flexibility, opt for simplicity and move step by step. We must be focused on the local situation and therefore be socially sensitive and responsive to the local human needs and wishes. Eventually, we can emphasise that development cannot take place in a vacuum. We need local structures created by the people to carry the development.

Participation, learning and ownership cannot take place within a chaotic situation. For this reason, all these activities must be structured. We must remember that the structures are there to serve the purposes already mentioned. They must therefore be appropriate for the task and they must be the means to an end, not the end in itself.

Participatory decision making is crucial. Local knowledge and skills should be used through participation. Local people are the experts on their own situation and this expertise should be used.

The public service, including the local government, is not the only development role player. The responsibility is shared with the private sector, community organisations, trade unions, other stakeholders and the community at large. Service delivery will therefore become developmental, will address the poverty situation of the people and will be founded on the creation of a government-community partnership or what is commonly referred as the public-private partnership.

9.2.3 Participation in projects

Participatory management of projects means that the people who are going to be affected by the change the project aims to bring, should be full partners in the initiation of the project and should play a leading role in the management of the project. When we look at the world around us, it becomes clear that local people have a much better understanding of their own circumstances, needs and aspirations than anybody on the outside. People can make better decisions within the framework of their own understanding of their situation. The mothers of the mountain community (see Case study 17: *Mothers of the mountain community*) knew and understood what constituted a good diet, but did not have the means to provide it. It was only through participatory processes with the superintendent that they were able to devise means to improve their situation.

However, this is only one reason why local people should participate. The other, more important, reason is that it is their democratic right to participate in decisions affecting their lives. Excluding people from participating in issues that affect their lives is a violation of their human right and therefore of their human dignity.

Community participation means that local people must take part in the management of their own lives and their own environments, in this instance within projects. The slogan 'nothing about us without us' is apt in this context. Community participation in project management includes:

- identifying and making decisions on issues, needs and problems they consider important or believe need to change
- implementing projects aimed at changing unacceptable situations in a positive way
- evaluating and adjusting the project and its processes in order to see if they are successful in addressing their needs and in changing their circumstances for the better
- taking full responsibility for and control over projects and processes on which they have embarked.

Community development practitioners (CDPs) are the enablers of this participation and, in being the enablers, they must make sure that the following aspects receive attention:

- *The people must have a need to address through a project*. They will not participate just because a project serves a good cause, and they will not participate just because the project looks interesting. People must have a real need before they will pledge themselves to do something (see Chapter 5). That need should be identified through participatory processes. It should not be imposed on local people by external people.

- *The people must be motivated.* One of the most important tasks of facilitation is to motivate. There must be a vision that the people share, and they must be eager to fulfil their aspirations (see Chapter 13). The people must be able to visualise the end product and what the future will look like to get motivated.

- *There must be as few hindrances to participation as possible.* Animosities, jealousy, favouritism and opportunism must be absent if a climate for participation is to be created. Also, from the official side, the people must be given the freedom to participate. Departmental rules and regulations and bureaucratic red tape can easily act as demotivators and can make it difficult or unpleasant to participate (see Chapter 13). While it is hard to manage and guarantee this in practice, every effort must be made to manage this process. Sometimes explaining bureaucratic processes well in advance might help to alleviate these demotivators.

- *There must be regular feedback to the people.* Not all people can directly participate in project management. For that reason, it is mostly an elected committee, a representative body, that does the day-to-day management on behalf of the people. However that does not mean that the bulk of the people must be disempowered by ignoring them. They must still have the power to call a halt to actions by their representatives and to contribute their ideas, meanings, concerns and suggestions to the process. Regular meetings must be scheduled well in advance to update and give feedback to the community. This should not be done on an ad hoc base. Community members participate well if they know that every last Sunday of the month, for instance, they have to congregate to get reports.

- *The project must eventually ensure concrete visible benefits to the community or to a group of people who have a common need.* One project that does not deliver anticipated benefits makes the acceptance of future projects by the people more difficult. On the other hand, a project with visible and obvious benefits acts as a motivator for future projects (see Chapter 13).

Management of a project consists of four discrete responsibilities or actions. They are planning, implementation, evaluation and control. Development management, though, does much more than that. Development management is the management of development that includes the management of the project, but reaches much further. We can say that development management differs from ordinary management in that it must:

- adapt to a dynamic, and therefore constantly changing, environment
- deal with a situation where new needs appear all the time
- ensure the effective participation of the people who are touched by the project
- include and support existing institutional structures in the development process.

This is a tall order and that is why development management is never easy.

A further very important aspect of development management is that it must integrate community and technical inputs. The fact that it must be integrated, immediately tells us that the two are not in opposition or that the one automatically nullifies the other. These two types of inputs are equally important and it is the task of development management to optimise both.

Community inputs consist of the following:

- *Participation*: In terms of input, participation in all aspects related to planning, implementation and evaluation is essential as it points to the process of community input and not as a once-off activity.
- *Local knowledge*: Local people are guardians of a wealth of information that, once unleashed, can work wonders. This local, indigenous information by far exceeds any academic or book-gained knowledge to which outsiders may have access. This information is a crucial aspect of community-based development management. For example, in Case study 17: *Mothers of the mountain community*, some mothers knew that there was a demand for broilers in their community and pursued this business with great success. An outsider would not have known this. This local knowledge cannot be underestimated.
- *Local skills*: While local people have access to indigenous knowledge, they also have indigenous skills that are not necessarily inferior to any technical skills and are quite often better suited to the situation than technical skills are. Many actions in any development project need the type of skills that can readily be found among local people.

In these instances, technical skills are unnecessary and can even be inappropriate. Participatory management does not mean that the community should be managed. The whole idea of participatory projects is that the community should not be managed from outside. Participatory management can therefore only mean to organise and to enable the community to take charge of its own affairs. This reflects specifically on sustainability, cost recovery and the implementation of government policy.

9.2.4 Important aspects regarding participatory management

Short- and long-term sustainability

Sustainability means the opposite of what frequently happens in development situations in Third World countries. We use sustainability here in the sense of 'able to last or continue for a long time'. Often, a sizeable amount of money is spent on projects, a number of arrangements are made and usually a lot of effort is put into the matter, just to find that the whole effort grinds to a halt before real benefits have been reaped.

Participatory management is meant to prevent this situation. This can only happen if development efforts are maintained through a system of management. Through this management process, the community must be put in a position where it can continuously take responsibility for what has been started. Sustainability can be realised through the involvement of community members in the committee, as they are able to defend the common goal and long-term interest of the project.

Sustainability is also dependent on a notion of long-term commitment. Quite often, in Third World situations, there is a strong realisation of the short-term needs of people. Projects are then aimed to bring relief as soon as possible and very few arrangements are made to sustain the benefits going forward into the future. As for long-term sustainability, people must be helped to see beyond their immediate needs. They must also realise that they cannot redress all their problems without having some patience. Although development should bear fruit in the short term, it is equally important to realise that the totality of the problem can only be addressed over an extended period of time. Sustainability therefore becomes extremely important to ensure that the problem receives attention in the long term. CDPs use *logical frameworks* to stagger the impact of projects over time, and it is crucial that communities are made aware of these project milestones. Monitoring and evaluation systems, discussed below, enable this process as communities are able to measure and see progress.

Further, what has been started should be successfully completed. An effort should therefore be sustained until it bears the fruit expected of it and must then be maintained in order to continue to bear fruit. Sometimes greater benefits of projects may be reaped by descendants of those who initiated them. These realities must be communicated with the community well in advance to avoid a situation where people feel discouraged to participate when results are not immediately visible.

Cost recovery

The initial financial outlay for and the continuous maintenance of any community project must at least be partially recovered by the users of the new service. A cost recovery mechanism must therefore form part of the planning of any project. This is one of the long-term aspects and is dependent on the sustainability of the project. An important reason for participatory management is to ensure a healthy cost recovery in the long term. Most communities do not value free services as they tend to abuse them. Where possible, a minimum fee should be paid for services as people value what they pay for. In south Africa we have seen how charging for plastic bags at retail stores has reduced plastic waste as people have become more aware of how many they are using and the cost, and are motivated to recycle.

Government policy

Government policy is dependent on long-term commitments and can only come to fruition over time. Government policy is also dependent on a well-organised system through which it can be implemented, and it sets the targets, determines the scope of and identifies the strategy through which development efforts are to be launched in deprived areas. Government policy must be implemented before it means much and for that reason, an organised community is necessary to put policies into practice (Mmakola 1996:20). Participatory management therefore helps to ensure that government policy is implemented.

Monitoring and evaluation

Sustainability must be maintained through a participatory management system that works. It is not enough to have a policy and strategy in place, to have the determination to do something about the situation and to announce the imminent launch of projects, and then to do nothing further. Monitoring and evaluation must play an important part.

It is only through monitoring and evaluation that we can really determine whether the initial plans have been put into practice and whether they are being carried out according to the plans. It is also the task of monitoring and evaluation to ensure that the direction is correct. In other words, monitoring and evaluation also ensure that the initial plans are on target and suggest course changes when necessary.

The most important condition for monitoring and evaluation is that they must be orderly. Together, they are a process, using previously selected and accepted criteria and indicators to tell us whether an effort is still on track, along with other aspects such as whether the time frame is being maintained and whether the project really addresses the problems as initially identified.

9.2.5 The benefits and value of participation

Planning and implementation without participation is a sure method to extend costs, stir up political unrest, ensure lack of progress and cause rifts in the community. Real participation adds quality and cooperation and eventually brings together (perhaps with a measure of strife) a number of diverse players in an issue-based process toward achieving acceptable solutions.

Not only does the Constitution indicate that the participation of communities and community groups in the matters of local government should be encouraged, experience in South Africa and elsewhere has shown that it is vital.

In summary, communities should participate in management of their projects for the following reasons:

- Through participation, both concrete and abstract needs of participants are fulfilled.
- It encourages a learning process and enables people to take the initiative from the start by assisting with needs identification and decision making.

- Collective action that includes collective decision making is stimulated.
- If communities do participate, development is needs oriented.
- Because communities work towards addressing needs, they focus on achieving objectives.
- It involves people at grassroots level and through this process provides an opportunity for ordinary people to be included.
- It brings about awareness among people about their own situation and their ability to address their situation themselves.
- It leads to community building by encouraging leadership skills, institutional development and organisational ability.
- People gain awareness and power for further developmental activities.
- It enables community members to identify and feel a connection with the project, enough to defend it from opportunistic individuals who may want to exploit them (Lederman 2019; De Dieu 2019).
- It is the people's democratic right to participate in decision making. Moreover, the participation of civic society organisations such as churches, NGOs, legal and political advocacy groups is seen to be related to democratic effectiveness (Tsobanoglou & Harms 2018). This is crucial as civil society participatory communication platforms can assist in resolving mistrust in social and political institutions.

9.2.6 Constraints to meaningful participation

Whereas participation promises to be a noble process with all good intentions, there are several constraints that make meaningful participation impossible. For instance, in cases where authoritarianism prevails, people feel reluctant to participate in leadership structures as they are perceived as ill-equipped to contribute to decisions based on their status (Munoz, Davila, Mosey & Radrigan 2021; Adzahlie-Mensah 2014). There are also instances where management control meetings (who is invited, who may speak and to what end) through a wide-ranging dimensional power, thereby directing both the course and outcome of deliberations (Munoz et al 2021). This has the potential to limit certain people's participation. For example, one study showed how homeless individuals were limited in presenting their true selves to others at a table of shared concerns due to their perceived position of inferiority in society, which dehumanised them (Kennelley 2018). It takes willing CDPs to ensure that members of the community feel confident enough to engage.

A modest but significant body of literature has demonstrated that marginalised youth participate in ways that liberal democracies undervalue as they prioritise formal interactions with the state such as voting (Godfrey & Cherng 2016; Kuttner 2016; Taft & Gordon 2013; Kennelley 2018). This becomes a problem in Global South contexts, where other forms of participatory mechanisms may be deployed to make their voices heard. Another form of constraint to participation includes creative editing of what marginalised communities have said to gain the sympathy of donors, authorities or the middle class section of society.

9.3 GROUP DECISION MAKING

Development-relevant institutions need group decision making, but it is necessary to manage the process. The one tasked with this responsibility should know that it has advantages and disadvantages. We will first look at the advantages (Massie & Douglas 1981:178):

- Individual specialists can approach a problem from different viewpoints in the group.
- Coordination of activities and decisions of separate departments can be achieved through interaction and joint decision making in groups.
- Motivation of individual members to carry out decisions may be increased by the feeling of being part of the decision-making process.
- Groups provide a means by which personnel members can be trained in decision making.
- Groups permit representation of different interest groups in the decision-making process.
- Groups provide the opportunity for experts from outside an organisation to be made part of the decision-making process.
- Groups may also be a way to democratise decision making by drawing members of the public into these groups so that their preferences, fears and knowledge are part of the process.
- Groups are good to use for creative thinking because fragmentary ideas from individuals usually start a chain reaction in the minds of others so that a decision is built like a jigsaw puzzle.

The disadvantages are the following:
- Considering the value of the time of each individual member, groups are expensive.
- Prompt decision making is difficult, if not impossibe, because of the length of time it takes a group to come to an agreement.
- Group action may lead to compromise and indecision.
- Group decision making can be a sham where very senior people or outside experts are present.
- Group decisions may lead to a situation where no one takes responsibility for a decision.
- The decision process can be time consuming for both the community and government, it can be costly and it may backfire 'creating more hostility to the government' or NGO (Irvin & Stansbury 2004:58).
- The outcomes may be worse for the community, may lead to outcomes that are politically sensitive and lead to a reduction of budgets for the actual project.

Some guidelines for successful group decision making are as follows (Massie & Douglas 1981:179–180):
- The physical layout, size of the group and general atmosphere are important factors determining the effectiveness of decision making.
- Threat reduction is an important objective in the planning of group action so that the group will shift from interpersonal problems to group goals. The golden rule should be: no personal attacks allowed.
- The best group leadership is performed by the entire group. It is not the job of the chairperson, the CDP or any formal leader. A group that functions well tends to function informally with no single person providing all the leadership.
- The group should explicitly formulate goals. They should not be fenced in by predetermined rules, but should rather be guided by their own predetermination of goals.
- The group should formulate an agenda, but it should never be regarded as a blueprint.
- The decision-making process should continue until the group formulates a consensus upon which it can formulate a solution. If the group action results in a minority opinion, the group has failed to

maximise its effectiveness. So, voting is not a solution if consensus cannot be found quickly.
- Any group should be made aware of the interaction process by which it arrives at solutions. The individual members must be made aware of their individual and collective role and responsibility. In this manner, the skill of being a member of a group becomes a distinguishable skill that can be developed.
- Group members should be made aware of problem-solving and decision-making models and then they can choose a model that suits their situation or they can devise their own process.
- It is important that a group obtains the necessary information that will enable it to make enlightened decisions.
- It goes without saying that a manager, executive or official may never ignore or override the decision made by a group.

9.4 THE NEED FOR INFORMATION IN DECISION MAKING

Nobody can make informed decisions without the necessary relevant information. For this reason, information dissemination is part of the mobilisation and empowerment drive. No community lives in isolation. There is a constant flow of information to a community. This information covers many aspects of life and can also be of an interpretative nature. In other words, the information explains something.

Information can also be of a motivational nature, and political information is usually of this nature. Development management could also carry motivational information. See Chapter 13 for more about motivational information.

In a development-relevant situation, a process of regular ongoing communication is required once stakeholders have been identified to ensure that effective linkages can be established for their participation. Both the mechanisms for communicating and the content of communication need to be based on the needs of each stakeholder group as well as on the particular stage of the process. Most of the information will be project-related, but with different objectives in mind. The different types of information are discussed in the sections that follow.

9.4.1 Motivational information

Information should not speak only to the minds of people, but also to their hearts. Their commitment to the project and their organisational obligations must be established and for that purpose, motivational information is needed.

9.4.2 Organisational information

People such as stakeholders find themselves within organisations and that one organisation exists within another. It is therefore necessary to know how organisations work and what organisational obligations exist for stakeholders, for example the obligation to attend meetings.

9.4.3 Management information

People who are stakeholders will fulfil certain managerial functions within development-relevant institutions. They will also have linkages with managers and management systems; they need to know and understand how these work.

9.4.4 Professional/technical information

Professional/technical information is needed by stakeholders because most of their decisions will be of a technical nature. This does not mean that the other types of information will not also contribute to their forming opinions and making decisions.

All this information must be channeled to the target audience, and for that, communication channels are needed. These channels must satisfy certain requirements. They must be without obstructions that hinder or stop the flow of information. They must not be too long, because long channels slow down the dissemination of information to a trickle. They must be clean, and no pollution of the information must be possible. Information gets polluted because the senders or handlers of information are not careful. Sometimes information gets polluted because someone has an ulterior motive, such as political or financial expediency. One of the most important requirements is that the channels must be connected to a source of information.

There are many information channels to a community – from mass media, such as television, radio and newspapers, to small interest groups with focused interests. In the context of community development, we would make use of mass media and other large distributors of information, such as schools, only at the beginning of entry to announce and introduce something to the larger public. However, as the development-relevant institutions become established and the stakeholders become involved, it seems that more specific channels, such as the stakeholder groupings and the various structures regarding development projects, would be the ideal information channels.

9.5 CONCLUSION

There may be easier ways of decision making than participatory. The local development environment (see Chapter 2) provides many stumbling blocks to community development and in particular to participatory decision making. Consider the situation with service delivery protests experienced in South Africa since 2004: local government fails to provide and local communities feel excluded, not receiving what they are owed. Because of that, it becomes tempting to take short cuts.

However, participatory decision making is so much part of the new-look development, so integral to adaptiveness and learning, that there is not really any short cut. Instead of looking for short cuts, CDPs should rather look for ways and means to manage this process so successfully that participatory decision making becomes the only way of decision making.

The CDP must champion the cause of the poor and as such must do everything to ensure that the poor will make enlightened and reasonable decisions.

Just as a water pipe can only provide water to the tap if it is connected to a reservoir, so communication channels can only provide information if they are connected to a source.

Problem solving can be tackled incorrectly from the start or many smaller things can go wrong during problem solving.

REFERENCES

Adzahlie-Mensah V. 2014. *Being 'Nobodies': School Regimes and Student Identities in Ghana*. PhD thesis, University of Sussex.

Alderson P (ed). 2002. *Young Children's Health Rights*. London: Routledge Falmer.

Bernardes A. 2015. Implementation of a participatory management model: Analysis from a political perspective. *Journal of Nursing Management*, 23(5):888–897

De Dieu KTC. 2019. Participatory management and organizational involvement of employees in sub-Saharan Africa. *European Journal of Business Management*, 11(36):128–136.

Godfrey E & Cherng HS. 2016. The kids are all right? Income inequality and civic engagement among our nation's youth. *Journal of Youth and Adolescence*, 45(11):2218–2232.

Irvin RA & Stansbury J. 2004. Citizen participation in decision making: Is it worth the effort? *Public Administration Review*, 64(1):55–65.

Kennelley J. 2018. Envisioning democracy: Participatory filmmaking with homeless youth. *Canadian Review of Sociology*, 55(2):191–210.

Kuttner P. 2016. Hip-hop citizens: Arts-based, culturally sustaining civic engagement pedagogy. *Harvard Educational Review*, 86(4):527–555.

Lederman J. 2019. The people's plan? Participation and post-politics in Flint's master planning process. *Critical Sociology*, 45(1):85–101.

Massie JL & Douglas J. 1981. *Managing: A Contemporary Introduction*. Englewood Cliffs: Prentice-Hall.

Matthew H. 2001. Citizenship, youth councils and young people's participation. *Journal of Youth Studies*, 4:299–318.

Mitchell R. 2017. Democracy or control? The participation of management, teachers, students and parents in school leadership in Tigray, Ethiopia. *International Journal of Educational Development*, 55:49–55.

Mmakola D. 1996. The place of policy analysis in South Africa. *Africanus*, 26(2).

Munoz CA, Davila AM, Mosey S & Radrigan M. 2021. Exploring participatory management in social enterprise practice: Evidence from Chile. *Voluntas*, 32:1096–1112.

Taft J & Gordon H. 2013. Youth activists, youth councils, and constrained democracy. *Education, Citizenship and Social Justice*, 8(1):87–100.

Thomas N. 2006 *Towards a theory of children's participation*. Paper presented at Choice and Participation Conference. University of Sheffield, England, July 4–6.

Tsobanoglou G & Harms H. 2018. Citizen's participation and the crisis of representation in Europe: Models of citizen participation and the quest for local democracy. *Journal of Regional Socio-Economic Issues*, 8(2):47–59.

SECTION C

Skills for Community Development

CHAPTER 10

Communication Skills

Frik de Beer

10.1 INTRODUCTION

Talking to other people, reading a book or newspaper, watching television, bargaining about the price of something, making an appointment, enjoying a joke with friends – these are all part of our daily communication that links us to our environment and makes our existence meaningful. Communication can be regarded as the activity humans do most and it can be seen as the activity that affects humans most.

It is quite obvious that communication is important to all of us. If we are good communicators, it will affect our lives and those of other people positively. In effect, it will shape our lives and when we have a hand in influencing other people positively, it will in turn help us to become more effective communicators. Communication is improved by discovering better and more effective ways of relating to others and having them relate to us. Human communication is the vehicle through which interpersonal relationships are developed and destroyed.

If communication is so important in our daily lives, we can imagine how important it is in development projects where a number of people, usually as an organised group, are actively and emotionally involved in decision making and executing those decisions. We can safely say that community development projects succeed or fail according the communication that takes place within them. That is why it is so important to spend some time on this aspect.

10.2 A COMMUNICATION MODEL

Let us look at the ingredients of communication in order to understand it better. First, there is a **sender**, or source, or origin, of communication. Communication must start from somewhere. I start talking to you.

The television announces a new programme. The newspaper has a heading that catches my eye. So, the communication originates with the sender.

Second, there is a **receiver** or target. Communication is directed at someone or at a group of people or at a certain type of person. If I say: 'How are you today, Margaret?' the receiver or target of my communication is Margaret. If a notice in the newspaper says: 'To all those who want to start a new career', the target is not only one person, but a certain type of person.

Third, there is a **message**. Communication without meaning is not really communication. Language has meaning, music has meaning – a certain kind of music conveys a certain kind of message. Even colour can have meaning; if I give someone a bouquet of red roses it means something and it conveys a certain message. If the traffic light shows green, it means something and tells the road user something.

Fourth, there is a certain **coding**. We use certain codes to convey our messages. I may say: 'Hello'. Someone else may say: 'Good morning'. A third person may say: 'Hi'. The message in all three cases is similar, but the coding differs vastly. Coding also includes non-verbal communication. Non-verbal actions (also called immediacy behaviour) include smiling, touching, eye contact, open body positions, closer distances and more vocal animation. According to López-Ozieblo (2015:14), immediacy

> ... refers to the perceived degree of physical or psychological distance between two (or more) people. We tend to distance ourselves from people we do not like and get closer to those we do like, or for whom we have positive feelings. We distance ourselves or get closer by a combination of verbal and nonverbal behaviour.

A smile while talking means something and a frown means something else.

Fifth, there is a **medium of communication**. The most common medium is the word of mouth, where people speak to one another, but writing is another medium and so is music, pictures or even body language.

Sixth, there are various **channels** that can be used. I can make use of a direct channel by talking to someone face to face, I can write the person a letter, I can send the person a message via someone else, or I can send an email message or an SMS to the person. In recent years, social media as a channel for communication has gained popularity: Facebook, X (previously Twitter), Instagram and YouTube are some of the well-known platforms. With increasing popularity of social media, a new type of communicator has emerged: the influencer. According to Geyser (2022), 'influencers in social media are people who have built a reputation for their knowledge and expertise on a specific topic'. Influencers are found in all aspects of life, even in community development. Several of them are listed here: https://klear.com/influencers/Community%20Development (Klear 2022).

The process of communication always takes place in a certain **context**. Communication in the cafeteria is different from communication in the boardroom; communication between friends is different from communication between business rivals; communication while we watch a football match is different from communication while we attend a funeral service.

Now that we have all the ingredients, we know what communication consists of, but we still do not have communication. It is now necessary to mix all these ingredients together. Communication may consist of a sender, a receiver and a message, but that does not really tell us how communication takes place. If I say to you: 'It is very hot today', I am the sender, you are the receiver and the message is that it is very hot today. You may respond by saying: 'Isn't it?', while you wipe your brow. Now you are the sender, using a different code and I become the receiver, decoding your code so that it means to me: 'Yes, it is very hot'. Now we are both senders and receivers, using different codes.

The process of communication is also unpredictable. You could have responded by saying: 'It is not really very hot', or 'Are you mad! It isn't hot! Have you got a fever?' Every time your response will be different.

Imagine the communication process at a party where four friends talk to one another while loud music is playing. Every now and then some other person passes the group of friends and may say hello or make some remark to one or more members of the group, to which one or more of them may respond. In this scenario, senders to one target may at the same time be receivers from another source. Different codes may be used even by the same source or sender. It makes for a very untidy situation, but also a very complex one in which communication becomes difficult. Most of the communication situations resemble this untidy scene where it becomes difficult to identify sender, receiver, message and codes.

All this simply means that communication is not linear. That means it does not take place in a straight line: from sender to receiver. Rather, it is cyclic, which means that, after the receiver has received the message, he/she becomes the sender and the sender becomes the receiver. These roles change all the time and at the same time different messages may be transferred between the participants and different forms of coding may be used.

10.3 BARRIERS TO COMMUNICATION

Because communication is complex, because it is unpredictable and because different participants use different codes, there are barriers in the way of successful communication. We can group these barriers together and say that there are barriers to receiving a message, barriers to understanding a message, and barriers to accepting a message. These barriers are serious because their presence disturbs any situation where the sender wants the receiver to receive the message, understand it and accept it. Communication is only successful if that happens. (Note that this section on barriers to communication is based on Swanepoel & De Beer 1996.)

10.3.1 Barriers to reception

Barriers to reception can include delays, a total breakdown of communication or influences causing distortion. The following barriers can result in the receiver not receiving the message, even though the sender has sent it:

- *The receiver may have anxieties.* The receiver may be scared of the sender or the message. The receiver may feel him/herself trapped and at the mercy of the sender. In such a situation the receiver does not really listen to the message and therefore does not really receive it.
- *The receiver may have expectations.* The receiver may think that the communication will lead to further good things and then pre-empt the message, therefore he/she does not listen properly and misses out some detail of the message.
- *The receiver may be preoccupied.* If you read a book on quantum physics, but your mind is really with the soccer match that will take place later today, you will not know what you are reading. Few people can really concentrate on more than one thing at a time. However, people's lives can be filled with something at a certain stage that preoccupies them and makes them poor receivers. If your child is seriously ill, you are preoccupied and will find it very difficult to listen to something that is not related to the illness.

- *The receiver may have a physical disability.* He/she may be feeling sick. A severe headache makes concentration difficult so that a message cannot be decoded properly. A common disability is of course that the receiver is deaf or his/her hearing is impaired.
- *The sender may have a physical disability.* He/she may stutter or have a very soft voice. Then the receiver does not really receive the message, even if he/she tries.
- *There may be environmental disturbances.* Circumstances such as noise or competing messages, for example the news being read on the radio at the same time that another message is conveyed, may hinder reception.

These barriers make the receiver hear or read the sender wrongly; in other words, they get the wrong message, or receive only part of the message. It is clear that if communication stumbles over this first barrier, there is no hope that the message will overcome the other two barriers, in other words, that the message will be understood and accepted. Receiving the message is therefore absolutely necessary and that does not mean snippets of it, but as much as possible if not the total message.

10.3.2 Barriers to understanding

Barriers to understanding are common among people of different cultures and/or languages or of different ages or between professional and lay people. They include the following:

- *The receiver may not understand the language used.* In a multilingual country such as South Africa, it can easily happen that the receiver understands nothing or very little of the language that the sender uses. The reverse is also possible, that is, that the sender does not know the language he/she must use.
- *The receiver may not understand the jargon used by the sender.* Jargon or official terminology permeates all languages more and more. Take, for example, the jargon attached to computers and their use. For somebody who does not have a computer or never uses one, it is difficult to understand a message regarding computers. For example, teenagers like to use jargon such as vague up (make less clear), mootville (irrelevant), a world of no! (definitely not), carbon-dated (very out of date) and all-dat (everything).

- *The receiver may have a problem listening intelligently.* People differ in intelligence and in concentration span. If a message comes to a receiver in a language that he/she does not use every day and if the message is also complex, it is difficult to really break through the obstacles and understand the message.
- *The receiver may have a poor knowledge of the subject of communication.* If someone talks to you about something that you know very little about, chances are that you will understand nothing or very little of the message. Any subject has its own jargon and if you are not familiar with it, you will not be able to understand. Each subject also has its own causality and if you do not know that causality, it can be difficult for you to understand. The meteorologist knows what causes rain, but the receiver of his message may not know that and therefore may find it difficult to understand.
- *The communication may be too lengthy.* A long message runs the risk of not being understood simply because the receiver loses concentration. Very few people can focus properly for more than about 18 minutes, implying that the longer the message, the less it will be understood.
- *The message may be garbled or coded.* The message may be presented in such a way that the receiver finds it difficult to decode. Again, this happens when the subject of the message is not known by the receiver and he/she therefore does not know the meaning of the jargon or does not know the causality typical of that subject.
- *The receiver may be anxious or preoccupied.* This will make it difficult for him/her to listen intelligently.

These barriers result in the receiver hearing or reading the message, the message is received, but the receiver does not understand everything, understands wrongly or does not understand at all.

10.3.3 Barriers to acceptance

Barriers to acceptance occur when political, social, cultural, religious, moral and even biological differences between communicating parties are marked. The following factors usually cause these barriers:

- *The receiver may have prejudices.* In fact, we can say that the receiver will have prejudices because it is human to have them. It is hoped that the prejudices will not form a barrier, but quite often they do.
- *There may be emotional conflict between the sender and the receiver.* Because we are human we have emotions and quite often those emotions can conflict with those of the other person.
- *The way the sender communicates may make the message unacceptable.* For example, the sender may be overbearing. Good manners and civility can go a long way in simplifying communication.
- *There may be a status clash or a marked status difference between sender and receiver.* In severe patriarchal situations, older men may find it offensive if younger women communicate with them. So-called 'hlonipa rules' in most of the traditional black communities in southern Africa create a situation which can make communication difficult and can often lead to communication failure. These rules regulate relationships between, for example, young women and older men, teenagers and grown-ups, daughters-in-law and fathers-in-law, and ordinary folk and tribal chiefs. In residential areas with marked social differences, we might find the same problem.
- *The values, ways of life and ethics of the sender and receiver may be in conflict.* This usually happens because of a difference in age or culture or simply because of a difference of opinion. People tend to think that their values and mores are universally acceptable and this can lead to a situation where the sender resents the receiver and the receiver resents the sender.
- *The message may be in conflict with the receiver's interests.* In this case, the receiver is hardly going to accept it just like that. People can be opportunistic. The common good is always subordinate to the individual interest. So, a message with a positive outcome for the society may still be unacceptable for the individual if it seems in conflict with his/her interests.

In these cases, the receiver receives the message and understands it, but rejects it on one or more grounds.

10.3.4 Reasons for barriers to communication

There are various reasons why barriers to communication exist. Various situations put up barriers that make communication ineffective. Some of these are as follows:

- *Different perceptions exist among communicating parties.* Because every human being is unique, our perceptions of things tend to be unique too. We see things differently from one another. This results in our giving different meaning to verbal and non-verbal communication.
- *Communicating parties quite often come from different situations.* They live under different circumstances and experience different inputs. Thus, communicating parties may have different realities that may differ slightly or vastly and may even be in conflict with one another.
- *Communication has got to compete with a lot of noise.* By 'noise', we do not mean only physical noise so that we cannot hear communication. We also include psychological 'noise' such as fear, social 'noise' such as prejudice, cultural 'noise' such as superstition, and political 'noise' such as opportunism.
- *Much of our communication has emotional content.* In such cases, we tend to respond to the emotion and not to the content of the message. By this we do not say that communication should be without emotion, but that we should be careful of how much emotion we allow in our communication and how we respond to emotion. We must also accept that communication can hardly be without some emotion.
- *Very few of us are prepared to trust another person unconditionally.* Distrust is really the poison for communication because, in communication, we do not only give a message, we give something of ourselves. We open up through communication, but if we do not trust the receiver of our message, we are loath to reveal anything personal. As long as communication is less than spontaneous because of distrust, it faces a plethora of pitfalls that can cause its demise.
- *Apathy is not very helpful to communication.* We may be apathetic about the message. That means that we are not worried about the message and do not regard it as important. As the receiver, we may also be apathetic toward the sender and disinterested in the other person's feelings, interests or wellbeing. If we do not care for the message or for the sender, it is impossible for communication to be successful.

- *It is human to feel* apprehensive *about change and even to resist it.* If a message contains a hint of impending change or emphasises the need to change, many receivers will close out the message. The situation becomes worse if the receiver is confronted with change, and if it becomes a matter of change or bust. It is easy to see why this is one of the most prolific barriers in development communication.
- *Culture determines the meaning of the world we live in.* Culture rationalises what we do and how we do it. It also causes a feeling of 'us and them'. The meaning that people from other cultures attach to things such as life, circumstances and situations, may not look rational to the receiver and this often leads to cultural snobbishness and prejudice. Communication on an equal footing where there is respect for the other person and his/her views becomes really difficult. According to Servaes and Lie (2003:11), culture does not only provide context but is becoming text. As text it constitutes the common, shared interest around which a community project evolves.

10.4 OVERCOMING BARRIERS TO COMMUNICATION

In community development work, it is important to be a good communicator, in other words, to overcome the various barriers to communication. The first thing on the way to overcoming the barriers is to admit that they exist, also within you, and to decide to do something about it. This is a sincere way of addressing the problem and an important starting point that must lead to tackling the problem at two levels: first, at a psychological level and second, at a technical, mechanistic level.

10.4.1 The psychological level

The first step toward effective communication with others is successful communication with oneself. Intrapersonal communication means messages sent and received within the same individual. It takes place whenever we evaluate and respond to internal and external stimuli. It reflects our physical, emotional, intellectual and social selves. In other words, it reflects our self-concept.

As we increase our self-awareness, we also tend to be willing to share that awareness with others. If we have reached this stage, we are on the brink of becoming a successful communicator because self-disclosure lies at the heart of communication. It is the vehicle by which others know what is going on inside us – our thoughts and feelings and what we care about. Self-disclosure opens a window through which others can look into one's soul. Self-disclosure is also the key to any long-term relationship, and most importantly, it leads to greater self-awareness because it works directly against the very negative natural tendency to hide feelings of incompetence, loneliness, guilt, fear and anxiety.

The Johari window is a model used to understand better and to enhance communication in a group. Good communication is promoted by a safe environment in which openness between members can prosper. The perception of individual members in the group of others can be improved by using the Johari model. The happiness of people depends on the extent to which the need is met for healthy social relations (a psychological need).

According to Osmanoglu (2019:76), there are two dimensions involved in the Johari model: 'what the person knows about himself/herself and what other people have learned about this person'. Form this interaction between two persons, four states of knowing information emerge: (1) an *open state*, where information about an individual's behaviour, attitude, emotions, experiences and so on is open and known; (2) a *special or hidden state*, which includes information known to a person but which he/she does not want to share, such as fears, jealousy and things about which he/she might be ashamed; (3) the *blind or suspicious state*, which includes information which is known by other people but not known, or rejected, by the person – this is the area of ignorance about oneself; (4) the *unknown state*, which includes characteristics like strengths, emotions and talents, which is not known to the individual or other people.

1. OPEN STATE	2. SPECIAL OR HIDDEN STATE
3. BLIND OR SUSPICIOUS STATE	4. UNKNOWN STATE

Figure 10.1 The Johari model represented by a window with four panes

The Johari window is a tool to help members of a group to understand themselves and the others better. In this model, the wider the open area is, the healthier communication will be. For the sake of communication, the main effort of community development groups 'should be to expand the open area of the individual member because open or free area [sic] can be seen as the area where good communication and cooperation take place'.

The less we feel threatened by communication, the easier it is to trust the other party. If we succeed in trusting someone else, we can really look forward to fruitful and productive communication because without that trust very little communication can really take place. Trust is seldom instantaneous. It takes a while to get to trust someone, simply because it takes time to get to know him/her. Trust in a person therefore develops over time and can be accomplished only with genuine effort. As this trust grows, it becomes reciprocal in most cases; in other words, the more we trust someone, the more that person trusts us. Only if that mutual trust develops can there be real communication between two people.

This process of real communication is boosted tremendously by feedback. If silence is the only feedback we get as a result of our communication, or if we respond apathetically to communication directed to us, the communication stops right there. Feedback takes place internally and externally. Internally we conform or correct our understanding of a message or our feeling about a message by external feedback such as asking questions and responding with feeling. Such feedback comes in the form of a message to the other party, who will again react externally by perhaps asking further questions or agreeing, and internally by shaping his/her behaviour or perspective accordingly.

10.4.2 The technical level

On the more practical or technical level, there are a lot of things that we can do to overcome the barriers to communication. As a starting point, we should follow a few standard guidelines:

- *Acknowledge barriers*. This means that we admit that barriers exist. This admission shows our honesty, without which we will never overcome any barriers. The CDP must also be honest in this regard. To acknowledge is not a sign of weakness.
- *Bring it out into the open*. It is not wrong to bring communication problems out in the open. We should even admit to the other party that there are barriers and try to persuade the other person to help us to overcome them.

- *Develop counteracting strategies to the barriers.* Admitting to their existence is not enough. We are then still in a negative mode. We must also do something positive to overcome them. In this regard the CDP's creativity can go a long way to ease the situation. If it is a language problem, the community can help the CDP to remember certain expressions and words from their language. In this, the CDP becomes dependent on the community and it shows them that they can also teach the CDP something important. If it is jargon problems, the community can help the CDP to get a word from the vernacular to explain the jargon.
- *Be aware of the context of your communication.* Take note of the circumstances and the situation because the context determines what barriers are present and how to overcome them. This context is both concrete (or physical) and abstract. It is a noisy room where people are coming and going all the time (physical) and it takes place between two people who do not know each other well (abstract). If CDPs disregard the contextual aspects, they are going to find very soon that they are talking to themselves.
- *Be honest.* That means that we should not lie to a person. Honesty will be the first step in breaking down barriers. A lie has the tendency to reveal itself as such – to the detriment of the communal effort.
- *Be sincere.* Sincerity means that we mean what we say. It invites a positive response from the receiver that makes it easier to overcome the barriers.

Let us now look at a number of specific aspects – the everyday things that one should do in order to overcome barriers and to make communication successful:

- *Be aware of the importance of perceptions.* Take special care in ensuring that perceptions are clear and correct. Start with yourself. Are you clear on the issue at hand and is your perception thereof generally acceptable? Then look at the other person. Is there consensus between your understanding and his/hers? Remember that you are not communicating with a computer or smart phone. You are communicating with a human being with a vast array of circumstances and views.

- *Consider the other person's point of view or frame of reference.* There can be more than one point of view about most issues in life. The other person's point of view is not necessarily incorrect because it differs from yours. The other person may have an altogether different frame of reference than you have. You are not communicating with an enemy or opponent, but with a person.

- *Use face-to-face communication if the communication situation is problematic or difficult.* Feedback and responses are direct and can be responded to directly, which obviates many potential problems. The only advantage of written communication is that you can take care with the phrasing of the message, but on-the-spot monitoring of the communication process can only take place in a face-to-face situation. In order to have the best of both worlds you can put the message in writing where you take care with the phraseology and then work through it with the other party in a face-to-face process.

- *Be sensitive to the other person's background and adapt to that background, culture and the person's circumstances.* If you are a good communicator, you will not regard the other party as an antagonist, but you will have empathy that will manifest in sensitivity for and an appreciation of the other person's background and circumstances.

- *Use direct, clear and simple language.* The clearer and less abstract the message, the better it will be received and considered. Symbolic meanings of words must be carefully explained so that there is no confusion as a result of cultural or background differences.

- *Use frequent repetitions to make sure that the message sinks in and is understood.* Repetition is a tried and trusted method used by educators. The rhetorical speaker, such as the preacher or the politician, does it too and usually with great effect.

- *Be supportive to counteract defensiveness.* If you want to make a success of your communication, you must support other parties in the communication situation. Let a person be comfortable in your presence and ensure that your communication is objective and descriptive rather than subjective and prescriptive.

- *Do not use racist or sexist terms, even if it is meant as a joke on yourself.* It could cause negative reactions and even start conflict. It may be perceived as disdain for other people rather than respect. Even if it is meant as a joke or a tongue-in-cheek remark, rather do it only if you know the other party very well.

- *Concentrate on the common ground and aims and avoid differences.* This does not mean that we should be blind to or ignore differences, but we should also not be blind to the common ground and the things that we agree about. A CDP should think like a politician and should make the other party feel comfortable.
- *Encourage a climate and atmosphere conducive to communication.* The best way to do this is to be friendly, honest and sincere. Do not preach to a person or people. It makes them uneasy and they fall quiet while you are the only speaker.
- *Try to establish a rapport between you and the receiver.* Having a rapport means to accept one another's bona fides, to accept that the other person will be civil, decent, honest and sincere.
- *Do not give a person the idea that you want something, but rather that you are willing to contribute and to make a sacrifice.* This is the secret of the successful tradesperson who makes you feel that you are the receiver of something good. The fact that you pay money for whatever you receive does not figure strongly.
- *Make sure that your body language corresponds with what you are saying.* If it does not, you are guilty of lying. If you are talking to a group of people about their poverty or the lack of health among their children and you do it while you are lounging in an easy chair with your legs stretched out, your body language will not support your communication. Inconsistency between verbal and non-verbal communication is picked up quite easily and has a negative reaction from the other party. On the other hand, if the verbal message and the body language agree, it is a sign of sincerity.
- *Be wide awake to the other person's body language.* Use that as a frame of reference for your participation in the communication process. In other words, observe the other person's body language, interpret it and adapt accordingly.
- *Avoid politics and religion because there are too many tricky nuances that can get you into trouble.* If these topics do crop up, do not give the impression that you are wary of discussing them, but ensure you are not prescriptive in anything you say.
- *Be prepared to admit your own mistakes and to take responsibility for them.* People appreciate it when you make yourself vulnerable and usually respond kindly to it. It also makes you more human, something

that can only be beneficial in a communication situation. It does also open yourself for outside scrutiny and shows some trust from your side.

- *Prepare yourself thoroughly if you have to explain a difficult or foreign concept and make sure that it is pitched at the right level – not too high, but not too low either.* Then let your empathy with the other person's weaker position guide you so that you can move at his/her pace and remain at his/her level.
- *Communicate with confidence.* This is of course only possible if you are well prepared and sure of your facts. Then it is also necessary to accept responsibility for the message that you convey.
- *Do not force the other person to communicate with you.* It is every person's right to choose with whom he/she wants to communicate. To force a person to listen to you will border on aggression, which you should never display. However, you should be assertive because otherwise you are no better than a lame duck. Therefore, you should state your case and explain your opinion, but coercion should not be part of your argument; this means bringing the horse to the water and forcing it to drink.
- *Keep your information lean.* Give optimal information, not maximal. An information famine is just as bad as an information overload. So, the appropriate information and the correct amount of information are very important.
- *A participant in communication should never feel threatened, therefore do not put a person on the spot.* Do not be overbearing, do not talk down to a person and do not make jokes at the expense of a person.
- *Never gossip* because the receiver will, rightfully, have anxiety that you will gossip about him/her too. Remember the importance of trust. Remember also that gossip breaks down trust.
- *Be trustworthy and reliable, consistent and honest.* Show your good intentions and demonstrate your integrity to the other party.
- *Regard yourself as a trainee communicator.* Therefore assess every activity of communication and learn from such an assessment.
- *Persevere.* Communication is not easy and we will encounter obstacles that hinder communication. However, obstacles are never insurmountable. They only provide huge challenges to our originality, our sincerity and our perseverance.

To a large extent these suggestions are meant for the sender, the initiator of communication. For the receiver, listening skills are important. Remember that the sender becomes the receiver once the receiver responds to the initial input and then the sender must apply listening skills to ensure successful communication. We can say that you must be an active listener. This includes the following:

- Listen to understand fully a speaker's remark before criticising or evaluating it.
- Listen in order to evaluate a message only after you know what has really been said.
- Listen to the complete message. Do not listen and then assume that you know the rest of the message.
- Listen to provide support for the speaker. In other words, identify whatever it is in the message with which you wholeheartedly agree.

10.5 DEVELOPMENT COMMUNICATION

Personal communication and personal skills impact directly on what is known today as development communication. Development communication can be described as a process by which people become leading actors in their own development, which allows people to go from being beneficiaries of external development interventions to generators of their own development (Barker 2001:4). The objectives of development communication are to:

- exchange information to help resolve a development problem
- improve the quality of life of a specific target group
- implement needs analysis and evaluation mechanisms in the communication process.

Ali and Sonderling (2017:84) identify factors that may affect the practice of participatory development communication. The CDP should consider whether these factors are applicable to the work situation, and how to address them (or limit negative impacts). For instance, a top–down development approach represents an institutional factor and cannot be directly addressed at community level. The factors identified are:

- economic perceptions of development
- top–down development approach

- short time span of the development project
- dependency on donor funding
- perceptions of participation as labour and material contributions
- dependency syndrome
- perceptions of development communication as information transmission
- lack of professionalism of communication
- lack of adequate manpower
- challenges or problems posed by the organisation's structure
- lack of adequate budget
- the absence of communication policy
- political interference and lack of democratic culture.

Most of the issues listed above are discussed in various other chapters of this book.

Development communication models emphasise two-way communication to disseminate messages and to transmit information or to motivate people. These models also allow for horizontal communication among people rather than traditional vertical transmission from the expert to an audience. Steyn and Nunes (2001:35) go so far as to suggest that the communication roles of the various stakeholders should be plotted and, if necessary, communication training should be given. Emphasis is not on the use of the media but on the process and strategies for participatory grassroots communication and an exchange of information through two-way media. Communication models will fail if they are not characterised by participation and the needs of the community, or if they are aimed at information transmission away from and not in harmony with community processes (Mersham, Rensburg & Skinner 1995).

The CDP should prompt the community to initiate the messages about their development needs. Individual circumstances must also be taken into consideration. In spite of the commonalities that link us into the social structure, no two lives are ever the same in terms of personal experience (Barker 2001:7).

Development communication is aimed at and includes the following applications (Barker 2001:8):

- An understanding of user needs through contact with target groups
- Target group analysis and message development
- Beneficial two-way communication relationship between participants
- Messages initiated and facilitated by the community
- Messages that are decipherable because of simplicity and clarity
- Participants as co-managers of communication
- Skills among all participants in communication technology and techniques
- A healthy internal culture and climate conducive to the dynamic flow of information
- Communication with meaning that depends on personal interpretation and collective agreement
- Internalisation and externalisation of the message
- Formulation of new ideas and directions through participatory action
- Messages relevant to inputs from the community
- Environmentally sensitive message
- Carefully chosen communication channels
- A well-planned and strategically motivated communication plan
- Objective-achieving communication (see Chapter 11).

10.6 CONCLUSION

By learning more about what communication is, we have also learnt about the obstacles or barriers in the way of successful communication. It is clear that communication is the life of community mobilisation and facilitation, that it runs through a project and that it determines the vitality and success of groups, but it is also clear that it does not come by itself. We have to work hard to become skilled and successful communicators.

Without this skill, we can hardly do our job successfully. Communication is such an important ingredient of our everyday task. It is therefore imperative that we give it top priority. See also Chapter 14 on operational writing and Chapter 16 that deals with public speaking.

REFERENCES

Ali AC & Sonderling S. 2017. Factors affecting participatory communication for development: The case of a local development organization in Ethiopia. *Malaysian Journal of Communication,* Jilid 33(1):80–97.

Barker R. 2001. Communication with communities: A South African experience. *Communicatio*, 27(1):3–14.

Geyser W. 2022. What is an influencer? Social media influencers defined. Available at: https://influencermarketinghub.com/what-is-an-influencer/ (accessed 15 December 2022).

Klear. 2022. Find Top 10 community development influencers. Available at: https://klear.com/influencers/Community%20Development (accessed 15 December 2022).

López-Ozieblo R. 2015. Cultural aspects of immediacy in an Asian classroom context. *ELIA*, 15:13–34.

Mersham JM, Rensburg RS & Skinner JC. 1995. *Public Relations, Development and Social Investment: A Southern African Perspective.* Pretoria: Van Schaik.

Osmanoglu DE. 2019. Expansion of the open area (Johari window) and group work directed to enhancing the level of subjective well-being. *Journal of Education and Training*, 7(5):76–85.

Servaes J & Lie R. 2003. Media, globalisation and culture: Issues and trends. *Communicatio*, 29(1–2):7–23.

Steyn B & Nunes M. 2001. Communication strategy for community development: A case study of the Heifer project – South Africa. *Communicatio*, 27(2):29–48.

Swanepoel H & De Beer F. 1996. *Communication for Development: A Guide for Fieldworkers.* Halfway House: International Thomson Publishing.

CHAPTER 11

Leadership and Group Facilitation in Community Development

Abel Mafukata and Frik de Beer

11.1 INTRODUCTION

Literature specific to community development and leadership has been burgeoning and getting popular in South Africa – especially since the 1990s when the apartheid regime made way for the new dispensation. In various disciplines, these concepts have been receiving comprehensive attention, and continue to do so. However, what has not been so widely covered is the integration of these two – leadership in/and community development.

This chapter reviews selected literature across disciplines to demonstrate the linkage and synergy between leadership and community development. The chapter points out how leadership relates to or alternatively integrates with community development for positive output. It begins with a discussion of the concept 'leadership', which is understood and defined differently by different people across disciplines. It considers numerous definitions to emerge with a 'compromise' meaning of how leadership will be defined for the purpose of this chapter.

To review the context of community development, refer to Chapter 3: *Stakeholders in community development*, and Chapter 6: *Principles of community development*. It is important to be reminded that community development is informed, often guided by community development and related policies and programmes as provided from the broader South African political and public administration environment. In South Africa, these include, among others:

- Reconstruction and Development Programmes (RDP)
- Growth, Employment and Redistribution Strategy (GEAR)
- Accelerated and Shared Growth Initiative for South Africa (ASGISA)
- The White Paper for Social Welfare (South Africa 1997)

- The White Paper on Local Government (South Africa 1998)
- The Local Government Municipal Structures Act 117 of 1998
- The Local Government Municipal Systems Act 32 of 2000
- Integrated Sustainable Rural Development Programme (ISRDP))
- Urban Renewal Programme (URP)
- Expanded Public Works Programme (EPWP)
- War-on-Poverty (WoP) and Comprehensive Rural Development Programme (CRDP).

These policies and programmes were meant 'to attend to the experience of material poverty of the majority' (Luka & Maistry 2012) in the context of a community development framework developed for the purpose of attending 'to poverty in its multifaceted reality consisting of, inter alia, lack of power, resources (including income) to make choices and take advantage of opportunities' (Luka & Maistry 2012). Chapter 25 pays more attention to the legislative framework for community development in South Africa.

The chapter defines leadership in the context of community development, by presenting the skills needed for successful leadership in community development, before a conclusion is given.

11.2 DEFINING THE CONCEPT 'LEADERSHIP'

The concept 'leadership' has been a growing enquiry in a few disciplines. Its study 'is a recent academic activity ... [although] ... the phenomenon of leadership has been ever present in human relations' (Fairholm 2015:1). Like any other concept, 'leadership' is understood by different people differently depending on the factors involved in its formulation. Established scholars across disciplines who study the concept 'leadership', among others Gary Yukl, John P. Kotter, Peter Northouse, Ruel Khoza, Wangari Maathai, Louise Kretzschmar, Elif Baykal, Shawon Jackson, Satoe Sakuma and Purva DeVol, understood and defined this concept differently. Many of these scholars agree that the concept is a complex one 'which, to date, still has no concrete definition' (Jackson, Sakuma & DeVol 2015). As with any other concept, 'leadership' is explained and understood according to its context, and as definitions of concepts emanate from several intertwined factors, certain concepts will continue 'to mean different things to different people' (Hyden & Court 2022).

For the purposes of this chapter, we rely on the work of the following: Northouse (2010:3), who defines leadership as 'a process whereby an individual influences a group of individuals to achieve a common goal'; Maathai (2009), whose conceptualisation of 'leadership' fits well with the essence of this chapter: her approach is defined as 'radical leadership ... engaging in transformative actions toward the common good in spite of the personal cost' (Ngunjiri 2014:123) in that it clarifies its meaning in relation to 'community'; and Yukl (quoted in Bogenschneider 2016:37), who defines the concept of 'leadership' as

> the process of influencing others to understand and agree about what needs to be done and how to do it, and the process of facilitating individual and collective efforts to accomplish shared objectives.

Linking these works (Yukl 2006; Maathai 2009; Northouse 2010), we find that leadership comprises several components, as described in Table 11.1.

Table 11.1 **Components of leadership**

Component	Description of component
Leadership involves influence.	Leadership is about the ability of leaders to influence those they are said to be leading. These could be subordinates and/or peers. Leadership is two-way, meaning that those who are being led in turn lead their 'bosses' or their leaders. Leaders rely on influence, which demands ethical considerations. In other words, leaders are expected to exercise their influence ethically.
Leadership is a reciprocal process.	Those who lead affect those they lead, while those who are led also affect those who lead them. This can be positive or negative. Leadership is an interactive process that goes beyond those who are formally recognised as leaders. Informal leaders can hold just as much influence.
Leadership involves directing followers who require motivation to attain a particular goal.	Leadership is the provision of ethical guidance and direction to those being led to achieve their set goals. Therefore, leadership is about accomplishment of a set task.
Leadership involves others and happens in the context of a group.	Leadership involves operations conducted in organised groups. Leaders must influence those in these groups.

Component	Description of component
Leadership is about driving the group to achieve a particular goal.	The group of people who are led have a common goal to achieve. The goal could involve development of a particular project in a community. For example, in a rural area where services such as water supply and access are hard to come by from government, a group of residents could mobilise themselves to provide this service with the common goal of improving water supply systems at the village. Leadership is required to influence them to achieve the set goal.
Leadership involves attainment of shared goals, not imposed goals.	Leaders and followers first and foremost share objectives, and one of those objectives could be to achieve a common goal. Following this imperative, both those providing leadership and those following, work in cooperation to achieve the set objectives (that they all share). Despite the challenges which could arise while working towards the goal, both the leader and those being led 'focus' on the shared goal. Cooperation between the leader and the group is key for successful achievement of the goal. Leaders should bear in mind that 'imposed' goals are harder to achieve and good leaders often develop their organisation's goals along with their followers.
Leadership is about bringing change by identifying opportunities and turning risks into opportunities.	Leaders lead groups to change(s). Leaders create organisations and put systems in place. These organisations and their systems allow for the groups being led to exploit opportunities to reach their goals. Leaders motivate those they lead to realise opportunities out of risk.
Leadership is not a characteristic or trait with which only a few people are endowed at birth.	Leaders can be developed. The notion that leaders are born has been widely challenged by many who study the concept of leadership.

Source: Adapted from Yukl (2006); Northouse (2010); Maathai (2009)

11.3 LEADERSHIP FOR SUCCESSFUL COMMUNITY DEVELOPMENT

Leadership is about bringing followers together with the purpose of directing them toward their desired goals (Ertosun & Adiguzel 2019:56). It occurs when one person induces others to work toward some predetermined objective. Leadership is an influential increment activity that goes beyond routine acts of supervision – it is the value added to the organisation or project by having an individual assume a role. This goes for all types of leaders, including managers of organisations from the private and public sector, group leaders in a project and also CDPs. The success of community development initiatives hinges on good leadership.

In community development, leadership grows out of an understanding of what needs to be done practically and what the situation or milieu demands. Kirk and Shutte (2004:235) call this type of leadership 'a phenomenon that grows out of, and is a product of its setting'. A community development leader is therefore not an individual managing people, but rather a member of a community of practice (Horner 1997, in Kirk & Shutte 2004:236).

The wellbeing of structures such as forums, project groups and committees is very dependent on the leadership. By leadership we do not refer only to a single leader such as a chairperson, but rather to a leadership corps such as an executive committee or governing body. The leadership of a group determines to a large extent the amount and calibre of communication; the amount and calibre of communication similarly determine the success of the leadership. We therefore have two interdependent items – leadership and communication.

Communication can only be successful in an open situation. This is especially relevant for heterogeneous groups. The openness of a group is determined by its leadership. Therefore, one of leadership's more important responsibilities is to see that there is an open situation in which communication flows freely. We can also say that a leadership with a balance between task orientation and relationship, or group orientation, brings maturity among both leadership and followers and this maturity leads directly to motivation.

Maturity is seen as follows:

- *The ability to set high, but achievable goals*: Maturity is obtained when goals will require effort, but not unduly so.
- *The willingness to accept responsibility*: Leadership must accept a leadership responsibility and the rest of the group must accept a participant responsibility.
- *Education and experience applicable to a specific task*: This is the outcome of the learning process that is foremost a capacity-building activity.
- *Work maturity and psychological adulthood*: This is the ability to do a job and having the will and confidence to do it.

11.3.1 The importance of leadership

There have always been contentions regarding the importance of leadership with some arguing that it was not necessary and important. Based on this, the critical question is therefore whether leadership was necessary or not. To shed some light in response, Massie and Douglas (1981:320) argued the following:

> There are at least four inescapable facts of organisational life that demand leadership. First, no matter how superior the planning, procedures and design, there is a fundamental incompleteness in organisations. Gaps appear, overlaps emerge and the segments would come apart if it were not for someone functioning as a leader. A second fact of life is environmental change. Few firms can isolate themselves from the external environment with its changes. Organisations need people to interpret these changes. The internal dynamics of organisations represent a third fact that requires someone in leadership. Organisations are composed of many parts or subsystems. If left to their own movement and energy, subunits may never become functional for the whole organisation. The last fact of life is that the nature of human membership in organisations is somewhat unpredictable. Human behaviour and subsequent responses vary so greatly that individual leadership is needed for adjustment and adaptation.

From this, it is evident that a manager should be more than a non-personal arranger of organisational functions. Leadership is interpersonal and a leader, be it the manager, the CDP or the group leader of a project, must realise that its essence lies with people.

Personality characteristics of people involved in the leadership act contribute a great deal to the effectiveness or ineffectiveness of the act itself. In the same way that personality characteristics of the leader are critical for effectiveness, the personality characteristics of those surrounding the leader must also be recognised and understood.

People in organisations carry different values, aspirations and expectations. A leader must be aware that these differences will affect any leadership attempt. To fully understand leadership the person factor must be acknowledged. This factor, including items like values and personality, appears in both leaders and followers.

Every person has some kind of an image of the way to act in a given position, and this image is called the role concept. Those who must come into contact with the position also have an image about how the person should act in the position, and this is called the role expectation. Both these images are important to the understanding of the human behaviour that flows from the position factor of leadership.

There are at least three sources of role expectations:

1. *Personal expectations*: These are the ways in which people expect the leader to behave. In every group, there is a pattern of expectations – the group expects the leader to do certain things and to refrain from doing others. The group expects certain patterns of behaviour from the formal leader. This applies especially with regard to the CDP and the leader of the project action group.
2. *Organisational expectations*: Many organisations have definite and specific expectations about the behaviour of their managers and leaders. These expectations are frequently written into formal position guides and job descriptions.
3. *Cultural expectations*: In addition to the specific personal and organisational patterns of role expectation that contribute to the shaping of the leadership role, there are also cultural expectations of many types.

There is no magic formula for becoming an effective leader. Management and leadership are not easy jobs, and the leadership function of a manager frequently requires many difficult decisions. The same goes for the CDP and the project leader. Not all people, obviously, have the physiological, psychological and sociological make-up to be leaders. Yet, there is a need and challenge for leaders.

11.3.2 Improving leadership behaviour

The following are some suggestions for how to improve leadership:

- *Believe the best about others*. The leader's behaviour and the response to his behaviour depend upon beliefs about the nature of human beings. The Theory X philosophy states that if you believe that people are lazy, hate work, do not want responsibility, work as little as possible, are motivated by money and fear, and are basically uncreative, you will tend to expect this behaviour from them. This belief and expectation creates just such behaviour in others. It is clear that there is no place for such an attitude in CDPs or any other person with leadership duties in community development. We should rather substitute this theory with Theory Y. According to Theory Y, the nature of people would suggest that they are intelligent, creative, want to work, want to achieve and to solve problems, and will initiate actions if given the opportunity (Massie & Douglas 1981:339). With this attitude, leadership can be successful.

- *Be yourself.* If you can find yourself and know yourself, the behaviour will take care of itself. It is true for communication too, as we have seen in Chapter 10. The good communicator, also the communicating leader, is the one who is at peace with him/herself.
- *Meet the needs of your fellows.* This is not so easy. What do you do with those whose needs do not seem to find satisfaction? The leader should at least show empathy regarding those unfulfilled needs. The leader can never appear to be uncaring about such things.
- *Use what is available.* Use personal experiences to form a simple, concrete, day-to-day working model. A logical and 'quiet' model is better than something grandiose and 'noisy'.
- *Employ an integration approach.*
- *Create support.* This behaviour will let others feel that they are of worth and importance to the leader.
- *Facilitate interaction.* This will encourage members of the group to develop close, positive, warm, satisfying relationships.
- *Emphasise goals.* This will stimulate an enthusiasm among people to meet the performance goals of the group.
- *Facilitate work.* This behaviour is related to goal attainment and includes scheduling, co-ordination and planning.

CDPs should pay attention to the above in terms of their own 'leadership' style, but they must also enable the project leadership to do the same.

Capacity building is meant for all participants, but leadership especially should engage in this activity to enable them to manage projects better. In order to allow participants to take on responsibility, responsibility has to be given to them. Capacity building is vital in this regard, particularly because, in the field where we all work together, there are enormous differences in education, status, wealth and self-esteem. (See Case study 25: *The smart community development worker.*)

Capacity building is often understood as a discrete period, such as a 10-day training course. This understanding of capacity building is a limited one and has limited results. Capacity building must be understood as an integral part of every effort to run a community development project. Capacity has to be developed in context, not in the offering of general once-off training courses in isolation from any other support that is of little use in the long run.

Capacity building is embedded in various growth points, for example in the issue of needs. Capacity building enables participants to recognise and express their needs. Without this foundation, there can be no constructive work towards a forum that truly reflects participants' needs. Other areas where capacity building is integral are creating autonomy, facing and dealing with conflict, prompting the ability to deal with change, working with diversity, growing trust and respect, encouraging responsibility, celebrating success, integrating local participants, creating strategies and encouraging flexibility. In every instance, the growth of these abilities and the capacity that makes them possible occurs as an evolution.

11.3.3 Leadership and communication

A central aim of capacity building is to enable participants to enter into a range of situations with stable abilities and self-confidence, allowing them to engage actively in seeking agreements and solutions that work for them and allow them to enjoy maturity. If this is true, then a leader should see communication as:

- a dialogue engaging members of the community in an open discussion with a view to discovering solutions and jointly determining the way forward
- an opportunity for capacity building for all involved
- a collaborative effort.

If the leadership takes action without informing or integrating the group members, or makes decisions without the knowledge of the other members, and if the members do not know what the leadership is doing, we have a closed situation. It is obvious that there can be no healthy, dynamic communication in such a situation. Here there is little or no sharing of ideas, little or no sensitivity for the feelings or the opinions of others, little or no transparency, and little or no concern from the leadership for group wellbeing.

This type of situation may often be the result of the leadership being overly task oriented. The result of this is an ever-widening gap between the leadership and the other members, and a loss of enthusiasm among the ordinary members who rightly do not feel themselves part of the action. This also leads to a drop in the numbers of ordinary members so that, over time, the executive becomes the group and the group as such disappears.

When communication is healthy and vibrant in an open situation, a certain cyclical dynamism is established between the leadership and the rest of the group. In this situation, the leadership maintains a balance between task and group orientation. The leadership receives inputs from the group and responds by making decisions. The group, being aware of the decisions being made because of continuous communication, responds to the decisions and this response is then the next input for the leadership to respond to. This process goes on and on, and the whole group becomes part of the decision making because everyone can influence decision making directly. In this situation, the leadership knows the needs and sentiments of the group so that it can respond to these, and the group knows what the leadership is doing about its needs and sentiments. This is sympathetic leadership and participatory management. This leads to a vibrant group that builds confidence and self-reliance, which strengthens the leadership.

If the leadership of development-relevant institutions is open and the cyclical input–output model works, we will reach our goal. But do stakeholder groups and leaders of these groups know how important this open model is? If they do not, it seems as if capacity building should take place on this matter, not only for the group leadership, but for all members of groups so that whole groups can become aware of the ideal situation that will ensure participatory decision making. Poor or ineffective participatory decision making is not always the fault of the leadership. Ordinary members and supporters are often unwilling to participate in decision making because they are unwilling to share the responsibility with the leadership or they are just too lazy to add to their responsibilities.

11.4   GROUPS

The groups that are busy with community development in various projects are the second role players that we can identify in this chapter. Civic duty, civic responsibility and civic action are usually the domain of groups, not individuals. These groups are relatively small. They can number as few as 10 people and never have more than 100 members. The small group is extremely important, and it is necessary to know something about group dynamics and how to facilitate these groups. In order to fulfil their civic duty successfully, small groups must be kept healthy and active.

Communication in these small groups is essential. It is interesting that the definition of small groups describes communication as being their central ingredient. It describes a group as: a number of persons who communicate with one another often over a span of time and who are few enough so that each person is able to communicate with all the others, not at second hand through other people, but face to face. The central place of communication is indisputable and that is why one cannot discuss group dynamics without looking at communication. That is also the reason why the topic of group dynamics goes hand in hand with the topic of communication.

11.4.1 Types of small groups

We are mainly concerned with the following types of small groups:

- *Governmental organisations*: Here we refer to councils and their committees. In metropolitan and other structures, there are policy committees, liaison committees and all sorts of other committees such as organisational and action committees. All these take part in civic action.

- *Non-governmental organisations (NGOs)*: NGOs are organisations outside the sphere of government that were created to serve some civic duty, for example the Red Cross, which fulfils a welfare task. We must be careful not to see the Red Cross with its many members across the world as a small group; the local branch consisting perhaps of around 30 members will, however, constitute a small group.

- *Community-based organisations (CBOs)*: CBOs can be divided into two types. The first is less formal. Burial societies, women's clubs, rate payers' associations and youth clubs fall into this category. The more formal types are school committees, clinic committees, water committees, project-steering committees, committees emanating from economic and other forums, and so on. We may be tempted to classify these last groups as governmental, but that would be wrong because they have autonomy to carry out specific tasks, quite often to advise and inform government organisations. There are also large CBOs such as mass movements and political parties. Because of their size, they cannot be regarded as small groups except if they are divided into branches. A branch will then constitute a small group in our view of the concept.

- *Ad hoc groups:* Ad hoc groups are tied to community development projects where a group of concerned citizens comes together to address a need or problem common to all those members. A good example of this type of group can be found in Case study 17: *Mothers of the mountain community* and Case study 18: *Food garden in Mapayeni.*

11.4.2 Group dynamics

Every individual person thinks differently from all other people, sees life differently and therefore does things differently. There may even be big differences in perceptions and beliefs, even if the people live in the same society. A group consists of a number of such individuals and therefore a group becomes a melting pot, with different ways of thinking, doing, perceiving and believing all thrown together.

The one thing that we can be sure of is that this melting pot will bubble and boil. A lot of activity and energy is generated within a group because people respond differently to one another, and these responses may change from one minute to the next. Conflict comes and goes, tensions rise and then dissipate, moments of happiness are followed by moments of unhappiness, laughter makes way for seriousness that makes way for laughter again, and hectic moments become serene. The ups and downs of a group, the active and the restful parts of the life of a group, and the differing and sometimes clashing personalities, are all part of normal group dynamics. The important thing is to understand the dynamics in order to work with groups successfully. It is also important to define and stay aware of the role of communication in this dynamism.

We tend to think that group activities should go smoothly, that harmony must exist at all times and that everything must be done in concert. That is not how a group normally works, however. On the contrary, if group members always agree on everything and always work in harmony with one another, we would have reason to be concerned because then that group may be experiencing 'group think', which is detrimental to the health and wellbeing of the group. In such a situation, members do not contribute their individual ideas, perhaps because they are not encouraged to do so. The other reason is simply that the more a group develops mutual trust and a sense of togetherness, the less individual members are inclined to 'rock the boat'. People do not want to disagree on anything because they are worried that it will harm the feeling of oneness. Further, as a group grows together it develops a common set of beliefs. 'The values of each person, the values of the group, and the values of the leader are all moving toward a balance and agreement' (Massie & Douglas 1981:140). Anyone who challenges that set of beliefs may be regarded as a rebel and disrupter. We can understand this trend in groups, but while it is good for group cohesion, it makes a group less innovative and the group then forfeits the energy, wisdom, enterprise and uniqueness of the individual. A group must always be busy investigating itself, seeking better ways of doing things, and looking for alternatives that may work better.

11.4.3 Group psychology

Group activities and dynamics are informed by group psychology. Originally a group of people come together with different psychological backgrounds, different psychological outputs and different psychological workings. One of the main characteristics of groups is that, over time, there is a tendency for the group to develop a group psychology. Members of a group tend to develop similar psychological processes, at least while they are together. They tend to feel happy about the same things, and sad about the same things, and certain things and situations tend to bring about the same response from them. However, this does not imply that individual members lose their personal psychological make-up. It simply means that the individual psyches move closer to one another and form a harmonious entity in group relations. Again, while this is a natural process and while it is good to get a group to function properly, it can carry the danger of group think and it can stifle synergy.

Morale is an important psychological factor that helps in making groups successful. Morale includes:
- confidence in what the group is doing
- optimism that tasks will be completed successfully
- resilience to carry on even in adverse conditions
- mutual trust and respect among members
- loyalty towards one another and the objectives of the group
- willingness to sacrifice for the good of the group (Peterson, Park & Sweeney 2008:23).

11.4.4 Group wellbeing

A group must be kept healthy and well. If it is not healthy, its functioning will also be poor, it will not reach its objectives and eventually it will be a great disappointment to itself and everyone else. The factors that can ensure group wellbeing are given below.

Group identity

A group must have an identity. This is obtained through regular meetings, preferably at the same venue, agreement among its members on their objectives, an acceptance of one another in the group and a common belief in the capability of the members of the group to stand on their own feet. There are also more formal aspects giving identity to a group. These are a name for the group, a group emblem and/or logo, a constitution, and a vision and mission. Some groups form an identity by having a uniform, preferred colour or a piece of clothing such as a distinctive headscarf, tie, shirt or dress.

Purposeful activities

If a group is not purposefully busy, the very reason for its existence falls away. In this case, members will each follow their own fancy: meetings will be poorly attended and will ultimately not be regularly held. The moment that poor attendance at meetings and gaps in the meeting cycle happen without some sort of sanction against it, the reason for attending meetings or holding meetings for that matter falls away. It is clear that such a group has only one way to go and that is down to its ultimate death. Therefore, a group must have an objective to achieve, must have a strategy to obtain its objective and must be busy doing that.

Even personal growth-oriented groups must attain that personal growth through task execution. The women's club will not continue to exist simply because all its members are of the same sex. They must have an objective and must have some project activity to reach that objective in order to remain a healthy group.

Objective achievement

A group without an objective, or without acceptable progress toward an objective, will suffer and may even eventually die. Therefore, a group must have an objective that is reasonable and attainable, and that falls within the group's line of function and within its reach. The best approach is for each group to have one objective so that each group can have a single aim that drives it forward. This objective will be the reason for the group's existence. This objective must be concrete and easily definable so that the group and the individual members can identify themselves with the objective. The more the members identify themselves with this objective, the healthier the group will be. That is why it is better to have separate committees for sanitation, water and other services rather than one committee for all service delivery. A focused view and activity are always better than a broad view and activities.

Group maintenance

Just as a motor car or machine must be maintained to remain functional, a group also needs maintenance. Therefore, if something goes wrong in a group, it must be put right. If the group lacks energy, the cause must be identified and addressed. If the group lacks cohesion, the cause must be identified and addressed. Conflict cannot go on unattended. Clique forming cannot be tolerated and free riders cannot be allowed to leech off the group. Regular group evaluation may help to timeously identify things that are not right (see Chapter 22 for more on this). Case study 13: *The club with two committees* illustrates how easily something can go wrong in a group.

Group leadership

The type of leadership determines the calibre of communication, as we have mentioned earlier. Leadership should therefore not only be strengthened, but, more importantly, the right kind of leadership should be established and the members of a group should be conditioned not to accept anything else. An open leadership style makes for open communication that means that all members participate in and are responsible for decision making. No other leadership model is acceptable.

Group strengthening

A group must become cohesive. It must be strong enough to withstand attacks on its integrity and identity. There is no better way to ensure this than to enable a group to achieve something. A CDP should encourage a group and help it to develop standards for its performance, and then a CDP should support individual members to abide by those standards and to be proud of them. The setting of high but reachable standards in itself leads to group strengthening. Success is the surest way to strengthen a group and if that success is measured by the group's own standards, it acts as an energiser to the group. Through success, a group also gains recognition which will help in the strengthening of the group.

Boundary maintenance

A group must have some boundaries that will keep it together and set it slightly apart from other groups. For this reason, a group must have some exclusivity. It must not be open for a constant stream of new members. Members must feel that they have earned their membership and must be proud of it. In the case of committees, membership is usually already closed. However, the problem with committees can be when members are permitted to nominate a delegate to represent them when they cannot attend meetings. Eventually, while the membership stays the same, the actual personnel changes all the time and very few boundaries remain and little exclusivity exists. There is scant evidence of any group life in this instance, and one should rather talk of events (meetings) than of a group. Eventually a group busy with a community development project should grow in ability and should improve the following aspects of the group's life:

- *Awareness, ability to reflect and taking action:* At the initial stage, 'awareness' arises on the need to solve the common problems faced, to overcome the feelings of exploitation and alienation, and to meet the felt common needs.
- *Capacity to exercise own abilities:* Normally, at the beginning of establishing a group or initiating an activity, only one or two individuals may be involved. They are the local activists and group or project leaders who have demonstrated their leadership capabilities to mobilise, organise, facilitate and influence their friends to participate in a group to achieve group goals.
- *Gaining control over their lives:* The people's capabilities to think about their problems and needs and to act upon them by establishing various types of community groups, conducting and sustaining group activities, and pressuring and negotiating with the relevant authorities in order to solve their problems and meet their needs, is part of the process by which people come to gain control over their lives.
- *Developing and enhancing confidence, skills and knowledge:* In the process of participation, individuals learn. This leads to increases in

confidence, skills and knowledge, which in turn further enhances existing abilities to organise, solve problems, initiate action and manage group activities.

- *Gaining and exercising power over another party*: An examination of people's empowerment should not be viewed only as individuals' abilities to put forward their effort by working together in a self-help fashion to meet their goals within the sphere where they live. People living in one community, at the micro level, also interact with the outside system, at the macro level, in the development process. The linkage between the two levels lies in the context of the living environment itself.
- *Self-evaluation*: Empowerment does not end when people achieve their group goals. Motivated individuals who possess the characteristics of empowerment begin to evaluate their activities. This self-evaluation process, facilitated by an empowering research approach, enables individuals to reconsider changing the dynamics of their group process in order to maximise benefits. They are able to see possibilities to improve the activity, the group and the whole working process that can promote members' involvement (Abu Samah & Aref 2009).

11.5 SUPPORT AND ENABLEMENT OF LEADERS AND GROUPS

We now come to the third role player in this chapter, the CDP, who is entirely charged with the enablement and facilitation of the first two role players.

11.5.1 Leadership support

The CDP should provide support to leadership, acting as guide, adviser, advocate, enabler and facilitator, just as he/she does for the project as a whole. Remember that the goals of the CDP and leadership are not the same. They want a successful project, and the CDP wants them to grow and develop into fine leaders. The CDP should be humble and regard him/herself as the people's servant (see Chapter 8).

One of the primary tasks of the CDP is to facilitate the input–output model between leadership and members. The CDP should ensure that this communication always flows richly and swiftly.

11.5.2 Group support

The CDP has the following roles to play when it comes to the support and enablement of groups (Continuing Education for Africa (CEFA) 2007):

- *Clarifying*: Ensure that there is clarity on the purpose of the group.
- *Contracting*: Facilitate a mutual agreement between the group and yourself as the CDP, specifying expectations, obligations and duties.
- *Motivating*: Facilitate members' motivation and ability to work in the group and put their expectations regarding the CDP's role in perspective.
- *Addressing ambivalence*: Ensure clarity so that there are no mixed or contradicting ideas about the whole venture.
- *Anticipating obstacles*: Possible obstacles in the group's way toward its objective must be identified.
- *Structuring*: The work of the group needs to be structured through the use of planned, systematic, time-specified activities.
- *Facilitating*: The final activity for the CDP is to help group members to participate fully in the process.

The CDP can do the following to facilitate participation and empower group members:

- Demonstrate faith and trust in the strength and ability of group members.
- Emphasise the group members' ownership and right to self-determination relating to the group and the group process.
- Acknowledge group members for reaching out to achieve their goals.
- Encourage group members to experiment with their project.
- Select activities that will enhance the learning process.
- Monitor and evaluate the group's progress. An excellent way of doing this is by the participatory self-evaluation method that is explained in Chapter 22.

11.6 THREATS TO GROUP AND LEADERSHIP SUCCESS

The CDP must be aware of any possible threats to the wellbeing of groups. The following are a few that must be dealt with.

11.6.1 Domination

A dominating individual demands attention, controls the discussion, keeps others from being heard, prevents the group from concentrating on its task, and frequently creates resentment and power struggles within the group. However, this person is not necessarily a troublemaker that must be thrown out. This person may care deeply about the group and its goals, and be frustrated if the work is not progressing smoothly. The dominator may have something important to contribute and may bring energy and enthusiasm to the team process, but this person must be channelled in order to become a positive resource.

11.6.2 Distraction

It is clear that distractions can become obstacles for group progress. On the other hand, distracting the group once in a while is a genuine service. Humour at the right moment or a slight side trip to break tension can be a healthy contribution to transactional and task processes. However, sometimes people dedicate themselves to distracting the group from its work. They may be playful distracters (like adorable puppies), or aggressive distracters (more like vicious attack dogs). One is more fun than the other, but both keep the group from its tasks.

11.6.3 Non-participation

People who consistently stare out a window, doodle, mutter monosyllabic responses to questions, or say 'whatever' to any suggestion may not seem to constitute a major problem, but they certainly reflect and create one. Non-participation reveals a problem in that the group's processes do not involve every group member. Full participation is needed to facilitate the group's development and task.

11.6.4 Irresponsibility

People who do not show up, show up late, and/or do not do their share of the work constitute the most serious threat to the group. Sometimes, irresponsible behaviour results from other issues, so we could think about the irresponsibility of a group member in the same vein as what has been indicated in relation to non-participatory group members experiencing legitimate problems.

11.6.5 Reprehensibility

Reprehensible behaviour implies consistent unethical action, dishonesty, conniving, sexism, racism, bigotry or nastiness – someone who enjoys making other people miserable, who has no conscience and prefers to take the immoral road. This individual constantly twists conversation into a negative rope with which he or she tries to 'hang' the group. The best way to solve this problem is to have the group sanction that person and if need be, exclude him/her from the group.

11.7 GROUP FACILITATION SKILLS

Facilitating a group where the members are not used to meeting procedures, where the chairperson is unsure of him/herself and where the secretary is slow in making notes of the activities of the group, is not an easy task. The CDP needs the following skills for this task:

- *Active listening*: The CDP attends to the verbal and non-verbal aspects of the communication without judging or evaluating.
- *Clarifying*: The CDP grasps the essence of a message on both the thinking and feeling levels. Simplify the person's statement by focusing on the core of the message.
- *Summarising*: By connecting the important elements of an interaction or session, the CDP makes sure that all members have a grasp of the activities and thereby ensures as little misunderstanding as possible.
- *Questioning*: The CDP asks open-ended questions that lead to self-exploration of the 'what' and 'how'.
- *Interpreting*: By offering possible explanations for situations, behaviour and activities, the CDP helps the group to understand the context.
- *Supporting*: The CDP creates an atmosphere that encourages members to continue with their work, especially if members experience difficulties. It should also create trust.
- *Empathising*: The CDP is not aloof from the group. Through empathising, the CDP fosters trust among members that enhances communication (Corey, in Gladding 1995; Kadushin 1979).

The CDP's most important skills are to know when to apply his/her skills and what not to do in groups, and then not doing it. Being aware of pitfalls (what not to do) can thus assist the CDP to avoid potential problems that could damage or end the relationship between the CDP and group members.

Groups usually start off as weak and flimsy structures without cohesion and with little identity. They need to be supported and enabled by the CDP, among others, to:

- hold meaningful meetings by getting and learning the basic rules and procedures of meetings
- make enlightened decisions by receiving appropriate information
- implement their decisions by receiving aid to interpret their plans in a practical way
- evaluate their actions by receiving simple and practical guidelines on evaluation
- resolve conflict in their ranks by getting support for problem-solving communication
- hold their own against outside threats by being supported by advocacy
- grow in confidence and self-esteem by enjoying a climate in which they can prosper.

11.8 CONCLUSION

This chapter focused on how leadership influences groups to facilitate success in community development. A community development project is usually only as strong and successful as the group that runs it. Whatever challenges and complexities are experienced in a particular community development project can inevitably be traced back to this group. CDPs should therefore concentrate on the group's health and running projects, and assist the group to reach their objectives. To a large extent, the life of a group reflects the communication taking place within the group, and it is therefore important that communication should be placed high on the CDP's priority list.

REFERENCES

Abu Samah A & Aref F. 2009. People's participation in community development: A case study in a planned village settlement in Malaysia. *World Rural Observation*, 1(2):45–54.

Bogenschneider BN. 2016. Leadership epistemology. *Creighton Journal of Interdisciplinary Leadership*, 2(2):24–37.

CEFA (Continuing Education for Africa). 2007. *Further Education and Training Certificate in Social Auxiliary Work*. Wellington: CEFA.

De Beer F & Swanepoel H. 2012. A postscript as an introduction: Do we know where to go with the professionalisation of community development In South Africa. *Africanus, Journal of Development Studies*, 42(2):3–13.

Ertosun OG & Adiguzel Z. 2019. Leadership, personal values and organisational culture. In Dincer H, Hacioglu U & Yuksel S (eds), *Strategic Design and Innovative Thinking in Business Operations: The Role of Business Culture and Risk Management*. Cham, Switzerland: Springer Nature.

Fairholm MR. 2015. *Defining Leadership: A Review of Past, Present, and Future Ideas*. Washington, DC: Center for Excellence in Municipal Management.

Gladding ST. 1995. *Group Work: A Counselling Speciality*. 2nd ed. Englewood Cliffs: Prentice Hall.

Hyden G & Court J. 2002. Governance and Development. World Governance Survey Discussion Paper 1. United Nations University. Available at: https://www.google.com/search?q=Hyden+and+Court...to+mean+different+things+to+ (accessed 29 November 2021).

Jackson S, Sakuma S & DeVol P. 2015. The complexity in defining leadership: How gifted students' backgrounds influence their understanding of effective leadership. *NCSSS Journal*, 2015:40–46.

Kadushin A. 1979. *The Social Work Interview*. New York: Columbia University Press.

Khunou SF. 2009. Traditional leadership and independent Bantustans of South Africa: Some milestones of transformative constitutionalism beyond apartheid. *Potchefstroom Electronic Law Journal*, 12(4):81–125.

Kirk P & Shutte AM. 2004. Community leadership development. *Community Development Journal*, 39(3):233–251.

Kotter JP. 1998. *What leaders really do*. In *Harvard Business Review on Leadership*. Boston: Harvard Business School Press, pp 37–60.

Kretzschmar L. 2019. An ethical analysis of 'big man' and 'inner ring' leadership in South Africa: The example of Jacob Zuma and the resistance of Thuli Madonsela. In Jung S, Kessler V, Kretzschmar L. & Meier E (eds), *Metaphor for Leading – Leading by Metaphors*. Gottingen, Germany: V&R Unipress, pp 17–27.

Luka S & Maistry M. 2012. The Institutionalisation of community development in a democratic South Africa. *Africanus, Journal of Development Studies*, 42(2):14–28.

Maathai W. 2009. *The Challenge for Africa*. London: Arrow Books.

Mafukata MA. 2020. Maximising the use of environmental and cultural resources for community-led entrepreneurship development in rural South Africa. In Mafukata MA & Tshikolomo KA (eds), *African Perspectives on Reshaping Rural Development*. Pennsylvania, USA: IGI Global, pp 164–192.

Massie JL & Douglas J. 1981. *Managing: A Contemporary Introduction*. Englewood Cliffs: Prentice-Hall.

Mazibuko S. 2020. *Reflections on Post-apartheid South Africa*. Pretoria: Staging Post.

Moyo D. 2010. Dead Aid: *Why Aid is not Working and How There is Another Way for Africa*. England: Penguin Books.

Ngunjiri FW. 2014. 'I will be a hummingbird': Lessons in radical transformative leadership from Professor Wangari Maathai. In Jallow BG (ed), *Leadership in Postcolonial Africa: Palgrave Studies in African Leadership*. New York: Palgrave Macmillan. doi: 10.1057/9781137478122_6

Northouse PG. 2010. *Leadership: Theory and practice*. 5th ed. Thousand Oaks, CA: Sage

Peterson P, Park N & Sweeney PJ. 2008. Group well-being: Morale from a positive psychology perspective. *Applied Psychology*, 57:19–36.

Yukl G. 2006. *Leadership in Organizations*. 6th ed. Upper Saddle River, NJ: Pearson-Prentice Hall.

CHAPTER 12

Development Projects, Change and Conflict Resolution

Francois Lategan

12.1 INTRODUCTION

The Project Management Institute (PMI) defines a project as a sequence of predefined tasks that need to be completed to achieve a particular outcome (Kerzner 2017). In line with this definition, it is important to understand that a project is also unique in its intended outcomes and has a definite beginning and end. In other words, it is focused on creating something that did not exist previously. We should also remember that projects are not processes.

A process is a series of routine, predefined steps to perform a particular function, for example to plant a crop. On the other hand, a project is not a once-off activity, but it specifies the implementation and performance of a set of specific functions every single time. Actions, activities and their sequences are specific to a particular project.

Development should also be understood as a process, not a product. Societies are continuously changing. Some improve, while others do not do so well. Development practice endeavours to provide tools and mechanisms that can be applied to assist entire societies or specific communities. Such interventions intend to guide communities or societies from a situation in which they are believed to be worse off to a situation in which they are perceived to be better off (Barbanti 2004).

Projects may be big or small, simple or complex. Depending on its nature, a project can be managed by a single person or many people, emphasising that it can also be participating, empowering and adaptive. Projects have the inherent potential to achieve a variety of outcomes, like economic growth, educational development, improved living conditions and enhanced human dignity through following a learning approach, and yet it can be gripped, and often destroyed, by conflict.

In fact, in projects following participative approaches, the chances for conflict are greater. Participants and stakeholders in more open societies, where there is greater freedom of speech and thought, will exercise this right, which then often creates tension and escalates into conflict situations.

Poor communication is, more often than not, the cause of such conflict. Once conflict arises in a given situation, it also ruins all hope for purposeful communication that might still have been present. Conflict and poor communication are therefore serious opponents. When conflict arises, it must be resolved, but to resolve conflict is not an easy skill. In fact, we nearly instinctively strive to avoid conflict situations. However, our natural tendency to avoid conflict situations causes us to miss the very interesting reality – that poor communication can cause conflict, but conflict can be resolved by good communication. This good communication normally occurs through the process of negotiation.

12.2 CONCEPTUAL UNDERSTANDING OF CONFLICT

There are a number of causes of conflict. Some can vary from minor disagreements between individuals or groups to major, extreme situations that can threaten life and limb. It is appropriate to make sure we understand the concept 'conflict' in the same way. The Merriam-Webster Dictionary defines 'conflict' in the following manner:

Definition of conflict

1: *FIGHT, BATTLE, WAR and armed conflict*

2a: *competitive or opposing action of incompatibles: antagonistic state or action (as of divergent ideas, interests, or persons), a conflict of principles*

  b: *mental struggle resulting from incompatible or opposing needs, drives, wishes, or external or internal demands. "His conscience was in conflict with his duty."*

3: *the opposition of persons or forces that gives rise to the dramatic action in a drama or fiction. The conflict in the play is between the king and the archbishop.*

Through understanding the causes of conflict, according to Adedeji (1999:10–11), it becomes possible to assess what type of solutions are possible. It is, therefore, necessary to probe the different causes of conflict and their relationship with each other. Adedeji (1999:10) explains it as follows: 'Understanding the origin of conflict means, therefore, developing a framework for comprehending ... how the various causes of conflicts fit together and interact'. We can identify a number of causes for conflict, but it is impossible to identify the relationship between these causes realistically, because of different situations and different scenarios. This means that conflict may vary from a simple cause (meaning one or simple reasons) to more complex causes comprising interrelated and complicated reasons and origins.

In the development arena, 'conflict' is often described and valued in different ways. Henkin and Singleton (1984), in their review of conflict as an asset, quote Coser's classic definition of conflict as being the 'struggle over values and claims to scarce status, power, and resources, a struggle in which the aims of opponents are to neutralize, injure or eliminate rivals' (Coser 1956:8). If status, power and resources are scarce – as, inevitably, they are, given the fact that they are, in part, relational constructs – it would seem that conflict is inevitable. He further refers to Cooley (1909:199), who maintained that conflict is an integral part of communities, since 'conflict of some sort is the life of society, and progress emerges from a struggle in which individual class, or institution seeks to realize its own idea of good' (also see discussion of Maslow's hierarchy of needs and Chambers' deprivation trap in Chapter 1).

It should not be confused with contradiction, competitive behaviour or competition, although all thrive on tension, often providing the pretext for a 'positive (constructive) conflict experience'. Ogharanduku and Tinuoye (2020:180) poses the careful description put forward by Deutsch (1973) of a *constructive conflict* as one resulting in 'mutually satisfactory experiences of the processes, relationships and outcomes associated with the conflict for all parties involved'.

Where 'competition' is normally associated with 'positive energy', which is essential in stimulating uplifting, innovative and productive behaviour, 'conflict' is mostly the result of an unsolved dissatisfaction with a particular situation. This dissatisfaction can be either because of the perceived existence of a real problem (such as crime or a lack of resources), or because of conflicting or opposing norms and standards requiring specific opposing forms of behaviour (such as religious, cultural or social conventions). This creates 'negative energy', mostly leading to destructive or unproductive behaviour that could easily destroy a project.

In this context, it is important to understand the role and importance of *'tension'*. The Merriam-Webster Dictionary describes it as follows:

> **Definition of tension**
> a: *inner striving, unrest, or imbalance often with physiological indication of emotion*
> b: *a state of latent hostility or opposition between individuals or groups*
> c: *a balance maintained in an artistic work between opposing forces or elements*

Ogharanduku and Tinuoye (2020) support the supposition expressed by Vallacher et al (2013) that, although opportunities for positive conflict exist in society, destructive conflicts often occur when parties experience dissatisfactions. In earlier work, Coser (1956:199–203) elaborates on this important possible 'positive effect' of conflict in society by describing how merely entering into conflict often establishes new relationships where none existed prior to the engagement. Other types of relationships follow when relations have been established through conflict. Conflict often revitalises existent norms and creates a new framework of rules and norms by modifying and creating laws as well as allowing the growth of new institutional structures to enforce these laws. Marx (1910, in Coser 1957:200) already made this important observation by stating that 'conflict leads not only to ever-changing relations within the existing social structure, but the total social system undergoes transformation through conflict'. This point of view is also cited in Henkin and Singleton (1984). Coser (1957:203) famously states that 'conflict may be the result just as much as a source of change'.

It will, therefore, be somewhat short-sighted to ignore the potential duality of conflict in conflict resolution strategies. Some researchers even view it as an ongoing class struggle between authority figures and their subordinates that never ends but is merely regulated. Regulatory mechanisms (read: conflict management) are most effective when all sides recognise the conflict, interest groups are organised, and the rules of the contest are clearly articulated (Dahrendorf 1959, cited by Henkin & Singleton, 1984).

As can be seen from reflections in the literature, conflict is considered a natural social phenomenon with a functional value. This section intends to focus more on the importance, role and management of conflict (and the associated presence of tension) as a potential force for stimulating or destroying projects focused on stimulating or bringing about improved social or community conditions, through human development activities, socio-institutional support programmes or economic-technological activities, processes and practices.

12.3 ORIGINS OF CONFLICT IN DEVELOPMENT PROJECTS

It is easy to see that, to spark or arouse disagreements which provoke individuals, groups or even nations to a conflict situation, is relatively easy to achieve. The art or actions taken to remedy or calm such occurrences (read: conflict resolution), on the other hand, is not an easy undertaking (Guan 2007). The following are common sources of conflict, especially in the project environment.

12.3.1 Poorly planned project schedules

Schedules that are not carefully planned, incorrectly implemented or which create confusion due to poor project management, often cause schedule and resource competition. An example, for instance, arises when datelines are imposed on the CDP, creating serious pressure to complete the project to meet the schedule on time. This stress on time often creates unnecessary conflict and distrust among community members and the CDP. Changing original information already communicated to the beneficiary communities is an important source of potential conflict.

12.3.2 Unresolved conflicts from the past

Prior unresolved conflicts are very often the source of serious conflict in communities. All information of such unresolved conflicts is often not openly declared, resulting in underlying tensions erupting at the least expected times. For the CDP, conflict resolution becomes extremely difficult in the case of old, unresolved conflicts, because the resolution does not lie only in the here and now, but also in the history. When we need to revisit the past over and over again in order to make some headway in the present, the situation becomes difficult.

12.3.3 Poor alignment between community expectations and project priorities

Project priorities and boundaries that do not seem to align with beneficiary community priorities and expectations, or which are often not well communicated, lead to distrust and accusations of hidden agendas and eventually to conflict situations. If role definitions in projects are not clear, it is also difficult to know what to expect from various stakeholders. This point is acknowledged by Mkandawire (2005:25) when stating that there is 'recognition that the axiomatic mapping of policies into performance was naïve and misleading' in many of the development projects implemented in African countries. This implies largely having underestimated the external constraints on policy and the vulnerability of African economies to them. Among other important shortcomings were overestimating the responsiveness of the economies and the private sector to the incorrect structuring of policies. All these errors had important impacts on eroding state capacities and responsibilities. Inadvertently, policy ownership did not materialise, resulting in serious misalignments between community expectations and project priorities.

In a situation where stakeholders influence each other and operate within the same set of boundaries, unclear role definitions also make for unclear role boundaries, which is bound to cause misunderstanding, friction and eventually, conflict. One way to address the issue is by coordinating as many of these stakeholders as possible and to ensure a vibrant network of communication among them (see Chapter 3).

12.3.4 Competition for project and other resources

Resource competition often creates conflict when regional community projects are not managed carefully to acknowledge resource difficulties (or imbalances) that may exist in the different communities competing to satisfy their basic needs (see Chapter 1). This factor places huge stress on the CDP to sustain interest and goodwill during the implementation process.

The significance of ethnic conflict management in Africa in the competition for growth and other resources is often underlined by the continent's so-called *underdevelopment* and sub-optimal economic growth. In his discussion on ethnic conflict management in Africa, Irobi (2005) argues that Africa should change its approach to conflict management to reflect a greater understanding of and urgency with its generally accepted viewpoint that peace in Africa is not the absence of war, but the provision of the people's basic human needs. Different outcomes and activities between communities participating in the same project often accentuate and attract deep concerns and can easily ignite conflict. There is a major responsibility on the CDP to take care in selecting similar communities when developing or implementing projects. Project experience is a major component of project success in communities.

12.3.5   Role dependency

If one role player depends on another playing its role, it is obvious that a conflict potential exists. This is especially true in the case of horizontal dependency, as is often found in communities. Various stakeholders have various tasks that influence one another. The one person or committee is dependent on another body to perform a function. Horizontal dependency can also occur in a development project or, more correctly, in a project steering committee. If one section of a project does not perform, for example, it can and usually does influence other role players which can cause animosity and open conflict. It is important that these dependencies are identified during the planning activity and that some checks and balances must be provided to obviate the possibility of conflict as a result of horizontal dependency.

This dependency does not only apply to persons, but also to institutions. The interconnectedness of development factors often causes further conflict escalation (Barbanti 2004). The administrative chaos in under-financed governmental bodies, for example, often causes the transference of responsibilities from the central state to NGOs, local governments and the private sector. The result is that such organisations assume duties that may go well beyond their capacities, which causes further conflict. For example, NGOs, local governments and the private sector often lack training in facilitation, mediation and negotiation as well as the theoretical knowledge of conflict resolution. This kind of misalignment and role dependency has often led to serious project disruptions, even closure of projects.

12.3.6 Cultural differences

In a comprehensive discussion on culture and conflict resolution, Avruch (1998) offers a functional explanation of culture as a learnt and socially inherited way of living shared and acquired by persons benefitting from their membership of social groups. This, in turn, offers groups and individuals a social identity (Haralambos & Holborn 2008). Multicultural societies are often considered to be the embodiment of cultural freedoms, as expressed in their values, norms, religion, beliefs and customs, without fear of persecution, discrimination, exclusion, conflict and violence. Vadim (2010) also offers evidence that in history multicultural societies exemplified tolerance, unity, trade and wealth.

The reality in the current era is, however, that 'cultural differences often impact negatively on conflict prevention and peacebuilding in multicultural settings by establishing barriers and instigating failures of these conflict resolution processes' (Ogharanduku & Tinuoye 2020:177). Modood (2002:46) is of the opinion that every culture is unique and therefore influences intercultural and multicultural relationships and communities. However, Habermas (1986:243) believes that culture and its traditions are selective in nature, and that they represent unique, fixed essences that make an ethnic group behave in its specific way, independent of context or intercultural relations. Abu-Laban (2002:461) believes the opposite is true, namely that the variety of (multicultural) networks tends to cross borders.

The awareness of different cultural and/or ethnic groups in a multicultural environment in particular is extremely important when dealing with conflict. There must be a search for a common denominator that will contribute to problem solving and conflict management that will benefit the whole community.

This is often an unfortunate but expected result of poor project development and communication, leadership and management processes coming together to create misunderstandings, dissatisfaction, social and political polarisation, and distrust in the project, leading to major conflict situations. The importance of good communication processes dealing with the pre-implementation and implementation phases are important to manage perceptions. If left unchecked, this oversight can lead to a high degree of misperception around the project or intervention, opening the door for conflict at different levels. It is not difficult to anticipate the problems this aspect creates for the CDP and all stakeholder concerned with the successful implementation and management of development projects.

12.3.7 Technical issues

Unskilled or incompetent dealing with the technical or social implementation process of the project (or any action, for that matter, that has the objective of initiating and establishing some degree of change in a community) will lead to some degree of dissatisfaction and conflict. Hansen (1987) puts this aspect clearly into focus by illustrating the following two significant approaches to the study of conflict in Africa:

1. The modernisation paradigm, which tends to see conflict as endogenously generated by factors such as the conflict between basic loyalties and the strains caused by the modernisation process
2. The structural approach, focusing on the economic and political linkages between African countries and more metropolitan countries as context against which to try and deal with issues of conflict. This approach shows that external factors lay down the parameters within which conflict occurs and they sometimes fuel them.

This puts important responsibility on the CDP guiding the project to ensure transparent, participatory and accurate implementation processes with careful consideration for the contexts and paradigm frameworks of all stakeholders. Accurate and strong leadership, both in project processes and community processes, are essential here. For the CDP it means active listening and intuitive support for the community participant leaders of the project.

12.3.8 Team or clique and the need for consensus

In a situation where consensus must be obtained before action can be taken, the potential for conflict is greater because no party can go it alone without regard for anyone else. The effort to try to obtain consensus can then lead to conflict, especially if communication is poor (eg as a result of factions inside communities). Consensus decision making accepts good communication as a given. If, however, the situation is different, the potential for conflict is very high. Decision making in development projects is usually meant to be by consensus and for this reason CDPs must be awake to the potential for conflict.

12.3.9 Conflicting personalities

It often happens that, inside a steering committee for a project, two or more clashing personalities are present. Usually this happens between senior people, or people with strong personalities, with the result that each opposing party will immediately have his/her followers, which increases the potential for devastating conflict. In developing communities there is also often the additional struggle for recognition between political and traditional representatives that often cause emotional personality clashes. Clashing personalities can therefore cause conflict that can spread far beyond the confines of two conflicting persons.

Conflicting personalities invariably result in conflicting interests and expectations leading to disagreements and conflicts. Conflicting parties would scarcely admit that the conflict is the result of the fact that they do not like one another. They will look for a reason at a higher level, such as clashing interests, viewpoints, political opinions or community agendas. The work of the chairperson of a committee in handling this potentially disastrous situation is obvious. The problem is that the chairperson is often also a learner and not sure of him/herself. It is then the task of the CDP, not to call the conflicting parties to order, but to assist the chairperson and the whole group as such to do it.

12.3.10 Insufficiently recognised community structures and institutions

This is often not only a project planning problem but also a community problem, especially where the faction or group negotiating the project with the project company is not recognised as representative or being a mandate holder from the community. It should be appreciated that projects are, by definition, intrusive and focus on bringing about change in existing systems, irrespective of whether those systems are efficient or not.

Projects also impact on efficient systems, meaning that it might be necessary to adopt, for the period of the project, alternative systems to complete the project. This is a process that has important conflict potential. This is particularly evident in situations where local authorities or other project implementing authorities implement projects under political leadership in traditional societies where traditional authorities very often are not sufficiently recognised. Without proper planning, consultation, management and communication activities into the target population, whether such matters are well conceptualised and managed or not, the conflict potential will be exponentially increased if not carefully managed.

We have seen that ALL projects have a conflict potential and project planning processes should make provision for it to be dealt with in advance. This conflict potential may be attached to specific aspects of the project intervention programme, each with a different polarisation potential and destructive impact. Frances Stewart, as quoted by Cenciarini (2020), also believes that conflict in developing countries can be explained by four different factors:

1. *Group inequality*: In a condition where resources are limited and governments are, most of the time, not providing measures to build political and economic stability, conflict is found as a solution to gain power and autonomy over oppressing authorities and access to resources.

2. *Private motivation*: Conflict can be destructive for a community, but can give benefits to individuals, mostly uneducated young men. Conflict can, also, create opportunities in illegal traffics and loots, motivating people to join conflicting factions, following their 'greed'.

3. *Failure of the social contract*: Where the social contract between the citizen and the government is weak and unstable, people stop following the public authority and, instead, the levels of conflict increase, and other rules are established by different leaders.

4. *The green war hypothesis*: Both the lack and abundance of resources in a region can ignite conflict. Conflict is a solution for some people to escape desperate situations or specific groups to gain power over prosperous areas.

These factors, we have seen, are not limited to the scale or the nature of the projects but are often responsible for escalations in the intensity of the conflict. Of course, this reality holds important consequences for the skills demands and attitudes (competence) of the CDP. Conflict resolution skills have become essential arrows in the quiver of the CDP.

12.4 COMMUNICATION BARRIERS CAUSING CONFLICT IN DEVELOPMENT PROJECTS

The process of intrusion has commenced with the introduction of projects and the social changes and conflicting messages that often accompany this phase need to be carefully managed. The purpose is not for the CDP to deliver motivational or polarising messages, but to remain in close contact with all communication processes occurring in the community and also in the project management team.

In this process, the CDP needs to identify carefully possible and probable potential barriers that could cause conflicts in development project implementation. The following are some of the more prominent barriers and causes of conflicts in communication that the CDP should carefully monitor:

- Lack or ineffectiveness of existing communication procedures may discredit the process.
- Non-adherence to communication procedures may lead to escalated conflict potential and feelings of distrust.
- Ensuring effective communication is a planning skills issue and should be dealt with early in the process. Effective communication will determine the success of anything done in the project process.
- Negligence in the management of the communication process should be avoided and the CDP should be particularly well skilled in identifying this negligence.
- An effective feedback system is important, not only for managing conflict but also particularly for assessing and ensuring positive project progress. The skilled CDP will also learn to use effective feedback systems to oversee the project process and timeously identify shortcomings in this system.
- Deliberate blocking of communication processes and the flow of important information is extremely detrimental for project progress and easily causes conflict situations. This process should be carefully monitored by the CDP.

During project implementation, accurate and properly aligned communication focused on demystifying the process of change initiated by the project implementation and the establishment of the new status quo (following the project implementation process) needs to be sustained, even after the completion of the project. The process of change can be very disruptive (even if it is considered to be 'beneficial for the community'), with the potential of escalating any degree of conflict that may arise. This may continue to any degree if not properly managed and contained.

Skilful and effective communication during the project implementation process cannot be overemphasised. We have seen that communication in the development project environment is complex and fragile and should be carefully managed. Common agreed-upon communication procedures are important strategies that can support conflict resolution. Setting such procedures assists in creating transparency and eases the levels of distrust and suspicions present in conflict situations. The CDP should be instrumental in setting up these mechanisms.

12.5 UNINTENDED CONSEQUENCES CAUSING CONFLICT IN DEVELOPMENT PROJECTS

The appearance of 'unintended consequences' and their contribution to the escalation of conflict potential and occurrence during project implementation is a reality for which there needs to be a contingency plan as a conflict resolution mechanism. This contingency plan will be contextual and should be planned and managed as such. However, in many instances, development interventions underestimate local politics, social realities and belief systems. These are strong factors affecting the opportunities for conflict resolution, which nevertheless have remained overlooked by those working in the field of development theory and practice (Barbanti 2004).

A poor understanding of this underlying sensitivity in communities or societies during the implementation of economic growth and development projects is bound to lead to serious conflict. It is not difficult to understand or foresee. It is unfortunate that all interests of all parties cannot be served at the same time. However, if the potential for conflict in this situation is identified in time, good communication can go a long way in preventing conflict. Good communication is present when a communication network exists. A communication network does not point only to a structure that may or may not be used, but rather to the functional structure, in other words, a working structure that can be used to negotiate interests and set participants' minds at rest. Case study 13: *The club with two committees* is a good illustration of conflict flowing out of clashing interests.

Misunderstanding

Misunderstanding is a direct result of poor communication. Misunderstanding leads to a situation where the different parties each have a particular perception that makes the other party suspicious. Different persons and different larger parties and groups can have vastly different perceptions of the same situation. In such circumstances, it might be better to follow a more unofficial, easy-going approach to make sure that everybody speaks the same language and agrees about perceptions.

It is natural for distrust to grow between the parties and that is bound to bedevil good communication, which is followed by accusations and so on – each new development making communication more difficult and bringing the situation nearer to conflict. All the barriers to successful communication discussed in Chapter 10 are present and everyone who is involved should be aware of this and should apply the suggestions made there for successful communication.

12.6 PREVENTION OF CONFLICT

Prevention is better than cure and therefore it is better to anticipate conflict and remove the cause timeously, so that conflict does not erupt. In as much as healthy conflict is a necessary evil in the implementation of development projects, prevention of conflicts, on the other hand, saves a lot of time and resources for the project manager, in this case often the CDP. Important skills and behaviour such as the following, when learnt by all team members, go a long way in helping prevent conflict:

- Active listening is important to create trust and confidence in the process.
- Conflict should not be allowed to become personal.
- There should be mutual respect for individual viewpoints.
- The focus should be on identifying and addressing a solution.

Management of conflict potential consists of the following actions:
- *Identify potential clashing interests.* While the potential for conflict cannot be avoided, it can be managed. Based on an evaluation of mandates, areas of activity, interest and needs of stakeholders, it is possible to identify beforehand which stakeholders will or might

have clashing interests, and then to work to mitigate it. In Case study 14: *The case of the community worker who met his match*, the CDP did not do his homework in this regard. For a relatively conflict-free environment and to ensure things run smoothly, the CDP should consider greed as a possible conflict source, the corresponding grievances and, in the background, the ever-present poverty situation.

- *Identify potential clashing personalities.* Clashing personality types can make management of an institution, especially a small one such as a project action group, particularly difficult and can impact severely on reaching consensus. Destructive conflict can often be avoided by depersonalising points of disagreement.

- *Identify potential high conflict situations in advance.* Conflict is seldom sudden and unexpected. Knowing the stakeholders and the potential areas for conflict well in advance can assist in avoiding or managing these situations. Remember that good communication can go a long way toward defusing any conflict. In Case study 13: *The club with two committees*, the CDP did nothing to manage a potential conflict situation.

- *Set clear mandates for role players.* There should be no unclear boundaries. Each role player should have its place and role clearly demarcated. If one stakeholder is unclear about its role, it can upset each and every other stakeholder – an ideal situation for conflict.

- *Improve communication skills.* If the communication skills of role players are strengthened, opportunities for misunderstanding will be minimised. The better the communication, the less misunderstanding there will be, and the less misunderstanding there is, the less conflict will erupt.

- *Organise the activities of different role players.* Activities of role players must be organised in such a fashion that dependency on one another is reduced as much as possible. This can be done with good programming and strategising and will definitely diminish the potential for conflict. Embuldeniya (2013) talks of policy to overcome the possibility of conflict on state level. It is similarly true that on the community level and in the project structure there must be policies to prevent conflict and to address the three basics of greed, grievance and poverty.

- *Set clear 'rules of order'.* It is advisable to have a standard set of agreed-upon rules of conduct for meetings and discussions. These may include 'rules of good manners' and 'rules of conflict avoidance'. While a goal-directed facilitative approach is most productive within an institutional context, it is essential that participants agree and adhere to clearly set rules and boundaries. In this way, the individual is safeguarded against personal abuse and violent conflict. Apart from the fact that it will diminish the potential for conflict, it will also give individuals and even groups greater confidence to participate in the activities.

- *Encourage and promote tolerance in a potential conflict situation.* The message must be loud and clear that the project is bigger than any of us and that we should be prepared to take a slight without wanting to retaliate.

12.7 NEGOTIATION AS CONFLICT RESOLUTION

Negotiation is a way to resolve conflict in which all parties come out as winners. The objective is to bring conflicting or opposing parties nearer to each other until they can declare common ground and resolve their conflict within the parameters of their common ground. In this way no party is the loser, because each has gained something and is relatively satisfied with the outcome.

Negotiation can be quick, or it can be a long-drawn-out activity that lasts months. Luckily, in development projects, negotiation is usually short and less formal, and often takes place to prevent rather than to resolve conflict.

As we can see, conflict is part and parcel of managing projects whether big or small, simple or complex. There are few institutions in most developing societies that understand or engage in the practice of conflict resolution. However, even when they do, they tend to work with inadequate win-win frameworks. In some cases, for example, negotiation through typical win-win processes is blocked because the powerful within poor communities are criminals or conflicting factions. Such elements are able to exert full control over large areas, from where they conduct criminal or other subversive activities. This is one of many reasons why traditional interest-based, win-win negotiation often does not work in developing countries.

Table 12.1 provides some insight into the different types of conflict resolution and their commonly expected results.

Table 12.1 Conflict resolution types and their common results

Conflict resolution type	Common result
❖ Forcing/directing Pushing one's viewpoint at the expense of others	Win/lose
❖ Smoothing/accommodating Emphasising areas of agreement; conceding one's position to the needs of others	Lose/win
❖ Withdrawing/avoiding Postponing the issue to be better prepared or to be resolved by others	Neutral/neutral
❖ Compromising/reconciling Searching for solutions that bring partial satisfaction to all parties	Moderate lose/moderate lose
❖ Problem solving/confrontation/collaboration Incorporating multiple viewpoints and insights from different perspectives	Integrative / win/win

Source: Adapted from PMI (2017:349)

In development projects, the role of mediator can be played by the CDP. The mediator is the person who facilitates a process of negotiation. A mediator is required when the negotiation is more formal and takes place to resolve some existing conflict. If negotiation is necessary during a meeting, it is the task of the chairperson to facilitate discussion.

The CDP must know and understand the position of mediator. The mediator is not the arbitrator, who has the task to decide who is right and who is wrong in a dispute. The mediator is entirely committed to bringing the opposing parties nearer and nearer to each other until they find common ground. Thus, no one is right, and no one is wrong, and no one is a lone winner and no one is a complete loser. The process strives towards a win-win solution where all parties will be relatively satisfied with the outcome. The mediator must be well prepared for negotiation.

The following five steps should be taken before and during the negotiations:

Step 1: Review the specific environment and conditions in which the conflict and communication take place, for example spatial arrangements, group size and leadership structures.

Step 2: Review the existing attitudes and perceptions of the parties by looking at, among others, personality traits, different needs and self-esteem. Do not forget the basic situation of greed, grievance and poverty.

Step 3: Define the problem. This includes determining the basic issues, stating the problem as a goal and depersonalising the problem.

Step 4: Facilitate a joint search for alternatives. This can be done through the nominal group technique, brainstorming and discussion groups.

Step 5: Facilitate the evaluation of alternatives and the reaching of a consensus decision by narrowing the range of solutions, evaluating them in terms of both quality and acceptability according to criteria previously agreed upon and through various means, such as sub-groups and sub-problems.

Out of all the conflict resolution types presented in Table 12.1, the most recommended is problem solving/confrontation/collaboration, which leads to a win-win solution for both parties.

Social values are also often undermined by the official educational system, since information disseminated by books in public schools is embedded with prejudice and stereotypes that, for example, overvalue conflicting viewpoints (Barbanti 2004). However, in many instances, development interventions underestimate local politics, social realities and belief systems.

These are strong factors affecting the opportunities for conflict resolution, which nevertheless have remained overlooked by those working in the field of development theory and practice. Table 12.2 illustrates the different conflict management strategies and their potential impact in managing conflict situations.

Table 12.2 **Conflict management strategies**

Conflict source	Description	Impact	Strategy
People-focused/ personal differences; interpersonal; relationship issues; personal traits	This conflict stems from incompatible values and needs, and differences in personalities, interpretations and expectations. The conflict grows due to a lack of understanding or inability to manage the various personalities encountered.	It is a high-level and emotional type of conflict that is difficult to resolve and can harm team members' relationships. It can increase absenteeism and turnover and lower team performance and work satisfaction. ➤ Mostly negative	❖ Diagnose the conflict early on and manage it constructively using a collaborative approach. ❖ Increase the level of trust and understanding; maintain open communication and psychological safety. ❖ Develop active listening skills to give people the opportunity to disagree and express their opinions. ❖ Encourage team building to develop beneficial coping strategies and learn to develop highly flexible behaviours.
Unresolved prior conflicts	This conflict occurs when people bring to the team past grudges and unresolved issues.	It creates a tense atmosphere and defensive behaviours among team members. ➤ Negative	❖ Use a collaborative approach to mend and strengthen people's relationships.
Issue-focused; task issues	This conflict is associated with the project's end results and performance requirements.	It generates new ideas and solutions because it is a rational approach to conflict. Its effect will depend on the type of task (routine or complex) and it is only beneficial up to a certain level. ➤ Mostly positive but can become negative if the conflict is too intense	❖ Foster a safe environment that encourages open communication and high levels of trust. ❖ Resolve disagreements through negotiations.

Conflict source	Description	Impact	Strategy
Goals and priorities; values, interests and objectives; intrapersonal	This conflict stems from diverging goals, objectives and priorities, or a lack thereof	This type of conflict is unproductive because it leads to task overlap, poor communication, and waste of resources. Project participants are driven by what benefits them instead of collaborating towards project goals. It leads to decreased personal motivation and performance because of unmet personal and professional expectations, but this type of interpersonal conflict may not affect the project team. Goal conflict is not as harmful as people-oriented conflict. ➥ Mostly negative	❖ Establish SMART (specific, measurable, attainable, realistic and timely) goals that are not incongruent with other organisational goals. ❖ Perform careful project planning and constantly communicate with all stakeholders. ❖ Ask team members where they see themselves fit into the project and assign roles accordingly, based on experience, competency and knowledge. ❖ Clearly delineate roles, responsibilities and authority at the beginning of the project and review them throughout the project lifecycle. ❖ Give the project manager the appropriate level of authority and punishment power. ❖ Create a balanced set of interests among stakeholders. ❖ Increase team commitment, cooperation and participation.

Conflict source	Description	Impact	Strategy
			❖ Allow the team to fully develop and provide the necessary resources to accomplish that goal, ie training, etc. ❖ Provide role clarification. ❖ Use self-managed or self-directed teams appropriately.
Authority based	This conflict stems from the uncertainty about who has the authority to make decisions.	It can result in high levels of stress, anxiety and frustration because of poorly defined roles, responsibilities and authority. ➤ Negative	❖ Clearly define responsibilities and authority at the onset of the project.
Administrative/ behaviour regulations	This conflict is connected with the organisation's management structure, philosophy and techniques. It is based on the definition of the responsibilities and authority for the project's tasks, functions and decisions.	It can lead to high levels of conflict and frustration because individuals may resist the limits placed on their actions. They may also experience anxiety because of their diverging views of the organisation's policies and procedures. ➤ Negative	❖ Increase team member involvement throughout the project life cycle.
Role incompatibility	This conflict stems from the perception that an individual's assigned role is incompatible because he/she is working in an environment with different bases of information.	It increases the level of confusion when people are required to communicate with various sets of people, work with different reporting systems and receive instructions from different supervisors. ➤ Negative	❖ Improve organisation processes. ❖ Define responsibilities clearly and avoid task overlap. ❖ Improve communication. ❖ Ensure that people are assigned to tasks that are related to their skills, experience and previous positions.

Conflict source	Description	Impact	Strategy
Organisation differentiation or specialisation	This conflict results from different individuals perceiving the same thing differently.	It increases misunderstandings and confusion because team members do not understand each other due to differing viewpoints, 'language', goals and ways of doing things. ▸ Negative	❖ Increase team-building activities to smooth out participants' differences in a non-threatening environment to become familiar with each other and to understand where others are coming from to create a common mindset.
Task interdependency	This conflict results from the dependency upon others to complete one's work (information, assistance, compliance, feedback, etc).	It increases misunderstandings, missed deadlines, and poor decision making because of a lack of information and feedback among team members. ▸ Negative	❖ Increase the level of trust among team members. ❖ Increase effective communication. ❖ Create shared goals and understanding.
Communication; information deficiencies	This conflict results from poor and ineffective communication as well as misinformation.	It creates high levels of dysfunctional conflict because of misunderstandings and misinterpretations. Team members lack common experience and knowledge about each other's responsibilities, which leads to a lack of collaboration and unreasonable demands because of ignorance. It causes friction, frustration and inefficiency. It makes negotiations and the explanation of differing viewpoints difficult. ▸ Negative	Include team-building activities to accelerate the integrative process to overcome the effects of differentiation. It gives team members the opportunity to communicate, interact and learn about each other on a personal and professional level.

Chapter 12: Development Projects, Change and Conflict Resolution

Conflict source	Description	Impact	Strategy
Culture	This conflict stems from different cultural values and norms.	It may hinder task execution and effective communication. The conflict resolution method is contingent on the culture and the level of conflict involved. ➽ Negative	❖ Provide training and experience to adopt resolution techniques that match the level of conflict. ❖ Be proactive and aware of important cultural offences.
Institutional	This conflict stems from differences in workplace norms, legal regulations and cultural values.	It creates misunderstandings as well as increased costs and delays.	❖ Requires training, experience and effective communication to determine the causes of the conflict and judge the relative ease to resolve it.
Environmentally induced stress; tension	This conflict stems from a fast-paced environment characterised by high levels of stress as well as unresolved and mounting interpersonal tensions due to high uncertainty.	It can lead to low morale and possibly staff turnover due to inconsistent demands, stress and identity crisis. ➽ Negative	❖ Plan social interactions at strategic project milestones to create a better atmosphere.
Termination/ reassignment	This conflict arises from poor project closeout procedures and inadequate reassignments.	It creates high levels of stress, anxiety and frustration. ➽ Negative, but it can be positive as it offers team members new opportunities and challenges	❖ Carefully plan the termination of a project. ❖ Provide guidance at a time of change; help with project reassignments and career opportunities, and offer emotional support.

➥

Conflict source	Description	Impact	Strategy
Interface; intergroup	This conflict involves the project team and groups that are outside of the project.	It creates dysfunctional conflict because of incompatible requirements from different social groups. » Mostly negative	❖ Increase the communication flow with affected groups and ensure that they are involved in the project planning process. ❖ Present accurate and detailed information during the initiation and planning phases.
Groupthink; need for consensus	This conflict stems from failure to generate diverse opinions through brainstorming.	It leads to flawed ideas and undetected inefficiencies because of collective rationalism, self-censorship, fear of separation, a need for unanimity, etc.	❖ Foster open and effective communication. ❖ Create a safe environment. ❖ Assign a devil's advocate to stimulate creativity.

Source: Adapted from Villax and Anantatmula (2010)

12.8 PERCEPTIONS OF CONFLICT IN THE DEVELOPMENT PROCESS

As has been mentioned earlier in the chapter, the potential for and probability of conflict is an intrinsic aspect of development projects and considered unavoidable. Both Henkin and Singleton (1984) and Ogharanduku and Tinuoye (2020) have shown from their research that, irrespective of the types of conflict that have occurred, the key message remains that conflict can be managed to avoid it becoming destructive. It is therefore appropriate to consider briefly the various viewpoints (or perceptions) that exist of conflicts in societies where change is occurring through project interventions. This plays an important role in developing attitudes towards conflict resolution (Knutson, Hwang & Deng 2000). More *traditional viewpoints* consider conflict as:

- bad and negative
- only caused by troublemakers
- something which should be avoided at all costs.

More *contemporary perspectives* hold the following views:
- Conflict is inevitable.
- Conflict is often beneficial.
- Conflict should be managed.

The underlying motivation for and focus of development projects are mostly the stimulation of economic growth and development in developing regions in an effort to overcome development challenges such as increasing poverty, inequality, poor economic growth, educational inadequacies, and inadequate human capital development and structural socio-economic development.

The seeming inabilities of communities and nations to structure, develop and grow economically has amplified the impact of conflict on the successes of development projects. Various researchers like Adedeji (1999), Barron, Smith and Woolcock (2004), Cenciarini (2020), Embuldeniya (2013) and McCandless and Karbo (2011) have, over a long period of research, described its complex nature and its impact on social, economic and technological processes that are designed to stimulate growth and development in projects. Conflict in itself is inherently a personal and social phenomenon, and can be pre-emptive, reactive or even manipulative as a tool.

Without denying the mentioned possible positive and negative influences of conflict, conflict management strategies and approaches should contribute to general positive outcomes. The basic premise is that the management focus in such situations should be that one is working with people with particular personal, social and political contexts; driven by aspirations, perceptions, needs, knowledge levels and cultural values, norms and standards, and mostly governed by contextual codes of good practice – institutionalised or socially accepted. They also function in a context best described as the deprivation trap (see Chapter 1).

This suggests that conflict management and resolution processes and practices should be managed at two levels:

1. *Strategic (primary) level*: Ensure that the project development and planning process already contain the necessary accurate and effective measures to limit, or even eradicate, the potential for conflict during the development or later in the implementation phase. This is typically a process management issue where generous and accurate attention should be paid to limiting the probability for the creation or manifestation of misperceptions and unrealistic expectations from the intended project. The objective is to ensure full and complete

buy-in from all stakeholders into the final product and process of project implementation and management. Buy-in is subject to the principles of community development, especially those of participation, empowerment and ownership (see Chapter 6). This is the first level of defence against proliferated and destructive conflict manifesting during project implementation and is mostly a pre-emptive process relying on forecasts and expectations.

2. *Operational (secondary) level*: Conflict at this level is more often than not the result of an inability to manage effectively or competently the probability and potential for conflict arising from human error or deliberate efforts to create conflict situations in whatever manner during the implementation phase. The management process may have been compromised during implementation, giving rise to situations where proper and professional project management activities are neglected. If dealt with professionally, such conflict situations are short-lived and possible to resolve through effective resolution, mediation or negotiation processes. This is normally a reactive process and requires skillful handling from the project management team. In the context of a community project, conflict at the operational level can arise between the CDP and other professionals, on the one hand, and leaders (traditional or natural) and/or interest groups from within the community, on the other. The competence of the CDP in this context is fundamentally important to resolve such conflicts.

The manifestation of conflict is not in itself the 'problem' but rather a reaction to a 'problem'. Dealing with conflict attracts different reactive approaches, mostly inspired by the understanding of the nature and origin of the conflict. An interesting and effective methodology of conflict management has been developed by the Japanese International Cooperation Agency (JICA). This method is essentially aimed at providing actual service delivery assistance to alleviate difficulties faced by people affected during and immediately after conflict, thus securing a stable environment to achieve stable development over the medium and long term. In such scenarios, JICA (2022) focuses its support in areas such as:

- the rehabilitation and reconstruction of socio-economic infrastructure to secure the platforms and networks for collaboration
- economic recovery to ensure the resources and the support for the process

Chapter 12: Development Projects, Change and Conflict Resolution

- governance for securing the integrity of the conflict resolution process and the continued implementation of the project
- security for the protection of all resources, equipment and human capital essential for the successful completion of the project.

This not only effectively structures the conflict resolution process but also provides clear indications of the critical aspects that need to be strengthened to secure continued success. Through the rapid restoration of basic social services, for example in the education and health sectors where dissatisfaction has in some areas led to violent and destructive protests, people's growing expectations can soon be met after achieving a peace agreement, and public confidence in the project can eventually be restored to continue the process of negotiation and conflict resolution. This provides important indications and guidelines to the CDP that, in conflict resolution, the process might be more important than the final result to secure a conducive environment for the successful implementation and finalisation of development projects.

See Chapter 11 for more about groups, their development and management.

THE ABC OF SUCCESSFUL OUTCOMES

The ABC of successful outcomes is a synopsis of the most important aspects of negotiation.

Aim for a specific result. Negotiation that does not aim for a specific, concrete result will flounder and discussions will tend to go round and round without moving in a specific direction. This means that merely to talk about a disagreement will not achieve much. Discussions must be aimed at coming to a conclusion that will be satisfactory for all.

Be positive. If you want negotiation to move forward towards a decisive conclusion, you must be positive. It serves no purpose to dwell on the negative aspects. Criticising the other party for not seeing things the same way will never bring an outcome.

Concentrate (see, hear, feel) on sensory data. In a negotiation situation all the barriers to communication that can possibly exist are present. To compound the situation, communication does not take place only through the spoken word. You must therefore be wide awake to both verbal and non-verbal communication so as to identify all the possible barriers, remove them in time and respond to positive and negative reactions from the other parties.

Dovetail desires. Dovetailing is the opposite of manipulating. Dovetailing desired outcomes ensures your integrity because it shows respect for the other parties' integrity. While you cannot decide on outcomes for the other parties, you can aid them in attaining what they desire. Dovetailing is the intelligent way to ensure your own outcomes.

➡

Entertain long- and short-term objectives. Negotiation is not only to bring harmony for the present. A win–win solution is also necessary for the long term otherwise you will soon have to gather around the negotiation table again.

Find rapport as soon as possible. Rapport is the most important ingredient of negotiation. Without it, negotiation can never be positive. Rapport is present when you experience a level of comfort and a sense of shared understanding. Only when rapport is present can you proceed towards the outcome. So, the first objective is to establish rapport. Once rapport has been established, it will develop and grow as the negotiation progresses.

Get as much information as you can. Information on the other parties and their positions will help you to know with whom and with what you are dealing.

Have extra alternative options ready. If your options are not accepted or if the situation changes, you will know that your options are no longer applicable.

Identify and keep outside influences in mind. This usually constitutes pressure from outside, either to come to an agreement or not to sacrifice certain interests.

Join the other party if they make suggestions or state viewpoints with which you agree. The objective is to move closer to one another, so if consensus or common ground is found, acknowledge it.

Know exactly what your manoeuvrability is. Know how far you can go and what you can sacrifice. This helps you to be sure of yourself and makes a good impression on the other parties.

Leave space in which you can move. In other words, do not move all you can the first time. If other parties are not satisfied, you cannot move any further or you may move so far the first time that there is very little for you to win and little for the other parties to forfeit.

Make sure that you are negotiating with someone who has decision-making powers. These decision-making powers should be at least at the same level as yours.

Never be insulting or accusing. This will put distance between you and the other parties instead of bringing you closer and it will also lead to accusations from the other parties. All this will just delay a solution and may even jeopardise a genuine seeking of solutions.

Obtain agreement from the other parties. Find out whether there is a basis for negotiation.

Prepare yourself properly. Decide on what you want the outcome to be with a best-case scenario (ideal outcome) and a worst-case scenario (the minimum that you will settle for).

Qualify your viewpoints and suggestions. State the reason for a proposal before you make it. The other parties must know why you say something and if your qualification holds water, it will be so much more difficult just to reject your viewpoint.

Remain flexible about sequence and options. Negotiation is by definition flexible and hard base lines just do not work in such a situation.

> **Stand** up for your principles. Do this by all means, but make sure that they are in fact principles and not unnecessarily rigid base lines.
>
> **Think** carefully about anything that is said. Take time out if you need to think about some new option. Rather spend some time in the first place to think about things than to rush it at first only to come back on your word later on.
>
> **Untie** the knots. That means that things must be straightened out. Arguments must be clear; facts must be on the table and verified and the standpoints of the different parties must be clear. One just cannot negotiate if there is still a muddle.
>
> **Validate** (confirm your understanding of) any proposal. You need to understand the other party's proposal before analysing and criticising it.
>
> **Work** towards consensus. It is no use to try and keep your original position. That is not negotiation. Try to stay as near to your original position as possible (best-case scenario), but use the space between that and what you can settle for (worst-case scenario).
>
> **X** represents the other parties who may be foreign to you or just unknown. Just remember, though, that they are human beings with the same emotions and fears as you; with the same belief in their position as you have in yours; and with the same sense of being right that you have.
>
> **'Yes'** is a better word than 'no' in negotiation. However, let your yes be yes and your no be no. In other words, be objective and trustworthy.
>
> **Zero** in. Concentrate on the problem from the beginning and do all you can to solve it.
>
> The ABC of successful outcomes is meant for negotiators, but gives the CDP a good idea of what is necessary in a negotiation situation.
>
> A good negotiator:
> - is a problem solver
> - separates the person from the problem
> - is soft on the person but hard on the problem
> - is more concerned with his/her interest than his/her position
> - obtains and maintains objectivity
> - gives in to reason but not to pressure
> - develops several options for later choice
> - avoids a rigid base line
> - investigates common areas of trust
> - portrays an image of trust.
>
> If the CDP can guide the participants in a negotiation to be true to these aspects, the process will be that much easier.

CDPs have an obligation to help others, especially leaders such as chairpersons of steering committees, to become knowledgeable about the potential for conflict and the methods to resolve it. They, as well as the leaders, should be prepared to use them in order to solve conflict situations.

12.9 CONCLUSION

Globally the design and implementation of development projects are essential interventions to assist countries, communities and even regions to access opportunities for economic growth and development. The interconnectedness of economic processes and networks makes it important for such projects to ensure that beneficiaries achieve the intended outcomes and the full benefit of the successes of such interventions.

An intrinsic characteristic of development programmes is the change that invariably occurs during the implementation of such projects and the, often negative, impact of such change on the project process through the conflict it provokes. The process and management of change therefore requires the skillful interpretation and management of this potential conflict with the objective to optimise its energy for the better. This is, however, not a guaranteed result and conflict resolution remains an essential and critical process that project managers, CDPs and other leaders in similar projects need to take careful cognisance of.

In this chapter, we have had a brief analytical discussion on the nature, origins, potential manageability and potential impact of conflict that is characteristically associated with development projects of all sizes, types and impacts. We have come to see how complex conflict potential is to manage, and that conflict resolution is often more prevalent than conflict avoidance. We have come to realise that some degree and intensity of conflict, with skillful management and resolution strategies, can be beneficial for the successful completion and embedding of project outcomes in societies. Conflict in development should not be feared, or even be indiscriminately suppressed, but CDPs should be sufficiently skilled in the analysis and interpretation of conflict situations to try and manage such situations to the benefit of the project.

Clear indications exist from research reports that the conflict episodes associated with development projects are also not uniform in their origins or their dynamic development. The types of conflict resolution strategies applied in particular situations have a definite impact on the dynamic flow and outcomes of the conflict – anything from win-win to lose-lose results. The matrix of possibilities of and reasons for such conflict highlight that conflict resolution should be a definite skill in the set of abilities associated with CDPs in project driven regions or locations.

It also stands to reason, from the discussions in the chapter, that conflict resolution should not simply be accepted as a finite process with conclusive outcomes. Lingering conflict within and between communities, underlying dissatisfaction and the, sometimes unintended, promotion of inequalities and discrepancies between communities and groups due to the outcomes of development projects are often important sources of conflict. Poor communication that exacerbates these discrepancies (often because of ineffective consultancy processes before and during the project) may also lead to community expectations either being neglected or not being met, adding to the reservoir of unfulfilled expectations, resulting dissatisfaction and the eventual failure of the project.

When CDPs start working with community members and recognised leaders as development partners with joint collaborative responsibilities, accountabilities and rewards from the project implementation process, conflict becomes a more positive contributing force that reacts more favourably to a variety of conflict resolution strategies. The complexities of the potential origins and reasons for conflict in development projects are not easy, or even simple, to fathom and mitigate. However, it does seem as if there are some basic conflict resolution skills and wise approaches that CDPs could follow to limit significantly any negative impact. This chapter highlighted some of these complexities, realities and approaches with the objective to offer some guidelines to CDPs involved in the management or leading of development projects in communities.

REFERENCES

Abu-Laban Y. 2002. Liberalism, multiculturalism and the problem of essentialism. *Citizenship Studies*, 6(4):459–483.

Adedeji A. 1999. Comprehending and mastering African conflicts. In Adedeji A (ed), *Comprehending African Conflicts*. London: Zed Books.

Avruch K. 1998. *Culture and Conflict Resolution*. Washington, DC: United States Institute of Peace Press.

Barbanti O Jr. 2004. Development and conflict theory. Available at: http://www.beyondintractability.org/essay/development-conflict-theory (accessed 11 May 2023).

Barron P, Smith CQ & Woolcock M. 2004. *Understanding Local Level Conflict in Developing Countries: Theory, Evidence and Implications from Indonesia.* Social Development Papers. Paper no. 19. Washington, DC: World Bank.Cenciarini L. 2020. The relation between conflict and development in developing countries. Discussion paper, University of Bologna. doi: 10.13140/RG.2.2.13505.99680

Coser LA. 1956. *The Functions of Social Conflict.* New York: The Free Press.

Coser LA. 1957. Social conflict and the theory of social change. *British Journal of Sociology*, 8(3):197–207.

Deutsch M. 1973. *The Resolution of Conflict: Constructive and Destructive Processes.* New Haven, CT: Yale University Press. doi: 10.1177/000276427301700206Embuldeniya D. 2013. Ethnic conflict, horizontal inequalities and development policy: The case of Sri Lanka. Doctoral thesis, University of South Africa, Pretoria.

Guan D. 2007. Conflicts in the project environment. Paper presented at PMI® Global Congress 2007 – Asia Pacific, Hong Kong, People's Republic of China. Newtown Square, PA: Project Management Institute.

Habermas J. 1986. *Autonomy and Solidarity: Interviews with Jürgen Habermas.* New York: Verso Books.

Hansen E (ed). 1987. *Africa: Perspectives on Peace and Development.* Tokyo: United Nations University.

Haralambos M & Holborn M. 2008. *Sociology Themes and Perspectives.* 7th ed. London: HarperCollins UK.

Henkin AB & Singleton CC. 1984. Conflict as an asset: An organizational perspective. *International Review of Modern Sociology*, Autumn, 14(2):207–220.

Irobi EG. 2005. Ethnic conflict management in Africa: A comparative case study of Nigeria and South Africa. Available at: https://www.beyondintractability.org/casestudy/irobi-ethnic (accessed 9 October 2023). JICA (Japan International Cooperation Agency). Peacebuilding. Available at: https://www.jica.go.jp/english/our_work/thematic_issues/peace/activity.html (accessed 11 May 2023).

Kerzner H. 2017. *Project Management: A Systems Approach to Planning, Scheduling, and Controlling.* 12th ed. Hoboken, NJ: Wiley.

Knutson TJ, Hwang JC & Deng BC. 2000. Perception and management of conflict: A comparison of Taiwanese US business employees. *Intercultural Communications Studies*, IX-2. Available at: https://web.uri.edu/iaics/files/1-Thomas-J.-Knutson-John-C.-Hwang.pdf (accessed 15 October 2022).

LeBaron M. 2003. Culture and conflict. Available at: http://www.beyondintractability.org/essay/culture-conflict (accessed 9 October 2023).

McCandless E & Karbo T (eds). 2011. *Peace, Conflict, and Development in Africa: A Reader*. Addis Ababa: University for Peace – Africa Programme. Mkandawire T. 2005. Maladjusted African economies and globalisation. *Africa Development*, 30:1–2.

Merriam-Webster Dictionary. nd. Conflict. Available at: https://www.merriam-webster.com/dictionary/conflict (accessed 23 May 2023).

Merriam-Webster Dictionary. nd. Tension. Available at: https://www.merriam-webster.com/dictionary/tension (accessed 23 May 2023).

Modood T. 2003. Muslims and the politics of difference. *Political Quarterly*, 74:100–115.

Ogharanduku VI & Tinuoye AT. 2020. Impacts of culture and cultural differences on conflict prevention and peacebuilding in multicultural societies. In Essien E (ed), *Handbook of Research on the Impact of Culture in Conflict Prevention and Peacebuilding*. Hershey, PA: IGI-Global.

PMI (Project Management Institute). 2017. *A Guide to the Project Management Body of Knowledge (PMBOK® Guide)*. Newton Square, PA: Project Management Institute.Stewart F. 2002. Root causes of violent conflict in developing countries. *BMJ*, 324(7333):342– 345. Available at: https://www.ncbi.nlm.nih.gov/pmc/articles/PMC1122271/ (accessed on 11 May 2023).

Vadim J. 2010. *The Social History of Achaemenid Phoenicia: Being a Phoenician, Negotiating Empires*. London: BibleWorld. Oakville, CT: Equinox Pub. Ltd.

Vallacher RR, Coleman PT, Nowak A., Bui-Wrzosinska L, Liebovitch L, Kugler K & Bartoli A. 2013. *Attracted to Conflict: Dynamic Foundations of Destructive Social Relations*. Peace Psychology Book Series. Berlin: Springer Science & Business Media

Villax C & Anantatmula VS. 2010. Understanding and managing conflict in a project environment. Paper presented at PMI® Research Conference: Defining the Future of Project Management, Washington, DC. Newtown Square, PA: Project Management Institute. Available at: https://www.pmi.org/learning/library/understanding-managing-conflict-resolution-strategies-6484 (accessed 11 May 2023).

CHAPTER 13

Mobilisation and Motivation

Marliane Owen

> A positive attitude may not solve all your problems but it will annoy enough people to make it worth the effort.
>
> *Herm Albright*

13.1 INTRODUCTION

When we implement projects, we work with people and it is likely that we want them to adopt new behaviours or change behaviours that they currently have to ensure the success of the projects. After all, if they were already doing what was required, the project would not be necessary. That means we need to have a basic understanding of what behaviour is, what influences it, what the barriers are to behaviour change and the tools we can use to help implement positive changes in our communities.

Our behaviour and decisions shape our everyday lives. They impact our health, our financial wellbeing, our interactions with our community and our futures. It is important to look at behaviour and motivation separately because we might be motivated to do something, yet never do it, or do something without explicitly pausing to think why or if it really fits with our personal motives.

Behaviours are not just influenced by our own rational thoughts and decisions but also by decision shortcuts we have evolved as a human race. These decision shortcuts streamline our thought processes but can sometimes get in the way of making the right decisions. We are influenced by the people around us, the environment we are in and how we feel in the moment.

We want projects to make changes for a better future so the actions we facilitate need to have long-lasting impacts and endure beyond the duration of the project. However, it is often hard for us to imagine how our behaviour now will impact what we will do later, how we will feel or how healthy we will be in the future.

Understanding what motivates behaviour will help us to form a framework on how to change or start a new behaviour. Motivation could be conscious or subconscious, intrinsic or external and there are a number of factors that influence it.

13.2 WHAT IS BEHAVIOUR?

Furr (2009:438) defines behaviour as 'utterances (excluding verbal reports in psychological assessment contexts) or movements that are potentially available to careful observers using normal sensory processes'. This means that behaviour is anything that someone does that can be seen, heard, touched, tasted or smelt. It must also have the ability to be repeated. Internal 'events' (such as dreaming, for example) are not included in this definition of behaviour (Bicard, Bicard & IRIS Centre 2012).

The *Collins Dictionary and Thesaurus* (Summers & Holmes 2004) describes *behave* as 'to act or function in a specified or usual way' and *behaviour* as 'response to a stimulus'.

Understanding what drives behaviour and how to change it, is important from a community development practitioner (CDP) perspective because when we talk about civic action what we really want is for a specific type of behaviour to change or to continue. Behaviours can change consciously or subconsciously, be a once-off change or a permanent one. When a new behaviour becomes a sustained change without someone having to choose to do it, it can be referred to as a habit. So, it is important to identify if it is a once-off change that we are trying to establish or, a continuous change in behaviour.

It is easy to believe that all humans need is information to make the right choices for ourselves, our families and, our communities. If we know how good something is for us, we will do it; if we know how bad something is for us, we will stop doing it. We also know that this is not true. If we think about people we know with a smoking habit; chances are that they know that smoking is not good for them. They know from the information campaigns and rules around what appears on packaging that their behaviour is damaging their lungs and, also the people around them, but they still smoke.

Have you ever gone to the cinema and ordered a large popcorn (because it is only a little bit more expensive than the size you really want) and then ate it all (even if you only really wanted a little bit)? Well, if you were really a rational human being the price of the popcorn or the size of the box would not make a difference in your choice. You would only buy the size you want and stop eating the moment you had enough.

13.3. WHAT IS MOTIVATION?

A number of theories of motivation exist which aim to describe why humans act the way they do. Motivation can be defined as brain processes that energise and direct behaviour (Mook 1987).

One of the original theories of motivation is that of Maslow, who describes human motivation according to their needs (also see Chapter 1). Maslow's hierarchy of needs is represented as a triangle and he posits that the needs at the bottom of the hierarchy, the bottom of the triangle, must be met before the higher-order needs become important (McLeod 2018).

From bottom to top the needs are as follows:
- *Basic order needs*: Physiological (food, water, warmth, rest) followed by safety and security
- *Psychological needs*: Belongingness and love needs (our need for relationships and friends) followed by esteem needs (prestige and feelings of accomplishment)
- *Self-fulfilment needs*: The need to fulfil our potential, including creative activities.

The theory is that unless our basic needs are fulfilled, we will not be motivated to fulfil the higher-order needs, as all our motivation will be directed to fulfil our need for food, shelter and security. Once those needs are met, our motivation turns to making sure that we are loved and belong. Maslow also expanded his original hierarchy of needs to include cognitive, aesthetic and transcendence needs.

Maslow's theory may feel like it makes intuitive sense, but its critics point out that he provided little scientific evidence for it. It was based purely on the analysis of the characteristics of people he deemed to have self-actualised. Furthermore, his study was highly biased toward educated, white males and although it included some females, they only comprised a small proportion of his sample. His findings therefore cannot necessarily be extrapolated to a broader population with diverse ethnic and social demographic backgrounds.

It is also not always the case that lower order needs must be met first before higher order needs can be addressed. It may be that the drive to fulfil higher order needs provides the drive to fulfil basic needs. For example, think of artists who buy paint instead of food to fulfil their creative desires ahead of satisfying their hunger. Once they have expressed themselves creatively and possibly sold the art they created, they can then buy food to fulfil the basic order need.

The search for a theory that explains motivation in greater detail continues. One such theory is the self-determination theory (SDT) (Ntoumanis, Prestwich, Quested et al 2021). SDT is also not new but, unlike Maslow's theory, it has more than 40 years of scientific evidence to support it. It builds on Maslow's theories and resonates with people's own experiences (Bucher 2020).

SDT defines six types of motivation:
1. Amotivated
2. External
3. Introjected
4. Identified
5. Integrated
6. Intrinsic

These types of motivation appear on a continuum ranging from controlled to autonomous. The more autonomous a motivation is, the less it is imposed by external sources and is generated from within a person. In other words, if we are intrinsically motivated to act, our motivation can be classed as autonomous. Whereas, if we need an incentive outside of ourselves to do something, that is described as controlled motivation. Motivation that starts as controlled can develop into autonomous motivation. The six motivational types are described in more detail below:

1. *Amotivation* is really the opposite of motivation. People in this category will be highly unlikely to engage in any kind of behaviour change. They are not motivated to do something (or feel something) and are unlikely to engage in the desired behaviour, potentially even under threat.
2. *Externally motivated behaviour* would be something that we really do not want to do but are forced to do by an external source. The moment that the external source is removed the motivation for doing

that behaviour disappears and the behaviour will stop. A financial incentive or nagging by a family member may motivate people in this category to act but it is not something they want to do or would do if left to their own devices. This is sometimes also referred to as motivation by fear, which could range from fearing to hear the nagging voice again or fearing for their life. It is not seen as true motivation. In the context of community projects, it is important to guard against this kind of motivation as it is not sustainable and behaviour would stop or return to previous ways if the external source were removed. In many community projects, the external motivation is tied up in the money or goods that are promised. Once the source is depleted, the motivation for the project dries up. Case study 6: *The parson who became a painter* demonstrates how external motivation can work initially but then, once it is removed, or when people stop fearing the outcome of the threat, the motivation disappears and the behaviour stops. The pastor threatened that the church would not be painted unless the garden were tidied up first. People were motivated by the thought of a well-maintained church, but then their sense of control over their own actions was removed when the pastor dictated the order in which the work had to happen. The pastor tried to motivate them by using a subliminal threat of the church not getting painted. That threat was not severe enough to change their motivation and, in the end, had the complete opposite effect.

3. *Introjected motivation* occurs when we internalise the expectation of other people and that then drives our behaviour. If we think we 'should' be doing something, that is, 'I should help out at the community day', it implies that the behaviour might not happen if we were not worried about what others would think of us. Again, when the source of motivation is removed, the motivation to act is likely to disappear too. If the person whose opinion we care about will not be at the community day to notice us, will we still help out? Case study 14: *The case of the community worker who met his match* is an interesting example of two potentially externally motivating factors clashing. At the very least, one external factor (the people had internalised the expectation of the headman) was greater than the internal motivation of the community to change their farming methods. Mr Dladla had neglected to identify the headman as a key stakeholder and a strong introjected motivator of the community. The expectation of the headman or other established community leaders can strongly drive

behaviour and motivation. In this case, the community wanted the approval of the headman or the leader, or may have feared retribution. It is therefore important for CDPs to identify potential sources of introjected motivation and think how that could influence the behaviour or motivation of the community. If Mr Dladla had gotten both the headman and Mr Kubheka onboard before talking to the community, he could have harnessed the introjected motivation (to please the headman) to support his project.

These three motivations (amotivation, external motivation and introjected motivation) fall within the 'controlled' category of motivations. They are all types of motivation that will influence behaviour only because of external sources and are not controlled entirely by a person's own thoughts or reasons. These types of motivation require the external sources to continue to influence behaviour.

Social norms, discussed in more detail below, fall within the controlled category of motivation. Even though it is external, the impact of this on behaviour should not be underestimated, particularly if the motivation then becomes internalised through either repeated behaviour or the desire to minimise cognitive dissonance. Cognitive dissonance is a sense of discomfort when a person's actions are not aligned to their beliefs or values (Harmon-Jones & Mills 2019).

Once we have acted in a certain way, we need to believe that it was our own choice. The story we tell ourselves then becomes one of trying to make our behaviour fit to the picture we have of ourselves. As we cannot change what has happened, the only way we can achieve this is by telling ourselves we wanted to do something in the first place. We will discuss social norms again later, as they are a strong motivating factor for behaviour change and, one that CDPs can put to good use when there are positive social norms to highlight.

The next three motivations move along the scale to autonomous motivation. These types of motivation relate to when people have their own reasons or motivations for engaging in a certain behaviour, regardless of external influences:

4. *Identified motivation* can also be described as 'stepping stone' motivation. This is when the behaviour is seen as a means to an end or a step toward achieving a bigger goal. Someone might not be that

interested in joining a stokvel, but has a bigger goal of opening a spaza shop. Joining a stokvel to help save would be a stepping stone to the bigger goal. Once he/she has saved enough money to open the shop, the motivation to be part of the stokvel will no longer be there and he/she will stop participating. However, as we will see later, it is not that easy to stop something – see the discussion on status quo bias and defaults in section 13.6.

5. *Integrated motivation* relates to a behaviour that someone sees as reinforcing a particular value or something that they see as part of their identity. It may be attending a religious service or meeting community leaders every Thursday. It is something that re-affirms what a person believes in.

6. *Intrinsic motivation* is the most autonomous type of behaviour. If we are motivated to engage in a behaviour purely for the enjoyment of doing it or, if we are devoted to a cause, self- or intrinsic motivation becomes a driving force. Something could start as identified motivation (running to lose weight), then become an integrated motivation (we believe it is good for us so we keep running) and then we grow to enjoy it so much we do it regardless of the health benefit or what others may think of it.

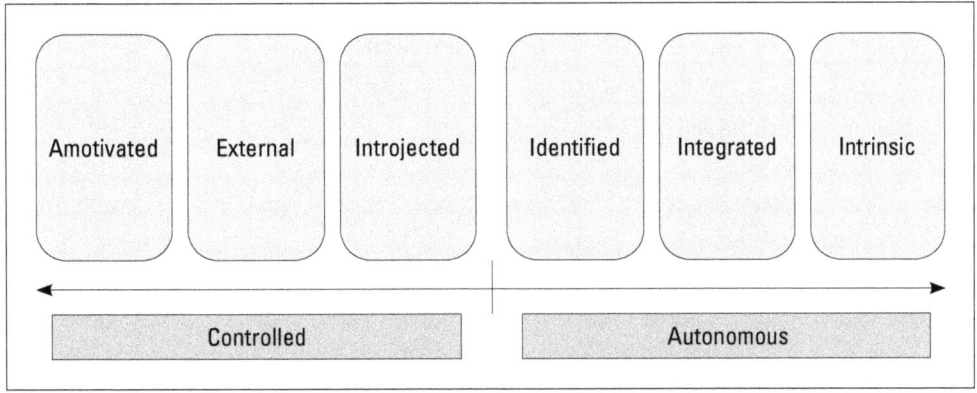

Figure 13.1 **The six types of motivation of SDT**

Source: Bucher (2020:12)

Figure 13.1 shows how motivation can move from amotivated, on the far left, to intrinsic motivation, on the far right. The first three motivations to the left are classed as controlled motivation and are weak. When the reasons for doing something become more personally meaningful to a person, their motivation becomes stronger and more autonomous.

For long-term behaviour change, intrinsic motivation is what we want to aim for. Changing behaviour is hard, so the more personal it is and the more it resonates with someone's personal values, the easier it will be to maintain. The role of the CDP would be to help people along the scale from controlled motivation (where it is mostly from external sources) to intrinsic motivation (where it is self-directed and sustainable).

So how can we move motivation up the scale? First, we will look at the relationship between behaviour and motivation, in particular what drives, or motivates, people to help. Then we will consider a behaviour change model that can be used as a framework for changing behaviours. Last, we look at insights from behavioural economics on how we can use behavioural biases and heuristics to help change behaviour and motivation. These are behavioural and judgement shortcuts. They help us make sense of the world and process information on an intuitive level, but they can also lead to 'errors' in our thinking. As these 'errors' are made systematically, we can use them to predict the impact they will have on our motivation.

13.4   RELATIONSHIP BETWEEN BEHAVIOUR AND MOTIVATION

Because there is a close relationship between behaviour and motivation, CDPs need to be aware of individual and group psychology. We can take note of the following aspects concerning this relationship (Massie & Douglas 1981:86–87):

- *One motive may result in many different types of behaviour.* For example, a person's desire for prestige may lead that person to run for political office, give money away, get additional educational training, steal or join a gang. It depends on other situational aspects, other realities, which of the behaviours will result from this motive. In other words, a person's desire for prestige (motive) will result in different behaviours if that person is in prison vs in the boardroom vs in the swimming pool, for example.
- *The same behaviour in different people may come from various different motives.* Consider the many motives different people could have for buying a certain car. For one person it may be to appear respectable, for the other to be accepted by his/her peers and for a third because

he/she wants to travel in relative comfort. We should therefore be careful not to read too much into a person's behaviour. We cannot say for certain what the motive behind the behaviour is. At best, we can suggest *possible* motives.

- *Behaviour can be used to estimate a person's motive.* This may sound contradictory to what has been said previously. However, it is possible after repeated observations of one person's behaviour to make an estimate of the cause of that behaviour. For example, some people always seem to feel insecure and thus behave continuously in a manner reflecting that feeling of insecurity. The key to this observation is that this estimation of a person's motive can only come over time when a continuous and recurrent behaviour takes place.

- *Motives may operate in harmony or in conflict.* Behaviour is frequently the result of the interplay of several motives. These motives may push a person in one direction or in a number of directions, for example a person may have to decide between a job that he/she would enjoy and a job that offers a higher salary.

- *Motives come and go.* It is rare that a motive has the same energy over a long period of time. This is important for organisational managers to remember because what motivates personnel today may not necessarily motivate them in two months' time. Good meetings may motivate an action group at the beginning of a project, but later meetings may lose their motivational power and now the group will be motivated by the attainment of their objectives.

- *The environment influences motives.* The situation at a particular time triggers or suppresses the action of a motive, for example we may not realise how hungry we are until we smell food cooking. In the same way, sociological needs or preferences become stimulated when we are in a situation filled with sociological factors that will lead to stimulation.

13.4.1 Why do people help?

What is required in community projects is a certain kind of behaviour, that of helping. Let us briefly look at different types of helping behaviour and why people may or may not help.

One theory for why people help is that of the *negative state relief model* (Batson, Batson, Griffitt et al 1989). This model proposes that we want to reduce our own negative mood, and helping others can elevate our mood and make us feel better. It is easy to link this to intrinsic behaviour because it is driven by our own mood. However, what if that mood changes? Would our need/desire to help change too?

When we believe someone is part of our group (ie the in-group) we are more likely to help than when we believe they are part of a different group (ie the out-group) (Levine, Prosser, Evans & Reicher 2005). For example, Jake is walking down the street wearing a Kaiser Chiefs T-shirt. He trips over a loose paving stone and falls, hurting himself badly. Because he is wearing a Kaiser Chiefs T-shirt, people who are fans of other clubs may be less likely to help him. However, if he were wearing a Bafana Bafana shirt, help may come from all football fans, not just that of his club.

The same can be true in communities, so finding what connects people (eg football fans) rather than placing them in different groups (or clubs) can be an important and useful tool.

13.4.2 What will prevent people from helping?

This is a true story. Early one morning in New York in 1964, a young woman left work after her shift ended. On her way home she was attacked and murdered. Her murderer was caught and convicted because the incident was witnessed by 38 people. Why did nobody, not one of the 38 witnesses, help the young woman?

The social psychologists Bibb Latane and John Darley have studied this intently and suggest the following (Latane & Darley 1968):

- *Diffusion of responsibility*: When there are many people present, the moral responsibility to help is divided among everyone there. People think either that someone else will help or, if no one helps, that the guilt will be shared. This happens in communities too – it is someone else's problem, or there are other people who can help. Being aware of this mindset will help community workers to find a way to show why being involved is everyone's responsibility.
- *Pluralistic ignorance*: Everyone is waiting for someone else to act first, or see people are not reacting and then assume that no action is required. This also links with social norms described in more detail below. In new or unfamiliar situations, we do not know how to act, so we are looking for a reference point, something, or someone, to show us what to do, how to act or how to behave. We are afraid to look silly

and be the first to support something that later is deemed not to be a worthy cause.
- *Audience inhibition*: When people feel that they are being watched, they may be too embarrassed to act for fear of doing the wrong thing. Women often have less confidence than men, particularly in new situations or with topics that are unfamiliar, and may not feel empowered to voice their opinion (Kay & Shipman 2014). Being aware of how the audience may impact participation will help CDPs facilitate meetings as they can take measures to ensure all members feel comfortable to speak.
- *Bystander effect*: As the number of bystanders increases, the likelihood of one person helping the victim decreases. In/out group behaviour, described in section 13.4.1, may help to overcome the bystander effect.

13.5 BEHAVIOUR CHANGE MODELS

If we want to change a behaviour, we need first to identify what it is we want to change. This might sound obvious but when we start analysing behaviours in detail it can reveal a surprising, unexpected, smaller constituent behaviour that is preventing the bigger behaviour change. For example, we might want more people to attend a meeting on a regular basis. If we start looking at the reasons why people are not coming, we might discover that childcare is actually the issue. Our intervention could then simply be to make sure people know they can bring their children with them or we could move the meeting to a more convenient time.

Start by making a list of all the behaviours you observe and then decide which is the one that you want to change.

Following that, look at the barriers that are preventing behaviour change and the opportunities available to effect the change. A number of behaviour change models have been developed to assist in this process. They include the following:
- Com-B model
- Fogg.

The type of project will usually determine the most appropriate model. We will discuss Com-B in more detail in this chapter as it pertains to the broadest range of situations with specific focus on long-term change and can be adapted with relative ease.

Identifying what needs changing can be the hardest part. It is not always obvious at first if it is a behaviour that needs changing or a barrier that needs removing. Barriers could also be internal or external.

The Com-B model defines the following factors to be identified for a behaviour change programme (Michie, Atkins & West 2014):

1. *Capability:* Do the people involved in the project have the necessary skills, strengths, knowledge or ability to achieve the required behaviour? Capability can be mental/psychological or physical.

2. *Opportunity:* This can be physical or social. For example, if there is no school, the opportunity to go to school does not exist. Otherwise, there may be a school, but it is not seen as socially acceptable – so the physical existence of the building does not provide the social opportunity.

3. *Motivation:* People need to be more certain of the benefits of behaving in a certain way as opposed to not. Motivation can be broken down into reflective motivation; conscious decisions, plans and evaluations; and automatic motivation, which is those things we do not think about, including emotional reactions, reflexive responses, and our wants and needs. Refer to Section 13.3 for a detail discussion of motivation.

The components do not just exist as freestanding elements, but interact with and impact each other on various levels. Motivation can be high, but if opportunity or capability is not present, then motivation alone would not achieve behaviour change. In our example of meeting attendance, people may be highly motivated to attend, but their physical ability to do so is hampered by a lack of childcare. Alternatively, it may be possible to give people a choice of which meeting to attend, allowing them to pick a time that works for them. This would make them feel more motivated to go. Having that sense of control, or choice, could also improve motivation.

Figure 13.2 shows how capability, opportunity and motivation interact with each other (Michie et al 2014).

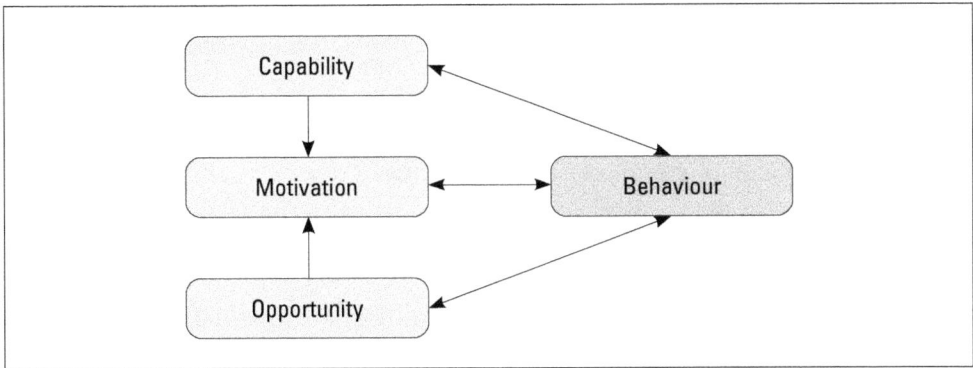

Figure 13.2 Interaction of capability, opportunity and motivation

Source: Michie, Atkins & West 2014

13.6 MOTIVATION AND MOBILISATION IN HUMAN DEVELOPMENT

It may be overwhelming trying to figure out where to start to increase motivation and influence behaviour. It is natural to want to provide more information, thinking we can convince people to be motivated or that if they have more information, they will understand the benefits and change automatically. However, by using the heuristics and biases that influence behaviour, CDPs can enhance their efforts to motivate the people they work with.

MINDSPACE is a framework focusing on nine strategies that can be used individually or combined to impact motivation and ultimately behaviour (Dolan, Hailsworth, Halpern, King & Vlaev 2011). It is an acronym for the following:

1. *Messenger:* We are often more influenced by who delivers a message or information than the information itself, or at least our judgement of the information is determined in part by our perception of the messenger. For example, if we believe someone is an authority in a certain subject, we will give greater weight to his/her opinion than someone we do not believe to be an authority. This can further be enhanced if the expert has something in common with the audience, be it demographic or behavioural. Although experts are important, we are also more likely to listen to our peers than people with who we have nothing in common. If someone gives us good advice, we may ignore it simply because we dislike that person. It is therefore important to consider the audience and who is delivering the message.

2. *Incentives:* Incentives are a strong motivator. For example, we usually go to work to earn money. However, incentives do not always have to be monetary. We may go to church to gain the respect of our community and experience spiritual joy; we may join a committee because we find fulfilment in doing good for the community. Interestingly, the thought of losing something is a stronger motivator than the possibility of gaining something. We sometimes also struggle to judge how much something is worth, which is why social norms become important – if our community indicates that something is valuable, it may also become more valuable to us as individuals. What one community perceives as an incentive may not be the same somewhere else. It may be money, food or status (Akbas, Ariely, Robalino & Weber 2016). We also tend to value smaller, immediate rewards over bigger, later rewards (McClure, Laibson, Loewenstein & Cohen 2004).

3. *Norms:* People often find it hard to know what to do; not only in new situations, but in daily life as well. So we look for clues from other people as to how to act. It removes some cognitive load – the thinking behind why and if we need to act in a certain way. Sometimes it is just easier to do what others are already doing. In a community setting, highlighting something that another group or community is already doing can act as a motivator. Beware, though, that highlighting an undesirable behaviour may make it easier for people to continue that behaviour (White, Habib & Hardist 2019).

4. *Defaults:* A default is something that is pre-selected as an option if a participant does not make a choice (Thaler & Sunstein 2009). It could be the default investment in a savings scheme or the tick box at the bottom of the email asking if we want to opt out of the newsletter, rather than opting in. Finding it hard to move from the default is partly the result of status quo bias. We prefer the position we are in at the moment and find it hard to move away from it or change for a number of reasons. It could be that we do not know what the other options are or we do not feel we have the skills or knowledge to make a different decision, or it might just be easier to stay with the pre-selected choice. We may have been telling ourselves for years that we have made the right choice not to move away from that. It could be all those reasons put together. When you bought your phone it most likely came with a pre-set security password. A default password. Have you changed yours yet? Most people will not, even though they

have the option. Do you still bank at the same bank you have always done? It may be that it is cheaper to go somewhere else, but it is easier to stay where you are.

Status quo bias is also why it can be hard for people to change. See Case study 14: *The case of the community worker who met his match*. The CDP had proposed a change to the committee but in the end, it was easier to keep the default, the current structure of the committee. Moving an individual from their current position is hard. Moving a group is even harder. Maybe the CDP could have suggested a subcommittee to focus on innovation rather than trying to change the committee that was already there?

CDPs need to be aware of the defaults that exist in their communities. They also need to think carefully about any new intervention as that will become the default of the future (see also the discussion in Chapter 18 about contact making).

5. *Salience*: This refers to stimuli that attract attention and can change someone's actions and motivations. Something can be salient (ie more noticeable, consciously or subconsciously) because it is new or stands out for any other reason, including placement, colour and smell. It refers to something that is brought to the forefront of the mind and through that influences decision making (Bordalo, Gennaioli & Shleifer 2021).

6. *Priming*: Priming refers to unconscious cues that influence behaviour. If something is subtly mentioned earlier in a conversation, it may influence how we feel about a certain topic now, without us even realising it has happened. We can be primed by any of our senses.

Related to priming is the 'mere exposure effect' – the more we are exposed to something, the more likely we are to grow to like it or at least tolerate it. In a community context, seeing how the environment has been mistreated may prime us to do the same or just accept it as the status quo. Some studies have shown that buildings with broken windows encourage vandals to do more damage (Steg, Bolderdijk, Keizer & Perlaviciute 2014). Our environment has an impact on our actions and motivations.

7. *Affect*: How we feel can shape what we do. If we are happy, we may be more comfortable making quick decisions. When we are unhappy, we may be more analytical. This is often described as the hot-cold

empathy gap. When we are in a hot state, our emotions are heightened. In cold states, we are more logical and considerate in our actions. The immediate moment can often be hot, so we may want to delay decision making to give ourselves a chance to cool down and logically assess the pros and cons. However, it is harder to motivate people when they are in a cold state. Consider how political leaders can ignite the passion of a crowd to act in a certain way in the moment that they might not individually do the following day.

8. *Commitment:* As human beings, we like to keep our promises. If we have said that we will be somewhere at a certain time, and have done so publicly, we are likely to show up at that time. However, the more time that passes between the commitment and the date that we promised to do something, the easier it will become to renege on that promise. See Case study 15: *The inspector whose help was dumped.* The inspector wanted to clear an abandoned area for a children's playground. He initially received a commitment from the boys to turn up to help him. What he failed to do was get a commitment from the children at the end of each day to come back the next day. He could also have sought commitment from the parents that the children would help with clearing the area.

   CDPs can use this human characteristic of wanting to stick to promises to their advantage by getting public commitments from the people they are working with to do something in the not-too-distant future. To strengthen that commitment, a reward can be offered to those who stay the course.

9. *Ego:* We like to act in a way that make us feel good about ourselves. When we achieve something good, we tend to credit ourselves for it, and when something does not go according to plan, we prefer to place blame elsewhere. This is called the attribution bias, when we attribute an outcome to someone's personality traits rather than the context of the situation (Ross 1977). Unwanted behaviour in communities can often be attributed to the drive for enhancing ego. People act in a certain way to achieve status and respect (Walker & Bright 2009).

The nine MINDSPACE strategies will not all be applicable in all situations. CDPs will have to identify the most appropriate strategies for their projects to motivate people to achieve a common goal or to change their behaviour. People may have lots of things in common, but it does not mean that everyone will react the same way to the same approach. The context and the environment play an important role and CDPs need to be able to adapt and change their approach as required.

13.7 CONCLUSION

Behaviour and motivation are interlinked and sometimes hard to untangle from each other. Acting in a certain way may increase our motivation to continue to do so and vice versa, being motivated may help us start a behaviour that previously we would not have considered.

However, neither behaviours nor motivations are always conscious and many external factors can have an impact. CDPs need to understand what the behaviours are that they may want to change or keep going in order to facilitate successful implementation of a project and, the context in which that behaviour needs to take place. The aim of this chapter was to provide an overview of what motivation is, how it interacts with behaviour and what strategies CDPs could use to influence both in order to have a higher chance of affecting meaningful, long-term change.

REFERENCES

Akbas M, Ariely D, Robalino DA & Weber M. 2016. How to help the poor to save a bit: Evidence from a field experiment in Kenya. *Discussion paper No. 10024*. SSRN. Available at: https://papers.ssrn.com/sol3/papers.cfm?abstract_id=2803856 (accessed 13 May 2023).

Batson CD, Batson JG, Griffitt CA, Barrientos S, Brandt JR, Sprengelmeyer P & Bayly MJ. 1989. *Negative-State Relief and the Empathy-Altruism Hypothesis*, 56(6):922–933.

Bicard SC, Bicard DF & IRIS Centre. 2012. *Defining behavior*. Available at: https://iris.peabody.vanderbilt.edu/wp-content/uploads/2013/05/ICS-015.pdf (accessed 13 May 2023).

Bordalo P, Gennaioli N & Shleifer A. 2021. Salience. *NBER Working Paper No. 29274*. SSRN. Available at: https://papers.ssrn.com/sol3/papers.cfm?abstract_id=3926955 (accessed 13 May 2023).

Bucher A. 2020. *Engaged: Designing for behavior change*. New York: Rosenfeld Media.

Dolan P, Hailsworth M, Halpern D, King D & Vlaev I. 2011. MINDSPACE: Influencing behaviour through public policy. Available at: https://www.instituteforgovernment.org.uk/sites/default/files/publications/MINDSPACE.pdf (accessed 13 May 2023).

Furr RM. 2009. The study of behaviour in personality psychology: Meaning, importance and measurement. *European Journal of Personality*, 23:437–453.

Harmon-Jones E & Mills J. 2019. An introduction to cognitive dissonance theory and an overview of current perspectives on the theory. In Harmon-Jones E (ed), *Cognitive Dissonance: Reexamining a Pivotal Theory in Psychology*. 2nd ed. Washington, DC: American Psychiatric Association, 3–24. doi: 10.1037/0000135-001

Kay BK & Shipman C. 2014. The confidence gap. *The Atlantic*. May, 1–18. Available at: http://www.theatlantic.com/features/archive/2014/04/the-confidence-gap/359815/ (accessed 13 May 2023).

Latane B & Darley J. 1968. Group inhibition of bystander intervention in emergencies. *Journal of Personality and Social Psychology*, 10(3):215–221.

Levine M, Prosser A, Evans D & Reicher S. 2005. Identity and emergency intervention: How social group membership and inclusiveness of group boundaries shape helping behavior. *Personality and Social Psychology Bulletin*, 31(4): 443–453. doi: 10.1177/0146167204271651

Massie JL & Douglas J. 1981. *Managing: A Contemporary Introduction*. Englewood Cliffs: Prentice-Hall.

McClure SM, Laibson DI, Loewenstein G & Cohen JD. 2004. Separate neural systems value immediate and delayed monetary rewards. *Science*, 306(5695): 503–507. doi: 10.1126/science.1100907

McLeod S. 2018. Maslow's hierarchy of needs. *Business*, 3–5.

Michie S, Atkins L & West R. 2014. *The Behaviour Change Wheel: A Guide to Designing Interventions*. Great Britain: Silverback.

Mook, D.G. 1987. *Motivation: The Organization of Action*. New York: WW Norton.

Ntoumanis N, Ng JYY, Prestwich A, Quested E, Hancox JE, Thøgersen-Ntoumani C, Deci EL, Ryan RM, Lonsdale C & Williams GC. 2021. A meta-analysis of self-determination theory-informed intervention studies in the health domain: Effects on motivation, health behavior, physical, and psychological health. *Health Psychology Review*, 15(2): 214–244. doi: 10.1080/17437199.2020.1718529

Ross L. 1977. The intuitive psychologist and his shortcomings: Distortions in the attribution process. In Berkowitz L (ed), *Advances in Experimental Social Psychology*. New York: Academic Press, 173–220.

Steg L, Bolderdijk JW, Keizer K & Perlaviciute G. 2014. An integrated framework for encouraging pro-environmental behaviour: The role of values, situational factors and goals. *Journal of Environmental Psychology*, 38:104–115. doi: 10.1016/j.jenvp.2014.01.002

Summers E & Holmes A. 2004. *Collins English Dictionary & Thesaurus*. New York: HarperCollins.

Thaler RH & Sunstein CR. 2009. *Nudge: Improving Decisions About Health, Wealth, and Happiness*. London: Penguin.

Walker JS & Bright JA. 2009. False inflated self-esteem and violence: A systematic review and cognitive model. *The Journal of Forensic Psychiatry & Psychology*, 20(1):1–32.

White K, Habib R & Hardisty DJ. 2019. How to SHIFT consumer behaviors to be more sustainable: A literature review and guiding framework. *American Marketing Association*, 83(3):24. doi: 10.1177/0022242919825649

CHAPTER 14

Operational Writing

Frik de Beer and Andries de Beer

14.1 INTRODUCTION

The goal of operational writing is to create a composition that is ready for action. There are various types, one of the most important of which is meeting minutes (see also Chapter 15). Another type of operational writing is the creation of a curriculum vitae (a work and educational history). However, in this chapter, we are primarily concerned with the following:

- Report and proposal writing
- Composition of a business plan or proposal
- Taking minutes.

A report is a vehicle or tool for transferring information. In section 14.2, we consider some of the questions we need to ask and answer before and during the composition of a report. Section 14.3 describes some of the main features of a proposal or business plan, presented as a typical example of a fundraising request. The business plan in this context is therefore an example for a request for funding of an organisation or project. In section 14.4, we look at taking minutes.

14.2 REPORT AND PROPOSAL WRITING

Report writing must serve a purpose. Its main purpose is to inform people who are not directly involved in what is going on in a project. The aim of the report is therefore to provide information not only about the outcome of a project (product) but also about what takes place during a project (process).

14.2.1 Preparing to write the report

Before writing a report, four types of questions must be answered:
- Why (the purpose of the report)
- What (the topic of the report)
- For whom (the target (audience) of the message)
- How (style and format).

These are explained in the sections that follow.

'Why' questions

Determine the purpose of the report. Is your report aimed at informing the community about progress or problems? Are you writing a submission to influence policy makers? Is your report a historical record of a specific action that took place? Are you evaluating a process or product and writing a research report?

Some reports, such as minutes, are recurring writing tasks. Others, such as information reports to the community, may not be 'compulsory', but your committee may decide on them as a good communication medium.

'What' questions

Determine the type of report you should write. Once the 'why' question has been answered, you will know this. It might be a historical record, a research report in which a problem is addressed, a discussion paper in which a new idea or strategy is introduced for reflection, or a proposal with definite recommendations on something of importance to you or your organisation.

Identify the issue or situation on which you want to report. You must be very careful and specific in your choice. Remember, the golden rule is to address only one main topic in a report. If the report is on a comprehensive issue, make sure that individual aspects are addressed separately and marked as such. In this instance, you must clearly indicate how the different issues relate to one another.

'For whom' questions

If you know the individual or group for whom the report is intended, you must use language and phrases that you know will be clearly understood. If not, your report must be in neutral language and as brief as possible.

'How' questions

Decide on the procedure to follow. What is the best way of presenting your message? Readers usually look for an introduction, a body, conclusion or summary, and recommendations. Select all the relevant material. You may need minutes of previous meetings, information brochures or even verbal accounts from witnesses or participants in a project. Organise the material logically in the form of the report. Answers to the 'why', 'what' and 'for whom' questions will dictate the form of your report.

A good report is one that clearly outlines the issue or problem, indicates what the objectives of the report are, discusses all the relevant information and makes clear and well-argued recommendations. In discussing the relevant information, stumbling blocks or problems must also be identified and acknowledged. Do you see how interrelated the 'why', 'what', 'for whom' and 'how' questions are?

14.2.2 Presentation of a report

When someone picks up a report and looks at it for the first time, it must make a good impression; therefore, it should be neatly set out. Headings must stand out, subsections must be logically numbered and the pages should not be too full.

When someone begins reading the report, it must also make a good impression. Therefore, sentences should be well formulated, and what you have written must be clear, specific, easy to read and easy to understand. The style must be suitable, sometimes more formal and sometimes more informal, depending on the type of report and who is going to read it.

When someone has finished reading a report, the good impression that it made earlier must continue. Therefore, the contents must be concise (do not tire your reader with a long, drawn-out report), but at the same time it must be complete (do not leave your reader hanging in the air). A lasting good impression is only possible if the structure of the report is correct.

A report must consist of at least:
- a title
- an introduction
- a main body divided into easily digestible and logically arranged chunks
- a conclusion.

Research proposals, research reports and discussion papers are all specialised reports and contain all the above. Yet, because of their specialised nature, they need more than ordinary reports. In addition to the above, they also need a discussion of the problem statement, objectives, literature study, research methodology, findings and recommendations.

The elements of a report are itemised below. Do not forget to sign and date your report and make a copy for your records.

Title

The title must be carefully formulated because it must, in a few words, summarise the essence of the report. A title should also not be ambiguous. The reader must know exactly what the report deals with, just by looking at the title. Usually it is best to formulate (or revise) the title after completion of the report.

Introduction

This is where you state why the report is being written and what you want to achieve with it. No argument is proffered yet, that will come in the main body.

Background

It is often necessary to provide the reader with some background to the report, for example socio-economic information of an area, typical problems experienced and types of resources and assets available. This information explains the context within which the problem occurs.

Problem statement

A clearly formulated problem, issue or challenge helps to focus the mind of the author and the attention of the reader. The problem statement provides the reason for writing – and reading – the report.

List of objectives

Once the problem has been formulated, the author should list the objectives of the report, that is, what he/she intends to achieve in the report with reference to the problem statement.

Literature study

Books and journal articles are consulted to gain a broader understanding of issues, models, approaches and historical information. Here, relevant publications are discussed to provide a historical and theoretical background to the problem.

Field research

Sometimes, especially when dealing with real-life socio-economic issues, the report should contain information that can only be collected through field research. For instance, a demographic and socio-economic profile may be needed; for this purpose, a survey needs to be conducted.

The report may need to provide information or reflect on the perceptions of a group, for instance teenage mothers, about the provision and quality of a service. In this instance, in-depth interviews or focus-group discussions may be required.

The main body

Do not call this section 'main body'. Give it a sub-title related to the contents. In this section, you discuss the information provided earlier in relation to the problem and objectives. In other words, here you show how the information helps to explain the problem, gives direction to the study and helps to find answers that may help address the objectives.

The scope of the body will be determined by the complexity of the issue and this will influence the number of subheadings used. Subheadings are used to subdivide text into smaller, logical units that make the report easier to read, understand and remember.

Findings and recommendations

This section provides the answers to the objectives stated in the beginning and makes recommendations on the way forward, with reference to the objectives and findings. Recommendations answer the questions that have been asked. They are the culmination or logical conclusion of the argument developed in the main body.

Conclusion

The whole report is summarised in a few paragraphs. The conclusion should show how the report addresses the problem and achieves the objectives. Never leave it to your reader to make the deductions, but guide him/her to accept your conclusions.

14.3 BUSINESS PLAN

A business plan is a well-thought-out financial proposal or plan for a company or project. A business plan outlines what the company intends to do and how it intends to achieve its objectives. It is appropriate for micro- and small business ventures as well as development projects. It cannot be a detailed planning document in the case of development projects (Tassiopoulos 2011). It can provide for detailed planning later on, but it cannot be used as a project blueprint, for all the reasons that will be discussed in Chapter 21. It should show how much money is required to start the business or project and/or ensure its success. The manner in which a business plan is written can have an impact on the receiver, who is usually a banker, donor or funder. Remember the following important points:

- A business plan should be written in a formal manner.
- It should have a clear subject line.
- It should be factual and clear.
- It should not be a begging letter.
- It should reflect need, yes, but always in a positive manner.

A business plan should indicate:
- what kind of business or project you want to start or are already working on
- how you are going to do it
- how you will pay back the loan or fund.

A well-thought-out, well-documented business plan shows that you know what you want and how you are going to achieve it; by showing this, you establish credibility with your potential funder.

Apart from its funding purpose, a business plan can also:
- be used to force yourself to take an objective, critical and unemotional look at your business or project in its entirety
- become an operational tool that, if properly used, will help you manage your business or project towards its success
- become a means of communicating your ideas to others and provide a basis for a financing proposal.

14.3.1 Proposed business plan format

Although the guidelines for a business plan focus on the start or beginning of a new business venture, the same principles apply for obtaining funding for special projects, Section 21 companies, trusts or non-profit organisations. Even though some of the headings might change, certain key aspects need to be addressed when compiling a business plan. The following are the most important items to be addressed in a business plan.

Cover sheet
- Full name of business, organisation or project (a project needs an appropriate name that will reflect the nature of Its business or activity)
- Physical and postal address
- Contact details
- Contact person
- Date of plan

Table of contents
- Main headings
- Graphs, charts and tables
- A map to indicate the physical location of the project
- The constitution of the organisation
- A copy of the registration certificate, if applicable
- Annual report, or a copy of a progress report or minutes of a meeting
- A recent bank statement
- Supporting letters that will reinforce your application

Executive summary
- Highlighting of the important aspects of the plan

Implementing agency

State the name and address of the organisation or organisations that will be responsible for the physical implementation of various aspects. You also need to indicate the legal status of the organisation: is it a Section 21 company, a legal trust or a non-profit organisation (NPO); does it have a constitution, and what are the dates of registration? Bank details must also be provided: when the financial year-end of the project is, and the name and contact details of the bank and account number.

Governance and membership

Donors need to know who is involved in the governance of the organisation (board members, directors or project participants) and the names of the management team. They also usually require a list of members of the organisation or project. If the beneficiaries of a project differ from its membership, a separate name list may be required. Sometimes, the donor may ask whether the project is made up of family members and will ask for a list of names.

Project description

The project description or funding request is the core component of the business plan. Describe exactly what you want to achieve and your plan to achieve it by starting with a problem statement. The more detail you give, the better. This will show the donor that you really know what you need for the project to succeed. The project description can be divided into three themes: training, equipment and material. For each of these, a separate budget can be provided (see cost estimates below).

To make a favourable impression, the project description should also describe the available expertise. A donor may, for instance, require information about the technical and business skills available and the rate of literacy and numeracy of those involved in the organisation or project.

Location

Describe the geographic area, as well as the political, social and economic area in which the project will take place or the business will operate, making specific reference to the target groups.

It may also be important to show the extent to which the organisation/project networks in the community. Does the wider community know of your existence, and do you have a relationship with and support from the local government, traditional authority, other stakeholders in the community and community development forums?

Objectives

Objectives are the measurable results that an organisation aims to achieve within the time frame of a specific project. They are those goals that you need to reach in order to realise your mission.

Scope of work

Explain how you are going to reach your objectives. Give a strategic plan and the implementation process with indicators to be used for monitoring and evaluation purposes.

Budget (cost estimate)

A budget is a planning instrument: it shows the expected income and expenditure of an organisation. A donor wants to see this document, at least the current one of your organisation, or they want a copy of the project's budget if this is separate from that of the organisation. Sometimes, they also require a bank statement and a report from the auditor or bookkeeper for the past year.

The budget must provide the would-be donor with as much detail as possible and make sure that estimates are realistic and verifiable (see project description above). This section must indicate the seriousness of your financial commitment. It should not only indicate what and when the would-be donor should contribute but should also show the use of other available or own funds. Where applicable, and to show the donor that you did your homework, two or three quotes from service providers should be attached.

Cash-flow plan

This section is important for two reasons. First, it shows when the donor should make finance available. Second, it concretises the plans and ensures that money will be available when needed.

Time schedule

Indicate when you plan to start and end the different phases of the project. If at all possible, make use of a graphic timetable.

Evaluation and reporting

Cuthbert (1995:141) makes the following very important statement: 'Thanking and recognition are the most important first steps in assuring a continuing and fruitful relationship with your donors'. Thanking and showing recognition are basic values in all cultures. It is common-sense good manners. However, to know who to thank and what for, information is needed. This is information gathered through regular monitoring and evaluation.

When preparing a business plan as a fundraising document, you will want to evaluate your success in raising funds. However, to do this you will need standards or benchmarks against which to do the evaluation. Though some guidelines exist, a firm set of benchmarks is not available. However, the benchmarks usually concern the achievement of project goals: completion of tasks and phases, spending of funding according to budget and timelines, achievement of training and empowerment goals, and so on. Through trial and error, you will have to develop your own set of benchmarks.

Reporting is a vital component of effective donor management as it keeps the donor informed about your activities and whether you are succeeding in what you have set out to do. In other words, it ensures responsibility regarding the use of funds. Because of its importance, reporting should be covered in the business plan, where at least an outline of the reporting procedure must be given.

> **Beneficiaries reached**
>
> In this section, you should provide proof that the business or project is satisfying or will satisfy the needs of the people who you intend to help. You can also include details of human resources development, specifically capacity building (training), the use of small local enterprises and affirmative action (see also governing and membership described above) under this heading.
>
> **Documentation**
>
> The following documents should accompany the business plan:
> - A map to indicate the physical location of the project
> - The constitution of the organisation
> - A copy of the registration certificate, if applicable
> - The annual report or a copy of a progress report or minutes of a meeting
> - A recent bank statement
> - Supporting letters that will reinforce your application.

Source: Nieman and Nieuwenhuizen (2014:121)

14.3.2 Fundraising: a special type of report and some pitfalls to avoid

One of the most important forms of operational writing is the preparation of a business plan to raise funds for the organisation or a project. Windell (1988) identifies 10 pitfalls that seriously hamper or even contribute to failure of fundraising attempts:

1. *Time schedules totally absent or not adhered to*: Not only will the organisation be unable to meet its financial and other commitments, but people will lose interest in the programme.
2. *No clear strategy*: Everyone involved in the NGO and CBO sectors knows that donor funding is needed to meet budgetary needs. Sometimes it happens that the chairperson announces that they now need a specific amount to fulfil a specific obligation. He/she may even propose a specific donor to be approached. Everybody agrees and leaves the meeting, satisfied that the financial need will be addressed by means of fundraising. However, without a clear strategy, without a sub-committee or person made responsible for carrying out the fundraising, nothing will happen. At the next meeting, the chairperson will most probably announce a serious shortage of funds needed to complete the project.

3. *A lack of enthusiasm*: Not being enthusiastic about raising funds is a sure recipe for failure. However, the fundraiser can be enthusiastic only if he/she approaches the matter with clear objectives, in a planned way that fits into an overall fundraising strategy.

4. *Dependence on the telephone and correspondence*: There are thousands of NGOs pursuing good causes, but the potential pool of donors is limited. The reply to a telephonic request for support may be a friendly (or unfriendly) NO. It is very easy to respond negatively over the phone because the eye-to-eye contact or presence of the fundraiser is not felt so intensely. Likewise, a 'begging' letter can be easily disposed of in the wastepaper basket.

5. *Lack of orientation and coordination of voluntary workers*: As indicated above, fundraising must be driven by a committee or preferably an individual. The tasks of this person with regard to the voluntary workers are threefold: to orientate (train) them with regard to fundraising; to motivate them – they may feel isolated and become despondent when the public responds negatively; and to monitor progress and coordinate the action of volunteers.

6. *An attitudinal problem*: An attitude of 'I have already lost the battle' means that you have already lost the battle. The attitude of the fundraiser must be friendly, open, sharing and willing to engage, as an equal, with a potential donor.

7. *Inability to ask*: The essence of fundraising is the ability to ask. The potential donor cannot read your mind. He/she will not know that your request is, for example, 10 per cent of the total cost from his/her organisation and not the full budget of R500 000. If you do not ask, you will not get.

8. *No targets*: Fundraising targets must be clear and above all realistic. Macro-environmental factors and personal factors determine what people can or will give. The need is bigger than the amount available in society for contribution to NGO and CBO funds.

9. *Inefficient and clumsy administration*: In the past, there was no expensive and sophisticated computer system to ensure an efficient administration. A card or filing system had to do. However, nowadays a computer with the appropriate software and trained staff to manage it are indispensable for efficient administration. Efficient administration is necessary in order to: monitor progress; know when to remind

contributors of their donations; know when to send birthday cards or other important 'thank you' gestures; keep a record of contributions and compare it with the targets referred to above.

10. *Unrealistic expectations*: 'We only have to find 10 people to donate R1 000 000 each then our target is met!' This is quite an unrealistic expectation. It will only succeed in making fundraisers despondent and unmotivated.

We are sure that more sins can be added from practical experience. Nevertheless, this list can be used as a checklist to measure the performance of the organisation, to identify shortcomings and to plan solutions to problems. With this list as a guideline, writing a business plan can be better planned and executed. It can also help the organisation to set realistic goals and achieve small, interim successes in fundraising.

14.4 TAKING MINUTES

The formal record of a meeting is the minutes. During a meeting, the secretary or recording clerk will take notes on the proceedings, which will later be formalised into minutes. The use of a tape recorder or cellphone should be considered for accuracy, but this must be approved in advance by the attendees of the meeting. Minutes should:

- accurately reflect the proceedings of the meeting (transcribe the notes taken at the meeting as soon as possible after completion of the meeting)
- be brief and factual (long proposals or submissions should, where possible, be included as annexures and not be made part of the minutes/report of the meeting)
- be written with the agenda of the meeting as background document
- be written in a formal manner
- be written in the active voice
- have numbered headings
- consist of short sentences
- have clear paragraphs
- indicate what action should be taken and who is responsible for taking that action.

When a decision is made it should be prefaced in the minutes with 'resolved that …'. The proceedings must be correctly captured and subjective opinion avoided.

The type of meeting will have an impact on the contents and composition of the minutes. Generally, minutes should reflect the following:
- A clear subject line, in other words, what the meeting is about
- Date on which the meeting was held
- Venue where the meeting was held
- Starting and closing times of the meeting
- Organisation/institution conducting the meeting
- Chairperson
- List of attendees.

Generally, the following headings are used:
- Opening and welcome
- Attendance and apologies
- Approval of minutes of the previous meeting
- Specific items carried over from the previous minutes
- Way forward (decisions)
- New matters
- Date of next meeting
- Closure
- Attendance list.

See Case study 25: *The smart community development worker.*

14.5　CONCLUSION

Community development never takes place in a vacuum, which is why reports and proposals are necessary. While projects may be quite simple and their planning based on trial and error, reports and proposals must have a professional look, and the CDP will probably have to play a major role in the writing of these documents. This does not mean that the CDP should 'take over the job'. It simply means that people who are not used to this type of writing will need guidance, and the CDP should provide as much as is needed.

REFERENCES

Cuthbert D. 1995. *Money that Matters: An Introduction to Fundraising in South Africa.* 2nd ed. Pretoria: JP van der Walt.

Nieman G & Nieuwenhuizen C. 2014. *Entrepreneurship. A South African Perspective.* 3rd ed. Pretoria: Van Schaik.

Tassiopoulos D (ed). 2011. *New Tourism Ventures: An Entrepreneurial and Managerial Approach.* 2nd ed. Cape Town: Juta.

Windell C. 1988. *The ABC of Fund Raising.* Pretoria: Serva.

CHAPTER 15

Meetings

Frik de Beer

15.1 INTRODUCTION

Meetings are a common activity in most organisations, with the goal of providing a means for decision making, goal setting, work scheduling, problem solving and information circulation (Geimer, Leach, DeSimone, Rogelberg &Warr 2015:2015). A meeting occurs when a group of people gather in the same location at the same time to discuss and, if necessary, resolve a mutual issue or issues. The meetings that groups, committees and organisations hold are what make them what they are. Consider what would happen to organisations if they never held meetings. They would probably lose their identity and cease to exist in their current form. However, meetings can also be unproductive and even counterproductive.

15.2 THE MEETING CYCLE

A meeting does not stand on its own. It is connected to the previous meeting and it leads to the next one. Meetings form a pattern or cycle that consists of three phases:

1. During the preparatory phase, the secretary (see section 15.7 for more on the various role players in meetings) has a specific task, but other members also have a certain amount of preparation to do. The basic documents used as guidelines for the preparation are the minutes of the previous meeting and the agenda for the next meeting.
2. During the meeting phase, the preparation comes to fruition.
3. During the follow-up phase, decisions made during the meeting are put into effect. This phase dovetails with the preparation phase for the next meeting.

15.3 TYPES OF MEETINGS

Meetings differ in type and in size. There can be executive meetings with only a few people present, small group meetings with a limited number of people, and mass meetings with many people attending.

Meetings vary in character as well. There may be information meetings where specific information is communicated. These are usually large gatherings where members of a community or voters in a constituency are updated on current events. These meetings are also known as report-back meetings. There are also decision-making meetings where various issues are addressed and decisions are made on each one. Because many of the items on the agenda represent problems that must be solved, decision-making meetings can also be problem-solving meetings. Problem-solving meetings usually take place on a lower level of decision making where subcommittees or committees must thrash out matters and make recommendations to higher councils.

15.4 COMMON PROBLEMS ENCOUNTERED IN MEETINGS

Why are meetings often a waste of time? Why are they so unproductive? Why does it seem that they will never end? The answer is because the following common problems are experienced in meetings of all kinds. Note that this section makes use of Doyle and Straus (1976).

15.4.1 The multi-direction syndrome

In the meeting, everyone scatters in different directions. The meeting lacks focus, and no one tries to get everyone moving in the same direction. This is implies a problem with the chairperson. Focus and organisation are two of the most important aspects of a successful meeting. A meeting will be hampered if they are not present.

15.4.2 Confusion about procedure

Because the participants have not agreed on a procedure for the meeting, questions about procedure are likely to arise while discussing the items on the agenda, or disagreements about the procedure to be followed will result in a deadlock. This, once again, indicates that the chairperson is failing. It is best to have established procedures that everyone understands and can be followed at every meeting.

15.4.3 Personal attacks

Individuals are verbally attacked when they say something that is not acceptable to all. The ideas of people are not the central focus, but rather the characters of people who dare to voice a different opinion. This is catastrophic for any organisation or group. Either there is conflict or the discussion dies down.

15.4.4 Traffic problems

In many cases, it is difficult to leap into the conversational flow and get a chance to participate. This can result in multiple conversations occurring at the same time, or some members not participating, allowing a few individuals to dominate the proceedings.

15.4.5 Unclear roles and responsibilities

In some situations, it is unclear what roles various participants will play during and after the meeting. Their position and power are also unknown. There is no agreement on who is accountable for what. Roles must be established, possibly over time, but these things must eventually be clear to everyone.

15.4.6 Manipulation by the chairperson

The chairperson may use meetings to rubber-stamp his/her decisions. Meetings become monologues by the chairperson, where the rest of the members merely nod their consent or agreement now and then. This is surely the worst problem a meeting can have because the very purpose of meetings, that is, to solve problems through debate, falls away.

15.4.7 Data overload

We receive so much written and oral information that we cannot remember it all and may become confused. It is usually easier for a secretary just to put a lot of documents together than to sort out the really relevant portions. It is then left to the members to decide what should be read and what not. Unfortunately, very few have the ability or inclination to do that.

15.4.8 Repetition and wheel spinning

Often, a meeting cannot gain momentum. It gets stuck in the same place and every speaker repeats the same old ideas. There are no new arguments presented, and no progress toward a decision is made. This usually happens when a meeting lacks focus. Then the members are not sure where they are and what has been decided. The result is repetition and lack of progress.

15.4.9 Win-lose approach

In such a situation, it is taken for granted that every time that there is a difference of opinion, one party must win and the other must lose. Instead of discussing matters thoroughly, everything is put to the vote as soon as possible. This is a way to save time and to progress quickly, but it introduces a sense of strife and competition which makes open debate impossible. It also means that there are winners and losers, a division that may be continued after the meeting.

15.4.10 Expectations and questions of power

There is sometimes misunderstanding about the purpose of the meeting and its authority. Is this just an informational meeting, or are participants expected to make decisions? Is the meeting able to approve things or does it have to recommend approval to another body? When there is confusion, it is often the fault of the chairperson, simply because it is nice to pretend that a meeting has certain powers and it boosts the chairperson's image.

15.4.11 Problem avoidance

People may avoid issues that could lead to a disagreement because they are afraid of conflict. This attitude does not lend itself to problem solving. One should warn against unbridled conflict, but this can be taken too far, causing conflict to be avoided at all costs. A difference of opinion, debate and speaking 'against' someone's ideas or points of view are not necessarily signs of conflict. It demonstrates maturity among the participants if they can express themselves freely without getting into conflict situations.

15.4.12 Poor meeting environment

If the room is, for example, too small, stuffy, noisy, draughty or dark, a meeting becomes unpleasant and even unproductive. This problem is, of course, relative. The person used to modern and sophisticated facilities may find the meeting environment poor, while other people are quite satisfied.

15.4.13 Pre-set ideas and assumptions

Sometimes the result of the deliberations is a foregone conclusion. The meeting can only decide in favour of this side. Everything that goes on before a decision is made is just window-dressing. This is the result of a lot of talking and caucusing among members before a meeting. Their ideas and perceptions are then formed before the meeting and nothing can happen to change it.

15.5 BASIC CRITERIA FOR A GOOD MEETING

The following criteria contribute to the chance of a successful meeting:
- There must be a common focus on content.
- There must be a common focus on process.
- The chairperson must ensure that there is an open and balanced conversational flow.
- The chairperson must protect individuals from personal attack.
- The meeting must agree on the basic principle that a win–win solution will be sought.
- Everyone's role and responsibility in the meeting must be clearly defined and agreed on.
- The meeting must be governed by a set of rules to which all participants subscribe and which all participants know.

A meeting is successful when its business is conducted within a reasonable time, discussion takes place in an unhurried but business-like fashion, and the objectives of the meeting are being met, for example decisions are made or information is disseminated.

15.6 MEETING PROCEDURES

Meetings are guided by a number of important procedural aspects.

Opening

A meeting must be formally opened. The fact that a meeting is formally opened distinguishes it from a general unstructured discussion. At a discussion, people talk about whatever they want and come and go as they please. In a meeting, however, certain rules of procedure govern the proceedings, the meeting is structured and focused, and has a legal status in the sense that decisions can be taken at the meeting which are or can be binding.

A meeting therefore starts the moment that the chairperson has declared it open. The meeting cannot be declared open if there is not a quorum of members present. If it is clear that a quorum is not going to be present, one of three things can be done:

1. Some of the absent members can be contacted and requested to come to the meeting as a matter of urgency so that the proceedings can start.
2. The meeting can be postponed to a later date.
3. Those present can decide to continue with the meeting, but without taking any binding decisions. All decisions taken at such a meeting will have to be ratified or condoned at a later meeting.

Application for leave of absence or apology for absence

When members of a committee cannot attend a specific meeting, they should send their formal apologies, or, more correctly, should request the meeting to be granted leave of absence. This should be in writing and should reach the secretary before the meeting commences. If a person is absent without application or apology, it should be recorded in the minutes that such a person is absent without permission.

Reading of previous minutes

The minutes of the previous meeting must be read and approved, preferably early on in the meeting. If all the members have received copies of the draft minutes well in advance of the meeting, it can be decided at the meeting to take it that the minutes have been read. The attendants at the meeting can then suggest and recommend necessary changes to the draft minutes to ensure that the minutes reflect the proceedings of the previous meeting accurately. Minutes cannot be changed because someone does not like or does not agree with what has taken place. They can only be changed in order to reflect better what actually happened. The meeting must approve all such suggestions of change and finally the minutes as amended must be put to the meeting for approval. The minutes are then adopted formally as correct and signed by the chairperson. The minutes are now the official record of that specific meeting.

Matters arising from the minutes

Not all matters are necessarily completed and closed at a meeting. It is sometimes necessary to look for more information or to make an inquiry. Sometimes a matter cannot be resolved and the meeting can then decide to refer the matter to a sub-committee for recommendation at the next meeting. All such cases must be identified by the secretary from the minutes and must be placed on the agenda under the heading: 'Matters from the previous minutes'. These matters are not discussed in toto again, but are looked at in terms of the new information obtained or the recommendation made by a sub-committee.

New matters or motions

New matters come to the attention of a meeting through correspondence, reports and requests via the secretary or sometimes the chairperson. Members can also table fresh motions for the deliberation of the meeting. All such new matters must be reflected in the agenda and preferably the agenda must contain appendices with more information on the new matters. Members should therefore also present their motions in writing to the secretary so that they can be placed on the agenda. If members want to table a motion orally at a meeting, the meeting will only take note of it and will rule that it be placed on the agenda of the next meeting.

General

Most meetings have an item under the heading of general. This item on the agenda is not an opportunity to place new matters for discussion and decision on the table. It is a chance for general announcements to be made and sometimes it is also used for personalia, in other words, to table motions of condolences, congratulations and best wishes that are not for discussion, but only for general acceptance.

Date of next meeting

The date for the next meeting must be set and announced. In certain instances, meetings take place regularly, for example every third Friday evening at 19:00. In such cases, the chairperson can refer to the actual date of the next scheduled meeting and the secretary can record it in the minutes.

Closure

Just as the meeting had to be formally opened, so must it be formally closed. What happens between the formal opening and the formal closure has a different meaning from what happens outside of this period. Therefore, no decisions can be taken by a meeting after it has been declared closed.

15.7 ROLE PLAYERS IN A MEETING

Meetings cannot carry unnecessary passengers. No person can merely be a silent co-traveller. Every person present at a meeting must play a meaningful role. There are basically three important roles at a meeting. They are those of the chairperson, the secretary and the members.

15.7.1 Chairperson

The chairperson is the most important role player, not necessarily because this position holds the power to dictate, but because, without a chairperson, a meeting would erupt into chaos. A good chairperson is someone who acts as a referee or traffic officer. The chairperson must ensure fair play in a meeting. This includes:

- giving everyone a fair chance to speak
- guarding against undue interruptions
- summarising the debate from time to time just to focus the meeting again
- ensuring that a decision is taken on a matter and that everybody knows what the decision entails
- managing the time allocated to the meeting
- seeing that the rules and procedures of the meeting are followed without blowing the whistle like a real referee every time that rules are broken.

Checklists for the chairperson

The following checklists can help a chairperson in the execution of his/her task. A chairperson should strive towards the point where he/she can answer yes to every question in the checklists. (See Case study 25: *The smart community development worker.*)

> **Checklist: The beginning of a meeting**
> - Is the objective of the meeting clear to everyone?
> - Is everyone present aware of his/her important role?
> - Is everyone aware of the rules and procedures governing the meeting?
> - Is the chairperson well prepared for the meeting?
> - Does everyone know that the goal of this meeting is a win–win solution?
> - Does everyone know the contents of the agenda?
> - Are the people present aware of constraints such as time?
> - Does the chairperson have eye contact with everyone present?

> **Checklist: During the meeting**
> - Is there an easy conversational flow?
> - Does everyone get a fair chance to make a contribution?
> - Is progress being made in the discussion?
> - Is the chairperson neutral and unbiased?
> - Is there order in the meeting?
> - Is the secretary keeping up with notetaking of the decisions made?
> - Is the chairperson dealing well with problem people?

> **Checklist: After the meeting**
> - Has the chairperson discussed the minutes with the secretary?
> - Has the chairperson seen to it that the minutes are being dispatched timeously?
> - Has the chairperson followed up the tasks that he/she was given during the meeting?
> - Has the chairperson made sure that the secretary has done the tasks given to him/her during the meeting?

Dealing with problem people

It is the chairperson's task to deal with problem people in a meeting. Problem people are the potential disrupters of meetings and their influence should be minimised. The following are some of these problem people (broadly based on Doyle and Straus 1976):

The latecomer

This person always arrives late at the meeting and causes some kind of commotion, from shaking everyone's hand and enquiring about their health, to bumping and shuffling to get to a seat. When the latecomer has eventually settled in, he/she wants to be brought up to date on the progress of the meeting. The handling of this problem person will be dealt with together with the next one.

The early leaver

By leaving early, this person drains the energy of the meeting. Early leaving is often accompanied by clockwatching, finger tapping, paper gathering, apologising in various directions, and saying goodbye to all and sundry, eventually exiting in a crouching manner.

It is very important to settle the matter of punctuality among a group who have regular and frequent meetings. It should also be noted in the minutes when someone arrives late or leaves early. In any case, common meeting rules require that the early leaver obtain the approval of the whole meeting before departing.

The broken record

This person keeps bringing up the same point over and over again. This person may not act in this way to be difficult, but rather because no one will listen to him/her or because he/she really needs more explanation before understanding. The chairperson should make sure that everyone present knows what the discussion is all about and, once a decision has been made, see to it that it is recorded. It is a good idea if the chairperson or the secretary reads a decision before the meeting moves on to the next item.

The head shaker

The head shaker uses non-verbal communication to disagree or agree in a dramatic and disruptive manner. Head shakers shake heads, roll eyes, pull faces, throw hands in the air as if in despair, and laugh soundlessly. The head shaker is either a very animated person, in which case he/she will probably not realise what he/she is doing, or has a low opinion of the rest of the participants and watches them as if they are acting in a comedy.

The best way to deal with the head shaker is to force him/her to translate his/her body language into words. Every time the head shaker makes a gesture, the chairperson should ask him/her to comment. In that way he/she will become aware of the mannerism and will have to defend his/her reaction to the rest of the meeting.

The dropout

The dropout sits at the back of the room, does not say anything, never looks up, appears to be reading something or doodles. The dropout is especially disturbing to the chairperson. It is the chairperson's task as facilitator to get the whole group to participate freely and the dropout is living proof that the chairperson is failing. First, the seating arrangement can encourage or discourage the dropout. There should be no 'back of the room' seating. No person should be able to hide behind anybody else. Second, the dropout must be brought into the discussion by being asked for his/her opinion.

The silent observer

Although not a dropout, the silent observer never says anything, although he/she follows the discussion and may even nod now and then. The silent observer is usually the shy person who is unsure of him/herself. The chairperson should assure this person that his/her contribution is also important and should help him/her to gain courage.

The Doubting Thomas

This person constantly diminishes everything. He/she is always negative. You are wrong until you prove yourself right. No solution will ever work. Although it is good to be critical, there is a difference between being critical and being aggressively negative. The Doubting Thomas must be kept honest. Every time he/she reacts negatively, he/she must be requested to substantiate the reaction.

The whisperer

By constantly whispering to the person next to him/her, the whisperer distracts the chairperson. Eye contact with a whisperer may cause him/her to stop, or else physical movement towards him/her may stop the whispering. To ask the whisperer to repeat to the whole meeting what has been whispered may also quieten him/her down.

The clown

This is another potential disrupter of a meeting. He/she usually tells jokes or makes funny remarks in an aside that is only heard by the people sitting close by. The clown enjoys the attention of at least part of the group. His/her remarks cause peals of laughter from the people nearby. A bit of humour in a serious discussion is good, but the problem with the clown is that his/her humour is meant only for the people nearest to him/her. This can lead to the beginning of a subculture in the vicinity of the clown. Establishing eye contact and forcing him/her to be serious by asking his/her opinion may change the mood.

The loudmouth

This person talks too much and too loudly, dominates the meeting and is seemingly impossible to shut up. In many cases, the loudmouth is more senior than the rest. He/she then regards it as his/her right to dominate. The loudmouth usually makes it difficult for other people to participate so that a meeting quickly degenerates into a dialogue between the loudmouth and the chairperson. The chairperson should simply say that he/she is not interested in contributions from only one person, thus forcing the loudmouth to keep quiet while other people have the floor.

The orator

The orator makes a speech instead of an input. A speech is time consuming and tends to deal with various matters that are not totally relevant. A speech also tends to stifle lively discussion. The chairperson has a very difficult task in finding the opportune moment to interrupt the orator and quickly give someone else a chance to speak. In any case, the rules of the meeting should stipulate that a contribution should not be longer than a prescribed period of time.

The attacker

This person launches personal attacks on other members in the meeting. This person is aggressive by nature and may even like conflict. Such attacks cause anger, shock and even fear. The attacker must be stopped and it is best if the chairperson can get the whole meeting to censure him/her. The rules of the meeting should also stipulate that no personal attacks may be made.

The gun jumper

The gun jumper does not wait until the chairperson gives him/her a chance to speak. When a discussion is really going well, it is inevitable that a few people would have indicated to the chairperson that they would like to make a contribution. The chairperson must keep a waiting list in his/her head so that everyone can have a fair chance to speak. The gun jumper ruins this orderly proceeding and the chairperson must be strict and not allow him/her to rob someone else from making a contribution.

15.7.2 Secretary

It is said that the secretary makes a good chairperson, and it is also true that the secretary makes a good meeting. The secretary is the scribe and the assistant to the chairperson. He/she must help the chairperson to keep track of the proceedings as well as keep to the agenda. The secretary, in particular, is the source of information for the meeting and must supply all relevant and needed information. The secretary must also note important points of the debate and must record decisions so that true minutes can be written later. The following are the tasks of the secretary:

Before the meeting
- Draw up the agenda in consultation with the chairperson.
- Arrange a venue for the meeting.
- Send out notice of the meeting and include the agenda.
- Gather all necessary information regarding the items on the agenda.
- Discuss the agenda, item for item, with the chairperson so that he/she can be fully prepared.
- Bring all the necessary documentation plus some clean writing paper to the meeting.
- Arrive an hour early in order to get everything ready for the meeting.

During the meeting
- Get everyone present to complete and sign the attendance register.
- Supply the meeting with the necessary information for each item.
- Advise the chairperson on an ongoing basis throughout the meeting.
- Take notes of all decisions made during the meeting.
- Ensure that every decision has a what, when, who and how item.

> **After the meeting**
> - Discuss the outcome of the meeting with the chairperson.
> - Write the minutes as soon as possible after the meeting.
> - Dispatch the minutes timeously.
> - Follow up all tasks directed to him/her.
> - Advise the chairperson of all tasks directed to him/her.
> - Start collecting items for the agenda of the next meeting.

15.7.3   Members

The ordinary members of a meeting are not spectators, but active participants with a great responsibility. They must:

- prepare for the meeting
- contribute to the common knowledge and insight of a meeting
- help the meeting to run its course productively and in an orderly manner
- help those present at the meeting to make good decisions
- carry out the tasks assigned to them
- be loyal to the decisions taken at the meeting.

15.8   CONCLUSION

Meetings are frequently ineffective, which is why we examined meeting problems and problem people in meetings and discussed ways and means to improve meetings. It is critical that meetings are productive and do not waste time. The beauty of it is that productive and orderly meetings can be a huge boost for a group or committee. They are transformed into showcases for the members. They can serve as milestones for the group and can help motivate it to achieve its goals. Meetings are communication exercises in which conflict resolution and negotiation occur on a regular basis, group dynamics and group psychology play a role, and problem solving occurs. Meetings thus put many communication functions to the test.

REFERENCES

Doyle M & Straus D. 1976. *How to Make Meetings Work. The New Interaction Method*. Ridgefield, CT: Wyden Books.

Geimer JL, Leach DJ, DeSimone JA, Rogelberg SG & Warr PB. 2015. Meetings at work: Perceived effectiveness and recommended improvements. *Journal of Business Research*, 68(2015):2015–2026.

CHAPTER 16

Public Speaking

Hennie Swanepoel and Frik de Beer

16.1 INTRODUCTION

Community development practitioners (CDPs) frequently have to give speeches in front of groups of people, despite the fact that it is still one of the most challenging kinds of communication. This is easy to see why, if one keeps the context in mind. Public speaking is about developing storytelling skills and the most effective presenters use storytelling as a strong technique. The communication model is a large element of this context, that is, it consists of sender–message–coding–receiver–feedback. This should be multiplied to account for scenarios when the sender addresses a number of receivers, each of whom may interpret the message differently and reply accordingly. This, while all the barriers that we discussed in Chapter 10 are also present.

As a result, there are many things to remember before giving a speech in front of an audience as well as many things to do and avoid doing. Apart from the fact that it is a difficult form of communication, very few people find it easy to address an audience and very few people have a natural talent for it. Whether or not we have the talent, it is important to stick to several basic principles and do thorough preparation, as everyone has the potential to become a good speaker, with enough practice.

16.2 BASIC CHARACTERISTICS OF EFFECTIVE VERBAL COMMUNICATION

There are a number of characteristics that make verbal communication effective. These are relevant to any verbal communication, but they are crucial in public speaking situations. These characteristics are described below.

16.2.1 Clarity

The best way to describe communication clarity is to liken it to a clear pane of glass. Effective communication is so clear that it allows the receiver/s to look into the sender's mind, to see and to interpret messages from the sender's viewpoint.

Clarity has to do with the way a message is encoded by the sender and decoded by the receiver. The encoding must be done in such a way that decoding is not too difficult and will not give a different meaning to the message that was not originally intended. This means that the public speaker must be careful of:

- *Sentences that are too long*: Short sentences are easier to digest.
- *Complex abstract and philosophical ideas*: These need explanation; rather use sentences that will not need explaining.
- *Jargon*: Do not try to impress an audience with big words – simple is better.
- *A muddled line of argument*: Proofread your presentation a few times and then get rid of any muddled lines of argument.
- *Byways and extras that are not part of the message*: The shortest way is a straight line between A and B.
- *Physical deterrents*: These include a voice that is too soft. If your audience cannot hear you, you have two options – shout or use a public address system. The latter is preferable.

16.2.2 Accuracy

Accuracy is the ability to represent things verbally as they are. We must be extremely careful to present a message as accurately as possible. The same word can have different meanings in different sentences. Combinations of words change the meaning of the individual words. 'Love' is a word with many meanings; it could, for instance, describe something like sexual attraction, but used in the sentence, 'I love fruit', it has a totally different meaning. Different emphasis can also change the meaning of a sentence, for example 'I *am* sick' has a different connotation from 'I am *sick*'.

Words and combinations of words also carry emotions and feelings, and we should make sure that the right emotion or feeling is transmitted. In this regard, we should use adjectives and adverbs carefully and even sparingly.

Sloppiness in speaking leads to a lot of misunderstanding, especially if the language used is not the mother tongue of those receiving the message. How often do we hear that somebody claims that he/she was misquoted?

Be consistent in the use of terminology and make sure that the first time a term is used the audience understands it in the same way as the speaker does. Do not call an apple a pineapple and then next time a pear. In other words, use the same term; not 'development' now and 'progress' later and then 'change' a little later. The audience does not know whether these are three things or one.

16.2.3 Completeness

Speakers cheat their audiences by not giving them the whole message, simply because they assume the audience has the same set of information that they have. This is a dangerous assumption because it takes for granted that all members of an audience are as well informed as the speaker. It is better to include all possible information in a message than to starve it of information so that the audience cannot make the same mental progress as the speaker.

Do not take it for granted that all members of an audience read the newspapers regularly or listen to the news bulletins on the radio. We may think something is common knowledge, but that is another dangerous assumption.

Speakers weaken their messages by giving incomplete messages. If their audience does not know that they base what they say on fact, simply because the fact is withheld from the audience, the latter cannot be blamed for underrating the message.

When we deliver 'to do' messages, in other words, if we must give guidance on a sequence of steps and we use the wrong sequence, or we do not complete the process, or we give actions different names from what the audience knows them to be, we cannot expect that our message will be successful. On the way, at least one of the barriers will put paid to the message.

16.2.4 Conviction

The first three characteristics were characteristics of the message itself. This and the next characteristic have to do with how the message is brought. The audience must always feel that the speaker regards it as worthwhile to convey the message. In other words, the audience must feel that the speaker is interested in the message, believes in the message and is enthusiastic about the message. We need to be passionate about our topic in order to truly communicate with others through speech. Without emotion, our words have no purpose. If we want our audience to be moved by our presentation, we must convey our emotions to them with a degree of authenticity.

This is done not only through words but also through body language. The public speaker must make sure that his/her body conveys the same message as his/her words. Nine times out of 10, a public address has a motivational function; the motivational message must be right for the audience to accept it, make the motivation their own, and internalise it. If the speaker uses emotive words like destiny, power, compassion and freedom, but his/her body is slumped over the lectern, the audience will very easily regard his/her speech as rhetorical nonsense. The speaker must convey to the audience that he/she is convinced that the message is right.

16.2.5 Tastefulness

Even if people do not like our message, they should accept the way in which we have conveyed the message. A public speaker must, therefore, never insult or offend the audience and never hurt their feelings or belittle them or that which they respect. Always respect human dignity. Thus, we must avoid making fun of them, speaking down to them, or addressing them in a paternalistic manner. Additionally, we must never underestimate their intelligence. We will come back to most of this later on in the chapter.

16.3 YOUR PRESENTATION

16.3.1 Preparation

Even talented and experienced speakers will admit that good preparation is the key to successful public speaking. It ensures confidence, and a confident speaker is someone who can deliver the message with conviction in a tasteful manner and can see to it that the message is clear, accurate and complete. The following are important aspects relating to the preparation.

Theme or message

You cannot start to prepare if you do not know what the theme, message or subject of the address is to be. If you are invited to address a group, confirm the subject with those who invited you. They can be very vague about a subject because they are not familiar with it.

If you are asked to choose your own topic, choose one that you can handle and one that will fit the group of people and the occasion. Remember that, in the final instance, you do not want to amuse a group of people, but you want to bring them a message that they should hear and which you want them to accept.

You will find it so much easier if you know beforehand what type of meeting it is that you must address – the organisation who is calling the meeting; what it wants to accomplish; who the audience will be; how many speakers there will be and who they are.

Objective

After you have established the theme or message, you must decide what you want to achieve. It is important to do this early on because that, together with the theme, will decide the contents of your speech. Your objective could be to convey information or to explain something. It can go further by convincing people of something; in other words, to get people to accept something.

Your objective is not only important for the contents of your address, but also for the way in which you bring it across. Never lose sight of the objective. Every word of a public address must be one step forward to get to the objective. Your speech must therefore be logical and well structured. It must be well thought through. An audience will typically find a speech that does not accomplish this to be nothing more than rambling, a waste of time and extremely boring.

Preparatory reading

You must know what you are talking about. A speaker who appears to lack knowledge or grasp of a subject will not be very persuasive. It is therefore necessary to make sure that you can speak with authority and that you understand the topic. This may necessitate reading documents, files, pamphlets, directives and books or websites.

Before you can read the material, you will first have to search for it and that may take some time, so do not wait too long before you get started. It is not necessary to know everything about a topic but just make sure that you have your facts right for the address and that you know and understand enough to speak to people on the topic. If you rely quite heavily on one source, you must acknowledge that source, otherwise you may be accused of plagiarism.

Studying the masters

One tip for public speaking that is often overlooked is that of studying great orators like Martin Luther King, Winston Churchill or Nelson Mandela. The aim of studying these greats is not so that you can copy them, but rather to learn what makes a speech effective and to get tips on how to carry over your message effectively. Your primary aim should be to develop your own voice, mannerisms and deliver your speech so that it projects your own personality first.

Writing it down

While a speech is all about talking, it actually starts as something in writing. Remember, however, that eventually, you will deliver the speech, not read it; therefore, you must write it down as if you are speaking it. There is written language and then there is a spoken one, and you should write your speech down in the spoken form otherwise, when you deliver the speech, it will sound as if you are reading it.

It is not necessary to write down every word that you are going to say. The first draft may be in that form, but the final text that you will use during your speech should only contain the main ideas. The secret to success is to stay in command of the situation right through your speech and for that you must be organised, such as having a text outline or framework that you can follow easily.

Your written text must help you when you deliver the speech. Your eyes move from your audience to your text all the time and, every time that you come back to the text, your sight must land at the exact spot. Therefore, the letters or print must be large enough for you to see the text easily while you are delivering the speech. A font size of 14 is usually sufficient. The writing should not overflow a page, because you will get lost. Use a space to separate different ideas from each other. Underline headings or use a larger print to make it stand out. Number your pages so that they cannot get mixed up and staple the pages together in one corner so that the wind cannot blow them off the table or lectern.

When you write your speech, make sure that you have it right from the start. An address must have a certain framework and you should write it down within this framework. It starts with an introduction where the theme of the speech is announced, sometimes in the form of a problem statement, and the objective of the speech is made known to the audience. The audience is now tuned in. They know what you are going to talk about and where you are heading.

After the introduction, you should start on the main body of the address. Try to mould your speech in the form of an argument and everything you say must then substantiate that argument. Try to keep your speech lean, in other words, no frills or little extras to take the attention away from the main argument. Try to see your speech as a trip from point A to point B (the place you want to reach at the end of your address). Try to reach point B in the shortest possible way. If you follow a 'highway' of logical argumentation, your audience will find it easy to follow you, but if you use little twisting and turning side roads to get there, you are going to lose at least some of your audience.

Divide your speech into sections. Each section must form a logical entity and the sections must follow in a logical sequence on the road to point B, your conclusion. The conclusion should be the high point of your address. Your conclusion must be the culmination of your argument. It must be strong and short, bringing together all the ideas expressed during the address. Some speakers use the conclusion to wind down their speech. That is wrong because it will cause the audience to switch off. Your conclusion should therefore be brief, but full of impact and must stop on such a high note that your last words will echo in the minds of your audience. When you travel from point A to point B, the best moment of your trip is when you arrive at point B. Your speech should be exactly the same.

Preparing visual aids

Visual aids should be aids to your speech and your audience, not stumbling blocks. If you do not prepare your visual aids well and practise using them, they can easily become stumbling blocks. Visual aids cannot contain your whole speech. They should only show the main ideas and rounded figures. Charts should never be cluttered. The more you put on a chart, the longer it takes for your audience to read it, which will cause pauses in your speech while you wait for them to finish reading. In this way, you lose momentum and you lose the rapport you have established with your audience. Further, the more you put on the chart, the smaller the print gets so that the audience cannot read it properly and then your visual aids have become meaningless. In order to remain organised, number your slides, charts or other aids, and indicate in the text when to use each of them.

If you want to use PowerPoint as a visual aid, you should ensure that PowerPoint's features add value and interest to your speech but do not overwhelm or distract the audience. Keep your PowerPoint presentation simple. Maintain your audience's focus on the presentation, rather than simply reading the screen behind you and ignoring those to whom you are presenting. Your speech should never be replicated on the PowerPoint, but rather should be filled with images/photographs or important charts or figures (depending on the nature of your speech). Use as few slides as possible and only include the bare essentials of your speech. You can use an automatic timer on your presentation, or you can advance the slides with a remote device. Try not to walk back and forth between your speaking location and your computer as this creates an unnatural or uncomfortable pause in your speech. Most importantly, practise your speech so that you do not have to rely on your PowerPoint presentation. If technical issues occur, this should not be a stumbling block to your presentation.

Rehearsal

You cannot go out and deliver a speech without prior practice. If you have rehearsed your speech, then rehearse it again. And then, once again. You need to do this over and over until you are completely comfortable. Practise in front of a mirror, read your speech to your family and practise standing up as if you were actually delivering the speech to an audience. This is important, especially if you have nervous tics. Practising helps you identify those tics, swaying motions of your body or loss of eye contact with the audience. This is important, especially if you are an inexperienced speaker. It is only after a few practice rounds that you will have the confidence to speak in front of an audience. Time yourself when you run through your speech because it must fit within the allocated time; it is very annoying when you go over your allotted time and perhaps use someone else's time for your speech. A speech should, in any case, never exceed 20 minutes because that is about the attention span of the average person. A 20-minute speech will fill about eight pages with 1.5 line spacing and font size 14.

16.3.2 Delivery

All the preparation in the world cannot ensure that you deliver the address successfully. It can only help to make it easier and to have a better chance of success. The following are specific aspects that require attention to ensure success.

Text dependency

If you are too dependent on the text in front of you, you are going to read the speech instead of delivering it. The main problem with this is that you will not be able to make and maintain eye contact with your audience. If you do not have eye contact, you do not really communicate with your audience. Rather, you transmit or broadcast and you have no way of ensuring that your message overcomes all the barriers that exist.

If you read to your audience, there is always a gap between you and them, but if you deliver your speech, the interaction is close and alive and the whole situation becomes dynamic. If you deliver your speech without being independent of the written text, you can pick up serious trouble if you forget what you wanted to say or if you leave out important aspects so that your argument becomes difficult to follow. So, you can only deliver your speech and stay afloat if you have prepared yourself well.

Dress

Your dress must be appropriate for the occasion. If it is not, you will feel out of place and the audience may pay more attention to your dress than to your address. Your clothes can set you apart from the audience, which can impede lively communication and the audience may even feel that you do not respect their dignity if you are inappropriately dressed. Your attire must, therefore, be appropriate to the occasion and the audience. Therefore, make sure beforehand what function it is and what kind of people will be present.

Stance

Remember that non-verbal communication is just as important as verbal communication. The problem is that people always believe in body language rather than verbal language. If your words are enthusiastic, but your body language portrays disinterest and boredom, the audience will believe your body language.

The way you stand or sit in front of an audience will tell them something about how you feel and how you approach the occasion. Your stance should therefore never portray nervousness, arrogance or boredom, three totally different traits but equally devastating to a successful speech.

Your stance must project confidence, eagerness and enthusiasm. Most importantly, your body language must match your verbal communication; otherwise, you will not be heard with a willing and sympathetic ear. The audience will also follow the example your body portrays. If your body looks tired or bored, the audience's bodies will portray the same, but if you look vibrant and energetic, the audience will also look vibrant and energetic.

Confidence

You cannot be successful if you do not believe in your own ability. In more formal gatherings where you might not be well known, listen to your CV summarised by the chairperson and tell yourself that the person he describes is you. That greatly helps with confidence.

Never begin a speech with an apology. Do not apologise for your lack of knowledge on the subject. If you apologise for your lack of knowledge, the audience will think it is pointless to listen to you. If you apologise for your lack of experience, the audience will rather wait for you to make mistakes than listen to what you have to say. Do not apologise for having only had a short time to prepare the speech. If you apologise for the short amount of time you had to prepare, the audience may conclude that you do not value them highly enough and will therefore hold a negative opinion of you.

Try instead to start with a few strong and well-spoken sentences. It will give you confidence and will impress your audience so that they will pay attention to what you are saying. Choose at least three short and strong sentences and learn them by heart so that your start can be fluent and impressive.

On stage, all you have to do is be yourself; there's no need to pretend to be someone else. No matter how strongly you feel about what you are saying or how well you have practised, if you do not act like yourself in front of your audience, they might think your speech is forced or insincere.

Enthusiasm

If you are not enthusiastic about your message, you cannot expect anyone else to be. Remember that enthusiasm is experienced in verbal and non-verbal communication. Your message has a much greater chance to be accepted if you are enthusiastic about it. There are words conveying enthusiasm and if you want to win your audience over, you must use them. Here are a few of them: shall, can, success/succeed, force, message, believe, dedicate, hope, compassion, destiny, transformation, utmost.

Rapport

The secret of successful communication between people is a good rapport. Rapport means positive feelings for one another. Therefore, it is imperative that you as a public speaker demonstrate that you are aware of your audience's circumstances, that you respect them, that you share their worries and aspirations, and that you have their best interests at heart. The audience must have positive feelings towards you, for what you are saying and for the way that you are saying it.

Try to encourage, even create, a feeling of 'us' between you and your audience; this makes communication much easier and, most importantly, more amicable. We are focusing here on your audience because, if you have established a rapport between yourself and the audience, you have captured their attention and they are truly your audience. The context of public speaking is such that there is always a gap between speaker and audience. Rapport can do much to address this situation.

Voice intonation or modulation

If you want to be a more engaging speaker, avoid speaking in a tone that appears overly prepared, but you should still consider the speed and inflection of your delivery when practising your speech. When we sing, we use different notes. We should do the same when we speak. If you want to carry your audience along with you and keep their attention, you must use your voice. A lower tone denotes seriousness or gravity, while a higher tone gives a feeling of lightness and happiness. An emphasis on certain words shows that they are important. By repeating a sentence or phrase, perhaps by speaking slightly slower or louder, shows that you regard it as very important and that you want the audience to remember it; this is how you underline a word or phrase, using your voice. A longer than usual pause after a sentence tells the audience that you want them to think about it and let it sink in.

While you can say certain things more loudly, it is not good to shout at your audience. They may consider you rude. Also, be careful of speaking too softly so that your audience cannot hear you properly. Remember, if they cannot hear you properly, you have not even broken through the first barrier to effective communication. (See Chapter 10.) Another problem, especially with inexperienced speakers who are nervous, is speaking too fast. This makes it difficult for the audience to follow and it makes it difficult for the speaker to use intonation to keep the audience captured.

Your voice has more purposes than only communicating. Additionally, it should be employed to keep the audience's interest and focus, while conveying excitement, importance and seriousness. When a voice is used as a mechanical means of conveying a message, it usually lulls an audience to sleep. However, if it is used as an instrument that can play beautiful melodies, you will have a captive audience.

Eye contact

Normally, when you speak to someone, you try to maintain eye contact. You should try to do the same with an audience. If you have eye contact with someone, it is like a channel that you have built, which you can use for communication. Without it, communication becomes that much more difficult. In the case of a large audience, it may be difficult to maintain eye contact with all members all the time, but at least try to stand in such a position that you can see all the faces and that every member of the audience can see your face.

Mannerisms

Be careful of mannerisms because they can annoy your audience and/or act as a distraction. Annoying mannerisms may include scratching yourself, standing with your hands in your pockets, or playing with money or keys in your pocket. Another annoying mannerism is to take your glasses off and put them on repeatedly, or to lift your water glass and to put it down continuously without drinking from it. Distracting mannerisms may be moving from one leg to the other in the same rhythm, all the time. Such a movement has a hypnotic effect on the audience.

Mannerisms in speech can also distract or annoy your audience. Be careful not to punctuate every sentence with an 'eeh' or a guttural throat cleaning. Avoid phrases like 'you know', 'sort of', 'on the other hand', 'seemingly', 'therefore', and 'etcetera'. Remember, you are on the highway between point A and B and these mannerisms are potholes in the road that could slow you down.

You can occasionally leave the lectern and walk a few metres away before returning. Just keep in mind that you cannot do this if you are paper-bound or using a fixed microphone.

Visual aids

Visual aids can be very helpful, but then you must know when you are going to use them and how you are going to do it. Visual aids should never bring your speech to a stop. This breaks the logical flow of your argument and disturbs the concentration of the audience. In this way, visual aids can have the exact opposite effect to what was intended.

Visual aids and your verbal message should become one, should be integrated so that the one never plays second fiddle to the other, or hinders the other's message. This can only be accomplished if you have practised your address with your visual aids. You must also be very clear in your mind about what role the visual aids will play. We often see speakers following a text until the first slide is shown and then starting to talk off the slide, only to later look through several pages of text to try to find the correct place when the slides have run out.

Outside influences

There are always some external influences that can act as disturbances. You should identify these quickly and try to counteract them. Noise from outside is usually one of the most serious external influences. If you cannot counteract it, for instance by closing a door or window, it will be better to stop altogether and first remove the source of the noise before you continue. Outside influences can also manifest themselves inside the hall or room where you are delivering your speech. Cellular phones, loud coughing, the creaking and clanging of chairs, the buzz of an air conditioner and the movement of people all belong to this category. From outside there are aircraft landing or departing nearby, traffic, lawn mowers, generators and, last but not least, thunderstorms. Outside influences need not be so disruptive if your audience is captured by your presentation and if you use all the tools available to you.

Response from the audience

If your audience does not react to your speech, your efforts are fruitless. An audience responds with laughter, a buzz after you have said something, interjections such as 'yes!' or 'right!' or just a nod of affirmation from a few people. You should respond to those reactions because then you have true and natural communication going. You must be wide awake to pick up these responses and then to respond to them by emphasis or repetition or by saying something differently. The better rapport you have, the easier it will be to internalise the audience's response.

16.4 CONCLUSION

Some people are better speakers than others. Therefore, we can say that public speaking is an art, and some people are born with the talent to do it. While this is true, it does not mean that those with fewer talents cannot be successful speakers. It simply means that some people will have to try harder, concentrate on avoiding the pitfalls and use as many of the tools as possible to make their public speaking a success. It is ultimately the better speaker who becomes the successful orator, and that is the type of communication we seek.

REFERENCES

The authors are accomplished public speakers with decades of experience in South Africa and abroad. This chapter is the result of their expertise, insight and experience.

We acknowledge the contribution by Prof Candice Livingston of the Cape Peninsula University of Technology. She provided valuable insights, especially into using PowerPoint and practising before presentation.

CHAPTER 17

The Community Development Practitioner and Technology

Andries de Beer

Technology is best when it brings people together.

Matt Mullenweg

17.1 INTRODUCTION

Technology has always been a part of human history, most notably when a small group of people living near the Sterkfontein caves in Gauteng tamed fire more than 100 000 years ago (Organ, Nunn, Machanda & Wrangham 2011:3; Berger, Hawks, De Ruiter et al 2015:1). In sub-Saharan Africa, works of art and ruins provide compelling evidence of the development of man and his use of technology. Mapungubwe, Great Zimbabwe and Southern Thulamela residents, for example, are relics of prehistoric southern African communities and their technological practices or advances (Huffman 2009:37).

The global village has expanded while the world has shrunk, making it simpler for us to interact and communicate with our friends, family and, yes, neighbours. The push of a button can change the course of events in tumultuous times of pandemics and service delivery turmoil. It is nevertheless crucial to handle technology wisely and not forgo face-to-face human interaction, despite the advantages it provides to our daily life.

This chapter reviews several viral platforms and other technological resources that are available to communities and community development practitioners (CDPs), as well as how to manage them. In the context of this chapter, the term viral refers to videos, images or written content that spreads quickly to a large number of web users, similar to how viruses spread. This is a common method of explaining how ideas, knowledge and trends disperse within and among human communities, however with focus on technological aids and platforms. An overview of the different uses, advantages and challenges that need to be considered, along with relevant legislation and ethics, will also be discussed.

17.2 RESOURCES AND PLATFORMS

In Chapter 1, we introduced Abraham Maslow and his hierarchy of human needs, these being physiological, safety, love, belonging, esteem and self-actualisation. Although Maslow's pyramid can be used as a foundation or blueprint when working with people, CDPs must be aware of the ever-changing environment and the impact that technology, or the lack thereof, may have on communities.

Although by no means scientifically tested or endorsed, Figure 17.1 mirrors Maslow's pyramid in the modern world and how technology has become a necessity in our daily lives. The correlation is clever and should be viewed as social commentary; it does not serve as a replacement for Maslow's pyramid. Yet, for the purpose of this chapter, indulge in the parody created for effect.

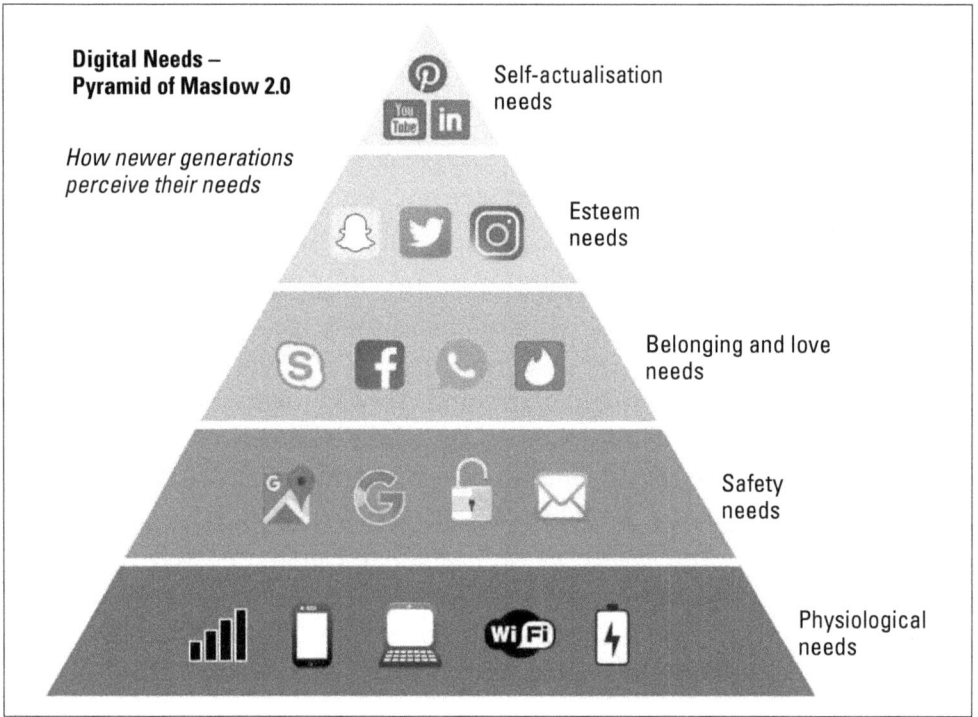

Figure 17.1   Digital needs – pyramid of Maslow 2.0

Source: Bhandari (2019)

In a digital age with computers and smartphones, the way we view and operate in the world has changed. People rely on technology to meet the needs described by Maslow. This includes not only applying for jobs but also, for some, working remotely. Other advantages of a digital presence are being able to do grocery shopping online and having improved educational possibilities in the form of distance learning. Through various social media platforms, the other needs of love, belonging, esteem and self-actualisation can also be met. This includes not only access to the internet but also reliable devices, sufficient electricity to recharge the devices and a reliable signal or connection; secure internet sites and a reliable email account; access to the world's largest library; social media applications and websites to connect with loved ones and like-minded people all over the world; and last but not least, boosts to esteem through people liking or commenting on content posted by individuals or groups.

17.2.1 Availability of resources

The resources available will differ from one community to the next, and it will be the responsibility of CDPs to know the circumstances of the community in which they operate. Access to electricity and/or the internet and a good cell phone signal would be starting points.

Although statistics indicate that the majority of people in South Africa accessed the internet via a smartphone in 2022 (Statista 2022), they do not specify how accessible and reliable the access is. Besides electricity (think of loadshedding and the effect it has on day-to-day living in South Africa), signal and devices, a cardinal ingredient to viral interaction is data and access to it. Since the COVID-19 pandemic, various telecommunication companies have lowered and/or sponsored data, in particular to various institutions and some communities (Vermeulen 2022; The Mobile Economy 2022).

Once again, the specifics will vary for each community. However, there seems to be a move in the direction of more general access to knowledge and communication. The community development practitioner (CDP) will need to assess the availability of the resources in the community but also their reliability in order to work out a technological strategy or approach and select the appropriate platform from which to operate. The checklist below can assist in the process. In addition, the CDP must assess whether the platform(s) meet the communication needs for the specific community.

RESOURCE CHECKLIST

RESOURCES	AVAILABLE	RELIABLE
Electricity		
Signal		
Data		
Costs		

17.2.2 Applicable platforms for the community development practitioner (CDP) and the community

There are millions of platforms and just as many applications available on the internet for day-to-day social interact. On a global front, the top 10 social media platforms are as follows:

1. Facebook
2. YouTube
3. WhatsApp
4. Instagram
5. TikTok
6. Snapchat
7. Pinterest
8. Reddit
9. LinkedIn
10. X (previously Twitter).

The above-mentioned, although the most popular, are not necessarily the most applicable to the community development context. For the purpose of this chapter, the main focus will be on the platforms and tools that can be utilised by the CDP. When dealing with communities, communicating and organising people and events is vital. The tools, platforms and applications selected must thus focus on achieving those goals or at least should aid the CDP in the process.

Although the CDP can and should explore the other platforms and applications at leisure, we will discuss WhatsApp, Instagram and Facebook in more detail.

WhatsApp

WhatsApp is a free smartphone messenger program that may be downloaded. WhatsApp sends messages, photos, audio and video over the internet. The service is quite similar to text messaging services, however because WhatsApp uses the internet to send messages, it is substantially less expensive than texting. Other features include group chatting, audio messaging and location sharing. The program can also be downloaded to desktop computers for the convenience of users.

Because WhatsApp requires a relatively small amount of transferred data, it is seen as data-lite. It will use less mobile data when separated from a Wi-Fi network and is thus cost effective. Plus, it is an easily accessible option, worldwide. It allows the CDP to communicate fast and efficiently with individuals and groups. Conference calls are possible and videos, documents and location pins for meetings or places of interest can be shared.

Instagram

Instagram is another free mobile application (app) that the CDP can use. It allows users to edit and upload photographs and short videos. Users can add a caption to each of their posts and utilise hashtags and location-based geotags to index and search for these posts within the app. Each post made by users appears in the Instagram feeds of their followers and can be viewed by the public when tagged. Users can also make their profile private so that only their followers can see their posts.

Instagram was developed for both individuals and businesses, thus leaving ample room for the CDP to utilise it as a tool for the community. Community initiatives, fund raising and collaborations between individuals and communities can be launched, promoted and managed from this platform.

Facebook

Facebook is a website that allows users to create free profiles and connect with friends, co-workers and strangers online. It enables users to share images, music, movies and articles, as well as their own views and opinions, with as many people as they choose. It is also the world's largest and most well-known social media network, giving it an ideal starting place for businesses or CDPs trying to establish their social media strategy.

All of the above-mentioned platforms have similar operating options, some more advanced than others, yet all three could and should be explored by the CDP.

However, when dealing with any platform and with people and their personal details, it is of cardinal importance to abide by the Protection of Personal Information Act 4 of 2013 (POPI Act) and regulations that govern the use of personal information (see section 17.5). While incorporating technology and applications, the CDP worker must always consider the resource checklist above and how it affects the community.

17.3 MANAGEMENT WITH TECHNOLOGY

Technology should be used as a tool and not as the rule – technology should never replace the human side of interaction. As a CDP, you are a human being, and the community consists of human beings, all with needs as described by Maslow, as a group as well as individually. In a development situation, these human beings are most often confined to the deprivation trap (see Chapter 1 for a discussion of Maslow and the deprivation trap). The community and individuals, with their various needs, do not always have sufficient, reliable and sustainable access to the tools that technology has to offer.

It is the responsibility of the CDP to know what types of resources are available, accessible and sustainable to the members of the community. Even when availability, accessibility and sustainability are assured, it does not mean that technology as a tool is fail proof or that it should be seen as a replacement for traditional methods of communication and face-to-face interaction. Technology should aid the CDP and the community and not alienate them.

By utilising the resource checklist, CDPs should be able to plan and manage their approach to the community with the use of technology. Where appropriate and feasible, training in the use of technology should be organised.

17.4 ADVANTAGES AND DISADVANTAGES

The appropriate use of technology on a day-to-day basis can save costs, and amplify and utilise networks and networking opportunities. It can be faster and more efficient in getting urgent messages across. Specific groups with shared interests can be created on the various platforms above, ensuring that ideas and messages have a wider and more instantaneous reach. Interacting with various stakeholders and other NGOs or sponsorships also becomes easier.

In a Utopian world, there would only be advantages. Yet, also in a Utopian world, there would be no need for CDPs or community development. The advantages mentioned above do not take into consideration the day-to-day survival strategies that members of the community have to employ, or the lack of sufficient and reliable resources. A lack of technology, or sufficient reliable access, is a reality that the CDP will need to acknowledge and manage.

One of the disadvantages of technology is the ever-present risk of falling prey to scams. The internet is full of predators and bullies, patiently waiting for an opportunity to pounce on unexpected victims. Knowledge is power and is the key to protecting the CDP and communities. Cyber-attacks can also take the form of victimisation, the spreading of false news and miscommunication, with devastating effects such as financial loss, job loss, social isolation and poor health.

In order to prevent the negative impacts that technology might have, the CDP must manage the use of technology carefully and stay informed. Various websites and online platforms provide training and guidance in avoiding falling victim to cyber-crimes. CDPs also need to familiarise themselves with communication skills (see Chapter 10) and the POPI Act, briefly discussed in the following section.

17.5 ETHICS AND THE POPI ACT

When communicating with people and/or dealing with their personal information, it is of vital importance to proceed in an ethical way. The core of ethics is to do no harm. CDPs must always uphold the highest standards of ethics and never do harm. There are many more technical aspects to it and considerations to make, but if our standard operating procedure is to do no harm, we are well on our way.

For further guidance in this regard, and especially on how to store, use and share personal information, the POPI Act should be consulted and adhered to. The POPI Act specifies the minimal requirements for accessing and 'processing' another person's personal information. The term 'processing' is used throughout the Act to refer to the gathering, receiving, recording, organising and retrieval of any such information as well as its use, distribution or sharing.

Personal information is any data that may be used to identify an individual, including name, surname, identity number, contact number, email address, religion, medical history, educational background, financial information and other particulars. The CDP must always remember, when forming a group or communicating with the community, that privacy needs to be respected and that consent must be obtained before any personal information of group members can be shared.

17.6   CONCLUSION

It has gotten simpler for us to connect and communicate with our friends, family and neighbours as the world has shrunk and the global community has expanded. The pressing of a button can change the course of events in tumultuous times of pandemics and service delivery difficulties. Despite the advantages that technology has for our daily lives, it is still crucial to control it and maintain face-to-face interactions.

This chapter discussed how to manage the various viral platforms and other technological resources that are available to communities and community development practitioners (CDPs). The various applications, benefits and considerations were outlined, along with pertinent legal and ethical frameworks.

REFERENCES

Bhandari S. 2019. Maslow's hierarchy of needs: The millennial perspective. Available at: https://yourstory.com/author/saakshibhandari-1548674689 (accessed 13 July 2022).

Berger LR, Hawks J, De Ruiter DJ et al. 2015. *Homo naledi,* a new species of the genus *Homo* from the Dinaledi Chamber, South Africa. *Elife,* 4. Available at: https://elifesciences.org/articles/09560.pdf (accessed 1 November 2022).

Huffman TN. 2009. Mapungubwe and Great Zimbabwe: The origin and spread of social complexity in southern Africa. *Journal of Anthropological Archaeology*, 28(1):37–54.

Mobile Economy, The. 2022. Available at: https://www.gsma.com/mobileeconomy/wp-content/uploads/2022/02/280222-The-Mobile-Economy-2022.pdf (accessed 25 October 2022).

Organ C, Nunn CL, Machanda Z & Wrangham RQ. 2011. Phylogeneticrate shifts in feeding time during the evolution of Homo. *Proceedings of the National Academy of Sciences (PNAS)*, 108(35):14555–14 559. doi: 10.1073/pnas.1107806108

Statista. 2022. Mobile internet user penetration in South Africa from 2018 to 2027. Available at: https://www.statista.com/statistics/972866/south-africa-mobile-internet-penetration (accessed 28 August 2022).

Vermeulen J. 2022. 10GB free data for every household – South Africa working on a plan. Available at: https://mybroadband.co.za/news/broadband/450208-10gb-free-data-for-every-household-south-africa-working-on-a-plan.html (accessed 22 August 2022).

SECTION D

The Life of a Project

CHAPTER 18

Contact Making

Andries de Beer

18.1 INTRODUCTION

Contact making is community development's most important phase, even though, at this stage, development has not taken place yet. The commuity development practitioner's (CDP's) initial contact with a community will make or break a development effort. It is of the utmost importance that it be done correctly.

In Chapter 8, we covered the CDP's attitude. It is at the initial contact-making stage that attitude is all-important. If the CDP appears to be a know-it-all or a 'superhuman', people may react in several ways, all of which are bad for community development. The community may develop a grudge against the CDP for disrupting their everyday lives or they may resent a patronising attitude and withhold their cooperation and support. Alternatively, they may be so impressed with the CDP's knowledge and contacts that they may assume that they have no place in finding solutions to their own problems. Initial enthusiasm will result from the great impression made by the CDP. However, it is misdirected, applauding the CDP's presumed excellence instead of the people's natural abilities. The attitude that generates unrealistic expectations is the most damaging of all, leading to inevitable disappointment and the demise of all enthusiasm.

The contact-making phase has three objectives. First, the people must get to know and accept the CDP; second, the CDP must get to know and understand the people and their circumstances; and third, the people and the CDP must get to the point where they can identify a need that they can address through a project. Figure 18.1 illustrates the contact-making process.

In this chapter, we are going to use a case study to illustrate how these three goals can be reached during the contact-making phase.

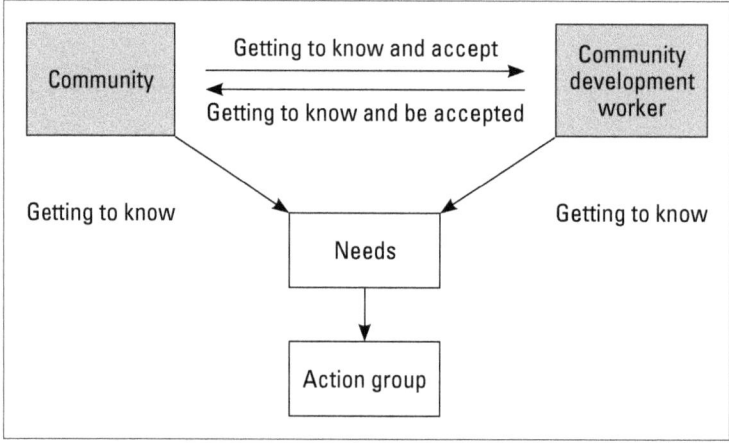

Figure 18.1 **The contact-making process**

18.2 CASE STUDY

In the excerpt from the case study that follows (King 1965), the dilemmas faced by the professional are well illustrated. We will call the case study 'The Story of Ms Najafi'. It took place about 60 years ago in the then Persia, now Iran. Ms Najmej Najafi was a young woman of a well-to-do family in Teheran. After studying in America, she returned to Teheran determined to help the villagers of her native Persia realise a better existence within the pattern of their ancient culture. The Ford Foundation granted her a small scholarship and complete independence of action. This is her account of how she gained the confidence of the village of Sarbandan where she decided to work.

> **Case study: The story of Ms Najafi**
>
> I clambered out of the ancient automobile that had brought me fifty-six miles from Teheran ... I looked over the rooftops of the village to the apricot and cherry orchards fanning up over the foothills; my eyes followed the clear stream of mountain water which we Persians (Iranians) called the jube as it flowed through the centre of the village. Along this stream, I could see people going and coming. My people. My heart shook for a moment! Perhaps, I thought, perhaps this is the place. Very near, there was a tea house ... In a moment, the owner stood before me.
>
> 'I would like tea,' I told him. 'Bring one for yourself too, so that we may talk together.'

Chapter 18: **Contact Making**

As we drank tea he told me that he was called Mash'hadi Mokhtar and that he was the owner of the place. ...

'You own a very fine tea house. But who owns the village?'

'Many own land here.'

'No landlords?'

'Some landlords. A few big ones. I am one of these.'

'You are a man of importance,' I told him. The man had taken my sincere words for dangerous flattery. Again his eyes were veiled.

'Another tea, my lady?'

'Another tea. A tea for each of us, please.' Again he came with tea. I curtained my eyes, too, and we were strangers.

'Well, Mash'hadi Mokhtar, what about the population of Sarbandan?'

'Almost two thousand – in the summer.'

'And in the winter?'

'They do not stay in this place ... they do work in the rice fields of Mazandaran. Only women and children and old men are left here.'

We talked for a time and I asked if the people had a bath.

'Bath? How could we have? Our forefathers made one about a hundred years ago but it is ruined now. Its pool is so unclean that no one has the desire to go into it.' Then he looked at me with a flash of anger. 'My lady, why do you ask these questions of me? Why?'

At this moment I loved Mash'hadi Mokhtar. I loved him because I saw the fear leap into his eyes, and I understood this fear. My people are proud and they have much to be proud of. How can they be happy when so many want to change them?

'Because I think I may want to make my home here, Mash'hadi Mokhtar,' I said very quietly. 'I think perhaps Sarbandan is the place for me.'

He left me and returned with his clopogh, a sort of long pipe. He drew on it two or three times. Then, wiping the mouthpiece first with his fingers then against his cheek, he handed it to me. I drew two or three suffocating breaths and returned it to him.

'Do you have a school, Mash'hadi Mokhtar?'

He smiled ... 'Indeed we do. Four years ago we built the school. We turned it over to the Ministry of Education. We have grades one, two, three and four. Next year, perhaps, we will have five and six. If not next year, at least some year.'

'And is there a school for the girls?'

'What are you talking about, my lady? A school for girls?'

I changed the subject. 'Tell me, does Sarbandan have a clinic?'

'Clinic? What is a clinic?'

'A place of care for the sick.'

'How would we have such a place when we have no doctor?'

'I am hungry, Mash'hadi Mokhtar. What can we eat?'

The CDP needs to establish rapport between him/herself and the people because with rapport communication is so much easier and meaningful. This rapport is established while the CDP learns more about the people and their area, and they learn to know him/her. Ms Najafi, not knowing the community, immediately started probing into the issues she knew to be important among developing people: a bath for hygiene, a school for education (especially for girls) and a clinic for treating the sick. However, Mash'hadi Mokhtar, an important man in the village, listened to her questions with suspicion. And for that you cannot blame him; in fact, Ms Najafi appreciated this attitude and detected her people's pride in it. Her attitude towards the individual she was talking to, the people of the little village she was visiting and the poor of her country in general, can be admired and followed.

> I wanted to work 'heart to heart', not in the mechanised way of organisations. Besides, I did not want to make a little America in the mountains of Persia (Iran). I wanted my people to stay as they were, keeping the feeling of security that goes with doing things the sweet, almost sacred way. I wanted to see if a better life could be built on a foundation of native customs and mores. For my people, I wanted happiness rather than that colder goal that is sometimes called progress (development).

Knowledge by CDPs of the poverty context is an important prerequisite to developing an **empathetic** approach toward assisting in the development of people. The ability to use such knowledge is, however, tested when the professional meets the poor face to face. Outsiders such as professionals seldom meet the poor or listen to them. In the words of Robert Chambers (2007:38): '[W]hose analysis and categories are to be privileged? These are largely "ours", those of professionals who are not ourselves poor, expressed in "our" language'. It is important for professionals to put themselves in the shoes of the poor and understand – feel – their reality.

> When Mash'hadi Mokhtar returned, I asked, 'Do you have a village council?'
> 'Yes, we have. But the members seldom see each other. When they meet there is nothing but quarrelling at the tea house.'
> 'Tell me, why do the old men quarrel?'
> 'My lady, in Sarbandan the people are divided into two factions. We even have two Kadkhodas.'
> 'Two Kadkhodas?' A Kadkhoda is a responsible man selected by the large landholders to keep order in the village. 'Two Kadkhodas? That is incredible.'
> 'But we have. You see, we are two tribes and our landholders ...'

Chapter 18: Contact Making

> The walls of the clinic and the school that I had just built in my mind crumbled away. Two factions. Two tribes. Co-operation, which is always hard to achieve with people as individualistic as my people, might be impossible. I would have to spend time and energy avoiding petty jealousies, ironing out petty disputes. I could not afford to waste myself that way. I was defeated before I began.
>
> 'Come,' he said, standing. 'Allow me to show you the village, my lady.'
>
> Half reluctantly, I followed him along the banks of the jube. Women were washing clothes along both sides. The crying of a lamb drew my eyes upstream. Two men were killing the little creature, and its blood was flowing into the water. Between the men and the women bent over their washing, a half-grown girl dipped a jug into the stream and lifted it, dripping, to her shoulders. Sarbandan needs me, I thought. I looked at the faces of the women and the children. Their skin was transparent; their cheeks like spring petals. Again my heart shook me.

Through talking and listening, a CDP can really get to know the community. Ms Najafi discovered very important aspects about the people and their area when she started to listen to one of the people, a leader from the community where she intended to work.

Let us continue the story of Ms Najafi. She moved to Sarbandan and rented a room to stay. First, she had convinced the elders that she was not from a development agency or from a government department but was a volunteer willing to teach at a school. She successfully introduced the idea of building a school but proposed that the council discuss it first. After settling in, she set out to meet the households and do a survey in an informal fashion.

> I knew that I had much to learn and that I had to learn as I worked, but I was determined to start out in an orderly way. Although I did not know the strange sea I had embarked on, nevertheless I needed to chart my course and decide upon my destination. Carefully I drew a map of the village. On it, I placed every home. Starting from the west and moving to the east, street by street, alley by alley, house by house, I would visit every home. Sometime, and that very soon, I would know the names of everyone in the village, I would know which families were rich, which ones were poor, which ones owned land ...

Ms Najafi used the contact-making period to get to know the people and their circumstances. In fact, while she had the idea of starting a school for girls, it was not uppermost in her mind. Her primary concern at this stage was to get acquainted. She was also concerned about her acceptance by the people as the following excerpt will show.

> Shortly after dusk I set out the things for supper: tea, rice, cheese, sugar. In the villages, a cone of sugar is considered the most desirable possession in the world.
>
> Three women, wrapped in their chadors, each carrying a lantern, were coming to call on me. They stood outside the doorway until I said, 'Won't you come in and have tea with me?'
>
> Glancing covertly about them, they came in and stood awkwardly just inside my house. 'I am breaking sugar,' I told them, not because they could not see me do it but because I must say something and could not speak the questions that were in my head: Who are you? What names do you have? Are your children healthy? Why do you not keep them clean? How much money do you have for food in a year? ... I thought of some of the ... social workers asking people who were almost starving for a handful of rice if they were serving their families the seven basic foods every day. So I might have asked, 'What do you know about nutrition?' I could ask none of these questions. Some would never be answered. Some would be answered later – much later. I said, 'I am breaking sugar.'
>
>   'May I help?' the youngest of the three, a woman of about thirty, asked.
>
>   'I would be so grateful. Now I can prepare the tea.' I turned the cone over to her.
>
> ...
>
> Many times I have knelt in a mosque at the closing month of Ramazan; but never in a simple mosque like this ... After the service I stood in the doorway with a reed basket filled with halva which I offered to the women as they left ... I heard one of them say as she turned away from me, 'She's young but she is a good Moslem.'
>
> I dressed carefully for my visits. I did not wear the dress of the women of Sarbandan; that would have been effrontery. The dress belonged to them and I was a stranger. I put on a full long skirt of bright print, a long-sleeved, high-necked blouse that matched it. Over my hair I put a kerchief. I suspect that one must have a feeling for matters of this kind and cannot follow a fixed rule. The only guide is probably a sincere sensitivity to the feeling of others.

Ms Najafi is extremely careful not to act with disrespect towards the people and the way they socialise, their religion and how they perform it, and their dress.

  No community is a homogeneous entity living in idealistic, caring harmony. The people are also not ignorant – they have survived without much help for generations – and they have cultural practices that assisted in their survival. Not all people will respond positively to professionals, or any other outsider entering a community. And not all responses will be equally honest. In situations of continued deprivation, any outsider can be viewed as a potential resource of goods, money or job opportunities. Therefore, the professional entering a poor community should guard against creating expectations or viewing him/herself as a redeemer, a superhuman who will save the community. In Ms Najafi's case she found the people decent towards her, but definitely not overenthusiastic or very friendly, for that matter.

In the excerpt above, Ms Najafi began to understand the pitfalls of getting acquainted with the community. Of course, the flipside of the coin is even more important: allowing the community to get acquainted with her. Ms Najafi realised that speaking to the leaders only would not make her fully acquainted with the community. She also needed to talk to the women, the children and men: at the river, in the market and other places. While doing the survey, she came to the house of Fatemeh …

> … I could hear the mewing of a sick child. I went around the back. A slender young woman, dressed in a bright cotton print, holding a whimpering child in her arms, was bent over a black kettle hanging above an open fire.
>
> 'Salaam,' I said quietly.
>
> She didn't turn, just kept stirring.
>
> 'May I help you?'
>
> She turned her face towards me. There was a look of complete despair in her red-rimmed eyes and I could trace the tracks of tears down her smoke-greyed face. I looked down into the child's yellowing face. He was six months old perhaps, but unbelievably thin and dry-skinned.
>
> 'He isn't going to die. Six I have that died, but Ali will live!' There was hysteria in her voice. 'I won't let him die!'
>
> 'What are you making?' I watched her rough hand, white-knuckled around the shapeless iron spoon.
>
> Her glance at me said, 'Why, you stupid woman! How is it that you don't know?' Her lips said defiantly, 'Medicine.'
>
> 'And what is this medicine?'
>
> 'The blood of a living raven boiled with crushed beetles.' Her eyes, wide with fear, came to my face for a minute. 'It is a good medicine?'
>
> 'No, no, no!' I wanted to cry out. 'It is not a good medicine!' Instead I said, as calmly as I could, 'It is a strange medicine for one so small, so helpless.'
>
> I did not know how to answer her. All I knew was that I must save this little one from that horrible brew. I moved to overturn the kettle, but I stopped myself. What right had I to do this? The baby's father had probably spent hours in snaring a living raven so that the blood could drip from it while it still lived. I reached for the child and the mother put him in my arms. Think of something, think of something, I told myself as I hushed him against my breast.

> In the tiny village of Japon, about five or six kilometres from Sarbandan, the government had opened a small, well-stocked clinic. I did not know who was in charge there. I didn't even know that I knew there was a clinic, but I trusted this moment of inspiration.
>
> 'Come,' I said. 'You hold the baby and I will go rent a donkey. We will take him to a doctor.'
>
> ...
>
> I described the cough. 'Croup,' he said, 'with a respiratory infection.' He studied the yellow face, the yellow eyeballs of the child. 'Give plenty of boiled water and as much milk as he will take.'
>
> The mother put her hands on her shrunken breasts, a mute gesture that said the milk had left her breasts and she could not feed the child. The doctor put a package of dried milk into my hands. 'You'll know what to do with this,' he said.
>
> Then he gave the mother a small bottle of medicine. 'When the child coughs, give him a dose of this every few minutes until he vomits,' he said.
>
> 'Vomits?' she questioned.
>
> 'Yes, that will clear his throat for breathing.'
>
> When I returned, my home was full of women with their children in their arms. 'You helped Fatemeh's child,' they told me. 'My child, too, needs help.'
>
> So now God had answered my question. I had asked Him where I should begin. Was it to be with education, with industry, with sanitation? Now I knew. Unprepared as I was in the field of medicine, I must begin with a clinic.

And so Ms Najafi came to understand the real need in the community. She also realised that, in spite of a good education and knowledge about developmental issues, she could not proceed without first gaining the confidence of those whom she passionately wanted to help. If we look at another case study dealing with contact making, Case study 14: *The case of the community worker who met his match*, we detect quite a different attitude and a different way of going about it. The objective of that contact making differs from that of Ms Najafi's case. The CDP is much more in the foreground, much more hands on, taking the initiative and accepting his superiority to those he works with.

18.3 PREPARATION FOR ENTRY

A CDP cannot just wade into a community and, from then on, act on the spur of the moment. CDPs need an operational strategy to guide their actions. We should not think that Ms Najafi just plunged without planning into the community. She made careful preparations, such as getting an organisation to support her, obtaining funds for the venture and deciding the way she wanted to approach the matter. She was not even sure whether she would work in Sarbandan.

The CDP must plot a strategy, leaving room for a good-, a bad- and a worse-case scenario. The CDP should discuss this draft strategy with his/her supervisor and colleagues and, taking their feedback into account, change and improve it where necessary. In fact, a team of CDPs with their supervisor can sit together and devise the operational strategy. Only after this has been done, can the CDP enter an area with the view to facilitate a project.

If the CDP uses the guidelines discussed above, his/her operational strategy will be an adaptive and milieu-sensitive tool. In compiling the strategy, the CDP should consider these questions about the following three aspects:

1. *Position of the CDP in the community*
   - What is the position of the CDP's organisation?
   - What are the organisation's mission and objectives?
   - What is the CDP's brief?
   - What resources can the organisation provide?

2. *CDP's own position*
   - What is the CDP's own position?
   - What is his/her objective?
   - How should he/she set about reaching that objective?
   - What time constraints must be kept in mind?
   - How much time can the CDP spend in the community?

3. *Position of the community*
   - What is the community's position?
   - How large is the community?
   - What type of leadership does it have?
   - What are the political, social, cultural, economic and psychological environments?
   - What aspects of the natural environment need special consideration?
   - Who will be the target group?
   - What resources will come from the community itself?

All these aspects must be considered and moulded within a structure containing the following:
- *CDP's goals*: What do you want to achieve?
- *CDP's plans*: How are you going to achieve your goals?
- *Time frame*: In what order and within what length of time are you going to work towards achieving your goals?

Side issues:
- How are you going to approach the various steps you are planning?
- What resources will you need?
- Where are you going to find those resources? (Note: this does not refer to sources needed by the community/organisation to achieve their aims.)

Important things for a CDP to remember:
- Be realistic in setting goals for yourself and in planning to achieve them. Do not aim too high because this will put you under pressure and if you cannot carry out your strategy, you will become frustrated.
- Write down your strategy so that you can refer to it regularly.
- Evaluate your actions in terms of your strategy regularly (preferably once a week).
- Discuss your strategy and your evaluation of your own actions with your colleagues or anyone with knowledge and experience. In fact, it would be better if the CDPs of one organisation could form a team who work out their operational strategy together and even with their supervisor present.

CDPs should remember that their operational strategy is not a blueprint that cannot be changed. It is an opportunity for them to learn how to devise and implement their plans better next time. CDPs should use their operational strategy as a guide for their own actions. This is the only way in which they are also going to be part of and benefit from the learning process.

18.4 ENTRY

The contact-making phase starts with the CDP's entry into the area. Entrance into a well-defined community is the exception, not the rule, although in the case study the village was rather well-defined although they had the trouble of two tribes sharing the same area. Usually, the CDP enters an area inhabited by a mass of people belonging to more than one community, representing various institutions and groupings, and subject to all the stratifications that a layered political, social and economic environment can provide (see chapters 2 and 7).

The CDP enters a rational social life experience. People naturally regard their daily activities as being the most appropriate to their circumstances. Therefore, the society's members regard the activities taking place as normal. People are also suspicious of change. This holds true for people trapped in poverty. Even when they suffer deprivation, they tend to adapt to it, becoming complacent rather than upsetting everything by effecting change. As McDermott and Vossoughi (2020:60) put it so vividly:

> The most obvious condition of poor people: they have little access to resources. ... The less obvious problem: poor people have to put up with being disparaged, distrusted, rejected, and theorized by those who are not poor. In the hands of social scientists, they become The Poor and have to face being described, spoken for, and explained by policy wonks. Being poor is awful, but being treated as poor might be, or might be felt as, the more disagreeable problem.

The CDP, therefore, should enter an area without broadcasting that he/she wants to bring about change. It is better and safer to display empathy with and interest in the people's situation, as Ms Najafi did. The people must come to a point where they realise that change is needed, usually through a process of awareness creation. It is not something that they should be told by a CDP who has just entered the area, as in Case study 14: *The case of the community worker who met his match*.

It is clear that the principle of learning is important in this situation. The many pitfalls facing a CDP can best be obviated by following the learning process approach. This approach requires that the CDP should enter an area without a preconceived objective or programme for the people to adopt and follow. Yes, he/she should have an operational strategy, but that only covers what the CDP's approach should be, not what the people should do. The CDP should keep an open agenda that he/she and the community will fill gradually as they get to know one another better. The CDP should be listening from the heart, as Ledwith (2022:137) says:

> Be interested in what people have to say. Listen, pay attention, empathise with the stories you are told. Step outside your own ego, and notice. Don't formulate responses, ask questions; be comfortable with the art of silence and don't crowd people with words. Hear your tone of voice …

This is the most natural way of coming to a point of needs identification. Ms Najafi was in danger of negating the learning process approach when she pre-empted the realities of the community by announcing to the council that she wanted to open a girls' school (not reflected in the excerpt above). However, the way she made contact from that point on helped her to become aware of the most important need in a natural way.

The unnatural way, which is most definitely not recommended, is for the CDP to establish contact with the community by way of a public meeting. Apart from it being unnatural, a public meeting showcases the CDP and he/she should only take a small step to become the community's redeemer. Case study 14: *The case of the community worker who met his match* illustrates this point nicely. No community development can or will take place if the CDP is cast in such a light.

18.5 GOALS OF CONTACT MAKING

We named the three goals of contact making in the introduction to this chapter. Let us now see what they contain.

18.5.1 Getting to know the CDP

The people must get to know and accept the CDP for what he/she is and has come to do. The CDP should remember that people are not obliged to be accepting. People are autonomous and they can therefore accept or reject a CDP. The community's acceptance must be earned. There are CDPs who think that people must and will accept them because of their position in government or NGO structures. Such CDPs will find that it is easy for people to say that they accept without any real commitment. Ms Najafi is an excellent example of earning acceptance. It was only when she took the seriously ill baby from its mother and told herself to do something that she started to earn acceptance. CDPs also cannot obtain acceptance through marketing themselves.

This part of the contact making should also not be rushed. Later it may be necessary to pick up speed, but at this stage enough time should be available so that people can accept the CDP's bona fides over a period of time. Ms Najafi took her time with her house-to-house visits. She wanted people to get used to her being among them.

This may also be a good time to make sure that there is no misunderstanding about the CDP's goal, his/her position and his/her role. Ms Najafi made sure that there was no confusion about her position. She was not from the government, she was not from a multinational NGO, and she had no logistical or financial backup other than the small scholarship. In other words, acceptance must be based on the correct understanding of the situation.

The people will not be receptive to development before they have become fully acquainted with the CDP. The CDP can help the process along by informal talks, friendliness, a keen interest in the people and their circumstances, and by just being present. These are the things that Ms Najafi did. A brief visit by the CDP once or twice a month will not win the people's acceptance. Regular and longer presence is needed to establish a strong relationship with the people. The CDP in Case study 14: *The case of the community worker who met his match* gave himself no chance for this. This also means that one CDP should not serve too many communities.

It is important that the CDP acknowledges the leaders in the area, especially the formally elected ones. The CDP must visit them and explain his/her role to them. Circumstances will dictate whether formal leaders will later participate in a community development project. At this contact-making stage, it is necessary only to acknowledge their position and to ensure that they know why a CDP is working in their area. Ms Najafi did the right thing to meet with the leaders on only her second visit to the village (not reflected in the excerpt above). It established her position and role formally there and then. The CDP in Case study 14: *The case of the community worker who met his match*, however, never got to the headman before it was too late.

A CDP should not pick champions early on in the contact-making phase. A person may act and look like a leader and may convince a stranger of his/her credentials as an accepted leader, but at the same time they could be mistrusted by many of the ordinary folk. If the CDP is associated with such a person, the mistrust and animosity directed toward that person can easily rub off on the CDP, making acceptance by the people nearly impossible. In this instance, Ms Najafi could have made a serious blunder by associating with the tea house owner from the first moment of entry, but luckily he was apparently accepted as at least one of the leaders. In Case study 14: *The case of the community worker who met his match*, the CDP picked someone who was not on a good footing with the headman, something that immediately made the CDP the headman's opponent – the last thing he wanted to be. Again, good observation skills are called for. A CDP must remain vigilant to avoid being associated with false or unpopular leaders.

CDPs must be open about their position with everyone they meet. Their bona fides will suffer grave setbacks if misunderstanding surrounds their role. If they are intentionally misleading from the outset and are later found out, it is even worse. The argument may be put forward that, because of this potential pitfall, it would be better to use a public meeting to introduce the CDP and inform the community of his/her role.

While there is merit in this suggestion, it is still fraught with danger. A political leader may try to make the most of the occasion and have the CDP in front or on the stage with the other leaders. Immediately, the association is wrong. The CDP should never be seen as a leader. Further, the leader may use the opportunity to impress those present that he/she has organised that the CDP now works in their area. Again, the association is wrong. The CDP is not in the service of the leader. The leader may even go further and try to show how many good things will flow from this arrangement and by doing so he/she makes the CDP a superhuman and raises the expectations of all those present that the CDP is going to save them from their problems. So, while a public meeting may be an opportune moment to inform the community of the presence and work of a CDP, there are just too many dangers attached to it to make it worthwhile.

It is good if from the outset the people regard the CDP as a compassionate person. People are easily affected by enthusiasm and motivated by compassion, and will be keen to return the friendliness – to the extent that they will be prepared to forgive the occasional blunder from the CDP. Compassion from the CDP leads to a deeper and more sincere relationship with the people and it makes community development so much easier. Ms Najafi's hospitality toward the women who visited her, her kindness at the mosque, and her total commitment to save the sick child's life, are indications of her compassion.

On the other hand, if the CDP is aloof and acts as an important government officer, people will accept his/her status and access to important people. That is not where a CDP wants to be. It creates a lot of expectations and places the CDP in a formal position where compassion will be slightly out of place.

18.5.2 Getting to know the people

The contact-making phase is the ideal time for the CDP to get to know the people and their circumstances. He/she must get to know the environment and all the social groupings sharing the environment. He/she must therefore make a demographic and sociological study of the area. In Chapter 19 we discuss ways to do studies and surveys in a fashion that is well suited to the principles of community development.

The CDP must augment information gained locally with information stored in government and agency offices and especially with the large amount of information on the internet. A Google search often finds valuable background information. Statistical data, which may be difficult to compile, may be readily available in some government office, or on the internet. Information from government offices should, however, never replace the local survey completely, because, as we will see in Chapter 19, the local survey is much more than only gathering information.

This is the time to start identifying resources and obstacles to their use. Not only is the physical environment important but all the environments discussed in Chapter 2. The CDP must know and understand the possibilities and constraints of these environments.

During this stage, the CDP must make contact with formal and informal groupings. These groups, more than individuals, will be interested in the CDP's presence and they might also harbour some reservations about the envisaged task. The CDP must dispel their fears, but must also analyse them with a view to earmark one or more groupings as project action groups.

18.5.3 Analysing the needs

During the contact-making phase, a CDP cannot help but notice the people's needs. Through observation, through listening to what the people say and through some sort of survey, a fairly clear picture emerges. In the case of Ms Najafi, the picture emerged quite clearly. In her mind, a clinic was not primary, simply because she was not medically trained. Her heart was set on a school for girls. However, because she did not push her ideas and rather let the situation dictate, it became quite clear where the need lay and what the people thought of it. It is also possible that previous research identified needs. This then, is the time for the CDP to find out how the people perceive their needs.

It is also an important time to start changing any negative feelings the people may have about their circumstances and their capacity to do something about them. In other words, the CDP must suggest to them that they can do something to meet at least some of their needs. Identifying needs can be a very negative activity; it can even be hypochondriacal. In itself, there is nothing positive about needs identification. It is necessary, therefore, that people be led to understand that they should not accept their humiliation, but should start thinking positively of using their abilities to do something about their needs. We will come back to this aspect in Chapter 20. Community development cannot start until at least some people have a positive attitude. They may still have doubts, but they must be prepared to try to alleviate their own poverty. This has a lot to do with mobilisation and motivation, discussed in Chapter 13.

The needs that come to the fore, people's perception of them, and groups identifying themselves with the needs will give the CDP a clear indication of who is going to comprise the action group once a development project develops out of the contact-making phase. Either an existing group (an interest group or club) will identify a specific need as its main concern, or a number of individuals will voice their concern about a certain matter. In the former case, the interest group will become an action group for project purposes and in the latter case, the individuals and others influenced by them will form the action group. It can also happen that a large part of a community at a public or mass meeting identifies a need and decides to launch a project to address it. They may then select a project steering committee that will be the action group for their purposes.

If there is a need for childcare, the group that will concern itself with it will comprise mothers and care givers of small children, for example. A farming problem will be addressed by people concerned with farming, and an education problem will be investigated and tackled by parents of children of school-going age.

Yet, even if the need identification is done as described in this chapter, the CDP can experience difficulties. In Case study 10: *The project that had its fences brought down*, it is shown how a CDP can break down initiative among grassroots people, in this case because of the mindset of his organisation. Case study 25: *The smart community development worker* tells the story of a CDP who is unprepared and fails in his task to listen to the community.

18.6 CONCLUSION

As it has been described here, the contact-making phase is a natural progression from entry to project. Unfortunately, all too often a CDP will enter an area with express orders to get a specific project going in the shortest possible time. Such projects never become the property of the people. They are agency efforts and, if there is some participation, it is only by casual participants and, more often than not, 'free riders'. What has been described in this chapter is a process that evolves naturally. Case study 10: *The project that had its fences brought down* illustrates the wrong approach well. The contact-making phase is never a waste of time. Besides obtaining all the knowledge that must be acquired, it is a crucial relationship-building period. It is a time in which the people get to know the CDP for what he/she is: not a miracle worker, an enforcer of innovations, but a concerned person who wants to help. It is an important time to start breaking down the attitudinal constraints of feelings of inferiority, fear of the unknown and apathy. It is a time of team building; a team consisting of a group of concerned people and the CDP – a group of people with enough interest, concern and willingness to do something about their needs. During this phase, the stage is set for community development to proceed.

REFERENCES

Chambers R. 2007. *Poverty Research: Methodologies, Mindsets and Multi-dimensionality.* Working paper 293. Brighton: Institute of Development Studies.

King C. 1965. *Working with People in Community Action: An International Casebook for Trained Community Workers and Volunteer Community Leaders*. New York: Association Press.

Ledwith M. 2022. Storytelling praxis. In Ledwith M & Springett J (eds), *Participatory Practice: Community-based Action for Transformative Change*. Bristol: Policy Press.

McDermott R & Vossoughi S. 2020. The culture of poverty, again. *Diaspora, Indigenous, and Minority Education*, 14(2):60–69.

CHAPTER 19

Participatory Research Methodology

Frik de Beer and Andries de Beer

19.1 INTRODUCTION

A rapid overview of publications dealing with community-based participatory research reveals a great number of variations and names applied by different authors to this type of research. In this chapter, we discuss a qualitative method of research called participatory rapid appraisal and planning (PRAP).

Over the last two decades, the Western and non-Western world saw an increase in interest in participatory mapping approaches, which have been used in a variety of fields of research and practice (Brown, Reed & Raymond 2020). The method is characterised by Sandham, Chabalala and Spaling (2019:1) as 'a family of approaches and methods that enable rural people to share, enhance, and analyse their knowledge of life and conditions, plan, and act'. The method is characterised as qualitative because it is based on the perceptions, opinion and insight of people, and not on formulas, working with figures and counting (quantifying) items. It is also characterised by participation because there is not a researcher *vis-à-vis* respondents, but all participants are researchers and respondents at the same time. In section 19.4, we briefly explain our choice of PRAP.

PRAP can be used for most facets of community development research: identification of community needs, surveying of resources in a community, recording of a history, measuring perceptions, and so forth. It is also a useful tool to assess community development progress.

The purpose of this chapter is to provide an overview of the methodology and techniques associated with PRAP. The reader may use this information to apply and experiment with PRAP in community development. Please note, however, in community development we work with people. Their emotions, knowledge and humanity need to be respected at all times. So do not make guinea pigs of them, especially not without their knowledge and permission. The aim of doing social research, especially in and with a community, should be about creating a mutually respectful, win-win relationship in which participants are pleased to respond candidly, valid results are obtained, and the community considers the conclusions constructive (Mcauley 2003:95).

19.2 ETHICAL PRINCIPLES

When engaging the community in PRAP, the community development worker (CDP) should be guided by at least the following ethical principles:

- Obtain voluntary and informed consent (to be given by the research participant/community).
- Ensure anonymity and confidentiality of the participants and information shared.
- Ensure that the research will do no harm to participants.
- Remember that participants should be entitled to withdraw from the study at any time without repercussions.

19.2.1 Informed and voluntary consent

Before starting a study, a researcher (in this case the CDP) must obtain informed voluntary consent from members of the community. This means that the participants are given all the relevant information about the research. The researcher must ensure that the participant understands the purpose and possible risks/benefits of participation. The participant must be free to participate, decline or withdraw from the research at any stage.

19.2.2 Anonymity and confidentiality

During a study, members of the community may reveal sensitive information, which, if linked to them, could cause harm. The researcher must ensure that they are protected, data and information remain confidential, and anonymity is maintained. Confidentiality is defined as 'a researcher undertaking not to publicly link a specific response or behaviour with a particular research participant' (Du Plooy 2000:112).

19.2.3 Do no harm

Members of the community must be treated with respect and consideration. In a study, people may be exposed to physical danger, emotional discomfort, emotional stress, embarrassment or humiliation. Researchers should be particularly sensitive when working with children or disadvantaged and vulnerable people. Du Plooy (2000:109) recommends that researchers deal with the issue of 'doing no harm' by 'reviewing our perceptions, values and judgements as researchers – and ensuring that all these are open to public review'.

Participatory research always takes place with the wellbeing of the community as its goal. Therefore, we agree with White and Pettit (2004:23) when they state: '… the key issue in participatory research is not so much the techniques used as the way in which the research is conducted and the relationships established between researchers and research participants'.

19.2.4 Participants' entitlement to withdraw

Participants will receive all the necessary information along with a consent form. They will always have the option not to participate or to withdraw, since participation is on a voluntary basis.

19.3 IDENTIFYING COMMUNITY NEEDS

The following list of need identification dos and don'ts must be carefully considered by the CDP. We place it here because we will show that these dos and don'ts conform perfectly to PRAP.

The 'Do' list

Do move among the people; their needs will be identified and discussed naturally.
Do help the people to believe that they can do something about their needs.
Do show the people that you believe in their ability to do something about their needs.

The 'Don't' list

Don't call a public meeting when you enter an area to do a needs identification exercise.
Don't ask the people what their needs are.
Don't tell the people what their needs are.
Don't take the lead in the identification of needs.
Don't regard your perception of needs as more important than theirs.

Having identified the needs of the people means that the CDP fulfils his/her role as a development generalist – but it does not mean it is his/her job to address all the needs. It does mean, however, that he/she must use the information to bring the community into contact with people who have the relevant knowledge and interest to address the need. For instance, if a need for a food garden is expressed by the community, the role of the CDP should be to bring the community in contact with the agricultural extension officer responsible for the area. An official from the education department should be brought into contact with the community in the case of a need related to skills development and education. The CDP can therefore act as broker in certain situations.

To return to PRAP, there are participatory tools that can be utilised to gain a better understanding of the community, determine and assess needs and plan, with community participation, development projects relevant to their needs. In the social sciences, new concepts and methodologies are continually created. The methodology discussed here is PRAP (Selener, Endara & Carvajalet 1999; Haldane, Chuah, Srivastava et al 2019).

The origin of this methodology can be traced to academic disciplines such as anthropology, development studies and agricultural extension. It is closely related to development approaches such as the basic needs approach and community development, with its added permutations of participatory development, adaptive administration and empowerment. According to De Beer and Swanepoel (1998:27), empowerment takes place in a milieu that emphasises 'community knowledge, resources, self-reliance, initiative and decision making'.

The research techniques utilised clearly qualify PRAP as qualitative methodology using action research techniques. PRAP evolved from the earlier rapid rural appraisal (RRA) and its successor, rapid and participatory rural appraisal (RPRA) (Chambers 1992:6 et seq). Bhatia (1995) refers to empowering rural appraisal. Participatory learning and action (PLA) is one of the more recently evolved interpretations within the broader 'participatory research' school of thought. It is said that: 'PRA (participatory rural appraisal) and the more inclusive PLA (participatory learning and action) are families of participatory methodologies which have evolved as behaviours and attitudes, methods, and practices of sharing' (Chambers 2007:03). The ultimate form of participation in PLA is self-mobilisation, where people take the initiative to change systems, independently of outside agencies (Pretty, Guijt, Thompson & Scoones 1995:61).

19.4 PRINCIPLES AND CHARACTERISTICS OF PRAP

To summarise, this 'basket' of related and overlapping approaches consists of the following:
- Rapid rural appraisal (RRA)
- Participatory rural appraisal (PRA)
- Participatory learning and action (PLA)
- Participatory rural appraisal and planning (PRAP).

From all the permutations, it becomes clear that these approaches (hereafter referred to as PRAP) are aimed at participation by the 'target group' in the action and appraisal, where learning and planning around the development issue should be a result of the process. The approach allows outsiders to learn from the people and make use of indigenous technical knowledge.

Chambers (1992:7) identifies the following principles of RRA:
- *Optimising trade-offs*: This principle has a dual meaning: that of optimal ignorance (knowing what is not worth knowing) and appropriate imprecision (not measuring more precisely than is needed).
- *Offsetting biases*: By being relaxed and not rushing, listening not lecturing, being unimposing and by learning about the concerns and priorities of the poorer people, biases are neutralised.

- *Learning from and with rural people:* Having first-hand access to technical, physical and social knowledge of a community will give a clear insight into local perceptions.
- *Learning rapidly and progressively:* This means not following a blueprint programme but rather a learning and adaptive approach.
- *Triangulation:* This means verifying data by cross-checking.
- *Planning with the people:* The advantages of community participation are many, among them strengthened collaboration with outside agencies and an affirmation of community ownership of a project.

While participatory approaches to development and research hold much promise, and are supported by us, we should be aware that the approach is not above critique and questioning. One important debate is whether participatory approaches are, or should be, a means to an end (a successful project), or whether participation be regarded as an end in itself. Put differently: is participation supported in order to get the job done, or is it acceptable that people participate regardless of the success of a project? An interesting discussion of this debate is provided by Hayward, Simpson & Wood (2004). To us, participation is a means toward promoting a learning process. Consequently, if participation contributes to the successful completion of a project, learning has also been achieved. However, should the project not come to a successful end, the learning that took place is still beneficial to the participants.

19.4.1 Advantages of PRAP

Selener et al (1999:4–5) identify the following 12 advantages of PRAP:

1. *Community mobilisation:* This empowers communities to solve those problems identified by them.
2. *Use of visual techniques:* The techniques used assist in information gathering in a way that activates and gives control to the community.
3. *Participatory community analysis:* This includes identifying problems and potential solutions.
4. *Promoting grassroots development:* This would ensure that development takes place among the neediest.
5. *Strengthening collaboration between the community and external organisations:* The resultant strategic partnerships contribute to sustained problem solving and community ownership of the project.

6. *Realistic proposals:* The formulation of realistic proposals must be allowed for.
7. *Promoting integration:* Diverse groups, including women and children, become part of the process.
8. *Speed and low cost:* Once the initial contact has been made with the local power structures and their cooperation ensured, the fieldwork can be done in three to four days per group, with insignificant resources. Prior training of the facilitator-researcher is probably the most expensive part of the exercise.
9. *CDPs 'waking up' to a new reality:* First-hand, community-based information is gathered that reduces the risk of 'desk-based' designs and increases the workability of the designed project.
10. *Control over project definition:* The community has control over project definition and this contributes to community ownership of the project.
11. *First-hand information:* Since it is carried out in and with the community, it is based on first-hand information.
12. *A systemisation process:* The collective memory and oral tradition of the community is used as source of information that can be systemised for future reference.

19.5 SOME PRAP TECHNIQUES

Selecting the most appropriate techniques from a long list is perhaps a bigger problem than applying the technique. Chambers (1992:8) identifies the following techniques:
- Direct observation
- Secondary data review
- Transect and group walks
- Do-it-yourselves
- Key informants
- Semi-structured interviews
- Group interviews and discussions
- Chains (sequences) of interviews
- Key indicators

- Workshops and brainstorming
- Sketch mapping
- Aerial photographs
- Diagramming
- Wealth ranking
- Other ranking and scoring
- Measurement and quantification
- Ethno-histories and trend analysis
- Time lines (chronologies of events)
- Stories, portraits and case studies
- Team management and interactions
- Key probes
- Calendaring
- Short, simple questionnaires
- Rapid report writing in the field.

The list above is not exhaustive, but gives an indication of techniques that can be used. In the next few sections, we discuss some of the techniques we have found most useful in doing PRAP. When using these techniques, we should be prepared and certain of what we want to know, which technique will bring the best results and how to record information. In direct observation, for instance, we will use a diary or make a summary for later use. With transect walks, participants must note or report and this information needs to be discussed to make sure that all understand what is meant. CDPs may also need to make notes for their own use and to remind the group later of its findings. The important thing to remember is to keep notes or summaries of information obtained, or the exercise will be futile. The discussion below is based on Chambers (1997:187–190) and Chambers (2004:1–13).

19.5.1 Secondary data review

Published and unpublished material, maps and aerial photographs give an overview of an area or community. Before entering a community or starting a PRAP exercise, a secondary data review should be conducted. While secondary analysis is adaptable and can be used in a variety of ways, it is also an empirical exercise and a method with procedural and evaluative steps, much like collecting and analysing primary data (Johnston 2014:1). This will help the CDP to become familiar with the community. It can also be done as part of PRAP and then it will not be an activity of the CDP alone and will include also discussing and interpreting.

19.5.2 Direct observation

This entails personal visits over time to areas to observe and identify dynamics and changes in the community. An observation checklist is a useful tool to keep track of observations. Direct observation is useful in getting to know the community and for the community to get to know the CDP (see Chapter 18). Observation over time also helps to turn around the snapshot effect of a single observation act. The primary goal of observation is to discover what people do; that is, this method of data collection focuses on the actions of participants in a specific setting. This also implies that observation is only an appropriate data collection method when there is something to observe: the actions or behaviours to be observed must be obvious (Denscombe 2003).

19.5.3 Transect and group walks

Walking through an area with local people frequently reveals resources and problems in an area. A transect walk in PRAP is typically led by a mix of locals and visiting professionals. It provides an opportunity for first-hand observation of the micro-environment. It means meeting people, listening, asking, discovering and identifying problems, resources, dynamics and many other issues. Participating community members are important in this exercise because this gives them an opportunity to reveal local knowledge. Transect walks can also be undertaken to verify information on a map or model. Apart from its verifying function, it can also be used as an assessment tool to observe changes in infrastructure and changes in life patterns.

19.5.4 Venn diagrams

A Venn diagram is useful to classify various objects into categories. It can be used to compare two or more objects or to identify and show links between a number of objects, for example stakeholders can be identified and their links to each other and/or the community can be visibly illustrated. This helps to form a picture of who is involved and how they relate to one another in a community.

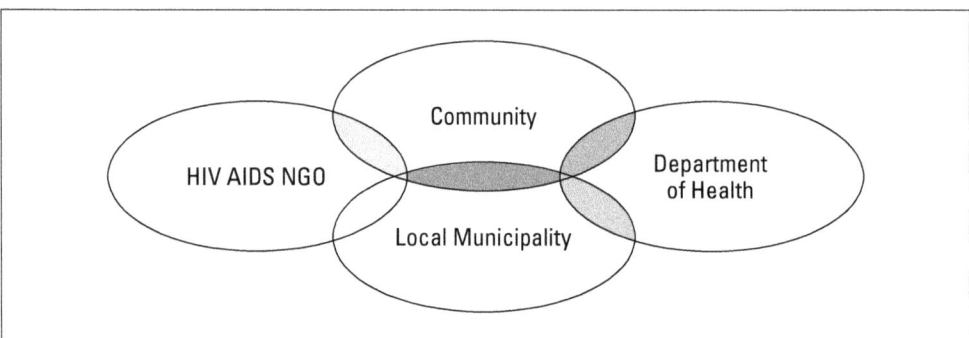

Figure 19.1 **Example of a Venn diagram**

19.5.5 Semi-structured interviews

A semi-structured interview is conducted with the aid of checklists but not a formal survey questionnaire. It is an open-ended technique which allows for probing and for participants to provide relevant information voluntarily. Interviews should be conducted with those key informants identified by earlier research.

19.5.6 Group interviews and discussions

These may be casual, taking place in the work place or a shebeen, or they may be structured to allow representations from concerned stakeholders. While group interviews and discussions should be conducted in an informal and relaxed manner, they should also be structured in some way. A checklist is a useful tool in doing this exercise. The group doing the research will often change hats and become the respondents in a group session where they will discuss what they have gleaned and try to make sense of it. The 'threat' of exposure can very easily be mitigated by the use of techniques such as the nominal group technique and brainstorming.

19.5.7 Sketch mapping

Maps are based on local observation and knowledge. They can be used to reveal physical as well as social information. It therefore provides a 'spatial visualisation and recording of the social, economic and natural dynamics of a given territory' (Di Gessa 2008:13). In a land claims project in North-West Province, South Africa, in which the authors of this book were involved, the community used mapping first to identify resources on the land. Once this exercise was completed, they did mapping to plan future use and development of the land. Eventually, through these processes, the participants gave life to the image so that it could become the basis of the community development project emanating from this exercise.

19.5.8 Time lines (chronologies of events)

A time line records the sequence in which history played out in a community. Remembered history provides 'anchors' to recall events. For example: the drought was just before the release of Mr Mandela; the chief got married a week after the train crash between Johannesburg and Durban. By using a time line with 'big' national or international events as anchors, histories and events in communities can be reconstructed.

19.5.9 Stories, portraits and case studies

In communities with a strong oral tradition, stories and case studies can reveal much about their history, practices and dynamics. Likewise, portraits or sketches bring out information that may otherwise not be revealed. Stories and case studies uncover histories of a family, crises in farming, environmental impacts and issues such as drought, and many other relevant themes. The application of stories, portraits and case studies will be further discussed in the workbook.

19.5.10 Seasonal calendars

Compiled by major season or by month, the seasonal calendar is used to show seasonal changes such as days and distribution of rain, food consumption, types of sickness and prices, income and expenditure; these are useful records for planning agricultural projects. Just think how long traditional research can take to obtain this information and how arduous a task it is. The information gleaned in this PRAP method may not be that accurate, but it is reliable and shows trends so that we can make our own judgement.

In Table 19.1, an indication is given in the first column of some of the types of information that will be gathered. In the second column, some of the techniques to be utilised are indicated, and the third column shows some of the results to be obtained.

Table 19.1 Types of information and techniques to be used with PRAP

TYPES OF INFORMATION	TECHNIQUES	PRODUCTS
General background of the community	Brainstorming in groups Observation Interviews	Matrix of basic characteristics
Spatial information	Mapping	Community map (a graphical representation of the community)
Time – history and trends	Time line Ethno-history Trend analysis	Community history (a chronological description of important events in the history of the community)
Socio-economic data	Venn diagram Trend diagram Income and expenditure matrix Migration diagram Ranking	Institutional relationships in the community Trend analysis (eg malaria-related illness over time) Types of livelihood, income generating activities and expenditure Impact of migration on community Identification of levels of wellbeing in the families
Production and technical information	Transects Flow diagram (of production system) Farming calendar	Information on the resources and technical aspects in the community
Identification of problems and solutions	Preference matrixes Problem trees Ranking	A list and description of issues of importance to the community
Project planning	SWOT analysis Programming matrix	Identification of strengths, weaknesses, opportunities and threats of proposed solutions Design of the project

19.6 APPLICATION OF PRAP

Action research through methods such as PRAP is used in various types of projects. In southern Botswana, the Kuru Development Trust uses this approach to establish a rural micro-finance scheme under the participant San communities (Dekker personal communication 2008). Lightfoot, Prein & Lopez (1994:22) write about 'dramatic results' achieved in a rural biological resource recycling exercise in the Philippines. In a Ugandan primary healthcare project, the utilisation of PRA resulted in, among other positive lessons, '... the local people (being) ... capable of assessing their own situation and mapping out strategies for improvement' (Osuga & Mutayisa 1995). The importance of action research such as PRAP is illustrated by a case study from Somalia. Research was undertaken into the reasons for the failure of an immunisation programme aimed at infants. One of the findings of the research was that no effort was made throughout the implementation of the programme to assess community needs or attitudes towards immunisation. The community had participated in the programme '... as the "object" rather than the "subject" of development efforts' (La Fond 1992:22–26).

Many other documented case studies can be quoted. The point is that, where sustained empowering development is the objective, PRAP has a proven record over many years in various types of projects. What remains for implementing agencies to make the approach succeed, is to demonstrate a willingness to accept the integrity of this approach and devote time and energy to its implementation.

19.7 SOME PROBLEMS WITH AND LIMITATIONS OF PRAP

In the PRAP process, the role of the implementing agency or the researcher should be: '... that of catalyst for social change as well as co-learner with the people. He or she does not pretend to be detached, as does the traditional researcher, in the name of objectivity and neutrality' (Selener 1997:12).

This very noble view on the role of the 'outsider' using action research such as PRAP is, however, difficult to attain. Development agencies have to deliver, and spend donor money according to agreed programmes so that new donor funds can be applied for. They have their mandate to which their constituency holds them accountable. In this situation it is hard to avoid agency-led development projects (Van Diessen 1998:46–47).

The client – a community where PRAP is applied – is usually caught in the deprivation trap characterised by poverty, powerlessness (including illiteracy), vulnerability, isolation and physical weakness (see Chapter 1). The implementing agency, on the other hand, is a government department, an NGO or private consultancy that has a political mandate and responsibility, is donor-dependent or pursues profit. All these agencies are to some extent task oriented and need to achieve certain benchmarks in pursuit of their goals. The implementing agencies make use of professionals and therefore presume superior knowledge and/or insight.

If the management and staff of implementing agencies are not aware of the difficulties inherent in bridging the gap between these two worlds, and actively pursue solutions to it, the following limitations to PRAP will soon become apparent and may mean the termination of a project. In Table 19.2, the limitations are indicated as well as the remedies that may be followed in a project. The limitations are listed by Selener et al (1999:6–7).

Table 19.2 **Limitations of PRAP and associated remedies**

LIMITATIONS	REMEDIES
Raising false expectations in communities, especially concerning financial aid.	Be open with the power structures and community members from the outset on the aims and limitations of the implementing agency.
Correct identification of problems and the design of feasible solutions do not automatically guarantee successful action.	The implementing agency must provide dedicated and well-trained staff that can provide the motivation through proper communication with participants.
Some information gained can be superficial and even false.	A variety of PRAP techniques must be used in order to validate information. Prior knowledge can also be used as a benchmark.
The speed of the PRAP process may leave insufficient time for establishing the necessary trust between the facilitator–researcher and the community.	Openness and honesty from the implementing agency generating goodwill and political commitment from the power structures must be aimed at from the start.
Individual interpretations and analysis may be lost during group discussions.	A selected number of open-ended interviews with key members of the community will overcome this limitation.
Lack of experience by the facilitator–researcher may result in him/her doing the PRAP for, and not with, the group.	Staff with the correct empathetic attitude and intensive training should be selected.
Very little experience exists in replicating the success achieved at community level at regional and provincial level.	There should be phased implementation, starting with a pilot project.
Language and cultural differences can result in communication problems.	Facilitators will be from the area, understanding the language and culture. Trainers of the facilitators will include individuals with knowledge of local language and culture.

LIMITATIONS	REMEDIES
Speed of the process can affect the quality of participation and inputs from the community.	Qualified and experienced facilitators will know when to halt the process and review proceedings to catch up any 'losses' in quality.
Some communities are simply not interested or have other more pressing issues to address.	The 'target' communities have something to gain from success. This will be communicated to them in clear terms.
An 'outsider' (agency or person) may 'steal' the information and use it for their benefit (eg for writing a thesis).	The implementing agency must make a specific decision on this issue and negotiate the need for further use of the information with the power structures.
Uneven representation or lack of representation of some groups in the community may occur.	The facilitator will actively endeavour to include all identified groups.
Using several methods of analysis or indicators may confuse the understanding by community members of the issues at stake.	The issues are clearly focused and should not contribute to misunderstanding. The facilitator will be sensitive to the group's reaction and 'body language'.

It is clear from this list that many of the limitations are true for all or most research methodologies, including those originating in a more traditional school. PRAP's limitations, therefore, do not put it in a bad position *vis-à-vis* these more traditional methods.

19.8 CONCLUSION

The objective of PRAP is to gather field data in a simple yet reliable manner and to analyse it by using local indigenous knowledge and perceptions of reality. However, it goes a big step further in that it wants to start something, it has a mobilising effect and it leads to further action. This fits in perfectly with our own idea of a contact-making period during which the CDP and the community get to know one another and identify the community needs. PRAP is part of the contact-making phase. The decision to launch a project is a natural outflow of what has been learnt through PRAP methodology. See Chapter 18 for detail on contact making. See also Chapter 22 on evaluation using PRAP principles.

REFERENCES

Bhatia A. 1995. Challenging the new professionals. Moving from participatory rural appraisal to empowering rural appraisal. Nepal Participatory Action Network Workshop. Dhulikhel, 20–22 January 1995.

Brown G, Reed P & Raymond CM. 2020. Mapping place values: 10 lessons from two decades of public participation GIS empirical research. *Applied Geography*, 116: 102156. doi: 10.1016/j.apgeog.2020.102156

Chambers R. 1992. Rapid and participatory rural appraisal. *Africanus*, 22(1&2):6–15.

Chambers R. 1997. Shortcut and participatory methods for gaining social information for projects. In Sepulveda S & Edwards R (eds), *Sustainable Development, Social Organization, Institutional Arrangements and Rural Development: Selected Readings*. San José, CA: Inter American Institute for Cooperation on Agriculture.

Chambers R. 2004. Notes for participants in PRA-PLA familiarisation workshops in 2004. Participation group. Brighton: Institute of Development Studies.

Chambers R. 2007. *From PRA to PLA and Pluralism: Practice and Theory*. Working paper 286. IDS: Brighton.

De Beer FC & Swanepoel HJ. 1998. *Community Development and Beyond. Issues, Structures and Procedures*. Pretoria: Van Schaik.

Denscombe M. 2003. *Observation*. In *The Good Research Guide for Small-scale Social Research Projects*. Philadelphia, PA: Open University Press, pp 192–212.

Di Gessa S. 2008. *Participatory Mapping as a Tool for Empowerment: Experiences and Lessons Learned from the ILC Network*. Rome: International Land Coalition.

Du Plooy T. 2000. Ethics in research. In *Research in the Social Sciences: Only Study Guide for RSC201H*. Pretoria: University of South Africa.

Haldane V, Chuah FLH, Srivastava A, Singh SR, Gerald C, Koh H, Seng CK & Legido-Quigley H. 2019. Community participation in health services development, implementation, and evaluation: A systematic review of empowerment, health, community, and process outcomes. Available at: https://journals.plos.org/plosone/article?id=10.1371/journal.pone.0216112 (accessed 17 May 2023).

Hayward C, Simpson L & Wood L. 2004. Still left out in the cold: Problematising participatory research and development. *Sociologia Ruralis*, 44(1):95–108.

Johnston MP. 2014. Secondary data analysis: A method of which the time has come. *Qualitative and Quantitative Methods in Libraries*, 3(3).

La Fond AK. 1992. Qualitative methods for assessing the acceptability of immunization in Somalia. *RRA Notes*, 16:22–26.

Lightfoot C, Prein M & Lopez T. 1994. Bioresource flow modelling with farmers. *ILEIA Newsletter*, 10.3, Oct 1994. Available at: http://www.agriculturesnetwork.org/magazines/global/wastes-wanted/bioresource-flow-modelling-with-farmers (accessed 2 March 2016).

Mcauley C. 2003. Ethics. In Miller RL & Brewer JD (eds), *The A–Z of Social Research*. London: Sage.

Osuga B & Mutayisa D. 1995. Use of PRA in programme reviews and evaluations: Key strengths, weaknesses and lessons. Unpublished paper.

Pretty JN, Guijt I, Thompson J & Scoones I. 1995. *A Trainer's Guide for Participatory Learning and Action*. London: IIED.

Sandham LA, Chabalala JJ & Spaling HH. 2019. *Participatory Rural Appraisal Approaches for Public Participation in EIA: Lessons from South Africa*. Basel, Switzerland: Multidisciplinary Digital Publishing Institute (MDPI).

Selener D. 1997. *Participatory Action Research and Social Change*. New York: Cornell University Press.

Selener D, Endara N & Carvajal J. 1999. *Participatory Rural Appraisal and Planning Workbook*. Quito: International Institute of Rural Reconstruction.

Van Diessen A. 1998. Keeping hold of the stick and handing over the carrot: Dilemmas arising when agencies use PRA. In Boog B, Coenen H, Keune L & Lammerts R (eds), *The Complexity of Relationships in Action Research*. Tilburg: Tilburg University Press.

White S & Pettit J. 2004. *Participatory Approaches and the Measurement of Human Well-being*. WeD Working Paper 08. Wellbeing in Developing Countries ESRC Research Group (WeD). Bath: University of Bath.

Personal communication

Dekker, R. 2008. Personal interview. 14 March, Pretoria.

CHAPTER 20

The Start of a Project

Frik de Beer

20.1 INTRODUCTION

All community development projects are built around resources and needs. The starting point of any project is therefore a resource or a need.

A community development project can be approached from a 'problem solving' or an 'asset building' angle. In the past, much emphasis was placed on identifying problems in communities and solving them. As a corrective to this somewhat negative approach (as we warn against elsewhere in this book), an asset-based approach emerged. The asset-based approach to community development (ABCD) wants to focus on what communities have, instead of what they need. The idea is to build from within, focusing less on what can be added from outside. According to Harrison, Blickem, Lamb, Kirk & Vassilev (2019:8), communities can 'start defining themselves differently, that is, what they are good at, what are their talents and skills, and so forth focussing on their assets'. An asset according to this approach is not only physical objects or money but also includes 'personal attributes and skills [and] … the relationships among people through social, kinship, or associational networks' (Mathie & Cunningham 2003:5).

ABCD is, according to Mathie and Cunningham (2003:6), 'a strategy for sustainable community-driven development – Beyond the mobilization of a particular community, ABCD is concerned with how to link micro-assets to the macro environment'.

We agree in general with the sentiment to identify what people have and build upon it, rather than focusing on what they do not have and try to supply it. Yet it is important to distinguish between resources and assets in a community. A resource is something that can be used to create an asset. Human resources, capital and infrastructure, land and entrepreneurship (or business and organisational skills) are resources. All communities possess some or all of these in varying degrees. Below we identify and list potential resources in communities.

Turning resources into assets – something that will produce a benefit of some kind (social relations, income, better services) – is what asset-based community development is about. According to the Cambridge Dictionary (2023), a resource is 'a useful or valuable possession or quality of a country, organization, or person'. In an economic sense, an asset is a resource controlled by a person or group (an entity) 'from which future economic benefits are expected to flow to the entity' (Advisory Expert Group 2006). Another view on an asset is to define it as an economic resource that 'has the ability to generate favourable cash flows to the entity' (International Accounting Standards Board 2014:23).

In communities we also find social and other resources that may generate favourable social and other gains. A stokvel, for instance, is a social grouping that represents some of the characteristics of a resource (see section 3.2 in Chapter 3). Using this social resource can lead to the development of an economic asset (a savings club, for instance) or may have a demonstration effect for others in the community to follow and become organised in a similar way (a social asset). A resource thus holds potential to become an asset to the community and to individuals.

20.2 RESOURCE IDENTIFICATION

Resource identification takes place before a project is started. It should be part of the PRAP exercise so that needs and objectives will be handled in terms of the available resources (see Chapter 19). A PRAP exercise, or any survey for that matter, should not only concentrate on the negative, on the needs and problems, but should have a positive side. The identification of resources will adequately fill this positive side. Because the identification of resources is a positive step, it influences people positively. If we define available resources in terms of the needs, those resources point to an outcome, a solution. Resource identification encourages people to pay attention to their objective and, by doing so, lays the foundations for a community development project.

No community development project can function without resources. It is ironic that the need addressed by a project is invariably the lack of some resource, but we must be careful not to see a poor community as without resources. However poor the people may be, they are never entirely without resources. There is a tendency to look for resources outside the community. People are very much aware of their needs and they can identify many when they are asked to do so. Yet, when asked to identify their resources, they find it difficult to identify more than a handful. We can also argue that it is terrible to use the few resources people have while there are abundant resources outside the community. Should we not use the abundant resources rather than the meagre ones? It is easy to sympathise with these views. The community resources are in any case seldom enough to run projects.

The big problem with external resources is that they usually come with strings attached. Donors of resources may have their own agenda and their own reasons for funding development. They may attach provisos to the use of their resources that are not in line with the principles that we discussed in Chapter 6. The dependency of communities on these external donors may also increase, which will work against their obtaining self-reliance and accepting ownership of projects. People can be manipulated by resource grants. They can be made to do things they do not want to do, or do not usually do. Donor dependency can be as bad as the deprivation trap and it can keep people in perpetual bondage. When decisions must be made regarding the use of resources, the community development practitioners (CDPs), their organisations and all levels of government service should keep this danger in mind.

20.3 TYPES OF RESOURCES

There are four types of resources of importance for community development projects: natural resources, manufactured resources, human resources and organisational (entrepreneurial) resources.

20.3.1 Natural resources

Natural resources are those provided by Mother Nature, such as water, a temperate climate, good soil, rainfall, vegetation such as trees, and minerals. These natural resources are especially important in rural areas. Harsh climates, low rainfall and poor soil types are serious obstacles to development.

Natural resources must usually be shared with other communities and with future generations. For example, a river that flows through a community is a natural resource and may be used by that community, but without unnecessarily depleting it and polluting it because it also flows through other communities who also have the right to use it. We also share natural resources with people still to be born. Many of the natural resources, such as water and vegetation, are finite and must be used responsibly and very carefully so that future generations can also use them.

A community development project that leads to the abuse of natural resources is a worse than futile exercise. Development cannot be sustained if a project harms the environment. It can bring short-term relief and long-term damage. The long-term disadvantages of such 'developments' are usually permanent and make nonsense of any short-term benefits. People and their environment are integrated, and harm to the one means harm to the other. Instead of abusing the environment, community development projects must enhance natural resources. In order to do this, CDPs should make use of expert advice. Using expert advice also enhances the learning process of the community and the CDP. CDPs may think that a proposed project will not harm the environment, but may be unaware of indirect or covert results that may be harmful to nature. CDPs cannot be too sensitive about this and must guard against good intentions leading to environmental degradation or even disaster.

20.3.2 Manufactured resources

Manufactured resources are all those that are artificially made and include roads, water reticulation, communication networks, shops, markets, electricity, buildings and sanitary systems. These are collectively called infrastructure and projects are dependent on at least some of them, but may also develop or improve them.

The existence of infrastructure does not necessarily mean that it is available and that it can be used for community development. Various questions must first be asked because the use of infrastructure is usually accompanied by some provisions. These questions are, among others, as follows:

- For whom are the resources open?
- How must the resources be shared?
- What will they cost?
- Who has authority over them?

CDPs must seek answers to these and other questions regarding the use of infrastructure. It is important to establish who manages and maintains a certain infrastructural item. It is also important to know whose permission must be sought for the use of infrastructure. In this instance, a bit of bargaining may be called for because special cases can be made out for community development projects so that infrastructure can be used at lower cost or even free of charge.

One of the most important manufactured resources is money. All community development projects need money. The community, even with poverty prevalent, will generate some of the necessary funds for a project internally, but only if they think that it will be worthwhile and not too risky. However, most of the money will have to come from outside the community. It is very important that the action group know the conditions under which they receive money for a project:

- Is it a loan or a grant?
- If it is a loan, what are the conditions for the repayment of the loan?
- Does the donor want some decision-making powers concerning the project?
- Does the donor know what community development is?
- Is it a once-off donation or is it a long-term financing of the project until completion?
- Will the action group be able to meet the terms of the financing?

Action groups are frail and vulnerable entities comprising poor people who must be assisted so that they do not fall prey to donors with ulterior motives or hidden agendas. On the other hand, action groups must also know what their obligations will be and what responsibility they must bear. They need to know the consequences if they commit themselves to a financial deal. They cannot make sound financial decisions if they do not have all the relevant and necessary information.

20.3.3 Human resources

We quite often regard people as the reason for certain needs. We see them as part of the problem and from there it is easy to treat them as if they are the problem. People become the beneficiaries of development efforts. External agencies start projects and the people who are the beneficiaries are supposed to be grateful. Because they are part of the problem and because they are the target, the people have no say in the matter of their development. If they are involved, it is usually to fulfil soft options, such as providing developers with wish lists and doing some manual work sometimes required in projects. The fact that people are also a vital resource is completely obscured. The fact that people can and should be a part of the solution is overlooked. Human faculties are important resources, and most people are potential contributors to development. It is therefore fitting to be reminded of the definition by Swanson (2022:4): 'Human resource development is a process of developing and unleashing expertise to improve individual, team, work process, and organizational system performance'.

Human skills are extremely important resources. In poor communities, there are always people who mastered a skill when they were employed. They may be out of work and not practising their skills, but they still retain knowledge about them and can easily take up such a skill. They represent a resource that 'provides an opportunity for organizations ... to enhance the potential capabilities of natural resources' (Yuesti & Sumantra 2017:96).

To make better resources of people, in other words to make assets out of them, is one of the objectives of community development. Community development is a learning process and far-from-perfect human resources will become better equipped if they are part of the process. The CDP must assist people to become better human resources by providing learning opportunities in the normal process of development projects. The road to self-reliance and self-sufficiency is the same as the road along which people become increasingly better human resources.

We tend to think that human resource development belongs to formal education and training. Education and training help in the process but are not the only means of developing human resources. Reflection, debate, decision making, experimental implementation and evaluation – all ingredients of the community development project – are part of resource development.

We can also regard norms and traditions as human resources. Again, we are more likely to see them as obstacles to development (which is quite often the case), but there are norms and traditions that can be used to tackle the poverty situation. Norms and traditions can bring stability and harmony, but may also pose stumbling blocks. As a positive influence, they may be very valuable in a project by, for instance, strengthening discipline; on the negative side, they may block the development necessary for people's health and safety.

Whether norms and traditions are a resource or an obstacle depends, to a large extent, on how they are handled. The CDP must handle norms and traditions carefully. If people see a CDP as someone with little respect for their norms and traditions, they will seldom accept such a person's bona fides. The situation of the poor is often so bad that their norms and traditions are the only guardians of their remaining dignity. To treat their norms and traditions with disrespect is to treat the poor as badly.

20.3.4 Organisational (entrepreneurial) resources

No resource is of use if organisational resources are absent. That is why this fourth type of resource is so important. The societal structures and external structures influencing a society are very important organisational resources. They make the use of all other resources possible. The ability to organise is an inherent part of the human species. Even the most unsophisticated and isolated society uses its people's organisational ability to structure its existence. This extraordinary resource must be identified and used. It must also be developed because it is a resource that cannot be depleted through use. In fact, the more it is used, the better it becomes.

Interest groups that are community-based organisations (CBOs) are important organisational resources. Because we easily overlook them, they warrant specific mention. Every community has several interest groups; in fact, often they have a great number of such CBOs. Every community has its burial associations, stokvels, ratepayers' societies, women's clubs, youth clubs and sports clubs. These are all valuable organisational resources. Normally, they are fairly well organised with clear membership and leadership structures. Members of an interest group with some experience can form an action group for project purposes. We could therefore find a group of young people, all belonging to the same youth club, forming an action group to pursue a specific objective or address a specific need.

Not surprisingly, Matsela (2015:8) states that '[w]ith their vigour and vibrancy, young people are a good resource base'. However, the presence of organisations and participation by the youth require training and continuous incentives to remain focused. We must be careful not to overlook the fact that when interest groups feel a project to be prejudicial to their interests, or if they foresee a project's spin-offs affecting them negatively, they can become huge obstacles in the project's path.

20.4 CONSENSUS ON NEEDS

A need is not an unspoken wish or a vague feeling of discomfort. A need is much more concrete, more definable; otherwise, a project could never be well planned. The people know their needs, but a project cannot address all or many of the people's needs at the same time. A project can only tackle one need at a time. A project will therefore evolve out of a problem, need or concern of a specific group of people. A project can only address a need if that need is properly identified, and if the people participating in the project can reach consensus on the definition of the need they are trying to address.

We saw in Chapter 18 that needs identification starts informally during the contact-making phase. We can therefore say that needs identification undergoes an informal phase during contact making and a more formal phase when a project is instituted. In fact, we can say that there must be an informal phase for the formal phase to develop naturally. PRAP lies between these two phases and is therefore a link or bridge from the informal to the formal (see Chapter 19). It is difficult to describe PRAP as either informal or formal. We must admit that there is something of both present. It may start more informally when discussions and brainstorms are held around the situation in which the participants find themselves. It becomes more formal when those discussions are followed by PRAP methodologies for learning more about the situation such as transects, calendaring and ranking (see Table 19.1 for examples of the application of these techniques). The informal phase of needs identification should be naturally followed by a more formal process according to PRAP principles and methodologies, to complete needs identification before a project starts. By then the need will be quite obvious. Formal meetings to launch a project will then be more concerned with need formulation and not need identification.

During contact making, the CDP may realise that different groups of people are concerned about different needs or they may have different perceptions about the same need. It is quite obvious that not all people will agree on needs. It is natural that different groups of people will identify different needs for attention. A group of mothers of small children, a group of maize farmers and a group of pensioners will differ in what they regard as urgent needs. When CDPs realise the existence of these different groups with different needs, they have taken the first step in establishing different action groups capable of launching different projects catering to their different and peculiar needs. In this regard, the only limitation is the capacity of the CDP who can facilitate only so many projects.

It is something else when people have different perceptions of the same need. It is obvious that conflicting views must be ironed out through informal and formal discussion before a project can be launched. The important thing is that the people comprising an action group charged to address a need within a project must enjoy full consensus on the definition of the need.

It is also important that a project is limited to a single need, especially if the action group and the CDP are unsure of themselves, or have a small base of skills or other capacities and capabilities. There is nothing wrong with admitting that there are several needs and to identify them. They must then be ranked in order of priority according to urgency or do-ability, or whatever other criterion is chosen so that they can be tackled one at a time.

A public discussion of needs is fraught with danger because the outcome cannot be anticipated. We have already seen in the chapters on contact making (Chapter 18) and PRAP (Chapter 19) what the proper way is to identify needs. It is most definitely not through a public meeting. We have established that needs identification should begin as an informal discussion progressing naturally to a more formal stage in which PRAP methodologies are followed. When this stage is reached, the participants will not be the public at large, but the people who have identified themselves with the specific concern; the action group in the making. The need will then not require formal identification. It will require formulation to bring more clarity to issues relevant to it, in other words, to contextualise the problem or need.

20.5 FORMULATING NEEDS

People often need assistance in formulating their felt needs correctly. A vaguely felt or broadly described or obscure need cannot successfully be tackled through a project. Obscurity is quite often the problem in coming to terms with the need. We need to clarify the issue and for that a causality and linkage exercise might prove to be valuable. It will help to streamline perceptions and it will put the needs in proper context so that a general understanding of the situation and milieu can be developed.

A causality and linkage exercise can be done with the help of a spider diagram, also known as a tree diagram. The best way of doing it is on a blackboard or flip chart where all present can concentrate on the same thing and experience the same visual effect. A causality and linkage exercise establishes the causes and the results of a felt need. It also establishes the linkages that exist between causes and results.

A causality and linkage exercise is not meant to identify a need. In logical framework exercises, we can start with problem areas and decide what the desired outcome should be if something is done about the problem areas. Between the problem area and the desired outcome, a logical sequence must be sought and on this logical linkage a subject or need can then be identified as focus for a project. However, it is not something that will ensure success in the fluid and unsure situation of the poverty context. It is thus much better to start with an identified need that can be more clearly formulated through such an exercise.

In Figure 20.1, the need is formulated as the root problem. Several causes of the problem are indicated in the branches of the tree. By discussing the causes, members of the group go deeper to identify the causes behind each cause – the root causes. Once the root causes are known, action steps can be identified. Through the causality and linkage exercise, the causes and possible actions are identified and then the context of the need – or problem – becomes clearer. It should be noted that a small community group may not be equipped or able to attempt to implement all the identified actions, for instance job creation. This is where the CDP should play the appropriate role required of the situation (see Chapter 8).

Chapter 20: The Start of a Project

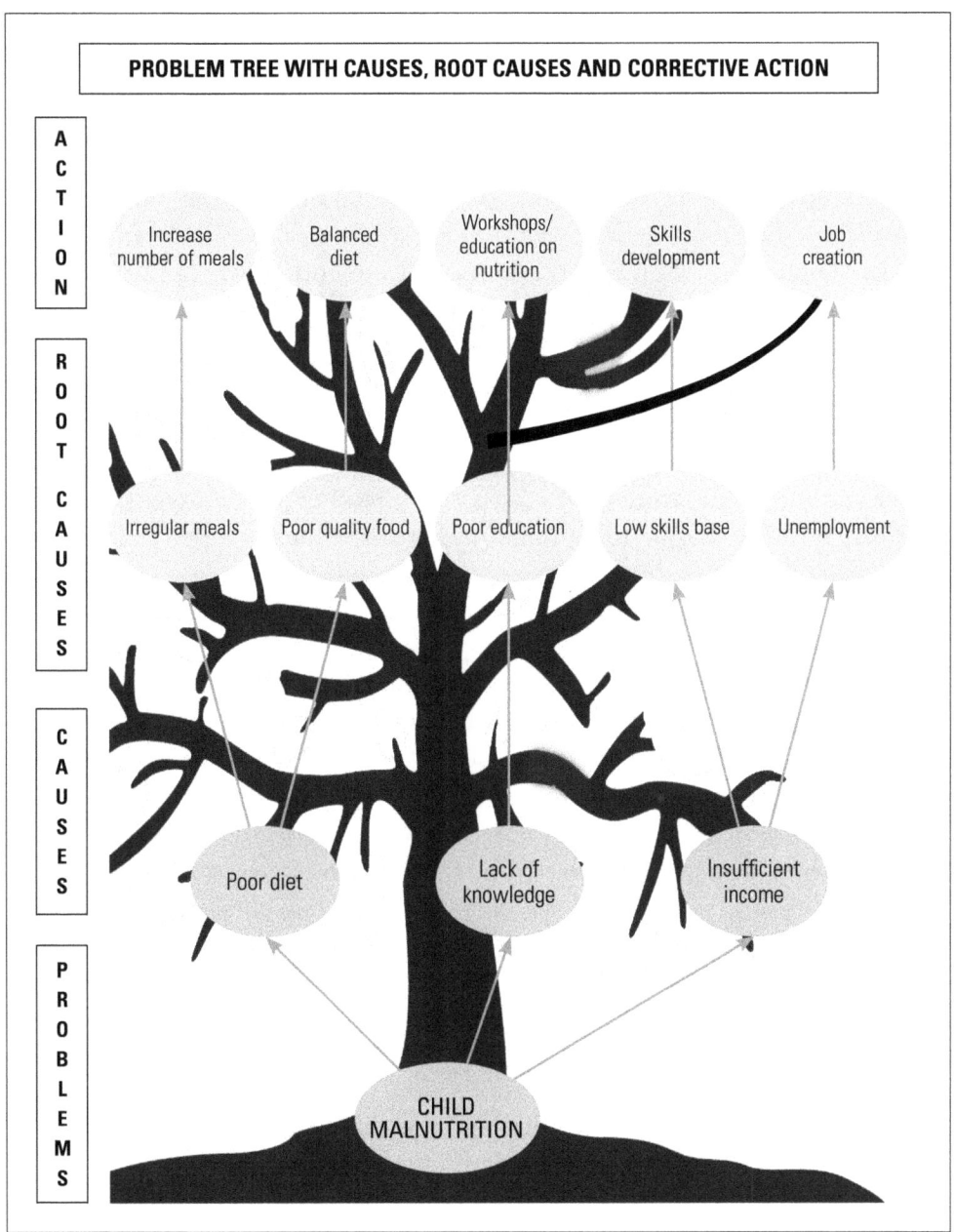

Figure 20.1 Problem tree with causes, root causes and corrective action

Source: Author's own depiction based on an image from https://www.conceptdraw.com/examples/cause-and-effect-flow-chart (accessed 7 January 2023)

20.6 FEELING A NEED

It is imperative that the people forming the action group should feel the identified need to be their own. In the development graveyard, there are many tombstones with the inscription, 'Here lies a community development project whose need was not felt'. People will rally together and will be prepared to contribute labour, time, energy and money only if they feel a definite need and if the need is a matter of concern to them. The poverty situation does not allow luxuries, which means that people are not seeking to indulge in 'interesting' or 'worthwhile' activities.

CDPs should be careful not to impose needs on people or to organise people for what they regard as a good cause. Nor should they regard community development as a hobby some people would like to pursue; as a pleasant and stimulating way to pass the time. People in a crisis situation have very little inclination to do something 'nice' or 'pleasant' while their crisis persists and confronts them daily. Community development is a constructive process in which people involve themselves to eradicate a serious need or solve a serious problem. They participate not because they enjoy it, but because they regard it as a last resort, as the only alternative left to them. Case study 18: *Food garden in Mapayeni* is a case in point. Many a community development project has floundered because of basic misconceptions surrounding this issue.

A CDP may think that after one or two visits to an area he/she can identify the main needs and even put them in order of priority, but in the final instance it is the people's conception of what constitutes the most important identifiable need that is paramount and should therefore receive primary attention. The secret of success is found in a great deal of informal discussion of the need. Through that period of relaxed discussion people's views can be honed so that they grasp the problem correctly. This discussion can run over into a PRAP phase of more formal surveying where the group as a whole gets to grips with the problem or need. Eventually, the need will have gained such a prominent place in their minds that they can, better than anybody else, formulate that need clearly.

People will not easily be moved to action if they do not feel a need, irrespective of the reality and urgency of that need. For this reason, the felt need must receive preference even if the CDP feels otherwise about the needs. It is necessary for the CDP to work through the felt need in order to bring the action group to the real need. When we consider that the eradication of a need is not the only objective of community development, but that it is also a learning process through which people's dignity is enhanced and self-reliance is strengthened, the time spent on a felt need that may not address the real problem cannot be regarded as wasted. See in this regard Case study 16: *The felt need and the real need*.

20.7 THE FIRST PROJECT MEETING

We have seen in Chapter 18 that the contact-making phase must be a natural process. For that reason, it must come to a natural conclusion. The contact-making phase results in the first project meeting. By this time, CDPs must be sure that they know the community and that the community knows them and have accepted their bona fides. CDPs know that the contact-making phase can come to a conclusion if they can identify a group of people, either individuals or an existing group, that is concerned about the same problem or need and, very importantly, is keen to do something about it. This means that the first project meeting must be the direct result of a consensus among the group of concerned people that something must and probably can be done about the identified need. It is the logical outcome of a spontaneous reaction by the people. It is the next logical step to be taken in a process that started when a CDP entered the area and it brings the contact-making phase to a natural conclusion.

It is quite possible that the first project meeting will not really be the first time that many of those involved have met. If the people concerned about a certain matter were part of the survey, as a group in conversation with the CDP or as a PRAP team, they would have met before. Yet, the nature and the goals of the first project meeting are different from previous gatherings and it can, therefore, be regarded as the conclusion of one phase and the beginning of another.

Invitations to the first project meeting should be extended only to those people who have already shown a clear concern for or have aligned themselves with the problem. This is not a public meeting. It is not a good thing to get 200 or 300 people together to discuss a problem identified by a small group of people. The identified need grows immediately because it is now not only the concern of a small group of individuals but has also become a topic for general discussion. It catches the eye of the politicians and other leaders and is therefore open to manipulation or, if the venture is regarded by some influential stakeholder or stakeholders as a personal threat, it can be destroyed. The group of individuals who have aligned themselves with the need may be a group of poor women. In a public meeting where elite and leaders are present, the women will not be heard. They will not even speak and, eventually, their concern and their initiative will be taken away from them and others will decide the issue. The principle of simplicity requires that we begin small. If the group is really small (less than 20), participants can be invited to bring along one or two other people who they know share the same concern and hold the same views on it.

This meeting does not have an open agenda. It is not a needs identification meeting. The need has already been identified. This meeting has a closed agenda with just one objective, which is to talk about a specific problem or need already identified by those concerned and to discuss what can be done about it.

20.7.1 The role of the CDP during the first meeting

At this first project meeting the CDP will, of necessity, play a prominent role. This poses a dilemma because the CDP does not want to play too prominent a role. Those present must realise from the start that it is their concern and that they must do something about it. If the group comprises members of the same interest group, the problem is not as acute because the existing leadership will also lead the meeting. The problem is more severe if an ad hoc group comes together. Who is going to set the ball rolling? Who is going to act as chairperson? Perhaps the CDP should start by stating the purpose of the meeting and by suggesting that a chairperson be chosen for that meeting. The role of the CDP will still be more prominent than is desirable because he/she will have to assist the chairperson who would not have had the opportunity to prepare for the job. The CDP must therefore be careful not to be domineering during the meeting.

It might be necessary for the CDP to do the secretarial work during this first meeting, but he/she must stress that it will be for this first meeting only. If there is someone present who is able to fulfil the secretarial function, he/she should be nominated to do it. In this case, the CDP can assist such a person.

The CDP must come to this meeting well prepared. He/she should:
- bring enough paper to write down the minutes of the meeting
- arrange for a board or flip chart to do the causality exercise

- be familiar with the presentation of the causality exercise
- prepare a ceremony for the people giving their commitment (see later)
- prepare well for the first short-term planning meeting in case the group decides to go without a committee (see later)
- prepare for an election of committee members in case the group decides to elect one at this meeting
- have a pro-forma constitution ready that could be used by the group as a working document to draw up their own constitution.

20.7.2 Contents of the first project meeting

At the first project meeting, the following should take place:
- The meeting should discuss the problem or need. This should be a free-for-all informal discussion with a view to formulating the need.
- The free-for-all discussion should culminate in a causality exercise.
- The outcome of the causality exercise should be a precise formulation of the need to be addressed.
- After the need has been formulated, the next step is to decide what is to be done about it. In other words, the meeting must decide on an objective.
- A discussion of the objective can only be meaningful if resources and obstacles to their use are also discussed.
- The next step is to do some long-term planning. This should comprise a scenario, drawn in broad terms and tied to roughly estimated dates and a roughly estimated budget. It serves no purpose to do detailed long-term planning, as we will see in Chapter 21.
- Now, some logistical arrangements must be made. These include the number and frequency of meetings, the duties and obligations of the various role players, the necessary registrations and approvals that must be sought and the working method that will be followed, for example the planning-cycle method and what methodology will be used to evaluate.
- An optional item at this stage, not earlier, is to get a personal commitment from every person present to join the group and the venture. This can even include a little ceremony. The CDP must obtain the names and contact details of all those who commit themselves.

- The group must discuss the possibility of a committee. It must decide whether one is necessary and (if yes) whether it wants to elect one immediately or postpone it to the next meeting. It must also discuss the functions and obligations of the proposed committee.
- If the group decides to elect the committee immediately, its election can take place.
- If the group decides to elect the committee later, they must decide on a date and place for the election to take place. Such a meeting should, preferably, take place within a week of the first meeting so that the momentum generated by the first meeting is not lost.
- If the group decides to go without a committee, the meeting can either constitute itself as a short-term planning meeting, or it can decide to hold such a meeting on a specific date in future.
- The CDP should be patient and allow free but focused discussion. Also be mindful of the length of the meeting. Some items, such as a causality exercise, may take a long time and much discussion to complete.

20.8 THE COMMITTEE

It must be a rule not to have a committee elected before the group has decided on the need it wants to address. The felt need is the most important and fundamental aspect of any community development project. It is also the most important binding factor. It is better, therefore, to have the whole group involved in the identification and formulation of the need than to entrust it to a newly elected committee. If a committee is elected too early, it may not know where to begin with the result that it may not start at all. This may lead to conflict between the committee and the group, but more often it will lead to nothing, which is just as bad. The election of a committee is often followed by a protracted period of inactivity. The very early election of a committee can also undermine the principle of participation because usually the group will wait for the committee to start the ball rolling, and if it does, the chances are that it will roll it alone.

Another reason for not electing the committee too early is that most of the members of the group may have no idea of what a committee should do or may have the wrong impression about it. If the committee is elected before the project is under way, the group or some of its members may expect from the committee activities falling outside the ambit of the project.

When the committee is elected after the need has been identified and formulated, its task will be much clearer. It will have a basis from which to work. More importantly, though, if the group has been involved in these tasks and others leading up to the election of the committee, it is doubtful that it will leave all subsequent actions to the committee. Because the action group already has an interest in the matter, it will maintain that interest and, in so doing, identify itself with the project. In such a situation the committee will fulfil a real leadership role. It will not do everything itself; the group will not allow this. Rather, it will lead a committed and concerned group which is as much part of the project as the committee. The CDP must guard against over eagerness to get a committee established. The committee exists to provide leadership; not to dominate a project.

A committee's election is also part of the learning process. Members of the committee will not necessarily start out as good leaders, but their participation in the learning process will make them better leaders. The CDP must encourage the climate and must continuously provide opportunities to learn.

The CDP can serve on the committee as an official adviser. Then the CDP is present in an advisory position only and the decision-making function lies with the committee. At the same time, the committee is not thrown into the deep end because the CDP is available as an adviser and a guide. It is obvious that this situation can easily go the wrong way. The CDP can become the wise oracle with everyone dependent on his/her wisdom. Then the committee no longer makes the decisions. It either offers suggestions which the CDP accepts or rejects, or it waits for his/her advice and promptly converts it into decisions. The best way to give advice is by offering the committee options and assisting it to work out the consequences of every option. With this as its background, the committee must then make the choices.

20.9 PROBLEM SOLVING

Groups make decisions by solving problems. How this problem solving is done can make a big difference to the wellbeing of a group. The wrong way of problem solving can and will adversely affect relationships in the group. We must remember that problem solving is the core business of most groups. If it is done wrongly, the whole group functions in a wrong way. Problem solving can lead to the wrong conclusion, which will also have a negative influence on the group. In any case, the problem will still be there because the solution the group had chosen was not the correct one.

We should therefore try and follow a pattern divided into discrete phases so that everything is done correctly and the group prospers as a result. Such a pattern will consist of the following different discrete phases. This section is based on Doyle and Straus (1976).

20.9.1 Problem perception

The problem perception phase is the time for the problem-solving group to try and get closer to the issue. It is not a very well-disciplined phase because the group will still be trying to get a grip on the problem. It has therefore been called 'the sniffing, groping and grasping phase', where ideas about the problem are brainstormed. The group must ask themselves questions such as 'Is there a problem?', 'Whose problem is it?', 'Where is the problem?', 'What does the problem look like?', 'What does it feel like?' and 'How big is the problem?'. This is all that is done in this phase. We only want to get a clearer picture of what we perceive as a problem. We want to make sure that we are all talking about the same thing.

20.9.2 Problem definition

Once we have perceived a problem, the next logical step is to define it. This is the phase where boundaries must be set around the problem. What is part of the problem and what is not? The problem must therefore be described – who, what, where, when and how. The importance of a definition is that it synchronises all the opinions about the problem so that all participants will describe the problem in the same way. It also determines the range of acceptable alternatives.

20.9.3 Problem analysis

In the analysis phase, the objective is to break down the problem into component parts and to examine how they fit together. This is how we try to learn more about the problem. Group members should now think what questions need to be answered in order to build a complete and detailed picture of the problem. Any problem can be broken down into smaller sub-problems until we reach a size that we can handle. This exercise is especially important if a problem is complex. As the problem is defined and analysed, it is usually found to consist of a number of sub-problems. Eventually it will be good if the group could reach consensus on how to divide the entire problem into sub-problems.

20.9.4 Thinking of alternatives

Now that the problem has been looked at from all angles, the first positive phase can commence. However, this phase should start only after the previous three phases have been dealt with to the satisfaction of the whole group. If not, we may be doing more harm than good by letting the group charge on to generating alternatives. Participants should come forward with creative ideas during this phase. Brainstorming is one of the best ways to solicit creativity and originality.

Part of this phase is to set criteria for alternatives. This is usually not done in a formal exercise. Reactions to ideas about alternatives will invariably contain criteria and if they do not, such criteria must be provided. 'That is not a practical idea because ...', 'That is an excellent idea because ...'. It is not permissible to only say that an idea is good or bad: the reasons for saying so (the criteria for alternatives) must also be given.

When thinking of alternatives, past experience is also drawn from. After all, it is not necessary to reinvent the wheel. 'So-and-so had the same problem and they did ... Remember when we last had a similar problem, we did ... Last time that we had this problem we tried to ... but it didn't work.'

Any one or all of the sub-problems identified during the problem analysis phase can now be placed on the agenda. Remember that we have not yet come to the planning phase where we will have to concentrate more on the central aspects. We are still not talking about what we are going to do. We are simply suggesting alternatives to the situation as it exists now. During this exercise members must learn how to work with other people's ideas and to admit that their own ideas are not necessarily correct or the best. It is important to work for agreement on common criteria before judging alternatives.

The development of explicit criteria has important benefits:
- It forces all group members to externalise their values and to re-examine them.

- Being clear about your personal criteria helps others to understand how you make your decisions.
- The procedure of developing criteria for evaluation causes a useful interlude between generating alternatives and the evaluation of alternatives.
- It is much easier to reach consensus on criteria before alternatives are discussed than to try this afterwards.
- If you cannot reach consensus on criteria, it is not likely that you will reach agreement on an acceptable alternative.
- If you can reach consensus on criteria, future decisions concerning the problem should be greatly simplified.

20.9.5 Decision making

During the previous phase, possible alternatives would already have been screened. Some would have remained on the table and some would have been discarded. During this phase a choice must be made between those that remained. Decision making is thus the making of a choice or choices. In order to do so, the consequences of each choice must be considered. This is an extremely important and necessary exercise and the people must realise why it is done. 'If we decide to do it this way, we will have to ... If we decide on this or that option, just remember that this or that will happen ... This option will cost us ... This alternative will mean that ...'. It is not necessary that only one alternative be chosen. In certain situations, two or more alternatives can be considered or there can be a plan A and a plan B. The important thing is that there must be consensus about the decision, and so, some negotiation may be necessary. In fact, if this whole process is followed, nothing but consensus can be the end result. It is when problem solving becomes a landslide instead of a well-thought-out exercise that voting must be done to see which alternative carries a majority and that is definitely not recommended.

20.9.6 Planning

The alternative has now been chosen. During the planning phase it must be decided how the desired result will be obtained. Planning is task oriented. Action must be taken in order to eradicate the problem. Planning decides what is to be done, when it is to be done, how it is to be done, and who is to do it. However, in the case of a community development project, the planning cannot be done in detail and only once. We will see in the next chapter (Chapter 21) that planning should take place incrementally.

20.10 CONCLUSION

The first project meeting is the first positive manifestation that people want to do something about a need. As such, it is the culmination of a process that has started with the entry of the CDP into an area. A very important process has taken place during this period. Relationships have been sorted out and established. The CDP's bona fides have been accepted and he/she has found a niche for him/herself. A group of people have become aware of a situation that they cannot tolerate and therefore are going to address through a project. That group of people have also committed themselves to an all-out effort through a project. They have set themselves a target and they have mapped out a rough path of action. So, we can say that this is the launch of a project.

The CDP must realise that the meeting following this first one will really show who is committed to participating in the project. It is natural that, during the first project meeting, the curious and the free riders will be present. People may even commit themselves during the first meeting not through conviction, but because of group pressure. Those who are really committed will attend the second meeting, and those who are not will fall by the wayside.

REFERENCES

Advisory Expert Group. 2006. Short report of the Fourth Meeting of the Advisory Expert Group on National Accounts, 30 January to 8 February 2006, European Central Bank Frankfurt. Available at: http://unstats.un.org/unsd/nationalaccount/AEG/papers/m4conclusions.pdf (accessed 3 March 2016).

Cambridge Dictionary. 2023. Resource. Available at: https://dictionary.cambridge.org/dictionary/english/resource (accessed 31 January 2023).

Doyle M & Straus D. 1976. *How to Make Meetings Work: The New Interaction Method*. Ridgefield, CT: Wyden Books.

Harrison R, Blickem C, Lamb J, Kirk S & Vassilev I. 2019. Asset-based community development: Narratives, practice, and conditions of possibility – a qualitative study with community practitioners. *SAGE Open*, 1(11).

International Accounting Standards Board (IASB). 2014. *A Review of the Conceptual Framework for Financial Reporting*. IFRS Foundation: London.

Mathie A & Cunningham G. 2003. From clients to citizens: Asset-based community development as a strategy for community-driven development. *Development in Practice*, 13(5):474–486.

Matsela T. 2015. Exploring Youth Participation in Community Development Organisations in the Western Cape. Minor dissertation submitted toward an MSocSci (Social Development). Cape Town: University of Cape Town.

Swanson, RA. 2022. *Foundations of Human Resource Development*. 3rd ed. Oakland: Berret-Koehler.

Yuesti A & Sumantra K. 2017. Empowerment on the knowledge and learning organization for community development. *Scientific Research Journal (SCIRJ)*, v(ix).

CHAPTER 21

Planning and Implementation

Frik de Beer

21.1   INTRODUCTION TO PLANNING

Planning is a process in which an individual or group of people decide on what to do in the future. Planning points the way to what must be done, when it must be done, by whom it must be done, and how it must be done to reach a certain objective. When dealing with planning for development, we must realise that there are serious differences in approaches. The two main and opposing approaches to planning can be identified as a **rationalistic** and **synoptic** approach versus an adaptive incrementalist approach. Whereas the rationalistic approach relies on rational decision making to plan and solve problems, the adaptive incrementalist approach argues that 'strategic decision making cannot be accomplished in a rational and straightforward manner, and it is coherently incremental and adaptive' (Methe et al 2000, in Ansari et al 2013:1). While we introduce the rationalistic, synoptic approach by way of background, we believe that the adaptive incrementalist approach is most suitable for community development projects as it provides for a space where the principles of community development can best be adhered to.

21.2   THE RATIONALISTIC, SYNOPTIC APPROACH

As a tool for decision making, the rationalistic, synoptic approach assumes the following:

- Decision makers are authoritative and objective. They are professionally trained and judge everything without bias.
- Exhaustive analysis will define problems. All problems can be analysed so that they can be described in detail.
- Models of social change can be constructed to aid in defining the problem and formulating the policy. The rationalistic approach is a great believer of models.

- There is a direct relationship between government action and the solution of social problems. The rationalistic approach needs a strong, capable and benevolent government.
- Plans must be carried out through hierarchical structures of authority. A hierarchical organisation ensures that decision making is situated where it should be.
- **Deviations** from preconceived plans are detrimental to achieving objectives. When you assume all the above, then this is obvious.
- Conflicts over goals or courses of action are adverse and irrational manifestations of politics. There is no place for this in rational planning.
- Planners and policy makers determine correct action for others to follow. It is clear that the 'others' are only involved in carrying out the plans of professional planners.
- Analysis should be systematic regarding:
    - cost–benefit
    - linear programming
    - network scheduling
    - planning–programming–budgeting.

This last point needs further criticism because it forms the core of this approach. Systems analysis requires a concise definition of goals and objectives, but it is impossible because they are expressions of social values. Concise definitions of goals are therefore the ideal, but very difficult to attain. This also goes for identifying and categorising inputs, outputs, costs and benefits because they are subjective, and analysts and interest groups disagree on them.

A further strong consideration is that government agencies lack administrative capacity to do analysis effectively and, further, it is impossible to obtain adequate data on which to base systems analysis and synoptic planning. We can therefore say that systems analysis ignores and discounts complex processes of social interaction. Because of this, it is quite clear why political leaders do not understand or are unwilling to accept results of systems analysis and comprehensive planning.

In the final instance, systems analysis is not always suited to the job at hand. It is difficult to make comparisons between programmes and policy options, for example. Another problem is that systems analysis and comprehensive planning are episodic and time consuming, whereas political decision making is continuous and cyclical. Finally, systems analysis is concerned with how to maximise utilities, whereas policy making is concerned with how to distribute public resources.

We can therefore conclude by saying that this approach:
- is difficult to operationalise
- is incompatible with how political decisions are made
- discourages analysts from understanding the complexity and uncertainty of problems.

It is part of our culture to strive toward excellence. The rationalistic synoptic approach believes the way to obtain excellence is to devise and to follow methodologies that bypass the human factor as much as possible. The approach regards people as subjective and irrational, and therefore to be kept away from the planning process or to be severely limited in the planning process – the more planning emulates a machine or the computer, the better. We therefore regard planning as a technological process where variables and task paths are brought into harmony through a rational and logical process. Reality, however, tells us that this tendency is a fallacy, that planning simply cannot be done in that fashion considering the situation that we work with.

If ordinary people with just a basic knowledge are responsible for the planning, the situation in which the planning takes place is fluid and therefore constantly changing, and the planning process is to be a learning opportunity for those involved, then rationality and logic are of little consequence and excellence can only be obtained through trial and error.

Human development approaches and projects are complex, dealing with uncertainty and involving many actors. In this situation, adaptive administration is an approach proposed by Janssen and Van der Voort (2016:3): 'Adaptive governance is an approach that is often used for dealing with complex societal issues in which there are many stakeholders with diverging interests, and uncertainty about the actions to be taken'. This is discussed in the section that follows.

21.3 THE ADAPTIVE INCREMENTALIST APPROACH

Incrementalism assumes uncertainty as a fact and is based on the following premises:

- More detailed planning should proceed incrementally. Planning must be viewed as an incremental process. It is also known as emergent planning (Collyer, Warren, Hemsley & Stevens 2010).
- Complex social experiments can be partially guided but never controlled. Certain parameters can be set, but only as guides.
- Methods of analysis and procedures of implementation must be flexible and incremental. A trial and error process is all that can work.
- Analysis and implementation should facilitate social interaction. They should encourage continuous learning and collaboration.
- Planning and implementation are mutually dependent activities. Experimentation with implementation reflects on the planning.
- Fundamental changes are necessary in the way governments plan and implement. The more the government becomes an enabler, the better. All role players' dynamic capability is of great importance (Collyer et al 2010:110).

It stresses the following about the real world situation:

- Information is always partial and often faulty. Perfect information is not obtained through perfect analysis, so why waste time on perfect analysis.
- Goals must often be left vague. We have said before that objectives must be as precise as possible and that still holds, but it is easier said than done.
- Choices are highly constrained by prior commitments. There are a lot of role players with various commitments among themselves. A perfect system of a clean slate is therefore not so easy.
- Consequences of action in a complex system are unpredictable. We are dealing with a very volatile substance because of the complexity of the situation.

- Interests are pluralistic and frequently contradictory. There are a lot of role players in a complex situation and therefore it would be naive to think that interests will always fit and enhance one another. The situation changes so rapidly that the 'big picture' is out of date. It is a volatile system and therefore forever changing.
- Only weak control exists over the instruments of policy execution.

The perception of development policies as experimental activities implies that new forms of analysis, planning and administration must be devised that are better suited to experimentation and to uncovering and coping with uncertainties and risks attending policy implementation.

The primary purpose of projects should be to gradually build up planning and administrative capabilities of people and organisations; to design and organise projects to reduce uncertainties and unknowns incrementally; to integrate planning and implementation; and to use acquired knowledge to alter and modify courses of action. The strategies based on this adaptive incrementalist approach reflect more sophisticated understanding of the dynamics of development, the constraints on economic and social change, and the political and social forces that influence processes of change.

21.4 CONCLUSION ON THE APPROACHES

We should be careful not to view planning as a technological process done by planners. Community development is human oriented and involves people with subjective notions of their needs and what they can do about them. People-oriented planning is therefore tinged with subjectivity, is incremental and takes place through a process of trial and error. It is a learning process, and can even be emotional. To force a rational planning mode onto an action group is not only impossible; it would effectively estrange the people from the process. The rational blueprint approach has serious flaws when used in community development. One of the most apparent flaws is the assumption that an institutional structure exists that will fit any current situation. Another flaw is the assumption that a fully operational institution exists that will be able to monitor all eventualities and address all needs. This simply is not so in the situation in which we work. We have seen in Chapter 6 that there are certain practical principles to adhere to. These principles of learning, adaptiveness, compassion and simplicity come to bear in the planning process. It is therefore much more than just a preferred way of planning. In fact, there is no other way to plan for development.

This means that project planning must be viewed as a gradual process of testing propositions about the most effective means of coping with complex social problems. For this to be possible, planning must be incremental and can only be short term; objectives must be attainable in a fairly short period; and planning must be simple and singular, involving all possible role players. To be fully able to support adaptiveness, all actors involved in projects must be able to deal with changes, introduce bottom–up and decentralised decision making, and plan to mobilise and use local, community-based talents and competencies (Soe & Dreschler 2018:323).

If planning is a participatory learning process, so is implementation. The two functions simply cannot be separated. Implementation is part of the experiment and makes evaluation possible. In fact, implementation can be regarded as the greatest test of planning. For this reason, implementation cannot be regarded as 'the mechanical execution of a plan'. Rather, implementation informs the plan and makes it necessary to go back to the drawing board (De Beer & Swanepoel 2013:83–84). Because of this close relationship between the plan and its implementation, because a specific plan is implemented, the mode of implementation differs from project to project. Like planning, implementation is a situation-specific, step-by-step affair, unique to each project. Let us give Rondinelli (1993:18–19) the final word:

> Attempts to plan in more detailed and precise fashion should proceed incrementally, as uncertainties or unknowns are reduced or clarified during implementation. Planning must be viewed as an incremental process that tests propositions about the most effective means of coping with social problems, reassessing and redefining both the problems and the components of development projects as more is learned about their complexities and about the economic, social and political factors affecting the outcome of proposed courses of action. Complex social experiments can be partially guided but never fully controlled; thus, analysis and management procedures must be flexible and incremental, facilitating social interaction so that those groups most directly affected by a problem can search for and pursue mutually acceptable objectives. Rather than providing a blueprint for action, allowing policy makers and managers to readjust and modify programs and projects as they learn more about the conditions with which they are trying to cope.

Confirming this approach, Collyer (2013) quotes a manager saying: 'I like to lay out the major phases / deliverables / milestones at the outset, but only plan the detail for the phase I'm about to start'.

21.5 THE PLANNING PROCESS

Planning means bringing together three elements: the need, the resources and the objective, and relating them to a fourth element, namely action. It is obvious that the planners must know the first three elements in order to decide on the fourth element of action.

Below we discuss two planning methods. The first, the logical framework, relates to the rationalistic synoptic approach. The second, the adaptive incrementalist approach, offers a planning cycle method that allows for change (adaptive) and for continuous step-by-step implementation.

21.5.1 A rational planning method: the logical framework as a planning method

Logical framework analysis was developed in the US during the 1960s and came into use in the early 1970s. The logframe, as it is popularly called, was not designed for use in development projects. However, its relative simplicity, its clarity and its rationality make it apparently a reliable device to make project kick-off possible. The logframe's main advantage is that its aim is to improve the way in which projects are prepared, planned, implemented and evaluated, and therefore managed. A logframe is, in summary, 'a project design methodology that provides a systematic structure for identifying, planning and managing projects' (Jensen 2010:2).

A logframe consists of a rectangular matrix that provides a full picture of the project. It has four columns, one for each project structure (narrative summary) or what is to be achieved, indicators of achievement, verification methods and assumptions (Wiggins & Shields 1995:3). An example is provided in Table 21.1.

Table 21.1 Example of a logframe

Project structure	Indicators of Achievement	Means of verification	Assumptions
GOAL: What the project seeks to achieve	What are the qualitative and quantitative measures that indicate achievement of the objective?	What sources of information can be used to be able to measure the goal?	What external factors are necessary to sustain the objectives?
PURPOSE: What are the intended immediate effects of the project?	What are the qualitative and quantitative indicators by which achievement of purpose can be judged?	What sources of information are available to make measurement of purpose achievement possible?	What external factors are necessary to ensure the purpose to contribute to the achievement of the goal?
OUTPUTS: What deliverables are to be produced to achieve the purpose?	What quantity of time is allocated for what quality deliverables?	What sources of information will verify the achievement of the outputs?	What factors outside project control may restrict the outputs?
ACTIVITIES: What activities are to be achieved to accomplish the outputs?	What kind and quality of activities are there and when will they be produced?	What are the sources of information to verify the achievement of the activities?	What factors will hinder the activities from creating outputs?

The fact that there is a hierarchy of objectives tells us that there are causal linkages between the various items. If the means are provided, the ends will be achieved. If the necessary inputs are provided, specific outputs will result. This will lead to a purpose being achieved and broader goals being met. We therefore have a column of purpose and intent with two rows or columns that give us the indicators and their sources that will be used for monitoring and evaluation. Finally, there is a column for a set of assumptions which state the conditions that must apply before causal linkages can be realised.

The logframe methodology is popular among project facilitators and project donors for the following reasons:

- The logframe model is rational, with clean lines of causal moments. Because of this, it shows when a project lacks internal coherence and external plausibility. If we look at the narrative summary, we can see whether the project is logical in terms of its stated objectives. It can also determine external plausibility by ensuring that the team responsible for project design clearly stipulates the assumptions that have been taken as the starting point.

- It helps project designers to define tasks and responsibilities and it clearly lists the indicators that will be used in monitoring and evaluation.
- It is a comprehensive document that obviates misunderstandings because of poor communication.

The logframe methodology also has its shortcomings:
- The most important shortcoming is that it does not always fit into a situation run by adaptive measures. Rondinelli (1993) emphasises that community development projects are experiments with no rigid lines, no step-by-step causality. The rigid nature of the logframe makes it difficult for it to fit and may lead to important principles of development being left by the wayside.
- The logframe is an imposed procedure maintaining a relationship of control and domination that goes directly against the principles of participation and empowerment.
- The conceptual starting point for the logframe is Western and therefore its parameters for planning and implementation are formal and thus fixed. It is culture specific and therefore it does not allow ownership of the logframe as an approach.
- Interestingly, the logframe is rigid in its approach, yet by itself it is not sufficient for management of a project. It cannot give guidance to the means of obtaining project objectives. It is therefore a tool to identify the what, but cannot answer the question of how.
- The creators of the logframe are usually a selective group, but without the participation of a broad community representation, the principles and priorities of each stakeholder will not be reflected. We can say that the different interests are concealed and therefore areas of conflict are ignored.
- The development environment that we have looked at previously is complex and unstable. This dynamism is not really accommodated by the logframe with its inflexible structure. It does leave space for assumptions, but it does not ensure that assumptions are realistic, nor does it offer alternatives in case they are not. The logframe is linear while the reality is not. It assumes that all contingencies can be foreseen and that the progress will be predictable. It sees a linear causality from activities to outputs to purpose to goal. Once this

linearity is logframed, there is no chance of adaptability; reflection is not an option. Yet, the situation is so fluid that continuous opportunity for rethink is needed.
- The logframe seems concerned with quantitative indicators. It lacks qualitative measures of progress. It is also critical of the learning process approach because it is seen as something that takes place before a project, not during it. If the expected progress is not made, it means that someone is at fault. Policing and upward accountability are therefore at the heart of the whole reporting system, not the opportunity to learn from the situation.

According to Floate, Durham and Marks (2019:91):

> Widespread implementation of the logical framework approach by international agencies provided a way for practitioners to view programmes along a causal pathway and to develop a programme theory of how an intervention's inputs and activities generate outputs, outcomes and impacts.

21.5.2 An adaptive incrementalist planning method: the planning cycle method

There are a number of important aspects to take into account in order for planning to be successful in a community development situation.

Planning must be incremental. Planning cannot be done only once because there are so many unknown and changing factors in most situations that precise planning for the long term is impossible. No committee or action group can have one planning meeting covering the whole process up to objective attainment. It must return to the drawing board. At most, broad guidelines can be drawn on how to reach a certain objective, but detailed planning can only take place on a step-by-step basis. Not only does the situation change frequently, but the people participating are unsure of themselves and unsure as to how to reach their objective. It therefore cannot be a blueprint, but is rather a learning process.

The fact that planning is incremental also tells us that it is a process of trial and error, of experimentation. Decisions on action are formulated in the light of an assessment of previous actions and in the light of an assessment of previous planning. Through the process of trial and error and experimentation, a process of learning takes shape.

Planning must and can only be short term. It is suggested that the planning body meet monthly to plan for the period up to the next meeting. This planning is done in the light of an assessment of the actions taken since the previous meeting. Each planning meeting is therefore also an evaluation exercise.

In this way people will be in a position to judge their progress step by step and adjust their course from time to time. Only in this way can the community development process be a continuous learning experience for those participating. The added advantage of regular assessment and planning meetings is that a project will not easily run out of steam. Every meeting is, in a way, a milestone and fresh planning for another month helps to keep the enthusiasm alive. In this way the project generates its own rhythm.

Objectives must be attainable in a fairly short period. Objectives only have value if they are achievable, acceptable, measurable, motivating, understandable and flexible enough to adapt to changing circumstances. Therefore it is almost impossible to work towards a goal that can only be reached in a fairly long time. If at all possible, achieving an objective should not lie further than one year down the line. If an objective cannot be reached in such a short time, it is necessary to set interim objectives. For example, if the objective is to own a building for a crèche, it might be impossible to realise it within a year. An interim objective must then be formulated, for example to get the crèche temporarily established in a house or another building.

Quick results therefore minimise the risk factor. Quick results have a further advantage in that those outside the group who doubt the practicability of a project, will be confronted with proof that something can be done. This will make them more inclined to follow the example of one successful effort and it might even lead to the replication of the first effort throughout the larger community. Case study 17: *Mothers of the mountain community* is a case in point.

Planning must be simple, with one objective at a time. It is always easier to plan for one project with one objective at a time. That objective should not tax the project to the extent that the project becomes complex. We should also guard against sophisticated projects. Their planning becomes so technical that it is difficult for ordinary people to participate meaningfully. We say that planning and implementation are participatory actions, but we must be aware of the fact that many projects are large and 'technical' and that these projects cannot be made participatory so easily. So, we are faced with a dilemma: what to do with the larger and more technical projects, especially when it comes to planning and implementation. We have in earlier chapters suggested that large, technical projects should be divided into doable chunks so that participation can still take place.

An approach of more recent origin, called humanitarian engineering, attempts to address this issue – how to make complex projects participatory. To achieve participation by communities, Mazzurco and Jesiek (2019:3–5) suggest the following five principles, based on a review of 49 journal articles dealing with the issue:

1. Collaborating with local champions
2. Harnessing local resources and expertise
3. Integrating ethics and social justice
4. Building trusting relationships
5. Creating competent multi- or interdisciplinary teams.

Planning must involve everyone. Planning is not the prerogative of the celebrated few. In a project where a group of participants is led by an executive committee, not even that committee can claim the sole right to planning. In one way or another, the whole group must be involved. The reason for this is simple. It is the right of all members of the group to make decisions and carry the responsibility for those decisions, but the most important reason is that the planning process is a learning opportunity that should be attended by as many of the group as possible. There is also a risk that the committee takes over the project from the action group so that the action group becomes either uninvolved or involved only with doing physical labour, while the committee makes the decisions. In this case, a project's abstract aims will not be met because the group will not be strengthened and will not gain self-reliance. The whole action group must remain an intrinsic part of any action, including planning. Regular action group meetings should therefore be held. At these meetings, the committee must inform the group of its actions and the larger group must have the opportunity to discuss them at length and even to reverse them or to send them back to the committee for a rethink. The action group must also have the right to task the committee with new matters. The committee's position in community development is slightly different from other executive committees. The committee does not act on behalf of the action group. It provides leadership, continuity, coordination and a certain measure of preparatory organisation to enable the action group to remain optimally involved. Community development practitioners

(CDPs) should explain this situation to their groups and should facilitate their making of practical arrangements to accommodate this position. Action group meetings, for example, could follow close on committee meetings – on the same day if possible, so that the action group can discuss and approve the planning for the next month. If the whole action group is small (ie not more than 25 members) the committee can hold a preparatory 'caucus meeting' before the action group meeting and this latter meeting then becomes the primary planning exercise.

Planning must be written down. During the entire planning process everything must be recorded in writing. At meetings minutes must be kept which specify what must be done, how it must be done, when it must be done and who is responsible for each task. This must be distributed among all persons involved in the process to keep them up to date with the situation.

The planning cycle method is a simple way of ensuring a meaningful relationship between monitoring (evaluation) and planning. Planning meetings should take place once a month (it can even be twice a month if the ability of the group to plan and implement is still weak). Every planning meeting should start by evaluating the actions of the previous month. The actions of the coming month are then planned using the previous month's actions as a frame of reference. In other words, the meeting evaluates its implementation in terms of its decisions. In this way it learns something of its ability to put plans into action, and it also learns something of its ability to plan – the failure to implement or operationalise plans can often be ascribed to incorrect planning. Only when this process of evaluation has been completed, does the meeting decide on the actions to be taken in the next month. Actions for the next month will be determined by what has taken place in the previous month. If a planned action for the previous month has not been done or completed, it must again appear on the planning for the next month, perhaps with a changed 'how' in the light of the evaluation and definitely with revised time frames. See Figure 21.1 for a diagrammatical illustration of the planning cycle.

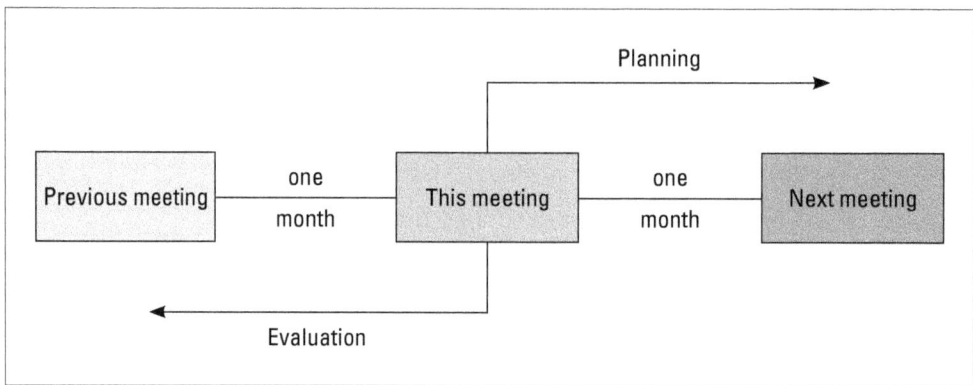

Figure 21.1 **The planning cycle**

The first phase of a planning meeting is to decide what action to take. The 'what' items should be separated from each other so that one 'what' item will comprise only one action. It is therefore necessary to break down an action into its smallest component parts. Each 'what' item is numbered separately.

The second phase asks when that action should take place. A timetable must be attached to planning. Action takes place sequentially because certain things cannot be done before others have been completed and certain actions enable others to commence. Attaching actions to dates helps maintain this sequence. In the minds of the planners, it gives a clear picture of how the various tasks will follow each other. A timetable ensures that each action is meaningful in relation to other actions and it prevents duplication and repetition.

The reaching of a milestone within the planned time is proof that the action was effective and that the action group was, up to that point, successful in its efforts. It acts further as a confidence booster that generates enthusiasm, and it acts as a barometer of the project's success.

This is all true only if a timetable is not cut too fine. The action group should not be under continuous pressure to meet the next deadline. Dates in a timetable should never be seen as deadlines, but rather as goals or targets. If a timetable is too tight, it is inevitable that most goals will not be reached within the set time. This may dampen the action group's enthusiasm. The unpredictability of the situation must also be acknowledged (see Rondinelli 1993 in this regard). It may even be wise to attach two dates to completion of each task; one in the event of everything going without a hitch (best-case scenario) and one taking unforeseen problems into account.

The third phase addresses who will be responsible for the planned action. Planning must tie every action to a person or group of persons who will be responsible for it. If this does not happen the chances are that nobody will attend to it. Either that or the secretary or even the CDP will have to do everything. Two people, the one not knowing about the other, may even undertake the same action and, apart from the duplication, it might also lead to quarrels and a host of other problems. Because every action in a project should be a learning opportunity, various people must be assigned to tasks affording them the opportunity to gain experience and knowledge.

Attaching actions to a specific person or persons enables the equal and fair distribution of the work. It helps to appoint people to tasks that they are equipped to do, thus using everyone's talents and skills optimally, or it appoints tasks to persons not skilled for those tasks, thus affording them the opportunity to gain first-hand experience. It usually also helps to identify those people who are really keen and those who tend to shy away from work. Finally, it shows who can go it alone and who needs assistance and guidance in carrying out tasks.

The fourth phase addresses how a certain action should be done. It is not enough to assign tasks to a person and tie them to dates for completion. The planning body must at least describe each task in more detail so that those tasked with it will know what the task entails and how much money can be spent on it. After a planning meeting a person assigned a task must have reasonable clarity on how to perform it. Tasks cannot be given only to those who know how to perform them. This would rob other people from learning through action. Although tasks must fit the persons who perform them as closely as possible, people must also be given tasks that they do not know how to perform. The problem is that, if a person does not know how to perform a task, he/she may be too shy to ask for clarification or assistance, and as a result not do the task or do it incorrectly. If this person is 'found out' it might be a humiliating and unpleasant experience. A discussion during the planning meeting detailing how a task is to be done will avoid this kind of problem. Even if the person assigned a task does know how to perform it, it might still be worthwhile discussing it, perhaps under the leadership of the designated person. Such a discussion can be a learning experience for the whole group and can bring new insights to the matter.

21.6 RECORDING PLANNING

Not only is the human memory amazingly short; it is also remarkable how different people interpret different decisions differently. This can easily lead to conflict in a group, and it can delay the whole process. For these reasons planning decisions must be recorded in writing. During planning meetings, minutes must be kept, especially of envisaged actions. They must indicate clearly what action has been decided, who is to be responsible for its execution, by when it should be performed, and how it should be done. If the planning cycle method is used, actions will obviously be undertaken between the current and the next planning meeting. Problems may arise if the decisions regarding those actions are recorded on a draft document that will only be ratified at the next meeting. Therefore, to have a correct and official written record from the outset, it is suggested that the minutes should be approved at the end of the meeting, rather than waiting to do so during the next meeting. Minutes can even be approved as a meeting progresses. Once a decision has been taken on a specific action, who should take responsibility for it, by when it should be performed and how it should be done, the minutes for that item can be read and approved and, at the end of the meeting, a decision can be taken to approve the minutes in their entirety. This method of looking at each decision via the minutes at that very same meeting can also help the secretary who is not sure of him/herself to correct mistakes and to do it better.

This cannot be done if minutes are written in 'story form', in other words, if the opening and welcoming are detailed and if the discussion leading up to a decision is recorded. Simplified minutes are needed. First, the minutes should reflect only the decisions taken and the 'who', 'when' and 'how' of it. Second, minutes can be kept in the form of a decisions register. For this, a sheet of paper with columns can be used instead of a minute book (see Table 21.2). The keeping of this type of record does not require many sophisticated skills or an education. Relatively unsophisticated groups with little schooling can handle this type of recording with minimal initial help.

Table 21.2 The minutes of a planning meeting

Action	Who	When	How	Evaluation
Item 2: **Buying of kitchen utensils**	Mrs A	10/8 15/8	15 bowls; 15 spoons; 1 large pot; 2 ladles; 2 trays; 1 bread knife; 2 knives. Buy at Cash & Carry. Don't spend more than R600.00. Minutes of this item approved.	Action on 12/8 Items bought at C&C. Mrs A. negotiated a special price – spent R500. Utensils now kept at her house until needed.
Item 3:				

21.7 INTRODUCTION TO IMPLEMENTATION

With planning done, the second step in the management cycle is the implementation process. Implementation should take place according to a plan. It is a plan that is to be implemented. It is the operationalisation of the plan. If it is not done according to a plan, it cannot be called implementation. Without a plan all we have are ad hoc actions or 'shots in the dark'. Implementation is a step-by-step process, addressing each separate task in the plan. Although the implementation process has a number of definite steps, the content is specific to each project and may vary greatly. Because a specific plan is implemented, the mode of implementation differs from project to project. Like planning, implementation is a situation-specific, step-by-step affair, unique to each project.

Because implementation reflects the plan, it is an important test of the plan. If implementation fails, it could be that the plan is incorrect. It could also mean that management is insufficient or that circumstances have changed so drastically since the plan was formulated that it is no longer relevant to the situation. In either case it means going back to the planning process. Alternative solutions must again be considered, and the best option and implementation requirements must again be chosen. The participants in a project, including the CDP, should accept this situation because projects are experiments and the planning process is a learning opportunity where we learn, among others, from our mistakes.

Circumstances do change between a plan and its implementation. For this reason, implementation must come as soon as possible after the plan. This is an important reason why it was suggested earlier that planning should be done for not more than one month in advance. Implementation will follow immediately after planning because there is only a month to do what should be done.

Changing circumstances do not necessarily present grave problems, especially if planning and implementation are strictly short term. However, if circumstances do change drastically over a short period, the plan must inevitably be scrapped and reformulated. The longer the period between plan formulation and implementation, the greater the chance that drastic circumstantial change will take place.

21.8 IMPLEMENTATION WITH STRONG COMMUNITY PARTICIPATION

All participants in a project must take part in the implementation of the plans.

Implementation is not for the management team alone. The people affected by a specific issue and committed to act on it, must participate in the implementation process as far as possible. People from outside a specific project can also be involved; for example, a driver with a tractor can be hired to plough a piece of land for a community garden. Some technical tasks needing specially trained people cannot be done by the ordinary participants, for example land surveying and soil sampling. It is important, though, that the tasks of such a person are prescribed in the action plan and that the prescriptions are adhered to. Such people or organisations must operate in accordance with a contractual relationship with the action group, where the latter is the client and they are the suppliers of services. Such a relationship has less of a chance to harm the participants' independence or self-reliance. It is advisable that at least some of the participants are present when people do something in a project, for them to learn, to make sure that the plan is adhered to and to show that they are in charge of the project, not the person or persons from outside.

Even with contractual arrangements in place, involving too many external contractors in a project tends to change its character and relegate the action group to a less important and less hands-on position. In such cases the action group's participation is eroded and the whole learning process comes under severe pressure. Case study 10: *The project that had its fences brought down* and Case study 11: *The project that was taken over* give an indication of how external participation can kill a project.

21.8.1 Implementation checklist

There are a few critical questions we have to ask ourselves when we are implementing a project:

- Does the plan address the issues? We can just as well ask whether the plan will lead to the objective that will mean the solution of the need or problem.
- Have tasks been identified and written down? Planning is about what to do and if this task is not done properly, implementation will meet with a lot of problems.
- Is there somebody responsible for each task? Neither the angels nor the fairies will do the implementation. Implementation is a human activity and specific members of the group must take responsibility for the various tasks.
- Do the people understand the finer details of the plan? There is no question of being empowered if people do not understand what they are doing. Explaining the finer points of the plan is the task of the CDP.
- Is the implementation being done step by step? There is no other way than taking small steps. We cannot take giant steps when implementing a plan. Either the implementation will go skewed or participants will miss out on the learning process.
- Have all tasks been completed? We cannot start with a new batch of implementation tasks before the previous tasks have been done. If this rule is not adhered to chaos will ensue and that is usually the end of the project.

21.8.2 The conclusion of implementation

Some projects are never concluded because what has been established must be managed and maintained. Yet, there comes a time when the main action comes to an end and a different type of action is necessary. This phase of a project is truly a high point for the action group and the most should be made of it. This is also the time to decide whether it is necessary to continue with the project. If the necessary maintenance and management can be done without a project in place, then so be it.

If the objective of a project is a physical facility such as a crèche or communal hall, and if the group of participants have involved themselves fully in the planning and implementation, the facility should never be handed over at an inaugural function to the group whose efforts have brought it about. How can something that is your own be handed over to you? The group should hand it over to the larger community or the mayor or another appropriate dignitary acting as a trustee. The self-esteem gained by a group when it can hand over the key to a building that was erected through its efforts, instead of receiving a key to a facility placed there by external agents, is of immense value.

The successful conclusion of a project must be celebrated. A celebration strengthens relationships among those involved; it underlines the importance of the action group's achievement; it advertises to the world that that group achieved something through its own efforts; and it is a statement that the group can stand on its own feet. It is, therefore, a terrific confidence booster.

21.9 THE ROLE OF THE COMMUNITY DEVELOPMENT PRACTITIONER IN PLANNING AND IMPLEMENTATION

The CDP should not regard it necessary to enforce blueprints onto the participating group to demonstrate a superior ability. A CDP cannot be judged by the time it takes an action group to reach its objectives, but rather to the extent that they have participated and have learnt from the project.

Interim, step-by-step and experimental planning is not the sign of a weak CDP, but instead the sign of a wise one, enabling the participants to learn as much as possible from their participation.

The most important task of the CDP in this experimental planning is to provide the planning group with relevant information. The group must make choices – that is what decision making is all about. Its members must know what options are available to them and they must know what the consequences of each option will be. By providing relevant information, the CDP enables them to identify the options, discuss their pros and cons in the light of their probable consequences, and make the best choice under the circumstances.

The CDP must always encourage broad participation in planning so as not to limit this fantastic learning opportunity to a privileged few.

The CDP's position in implementation is, at best, a delicate one, but usually also a difficult one. If the CDP becomes too involved, he/she may be accused of not trusting the action group with the work. If the CDP does not become involved enough, he/she may be criticised for being aloof and 'above the ordinary people'. A CDP should not try to be ever-present. Most CDPs are involved in more than one project, with the result that they cannot spend all their available time on one project. The CDP's presence is more important during the planning meetings. His/her most important task during implementation is to help the group to translate decisions into action and then to orchestrate the action. However, it does act as a morale booster if the CDP sometimes gets involved in physical action. It at least shows the group that the CDP believes that their plan is correct and can be implemented.

One thing a CDP should never do is to take over a job from someone who has been nominated by a planning meeting to do it. Apart from it giving people the opportunity to avoid their responsibilities, it may also be interpreted as a vote of no confidence in that person. It may be necessary that a certain job or task be demonstrated to a group or an individual. This can be done by the CDP or any other competent person, but then it must remain a demonstration. See Case study 18: *Food garden in Mapayeni*.

It may be necessary to assist a person initially in a certain task until it is clear that the person can do it properly, for example helping someone with the secretarial duties. A CDP should be extremely careful not to show paternalism in this situation. He/she is not there to teach, but to assist. His/her competency level is not to be a yardstick for the group. He/she is not a quality controller, but a partner in an endeavour that is new to the person and the group.

CDPs often complain that, if they do not do most of the implementation work, nothing gets done. In such cases something is seriously wrong. Either the action group tends to take a backseat because the CDP was too prominent from the start (and therefore perceived to be the de facto leader); or the group lacks enthusiasm; or it does not realise that it owns the project and therefore also the responsibility to see it through to its successful conclusion. It is usually a sign that the approach from the start, especially during contact making, was not right. To 'fix' such a project is extremely difficult because a pattern has evolved and has settled, and this pattern has already solidified roles and positions.

21.10 CONCLUSION

Planning in community development is a positive action. People who are the victims of deprivation are given the chance and opportunity to plan a route out of the deprivation trap. Planning should not be a mundane technical affair that most of the participants do not understand. The CDP should be open-minded about planning. A few 'musts' were given in this chapter. As long as planning adheres to them, the rest of the planning action can be quite unorthodox. It must be a discovery. It must be adventurous. Why plan in a room around a table? Planning can just as well take place *in situ* – where the action takes place. Why follow strict meeting procedures during planning meetings? A bit of 'free-for-all' can be highly productive and people not used to strict meeting procedures may feel more inclined to participate in an informal discussion. Why plan with paper and pen? Use other items to 'build' plans; just make sure that it gets recorded (see Chapter 19). Planning must be a monthly high point. It is the best way to maintain momentum and to generate an even greater enthusiasm.

Implementation should hang on to the planning and at the same time fulfil it. It is part of the learning process and just as in planning, it is out of the question to expect excellence. Mistakes are also going to be made during implementation, and they are to be treated as all mistakes in community development, as opportunities to learn. By treating implementation as a learning opportunity, it becomes more than just the operationalisation of the plan. It also serves to instill confidence in the participants; it is an abject lesson to all who want to take note; and it is the basis for further action.

People who take their first steps in community development lose heart easily. For this reason, they must realise results quickly, even if these results are small in the eyes of the CDP. Quick results act as incentives for the group to strive harder toward its next objective. Further, poor people are vulnerable to circumstance and a prolonged effort to reach an objective makes them even more vulnerable.

REFERENCES

Ansari F, Fathi M & Seidenberg U. 2013. Combining synoptic and incremental approaches for improving problem-solving in maintenance planning, monitoring and controlling. 9th Interdisciplinary Workshop on Intangibles, Intellectual Capital and Extra-Financial Information, Copenhagen, Denmark, 26–27 September 2013. Available at: http://www.wiwi.uni-siegen.de/wiwi/ prod/downloads/ansari_fathi_seidenberg.pdf (accessed 24 August 2015).

Collyer S. 2013. Management approaches for dynamic environments. Available at: http://www.dynamicmanagement.info/2013/02/emergent-planning.html (accessed 17 February 2023).

Collyer S, Warren C, Hemsley B & Stevens C. 2010. Aim, fire, aim – project planning styles in dynamic environments. *Project Management Journal*, 41(4):108–121.

De Beer F & Swanepoel H. 2013. *The Community Development Profession: Issues, Concepts and Approaches*. Pretoria: Van Schaik.

Floate H, Durham J & Marks GC. 2019. Moving on from logical frameworks to find the 'missing middle' in international development programmes. *Journal of Development Effectiveness*, 11(1):89–103.

Janssen M & Van der Voort H. 2016. Adaptive governance: Towards a stable, accountable and responsive government. *Government Information Quarterly*, 33(2016):1–5.

Jensen G. 2010. The logical framework approach: How to guide. Bond. Available at: https://www.bond.org.uk/resources/ (accessed 18 February 2023).

Mazzurco A & Jesiek BK. 2019. Five guiding principles to enhance community participation in humanitarian engineering projects. *Journal of Humanitarian Engineering*, 5(2):1–9.

Prinsen G & Nijhof S. 2015. Between logframes and theory of change: Reviewing debates and a practical experience. *Development in Practice*, 25(2):234–246.

Rondinelli DA. 1993. Development projects as policy experiments: An adaptive approach to development administration. 2nd ed. London: Routledge.

Soe RF & Dreschler W. 2018. Agile local governments: Experimentation before implementation. *Government Information Quarterly*, 35(2):323–335.

Wiggins DA. 1993. *Development Projects as Policy Experiments: An Adaptive Approach to Development Administration.* 2nd ed. London: Routledge.

Wiggins S & Shields D. 1995. Clarifying the 'logical framework' as a tool for planning and managing development projects. *Project Appraisal*, 10(1):2–12.

CHAPTER 22
Monitoring, Evaluation and Control

Frik de Beer

22.1 INTRODUCTION

There are many good reasons for doing evaluation. One of the most important is that, without evaluation, community development cannot be a learning process. We can assume that mistakes will be made and that the identification and analysis of those mistakes will help make future efforts more effective. A mistake can perhaps be seen without delving too deeply for it, but it needs a deeper scrutiny to get clarity on the context in which the mistake occurred. Monitoring and evaluation together are a tool that supports the learning process, helping organisations to become more effective, more efficient and to expand through asking the *so what questions* (Görgens & Kusek 2009:1).

Community development is a learning process and it strives toward clear concrete goals within a gloomy reality. By asking the so what questions, implementation of the project is monitored. For instance, when a training session is approved, the so what questions to ask would be when, where, who? From the answers, course adjustments might be needed during the project from time to time. This is the control part of project management.

The principle of adaptiveness is of importance here. Community development usually takes place within an environment of uncertainty. It is usually not very clear what must be done to achieve the desired results or what people's responses to a project will be. It is therefore inevitable that things will not always go as planned. Course adjustments as part of the control function will be necessary, but a course adjustment is impossible if the degree of course deviation is not established first. If monitoring and evaluation are not a continuous part of the project, assuring that timely course adjustments can be made, the chances are good that the deviations will become so severe that nothing will bring the project back on course again.

The debate on the evaluation of community development is very much an ongoing one. This debate has run for many years and has resulted in a lot of soul searching. Despite many years of discussion, debate and associated examination have not found comprehensive answers to the many problems experienced in evaluation. What is generally agreed is that '[e]valuation is a process that critically examines a community project or a programme. It involves collecting and analysing information about a project's activities, characteristics and outcomes' (Ardle & Murray 2021:434).

22.2 THE EVALUATION DEBATE

Traditionally, evaluation sought to answer the question: did this project accomplish what it set out to do? In other words, the so what questions. Ardle and Murray (2021:433) say that '[i]ndeed, the matter of measuring impact is complex and can be misconstrued and misunderstood'. They go on to quote Motherway (2006:36): 'There is no simple, universal, magic solution to the challenge of measuring community development impacts'.

Indeed, Whelan, McGuinness and Delaney(2019:43) reiterate that the diversity and complexity of group functioning and social relationships within communities make evaluating outcomes and success of community development difficult. Furthermore, to measure achievement and evaluate success of abstract constructs such as empowerment and participation is challenging.

The point of departure in evaluation is always the goal or goals of a project and whether they were realised – results-based project management. This type of examination was firmly based on providing a numerical value to project outcomes by quantifying the input–effort–output sequence. In other words, evaluation of community development worked on the premise that all projects should meet requirements of economy, efficiency and effectiveness, thus minimising cost and maximising impact. The International Labour Organization (ILO) (ILO 2007:3) puts it as follows:

> The key idea underlying project cycle management, and specifically monitoring and evaluation, is to help those responsible for managing the resources and activities of a project to enhance development results along a continuum, from short-term to long-term. Managing for impact means steering project interventions towards sustainable, longer-term impact along a plausibly linked chain of results: inputs produce outputs that engender outcomes that contribute to impact.

Even now, the tendency remains to regard evaluation as a measurement, and literature on the subject is concerned with giving a numerical value to the supposed results of a project. The emphasis is placed on the effort expended, the effect of the project and efficiency of the use of resources. Economic performance becomes a major criterion in evaluation, neglecting the issues relating to the principles of community development. However, if we are supporting the general debate on development with its specifically human focus, we tend to develop some negative reaction to the strong economic focus on project evaluation.

We will agree with the concern that the social dimension of development efforts cannot properly be measured by the traditional tools used in evaluation. In fact, it is doubtful whether we are still interested in the traditional answers obtained through evaluation, that is, the effectiveness of project outcomes in terms of the input–effort–output sequence. To repeat our earlier reference to Whelan et al (2019): in community development projects, the central issues for evaluation are participation, capacity building, sustainability and empowerment. It is argued that it cannot be expected that all the effects of development projects be given a numerical value.

This viewpoint on how evaluation should be done and what should be evaluated is embodied in the radical interpretative approach, which is based on the assumption that evaluation cannot be neutral, that evaluation is fundamentally about control over direction and resources, and that its main aim is to address the issue of power (Marsden & Oakley 1991:321). It therefore questions the conventional view of evaluation, in the words of Marsden and Oakley (1991:328):

> For evaluations to become instruments for liberation and tools for empowerment ... they must transcend the old dichotomies which separate subjective from objective, and which consign insiders and outsiders to separate sides of the fence.

Another dimension of the interpretative approach, that is a logical continuation of the basic premise, is that evaluation must be participatory. Collaboration by project beneficiaries in the evaluation of projects (ie analysing results and making judgements on the direction and outcomes) should be a tool of empowerment. Participatory evaluation is given a solid foundation by the principle of learning. While this principle is as old as community development itself, this can be regarded as a genuine effort to concretise it in a way that will ensure that learning leads to empowerment. Evaluation then becomes part of an educational process, and, because the whole project is then an educational process, evaluation becomes part of the basic dynamic of the project. The motivation for evaluation then becomes empowerment and learning from experience (Swanepoel 1996:56). People involved in the project develop a methodology for reviewing their own experience, and all conclusions are obtained from the collective reflection that is part of the learning process. Consequently, community participants in projects also become co-creators of relevant evaluation frameworks (Ardle & Murray 2021:442). In this fashion, a participatory evaluation approach is not only an evaluative but also an educational approach: 'It should be an empowering experience with all those involved having their say in setting the criteria and analysing the findings' (SCCD 2001:13).

We thus arrive at a further dimension which we can call participatory communication and which can, and should, contribute significantly to the methodologies used in evaluation (Swanepoel 1996:57). Through participatory communication, people can gain a better perception of reality – a fundamental part of evaluation. By encouraging people to question and understand their reality, participatory communication contributes to a more active role of the poor in projects and their evaluation. It is a process based on people's creative potential. 'The idea of mutual learning is at the heart of these processes, with communities in control and decisions made by agreement or consensus' (Ardle & Murray 2021:444).

We agree with the main ideas of the radical approach to evaluation. Evaluation must be part of a process of discovery in which the local people participate entirely. Through this process of discovery, an understanding of reality is gained and this understanding is the main impetus for the participants to enjoy a learning experience, to give them a further opportunity for capacity building. According to Ardle and Murray (2021:444), the learning experience should result in the designing of research questions and methodologies by community members. In this process, people get a better understanding of what has been done, why it was done and how. Evaluation should be regarded as participatory research in which the people, the development agency and/or the donor, and one or more researchers are involved.

The features of the participatory research technique as identified by Vaughn and Jacquez (2020:1) should be guiding principles for all involved in evaluation. They identify the following important aspects of participatory research:
- It should emphasise direct engagement of local people and their priorities.

- Construction of questions and methods should take place with the involvement of community members and researchers in a collaborative fashion.
- Consequently 'subjects' of research become partners in research.

22.3 MONITORING AND EVALUATION

Evaluation is an integral part of a project. It forms part of the survey – it evaluates the reality or situation through the information obtained and it evaluates the information to ensure that it is legitimate and correct. It is also tied up with needs and resource identification by seeking the fit between needs and resources. It is an important part of planning – it tests the situation specificity and the feasibility of the planning. It is necessary during implementation – it assesses the action group's ability to operationalise the plan.

It is clear that a large portion of evaluation takes place throughout the life of a project and only a small part has to do with a final, after-the-fact evaluation. This larger continuous part can be regarded as keeping the finger on the pulse of a project and is called monitoring. The second type is an action performed at the end of a project. It is the final opportunity, with the benefit of hindsight, to identify weaknesses and mistakes made during the lifespan of a project. It seeks to establish whether the project was successful in terms of obtaining its objective and whether it was successful as a learning process; whether the action group gained more than only the physical results for which it was aiming.

22.3.1 Criteria for monitoring and evaluation

Three main criteria are used in monitoring and evaluation, namely appropriateness, feasibility and effectiveness. Using the criterion of *appropriateness*, it must be established whether the needs, objectives, plan of action and the action itself fit one another. The following questions must be asked:

- Will the attainment of the set objective satisfy the identified need? (Does the objective fit the need?)
- Have we identified the correct resources to reach the objective? (Do the resources fit the need?)

- Will the plan lead to the attainment of the objective? (Does the plan fit the objective?)

The second criterion is that of *feasibility*. It concerns itself with the claims a project will make on resources, including human resources. These questions must be asked:

- Is the objective within reach of the action group?
- Are there sufficient resources to attain the objective?
- Is the project completely dependent on external resources to attain the objective?
- Can human assets be developed during the project?

The community development practitioner (CDP) has a special duty regarding this part of the monitoring and evaluation process. He/she must be honest with a group if it is apparent that they are aiming too high. In a diplomatic way, the CDP should help the group to realise that their objective is beyond their means by assisting them with mapping out the consequences of their decisions. It is much better to help the action group establish the costs in terms of time, money, experience and effort. It is also feasible to help the action group identify alternative choices and assist them in exploring the consequences. This method of confronting a group with choices, rather than telling them what to do, is a good way of letting them take the initiative and accept the responsibility. Eventually, it is a great opportunity of learning and must lead to greater self-reliance.

Questions using the criteria of appropriateness and feasibility must also be put in the past tense. In other words, these criteria must be used for monitoring and for evaluation. It is necessary in monitoring and in the final evaluation to establish whether decisions taken interpret(ed) feasibility and appropriateness correctly.

Finally, the criteria of appropriateness and feasibility both point to the criterion of *effectiveness*. The action group wants to establish through evaluation whether its actions during the lifespan of a project were (are) effective. However, effectiveness in terms of the principles discussed earlier, must also be established. How effective was the project in

- fulfilling abstract human needs?
- providing a learning process for the participants?
- establishing ownership in the action group?

- empowering the action group?
- releasing the people from the deprivation trap?

These questions must be answered truthfully because the danger exists that the CDP and the committee may rush toward the objective with a lot of external help while the group of participants are left behind and find themselves mostly outside of the important activities. In terms of effectiveness, a project may score highly because the principles were ignored. In order to obviate this possibility, effectiveness must therefore also be evaluated in terms of the principles.

Many questions can be suggested to evaluate effectiveness. Some of these assess effectiveness in objective attainment without taking community development principles into consideration. Others evaluate effectiveness only in terms of the principles (see Chapter 6). Both these types should be used. For ease of use, the two types appear in two separate lists of questions.

List 1: **Questions to establish the effectiveness of objective attainment**

Technique Was a survey done before a need was identified? Which research techniques were used in the survey?	
Needs and objectives Was a need eventually identified? Was the need contextualised? Was the objective specified concretely? Was the objective within reach of the action group? Was the objective to alleviate the whole or only part of the identified need? Was the objective fully attained? Was the objective attained within the planned time? Did the attainment of the objective satisfy the identified need?	
Resources Was a survey of resources undertaken? Were the right resources identified to reach the objective?	

Planning	
How often were planning meetings held?	
In what way was the planning done?	
Did the planning specifically appoint certain people to certain tasks?	
Did the planning attach a timetable to action?	
Did the planning address how to do certain tasks?	
Was the planning appropriate to the identified need and the set objective?	
Were measures taken to institutionalise and maintain the objective?	
Monitoring	
Was the project monitored?	
What monitoring techniques were used?	
Finance	
Was money handled correctly?	
Was bookkeeping done correctly?	
Record keeping	
Was a record kept of the planning?	
In what way was recording of planning done?	

List 2: Questions to establish whether the objective was attained successfully in terms of the principles

Formation of the action group	
How was the action group for the project formed?	
Was the committee elected by the action group?	
Activities and responsibilities of the action group	
Did the action group accept ownership of the project?	
Did the action group accept responsibility for the project?	
Did the action group take more initiative as the project progressed?	
Did attendance at action group meetings increase or decrease?	
Did the action group have the power of decision making regarding the project?	
Did the project lead to the action group identifying further needs?	
Is the action group now better able to identify its needs?	
Is the action group now better able to plan?	
Is the action group now better able to organise itself?	
Is the action group now better able to tackle a project?	
Is the action group now desirous of tackling further projects?	
Is the action group now less dependent on external aid?	

Activities and responsibilities of the action group (continue)	
Is there any notable change in the attitude of the action group regarding its situation?	
Is there evidence that the larger community wants to follow the action group's example?	
Needs Identification	
Did the action group decide on the need?	
To what extent did the action group participate in the survey?	
Role of the CDP	
What was the role of the CDP in deciding the need?	
What was the CDP's official position on the committee?	
To what extent was the CDP involved in monitoring and evaluation?	
Did the CDP's role diminish as the project progressed?	
Action group meetings	
How often were action group meetings held?	
Did the committee report back to action group meetings on its activities?	
What percentage of action group members attended the action group meetings?	
Was enough time allowed in meetings for action group members to participate in the discussion?	
Were members encouraged to participate in discussions during meetings?	
Project planning	
What part did members play in project planning?	
What part did the CDP play in project planning?	
Implementation	
What percentage of the action group members were involved in the implementation?	
In what way were persons/organisations from outside involved in the project?	
Monitoring and evaluation	
To what extent did members participate in monitoring and evaluation?	
Were the benefits of the project distributed equally among participants?	
To what extent was the larger community advantaged by the project?	
Leadership	
Was leadership strengthened during the project?	
Were new leaders identified and involved in leadership activities?	

Some of these questions can be asked during a project and some only at the end of a project. There are, therefore, monitoring questions and evaluative questions. Most can be dealt with by the participants, but some of the questions in the second list will have to be answered by the CDP.

22.4 RECORD KEEPING AND MONITORING/EVALUATION

One of the most glaring shortcomings of projects is that they are seldom systematically recorded. As a result, extremely valuable information is lost and cannot be used as a learning experience for future projects. Good record keeping enriches the process of evaluation and, because evaluation is one of the cornerstones of the learning process, we can say that well-kept records enhance the learning process.

In this section, we discuss a number of formats of record keeping. When we talk of reports or event cards further down, we propose the nature and format of the contents. However, the means of recording are dictated by circumstances. If the group or project committee members have cell phones, 'event cards' can, for instance, be created as an SMS or WhatsApp message. If computers are generally available, event cards and reports can be created on a word processing program and forwarded by email. Whichever way event cards and/or reports are created and distributed, copies need to be kept centrally, either as a hard copy on file or as an electronic copy in a dedicated electronic filing system.

Creating event cards and reports is creating the project memory, which is all-important for project evaluation and control.

22.4.1 Records of planning meetings

In Chapter 21, we saw that planning meetings should also be an evaluating exercise. Every planning meeting should start with an assessment of the activities undertaken since the last meeting, and then planning takes place in the light of that evaluation. If records are kept of both the evaluation and planning sections of each meeting, a complete picture will evolve and be available by the time the final evaluation is reached. This record should start with some broad guidelines on how to reach the objective (decided on at the first meeting), followed by detailed planning for one month. This should be followed by an evaluation, first, of the implementation of that detailed planning and, second, of the 'implementability' of the detailed planning; in other words, an evaluation of the planning. This in turn, is followed by detailed planning for the next month in the light of the evaluation of the previous month, and so on. We would therefore have a record of every step we decided on (the what), a time frame attached to it (the when), a person or persons responsible for that step (the who), the way we think that step should be carried out (the how) and what happened, reflected in the right-most column of the minutes.

22.4.2 Reports

Another way of keeping records is to request full reports at planning meetings by key participants on all activities engaged in since the previous meeting. These reports can be written (in which case they can be attached to the minutes) or they can be oral (in which case detailed notes must be made of them in the minutes). The advantage of this method is that the correctness of the reports is verified when the minutes are approved, and the records are kept in a central place with other documents and correspondence. The disadvantage is that it places a heavy burden on the secretary if the reports are delivered orally. Further, participants may find it difficult to write reports on their activities and, lastly, the tabling of detailed reports may lengthen planning meetings considerably.

22.4.3 Event cards

In order to spread the burden of record keeping more evenly, the key persons in a project may be given event cards.

Each of them completes an event card each time they are involved in some action pertaining to the project. The completed cards are then left to be categorised and filed at a central place or with someone such as the secretary or CDP. The advantage of this method is that the work of record keeping is shared by several people. Another advantage is that the event cards are completed immediately after the event. The reports are therefore fresher than an oral report at a meeting perhaps three weeks after the fact. A further advantage is that several reports of the same event may be received because several people are usually involved. It means that more than one person's perception and experience of the same event is recorded. A final advantage is that records are short and precise, and will not take much time to fill in, compile or analyse.

The disadvantage of this method is that no one is really responsible for writing down the events, and it may happen that it is not done at all. If all or some of the key people are illiterate, this method cannot be used. The purpose of these event cards is not to table them at the next meeting. They form a separate and parallel record of the project. A comparison between this and the official record can be interesting. See Figure 22.1 for an example of an event card.

```
DATE OF EVENT:
REPORTER:
DESCRIPTION OF EVENT:


ROLE OF REPORTER:

REMARKS AND PRELIMINARY ASSESSMENT ON REVERSE
```

Figure 22.1 **Example of an event card**

The use of WhatsApp photos and voice notes should also be considered as an additional or a supportive tool in record keeping. However, such records should be carefully monitored and recorded so that they do not get lost.

22.5 DISCUSSION AND OBSERVATION AS MONITORING/ EVALUATION TECHNIQUES

For monitoring and evaluating purposes, written records must be augmented by observation and discussion. The CDP must keep his/her eyes and ears open to observe not only physical detail but also the attitudes and perceptions of those participating in the project. This observation is not of an isolated event, but happens over time so that progress and growth in attitude and approach can also be noted. Discussions can be formal or informal, between groups or individuals. There is no best way. The circumstances and the situation will decide which method is most fitting for the moment. The important aspect regarding this type of monitoring and evaluation is that we should not treat it as a careless way of research. It is not a second-rated way of doing things; it is just another, equally trustworthy way. We should realise that both objectivity and subjectivity are present in any given situation. The one is not more important than the other. Both are present and therefore both must be considered.

Just as in any other 'scientific' research the CDP and the participants must use triangulation (see Chapter 19) to verify the information received. The other important aspect that must be adhered to is that the CDP, who is part of the monitoring and evaluating process, can never stand aloof and view matters from a bird's eye vantage point. The view is strictly lateral, sometimes even worm-like, regarding the process from underneath. We looked at the evaluative, interpretative approach earlier on, therefore suffice to say here that we must have extremely open minds geared toward adaptiveness (Chambers' new professionalism, see Chambers & Pretty 1993) when dealing with evaluation and monitoring.

CDPs must consider the possibility of keeping a diary in which they can record from time to time (not necessarily every day) their observations, specifically subjective ones such as attitude, animosity, keenness, belief and self-reliance. All of these observations can be valuable inputs in a final evaluation of a project, especially when dealing with the second list of questions above.

22.6   DOS AND DON'TS REGARDING EVALUATION

Evaluation tends to have negative connotations. People do not like to be evaluated. In most people's minds it is like writing an examination – it is never pleasant. For this reason, the CDP should handle evaluation carefully. The following aspects require special attention:

- *Evaluation should never be presented as a test*. It is not intended to establish whether a person or group has succeeded or failed. Evaluation tries to establish whether an action had the desired result and to determine the reasons for its outcome.
- *Evaluation should never be personalised*. It is not a person or even the group that is evaluated, but an action. If the 'how' aspect is thoroughly discussed in a planning meeting, the individual cannot, in any event, be blamed if an action fails or has a less positive outcome.
- *Never tie evaluation to a penalty*. A less than successful outcome is already a letdown. A penalty will only have negative results under these circumstances.

- *Evaluation should be done openly.* It is not the prerogative of the CDP or the executive of a group. When evaluation becomes something done by an individual or a few individuals after they have distanced themselves from the rest of the participants, all the negative perceptions will find fertile soil to proliferate.
- *All participants must also participate in evaluation.* No one is to be excluded from it because apart from the elitism engendered by it, it also keeps certain people away from the learning opportunity offered by evaluation.
- *Evaluation should be simple.* Complex, so-called scientific methodologies require great skill that makes it impossible for most participants to participate or at least understand what they are doing. Such complexity and sophistication can only have negative reactions from ordinary people, to the extent that they do not understand the data and even less the analysis of the data, and that they therefore develop distrust in the activity of evaluation and the results it produces.
- *Evaluation should always be presented as a learning opportunity.* When evaluation shows a negative result, two questions must immediately be asked. What have we learnt from it? What should we do now? Every negative result must be turned into a positive learning experience. It must always be accompanied by planning or replanning, which is a positive expression.
- *CDPs should not distance themselves from a negative result.* CDPs should never be critical of a person's or the group's actions. If something goes wrong, CDPs must accept responsibility for it along with the group. Success must be ascribed to the action group, but for the mishaps CDPs must accept joint responsibility.

22.7 CONTROL

Control sounds like an important function and one to which we would want to attach authority. Only those with authority can control a project. Because of a lifelong preoccupation with amorphous figures of authority, we also tend to turn away from the community, from ordinary people, when we are seeking those figures of authority. Yet, when we speak of control as a management function in projects, we do not have other role players in mind than those with whom we are familiar. Those people who were participating in needs identification, who were present at the planning meetings and who are actively involved in implementation, are also the ones who control a project.

The control function is an important one, but we should be careful not to tie it to supervision and executive discretion, as in the case of organisational management. Yes, it has to do with supervision and discretion, but not that of one person over others. The supervision and discretion in our context lie with the participants who must supervise their own actions and exercise discretion over their own plans. If they realise through the learning process that a project needs adjustment, then they adjust accordingly and that is what is meant by control. Every planning meeting, therefore, is also a mechanism of control and every evaluation activity informs the control function. We can therefore conclude by saying that control is an everyday function, and it is situated in the project with the participants, not outside with some vague figure of authority.

22.8 CONCLUSION

Objective, quantifiable evaluation is not the only good evaluation. Some things that must be learnt through evaluation cannot be established in an objective, quantifiable way. Many of the questions in the two lists detailed earlier, require a subjective evaluative assessment of the situation. The intention of monitoring and evaluation is to afford the CDP and the group an opportunity to learn, and continuous evaluation will establish a critical disposition in the action group that will enhance the learning process. This type of evaluation relies on two factors for reliability and correctness. The first is honesty – dishonesty will lead to the evaluators bluffing themselves. The second is verification. No evaluation result stands on the opinion of one person. That is the reason for group evaluation rather than evaluation by a person. That is also the reason why PRAP (see Chapter 19) relies so heavily on triangulation.

It is important to accept that qualitative interpretative evaluation is as important as quantitative evaluation and that ideally they are combined. A lot of information necessary for community development can be gleaned in this way. In fact, Ardle and Murray (2020:13) state the following:

Evaluation should offer insight into an initiative so as to enable reflection that assists in the identification of pathways towards future change. Recommendations emanating from the evaluation should be linked to evaluation findings whether qualitative or quantitative, outlining who is responsible for the next steps and in what time frame. Active participation in monitoring and evaluation, including analysing data and describing concerns should be core to – rather than alongside – the process of community development evaluation and can in itself lead to community empowerment.

Marsden and Oakley (1991:325) come to the conclusion that 'the way forward lies in the construction of a practical evaluation that embodies many of the central concerns of an interpretative enquiry'.

The evaluation discussed in this chapter can be regarded as an alternative, even radical approach. It is in sympathy with and tries to give substance to the ideas of monitoring and evaluation as opportunities for participation and learning: it allows for the collective wisdom of community members and those of researchers to emerge and may lead to more meaningful findings translated to action (Vaughn & Jacquez 2020:7).

In dealing with participation, we are not only concerned with results (which are quantitative). More importantly, we need to understand processes (which are qualitative). Evaluation must be a process of discovery through which an understanding of reality is attained or enhanced. This understanding allows the participants to enjoy a learning experience providing further opportunities for capacity building – an absolute prerequisite for empowerment (Swanepoel 1996:57).

REFERENCES

Ardle O & Murray U. 2021. Fit for measure? Evaluation in community development. *Community Development Journal*, 56(3):432–448.

Chambers R & Pretty J. 1993. Towards a learning paradigm: New professionalism and institutions for agriculture. In Scoones I & Thompson J (eds), *Beyond Farmer First: Rural People's Knowledge, Agricultural Research and Extension Practice*. London: IT Publications.

Görgens M & Kusek JZ. 2009. *Making Monitoring and Evaluation Systems Work: A capacity Development Toolkit*. Washington: World Bank.

ILO (International Labour Organization). 2007. *Technical Cooperation Manual (Version 1). Geneva: ILO. (Accessed on 24 May 2023 from* https://www.ilo.org/wcmsp5/groups/public/---dgreports/---exrel/documents/genericdocument/wcms_172679.pdf.

Marsden D & Oakley P. 1991. Future issues and perspectives in the evaluation of social development. *Community Development Journal*, 26(4):315–328.

SCCD. 2001. *Standing Conference for Community Development: Strategic Framework for Community Development*. Sheffield: SCCD.

Swanepoel H. 1996. Evaluation of community development projects: A human development approach. *Africanus*, 26(1):53–64.

Vaughn LM & Jacquez F. 2020. Participatory research methods – choice points in the research process. *Journal of Participatory Research Methods*, 1(1).

Whelan A, McGuinness S & Delaney JM. 2019. *Valuing Community Development Through the Social Inclusion Programme (SICAP) 2015–2017: Toward a Framework for Evaluation*. Research Series, No. 77. Dublin: Economic and Social Research Institute (ESRI).

SECTION E
Training for Community Development

CHAPTER 23

The Training Dialogue

Frik de Beer and Andries de Beer

23.1 INTRODUCTION

The community development practitioner (CDP) has many tasks and roles. We have seen throughout this book how the CDW is involved in every part of development and poverty eradication. The next important task that we would like to discuss is that of trainer, because the CDP will have to train people to become motivators, mobilisers and advisers for people who want to take charge of their own lives (De Beer 1995). 'Since the learning process is a vital aspect of community development, it is important that as many role-players as possible are exposed to and share the same type of training input' (De Beer & Swanepoel 2013:112). Ledwith (2022:196–197) posits that transformation at which community development aims is not possible without curiosity and imagination. These traits require more than training in mechanical actions, to 'tick the boxes', as it were. It requires training for critical consciousness which 'stimulates curiosity from apathy, inspires confidence and frees the imagination to act'.

This chapter and the next (Chapter 24: *Planning and facilitating a training workshop*) have been written with reference to De Beer (1995), De Beer and Swanepoel (1996; 1998; 2013) and Swanepoel & De Beer (1994).

The United Nations (UNCHS 1984:17) states as follows:

> Training requires special skills and talents that are not common, and competent persons with a good deal of practical experience are required. It is often difficult, however, to attract such persons to the job of training and to reward them sufficiently to keep them on the job and improve their performance.

The teaching model supported by the authors may be described as a model of 'teaching by discovery' or as capacity building (workshop). This method of training, which the authors follow and is described in this book, should be used by the student trainers, such as CDPs, who undertake the training of people involved in the development of communities.

This workshop or capacity-building method is not easy, however its advantages (and the disadvantages of the direct or lecture method) outweigh its relatively difficulty. Opportunity for interaction is encouraged and a dialogue between trainer, trainee and material can be established to the extent that the trainer becomes a facilitator of a process of knowledge creation by the trainees. We therefore use trainer and facilitator interchangeably in chapters 23 and 24. Trainers are required to accept the challenge with an open mind, a willingness to experiment and, above all, openness to regard every training episode as an opportunity for themselves and the trainees to learn.

The trainer must become a 'dialogical man', as Freire (2006:90) puts it – a story weaver. Trainers must first of all have faith in humankind, in their 'power to make and remake, to create and recreate, faith in their vocation to be more fully human' (Freire 2006:90–91). Facilitators who enter into dialogue with the community must show humility, because without it dialogue cannot take place. 'How can I dialogue if I always project ignorance onto others and never perceive my own … How can I dialogue if I am closed to – even offended by – the contribution of others?' (Freire 2006:90).

The stories of the facilitator and the community matter, and they help to shape the approach and outcomes. Randall (2012) as well as Lindner and Garcia (2014) view the theory of autobiographical learning and the development of critical cultural competence as closely relating to teaching through stories (Rossiter, Derwing, Manimtim, Thomson 2010; Sandelowski, 1991:165). Stories are formulated through dialect or conversations, the key word being conversations, indicating more than one voice. It is not the facilitator that must be heard but rather the voices of individuals and the community as a whole. More specifically, it is the experiences of a community that should be heard, shaped around their stories. Their stories are invariably about interesting places, people, challenges and victories. People thrive in environments where there is a web of interconnectedness between the individual and the community as well as between the community and nature. The interconnectedness that links us all is reflected in the stories that we share. This implies that everything is connected, and that attending or listening to the stories allows us to attend to the whole. As a result, an individual can only be known as a member of a recognised community, through their stories. This connection includes our connection to the land and the places where we were born and live (Ledwith & Springett 2022:73–47).

It may take time and practice for the facilitator, especially the person who starts anew, to handle the workshop method efficiently. The results, once the method is mastered, are extremely rewarding.

This chapter provides a broad framework, using some ideas and approaches that have proven successful in practice. Facilitators are advised to use them as guidelines and not as gospel. The reality and the challenges facilitators face will differ and will require adaptation and experimentation. Ideally, the guidelines should be used as part of a training package. However, student trainers can also use them as a manual for self-training. Not all CDPs will necessarily be facilitators, but they should still take note of these two chapters (23 and 24) because they will come across training packages for development projects. They will then have the opportunity to evaluate those in the light of these chapters.

23.2 TRAINING AS A DIALOGUE

23.2.1 The concept explained

To be optimally successful, development training should be a dialogue between the three key elements in a training situation: material, trainer and the trainees.

The material may be a textbook or journal article, a video or audio clip, a PowerPoint presentation, equipment for simulation games or ideas in the head of the trainer: usually it consists of a combination of the items mentioned.

Trainers may be experts, and their task is to transfer their knowledge to the trainees. They come with skills, norms and attitudes and, because of their position, with authority, if not power. Sometimes trainers are not experts, but know how to facilitate a group to create their own knowledge, or know where to find and how to involve an expert when the subject is very technical.

Trainees are adults with some life experience and probably knowledge applicable to the theme they are about to be trained in. They also bring along norms and attitudes developed during their lives. These elements – material, trainer and trainees – form the 'raw material' with which to carry out a training session. The modes of training according to which the process can be conducted are action, discussion and presentation.

Action training is experiential in that it allows trainees to 'do' and therefore experience certain situations. From their experience, they are able to discover knowledge, learn a skill or identify and improve attitudes. Work integrated learning (WIL) or practicals provide one way of 'to do' training. WIL, in collaboration with contact session ('theory') training, provides the optimum situation for adult learning to take place. A diagram of action training is shown in Figure 23.1.

The role of the trainer is to choose an activity or topic and then to manage the action; the trainees engage directly with the topic and explore, discover and solve problems through the experience afforded.

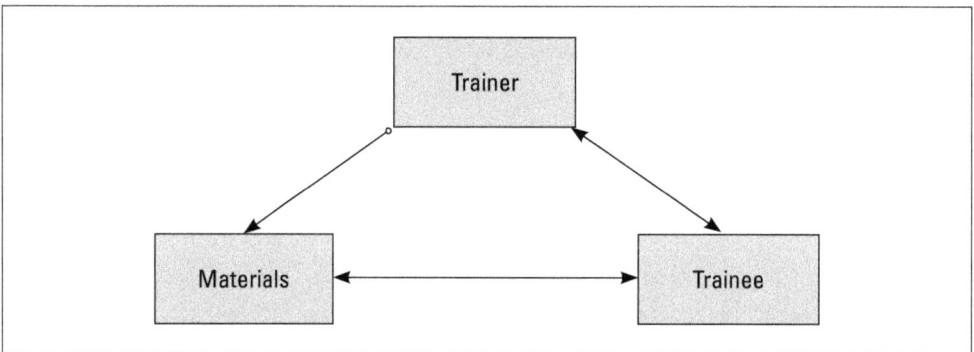

Figure 23.1 **Action training diagram**

Discussion is a method of training also called reflective learning. In this method, both the trainer and trainees engage in the 'dissecting' of material – be it a pre-read article or the material generated by the group in a workshop. They raise issues, analyse and come to conclusions by participating in the discussion (see Figure 23.2).

The trainer must decide on the topic or material and generally, 'regulates the traffic of discussion'. However, in some situations it may be wise, even preferable, for trainees to select a topic. The activity to debate and select a topic may in itself become a powerful learning experience (see the discussion on the use of participatory rapid appraisal (PRA) in Chapter 20). While this provides for a truly interactive learning episode, the trainer must be skilful in handling group interaction and dynamics. The trainer must allow the group members to voice their own experiences or perceptions of the material or topics selected. The stories need to be told, and in the telling become a powerful tool of learning. As Hong and Crowther (2016:64) put it:

Chapter 23: **The Training Dialogue**

A central axiom of community education is 'working where people are at' in the sense of meeting people on their own territory as well as engaging them educationally around their own expressed concerns and interests.

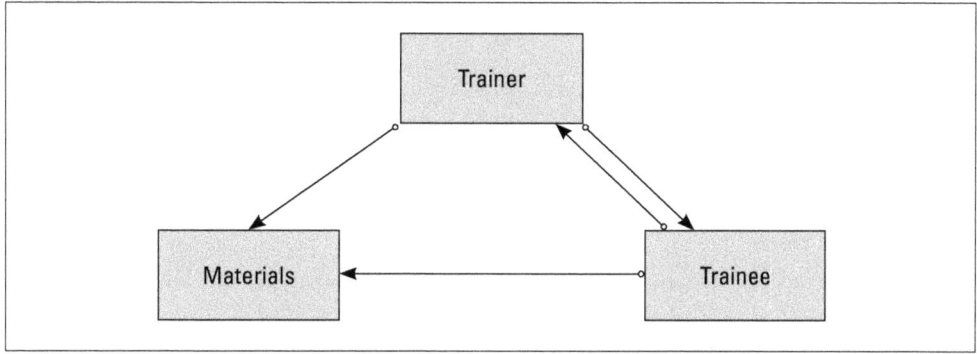

Figure 23.2 **Discussion diagram**

Presentation is a formal lecture in which the trainer relates the material to the trainees. He/she is a filter and in this situation the trainees have very little, if any, direct contact with the material. A diagram of presentation is shown in Figure 23.3.

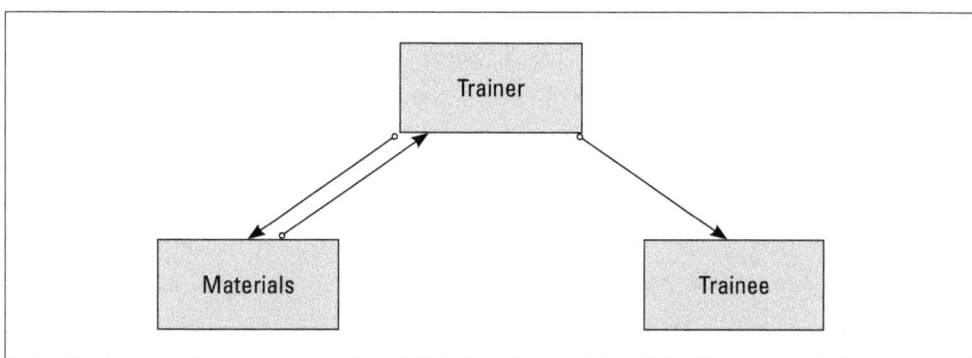

Figure 23.3 **Presentation diagram**

During a training episode, more than one, if not all three, of these methods are often used. For optimal learning to take place, the facilitator must plan a properly balanced learning episode in which, through action, discussion and presentation, the facilitator, material and trainees are continuously in dialogue.

23.2.2 The meaning of participation in training

Can we talk of participation when trainees are only allowed to answer questions posed by the trainer? Certainly not, though it may be a small part of participation. Participation in training means, among others, that:

- *trainees*:
  - are expected to, and must be encouraged to, help set the 'training agenda'
  - must contribute their practical experience to the process taking place in the workshop
  - must 'create' their own understanding of and solutions to problems.
- *facilitators*:
  - must be flexible in their approach, willing to be challenged by trainees and able to deal with the situation without causing tension or animosity among the trainees
  - must be capable of integrating and interpreting contributions by trainees so that they contribute to and become part of the process taking place in the workshop
  - must accompany and guide trainees in the process of gaining understanding of and solutions to problems.

Participation in training means that the facilitator encourages an atmosphere in which the trainee, facilitator and material engage in a dialogue to find applicable answers. It is, in other words, not an ordinary classroom situation in which an 'expert' shares his/her wisdom with passive students. It is taxing on the facilitator and requires practical experience, knowledge of the subject and a non-threatening disposition. It also requires of the facilitator a maturity to handle difficult situations and adult people. The rationale is that when confronted with critical analyses of their own personal situation, the focus of the community members can be shifted from identifying problems to finding solutions.

23.2.3 Setting the climate for learning

All people fear the unknown and all have expectations regarding specific situations they may experience. Fear and expectations are the two main issues to be addressed in order to set a relaxed and purposeful climate for learning.

In a classroom situation, people fear:
- the trainer, because he/she has power stemming from knowledge and position
- other participants, for they may be better qualified to voice their opinions
- their own inability to be assertive
- the environment in which teaching takes place
- failure.

Facilitators should address the trainees' fear in the following ways:
- They should make themselves vulnerable by sharing their own stories.
- They should acknowledge their shortcomings and emphasise the potential contribution of the trainees – the facilitator is not a know-all and the trainee not an empty slate.
- They should address the fear of other trainees by introducing them to one another informally, talking about their background.
- They should address the fear of lack of assertiveness by treating each trainee as an individual and providing an opportunity for each to make his/her viewpoint known.
- They should cultivate a relaxed attitude and use the applicable seating arrangements to reduce fear of the environment.
- They should emphasise the mutual learning experience and adopt an approach that is not aimed at examination and 'passing a test' to reduce fear of failure.

Expectations are often determined by factors that are not controlled by the facilitator. The community whom he/she represents may 'impose' their expectations on the trainee. The general political climate in the country may create high and unrealistic expectations. Trainees themselves may view any kind of training as an opportunity for personal growth and, often, as a guarantee of future employment opportunities. Above all, they may expect the training to empower them to move the world or, conversely, they may expect that they would in any case fail. By allowing expectations to surface, we are in a better position to deal with them.

Address the expectations of trainees by explaining the composition and objectives of the course very clearly. Discuss the organisation of the training. Allow trainees to explain and discuss their problems, expectations and aims.

23.2.4 Ensuring participation

The capacity-building approach is extremely dependent on the full participation of the trainees. However, participation does not always happen easily. Those who are supposed to participate always have some reservations. The main reason for this is that participation increases vulnerability (remember the fear factor). It is safer to keep quiet and look interested than to participate and be challenged or even be criticised. The facilitator can also be fooled by a quasi-participation which in the end contributes nothing to the process. Head nodding and phrases such as 'I agree', 'yes, yes' and 'that is so' fall into this category. It is acceptable for everyday conversation and makes it lively, but it is not participation in discussion.

Participation must be invited, made possible and made worthwhile. An important prerequisite for participation is an atmosphere conducive to participation, and this ties in closely with the attitude and ability of the facilitator. The trainees must be convinced that the facilitator is dependent on their contributions; that he/she is interested in their contributions; that he/she regards their contributions as valuable; and that he/she views their contributions as giving momentum to the process. The facilitator must also have the ability to give every trainee a fair chance to participate; to regulate the discussions so that no one person will dominate; and to make sure that every trainee is safeguarded against personal attack.

It is important that the discussions have relevance and that they deal with practical aspects. Trainees will feel it unnecessary to contribute, or feel themselves incapable of contributing, if the discussion does not affect them or their work situation directly. Many trainees also feel themselves incapable of contributing to theoretical discussions while they are quite competent to talk about practical issues. The feeling and attitude among the trainees may also work towards discouraging or encouraging participation. A few overly critical trainees may dampen the appetite for contributions to the discussions. If the training programme is for a multi-level group, the more junior members may feel incompetent (or intimidated) to talk in front of more senior personnel. The facilitator must nullify these negative aspects by playing the role of catalyst and enabler. He/she must be a competent and fair 'traffic' officer who will give everybody a chance to contribute. He/she will regard every contribution as important and will show it through his/her gratitude for every contribution. The trainees' understanding of the capacity-building approach is also very important. The trainees must realise and believe that no knowledge transfer is going to take place from the trainer to them; that they are responsible for finding solutions to their problems, and that it will not be rude to say what is on their mind.

Many trainees are used to the presentation (lecture) method – the talk-and-chalk approach. They had years of experience of lectures in school, college and university. In that context, participation is to ask at the end of the lecture if there is something that they do not understand. It may be difficult for them to make the leap to the type of participation required by the capacity-building approach.

A usually successful solicitor of contributions is a discussion on the needs of the trainees. A need orientation is therefore very important. People like to talk about their needs and problems, and it is the task of the facilitator to steer the discussion from this topic to the possible solution to the needs and problems. However, make sure that the discussion remains focused, or at least returns to the main theme under discussion.

23.3 INTERACTIVE (WORKSHOP) TECHNIQUES

Many interactive training techniques exist and more are developed by facilitators as they gain experience and face new challenges. Some of the techniques are mentioned below. However, CDPs are encouraged to investigate on their own and to learn more. Because group dynamics and background may make certain approaches more appropriate than others, CDPs or facilitators should be flexible and able to interchange techniques to suit the context.

23.3.1 Open session discussion

The input that the facilitator provides must never be regarded as gospel. The facilitator must submit it for the scrutiny of the trainees. Do not be satisfied with a simple reaction that they agree with the input. Ask the 'yes, but' questions if they do not do it. This scrutiny of the input takes place mostly through an open discussion by all the participants. The same applies to report-back sessions. Impress upon the trainees that reports from groups must also be discussed.

23.3.2 Group work

It is often taken for granted that work in small groups is better than in plenary sessions, and that it is the best way to involve all trainees. This is not necessarily true. Small groups can have various disadvantages, with the following being the more important ones, among others.

Loss of synergy

The facilitator's objective is to establish synergy, in other words a combined energy that is greater than the sum total of the energy of the individuals. Fragmentation into smaller groups can work against this objective. Breaking into smaller groups entails a stop to proceedings in plenary session, movement of people to other rooms or another place in the same room, some people rushing off to the toilets or smoking a quick cigarette, chats between people on any subject, sitting down for the small group discussion, and breaking the ice in order to start the work. In other words, the momentum of the workshop is lost, and with it, also the building up of synergy. Another cause of synergy loss is that groups do not finish their work at the same time. Some groups finish sooner and loiter, while others are still busy.

Duplication

Group work can be so structured that groups do the same work and come to the same conclusions. During the report-back session, the one group repeats what the other group has already said and this can happen three or four times, depending on the number of groups. This is not the most productive way to use limited time.

Time consuming

It takes time for groups to move to their places of work and to move back to the main centre for report-back. It can take as long as 20 minutes and breaks of 30 minutes are not uncommon. A report-back session can also be time consuming. If there are three groups, it cannot be completed in less than 20 minutes.

Competitive behaviour

Groups tend to compete with each other. Basically, there is nothing wrong with this – a critical disposition towards each other can have good results – but a lot of energy can be spent on the competition, that is, on peripheral foci. Competition between groups can also work against the unity of the larger group. It can therefore spoil its dynamics. Competition can also waste time and misdirect attention when groups try to catch each other out during report-back.

Possible lack of involvement

Group work does not ensure better involvement of the individual trainee. It is generally accepted that the shy, unsure of him/herself trainee will participate better in the small group. There is some merit in this belief, but it is not universally true. The leader of the small group may lack facilitation skills and the very people who cause the trainee's shyness and reluctance to participate may be with him/her in the small group. This is not going to help his/her participation in the least. On the contrary, he/she is in more of a face-to-face position with them than in the larger group.

Facilitation by group leader

Facilitation is taken out of the facilitator's hands. One of the most serious disadvantages is that the success of the small group depends on its leader. The facilitator has very little control over who will be nominated as leaders and they can have all the flaws a group leader can possibly have. They can be steamrollers, not allowing the group to participate. They can be biased toward certain people. They can be incapable of maintaining a free flow of ideas or of getting a group going. Group work can therefore be a low point with not much going on. Animosities and bad blood in the small group can also be brought to the larger group.

All these weaknesses must be kept in mind and the facilitator must try to prevent them from weakening the workshop. If group work is done, then the following should be kept in mind:

- The task must be precisely described so that the group can operate within well-defined parameters.
- It must be ascertained whether the group understands its task before it starts its group work activity.

- Enough time must be allocated (less than 30 minutes for group work is counter-productive).
- Groups must not be overloaded with a number of tasks for a single work session.
- Report-back must lead to discussion.

Group work can be of value if different groups give attention to different aspects to save the larger group's time. Not more than four groups should be operative because it taxes workspace severely and because it makes report-back too long.

The division of the trainees into groups can follow one of two points of departure, namely to put together what belongs together or to make each group as diverse as the large group is. People belong together if they share the same workplace, do the same job, and find themselves at the same level of the hierarchy or when they are friends. It is better if the small group reflects the composition of the large group. The best way to get this diversity in the small group is simply to give trainees a number in repetitive sequence – such as 1, 2, 3, 1, 2, 3 – starting at one point and running through to the end. It ensures the breaking up of friends or colleagues from the same office, who usually sit next to one another.

23.3.3 Buzz groups

Buzz groups may be a better option than larger groups, although the one cannot replace the other. Buzz groups consist of two or three people sitting next to one another. The aims with buzz groups are not to let them work out things in detail and to report at length. Therefore, a buzz group session lasts a maximum of fifteen minutes. The idea is to get a few ideas from every buzz group, and then to work with that 'raw material' until some refined product is achieved. Buzz groups are also less formal than small groups.

It is not necessary for all buzz groups to report back. The primary aim is to get a discussion going. Therefore, the facilitator uses inputs to solicit reaction and then invites only inputs that will represent a counter reaction. Alternatively, he/she takes up an idea from a buzz group and develops it up to a point and then invites inputs that will develop it further. It can be quite a hectic session, with buzz groups clamouring for attention or aggressively opposed to one another's inputs. Later, the inputs are not all from buzz groups, but individuals make inputs. This is fine, as long as the argument develops at a fast pace. The facilitator is therefore more than a chairperson who gives everyone a fair chance to report back. He/she manipulates inputs to get a discussion going and even plays devil's advocate to make the discussion livelier.

23.3.4 The nominal group technique

The purpose of the nominal group technique is to ensure equal inputs from all trainees. The method is briefly as follows. A question is put to the trainees. This can emanate from the facilitator or can come out in discussion, for example: what are the most serious problems you encounter in your work? What are the most serious constraints in your communication with the public? The questions need not only be so extreme. One can also ask questions such as: what are the solutions to the credibility crisis you experience? How can communication between you and your supervisor be improved?

Trainees must draw up a list individually, without consulting with anyone, in which answers or solutions to the question or problem are given. When all the trainees have done that, the facilitator starts at a point and each trainee gives the first item on his/her list which is then written down on a board or preferably on a flip chart. The contributor's name is not written next to his/her contribution. When every trainee has had a chance to contribute one item, the facilitator goes back to the starting point and gives every trainee a second chance to contribute an item. This he/she continues to do until no trainee has any item left.

An important rule of this technique is that no item is discussed or criticised as it appears on the flip chart. After all contributions have been received and have been written down, the list is purified. This is done by discussing the different contributions one by one; not in relation to their importance, but to their truth and relevancy. Items that are related may be consolidated and wording may be changed slightly to better bring out the meaning. A fresh list can be drawn up to reflect the purification and improvements.

This technique has two real advantages. The first is that every trainee is obliged to make a contribution without being held directly responsible for it. Because discussion is postponed to after the completion of the list, trainees are no longer sure who contributed which items. An item becomes removed from its contributor and is discussed without the contributor having to defend it, which he/she can do, of course, if he/she wants to.

The second advantage is that all possible answers are given to a question. Any question or problem can therefore be discussed with all viewpoints or suggestions on the table. In this way the trainees experience that they are creating knowledge: it is their own answer to an issue, not that of the trainer, that they must accept.

The disadvantage of the technique is that it takes a great deal of time and therefore is impossible to use regularly. It is also not very effective with large groups. If the group is too large, say more than 20, the trainees can be paired and then the two people must decide on their combined contribution; they are then regarded as one person.

The nominal group technique is ideally suited to get a group going. It is therefore especially good for early on in a training session. After the first contribution by a trainee, the ice is broken for him/her and he/she will from then on participate more easily.

The following are alternatives to the full exercise:

- The facilitator lists only the first contribution of each trainee before the list is closed, irrespective of whether there are more contributions to be made.
- The facilitator requests the trainees to prioritise their contributions and to submit only the number one priority on their list.

23.3.5 Brainstorming

Brainstorming is an unstructured discussion that may seem confusing (especially at the start of the process) but which, if carefully conducted, will lead to a synergy of inputs into original and often new ideas. Brainstorming is used to break new ground, to overcome what seem like insurmountable stumbling blocks or to find a way out of a stalemate situation. This technique is also time consuming, perhaps more than others because of the absence of structure. An added problem is that it can end in total confusion, causing bigger problems than those it intended to overcome. The facilitator must therefore be attentive to what is said: he/she must pick up the positive contributions, integrate ideas and in an ongoing fashion structure the debate, without monopolising it.

The aim of brainstorming is to get a lot of ideas on the table and then to look for the 'rough diamonds' and to polish them until they can be used. It is a creative exercise, but also hectic because it is the group mind at work, not the minds of the individual trainees. (See Case study 26: *The trainers who thought they were teachers*.)

23.4 TEACHING AIDS

The trainer must be creative in identifying, using and sometimes creating new teaching aids. The core teaching aids of games, role play and case studies are well known and often used. In addition to these, trainers should identify and use relevant video clips available on the internet. TED Talks (https://www.ted.com/talks) and some YouTube clips (https://www.youtube.com) are very useful.

Training material can also be generated by trainees by making use of PRA methods such as mapping and transect walks (Kar 2010:20). (See Chapter 19.) Kar (2010) uses PRA extensively in training for what he calls 'community led total sanitation'. By gathering material through PRA exercises, information is obtained which leads, according to Kar, to identification of the problem – he calls it triggering. The training creates awareness of sanitation problems which triggers the community into finding a solution (often with help from outside).

23.4.1 The relevance of games, role play and case studies for training

The use of games, role play and case studies as methods of experiential and participatory learning, fills a definite niche in the training of people involved in development at grassroots level.

Among others, they have the following specific advantages:
- They can be used to convey facts, teach concepts, promote attitudes and foster ideas.
- They are extremely flexible both in time and content.
- They can be adapted easily to meet changing circumstances and needs.
- Learning is enhanced because they are fun and participation is maximised.

- They provide a safe environment within which to experiment, be exposed to new ideas and attitudes, and take risks.
- High levels of literacy and numeracy are not prerequisites.

23.4.2 The rationale for using games, role play and case studies

Before making the decision to use one of these teaching aids, we must keep in mind that they represent only a single component in the learning process and can never convey all the knowledge on a particular topic. Ideally, these methods should be supplemented with other adult and non-formal educational aids such as posters, film/video shows, informal discussions and formal lectures.

The principal advantage of the teaching aids discussed here over other instructional methods is that they represent an optimal experiential and participatory learning activity in which participants take control of their own learning. They also tie in well, therefore, with current development theories and approaches, such as participatory development, human-centred development and the learning process approach.

Advantages of using games, role play and case studies (Cornwell 1996:9)

Most people have been exposed to the formal classroom situation only and find the use of different teaching/learning experiences stimulating. This, in itself, enhances learning and the retention of information. Other advantages include the following:

- Learning that has already occurred through other informal or non-formal methods is reinforced.
- People are active participants in processes and activities that reflect real-life situations and problems.
- Skills such as problem identification, relating cause and effect, identifying alternative courses of action and problem solving are practised through these teaching aids.
- Active learning is more effective than passive learning.
- Empathy and increased awareness of and insight into major societal factors affecting the lives of participants are developed.
- They provide a safe learning environment because the actions and outcomes are fictitious.

- Participants are given the chance to discuss and apply different courses of action and experience their outcomes.
- Opportunity is provided for experiencing situations which, in real life, would be too time consuming, costly or dangerous.
- Games, role play and case studies involve a move away from one-way communication between teacher and learner, and become an interactive and mutual learning process.
- The result of actions is visible almost immediately.
- Feedback is provided in which information is given on the effectiveness and the cost of certain decisions.
- The environment is non-threatening and participants have the chance to try again, or to correct mistakes, within a short space of time.
- The content is flexible; a broad range of issues and concepts can be addressed.
- The duration is equally flexible. Games taking less than 30 minutes are available, others may last for three days.
- Some are played for one hour per week over a period of months.
- Some games (such as *Exaction*) enable participants to see the different facets that make up the whole.
- Other games extract only one aspect of reality, enabling participants to study/experience it in detail.
- The ideal mechanism is provided for compressing time, for example several 'years' can be simulated within the course of a day. It is also possible to draw out time or even suspend it.
- The facilitator is provided with an opportunity to use his/her initiative and design a game, role play or case study to illustrate a specific situation, or to choose a case study through which certain situations can be explained.
- Possibly the most important advantage is that these activities are fun and usually enjoyable for most people.

Limitations to using games, role play and case studies (Cornwell 1996:11)

The teaching aids discussed here may prove to be dysfunctional if it is not ascertained right at the outset that this is the best or most effective way to meet learning objectives. There are other limitations:

- Only some of the variables contained in reality are extracted – reality is edited or filtered.
- Some participants may regard the 'playing of games', or the adoption of roles, as beneath their dignity and may refuse to enter into the spirit of a simulation/game or a role play.
- It is possible for the competitive element to dominate the learning experience. Games designed to develop empathy may be particularly susceptible to this.
- Participating in such exercises can be an emotional experience. This can even prove traumatic and have a lasting effect if not handled correctly by the manager or facilitator.
- Case studies used reflect only a condensed version of reality. Some influencing factors may not be accounted for, leaving an incomplete picture.

These are some of the limitations of games, role play and case studies. There are others; for example, that the 'wrong' lessons may be learnt. Many limitations can be removed by a well-trained and sensitive facilitator. This is covered in section 23.4.4.

23.4.3 Case studies

A case study usually describes a facet of, or the process related to, a particular phenomenon or action. The case study may be used to illustrate attitudes, to highlight problems or to point to solutions to particular problems. Case studies may be lengthy, but many are short and concise. In using a case study, the facilitator must ascertain whether it addresses the issue he/she has in mind, is clear and easy to understand and relates, to some extent, to the life experiences of the trainees. Trainees with inadequate literacy skills will need access to case studies that are short and written in a simplified style.

One of the most important advantages of the case study is that it allows trainees the opportunity for 'group learning'. Trainees from disadvantaged communities in particular benefit from discussion of cases in smaller groups.

23.4.4 Facilitating role play and games

Each role play and game is different, and even when only one exercise is used repeatedly, no two sessions are ever identical. All exercises start with a briefing session led by a manager or facilitator (the trainer) in which the rules, constraints and possible courses of action are explained to the participants. The role play/game is then played for the stipulated time, or the period agreed upon by the participants. At the completion of the exercise itself, an extensive debriefing has to take place, led by the facilitator. This is one of the most important aspects of the entire exercise.

Because of the importance of the facilitator or manager (who is usually also the trainer) in role playing or gaming, this section is devoted to this person's position and prerequisites for fulfilling this role.

Facilitators have to be trained well in the uses and effects of role playing or gaming. Apart from understanding the broad principles of games, they need knowledge of the specific game they are dealing with: they need to know its background and aims, and how participants may respond to the process portrayed in the exercise. Ideally, they themselves need to have been ordinary participants in the game and should also have practised managing it in a safe environment.

In a role play, the facilitator must clearly know what he/she wants to illustrate. Practical experience of a situation similar to that portrayed by the role play will be to the benefit of the facilitator in his/her role of 'director' and in the debriefing period. To optimise the learning effect, he/she needs to be able to relate the lessons from the role play or game to the real-life circumstances of the trainees (Cornwell 1996:13).

Facilitators need to be flexible and able to adapt to different exercises and a wide range of participant responses. Most role plays/games expect facilitators to be neutral and totally divorced from proceedings. They should never be seen to take sides or become another variable in the learning process. Above all, they must allow participants to make their own decisions, irrespective of whether the facilitator believes these to be wrong or unwise.

Depending on the nature of the exercise, facilitators must have the courage to either let the role play/game or the participants themselves dictate the pace. The point was made earlier that one of the advantages of role playing or gaming is that participants take control of their own learning.

Because debriefing is one of the most important aspects of the process, trainers (as the facilitators) should be proficient in leading and managing it.

Facilitators need to practise skills required in debriefing, as they may initially experience the task as threatening.

In conclusion, facilitators need to be able to handle the conflict, anxiety, frustration and anger that may result from playing games. It is important to realise that a role-playing or game-playing experience may be extremely traumatic. Facilitators need to accept that this is one of the dangers of role plays/games and that they need to provide sufficient time for people to 'unpack' much of what they have experienced. Only then will participants be confident and eager to experiment with other game-playing exercises. (See also sections 23.4.5 and 23.4.6.)

23.4.5 Video and audio clips

Video is a very useful tool to illustrate concepts and ideas visually. For instance, the YouTube video, *Gramya: participatory monitoring and evaluation (PME) in UDWDP* (https://www.youtube.com/watch?v=w1sSs8XN9cU) illustrates in a practical manner how PRA is utilised for monitoring and evaluation. The clip is short – less than 10 minutes – and shows real people in the process of conducting PRA. Another video clip, *Participatory rural appraisal* (https://www.youtube.com/watch?v=DWbeGmjLIYo) puts the use of PRA in context for trainees. Likewise, audio clips that are short and focused introduce concepts and expose trainees to views from different places and contexts.

23.4.6 PRAP exercises

In Chapter 19, we discussed a number of participatory rapid appraisal and planning techniques. Among the many techniques proposed, we focus on mapping, transect walks and Venn diagrams as examples of valuable techniques in a training situation.

Mapping is useful to get to know the community – the layout and physical resources and stumbling blocks can be easily identified and mapped. During the exercise, students are required to do a 'walkabout' in a specific area and note issues to be included in a map. The walkabout – or transect walk – is an interesting activity to collect information but also to expose students to the development context. After the transect walk, a debriefing discussion is often needed to put observations and emotions in context.

A Venn diagram is useful for identifying and plotting role players in an area and to show relationships between groups. To the keen observer, the transect walk can reveal information about stakeholders in the community. The Venn diagram is a tool that is helpful in drawing a type of mind map and to come to a better understanding of the often unobserved organisation within a community.

23.5 CONCLUSION

Umuntu ngumuntu ngabantu is an old Zulu proverb that means 'human beings need each other to be human'. Our stories contain the essence of ubuntu ('I am because we are') because of our ability to tell stories, but more importantly, to listen to them. This is because stories are alive and mobile, made up of clogs of various grips or parts that are and function in a constant state of change and interpretation (De Beer 2020:42).

CDPs are tasked with the job of weaving these stories together, through facilitating and training. It is a daunting challenge, yet it can be one of the most stimulating jobs that they have to do. They must remember that '[E]mpowerment of communities is the objective of people-centred development and training simply becomes a tool in that process' (De Beer & Swanepoel 2013:114). Although it may be relatively safe for them to follow the old, discredited lecture method, the rich rewards of capacity-building training should convince them to walk the more difficult road of sharing and listening. Commitment is necessary for success, so that none of the techniques briefly discussed in this chapter may be rushed over or totally ignored. For success, it is also important to be creative, because the learning process here is a creative one.

REFERENCES

Cornwell L. 1996. Using simulation exercises and games in teaching development. *Africanus*, 26(1):5–20.

De Beer FC. 1995. Training for community development: Some guidelines for the literature, some lessons from experience. *Social Work/Maatskaplike Werk*, 31(4).

De Beer F & Swanepoel H. 1996. *Training for Development: A Manual for Student Trainers*. Johannesburg: International Thomson.

De Beer FC & Swanepoel HJ. 1998. *Community Development and Beyond: Issues, Structures and Procedures*. Pretoria: Van Schaik.

De Beer F & Swanepoel H. 2013. *The Community Development Profession: Issues, Concepts and Approaches*. Pretoria: Van Schaik.

De Beer MA. 2020. *'n Driepootpotverhaalbemarkingsmodel vir Kleindorpse Toerismebestemmings*. PhD Tourism Management. Pretoria: UNISA.

Freire P. 2006. *Pedagogy of the Oppressed*. New York: Continuum International.

Hong P & Crowther J. 2016. Learning citizenship in the community. In Evans R, Kurantowicz E & Lucio-Villegas E (eds), *Researching and Transforming Adult Learning and Communities: The Local/Global Context*. Rotterdam: Sense.

Kar K. 2010. *Facilitating 'Hands-on' Training Workshops for Community-led Total Sanitation: A Trainers' Training Guide*. Geneva: Water Supply & Sanitation Collaborative Council.

Ledwith M. 2022. Transformative practice. In Ledwith M & Springett J (eds), *Participatory Practice: Community Action for Transformative Change*. Bristol: Policy Press.

Lindner R & Garcia MDCM. 2014. The autobiography of intercultural encounters through visual media: exploring images of others in telecollaboration. *Language, Culture and Curriculum*, 27(3):226–243. doi: 10.1080/07908318.2014.977910

Randall W. 2012. Composing a good strong story: The advantages of a liberal arts environment for experiencing and exploring the narrative complexity of human life. *The Journal of General Education*, 61(3)(Special Issue: St Thomas University):277–293.

Rossiter MJ, Derwing TM, Manimtim LG & Thomson RI. 2010. Oral fluency: The neglected component in the communicative language classroom. *The Canadian Modern Language Review/La revue canadienne des langues vivantes*, 66(4):583–606. doi: 10.1353/cml.2010.0010

Sandelowski M. 1991. Telling stories: Narrative approaches in qualitative research. *Journal of Nursing Scholarship*, 23(3):161–166. doi: 10.1111/j.15475069.1991.tb00662.x

Springett J. 2022. The participatory worldview. In Ledwith M & Springett J (eds), *Participatory Practice: Community Action for Transformative Change*. Bristol: Policy Press.

Swanepoel HJ & De Beer FC. 1994. *Guide for Trainee Community Development Workers*. Johannesburg: Southern.

UNCHS (United Nations Centre for Human Settlements). 1984. *A Systematic and Comprehensive Approach to Training for Human Settlements*. Nairobi: United Nations Centre for Human Settlements (Habitat).

CHAPTER 24

Planning and Facilitating a Training Workshop

Frik de Beer and Andries de Beer

24.1 INTRODUCTION

We discussed the principles underlying facilitating training and the role of the facilitator in a training set-up in Chapter 23. The emphasis in this chapter shifts to the more practical aspects of organising and facilitating a training workshop. It is also critical to make the planning and presentation relevant to the training's contents, specifically themes such as getting to know the community and evaluating resources; planning and executing projects; organising and communicating; and – finally – understanding the meaning and process of community development (De Beer & Swanepoel 2013:116–117).

24.2 TRAINING AS A WORKSHOP

The approach to training that we recommend community development practitioners (CDPs) use is that of capacity building. That means that CDPs do not deliver lectures, but that they facilitate the trainees to participate fully and to create their own knowledge. This takes place in a workshop. A workshop is usually a short training session, from 45 minutes to four or five days. Trainees are introduced to skills, techniques and ideas, and share their own experience and insights as a contribution to the learning environment. The environment should be participatory and reflective for participants, affording them an opportunity to experience a catalyst of change. We use 'trainee' for lack of a better word and not to suggest distance between the trainee and facilitator. In the true spirit of training or capacity building as a dialogue, trainee and facilitator become partners discovering (and sometimes creating) knowledge, skills and attitudes relevant to their situation. According to the Community Toolbox (University of Kansas 2023):

Most workshops have several features in common:
- They're generally *small*, usually from 6 to 15 participants, allowing everyone some personal attention and the chance to be heard.
- They're often designed for people who are working together or working in the same field.
- They're conducted by people who have real experience in the subject under discussion.

24.2.1 Workshop setting

The workshop setting is the ideal one to promote the dialogue between facilitator, material and trainees. 'Workshop' is a concept usually associated with the manufacturing of an article. In the workshop, raw material is taken through a process which leads to an end product. In a training workshop, the same elements are identified: raw material, a process and an end product.

- The *raw material* comprises the learning material provided by the facilitator (guides, articles or videos), experience, knowledge and ideas contributed by the trainees and facilitator.
- The *process* is the action and interaction between facilitator, trainees and material taking place during the workshop: problem identification, discussion, argument and doing assignments.
- Through the process, specific problems are solved, definitions formulated or strategies developed. This is the *end product*.

To make a training workshop succeed as a place where raw material is processed into an end product requires the careful hand of a well-trained and experienced facilitator. The rest of this chapter is devoted to giving an idea of the facilitator's role.

24.3 RAISING ISSUES

24.3.1 Adult learners

When facilitating training of people involved in development, it must be kept in mind that the trainees are adults, that they are already in a sense practitioners, and that they ought to be participants in the learning episode. As Smith (2017:22) puts it: 'Adult learners do not want to be taught.

They want to play a part and need to perceive training as something that will improve them as individuals.'

In teaching, the following three spheres of learning are important: knowledge, skills and attitudes. These three spheres are interrelated: we want to increase knowledge, develop skills and influence attitudes.

- *Knowledge* may refer to concepts, ideas and explanations of phenomena which may be regarded as necessary for trainees to have in order to learn about a theme. Knowledge of the pathology of poverty is, for instance, needed to be able to identify development needs and solutions.
- *Skills* refer to an ability to do things. The skills may include tangible abilities like writing reports, or intangible skills like communication.
- *Attitudes* that may need to be influenced are those related to and informed by the trainees' environment: the community, other role players, themselves. To some extent, the attitude expressed by trainees during the training session is an indication of their ability to be involved in the development at grassroots level and of their ability to change their attitude if it affects their role negatively. The expectations with which trainees arrive at the training session may cause an 'attitudinal problem'. The facilitator may encounter expectations of, for instance, an accredited diploma or immediate access to employment after completion of the course. Such an attitude must be corrected immediately, but preferably even before it starts, when trainees are invited to attend the training course.

Trainees bring along previously acquired knowledge and skills, pre-shaped attitudes and practical, everyday experience. Trainees also come to a training episode with their own source fields. See Chapter 13 for a discussion of motivational types.

For training to be a truly capacity-building experience, the facilitator must concentrate on making it possible for trainees to give their input to the fullest extent possible. This fact holds implications for the training situation regarding:
- perceptions
- confidence
- unlearning
- experience as a learning source
- varieties of experience
- learning styles.

Perceptions

Trainees (just as facilitators) will see all new material through the 'spectacles' of their existing experience. Constant feedback is necessary to determine how trainees' perceptions 'distort' or influence their understanding of the material.

Confidence

New learning must be linked to existing knowledge and experience in order to contribute sensibly to the acquisition of knowledge and skills and the adaptation of attitude. Often, however, trainees lack confidence regarding their own potential contribution, in spite of having acquired practical experience.

Unlearning

'Unfreezing' trainees from a narrow and perhaps non-participation-oriented approach may be necessary – especially for trainees from a strict professional background or those with a strong ideological base to their beliefs and attitudes. Existing knowledge, skills and attitudes may therefore have to be 'unlearnt'. Direct challenges **exhorting** trainees to change seldom succeed. Case studies probably offer the best opportunities for unlearning, providing an opportunity for trainees to come to their own conclusions and to realise the need to discard or adapt existing knowledge, skills and attitudes.

Experience as a learning source

Having indicated the need for unlearning, it is as important to remember that experience can be an important source of knowledge. Especially when 'theoretical' or 'academic' concepts are explained, the facilitator is well advised to link the discussion to previous experience of the trainees.

Varieties of experience

The 'packages' of experience trainees bring along vary in depth, breadth and weight. The result is that the trainees are at different levels of experience. By using tried and trusted techniques and developing new ones as you go along, an opportunity must be provided to allow for learning from the existing variety of experience.

Learning styles

Limited exposure to learning (and even illiteracy) complicates the issue of learning. At school, 'spoon feeding' is the learning style used. In a capacity-building approach, the learning style is totally different and may require time for the adjustment of trainees. Here, too, facilitators must experiment and adapt their approach to allow for the development or change of learning styles.

'Group learning', especially where trainees are semi-literate, is a learning style that needs to be experimented with. In small groups, case studies or relevant articles may be discussed with the aim to transfer knowledge or skills or to influence attitudes. In the small group, group learning allows for the fluent to read, the quick-witted to explain and the 'slower' trainees to benefit by asking questions and contributing practical examples in the safe environment of a smaller group.

24.3.2 Establishing a teaching agenda

Establishing and coping with a teaching agenda may be difficult for a facilitator new to the situation. With careful planning and a little experience, problems may, however, be overcome. The teaching agenda may have one or both of the following aims: to establish the expectations of the trainees and to establish the problems experienced by the trainees in carrying out their duties. A list of expectations may be useful to the facilitator to get to know the group better; if, however, he/she has made prior contact and knows the trainees, it may be a waste of time to do this exercise again. A problems agenda can be compiled to determine training needs experienced by the group. As the training proceeds, the facilitator ought to refer back to the problems agenda and link the training to it.

The list of expectations and the problems agenda provide the opportunity for trainees at an early stage to contribute to the learning from their own experience. In using either a list of expectations or a problems agenda, the facilitator must take care to 'weed out' immediately unrealistic/unattainable expectations and problems that do not fall within the ambit of the course (eg expectations of employment, transport problems). The facilitator must carefully consider the situation before deciding on the type of agenda he/she wants to compile. Some prior knowledge of the trainees and their situation may help to make the correct choice.

A list of expectations will assist the facilitator to understand something of the attitude with which trainees arrive: is it personal gain, is it community-oriented expectations, or is it interest/curiosity that brought them together? Do they fear the learning episode or are they positive? The list of expectations gives the facilitator some prior 'warning' of what may be expected from the particular group of trainees.

Compiling a problems agenda may be a worthwhile exercise, but taxing on the facilitator. The perception trainees most often have of a problems agenda is that it is a list of problems (needs) experienced by the community. Thus, items such as community needs for employment, schools and clinics are put forward as problems experienced by the trainee. Before compiling a problems agenda, the trainees must be well informed of its nature and place in the exercise. A few examples will illustrate to the trainees what is looked for: conflicting political groups, indecisive leadership, personal transport, and so on. These are examples of problems that a person involved in development experiences in doing his/her work.

Establishing a problems agenda is not merely a means to fill a time slot: it is a means of providing for the integration of the trainees' contribution into the workshop. The facilitator uses the agenda as a point of reference, referring back to it during discussions. This means that the agenda must be put up where it is visible to all. It also means that, while the trainees are busy with practical assignments, the facilitator must study the agenda and determine points to 'hook on' as the workshop progresses. As the facilitator becomes more expert, he/she will be able to 'hook on' to items on the agenda during a discussion session.

While the problems agenda can make a valuable contribution toward integrating the trainees' input, it holds the danger of creating expectations among the trainees. To avoid this, the facilitator must be absolutely clear on the place and role of the problems agenda in the workshop. Unrealistic expectations and problems (eg finding money for projects) clearly not fitting within the scope of the workshop, must be pointed out. Though not all expectations will be met, nor all problems solved, the trainees must be sensitised to the fact that with their input, some of these issues may be addressed during the workshop.

To balance the list of expectations and/or problems agenda, facilitators must also make their objectives or agenda known to the trainees. By doing this, they start encouraging a relaxed atmosphere, and can also indicate where their ideas and those of the trainees meet or complement one another.

Finally, in concluding the workshop, the problems agenda can be used as a tool of summary. The facilitator on his/her own, or with input from the trainees, can conclude the workshop by running through the problems agenda.

24.3.3　Drawing a picture of the milieu

Drawing a picture of the milieu and establishing problems and resources in the community may seem awkward when the trainees come from the community and supposedly know it. Milieu in this context means the particular people and society that surround you and that influence the way you behave. Yet this exercise has a number of advantages that cannot be overlooked, such as the following:

- It puts some distance between the trainee and the milieu.
- It allows the opportunity to illustrate the integrated nature of the problem.
- It allows trainees the opportunity to demonstrate their practical experience and knowledge.
- It allows trainees the opportunity to 'clear the air' and vent their frustration.
- Finally, by also identifying resources available, it brings a positive note to the training episode and gives some hope to trainees who may be overwhelmed by the perceived hopelessness of the situation.

The aim of this exercise is to allow trainees to see their situation in a wider perspective, and to realise the integrated nature of the problem – and of the solution. As an organising tool for drawing a picture of the milieu, the 'deprivation trap' as described by Robert Chambers (1983:103 et seq) is ideal. See Chapter 1.

The clusters of poverty, isolation, physical weakness, powerlessness and vulnerability – the deprivation trap – can be explained with reference to examples provided by trainees. How inadequate housing relates to poverty and to physical weakness can, for instance, be explained by referring to examples given by trainees. The interrelationship between these clusters and its causal relationship is illustrated with examples from the milieu known to the trainees. In this way, the trainees are assisted in understanding their work situation; they are also equipped to analyse the situation better and to find solutions. See De Beer and Swanepoel (2013) for an exposition of the urban poverty situation.

Time spent on raising issues is time well utilised. It allows trainees the opportunity to bring into the training session themes that are important to them and it makes it easier for them to relate to and participate in the training.

24.4 TRAINING AS COMMUNICATION

Teaching skills revolve around the ability to communicate. The facilitator needs not only knowledge about communication but also practice in applying it. It is only through applying knowledge that the skill of communication is developed. Once this skill is mastered, motivation of trainees, dealing with group dynamics and coping with troublemakers become manageable.

24.4.1 Communication

Communication is not simply sending and receiving messages. More things are at play than a speaker (sender), a message and a listener (receiver). It is therefore wrong to think of communication as linear. Communication is rather a circular process, with an in-built dynamism. When the communication circle is completed, it may set off another round of communication; it is therefore perhaps best depicted as a spiral of communication. The spoken language, body language, environmental influences (noise, climate), culture, the social position of the speaker and receiver, all interact to give meaning to the communication taking place. See Chapter 10 for a detailed discussion.

It is common knowledge that communication entails more than the spoken word: non-verbal communication (or body language) is increasingly recognised as an important part of communication. People in a lift communicate – without having to say anything! Chapter 10 explains the communication model in detail.

Training poses an opportunity and a challenge for communication. Trainees from poor communities are often illiterate, unsure of themselves and suspicious of other people. Their illiteracy is compounded by poor language skills and often an inadequate knowledge of the language used by the facilitator. The facilitator's presence may on its own pose a threat to the trainee: being an official from government (or maybe a professor from a university), he/she has power, has proper training and may therefore appear to be too 'wise'; alternatively, the facilitator may be young and inexperienced, therefore not accepted as a person who speaks with authority. These are some of the challenges faced even before the facilitator has spoken a word.

In a training situation, the environment is a crucial, sometimes a determining, factor for the success of communication. Noise of lawnmowers, people talking outside the room or music in the distance hampers communication. The climate may be too hot – making trainees sleepy – or too cold – disturbing their concentration. Seats may be too soft or too hard, the distance between facilitator and trainee too far to facilitate proper communication. Outside observers may come and go, each time distracting the attention of trainees; worse, they may make an unsolicited contribution and then leave the facilitator to win back the attention of the trainees.

Since this chapter is mainly about the skills and attitudes of facilitators, we deal only with direct communication between facilitator and trainees, in a one-to-one or a classroom (workshop) situation. 'Mass communication', reading, viewing and other forms of communication will not be discussed.

The spoken word is the means by which to communicate, but may also be the stumbling block to communication. The message will not be heard if the facilitator speaks too softly or is unclear. The facilitator who occupies the floor and undertakes a one-way conversation will soon lose the attention of trainees. Successful communication requires active and creative listening, both by the trainer and trainee. It is, however, the duty of the trainer to create the atmosphere in which active and creative listening can take place.

Body language is an important means of communication. Body language will tell the trainees a lot about the facilitator and his/her attitude. It may, however, also be misinterpreted. Shyness may be 'received' as unfriendliness; an overbearing approach may be viewed as a know-all. Direct eye contact should be used to establish rapport between facilitator and trainee. By not looking trainees in the eye, as facilitator you make them feel that you have something to hide or, perhaps worse, that you want to keep your distance. A hurried presentation will cause anxiety, while a relaxed approach will make the trainees feel comfortable.

Culture and body language may cause confusion. Arabs use a backward jerk of the head to indicate 'no'; we may interpret it as a 'yes'. In South African society, the matter of greeting is sometimes a cause for miscommunication. Where a facilitator meets trainees from a different culture (and social standing), he/she should acknowledge the pitfalls, discuss them with the trainees and elicit their help in teaching him/her when necessary.

Training communication should take the form of a dialogue. If we follow Freire's vision of dialogue, then the relationship required puts a great burden on the facilitator. 'Founding itself upon love, humility and faith, dialogue becomes a horizontal relationship of which mutual trust between the dialoguers is the logical consequence' (Freire 2005:91). The facilitator is not a know-all and should not pretend to be one. He/she should rather be a conduit (or link), putting the trainees in touch with the training material. Remember, the trainees bring along some knowledge and experience, and if we allow the opportunity, some valuable wisdom will come from the group. Their own 'body of knowledge', the training material and the facilitator's input should be in constant dialogue in order to create their own knowledge. If we succeed in establishing this cycle of communication, the trainees will find their training episode a worthwhile experience and will learn much more than in a linear, one-way type of communication.

24.4.2 Motivation and group dynamics

The most important principle in motivation is recognition of the individual. This may take a number of forms. By simply remembering (and using) people's names when addressing them shows them that they are regarded as someone distinguished from other persons. Acknowledging the contribution made by individuals tells them that the trainer (a powerful person) regards their input as important. Allowing individuals and the group as a whole to voice their fears, articulate their expectations and share their ideas builds a foundation for motivation. Taking them and their inputs seriously, and showing earnest interest, builds mutual trust and contributes to motivation.

It is most important to provide opportunities for individuals and groups of trainees to taste a sense of achievement. The trainer should challenge them, give assignments and make it possible for them to experiment and solve problems or master skills; few things motivate better than a sense of achievement.

On a practical note, motivation is supported by the physical wellbeing of the individual: a hungry and thirsty person is demotivated; a person enduring an uncomfortable bed and cold water on a winter morning will find reason to complain. If the facilitator does not allow time for breaks in between and during training episodes, the trainees tend to lose concentration and become demotivated.

If the individual trainee does not have the capacity or mechanism for self-motivation, these peripherals will be of little value to get him/her motivated, however well the facilitator handles the factors that contribute to motivation. In exceptional cases, individuals may be found without the capacity to motivate themselves. Such individuals often revert to 'trouble making' and can only be handled effectively by the group (see section 24.4.3).

Group dynamics is influenced, and sometimes shaped, by the type of characters present. In most groups one finds, among others, the clown, the snob and the know-it-all (see section 24.4.3). These characters can make or break a training episode. The communication skills of the facilitator will be taxed to the full to avoid serious disruption. An important partner in handling these characters is the group. By harnessing the group to act as adjudicator, disciplinarian and memory, group dynamics are used positively in the communication situation. Some suggestions in this regard are provided below. See also Chapter 11 regarding groups.

It is the nature of groups that the potential for conflict always exists. A few rules of thumb to manage conflict are provided, but the facilitator will always have to explore new ones and use his/her initiative in finding solutions. Chapter 12 deals in more detail with conflict resolution, but the following set of rules will also assist with managing conflict in the classroom:

- Concentrate on the issue, not on the person.
- Avoid personal accusations and the forming of opposing groups.
- Avoid muddling the discussion by rhetoric and side issues.
- Allow for difference of opinion, feelings (emotions) and ways of doing things.
- Have self-respect, respect for others and set the example.
- Allow people to speak their minds, but emphasise the importance of also listening to others.
- Do not apportion blame.

24.4.3 Discipline and coping with problem people

The capacity-building method of training is more prone to disruption by problem trainees than the lecture method. The discussion is much freer and therefore problem trainees have a good opportunity to affect the process negatively. The capacity-building method is very dependent on a continuous discussion and therefore it is imperative that the negative effects of problem trainees be minimised. The facilitator's handling of problem trainees should be experienced by the group as firm, fair, consistent and to the benefit of the whole group.

Doyle and Straus (1976) have identified a number of problem types at meetings. Their list has been used for discussion on discipline in meetings in Chapter 15. However, we are again using it in this discussion for its appropriateness, although a few more types have been added and the suggestions for handling the types do not necessarily follow Doyle and Straus. The typology of these problem trainees is perhaps an overstatement. We should keep in mind that problem types manifest in varying degrees. We should also remember that something of these types is present in most people. The original authors (Doyle and Strauss) discussed this list in relation to meetings; we change the scenario somewhat to a training situation.

The latecomer

Latecomers always arrive at the discussion late, making some commotion, from greeting everyone with the hand, enquiring about their health, to bumping and shuffling to get to their place. The handling of this problem trainee will be dealt with together with the next type.

The early leaver

Early leavers drain the energy of the session by leaving early. It is important to settle the matter of punctuality early in a training session. The group should decide on starting and break-up times, and the facilitator and trainees must abide by this. The only way to start on time is by starting on time, whether one trainee or half of the trainees are still not at their places. One way of keeping discussions punctual is to let the group appoint a person or persons to take responsibility for this aspect.

The broken record

Broken records (sometimes they are simply 'slow thinkers') keep bringing up the same point over and over again. The facilitator should make sure that the point has been noted and recorded. Broken records may act this way because no one will listen to them or because they need more explanation before understanding. The use of group memory, transparencies and slides also helps to get rid of broken records.

The Doubting Thomas

Doubting Thomases constantly put down everything. They are always negative. You are wrong until you prove yourself to be right. No solution will ever work. There is a difference between being critical and being aggressively negative. Criticism keeps a group on its toes, but aggressive negativism puts a damper on creativity. First, Doubting Thomases must be kept honest. If they react negatively, they must substantiate their reaction. Second, exercises such as the nominal group technique and brainstorming where no comment or evaluation is at first allowed, may quiet them down and give an ideal time to gain support for solutions before they are criticised.

The head shaker

Head shakers non-verbally disagree in a dramatic and disruptive manner. They shake their head, roll their eyes, cross and uncross their legs, pull faces, throw their hands in the air and/or laugh soundlessly. The best way to deal with head shakers is to force them to translate their body language into words.

The dropout

Dropouts sit at the back of the room, do not say anything, never look up, read something or doodle. They are especially disturbing to the facilitator. First, the seating arrangement can encourage or discourage the dropout. There should be no 'back of the room' seating. No person should be able to hide behind anyone else. If every person sits in a position where he/she is very much part of the group, it is difficult not to participate. Second, dropouts must be brought into the discussion and that can only be done by the facilitator asking dropouts specifically what their views are. They should know that the facilitator is aware of them and does not like their behaviour.

The silent observer

Silent observers are not dropouts. They follow the discussion and may nod or shake their head now and then, but they never say anything. They are usually shy or lack self-confidence. It is the task of the facilitator to show them that their contribution is also necessary by asking them to comment, perhaps at first on a fairly simple issue, and then congratulating them on their contribution. Silent observers must gain courage and the facilitator must help them to do it, also by talking informally to them during breaks.

The whisperer

Whisperers are constantly whispering to a neighbour. Eye contact with whisperers may cause them to stop or else physical movement toward them may interrupt them.

The clown

Clowns are also potential leaders of a sub-culture within the group. They usually tell jokes or make funny remarks in asides only heard by the people sitting near to them. Again, eye contact and forcing them to be serious by asking them to contribute, may change the mood. Seating arrangements should also discourage anyone taking the role of clown.

The loudmouth

Loudmouths (sometimes they are simply manipulators) talk too much, are too loud, dominate the discussion and are seemingly impossible to shut up. Their actions can cause two negative results: (1) they can establish a communication link between themselves and the facilitator to the exclusion of the other trainees, and (2), because they tend to react to every input, they can take over the role of facilitator, or at least take the initiative away from the facilitator. The nominal group exercises and brainstorming exercises will go a long way to quieten a loudmouth and to ensure that the initiative remains with the facilitator.

The orator

Orators make a speech instead of giving input. A speech is time-consuming, contains clichés and peripheral matters, and expresses various ideas strung together. For all three of these reasons a speech is not conducive to lively discussion. The orator must be stopped, but how? People feel reluctant to interrupt in the middle of the speech because it is considered rude. It takes an experienced facilitator to wait his/her chance to pounce, grab an idea expressed by the orator, comment on it with great interest, turn away from the orator, and throw the idea to the group as a delicate **morsel** to be savoured.

The orator has been silenced, but also noted and the last fact should make up for the interruption.

The attacker

Attackers launch personal attacks on other trainees or on someone in the organisation, usually someone in management. They are aggressive by nature and can even be one of the rare breed of people who thrives on conflict. Attackers must be censored and facilitators must get the group behind them for it to be effective. Group censure is needed. For the sake of the group and the discussions, it is imperative that attackers do not get away with it. Every trainee must know that he/she is safeguarded against personal attack.

The know-it-all

Know-it-alls use credentials, age, length of service and professional status to argue a point. Usually, they are more senior people and therefore more difficult to handle. A variation on this theme is benevolent know-it-alls or rescuers. Their intention is pure, merely helping a fellow trainee whom they regard as being in need of assistance to make a contribution. Know-it-alls and rescuers should be reminded that, in spite of their superior knowledge, they are part of a learning process, just like the facilitator and that all inputs, also those from trainees without credentials, are important to keep the learning process going.

The busy bee

Busy bees are always ducking in and out of the discussions, constantly receiving messages or rushing out to take a phone call or deal with a crisis. Having the training session at a venue away from the office is about the best way to pin down the busy bee.

The interrupter

Interrupters start talking before others are finished. Interruption and double talking are quite normal in any discussion, but it can be tolerated only up to a point. The facilitator is responsible for a smooth flow of contributions, and he/she must stop interrupters if they start making a habit of it. If a group memory is used, the facilitator has the good excuse that an idea which gets interrupted halfway cannot be recorded properly.

The gun jumper

Gun jumpers are worse than interrupters. They do not wait until the facilitator acknowledges them. When a discussion is really going well, it is inevitable that a few people will indicate to the facilitator that they wish to contribute. The facilitator must keep a waiting list in mind so that he/she can acknowledge the next speaker in the sequence. Gun jumpers must await their turn like all the other trainees.

The teacher's pet

The teacher's pet spends more energy looking for approval from the facilitator than concentrating on the contents of the training. The teacher's pet should not be given the slightest notion of encouragement. The facilitator does not want anyone of the trainees to become dependent on him/her.

The snob

Snobs are a rare species that regard themselves as better educated and better informed than the other trainees. They will inform the facilitator and the group of their superiority. The facilitator must deal with them by keeping them honest: let the group respond and show to them that their superior knowledge has shortcomings. Above all, remind them that this is a learning experience to the educated and well informed as much as to the uneducated and uninformed.

Nibblers

Nibblers are equally annoying. Their habits cause discomfort and distraction to both the facilitator and fellow trainees. Rules on eating during sessions should be determined at the outset and enforced by the group and the facilitator.

The peace keeper

Peace keepers can play an important role when arguments get heated. Yet their anxiety to restore peace can interrupt a challenging and important debate. The facilitator should allow them to make a contribution, but nevertheless let the debate proceed.

The invader

Invaders are either officials responsible for organising the training or people who have to report back to superiors on progress. Such people may sit and read a newspaper, come and go as they please and generally disrupt the proceedings. They may be made part of the workshop or asked by the facilitator to be unobtrusive and not to disturb the proceedings.

The most important precondition for successful capacity building is a free-flowing discussion. All of the above problem trainees can cause a breakdown in this free flow. It is therefore imperative to deal with these people. The best possible position facilitators can wish for is that these people are censured by the group. Facilitators need strong group cohesion for that and it is their task to promote group cohesion and to channel group dynamics.

24.5 PLANNING AND PRESENTATION

No facilitator can walk into a training situation unprepared. As trainers/facilitators, we must plan for a training session. Planning consists of establishing the aims or goals of the session. We write them down and after we have completed our preparation, we check if we have kept to those goals.

The best is to have a written plan of the presentation of a session. This must include contents, timing, techniques and tools. We must make sure that we know the plan by heart and must take it along to the classroom. We must put it at a special place on the front desk or podium so that we can refer to it when necessary.

Take note: a facilitator with a cluttered desk or podium will have cluttered training sessions. It also makes a bad impression if a facilitator must stop everything and hunt for some document on his/her desk while the trainees look on. The session plan must be in a specific place where it will not be covered by other papers. The laptop and overhead projector must be connected and the PowerPoint presentation(s) in sequence and easily accessible. If transparencies are used, they must be in sequence and there must be a place to put down the transparencies already used. Facilitators must have their notes in such a position that they can easily read what they have written. The flip chart must be clean and the pens close to it. The overhead projector must be switched on at the wall socket and focused.

24.5.1 Timing and time management

Facilitators have previously established time frames and time limits within which they must complete their work. It is therefore necessary to plan the presentation within a time frame. It is better to plan time liberally. Facilitators should rather have time free than find themselves hopelessly behind schedule.

As facilitators progress through the programme, it is their task always to keep an eye on the time. According to these regular time assessments, they will make changes in the programme in advance and use plenary session breaks to assess time use and to adapt the further programme. Remember that certain breaks, such as for tea and lunch, are previously arranged and cannot be altered. Facilitators must plan the programme with these compulsory breaks in mind.

The time issue should not, however, be in the forefront during the training. The trainees should not be constantly aware of the fact that the facilitator is trying to fit everything into a previously decided time frame. It is good to refer to the time issue now and then. That reminds the trainees that they cannot continue discussions for an unlimited period. However, the ever-present time constraints in most of these training situations should not be uppermost in the minds of the trainees. The programme is in service of the workshop, not the other way around.

24.5.2 The venue and seating arrangements

Facilitators will seldom find a perfect room for their training sessions. Rooms will invariably be too large, too small, too noisy, too hot, too cold, too draughty or too far from other facilities.

It is important that the room can be used for both plenary discussions and group work. If smaller rooms for group work are not available adjacent to the training room, the latter must be large enough to accommodate at least three groups at work at the same time. It must also have enough space for simulation exercises.

Keeping in mind the size of the group, an auditorium is not suitable for training purposes. Sound tends to disappear or reverberate in such a large room. The smallness of the training group amid the vastness of the hall tends to have a negative psychological effect. On the other hand, a room must not be so small as to only allow the necessary tables and chairs with no

Chapter 24: Planning and Facilitating a Training Workshop

space to move about. Such a situation can become **claustrophobic** and the inevitable stuffiness leads to drowsiness and consequently to an energy loss. The seating arrangement is of crucial importance.

A few general rules can be stated:
- The facilitator must be able to communicate with the group and with individual trainees.
- Each trainee must be able to communicate with the group, with the individual trainees and with the facilitator.
- The facilitator and the trainees must be able to move around easily.
- The facilitator must be able to look every trainee in the eye.
- The facilitator must be able to see the whole group without having to move his/her head more than 20 degrees in any direction.
- Trainees must be able to see the screen and the flip chart without turning their bodies in their chairs, or straining their neck muscles, and without playing a dodging game with a head in front of them.
- Trainees must have a desk in front of them for their note paper and they must be able to write without difficulty.
- The seating arrangement should never make obvious divisions in the group.

With these general rules in mind, a few arrangements are clearly preferable and a few are decidedly not.

Desirable seating arrangements

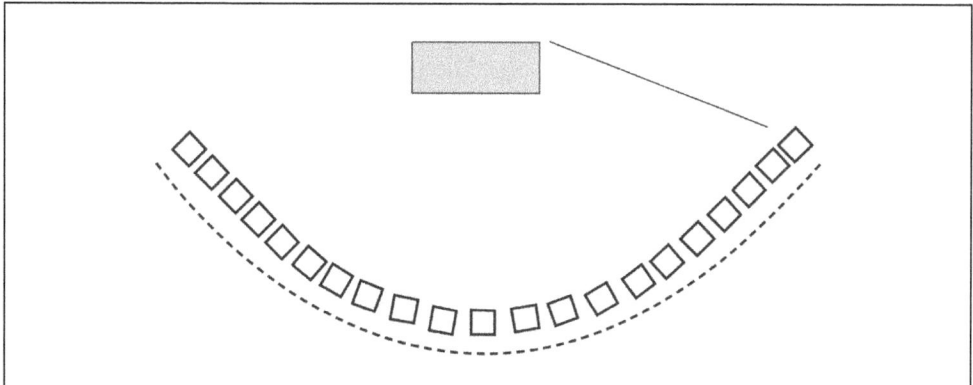

Figure 24.1 **The flat horseshoe**

The flat horseshoe is one of the most appropriate seating arrangements. Trainees can see and communicate with one another. The facilitator can move about on the inside of the horseshoe. No trainee is too far from the screen and flip chart stand.

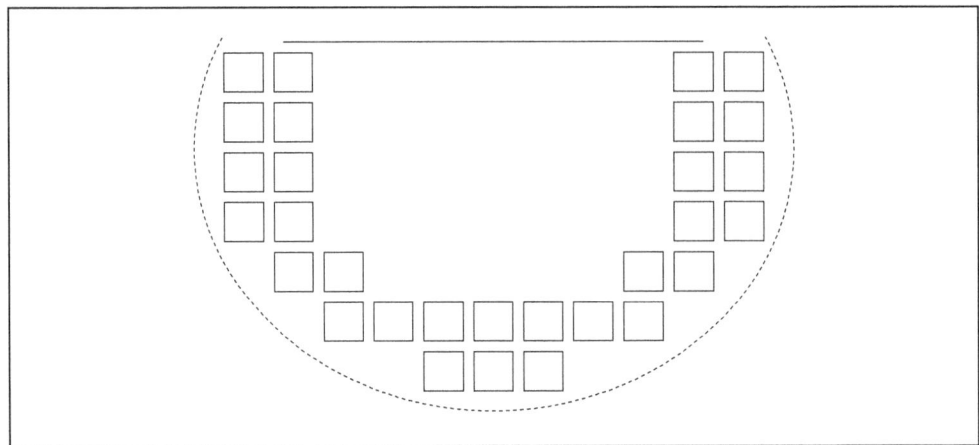

Figure 24.2 **The semicircle**

The semicircle is definitely the best seating arrangement. Unfortunately, not many trainees can be accommodated.

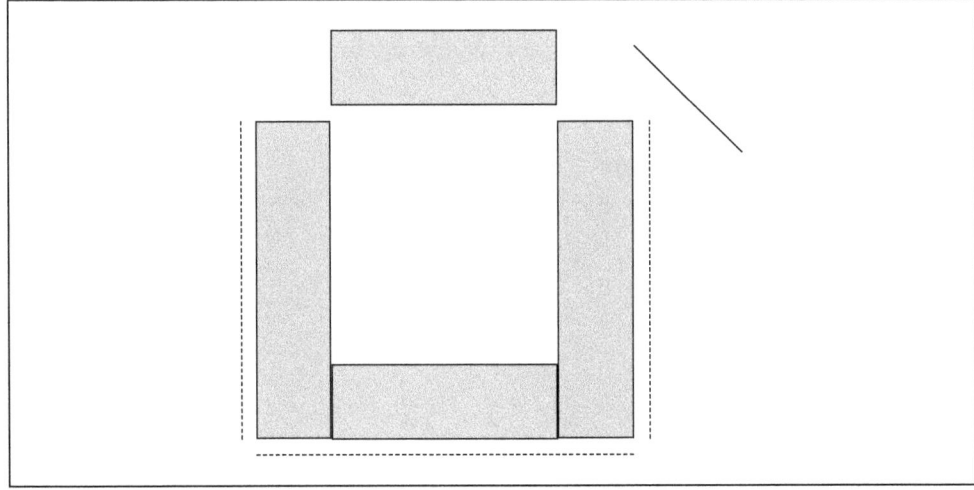

Figure 24.3 **The open U with outside seating**

The open U with outside seating is also one of the better arrangements. The trainees at the bottom side of the U may, however, be too far from the screen and the flip chart stand.

Undesirable seating arrangements

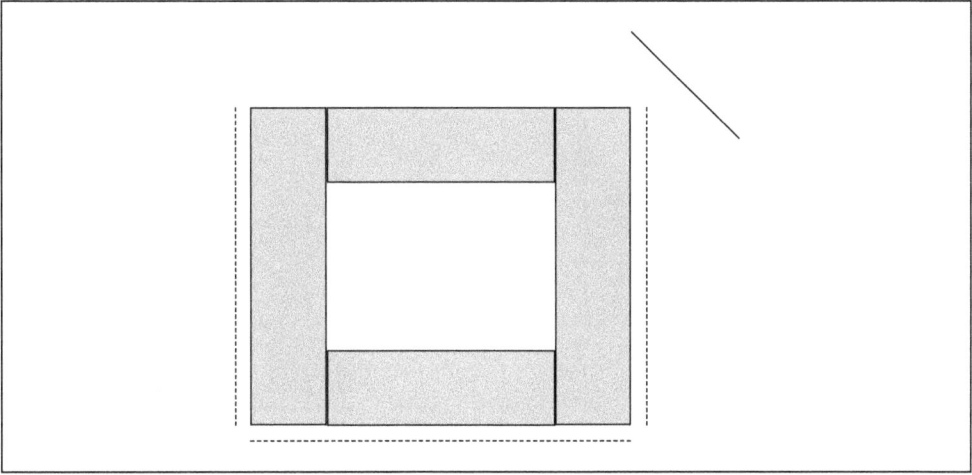

Figure 24.4 **The closed U**

The main problem with the closed U arrangement is that the facilitator can only move about behind the trainees. The whole space in the centre is wasted.

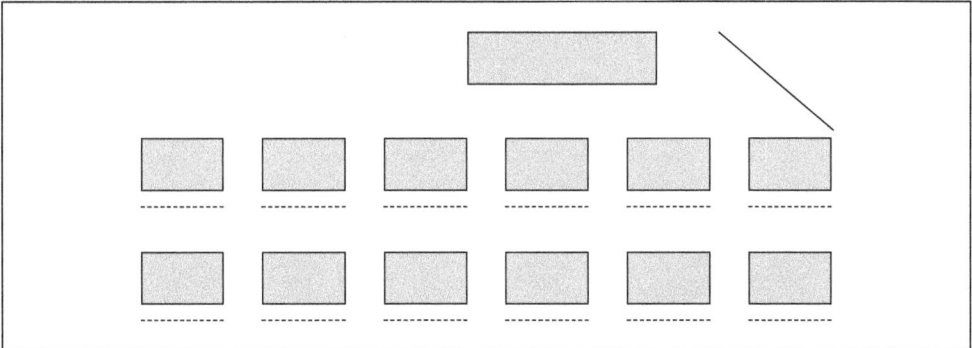

Figure 24.5 **The classroom**

The classroom seating arrangement is totally unacceptable for a number of reasons. Communication except with the person next to you is virtually impossible. A trainee in a row behind may address a trainee in front of him/her who will turn around and in so doing will sever all contact with the facilitator and the screen and flip chart stand. Trainees in back rows have a problem seeing the facilitator, screen and flip chart stand, and will be dodging heads in front of them all the time. The back row syndrome is bound to be present. That is that the trainees in the back row will either drop out or form a subculture. The movement of the facilitator is also restricted and so is that of the trainees in the inside rows.

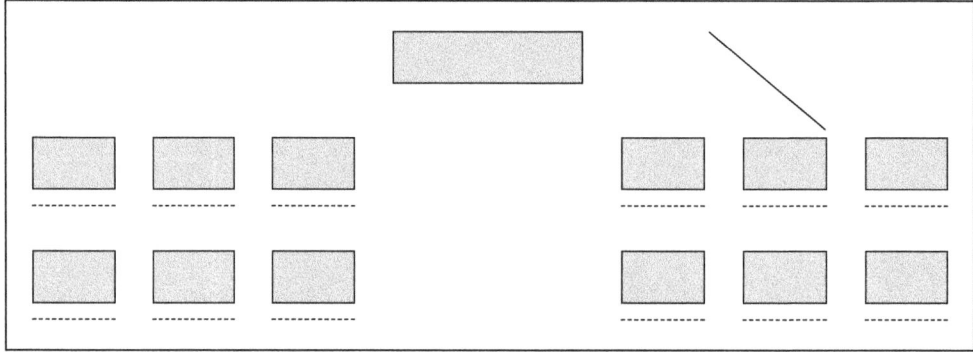

Figure 24.6 **The classroom with division**

The classroom with division arrangement is also unacceptable for the same reason as the previous one, with the added problem of a natural division that will inevitably lead to the formation of two subgroups.

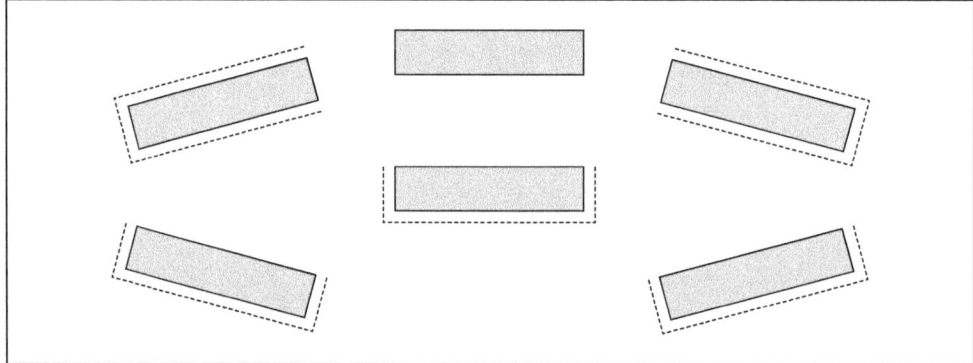

Figure 24.7 **The random tables**

The random tables arrangement is popular but is unacceptable. The facilitator finds it extremely difficult to maintain eye contact with all the trainees; many of the trainees have their backs to the facilitator, screen and flip chart stand. Free communication between the trainees is impossible. Subcultures will tend to form around each table.

The training room

There are other aspects of the training room that merit attention. Room temperature is one of the most frequent and annoying problems. Part of this problem can never be solved. People experience temperature differently. What is hot for one may be chilly for another. However, a too hot or stuffy room saps the energy of the group and makes them sleepy. Air conditioning has a negative effect on some people, apart from the noise it makes.

Stuffy rooms can be aerated by opening the windows, but often outside noise or a strong wind makes this impossible. In such cases, more breaks should be taken.

It is imperative that training take place with the minimum disturbances from outside. If the door of the training room is constantly opened by people looking for an office or a person, it is not only annoying, but counter-productive too. Therefore, a note must be pinned to the door with the words: Training session in progress. Don't disturb.

A tea facility too far removed from a training room is a time waster. A group of people move much slower than an individual. It takes a group of people a minimum time of 20 minutes to drink a cup of tea. Another 10 minutes can be added if the toilets are not on the same route or adjacent to the training room. So, 30 minutes are necessary if the tea facility is not very near the training room.

24.5.3 Study and relaxation

A training session of five days' duration needs a balanced pattern of study and relaxation. Even if the trainees are eager, the subject of training extremely interesting and the facilitator excellent, trainees can concentrate and work for limited periods of time only.

A day session should last from 08h00 to 16h00 (08h30 to 16h30; 09h00 to 17h00). During a day session there must be a tea break in the morning of 15 to 30 minutes, a lunch break of 45 minutes and an optional tea break in the afternoon of 15 to 30 minutes, plus a few short leg-stretch breaks. In all, about an hour and a half per day is necessary for relaxation.

Leg-stretch breaks are essential, especially when it is hot or when the room is stuffy. However, leg-stretch breaks have the tendency to stretch. A three-minute break will always end two or three minutes later than it should. If the toilets are some distance from the training room, no break can be shorter than 10 minutes.

There should be discipline in a group regarding the time. It must be stressed during the ice-breaker session that starting times and break times will be strictly adhered to and this must then be carried out.

Relaxation can also come from certain activities other than the ordinary breaks. A simulation exercise usually provides some relaxation. The same is true of group work where something must be created. Even an amusing case study can provide a break from the more disciplined way of concentration and work.

24.5.4 Visual aids

Traditionally, the overhead projector, with a screen and a long extension cord, and a flip chart with pens were the best visual aids available. However, with technological advancements and wider accessibility to all, PowerPoint presentations and video clips from the internet are surpassing all other types of visual aids. A flip chart remains, of course, an indispensable tool for visual presentation and making notes during training sessions. With a flip chart, the facilitator and trainees can keep record of proceedings and later rework information into useful records and guidelines. Filled sheets must be numbered to ensure that they remain in sequence, removed and stuck to the wall so that everybody can refer back to them.

PowerPoint presentations require prior planning and assembly; with such a presentation the facilitator has at his/her disposal colour and animation, and sound can also be added. A PowerPoint presentation can work well for a short lecture or giving information in an uninterrupted way. The facilitator should plan the use of this tool carefully. It is more structured and rigid, but cross- and back-reference to other slides can still be made. The facilitator must also be well trained and familiar with this tool not to get lost or confused; as with most things in life, practice makes perfect when using PowerPoint presentations.

PowerPoint slides are excellent visual aids, but there are a number of dos and don'ts when using them:

- A slide should only reflect the main idea or information regarding a matter.
- Words, phrases, brief sentences or simple diagrams are used. The slides do not carry the whole text.

- The typing on a slide must be large enough so that all trainees read it easily.
- Illustrations on slides must be as simple and clear as possible.
- A slide must look professional.
- Animation must contribute to a better product, not used just for entertainment.
- The more entertaining the presented information is, the better trainees will relate to and remember the contents.
- When not in use, the slide should be covered or switched off, or else the image on the screen may distract trainees from the discussion/debate about the issue.

Video clips on almost any topic discussed in this book can be easily accessed from the internet. Sites such as TED Talks and YouTube offer a wide variety of short and useful video clips. However, the abundance of products requires the facilitator to take care to select those video clips that are specifically appropriate and relevant for the training session. Video clips should:

- relate directly to the topic
- be short and focused
- present the material in an interesting and visual way.

It goes without saying that issues and lessons to be drawn from the video clip must be unpacked and discussed after the viewing.

Although technological advancements have opened new possibilities via the internet, with an extensive assortment of videos and online platforms to aid any facilitator, certain constraints such as loadshedding or theft might influence a well-prepared session negatively. The key to the success of any presentation is for the facilitator to be observant, innovative and vigilant. A technical difficulty as a result of a power failure or theft might be used to the advantage of the facilitator and/or the group. Instead of being in despair over an uncontrollable situation, a facilitator could ask the trainees to reach into their pockets and take out their smart- or feature phones (cell phones with access to the internet) if they have them. The facilitator can also use his or her own phone as an aid if none of the trainees has access or data available.

Besides sharing and showing videos, the cell phone can also be utilised as a communication tool between trainees and facilitators. Voice notes can be recorded along with photos or other relevant material can be circulated via SMS or WhatsApp. The use of the cell phone should not be regarded as a replacement for traditional or conventional teaching methods, but rather as an extension. (See Case study 26: *The trainers who thought they were teachers.*)

24.6 ASSESSMENT

Assessment and monitoring are two of the most crucial, yet often neglected, aspects of a training situation. What is meant by these terms? Assessment is used to refer to the 'testing' at the end of a definable module or training episode (eg a learning outcome or objective). Monitoring takes the form of a process – it is continuous and need not be formalised. For the facilitator, monitoring means to 'keep an eye' on the trainees, to see that all have an opportunity to participate, to detect when a trainee falls behind, to know when a trainee is not following the discussion or does not understand concepts, ideas or phenomena under discussion. With monitoring goes remedial action: to elicit participation, to repeat key points and to rephrase concepts, ideas and phenomena.

It is not only the facilitator who does assessment and monitoring. In an interactive, capacity-building training exercise, the trainee should be allowed an equal opportunity to monitor and assess. The trainee should assess and monitor his/her own progress and also the input and performance of the facilitator. By allowing for self-assessment and facilitator assessment, the capacity-building experience is enhanced and strengthened.

24.6.1 The role of assessment in training

Assessment must be conducted according to a kind of relationship – an ethos – which reflects the spirit of participation. This means the following:

- Not only the facilitator is responsible for assessment. He/she is in dialogue with the trainees, who assess their own learning.
- It is not only the product that is assessed but also the process.
- The product is not only assessed through the conventional examination method. The portfolio, test or examination as a reflection of the amount of knowledge and skills successfully transferred, forms only a small part of assessment. How the trainees assess their progress is equally important.

- It is also necessary to assess the training process: what the aspirations and expectations of the trainees are, how they progress towards fulfilling them and how the input of the facilitator relates to addressing their aspirations and expectations. The most important aspect of process assessment is that it engages the trainee in self-assessment.
- The trainee assesses the course contents, its presentation and the attainment of his/her goals against the objectives set for the course.

24.6.2 Monitoring and assessment of progress

As with all things in life, training is also subject to monitoring and assessment, measurement and setting of standards. In an ordinary educational setting (schools or universities), the paradigm used is standard tests, examinations and perhaps also orals and portfolios. In interactive or capacity-building training, we operate in a different paradigm; a paradigm in which simple 'wrongs' and 'rights' cannot determine levels of competency. We deal, in this type of training, with knowledge, skills and attitudes of adults who may be illiterate or semi-literate but who in many instances have acquired skills through experience. In this instance, tests and examinations may be of use but they can definitely not be used as the sole mechanism for monitoring and assessing progress. The facilitator, in planning a training episode, must also determine his/her learning objective and ways and means of measuring success.

Knowledge can be determined through essays, written tests and examinations. Yet, the trainee with knowledge but no or underdeveloped writing skills will most certainly fail. It is up to the facilitator to be inventive and apply other methods of monitoring and assessment. In discussion, small groups and practical assignments, trainees can demonstrate their knowledge. The facilitator must be sensitive to it and somehow devise a mechanism to keep record of such informal evidence of knowledge.

How does one monitor and assess the acquisition of skills? Skills cannot really be tested in a written test or examination. Depending on the type of skills, an appropriate mechanism – a game, case study or role play – should be used or developed. Once again, the ingenuity of the facilitator will be tested severely.

To monitor and assess attitudinal changes is perhaps the most difficult of all. Change or influence of attitudes is in any case seldom an overtly expressed aim or learning objective in training. Yet in development training, it is most often a crucial ingredient to the success of the exercise. Monitoring and assessment of attitudinal change should start with the facilitator. What is his/her attitude towards the trainees? Is it paternalistic, know-all or dominating? Or is it inviting, reassuring and relaxed? His/her attitude will create an atmosphere in which attitudinal change is either possible or smothered.

Observation by the facilitator is one, yet a subjective, way of monitoring and assessing attitudinal change. A more accurate measure is perhaps to use the group as barometer. In all groups, we will find the troublemaker, the know-all or the clown. It is hoped that, as the training progresses, their attitude will change. If it does not, the group reaction to their **antics** will tell. If it does, it will be noticeable in the way in which the group deals with and accepts the person. Attitudinal change can also be monitored in **subtleties** such as enthusiasm, concern and dedication. The way a person responds to an input can also be an indication of attitudinal change.

24.6.3 Product and process assessment

For an assessment to be thorough, both the product and the process must be evaluated.

Product assessment means to determine what has been learnt. Is there a change in behaviour of the trainees? Have the learning outcomes or objectives been met? Product evaluation can be for the sake of the trainees – to monitor their own progress; it can be for the sake of the facilitator – to determine the success in achieving the set outcomes or objectives; or it can be for the sake of the agency – to ascertain a basis for accreditation.

In short courses such as we are dealing with, assessment of the first two kinds mentioned above (discussion and small group) is of particular importance. By involving trainees in assessment, an additional learning opportunity is provided. Being subjective, their self-assessment is bound to be more rigid than that of the facilitator. The facilitator needs, however, to know how successful he/she was in achieving his/her objectives; it is, after all, also a learning opportunity for him/her and an opportunity to improve his/her next presentation.

In almost every training episode, an opportunity exists for product assessment through trainee involvement. Writing case studies, conducting surveys, doing simulation exercises and presenting (group) reports, all provide opportunities for participatory assessment. It is, however, important to structure the assessment carefully, work within clearly defined parameters and ensure the trainees fully understand their role and why it is important.

Process assessment relates to the following:

- *How the learning has been facilitated*: To what extent can the design and implementation (teaching) of the training account for the degree to which learning objectives have been met?
- *How the trainees have made use of the training*: To what extent have the trainees understood the material, availed themselves of the opportunity to gain knowledge and insight, and made use of the interactive method to create knowledge?

In assessing the process, trainees act as a 'sounding board' for the facilitator. They are given the opportunity to share their experience and perception of a particular training episode: the contents, the presentation and the training techniques used. Their assessment may initially be polite and reserved, for fear of **antagonising** the facilitator. If, however, the 'ice-breaker session' is successful and through proper communication a welcoming atmosphere is created, the response will soon become open and unrestricted. Throughout the training, the facilitator should stress (and make possible) assessment as a cooperative venture between him/her and the trainees; their input is for the common good, to jointly find flaws and strong points, and improve the training experience. At the same time, and without the trainees even being aware of it, the facilitator can ascertain the second point, that is, how the trainees have made use of the training.

If this type of understanding and relationship is not established, some trainees may interpret the assessment as an opportunity to 'get back' at the facilitator, and he/she may experience the assessment personally and negatively.

24.6.4 Feedback

All people are curious about their performance. They have, in any case, the right to know the results of their evaluation. Assessment is not only meant as an opportunity to score marks; it should above all be treated as yet another learning opportunity. Therefore, it is vital for the facilitator to provide trainees with feedback on their assessment. Continuous feedback not only underscores the learning process but it also reinforces a relationship of trust and openness in the group. Feedback is the final and ultimate product of a training session. It should never be ignored or neglected.

24.7 CONTENTS AND RELEVANCY

The most important aspect of training for development is that the contents must be relevant. If the CDP acts as a facilitator, he/she should have a good idea of what information the different role players in projects need by way of training. With this internalised knowledge, the CDP can discuss the various training needs with the various role players and try to marry his/her knowledge of training needs with their perceptions of what is needed in their **armoury**. What follows here is only a framework divided into three 'modules'. What the detail of these fields of study or training should be and where the emphasis should lie, is something to be sorted out with the role players.

Introductory training course for beginners

Module 1: Community capacity building

Poverty – the problem to be addressed

The development environment

The basic principles of community development

The role of the CDP

An operational strategy

The community development project

Evaluation

Module 2: Community-based development management

Principles of management

Mobilisation of community-based structures

Basic record keeping

Basic bookkeeping

> **Module 3: Communication for development**
>
> Communication and its importance for development
>
> The characteristics of motivation for community development
>
> Conflict resolution and negotiation
>
> Problem-solving mechanisms for development projects
>
> Group dynamics and group work
>
> Public speaking
>
> Operational writing
>
> The dynamics of meetings – making them more productive

We also suggest an advanced course although we realise that perhaps one needs more experienced facilitators than CDPs for this.

> **Advanced course for role players in community development**
>
> **Module 1: Development context**
>
> Sustainable development
>
> The politics of development
>
> The economics of development
>
> **Module 2: Advanced skills**
>
> Advanced management techniques
>
> Advanced negotiation techniques
>
> Advanced problem-solving techniques
>
> Advanced planning techniques
>
> Advanced evaluation techniques
>
> Advanced office management and bookkeeping

24.8 CONCLUSION

Facilitating training for community development is directed at project staff, community facilitators, communities or CBOs, or a combinations of these (De Beer & Swanepoel 2013:112). The single most serious problem, though, is the scarcity of facilitators. For this reason, it is necessary to view the

CDP as a potential facilitator. This potential is achievable because of the commonality between the work done by CDPs in their communities and the type of training espoused here. The training discussed in the previous pages is part of the process of learning and adaptation toward the breaking of the cycle of poverty.

REFERENCES

De Beer F & Swanepoel H. 2013. *The Community Development Profession. Issues, Concepts and Approaches*. Pretoria: Van Schaik.

Chambers R. 1983. *Rural Development: Putting the Last First*. Essex: Longman.

Doyle M & Straus D. 1976. *How to Make Meetings Work. The New Interaction Method*. Ridgefield, Connecticut: Wyden Books.

Freire P. 2005. *Pedagogy of the Oppressed*. New York: Continuum.

Smith SP. 2017. Adult learners: Effective training methods. *Professional Safety*, 62(12):22–25.

University of Kansas. 2023. *Community Toolbox*. Kansas: Centre for Community Health and Development.

SECTION F

Overview of the Professionalisation Context

CHAPTER 25

Legislation and Policy Frameworks Associated with Community Development in South Africa

Cornel Hart

25.1 INTRODUCTION

This chapter aligns with and presents more detailed descriptions of aspects discussed in chapters 3, 6, 8 and 13. The South African Constitution stipulates that people's needs must be addressed, and hence they must be encouraged to participate in policy making. South Africa is confronted with the triple challenges of unemployment, poverty and inequality and, as such, policy is used to promote employment creation and improve the socio-economic conditions of citizens. It is for this reason that legislation and policy frameworks are a critical component in community development practice.

Legislation and policy guide the practice of community development and direct the roles and responsibilities of community development practitioners (CDPs) when working with communities. Development is thus guided and guarded by legislative and policy frameworks. South Africa's National Policy Development Framework (NPDF) (Republic of South Africa 2020:10) provides nine reasons for policy:

1. It directs and guides the actions of all role players.
2. It provides a mandate to role players.
3. It clarifies the roles and responsibilities of role players.
4. It ensures consistency in the actions of those who implement policy.
5. It facilitates uniformity in decision making and the application of rules.
6. It ensures uniformity in the application of rules and it prevents confusion among those who implement it by clarifying the meanings of the mandate of the minister responsible as well as the terms used.

7. It improves the accountability of the people and organisations responsible for policy and its use.
8. It protects the public against the improper utilisation or exploitation of people and their resources.
9. It reduces unnecessary conflict among role players.

Community development is practised by people from different disciplines and sectors. It is thus cross-cutting, so that its implementation and practice are influenced by a plethora of legislation and policies that can be overwhelming for CDPs. This chapter aims to provide a guideline to the strategic and most pertinent legislation and policies impacting on community development practice.

25.2 POLICY TYPES AND PURPOSES

There are different types of policies. The NPDF (Republic of South Africa 2020:10) provides the following policy categories: regulatory, distributive, redistributive, transversal, department specific and directives. Table 25.1 links policy categories to policy types.

Table 25.1 **Policy categories linked to policy types**

Policy category	Policy types and examples
Regulatory policies	These policies have control over individuals and corporations by putting limitations on actions or behaviour. These policy types are typically 'protective' of consumers and the environment. *Examples:* The National Consumer Protection Act 68 of 2008 and the Protection of Personal Information (POPI) Act 4 of 2013 At a business level, these policies control pollution and transportation. Their purview includes affirmative action, gun control and standards setting, such as quality of drug manufacturing. *Examples:* The national traffic regulations, health regulations, and export and import regulations.
Distributive policies	These policies include direct government benefits to individuals, groups and the private sector linked to the use of public funds to assist the aforementioned. *Example:* Subsidies to farmers, public healthcare facilities and the National Student Financial Aid Scheme (NSFAS).

Policy category	Policy types and examples
Redistributive policies	These policies provide social benefits to specific groups and are aimed at redistribution of wealth and resources to different societal groups. *Examples:* Social security schemes/grants to the elderly, children and vulnerable groups, and the Broad-based Black Economic Empowerment Act.
Transversal policies	These policies are enacted at a departmental level and have the mandate to develop and apply a relevant/respective policy that affects other government departments throughout all spheres of government. *Example:* Policies related to the Public Service and the Public Finance Management Acts.
Department-specific policies	These policies have an operational focus linked to internal procedures, guidelines and protocols that must be observed by departmental employees. They do not necessarily originate directly from national policy or legislation but could be indirectly linked to national policies. *Example:* The school's admission policy developed by a school governing body but which must be in line with the Admission Policy for Ordinary Public Schools, National Education Policy Act, 1996 and South African Schools Act, 1996.
Policy directives	Directives are technical in nature and do not require changes to higher level policies or to legislation. They are formal instructions and can take on many forms. Their purpose is to communicate the changes, interpretation or application of their respective policies and legislation.

Source: NPDF (Republic of South Africa 2020:10)

Being knowledgeable of pertinent definitions relevant to legislation and policy is a key requirement for all practitioners working in community development. Table 25.2 provides important definitions from the 2020 NPDF that are especially relevant to community development, as a quick reference.

Table 25.2 **Important definitions**

| **Act of Parliament** – 'refers to a final legislation which originally assumed a status of a Bill and was subsequently passed by Parliament to become a law. The Act of Parliament will have a force of law once the President has assented to it and published a date for its implementation through a proclamation'. | **Legislature** – 'is a body of persons who have been elected and who make laws. The collective name for these laws (statutes) is legislation. In South Africa there is the national legislature (Parliament) which makes laws for the whole country on any subject'. | **Promulgation** – 'refers to the publication of regulations as final step of implementation. This is usually done by Executive Authorities'. |

Bill – 'refers to a draft law or legislation (eg Health Practitioners Bill) that is subjected to public consultative processes, parliamentary debate, voting and enactment. Once Parliament passes the Bill into law, the piece of legislation is sent to the President for assent and signature'.	**Monitoring** – 'involves continuous collecting, analysing and reporting data on inputs, activities, outputs, outcomes and impacts as well as external factors in a way that supports effective management. It aims to provide managers, decision makers and other stakeholders with regular feedback on progress in implementation, results and early indicators of problems that need to be corrected. Monitoring usually reports on actual performance against what was planned or expected'.	**Public Policy** – 'is an authoritative statement by policy makers in response to a societal problem, opportunities and changing circumstances the population is faced with at any given time. Policy contains goals to be pursued and the course of action needed to achieve the goals. Public policy becomes implementable provided the elected policy makers and senior government officials have authorised and legitimised it through a formalised policy development process'.
By-law – 'is passed by a Municipal Council since the Constitution bestows both the executive and legislative authority on this body in terms of Section 151(2), read together with Section 156(2) of the Constitution. A by-law serves as an original legislation in the context of a municipality. Municipal Councils are constitutionally empowered to pass and administer by-laws on matters listed in Part B of Schedule 4 and Part B of Schedule 5 of the Constitution'.	**Notice** – 'is usually issued to ensure that there is compliance with laws operating under the auspices of a government department, for example, the Environmental Affairs, Water and Sanitation, Mineral Resources and Energy departments. The overall aim of a compliance notice is to bring noncompliant actors into compliance with environmental legislation or with the conditions of permits, authorisations or other regulatory instruments'.	**Regulation(s)** – 'flows and derives from an Act of legislatures. It is intended to amplify the content of the original legislation for the purpose of implementation on the part of the policy implementers (ie bureaucrats). A designated Minister would be responsible for developing a regulation or regulations based on the content of a piece of legislation. For example, the Minister for Health may decide to develop a regulation based on the Health Practitioners Act'.
Evaluations – 'are the systematic collection and objective analysis of evidence of public policies, programmes, projects, functions and organisations to assess issues such as relevance, performance (effectiveness and efficiency), value for money, impact and sustainability and recommend ways forward'.	**Policy** – 'can be defined as the organisation's stated position on internal or external issues. It provides the written basis for an organisation's operations and informs legislation, regulations and the organisation's governing document. A policy is typically based on a government's political priorities, usually contained in the governing party manifesto and part of its programme of action'.	**Repeal** – 'refers to the process whereby legislation is deleted, in other words, removed from the statute book. Elected legislatures and persons or other bodies so enabled by primary legislation, are competent law-makers, and they may repeal legislation'.

Evidence-Based Policy Making – 'is the process that assists policy makers to make better decisions and achieve better outcomes. Evidence refers to the knowledge base and body of knowledge that is being drawn on and used to inform policy decisions'.	Policy Development – 'is the activity of developing policy [and] generally involves research, analysis, consultation and synthesis of information to produce recommendations. The end product of this process is a policy document reflecting on the policy issue to be addressed, procedures and mechanisms aimed at achieving the strategic thrust of the policy'.	Socio-Economic Impact Assessment System – 'refers to an ex ante policy analysis tool for assessing impacts and likely costs and benefits of the proposed regulatory propositions including, public policies, legislation, regulations and other highly impactful regulatory instruments'.
Green paper – 'refers to a draft (ie proposed) policy document on a specific government position ... It is important to bear in mind that a Green Paper is not considered a law since it is merely reflecting an official government policy position on a specific matter of public concern'.	Policy Framework – 'is an overarching structure tabulating a set of steps, procedures, principles, values and standards that officials ought to comply with to ensure the realisation of an organisation's adopted policy. It provides broad and detailed guidelines that are crucial to proper implementation of a policy'.	Statutory law – 'refers to law written down in statutes, parliamentary and provincial Acts, by-laws, proclamations, regulations and other subordinate legislation'.
Invalidation – 'happens when legislation is declared to be legally unacceptable. The legislation may no longer be applied, but remains on the statute book until removed by a competent law-maker. Courts may not and do not repeal legislation. However, they may invalidate legislation. Courts invalidate legislation on constitutional grounds'.	Proclamation – 'refers to when the President makes a public announcement in the Government Gazette about the commencement date of an Act or legal action'.	White Paper – 'represents a final comprehensive government policy position on a specific matter. A White Paper flows from a Green Paper endorsed by Parliament following a debate and voting. The White Paper does not have any force of law since it merely reflects a government official policy position on a specific matter of public concern'.

Source: NPDF (Republic of South Africa 2020:8–9)

Effective policy making depends on the following principles: necessity, simplicity, proportionality, predictability, accessibility, time frame, coordination and consistency as well as competitiveness (Republic of South Africa 2020:18). Additionally, several aspects influence policy making directly and indirectly. At a country (national) level, development and its required policies are directly influenced first by the country plan (eg in South Africa by the NDP: Vision 2030), then by the national and provincial departmental strategic plans as well as the Integrated Development Plans (IDPs) drafted in collaboration with community members by local government.

National and local plans are in turn indirectly influenced by developments at a continental (regional) level, for example the African Union Commission (AUC) 2015: Vision 2063, and at global (international) level, for example the United Nations (UN) 2015: SDGs 2030, as well as the many drafted and enforced global regulations on health and trade by the World Health Organization (WHO) and the World Trade Organization (WTO). Thus, policy making is influenced at varying levels by political, economic, social, technological and environmental factors as well as by legal and international obligations such as treaties and conventions (Republic of South Africa 2020:18).

The purpose of legislation and policy is to inform the public about the vision and intention of government's response to societal challenges, together with the 'rule of law' and democratic values to be respected and maintained. Thus, the public policy process aims to:

> ... a) Direct and guide the actions of role-players; b) Provide a mandate to role-players; c) Clarify roles and responsibilities of the different players; d) Ensure consistency in the actions of persons expected to implement policy; e) Facilitate uniformity in the application of rules and in decision-making; f) Clarify the meanings of terms used in the process of undertaking the mandate of the Minister, in order to avoid confusion among policy implementers, and to ensure uniformity in the application of rules; g) Improve the accountability of persons and organisations; h) Protect the public against the improper utilisation/exploitation of people and resources; and i) Reduce unnecessary conflict among role-players ... (Republic of South Africa 2020:10).

The post-apartheid democratic constitution reform impacted on all spheres of government and related legislation and policies. Most of the competing definitions are derived from the seminal work of Lasswell and Kaplan, both regarded as pioneers of 'policy science'. Lasswell and Kaplan (1970:71) define public policy as 'a projected programme of goals, values, and practices'. Weible, Heikkila, DeLeon and Sabatier (2012:2) are proponents for the plethora of public policy definitions because in their view it provides the opportunity to look at the policy process from multiple perspectives and prevents bias toward a single process with its related aspects or purposes. Instead, these authors propose that there should rather be a definition for 'process' which will guide public policy formulation, especially because of the different levels (ie spheres) of government at which public policies are formulated. Howlett (2014:199) proposes the need for a stronger focus on the 'method' of policy formulation, which is similar to the 'process' focus proposed by Weible et al (2012). The earlier quoted public policy definition in the 2020 NPDF not only provides a process/method definition to which the South African public sector subscribes but also mitigates the interpretation challenges and debates experienced with the plethora of competing definitions.

The CDP acts as the link between the state and the community in order to ensure that the different policy types and purposes are not only well communicated but that they also achieve their purposes in a participatory and inclusive manner involving all stakeholders, role players and community members.

25.3 THREE SPHERES OF GOVERNMENT

Legislation and policies are directly linked to the three spheres of government in South Africa: national, provincial and local (see also Chapter 26). CDPs' scope of work falls within these three spheres and their responsibilities are governed by the legislation and policies of these spheres. Additionally the CDP must ensure not only that community members understand the three spheres of government and their relevant legislation and policies but also that they are empowered to contribute to, and influence the drafting and operationalisation of, their policies and legislation.

The three spheres are autonomous, but in terms of Chapter 3 of the South African Constitution they have to work together and coordinate matters such as budgets, policies and activities, particularly those that cut across all the spheres. At national level, parliament makes laws called 'Acts of Parliament' that must be implemented throughout the entire country (see Chapter 4 of the Constitution). Economic, health and safety legislation are examples.

Provincial governments are responsible for matters at provincial level, as explained in Chapter 6 and listed in Schedule 5 of the Constitution. Each provincial legislature can draft its own laws, called ordinances, that apply to the people living in the relevant province. Additionally, some issues (listed in Schedule 4 of the Constitution) are relevant to both national and provincial government and for which both spheres of government can make laws, but national government remains responsible for setting the national standards for these laws and the provincial legislatures must then follow them when drafting their legislation.

Local government is responsible for matters that affect people at the local levels, which they control and which are determined by municipal and district boundaries. Positioned as an interdependent and interrelated sphere of national and provincial government, Schedules 4 and 5 of the Constitution list the responsibilities of local government. Examples are the provision of infrastructure (water, sanitation, electricity, recreational parks and facilities, and refuse removal) as well as local economic development. Section 152 of the Constitution, 1996, stipulates the new mandate for local government, whereby it no longer only provides basic services but is also required to promote social and economic development of communities. In terms of Section 152, local government is now mandated to: a) provide democratic and accountable government for local communities; b) ensure the provision of services to communities in a sustainable manner; c) promote social and economic development; d) promote a safe and healthy environment; and e) encourage the involvement of communities and community organisations in the matters of local government.

The Intergovernmental Relations Framework Act 13 of 2005 focuses on the system of inter-governmental relations in order to coordinate the structures between the different spheres of government. The Act provides for the integration and coordination of development efforts by government as well as, by its decentralisation, to promote local level decision making and control in a collective manner between government and citizens (ie community members).

Government's most significant example of decentralisation is evident in the Local Government White Paper of 1998 which states that 'local government is committed to working with citizens and groups within the community to find sustainable ways to meet their social, economic and material needs and improve the quality of their lives'. This example further emphasises the role of CDPs and their responsibility to work with communities in order to understand and contribute to the legislative and policy frameworks relevant to community development, because the operationalisation thereof is dependent on community members and their associate stakeholders.

The Constitution of the Republic of South Africa, 1996 is the ultimate law of South Africa. It consists of a preamble, 14 chapters, 224 sections and 8 schedules, all of which set out the ethos, responsibilities and rights that everyone must uphold. The lay-out of the Constitution is as follows: *Amendments*, *Preamble*, Chapter 1: *Founding Provisions*, Chapter 2: *Bill of Rights*, Chapter 3: *Co-operative Government*, Chapter 4: *Parliament*, Chapter 5: *The President and National Executive,* Chapter 6: *Provinces*, Chapter 7: *Local Government*, Chapter 8: *Courts and Administration of Justice*, Chapter 9: *State Institutions Supporting Constitutional Democracy*, Chapter 10: *Public Administration* Chapter 11: *Security Services*, Chapter 12: *Traditional Leaders*, Chapter 13: *Finance*, Chapter 14: *General Provisions*.

The Bill of Rights in chapter 2 of the Constitution is a cornerstone of South African democracy. Applicable to all law, it binds the legislature, the executive, the judiciary and all organs of state. Chapter 2 is thus one of the key chapters that influence the CDP's roles and responsibilities. The Bill of Rights lists 27 basic human rights that belong to all South Africans regardless of race, sex, socio-economic status, age or other differentiation. Although most people support human rights, not all people agree on the interpretation of it. Some of the key human rights are equality, the rights to dignity and life, freedom of religion, belief, opinion and expression, freedom from slavery and forced labour, freedom of association and movement – as well the right to basic housing, healthcare, food, water, social security and education.

The 1996 Constitution requires the state to achieve realisation of these human rights progressively from within its available resources, thereby establishing a rising base level of development rights. These rights are the 'building blocks' of human entitlements within communities upon which to build up the assets that support community development. The Constitution requires that: a) public administration must be development-oriented; b) services must be provided impartially, fairly, equitably and without bias; c) people's needs must be addressed; and d) the public must be encouraged to participate in policy making. It thus provides the framework for the 'developmental state' that government seeks to create through laying down the basic requirements for government actions in support of all citizens, their communities and their development.

In summary, the development focus areas of the different legislative and policy frameworks of the three spheres of government, that is, local economic development (LED), embrace health, social welfare, human settlements, free basic services, water and sanitation, land and agrarian reform, the environment and the criminal justice system. These focus areas drive the roles and responsibilities of CDPs and the related policies with which they must be acquainted. The 2014 (Draft) Community Development Practice

Policy Framework (CDPPF) presents a useful and quick access table of the legislation and policy frameworks associated with community development (Republic of South Africa 2014:31–33). This is provided as Appendix 25.1 at the end of the chapter.

25.4 ACTIONING AND DRIVING POLICIES FOR AND IN COMMUNITY DEVELOPMENT

At national level, the Department of Social Development (DSD) is responsible for the coordination of community development programmes and interventions because of the manner in which the parliamentary clusters are set up. The following five clusters currently exist: (1) Economic Sectors, Employment and Infrastructure Development; (2) Social Protection, Community and Human Development – headed by the ministers of the DSD and Cooperative Government and Traditional Affairs (CoGTA); (3) International Cooperation, Trade and Security; (4) Governance and Administration; and (5) Justice, Crime Prevention and Security. The DSD will, in partnership with other government departments, civil society and the private sector, design and review community development sectoral policies of technical departments.

While most government departments are responsible directly or indirectly for community development, there are some that must play a key role, as mandated by their policies, by ensuring quality, people-centred and integrated service delivery. Examples, other than the DSD and CoGTA, are the Department of Public Service and Administration (DPSA) and the Department of Provincial and Local Government (DPLG) because of community development that is actioned at local community level. The DPSA has four important functions regarding community development practice: (1) to integrate community development efforts to promote efficient public service and management; (2) to create a single public service for public service provision to communities; (3) to instil an ethos of community development that governs public service and administration in South Africa and to use it in measuring public service performance; and (4) to encourage greater harmony among the various practitioners in government responsible for community development.

The 2020 National Policy Development Framework provides a useful diagram of the policy-making cycle (see Figure 25.1). Earlier it was stated that a key responsibility of the CDP is to capacitate community members with regard to legislation and policies that are linked to community development. The second responsibility is to educate communities about the 'cycle' of policy making, together with some of the key definitions presented in Appendix 25.1.

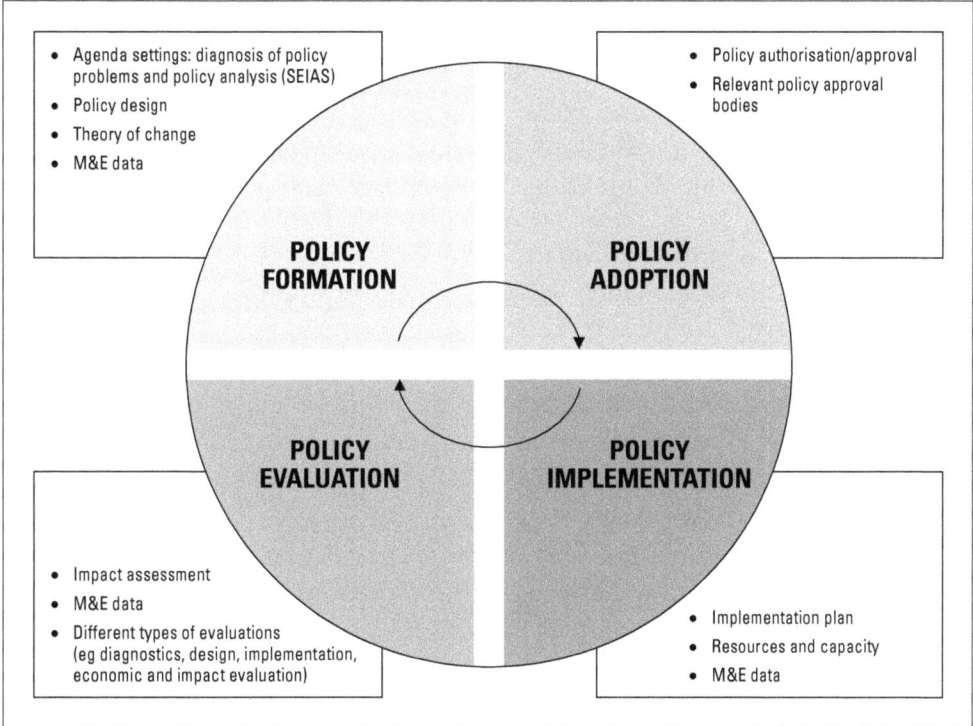

Figure 25.1   **Policy-making cycle**

Source: NPDF (Republic of South Africa 2020:13)

The policy cycle starts with the '**policy formulation stage**', also referred to as the **'diagnosis phase'**, which links with the sphere of government for which the specific policy will be developed. This stage of the cycle includes the following aspects (Republic of South Africa 2020:13–14):

- *Problem and root cause analysis:* This aims to understand the problems and their root causes so that an evidence-based and relevant intervention can be formulated.
- *Evidence use*: This informs the use of scientific research methodologies that focus on (a) citizen participation while collecting evidence, and (b) evaluation research methodologies that are also participatory in

approach when conducting an evaluation of past interventions that were implemented.
- *Option analysis*: This is done to weigh up the different options available to address the identified problems. It includes a theory of change (ToC), developed by the practitioner in collaboration with the community and relevant public and civic stakeholders. This is so that all parties can conceptualise the process and its intended outcomes via the policy that will be formulated to address the identified problems.
- *Early consultation and policy co-creation*: This is linked to, and following on from, option analysis, and is one of the most crucial aspects because it allows for inclusive consultation and policy co-creation.

The second stage is '**policy adoption**', which includes the different structures through which the draft policy must be taken for approval. It starts with a preliminary internal approval from the minister, premier or mayor, depending on the government sphere where the policy was initiated prior to engagement of the intergovernmental structures (eg ministerial cluster, or a committee consisting of a cabinet member and provincial members of the executive council for a functional issue, called MinMECs and district mayor's forum). If it is a national policy, such as education or health, that cuts across all spheres of government, then Cabinet must also be informed of it via the respective minister. Thus the order of the critical policy approval structure is as follows (Republic of South Africa 2020:14):

- Ministerial clusters
- MinMECs (for concurrent functions)
- Premier's coordinating forums
- District mayor's forum
- Forum of Director-Generals South Africa (FOSAD)
- President's Coordinating Council (PCC)
- Cabinet committees
- Executive councils of provinces
- Forum for heads of department
- Cabinet
- Council (in case of the local government by-laws)
- Member of Executive Council for Local Government.

The third stage of '**policy implementation**' is about translation of the policy into its implementation by the designing of a programme with activities and the provision of the resources required so that institutional arrangements can be made for its roll-out. This is again a crucial time for the CDP, who must ensure that the community is both correctly informed about this stage and has insight and inputs into the implementation planning that is taking place to action (translate) the policy. Additionally, a process of programme overlap must be assessed to both prevent duplication of initiatives between departments and ensure integration and coordination between them so that ultimately, progress of the National Development Plan (NDP): Vision 2030 priorities is assured (Republic of South Africa 2020:14–15).

The fourth and final stage is '**policy monitoring and evaluation**', which includes the appraisal of the policy content against the performance of its implementation. This is so its effectiveness and value can be determined, thereby contributing either to its future amendment requirements and/or to new or additional policy or policies of a similar nature. Most policies and programmes have 'sunset clauses' that indicate their time frames and lifespans, together with programme monitoring, evaluation and 'policy review'. The 2011 National Evaluation Policy Framework (NEPF) provides detailed guidance on the evaluation of policies, inclusive of a list of policy evaluation requirements (Republic of South Africa 2020:15).

25.5 POLICIES GUIDING COMMUNITY DEVELOPMENT PRACTICE QUALITY

Community development practice has some direct policies that specifically guide the practice of CDPs. These policies prescribe the CDP's purpose, goals, scope, values, principles, roles and functions as well as the operating norms, standards and ethical conduct to be adhered to by all CDPs. Currently the following policies guide and assure the quality of the professional and standardised practice of community development:

- 2014 (Draft) Community Development Practice Policy Framework (CDPPF)
- 2017 Policy for Social Service Practitioners
- 2020 Social Service Professions Bill (2021).

The 2014 Draft CDPPF is an example of how long the finalisation of a policy can take, in the absence of a statutory body that is responsible for its endorsement and enforcement. Thus, once the proposed Community Development Professional Board (ie the statutory body for the Draft CDPPF) has been elected and inaugurated (estimated target date of 2024), the draft framework can be approved and enforced in practice.

The 2014 CDPPF describes the rationale and purpose of the legislative and policy framework for community development practice, community development values and principles; the legislated definition for community development in South Africa; the unique and distinctive form of community development practice; the different levels and types of CDPs and their roles; the seven key norms and 25 related standards against which to standardise and assure the quality of community development practice; the code of ethics and conduct for practitioners; the skills, knowledge and attributes required of practitioners, their qualifications and continuous professional development; the institutional structures which coordinate and integrate community development; and the different stakeholders in community development (Republic of South Africa 2014:1–87).

The 2017 Policy for Social Service Practitioners has seven chapters which describe their policy, purpose, goals, mandate, application and objectives. This is inclusive of defining the SSP sector; the situation analysis of the end users (target groups) with whom Social Service Practitioners (SSPs) work; the contextual analysis describing the relevant legislative frameworks and policies; the overview of SSPs; the practice requirements of SSPs; the institutional and regulatory requirements of SSPs; and the behavioural norms and standards of the SSP sector (Republic of South Africa 2017:1–100).

The 2021 Social Service Professions Bill consists of nine chapters which prescribe the definitions and objectives of the South African Council for Social Service Practitioners (SACSSP), its establishment, powers functions and duties, composition of the SACSSP and its committees, the registrar and the administration of the SACSSP, the Social Service Boards (of which community development is one) and the SSPs (of whom CDPs are one), the registration of SSPs, the education, training and development of SSPs, and the SSP code of ethics and professional conduct (Republic of South Africa 2021:1–109).

The Policy for Social Service Practitioners describes each of the social service professions, namely social work, child- and youth care, community development and caregivers, against the earlier mentioned policy chapters.

The Social Service Professions Bill describes the powers, functions and duties of the professional boards under the SACSSP for each of the aforementioned social service professions. The policy and Bill therefore contextualise, define, describe and prescribe the practice of community development as well as the regulation of CDPs.

25.6 THE COMMUNITY DEVELOPMENT PRACTITIONER'S ROLE IN POLICY

The CDP's four key roles described in the CDPPF (Republic of South Africa 2014:41–42) are directly associated with the legislative frameworks and policies for community development. CDPs are:

- *change agents* who are required to identify the gaps in services and concerns of communities. They therefore have to know the human rights charter as well as the provincial and local government policies that deal with service provision and poverty alleviation. This is so that they can work with communities to enable policy to work for them when they identify their community assets, the stakeholders and the statutory authorities with whom they need to partner to integrate and coordinate the development interventions for poverty alleviation.

- *service developers* who must ensure that people and organisations working in communities are informed about the education, training and capacity building available to them. This so that community development practice is of the highest quality and standards, and that it remains a sensitive proponent of diversity and social justice when establishing partnerships between statutory and community services stakeholders.

- *access facilitators* who are responsible for the empowerment of communities regarding the services, volunteering, finances and initiatives available to them. This requires CDPs always to be up to date with the different plans and programmes initiatives derived from the policies at the provincial and local government spheres, so that they can guide communities with regard to accessibility and participation in those initiatives. Additionally, they are responsible for facilitating feedback to the relevant spheres of government regarding the feasibility of their plans and programmes from the community's perspective and context – thereby ensuring participatory and inclusive principles of democratic policy development and implementation.

- *capacity builders* whose key purpose has been highlighted in several sections of this chapter and book. CDPs must ensure inclusivity of communities at all times via community leadership and organisational structures capacitated as to the legislative frameworks, policies and programme initiatives for poverty alleviation, social transformation and community wellbeing. This so that these structures are informed and enabled (capacitated) to empower their community members to participate fully as equal partners in their own development.

In addition to their four key roles, CDPs also have six distinctive responsibilities in their practice which also requires that they are knowledgeable about the legislative and policy frameworks, and that they are skilled in transferring that knowledge to communities. Listed in the CDPPF (Republic of South Africa 2014:39–40), these responsibilities are as follows:

1. To help people realise the commonality of their concerns regarding local and public matters, so that they can work together and lead the process of their development.
2. To mobilise community members to work together and establish community structures that will represent and lead processes on behalf of the community.
3. To ensure ethical practices in and between community structures, so that equal and inclusive networks and partnerships can be established with government and all other stakeholders.
4. To promote values of equity, inclusiveness, participative citizenry and cooperation throughout the community development process – all of which directly link with the Constitution and its related sections.
5. To empower community members and their organisations to influence and transform public policies and services that affect their livelihoods.
6. To advise and inform public authorities about the community's perspectives, facilitation and strengthening of community partnerships.

25.7 CONCLUSION

The Constitution of the Republic of South Africa, 1996 in Chapter 3, Section 41, outlines the principles of cooperative government and intergovernmental relations which are binding on all spheres and structures of government. The South African Presidency's Intergovernmental Relations and Service Delivery Framework (13 of 2005) sets out the plan of government to transform South Africa and its government by integrating all spheres of government and by decentralising development. Thus the objective is to establish a system wherein all spheres of government plan together to provide a coherent approach to community development, which in turn requires intersectoral collaboration, coordination and action among all relevant key stakeholders to improve community development outcomes.

This summarises and prescribes the roles and responsibilities of CDPs in a systematic manner because they must first ensure that intersectoral collaboration includes the horizontal management of community development issues via the collective identification of common goals among sectoral partners, and then ensure the coordinated planning, development and implementation of related and required policies, programmes and services. Only if CDPs take up their responsibilities from an informed, ethical and quality assured position, based on common standards, will community development be participatory, inclusive and empowering for communities within the legislative and policy frameworks that prescribe and guide the community development process.

REFERENCES

AUC (African Union Commission). 2015. *Agenda 2063: The Africa We Want A Shared Strategic Framework for Inclusive Growth and Sustainable Development. The first ten-year implementation plan (2014–2023)*. Addis Ababa, Ethiopia: The African Union Commission.

Howlett M. 2014. From the 'old' to the 'new' policy design: Design thinking beyond markets and collaborative governance. *Policy Sciences*, 47(3): 187–207.

Lasswell HD & Kaplan A. *1970. Power and Society*. New Haven, CT: Yale University Press.

Republic of South Africa. 1996. *Constitution of the Republic of South Africa, 1996*. Pretoria: Government Printer.

Republic of South Africa. 1998. *White Paper on Local Government*. Pretoria: Government Printer.

Republic of South Africa. 2005. *Intergovernmental Relations Framework 13 of 2005*. Pretoria: Government Printer.

Republic of South Africa. 2021. *Social Service Professions Bill*. Pretoria: Government Printer.

Republic of South Africa. Department of Performance Monitoring and Evaluation (DPME). 2011. *National Evaluation Policy Framework*. Pretoria: Government Printer.

Republic of South Africa. Department of Social Development (DSD). 2014. *(Draft) Community Development Practice Policy Framework (CDPPF)*. Pretoria: Government Printer.

Republic of South Africa. Department of Social Development (DSD). 2017. *Policy for Social Service Practitioners*. Pretoria: Government Printer.

Republic of South Africa. The Presidency. 2020. *National Policy Development Framework (NPDF)*. Pretoria: Government Printer.

Republic of South Africa, The Presidency, National Planning Commission (NPC). 2012. National Development Plan 2030: Our future – make it work. Available at: https://www.gov.za/sites/default/files/gcis_document/201409/ndp-2030-our-future-make-it-workr.pdf (accessed 23 June 2022).

UN (United Nations). 2015. The United Nations Sustainable Development Summit 2015. New York: UN. Available at: http://www.un.org/sustainabledevelopment/summit/ (accessed 23 June 2022).

Weible CM, Heikkila T, DeLeon P & Sabatier PA. 2012. Understanding and influencing the policy process. *Policy Sciences*, 45(1):1–21.

Appendix 25.1: Legislation and policy frameworks associated with community development

THEME	LEGISLATIVE AND POLICY CONTEXT	THE APPLICATION OF A COMMUNITY DEVELOPMENT APPROACH
Working with ...		
Children	Children's Act, 2005	Reduce levels of child hunger and malnutrition
		Expand access to ECD programmes
Youth	Youth Development Policy	Empowerment of the poor and vulnerable to promoting the voices and participation.
	Youth Development Strategy	
Women	Domestic Violence Act, 1998	Community engagement and true representation within communities.
People with Disabilities	Disability Policy	Creating a climate where people can participate fully in decisions which affect their community.
Older Persons	Older Persons Act, 2006	Community involvement in developing services which meet the needs of specific groups.
Families	Draft White Paper on Families	
		Promoting community cohesion and understanding.
		Engage more effectively with communities to develop strategies which are responsive to their needs and issues.
		Develop capacity of local voluntary activists to engage more effectively in community planning.
		Empower local communities to engage with statutory bodies.
		Promote equality among all sections of society.
Working in the context of ...		
Community Safety	Prevention and Treatment of Drug Abuse Dependency Act, 1992 as amended	Supporting community partnerships and crime prevention programmes to improve social cohesion.
		Developing initiatives which reduce a community's fear of crime.

THEME	LEGISLATIVE AND POLICY CONTEXT	THE APPLICATION OF A COMMUNITY DEVELOPMENT APPROACH
Working with ...		
Food Security	Food and Nutrition Security policy, 2012 Integrated Food Security Strategy (IFSS) Household Food and Nutrition Security Strategy	Promoting household food production to improve access to nutritious and affordable food.
Local Government	Public Service Act 103, 1994 White paper on the Transformation of Service Delivery (Batho Pele) Municipal Demarcation Act 27, 1998 White paper on Local Government, 1998 Municipal Systems Act 32 of 2000 White Paper on Traditional Leadership and Governance National Policy Framework for Public Participation, 2007 National Policy on CDWP, 2009	Promoting and encouraging public participation. Advocating integrated development planning and transformation. Linking communities with the many services and programmes of public sector. Assisting citizen with access to main services such as health, welfare, housing, agriculture, economic activities, education & training and employment. Determining the needs of communities and communicate it to government (community profiles). Promoting networks between community workers and projects for improved service delivery. Assisting in removing development deadlocks. Strengthening democratic social contract. Advocating an organised voice for the poor and social excluded. Promoting principles of transformation (Batho Pele). Maintaining ongoing liaison and collaboration with various CBOs and other cadres of community-based workers. Ensuring intersectoral action for comprehensive development by involving all sectors, disciplines, agencies and departments. Prioritising programmes that are identified by the beneficiaries themselves and lead to the improvement in the lives of everyone with an emphasis on the most vulnerable, disabled and disadvantaged.

THEME	LEGISLATIVE AND POLICY CONTEXT	THE APPLICATION OF A COMMUNITY DEVELOPMENT APPROACH
Working with ...		
Education	White Paper: Education and Training in a Democratic South Africa: First Steps to Develop a New System, 1995 National Education Policy Act (NEPA) (1996) The South African Schools Act (SASA) (1996) The Education White Paper on Early Childhood Development (2000) Education White Paper 6 on Inclusive Education (2001) General and Further Education and Training Quality Assurance Act (Act 58 of 2001) Higher Education Qualifications Framework in the Government Gazette, 2007 (No 928, 5)	Developing skills and knowledge within a CommDev setting. Community action to increase access to education and learning at local level. Developing mainstream education. facilities as community venues for learning and other development activities. Supporting community settings such as local schools, adult education, and lifelong learning opportunities. Creating opportunities for people to advance their personal and professional development through education programmes.
Sports	National Sport and Recreation Act, 1998 (Act no 110 of 1998 as amended	Working with the community to identify opportunities, planning and delivering sporting and leisure activities at a community level.
Health	National Health Act, 61 of 2003	Engaging communities in activities which promote better health. Supporting locally based health and well-being initiatives which are community led.
Arts and Culture	Culture Promotion Act, 1983 White paper on Arts, Culture and Herritage, (Rvised Draft, 2013)	Nurturing the potential that exists in all communities to be creative. Finding a voice for communities to express their concerns through and using the Arts.

THEME	LEGISLATIVE AND POLICY CONTEXT	THE APPLICATION OF A COMMUNITY DEVELOPMENT APPROACH
Working with ...		
Economic Development	Industrial Development Corporation Act, 1940 The Competition Act, 1998 The International Trade Administration Act, 2002 Framework for SA's response to the International Economic Crisis The New Growth Path framework Social Accords on Skills Development, Green Economy	Community projects which help people into work. Developing skills in a community setting. Developing social enterprises as vehicles for economic development and community regeneration. Developing community led local tourism initiatives celebrating local distinctiveness.
Rural Development and Land Reform	Abolition of Racially Based Land Measures Act, 1991 (108) Communal Property Associations Act, 1996 (28) Development Facilitation Act, 1995 (67) Extension of Security of Tenure Act, 1997 (Act 62) Land Reform: Provision of Land and Assistance Act, 1993 (126) Spatial Data Infrastructure Act, 2003 (54)	Promoting community led projects in support of the rural economy. Supporting actions which sustain the viability of rural communities. Supporting local capacity to engage in rural economic activity.
Environment	White Paper on Environmental Management, 1998 National Framework Strategy for Sustainable Development, 2009 National Strategy for Sustainable Development, 2011 The National Environmental Management Act s (all 1998, 2003, 2004, 2008 & 2009).	Promoting local activity that combats climate change, the more sustainable use of resources and improving environments. Supporting local distinctiveness and sense of place. Encouraging the community to support the protection of the natural environment.

THEME	LEGISLATIVE AND POLICY CONTEXT	THE APPLICATION OF A COMMUNITY DEVELOPMENT APPROACH
Working with ...		
Agriculture, Forestry and Fisheries	Food and Nutrition Security policy, 2012 Integrated Food Security Strategy (IFSS) Household Food and Nutrition Security Strategy Small Scale Fisheries Policy, 2012 no. (474)	Promoting community led projects in support of small-scale fisheries economy and household food security. Broadening access to communities for food security. Promoting partnerships and joint management of limited marine resources. Support job creation for poor coastal rural communities. Supporting household food production to improve access to nutritious and affordable food.
Human Settlements	Housing Act, 1997 (107) Comprehensive Plan for the Creation of Sustainable Human Settlements The Social Housing Act, 2008 (16) The Rental Housing Act, 1999 (50) Inclusionary Housing Bill Sectional Titles Scheme Management Bill	Supporting tenant led initiatives around choice, improving conditions, influencing design, tenants self-build and other sustainabilities. Mobilising vvarious entities involved in housing provision. Community residents developing facilities and services. Developing Community Land Trusts and other innovative solutions to rural housing issues.
Transport	National Land Transport Act, 2009 (5)	Supporting community transport schemes. Improving access, eg rural areas.

Source: Republic of South Africa (2014:31–33)

CHAPTER 26

Challenges of Community Development Practice at Government and Non-Government Levels: A Case Study from South Africa

Ndwakhulu Tshishonga

26.1 INTRODUCTION

This chapter focuses on the practice of community development as an integral part of development intervention and community transformational change. Practice is the best way for CDPs to learn and improve their practice of community development, with experience forming their knowledge base. Swanepoel and De Beer (2016) differentiate professionals into two categories, namely specialists and generalists. Specialist professionals are those found in the mainstream occupations and hold occupational titles such as social workers, teachers/lecturers, nurses and doctors, engineers and others (Swanepoel & De Beer 2016). However, despite that this category of professionals does not include CDPs, in one way or another CDPs engage communities and their stakeholders using processes, values and principles embedded in community development practice. Generalist professionals, on the other hand, fall within the broader but key category of community activists, traditional leaders and healers, and indigenous knowledge holders as well as mobilisers of people for integrated community development.

Essentially, community development practice is reflective of both individual and collective agency with processes, strategies and techniques, and a set of values and principles for building strong, sustainable and healthy communities. In this regard, Vincent (2014) defines the practice of community development as an aspect of managing community change based on a dialogical engagement by citizens in creating a shared future vision and strategising on how to actualise such vision. Thus, demand for civil engagement and citizen empowerment and participation in community development processes (Silverman & Patterson 2014) compels practitioners to be active and radical change agents (also see discussion on principles of community development in Chapter 6). It goes without saying that community professionals and developers use practice approaches and models to engage people and community stakeholders in order to influence the outcomes of community change initiatives (Kahl & Hains 2020).

For community development practice to bear fruit, practitioners need to create a conducive environment for communities to develop shared vision and learning through sustained participation. Core to community development practice is the alleviation of poverty and deprivation, while minimising dependency through community empowerment, community building and grassroots sustainable intervention (Chitonge & Mazibuko 2018). Through community engagement, communities in partnership with practitioners and other stakeholders enhance community development practice as the cornerstone of community development work (Stanard, Goodman & Reddy 2020). Viewed from a radical perspective, community development practice engenders praxis, an integration of theory and practice as the knowledge foundation for critical consciousness and action (Ledwith 2020). Therefore, this chapter is a critical reflection of community development practice within the context of South Africa. In particular, the place and role played by CDPs and local government and non-governmental organisations are given priority. Given the history of social community activism and struggles, South Africa provides an interesting case for reflective community development practice. As mentioned earlier, CDP is used in this book as a generic term for professionals and workers in community development.

26.2 COMMUNITY DEVELOPMENT BACKGROUND

Community development is known to be an interdisciplinary and intersectoral field of study (see also chapter 27). Its interdisciplinarity saw the integration, influence and borrowing of some theoretical discourses and pragmatic frameworks from fields such as sociology, anthropology, political sciences and management (Ife 2016; Vincent 2014). This is reaffirmed by Maistry (2012), who grounds community development as a comprehensive, multisectoral and multidisciplinary field. Thus, from a multisectoral perspective, community development could be comprised of practitioners from the sectors of health, education, agriculture, political science, housing and social work (Garkovich 2011). As an emergent professional discipline in South Africa, community development draws its knowledge discourses from a multitude of disciplines such as economics, sociology, agriculture, community psychology and political science (Gray 1998, cited in Maistry 2012:34). As both a method and a process, community development has been adopted in health, education, welfare, environmental and tourism sectors. Due to the persistence of poverty, exclusion and marginalisation nationally and internationally, community development has shifted from traditional to participatory, liberatory and emancipatory approaches. This shift is in line with the international community development trends toward theoretical radicalising of community development for meaningful interventions and practice (Ledwith 2020). Thus, discourses on community development embrace a multi-professional approach in dealing with social justice, social exclusion and social cohesion-related issues (Larsen, Sewpaul & Hole 2014).

Because of community development's long and sometimes controversial history, there are various connotations attached to its conceptualisation, theorisation and practice. Central to community development are the planned efforts aimed at (1) producing community assets, (2) taking collective action, and (3) challenging the oppressive and unjust structures in society (Phillips & Kraeger 2018). In this regard, Liguori and Winkler (2020) argue strongly for an integration between theoretical discourses and deliberate practice in community development. The phrase 'community development', which has roots in the 18th century, is a general one that refers to a wide range of social sciences (Hart 2012:56) (also see Chapter 4 on the origins of community development). Community development has always attempted to improve a community's quality of life. Warren and Harper (2017) define community development as a process by which government officials and the general public work together to better the economic, social and cultural conditions of communities, and enable individuals to contribute fully to it.

South Africa has a long history of community development. Given the history of community activism and struggles, South Africa provides an interesting case for reflective community development practice. During the apartheid era, community activists and professionals played a decisive role in demanding and providing essential services for the people. This chapter in particular acknowledges radical community development work and practice embarked on by the Black Consciousness Movement and other religious formations in the 1970s, partaking in the 'struggle politics' against social injustices, economic inequalities and political change (Davids & Waghid 2021:xiv). Being influenced by ubuntu-based communalism and the spirit of self-reliance, Black Consciousness managed to mobilise and reawaken the power of collective solidarity (More 2017).

In this chapter, the various roles and functions of community development practitioners are identified and discussed within the context of community development practice. Their roles range from change agent and community capability builder advocating for social justice, to community activist, to scholar. For CDPs to achieve sustainable outcomes and benefits for people and communities, they need to make use of context, principles and perspectives to determine, adapt and consider their position. They must stand on the border between empowerment and disempowerment, being neither too specific nor directive (Ife 2016), but remaining steadfast in 'putting people first' in their development.

Figure 26.1 depicts how community development professionals engage with communities in many different ways, including door-to-door outreach, awareness campaigns, izimbizo (forums organised for social and political purposes) and other community meetings (Kenny 2016).

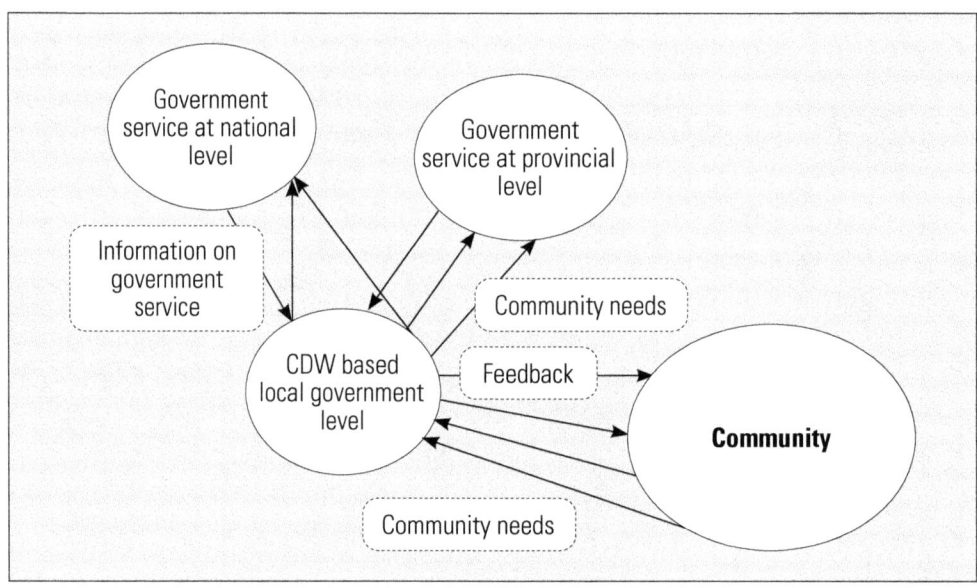

Figure 26.1: **CDWs' relationship with government and the community**

Source: Ministry of Public Service and Administration (2007:22)

Community workers or agents of change discover community issues, projects and gaps in service delivery and forward these cases to the relevant government departments, who ought to respond and take the necessary action (Abebe,

Kebede & Alemie 2019). Therefore, CDPs make sure that the community's issues are properly addressed and follow-ups are done. CDPs, communities and the government are constantly in communication with one another.

26.3 COMMUNITY DEVELOPMENT PROFESSIONALS AS CHANGE AGENTS

CDPs are known as participatory change agents, or community development agents, whose labour gives back to their local communities (see Chapter 19). CDPs are supposed to assist locals in understanding how to participate and strategise for neighbourhood development (Moeti & Mokoena 2017). They are entrusted to encourage community involvement in delivery of services, implementation of policy and in policy making (Heathershaw 2016). Change agents must promote community participation according to their understanding of the context that gives meaning to participation, in which 'people's needs are shaped by the political, economic, and social conditions in which they live' (Martin 2014:40). The environment of change agents also influences their work, with a supportive environment enabling them to be more effective and a prohibitive environment resulting in the opposite (Gwala & Theron 2012). CDPs as change agents also facilitate and advocate for a decentralised administrative structure. A change in goals and bureaucratic reorientation are characteristics of a helpful and enabling environment (Wilson 2019:3). CDPs therefore encourage development that will foster independence and promote a working atmosphere conducive to effectiveness.

Community interventions through change agents, in general, refer to actions that address social problems or unmet community needs in a neighbourhood, community or other setting (Maya-Jariego & Holgado 2019:7). A community intervention programme for change is thus an intentional action to promote change that can take various forms depending on the needs of the community. A professionally led intervention is more explicit as it involves a programme planned and implemented by professionals for community needs (Jason, Glantsman, O'Brien & Ramian 2019). Change agents are instrumental in facilitating community interventions and programmes designed for meeting the communal needs.

26.3.1 Community development practitioners as community and capacity builders

CDPs are community builders that inform local residents and aid in empowering both people and communities. One of the key responsibilities of community builders is to mentor and assist locals engaged in community-based projects, such as those that promote small business development, help people in finding employment, or enhance neighbourhood resources and assets (Moeti & Mokoena 2017). Community builders are also instrumental in promoting and easing the suffering of the poor and enhancing government ties with the community. CDPs as community builders also envision 'strengthening the democratic social compact and developing citizenry' and 'reducing the gap between the first and second economies' (Martin 2014:42). One of the reasons behind implementation of CDPs was to engage more in participatory governance; facilitate community development at local grassroots; and strive for elimination of bureaucratic bottlenecks across and within service delivery sectors (Parliamentary Monitoring Group 2007; Dupuy 2014). Through community building, communities are able to form an alliance with one another to allow more fluid neighbour-to-neighbour community engagements to foster a sense of belonging and to establish a power base that nurtures solidarity and power at the neighbourhood level.

Communities are among the key and fundamental stakeholders in local government. Empowerment of communities and their participation in government programmes and projects remains one of the measures for developmental local government as espoused by the White Paper of Local Government (Republic of South Africa 1998). Within local government, empowered and sustainable communities are an asset for effective practice, hence the National Development Plan (Republic of South Africa 2012) postulates that government has to act with the people in collaboration with other state organs for the provision of services. Imperative to this collaboration is the creation of spaces for the development of the communities (Ndevu & Muller 2018). The South African government's Department of Local Government and Traditional Affairs (CoGTA) has employed community development workers (CDWs), operating under the auspices of the Community Development Workers Programme (CDWP), across the country to expedite service delivery and community development through connecting people to government and government services. Introspectively, as a way of thinking and a philosophy of practice, Ife (2013) argues that community development should transcend being merely a process of building stronger communities to empowering all community members and organisations.

Primarily, this cohort of public servants are designated to be community builders in order to promote communities' and other stakeholders' self-reliance and ultimately interdependency. Accordingly, community builders are central in terms of building capacity and community development through promoting a culture of self-reliance and informed decision making in policy and programme processes (Khumalo & Tshishonga 2018). It is without doubt that people and communities can only become self-reliant when they are in charge of their situation and are empowered to work in solidarity with each other for their common good. In essence, community building entails empowering and strengthening communities through sharing of information and knowledge, facilitation of critical thinking and utilisation of multi-agency platforms for dialogue (Blewitt 2015). Without building the capacity of community development practitioners (CDPs), either through formal academic or informal training, CDPs remain weak and vulnerable to defend and represent community stakeholder-related issues and expectations. The role of community builder is a multifaceted one which demands community development practitioners, whether or not they are employed by the state, to possess skills of guiding, networking and providing professional expertise.

Community building is by nature confrontational, especially when based on the transformative agenda of 'conscientisation' – education for liberation as envisaged by Freire (2021). Despite the pronouncement of political freedom in 1994, due to the apartheid era's spatial exclusion, some South African communities are still divided along racial, class and gender lines, with townships, rural, semi-urban and informal settlements bearing the brunt of the racially discriminatory planning. Active and effective communities and community structures could be instrumental in helping municipalities toward executing their utilitarian role of providing services, and further force local government to be accountable to the citizens rather than to provincial and national spheres of government (World Bank Group 2018).

26.3.2 Community development practitioners as advocates for social justice

The history of South Africa is a critical component in understanding the current social justice issues (Smith 2020:35). Colonialism as well as apartheid shaped the advancement of injustices in South Africa (Watson 2017).

South Africa's unique history was decisively shaped by coloniality; hence the community development practitioners act as social justice professionals to help communities realise opportunities and withstand hardships. As the South African Constitution (Republic of South Africa 1996) forbids discrimination on the grounds of race, culture, gender, language or sexual orientation. According to Chipkin and Meny-Gibert (2013:8), the advocators for social justice are tasked to alleviate community or societal problems and transform communities into a just society that values freedom, equality and human dignity.

In a society saturated by inequalities and social injustices, CDPs emerge to challenge the prevailing oppressive systems by undertaking advocacy for social justice. Vital to an accountable and transparent government, is the strengthening of a developmental state and its institutional capacity through CDPs assuming the advocacy role. For social justice to prevail at both local government level and within communities, professionals and practitioners should invest their energy in educating people about their rights, including the strategies to bring about social change. In this regard, Loewen and Pollard (2010:5) argue that:

> [c]ommon threads bind the struggle for basic human rights among disenfranchised groups, offer experience and approaches to facilitate change, and move society towards social justice. Activists involved in social justice movements believe that oppressed people have a right to fair treatment and a share of the benefits of society based on their human rights and equality of all people.

Through the Constitution (Republic of South Africa 1996), government is committed to the creation of a democratic society based on the Bill of Rights underpinning democracy, human rights and good governance (World Bank Group 2018). However, this dream remains elusive while poor and deprived communities are still subjected to an oppressive environment that perpetuate socio-economic and political exclusion and marginalisation. Social justice is the product of self-reflection based on critical analysis of the prevailing situation and interventions aimed at addressing inhumane and unjust experiences and policies (Davids & Waghid 2021). Thus, social justice in the context of community development practice and engagement demands ethical accountability and responsibilities on the side of government as well as non-governmental organisations (NGOs).

South Africa is a troubled nation with prevailing structural poverty and underdevelopment, limited service delivery, lack of social capital, health deficits and social inequalities (Cebekhulu 2018). The situation as it stands does not only require professionals and practitioners to demand social justice, but also to be part of deprived and struggling masses. The perpetual challenge of unfair distribution of resources along with corruption by officials and politicians, especially at local government level, makes advocates for social justice demand redistributive justice. Zulu (2022:25) succinctly captures the implications of neoliberalism in the South African situation by adding that:

> [n]eoliberal capitalism has increased inequality and financial precarity, retained and expanded exploitative labour relations, stagnated wages, pushed multitudes into lifelong debt, intensified unemployment, ravaged the natural environment and severely weakened democracy by concentrating wealth in the hands of a few ...

Operating within the social justice framework, compelled professionals and practitioners to challenge the status quo in their quest for creating a better and fairer society (Ife 2016). A rich society is one whose people and communities are able to reach their full potential in realising common humanity. Community development practitioners with an interest in the development and redevelopment of a community are known as community advocates (Green & Haines 2015). They are eager to join block clubs, neighbourhood planning activities, and religious and social gatherings. Local community advocates fight for neighbourhood residents and are concerned about the health and wellbeing of their community (Gilchrist & Taylor 2016). The community advocates are not only concerned with but also involved in fighting for community justice. Community advocates provide a direct connection to the neighbourhood. Tompkins (2014) also mentions that community advocators for social justice are generally well-liked by their neighbours and are eager to serve on steering committees, action committees, community-based planning teams and other local boards, commissions or neighbourhood improvement groups. Community advocates have the power to influence people and communities by further enabling them to persuade other residents to join in neighbourhood redevelopment efforts (Molope & Oduaran 2020). An effective activist can obtain a strong local participation in neighbourhood planning and development meetings.

26.3.3 Community activists as development professionals

It is acknowledged that activism involves effort and time outside of regular business hours in order to 'act' or bring about change in circumstances that are never one-dimensional. Most community activists engage in public spaces with a collective group, thereby constructing 'communities' in one form or another (Benit-Gbaffou, Kara, Mbuyi, Molopi & Tunce 2013). The term 'community activist' or 'leader' refers to someone who works at the neighbourhood or grassroots level and claims to speak for the interests of the local community, which activists or leaders may create on their own (Asad & Le Dantec 2015). Community activists are also called social activists. Social activists are associated with 'people asserting their capacity to enact social change on behalf of a cause, often from outside the conventional politics' (Caliskan & McGregor 2019:628). They do this by enshrining common goals and values for the neighbourhood where they live together or that they use jointly. The goal of all community activists is to change the city and rural areas, how they function and how they are structured, primarily at the neighbourhood size but occasionally on a metropolitan scale (Zanbar & Itzhaky 2018). Therefore, community activism is about changing people's negative attitudes and empowering them. By employing suitable, cost-effective technology (see Chapter 17) to promote job creation and equitable resource distribution, community activists as CDPs promote democracy and encourage participation while being sensitive to cultural differences (Martin 2014; Wlokas, Westoby & Soal 2017). Additionally, they prioritise the programmes that the beneficiaries have picked and encourage efficient collaboration between all parties involved in development (see also the discussion on the roles of the CDP in Chapter 8).

Social or community activism has given rise to people who are called community activists. Community activists played a decisive and vanguard role during the struggle for political liberation, and they still play a vital role in terms of conscientising communities about issues that hinder their socio-economic and political progress in society. Unlike the employed and professional workers within various sectors, community activists operate actively within the non-governmental sectors such as the NGOs, CBOs and other civil society organisations, including labour movements. For socio-economically and politically deprived community people, the work of community activists is imperative for community empowerment, consciousness raising and community transformational change. Community activists are often unpaid and have accumulated organising skills, experiences and competencies through their active involvement in community issues and activities. According to Ife (2016:352), this cohort of workers is committed to working toward an alternative society. For them, community development is an ongoing process of improving communities and enabling them to participate in their social, economic and political life by gaining confidence and managing their own affairs, while at the same time protecting the environment (Abugu 2014).

Community activists are action orientated and employ popular and radical strategies to engage communities and community groups. Since community activists are often confrontational toward governmental authorities and political elites, their work results in massive harassment, marginalisation and exclusion in mainstream governmental politics. However, in the case of deprived and fragmented communities, the activist role can be fundamental in building unity, social cohesion and self-determination (Ife 2016). It is thus critical to addressing issues related to community development in order to improve quality of life within the communities (Phillips & Pittman 2015).

What becomes apparent in the context of efforts to improve quality of life is that community development can be viewed as a process meant for transforming marginalised communities and empowering them to work together when dealing with external forces that undermine their unjust conditions (Quimbo, Perez & Tan 2018). Community development as a process allows for communities to act collectively for their self-empowerment and improvement in the political, economic and social aspects they desire (Phillips & Pittman 2015). Within community development practice, community activists are resourceful for community mobilisation, cooperation and collective action. It could be argued that community development practice is often used to empower communities for collective control and responsibility for their own development. In the prevalence of oppression and hegemonic structures and systems (More 2017), the power and influence of community activists to transform society and communities alike cannot be underestimated. Hence, community development can overcome some of the challenges faced by wider government institutions, such as policies failing because they do not translate well, in the sense that CDPs/activists work on a smaller scale and are closer to the communities needing help (Goel 2018).

By confronting the status quo, community activists commit themselves to bringing about change in the oppressive powerful state structures. A typical example of social action and resistance is demonstrated by the formation of the Landless Movement, Treatment Action Campaign

(TAC), People Against Women Abuse (COWA), Anti-Eviction Campaign, Abahlai-base Mdlondolo (AbM) as social movements championing issues such as land, HIV/AIDS, women abuse and housing in South Africa. Despite all odds and tribulations suffered by these grassroots social movements, community/organisational activists have shown revolutionary resilience in challenging the powerful and corrupt governance system at both national and local government level (Sacks 2022). The emergence of this new breed of community-based social movements throughout South Africa has brought a fresh wave of a struggle for social change, inclusive democracy and citizenship, service delivery and struggle for human dignity (Amtaika 2013; Duncan 2016). New social movements such as AbM have carried the struggle against social injustices and socio-economic marginalisation (Booysen 2023). Mottiar (2014) adds that extremely uneven urban development is a major contributor toward the formation of new social movements. Community movements such as Abahlali are committed to challenging the boundaries of formal policies through engaging in what Avritzer (2002, cited in Friedman 2018: 199) calls 'participatory politics' in order to restore human dignity of excluded masses in the urban peripheries (Heller 2017; Friedman 2018).

At the heart of community activism is the notion of social capital, or social capacity, as a form of resource located within relationships between people and organisations that help facilitate collaboration and cooperation, something that is broadly recognised by both researchers and practitioners (Phillips & Kraeger 2018). Viewed from the self-help approaches to community development, community activists put more emphasis on people within communities working collaboratively for the improvement of their situation (Garkovich 2011). Working in this context, community workers often furnish community people with valuable information and facilitate the sharing of development skills and knowledge for local people to act in their own interests and for their own benefit.

Community activists, who are sent out to act as grassroots development workers, form the fundamental link between the government and the people it serves (Ziervogel, Enqvist, Metelerkamp & Van Breda 2022). The local government created this link so that community development professionals could encourage greater community involvement in order to improve community effectiveness and promote sustainable development (Rafferty 2020). Therefore, community activists ensure that it is everyone's responsibility to cooperate and work together for the good of their own communities. Community activists are connected to existing programmes like the free basic services, expanded public works and local economic development programmes, among others (Van Pinxteren, Colvin & Cooper 2022). Community activism is founded on a sense of place, a grounded expertise derived from routine activities, observations and experiences recorded in a nearby, accessible environment, through networks and interactions with a subset of individuals who can be identified. Community activism provides people the opportunity to respond, be inspired, be involved in their immediate daily surroundings and to try to improve them (Belfield 2020). It gives the impression that change is possible, that change is within reach and that people may access, organise and mobilise others around them in order to have an impact on how they utilise and design the shared spaces (Ziervogel et al 2022). However, Caliskan and McGregor (2019:628–629) criticise social activism in neo-liberal government contexts for (1) pushing activist organisations toward a business-like model, (2) professionalising social activist roles, and (3) viewing individuals as responsible for creating social change (Caliskan & McGregor 2019:629). See section 26.4 for more on how 'commercialising' NGOs affects community development.

26.3.4 Building social capital

One of the fundamental roles of professionals and practitioners is to strengthen and build social capital within communities and among community stakeholders. Maclure (2022:6) emphasises that social capital is based on the mobilisation of local associations, community vision development and collective action based on 'power with', often realised through cooperative power and relationships. It is about building networks to uplift communities. Social capital is about working together and sharing benefits equally (Mengesha, Meshelemiah & Chuffa 2015). Phillips and Pittman (2015) succinctly describe social capital as a way of bonding, bridging or linking up groups of people for the common good. Leonard (2004, cited in Mengesha et al 2015:167) asserts that bonding is exclusive as it only includes people with shared vision, while bridging is inclusive of all regardless of their social status or beliefs. This means that bridging connects people from diverse environments, who may not ordinarily interact with each other, to work together, increase their resources and broaden their identity (Magis 2010). Putnam (2000) states that 'bonding is for getting by while bridging and linking are for getting ahead'.

An effective community development practice can only work when people trust each other and are willing to cooperate (Henderson 2005, cited in Mengesha et al 2015) as it emphasises community asset mobilisation and utilisation (Mathie & Cunningham 2003) (see also Chapter 11 on leadership and group motivation, and Chapter 13 on mobilisation and motivation). This means that social capital can also be used as an asset in terms of structural and cognitive assets (Mattessich 2009). Mattessich (2009) further states that social capital assists community members to utilise their abilities to advance and maintain strong relationships, resolve issues that affect their community and come up with inclusive decisions, while working together to find aims and main concerns, construct development plans, distribute resources and implement the plans together as a group. The core of asset based-community development (ABCD) is its focus on social relationships (Putnam 2000) (see Chapter 4 for more on ABCD).

In addition to empowering communities, the assets/strengths-orientated approach also focuses on building interactive relationships through social capital even in a culturally diversified milieu (Schenck, Nel & Louw 2010). Such relationships are seen as assets which promote sensible and relevant application of social relations. Mathie and Cunningham (2002:479) state that at the core of ABCD is its focus on social relationships. Formal and informal associations, networks and extended families are treated as assets and also as a means to mobilise other assets of the community. Thus, by treating relationships as assets, ABCD becomes a practical application of the concept of social capital (also see Chapter 4 on asset-based community development). Social capital together with community economic development and appreciative enquiry are therefore the foundation for the asset-based approach. Social capital has become a cornerstone to community development and is underpinned by the informal rules, norms and long-term relationships that facilitate coordinated action and enable people to undertake co-operative ventures for mutual advantage (Halstead, Deller & Leyden 2022). Social capital is present in the networks, norms and social trust inherent in associations whose members work together in concerted collaborative action. It is also the store of goodwill. It enables people to 'get by'; bridging social capital enables people to get ahead. More importantly, Putnam, Leonardi and Nanetti (1993:35) associate social capital with features of social organisations such as networks, norms and trust that facilitate action and cooperation for mutual benefits. In addition, Putnam et al (1993) differentiate three types of social capital, specifically bonding, bridging and linking social capital:

- *Bonding social capital*: Bonding social capital is evident in the close-knit relations of friends and families who can be depended on for basic survival in times of stress. Through bonding, connections between people with similar characteristics and interests are forged and this can reinforce homogeneity and exclusivity (McGonigal, Doherty, Mills et al 2005). Group relations are key among members of the group and can be attributed to race, gender and socioeconomic status (Yunus 2017). Communities have inherited weak bonding social capital, with ubuntu values having been eroded.

- *Bridging social capital*: Bridging social capital provides leverage in relationships beyond the confines of one affinity group, or even beyond the local community. This type of social capital has the potential to connect people from diverse contexts and is seen as inclusive (McGongal et al 2005). Accordingly, bridging social capital concerns itself with group relations, and the individuals involved are more dissimilar to each other (Grewe 2003). In essence, this type of social capital underlies community development and engagement based on active citizenry and social compact. The National Development Plan (NDP) (Republic of South Africa 2012) considers bridging social capital as vital in promoting values of responsible citizenship and solidarity.

- *Linking social capital*: Linking social capital focuses on forging relationships between people with different powers and allows access to resources, ideas, information and knowledge within a community (McGonigal et al 2005). The essence of social capital was captured by the World Bank (1997) when it asserted that social capital was a 'missing link' in the development equation. This approach gives the poor and disadvantaged communities the chance to see problems and sort them out for themselves with little help from outside, as opposed to being needs based, where communities rely heavily on the leaders and outside assistance to elicit problems within their communities. Viewed from an ABCD perspective, linking social capital is key for socio-economic and political advancement of any community. The NDP (Republic of South Africa 2012:2) considers strong leadership throughout society, national consensus, social cohesion and a capable state to be the key enablers for linking social capital. Linking social capital consolidates the bonding and bridging social capitals in terms of expanding the networks of CDPs.

26.4 POLITICAL CHALLENGES TO THE PROFESSION

Along with its rewards, the community development profession also has its challenges, mainly stemming from the socio-economic and political environment in which CDPs work. Politically, CDPs (whether employed within government or NGOs, or unemployed) have no power to influence policies and budget allocation. Their powerlessness renders them vulnerable to bureaucratic government and community structures. In general, they operate in a highly politicised environment, with party politics playing a big role. More often than not, those working for local government are recruited on the basis of their political affiliation. As officials of government, their political affiliation compromises one of the key principles, that of impartiality. This is especially so when it comes to providing services or undertaking community development practice and engagement. Unlike the unpaid CDPs, paid CDPs are forced to comply with policies and political decisions imposed on them from local elites and political structures. Equally disturbing is that such decisions and policies are often in direct opposition to the community development principles of accountability, participation, transparency, social justice and empowerment. Without expert or professional power, CDPs are ignored in government departments and their remuneration suffers compared to other professionals such health workers and social workers in South Africa.

Another underlying challenge faced by CDPs is working within and under the bureaucratic structures and institutions of government. Partisan politics can infiltrate spaces for public participation and engagement by people and communities. This is especially prevalent at the local government level, creating a hostile environment for interaction and participation in the policy-making process (Nwauche & Flanigan 2022). It is important to create spaces for dialogue, but the nature of these spaces for interaction also needs attention. The use of these spaces by partisan politicians prevents NGO leaders from actively participating in the consultative process and engaging in dialogue about their services during the planning process (Salamon & Toepler 2015).

There are numerous issues confronting the South African NGOs and local government sector at present. One of the issues raised by Botha (2018) is the perceived corporatisation or commercialisation of the NGO sector. While NGOs that successfully professionalise increase their chances of receiving donor funding, it has had an impact on the organisational culture of NGOs. Kita (2017) ascertains that, because of donor conditionality, the emergence of a 'report' culture in which organisations do everything specified by the donor may sometimes result in organisations losing sight of their original purpose or objective. The CDP becomes more concerned with specific outputs or performance indicators, and frequently overlooks the actual impact or difference that these programmes/projects are making within the community. This, in turn, can result in the unintended effect of distancing CDPs from the communities they serve (Stuart 2013).

The issues of accountability and transparency are double-edged swords that can haunt both CDPs and stakeholders, such as local government and NGOs, alike. Through social contact, government, especially local government, is obliged to be accountable to the citizens who gave the legitimate power to elected representatives to govern on their behalf. However, due to the proportional representation (PR) electoral system, politicians end up being accountable to their political parties. Considering that democracy is not just about electing government, Mangcu (2017) posits that while elections are a crucial means of democratic accountability, much more is needed to achieve a democratic political culture. Elections at national and provincial as well as local government level should be understood as one of the mechanisms for citizen participation. Achen and Bartels (2017:35) make it obvious by arguing that citizen participation in a democracy happens through voting in elections. This calls for radical reform to the South African electoral system in order to enforce accountability to the people as the primary stakeholders in democratic governance.

Similarly, CDPs operating within the NGO sector pay their allegiance and are often accountable to the organisations which employed them. This at times leaves communities to fend for themselves without power in decision-making processes in the political arena and NGO sector. As such, most practitioners are calling for more explicit political agendas in order to put pressure on reaching and activating citizens through political consciousness and community power mobilisation (see also Stoecker 2012). In this context, Ledwith (2020) posits that poverty is often accompanied by relatively low levels of literacy, formal education and communication, which can in themselves hinder the ability of the poor to influence political processes designed and governed by elites (see also Chapter 1 toward understanding poverty and deprivation).

26.5 CHALLENGES TO THE PROFESSION

The disorganised nature of local government and the NGO sector makes CDP participation in policy planning difficult. According to Boitumelo (2017), local government and the NGO sector are so disorganized that it is difficult for CDPs to mobilise communities effectively for services, even through coalitions or other representation. The community development profession in South Africa is also failing because of improper implementation of public policies due to corruption and a general lack of managerial expertise (Shava & Thakhathi 2016). Although good policies were developed during the first five years of democracy, this has been the country's major challenge. According to Shava and Thakhathi (2016), the low sustainability of development initiatives was caused by a lack of well-defined and implemented training programmes that linked medium- to long-term development plans, inadequate budget implementation, and high levels of politicisation. Community development is often confronted with serious problems such as a lack of skilled workers and the deployment of a political party's minor cadres, who use development initiatives to their own advantage for political gain (James, Kwame, Albert & Justice 2013). Such complexity necessitates a paradigm shift in political circles, where development should be universal, and leaders of community development initiatives should be chosen on the basis of merit rather than on the basis of politics. This is a necessary condition for the creation of effective NGOs and local government that promotes development (Lassa 2018).

Community development takes place within a social environment of which CDPs are an integral part. Since social challenges are interwoven with the politics and economics of any country, so too are its challenges, which warrant an integrated and interdisciplinary approach. Unlike other members of the health and social work fraternity, CDPs are not yet recognised and are not professionalised. Since 2009, the National Department of Social Development has consulted widely with various stakeholders, including universities, in an attempt to rectify this. Both qualitative and quantitative progress has been made in assisting institutions of higher learning to establish a four-year degree aligned to South African Qualifications Authority (SAQA) requirements and protocols. The outcome of such engagements has been the establishment of community development degree programmes in universities in Gauteng, the Free State and the Western Cape (see also Chapter 27).

These institutional formations are a milestone toward professionalisation of community development with its own curriculum, knowledge base and practice frameworks. Greater efficiency, especially in mobilising resources, and greater perceived legitimacy are some of the benefits of professionalisation based on 'credentials and standards of practice' (Caliskan & McGregor, 2019:7). However, other scholars are critical of professionalisation for bringing the conventional forms of action such as lobbying and service provision. These differing views of professionalism affect South Africa's long history of community, social and political activism. For example, on 30 September 2022, the Cornerstone Institute based in the Western Cape hosted a seminar, 'Professionalising community development: is this the end of community-based activism?', where speakers questioned the standardisation and regulation of community development practise under professionalisation. They argued that the demand for professionalisation had the potential of ostracising most activists through its training and other statutory requirements, and as such the move from occupation to profession could see the disappearance of community activism. In line with this argument, Caliskan and McGregor (2019) envisage professionalisation as a method of disciplinary control and commitment, with less approval of activism in general.

Community development practice is an outdoor intervention and as such, CDPs are exposed to vulnerable and more often violent environments. They become the victims of crime, harassment and at times hijackings. CDPs, especially those employed by local government and for social development at provincial and municipal levels, are foot soldiers who move from door to door to mobilise or organise events within designated communities. Their being on the state payroll, along with their duplication of community development work already undertaken, causes resentment among, for example, ward committees, who are not remunerated yet do almost the same work in communities.

South Africa and its communities are known for having major social problems such as unemployment, poverty, inequality, crime, substance abuse and domestic violence (Hagg & Pophiwa 2019; World Bank Group 2018). In the community development profession, these challenges are overwhelming considering that most of practitioners are not well trained to tackle such issues holistically. However, for the profession to navigate through all these social problems, Ife (2016:115) advocates for a paradigm shift away from providing individualised service to an alternative community-based model that empowers communities in identifying their own problems and solutions by themselves (see also Chapter 18 on contact making and Chapter 19 on participatory research methodology). Therefore, for the profession to thrive, CDPs have to lead through and learn from this environment of volatility, uncertainty, complexity and ambiguity (coined as a VUCA world) (see Elkington, Van der Steege, Glick-Smith & Breen 2017). The profession still suffers from a social capital deficit, and CDPs should build and access networks within and across communities in order to address this challenge (Halstead et al 2022).

A major concern about local government and NGOs relates to the ability of NGOs to pursue their advocacy or lobbying responsibilities while working closely with government agencies (Vincent 2014). One of the reasons for the skills shortage in South African local government is the inability to attract people with the necessary qualifications and experience, coupled with a failure to pay what people in these positions truly deserve (Healy & Link 2011; Goel 2018). The reality is that there are currently too few willing people with the critical knowledge, skills and competencies to staff local government and NGOs. This effectively means that community development profession vacancies are filled by people who are not qualified to do these jobs well (Raga, Taylor & Gogi 2012). The result is that the quality of service provided to disadvantaged communities suffers, and millions of rands in donor funds are wasted in the process.

26.6 ECONOMIC CHALLENGES TO THE PROFESSION

The global economic crisis had a negative impact on South Africa, and it created additional funding challenges for government and NGOs operating in the country, as donations from private donors were significantly reduced (Botha 2018: 57). In preceding years, corporate social investment (CSI) also decreased, resulting in a rise in the number of NGOs seeking government funding and creating fierce competition among NGOs (Kobo & Ngwakwe 2017) (see also Chapter 14, section 14.3.2 on business plans for fund raising). Being so reliant on government funding has called into question the impartiality of these NGOs, despite the fact that being outside the government was one of their key strengths in the past (*Sunday Times* 2017:7). Due to lack of financial control and management, budgets earmarked for particular projects are redirected to projects that were not in the plans. One of the major issues confronting South African CDPs working in the NGO and local government sector is poor financial budgeting (Neary & Winn 2017). Another constraint is a lack of narrative and financial reporting skills within organisations.

Community development agencies often lack the commitment and manpower necessary to carry out community development services, negatively affecting the expansion of development initiatives. Due to this shortage of qualified individuals to oversee development programmes, many community development projects fail (Shaffer 2020). Poor leadership, management and public policy formulation, according to Khumalo (2014), are the main causes of ineffective monitoring and assessment of community economic development programmes. According to Stone, Cox and Gavin (2020), the lifespan of some community development projects has decreased due to the local government's failure to train staff members (community professionals) in project management, market awareness and business understanding, and to create conducive environments for NGOs to thrive. According to Kiggundu and Pal (2018), managers of community development initiatives struggle with weak managerial abilities, uncompetitive economic literacy, a lack of business expertise, and ineffective teamwork and coordination.

26.7 CONCLUSION

Community development plays an important role in the empowerment of South African communities. Central to community development practice are CDPs employed within formal and informal government institutions and departments. South Africa's local government and NGOs sectors are used as referral institutions for community development practice by CDPs. Local government, as the government at grassroots level, represents community interests. Municipalities are mandated to address local needs, interests and expectations, and involve communities in planning and implementing municipal programmes (Koma 2010). Those employed as community development practitioners are obliged to support in actualising local government as stipulated in the Constitution.

There is no doubt that local government plays a central role in promoting local democracy. It is within the governance framework that NGOs and other organs of civil society could play a developmental role, especially in augmenting government capacity by providing services and holding local government responsible through advocacy and oversight. With the primary goal of representing community interests within municipal councils, the local authorities should encourage communities' involvement in the formation and delivery of municipal programmes (Reddy & Maharaj 2008). Municipalities must be aware of the divisions within local communities and seek to promote the participation of the marginalised and excluded groups in community processes (Thornhill 2008). Therefore, this chapter recommends that municipalities should be inclusive in their approach and aim their strategies at removing obstacles in order to encourage community participation and community development.

REFERENCES

Abebe A, Kebede W & Alemie A. 2019. Roles of ego social networks for community development in southern Ethiopia: The case of Tullo Community. *International Journal of Community and Social Development*, 1(4):332–349.

Abugu SO. 2014. The role and challenges of local government in community development: An insight. *Review of Public Administration and Management*, 400(3615):1–11.

Achen CH & Bartels LM (eds). 2017. *Democracy for Realists: Why Elections do not Produce Responsive Government*. Princeton, NJ: Princeton University Press.

Allan J, Buckel C, Catts R, Doherty R, McDonald A et al. 2005. *Social Capital Theory: A Review*. AERS: Occasional Publications.

Amtaika A. 2013. *Local Government in South Africa since 1994: Leadership, Democracy, Development and Service Delivery in Post-Apartheid Era*. Durham, NC: Carolina Academic Press.

Asad M & Le Dantec CA. 2015. Illegitimate civic participation: Supporting community activists on the ground. In *Proceedings of the 18th ACM Conference on Computer Supported Cooperative Work & Social Computing*, pp 1694–1703. Available at: https://dl.acm.org/doi/proceedings/10.1145/2675133 (accessed 26 June 2023).

Atkinson D. 2007. Taking to the streets: Has developmental local government failed in South Africa? In Buhlungu S, Daniel J, Southhall R & Lutchman J (eds), *State of the Nation South Africa*. Cape Town: HSRC Press.

Belfield H. 2020. Activism by the AI community: Analysing recent achievements and future prospects. In *Proceedings of the AAAI/ACM Conference on AI, Ethics, and Society*, pp 15–21. Available at: https://dl.acm.org/doi/proceedings/10.1145/3375627 (accessed 26 June 2023).

Benit-Gbaffou C, Kara M, Mbuyi T, Molopi E & Tunce L. 2013. *Community Activists Tell Their Story: Driving Change in Johannesburg and Ekurhuleni*. Technical Report. CUBES & NRF SARChI: Development Planning and Modelling, Wits University.

Blewitt J. 2015. *Understanding Sustainable Development*. New York: Earthscan.

Boitumelo L. 2017. Combating poverty in South Africa: Understanding the informal sector in the context of scarce opportunities. In Vyas-Doorgapersad S, Tshombe L-M & Peprah EP (eds), Ababio *Public Administration in Africa: performance and Challenges*. Routledge, pp 97–116.

Booysen S. 2023. The nexus of citizen, party and state in accumulating protest repertoires in South Africa. In Brooks H, Chikane R & Mottiar S (eds), *Protest in South Africa: Rejection, Reassertion, Reclamation*. Johannesburg: Mapungubwe Institute for Strategic Reflection (MISTRA).

Botha CE. 2018. The role of the NGO in local government: The case of world vision in Ubuhlebezwe Municipality. Doctoral dissertation, Stellenbosch University, Cape Town.

Caliskan G & McGregor AJ. 2019. 'You can change the world. We're just here to help': Activist consultancy firms as forms of neoliberal governmentality. *Globalisation*, 16(5):625–643.

Cebekhulu A. 2018. *Umhlaba Uyahlaba: The World is Thorny*. Wandsbeck: Reach.

Chipkin I & Meny-Gibert S. 2013. Understanding the social justice sector in South Africa. Report to RAITH Foundation and Atlantic Philanthropies. Available at: http://www.raith.org.za/docs/Report-Social-justice-Sector-7Feb2013-FINAL (accessed 20 November 2022).

Chitonge H & Mazibuko N. 2018. *Social Welfare Policy in South Africa: From the Poor White Problem to a 'Digitalised Social Contract'*. New York & Brussels: Peter Lang.

Davids N & Waghid Y. 2021. *Academic Activism in Higher Education: A Living Philosophy for Social Justice*, vol 5. Dordrecht: Springer.

Dupuy KE. 2014. Community development requirements in mining laws. *The Extractive Industries and Society*, 1(2):200–215.

Elkington R, Van der Steege M, Glick-Smith J & Breen JM (eds). 2017. *Visionary Leadership in a Turbulent World: Thriving in the New VUCA Context*. United Kingdom & Japan: Emerald.

Freire P. 2021. *Education for Critical Consciousness*. London: Bloomsbury.

Friedman S. 2018. *Power in Action: Democracy, Citizenship and Social Justice*. Johannesburg: Wits University Press. doi: 10.18772/12018113023

Garkovich LE. 2011. A historical view of community development. In Robinson JW & Green GP (eds), *Introduction to Community Development: Theory, Practice and Service Delivery*. London & Washington DC: SAGE.

Gilchrist A & Taylor M. 2016. *The Short Guide to Community Development*. Policy Press.

Goel K. 2018. Understanding Community and Community Development. Doctoral dissertation. Available at: https://find.library.unisa.edu.au/primo-explore/fulldisplay?vid=ROR&id=9915910114201831 (accessed 31 May 2023).

Green GP & Haines A. 2015. *Asset Building & Community Development*. Newbury Park, CA: SAGE.

Grewe NR. 2003. *Social Capital and Local Development: An Exploration of Three Forms of Community-based Social Capital*. Ann Arbor, MI: ProQuest Information and Learning Company.

Gwala M & Theron F. 2012. Beyond community meetings: Towards innovative participation in developmental local government. In *13th International Winelands Conference, Stias*. Stellenbosch 2–4 April 2012, pp 2–4.

Hagg G & Pophiwa N. 2019. Tradition meets modernity: Bafokeng approaches to overcome poverty an inequality. In Soudien C, Reddy V & Woolard I (eds), *Poverty & Inequality: Diagnosis Prognosis Responses*. Cape Town: HSRC Press, pp 186–213.

Halstead JM, Deller SC & Leyden KM. 2022. Social capital and community development: Where do we go from here? *Community Development*, 53(1):92–108. doi: 10.1080/15575330.2021.1943696

Hart CS. 2012. Professionalisation of community development in South Africa, issues and achievements. *Africanus*, 42(2):55–66.

Healy LM & Link RJ (eds). 2011. *Handbook of International Social Work: Human Rights, Development, and the Global Profession*. Oxford: Oxford University Press.

Heathershaw J. 2016. Who are the 'international community'? Development professionals and liminal subjectivity. *Journal of Intervention and Statebuilding*, 10(1):77–96.

Heller P. 2017. Development in the city: Growth and inclusion in India, Brazil and South Africa. In Centeno M, Kohli A & Yashar DJ (eds), *States in the Developing World*. Cambridge: Cambridge University Press.

Henderson P. 2005. *Including the excluded: From practice to policy in European community development*. London: The Policy Press.

Ife J. 2016. *Community Development in an Uncertain World*. 2nd ed. Cambridge: Cambridge University Press.

James KM, Kwame AD, Albert A & Justice NB. 2013. Policy and institutional perspectives on local economic development in Africa: The Ghanaian perspective. *Journal of African Studies and Development*, 5(7):163–170.

Jason LA, Glantsman O, O'Brien JF & Ramian KN. 2019. Introduction to the field of community psychology. In Jason LA, Glantsman O, O'Brien JF & Ramian KN (eds), *Introduction to Community Psychology: Becoming an agent of change*. Available at: https://press.rebus.community/introductiontocommunitypsychology/ (accessed 1 June 2023).

Kahl D & Hains K. 2020. Community Development Society (CDS) Fellows Program: A purposeful exploration to strengthen community. *Community Development Practice*, 24(1):1.

Kenny S. 2016. *Changing Community Development Roles: The Challenges of a Globalizing World*. Bristol: Policy Press.

Khumalo P. 2014. Improving the contribution of cooperatives as vehicles for local economic development in South Africa. *African Studies Quarterly*, 14(4).

Khumalo P & Tshishonga N. 2018. Women's participation in planning and constructing of their houses: A case study of the Piesang River People's Housing Project at Inanda, Durban. In Szell G & Chetty D (eds), *Making Popular Participation Real: African and International Experiences*. Berlin: Peter Lang.

Kiggundu MN & Pal SP. 2018. Structure and management of formal and informal business activities in entrepreneurial family and small firms in Africa. *Africa Journal of Management*, 4(3):347–388.

Kita SM. 2017. 'Government doesn't have the muscle': State, NGOs, local politics, and disaster risk governance in Malawi. *Risk, Hazards & Crisis in Public Policy*, 8(3):244–267.

Kobo KL & Ngwakwe CC. 2017. Relating corporate social investment with financial performance. *Investment Management & Financial Innovations*, 14(2):367–375.

Koma SB. 2010. The state of local government in South Africa: Issues, trends and options. *Journal of Public Administration*, 45(si-1):111–120.

Larsen AK, Sewpaul V & Hole GO. 2014. *Participation in Community Work: International Perspectives*. London & New York: Routledge.

Lassa JA. 2018. Roles of non-government organizations in disaster risk reduction. In *Oxford Research Encyclopedia of Natural Hazard Science*. Oxford: Oxford University Press.

Ledwith M. 2020. *Community Development: A Critical Approach*. Bristol & Chicago: Policy Press.

Leonard M. 2004. Bonding and bridging social capital: Reflections from Belfast. *Sociology*, 38(5):927–944.

Liguori E & Winkler C. 2020. From offline to online: Challenges and opportunities for entrepreneurship education following the COVID-19 pandemic. *Entrepreneurship Education and Pedagogy* 3(1). doi: 10.1177/2515127420916738

Loewen G & Pollard W. 2010. The social justice perspective. *Journal of Postsecondary Education and Disability*, 23(1):5–18.

Maclure L. 2022. Augmentations to the asset-based community development model to target power systems. *Taylor & Francis*, 54(1):4–17.

Magis K. 2010. Community resilience: An indicator of social sustainability. *Society and Natural Resources*, 23(5):401–416.

Maistry M. 2012. Towards professionalisation: Journey of community development in the African and South African context. *Africanus*, 42(2):29–41.

Mangcu X. 2017. Shattering the myth of a post-racial consensus in South African higher education: 'Rhodes Must Fall' and the struggle for transformation at the University of Cape Town. *Critical Philosophy of Race*, 5(2):243–266.

Martin W. 2014. The effectiveness of community development workers (CDWs) as change agents in their pursuit of a holistic approach to development: A case study of CDWs in the Western Cape. Doctoral dissertation, Stellenbosch University, Cape Town.

Mathie A & Cunningham G. 2003. From clients to citizens: Asset-based community development as a strategy for community-driven development. *Development in Practice*, 13(5):474–486.

Mattessich RV. 2009. FASB and social reality: An alternate realist view. *Accounting and the Public Interest*, 9(1):39–64.

Maya-Jariego I., & Holgado D. 2019. Community interventions. In Jason LA, Glantsman O, O'Brien JF & Ramian KN (eds), *Introduction to Community Psychology*. Available at: https://press.rebus.community/introductiontocommunitypsychology/chapter/communityinterventions/ (accessed 31 May 2023).

McGonigal J, Doherty R, Mills S et al. 2018. Operationalising performance management in local government: The use of the balanced scorecard. *SA Journal of Human Resource Management*, 16(1):1–11.

Mengesha SK, Meshelemiah JC & Chuffa KA. 2015. Asset-based community development practice in Awramba, Northwest Ethiopia. *Community Development*, 46(2):164–179.

Ministry for Public Service and Administration. 2007. *A Handbook for Community Development Workers*. Pretoria: Government Printer. Available at: https://www.dpsa.gov.za/dpsa2g/documents/cdw/SDR_vol_5_no_2_2006.pdf (accessed 26 June 2023).

Moeti K & Mokoena S. 2017. Community development workers as agents of change and conduit of authentic public participation: The case of Mpumalanga Province in South Africa. *TD: The Journal for Transdisciplinary Research in Southern Africa*, 13(1):1–9.

Molope M & Oduaran A. 2020. Evaluation of the community development practitioners' professional development programme: CIPP model application. *Development in Practice*, 30(2):194–206.

More MP. 2017. *Boko Philosophy, Identity and Liberation*. Cape Town: HSRC Press.

Mottiar S. 2014. Protest and participation in Durban: A focus on Cato Manor, Merebank and Wentworth. *Politikon*, 41(3):371–385.

Neary M & Winn J. 2017. There is an alternative: A report on an action research project to develop a framework for co-operative higher education. *Learning and Teaching*, 10(1):87–105.

Ndevu ZA & Muller K. 2018. Conceptual framework for improving service delivery at local government in South Africa. Stellenbosch University, South Africa. Available at: https://journals.co.za/doi/epdf/10.10520/EJC-134c43edbc (accessed 21 March 2023).

Nwauche S & Flanigan ST. 2022. Challenges to nonprofit organization participation in social and development policy planning in South Africa. *Nonprofit Policy Forum*, 13(2):119–139.

Parliamentary Monitoring Group (PMG). 2009. Questions & replies. Available at: http://www.pmg.org.za/questions-and-replies/2009/11/25/question-replies-no-2176-2200 (accessed 26 September 2022).

Phillips R & Kraeger P. 2018. *Community Planning and Development*. London & New York: Routledge.

Phillips R & Pittman RH. 2015. A framework for community and economic development. In Phillips R & Pittman RH (eds), *An Introduction to Community Development*. 2nd ed. London & New York: Routledge.

Putnam RD.1993. The prosperous community: social capital and public life. *The American Prospect*, 13.

Putnam RD. 2000. *Bowling Alone: The Collapse and Revival of American Community*. New York: Simon & Schuster.

Putnam RD, Leonardi R & Nanetti RY. 1993. *Making Democracy Work: Civic Traditions in Modern Italy*. Princeton, NJ: Princeton University Press.

Quimbo MAT, Perez JEM & Tan FO. 2018. Community development approaches and methods: Implications for community development practice and research. *Community Development*, 49(5):589–603. doi: 10.1080/15575330.2018.1546199

Rafferty R. 2020. Conflict narratives, action frames, and engagement in reconciliation efforts among community activists in Northern Ireland. *Peace and Conflict: Journal of Peace Psychology*, 26(1):9.

Raga K, Taylor JD & Gogi A. 2012. Community development workers (CDWs): A case study of the Bitou Local Municipality. *TD: The Journal for Transdisciplinary Research in Southern Africa*, 8(2):235–251.

Reddy P & Maharaj B. 2008. Democratic decentralization in post-apartheid South Africa. In Saiko F (ed), *Foundations for Local Governance: Decentralization in Comparative Perspective*. Heidelberg: Physica-Verlag, pp 185–211.

Republic of South Africa. 1996. *Unemployment Insurance Act 30 of 1966*. Pretoria: Government Printer.

Republic of South Africa. 1998. *White Paper of Local Government*. Pretoria: Government Printer.

Republic of South Africa. 2012. *National Development Plan: Vision for 2030*. Pretoria: Government Printer.

Sacks J. 2022. The unseen massacre of Durban shack dwellers. *Mail & Guardian*. Available at: https://mg.co.za/thoughtleader/opinion/2022-08-23-the-unseen-massacre-of-durban-shack-dwellers/ (accessed 31 May 2023).

Schenck R, Nel H & Louw H. 2010. *Introduction to Participatory Community Practice*. Pretoria: Unisa Press.

Shaffer TJ. 2020. Democratic professionals in civic life: Cultivating civil discourse in community development. *Community Development*, 51(3):196–211.

Shava E & Thakhathi DR. 2016. Non-governmental organizations and the implementation of good governance principles. *Journal of Social Sciences*, 47(3):218–228.

Silverman RM & Patterson KL. 2014. *Qualitative Research Methods for Community Development*. New York: Routledge.

Smith ME. 2020. Social justice vulnerabilities and marginalised communities: A case study of day labourers in Mbekweni. Available at: https://etd.uwc.ac.za/xmlui/handle/11394/7686 (accessed 31 May 2023).

Stanard V, Goodman A & Reddy M. 2020. Creating a learning community for community engagement for Detroit practitioners. *Community Development Practice*, 24(1):5.

Stoecker R. 2012. *Research Methods for Community Change: A Project-based Approach*. Thousand Oaks, CA: SAGE.

Stuart L. 2013. The South African non-profit sector: Struggling to survive, needing to thrive. *Sangonet Pulse*. Available at: https://www.polity.org.za/print-version/the-south-african-non-profit-sector-struggling-to-survive-needing-to-thrive-2013-04-03 (accessed 31 May 2023).

Sunday Times. 2017. Putting hearts to work. 10 September, 7.

Swanepoel H & De Beer F. 2016. *Community Development: Breaking the Cycle of Poverty*. 6th ed. Cape town: Juta.

Thornhill C. 2008. The executive mayor/municipal manager interface. *Journal of Public Administration*, 43(si-1):725–735.

Tompkins R. 2014. Overlooked opportunity: Students, educators, and education advocates contributing to community and economic development. In Gruenewald DA & Smith GA (eds), *Place-based Education in the Global Age*. New York: Routledge, pp 197–220.

Tshishonga N. 2018. The war room as a platform for public participation: Views from stakeholders. In Szell G & Chetty D (eds), *Making Popular Participation Real: African and International Experiences*. Berlin: Peter Lang.

Van Pinxteren M, Colvin CJ & Cooper S. 2022. Using health information for community activism: A case study of the movement for change and social justice in South Africa. *PLOS Global Public Health*, 2(9).

Vincent JW II. 2014. Community development practice. In Phillips R & Pittman R (eds), *An Introduction to Community Development*. 2nd ed. New York: Routledge, pp 125–144.

Warren JI & Harper MG. 2017. Transforming roles of nursing professional development practitioners. *Journal for Nurses in Professional Development*, 33(1):2–12.

Wilson PA. 2019. *The Heart of Community Engagement: Practitioner Stories from Across the Globe*. New York: Routledge.

Wlokas HL, Westoby P & Soal S. 2017. Learning from the literature on community development for the implementation of community renewables in South Africa. *Journal of Energy in Southern Africa*, 28(1):35–44.

World Bank. 1997. Social capital: The missing link? In *Monitoring Environmental Progress – Expanding the Measure of Wealth*. The World Bank: Indicators and Environmental Valuation Unit, Environment Department. (Draft, revised January 1997.)

World Bank Group. 2018. *An Incomplete Transition Overcoming the Legacy of Exclusion in South Africa*. Cape Town: UCT Press.

Yunus M. 2017. Social business entrepreneurs are the solution. In Hafenmayer J, Hafenmayer W & Yunus M (eds), *The Future Makers*. London: Routledge, pp 219–225.

Zanbar L & Itzhaky H. 2018. Community activists from different cultures: Implications for social work. *Journal of Social Work*, 18(6):732–751.

Ziervogel G, Enqvist J, Metelerkamp L & Van Breda J. 2022. Supporting transformative climate adaptation: Community-level capacity building and knowledge co-creation in South Africa. *Climate Policy*, 22(5):607–622.

Zulu A. 2022. Inequality defines our economy. *Mail & Guardian*, 26 August to 1 September 2022, p 25.

CHAPTER 27

The Professionalisation of Community Development in South Africa

Cornel Hart

27.1 INTRODUCTION

This chapter discusses the requirements of professionalism for community development practice. It also outlines the manner in which practice is regulated and quality is assured by means of standardised knowledge, skills and attributes of practitioners who must subscribe to an ethical code of conduct. All of which is driven by the purpose of providing better professional and impact 'service' to the 'end user' (the community).

Community development continued for some time without a comprehensive theory, mainly because practice preceded theory. It was practised without a well-articulated paradigm and with just a few general principles, supported simply by models and theories borrowed from the social sciences and philosophy. In the 1950s, the United Nations attempted to define, describe and implement a global approach to community development. However, community development practice is a complex activity which involves many elements, thereby challenging definition and description. Additionally, community development is integrative and holistic, rather than sector specific, both in theory and practice.

The term 'community' has by several scholars consistently been associated with the physical, social and moral aspects of people and their collective lives (Chile 2012:43; Maistry 2012:33; Fraser, 2005:286–287; Bhattacharyya 2004:9; Fiol & O'Connor 2002:532) (see also chapters 3 and 6). The related literature on community development also indicates that its comprehensive interpretations are too rigid. This has hampered descriptive elaborations of norms and standards that are applicable to the multidisciplinary character of community development and its approaches applied by those working with, and in, communities.

Additionally, community development as an 'approach' has been followed by several occupations and disciplines for many years in South Africa as well as internationally. This has been a huge contributing factor in the 'identity crisis' of community development because for decades it has not been described as an explicit and specific practice but rather as an all-encompassing and comprehensive 'concept'.

Between the 1950s and 1970s, several countries such as the UK, New Zealand, Australia, the US and Canada began to formalise community development, both as a practice and an academic discipline (Chile 2012). This started the global move, over the past five decades, toward some form of formalised, professionalised practice linked to a standardised and quality-assured procedure.

Meanwhile, the academic debate continues about the desirability of professionalism. There are two distinctive schools of thought: (1) those not supporting professionalisation but who are proponents for quality-assuring community development practice for the benefit of communities; and (2) those supporting professionalisation for regulatory quality assurance, standardisation of community development as well as professional recognition and ethical practice by community development practitioners. This professional recognition must not be driven by a need for practitioner 'elitism' but rather should be founded on an ethical code of conduct with quality-assured standardised practice, because of the principles of inclusion, equity and empowerment to which community development subscribes. Fitzsimons (2010) indicates that the need to raise practice standards is what drives professionalisation, and this is indeed what has driven the professionalisation of community development in South Africa.

27.2 PROFESSIONALISATION OF COMMUNITY DEVELOPMENT IN SOUTH AFRICA

Community development is an emerging discipline, with a unique form of practice that only recently is becoming fully recognised as one of the Social Service Professions (SSPs) and which therefore needs to become an accredited profession in South Africa. Community development has an intrinsic orientation towards participatory and democratic outcomes for equality, inclusion and collective change. The plethora of policies, definitions and approaches is due to the multisectoral nature of community development, further resulting in a lack of standardised concepts and quality-assured knowledge, skills and attributes among those working in communities – all due to the lack of a professional career path in community development (see also Chapter 25).

The process for an accredited professionalisation of community development, licensed by government in the same way as other professions, started in 2010. The licensed accreditation of professions follows a specific process in South Africa, but it is locally and globally not well written up and published, resulting in a lack of clear guidelines for professionalisation of an occupation. When working with communities, a statutory profession applies a legislated regulatory framework that ensures quality, standardised skills and ethical practice.

Until 1994, community development in South Africa was spearheaded by activists, who mobilised communities against apartheid and were the voice of the excluded, disenfranchised and marginalised communities who were also being left out of decision making and local development leadership. Then came liberation – and freedom from the claws of apartheid, law-enforced inequality and underdevelopment. Meanwhile, the need to ensure equality, human rights and dignity, as well as freedom from want or need, still remains a critical goal of a non-racial, democratic South Africa.

Central to this goal is the enhancement of social capital and human capabilities as well as ensuring that development is people driven and not technocrat imposed. This emphasises the need for, and the important role of, community development practitioners (CDPs), who are well placed to bridge the gap between civil society and all stakeholders in community development. This important role requires of CDPs to have the necessary knowledge, skills and attributes for the start of the community development professionalisation process, founded on the regulation of ethical conduct and quality-assured practice measured against standardised norms and standards.

It was decided right from the onset of the professionalisation process, 'not to exclude anybody'. This decision required a recognition of prior learning (RPL) framework that was designed in 2012 as part of the training standards and career path development for community developers.

27.2.1 Professionalisation purpose and process

The purpose of professionalisation, or professional recognition, is to unify, consolidate, standardise and quality assure (eg norms and standards) the practice of a qualifying occupation with an ethical code of conduct. Obtaining a professional title (ie an occupational designator) is needed for unified participation in continuing professional development (CPD) regulated by a legislated professional body.

Figure 27.1 presents the two professionalisation operationalisation options from which to select when embarking on an occupational legislated professionalisation process. Option 1 starts with the development of standardised and legislated qualification frameworks and ends with the establishment of a professional regulation entity (eg professional board), while option 2 follows the opposite order to option 1. The occupational legislated professionalisation process of community development in South Africa followed 'option 1' (as indicated on the right-hand side of Figure 27.1). The South African professionalisation of community development therefore was:

> to achieve coherence and harmonization of community development practice across Government, NGOs, CBOs, FBOs and the private sector, with clarified roles of key stakeholders in an institutional mechanism that delivers effective and efficient community development processes towards building vibrant, equitable, cohesive and sustainable communities within the developed and developmental disjuncture context of South Africa (Republic of South Africa 2014:23).

Chapter 27: The Professionalisation of Community Development in South Africa

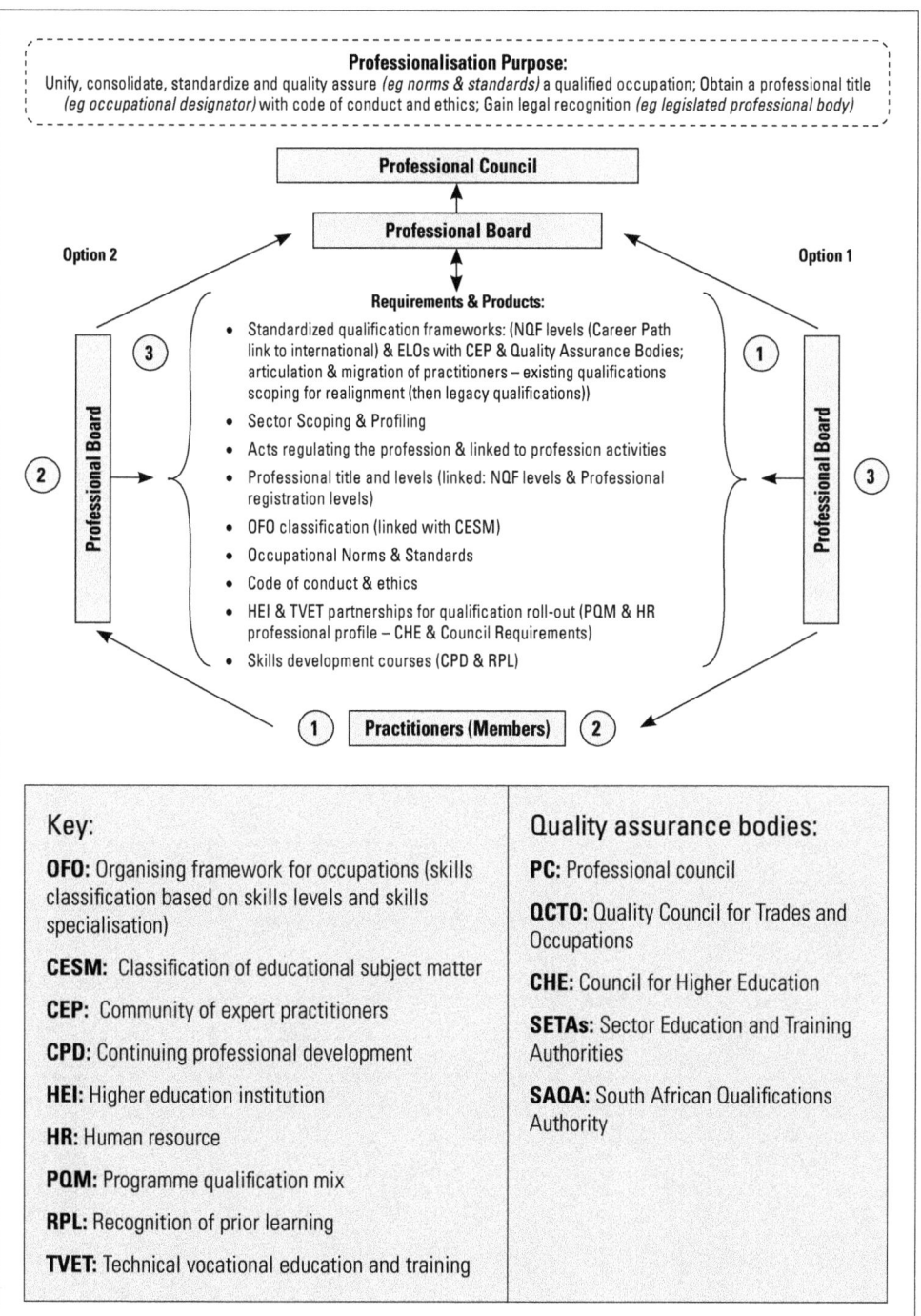

Figure 27.1 Professionalisation process options

27.2.2 Standardised legislated qualification frameworks

The professionalisation and operationalisation of community development in South Africa started between 2010 and 2011 with the development of three standardised and legislated community development qualification frameworks. This was done to ensure that practitioners: (1) know the community development theories, approaches, principles and processes, and have an ability to examine and follow relevant legal and regulatory frameworks; and (2) are skilled in conducting community-based research to inform interventions and are able to utilise existing community networks and stakeholder partnerships during the planning, design and implementation of community development interventions – all embedded in the transformational leadership attributes required for being a 'change agent' for community development.

The three legislated community development qualification frameworks are as follows:

1. *NQF L4*: Occupational Certificate: Community Development Worker (SAQA ID: 97708). Entry-level requirements for enrolment in this qualification are: (a) NQF Level 2 with communication; or (b) a Grade 11 and national (vocational) certificate NQF level 3 qualification.
2. *NQF L5*: Occupational Certificate: Assistant Community Development Practitioner (SAQA ID: 97691). Entry-level requirements are: (a) a successful completion of the Occupational Certificate: Community Worker (CDW) at NQF level 4; or (b) a Grade 12 certificate; or (c) a Grade 12 and NSC and national (vocational) certificate NQF level 4 qualification.
3. *NQF L8*: Bachelor of Community Development (SAQA ID 79706). Entry-level requirements are: (a) an NSC with appropriate subject combinations and levels of achievement, which grants entrance to a bachelor's degree, as well as being competent in communication and mathematical literacy at NQF Level 4; or (b) a minimum NQF level 4 qualification equivalent to NSC with full exemption; or (c) an appropriate access-route qualification approved by the Higher Education Institution. Additionally, learners with the Occupational Certificate: Assistant Community Development Practitioner (ACDP) (NQF 5) will gain access to the degree.

Each respective qualification framework aligns with the three professional practitioner registration levels of the professional body: (1) Community Development Worker (CDW) – NQF L4 qualification; (2) Assistant Community Development Practitioner (ACDP) – NQF L5 qualification; and (3) Community Development Practitioner (CDP) – which is linked to the NQF L8 qualification, as well as to subsequent Master's (NQF L9) and PhD (NQF L10) qualifications, which are also available to practitioners.

27.2.3 Community development sector scoping and profiling

Each of the three professional registration levels has a prescribed scope of practice. CDWs are trained with the NQF level 4 qualification to ensure that they are able to explore and coordinate networks and partnerships and conduct community-based research to inform the planning, design and management of community interventions. ACDPs are trained with the NQF level 5 qualification so that they are able to collect and provide relevant information from, and to, communities to build social cohesion, as well as to assist and support the development and implementation of development initiatives and processes. CDPs are trained with the NQF level 8 qualification so that they are able to facilitate collective processes in communities to effect psycho-social and economic development to enable households and communities to manage their own development to achieve sustainable livelihoods (Republic of South Africa 2014:63–55).

27.2.4 Norms and standards for community development practice

The aforementioned scopes of the three practitioner levels are quality assured with seven key norms, and are assessed against 25 respective quality standards. Table 27.1 presents these norms and standards, which are also aligned with the international norms and standards of the International Association of Community Development (IACD). Several of the preceding chapters discussed some of the pertinent knowledge and skills relevant to community development norms and standards, such as the various stakeholders and role players in community development (chapters 3 and 7), the different actions and approaches in community development (Chapter 5), the ethical and practical principles of community development (Chapter 6). Section C (chapters 10–17) discussed skills for community development, while Section D (chapters 18 to 22) dealt with all aspects and components relevant to the 'life of a project'.

Table 27.1 Norms and standards for community development (CD) practice

Norms = N		Standards = S	
N1	Understand and practise CD.	S1	Integrate and use the values and process of CD.
		S2	Work with the tensions inherent in CD practice.
		S3	Relate to different communities.
		S4	Demonstrate competence and integrity as a CDP.
		S5	Maintain community development practice within own organisation.
N2	Understand and engage with communities.	S6	Get to know a community.
		S7	Facilitate community research and consultations.
		S8	Analyse and disseminate findings from community research.
N3	Take a CD approach to group work and collective action.	S9	Support inclusive and collective working through CD practice.
		S10	Organise community events and activities.
		S11	Respond to community conflict.
		S12	Support communities to campaign for change.
N4	Promote and support collaborative and cross-sectoral working.	S13	Promote and support effective relationship between communities and public bodies.
		S14	Encourage and support public bodies to build effective relationships with communities.
		S15	Use CD approach to support collaborative and partnership work.
		S16	Apply CD approach to strategically coordinate networks and partnerships.
N5	Support community learning from shared experiences.	S17	Promote and develop opportunities for learning from CD practice.
		S18	Facilitate community learning for social and political development.
N6	Provide CD support to organisations.	S19	Advise on organisational structures using CD perspectives.
		S20	Plan and gain resources and funding for sustainability through CD practice.
		S21	Strengthen groups using CD approaches and practices.
		S22	Use a CD approach to monitoring and evaluation.
N7	Manage and develop CD practice.	S24	Supervise CDPs.
		S25	Manage internal organisational development and external relationships to support effective CD practice.

27.3 REGULATION OF PROFESSIONAL COMMUNITY DEVELOPMENT

Chapter 25 made brief reference to the policies guiding the quality of community development practice. In this section, we assess in greater detail the regulation of professional community development practice with a more elaborative description of three pertinent legislative and policy documents: (1) the 2017 Policy for Social Service Practitioners; (2) the 2021 Social Service Practitioners (SSP) Bill; and (3) how they link with the 2014 Community Development Practice Policy Framework (CDPPF).

27.3.1 Policy for Social Service Practitioners

Mention was made in Chapter 25 of the seven chapters of the 2017 Policy for Social Service Practitioners. In this chapter, the specific details are provided regarding community development in each of the seven chapters. It is a product of a long-drawn-out process to review the Social Service Professions Act 110 of 1978, as amended in 1998. The aim of the 1998 amendment, and of subsequent amendments, was first, to transform the social services sector, and second, to make the legislation more inclusive of a broader range of social service practitioners (SSPs) – for example, the inclusion of child and youth care workers as well as community development practitioners. The process of 'policy making' precedes the amendments and review of a Bill and its Regulations.

The aim of the SSP policy is to unite the social development sector and regulate it in a single professional body – the South African Council for Social Service Professions (SACSSP) – while recognising the unique and critically important roles that the different social service practitioners play in South African social development (see Figure 27.2). Additionally, the SSP policy aims to acknowledge the need for a social service workforce that is professional, recognised and regulated by the respective SSP boards to provide quality services to those communities, entities and members of society whom they serve. The policy therefore provides an overarching framework to guide and integrate all social development legislation linked to the social development context and profile of those whom the SSPs serve.

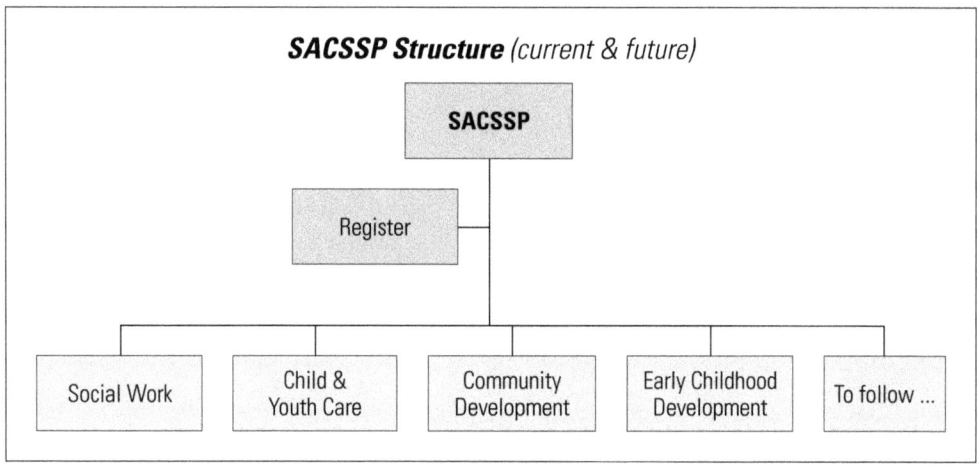

Figure 27.2 **SACSSP and respective SSP boards**

The SSP policy lists and describes existing and prescribed legislation relevant to SSPs. Legislation relevant to community development practice has been indicated in Chapter 25 – and has been provided as a tabulated appendix: 'Legislation and policy frameworks associated with community development'.

The SSP policy also describes the different scoping profiles of the social service practitioners as well as the regulatory requirements for the establishment of a regulatory body (ie institution) to regulate the social service workforce. Additionally, it lists a set of minimum requirements to establish a regulatory institution, namely: (1) the 'need' for having a regulatory institution linked to whether it requires a legal framework – endorsed via parliament, or only a policy directive for its establishment; and (2) its purpose and functions as a regulatory institution, as well as its governing and leadership structure for the execution of its responsibilities and tasks.

In the case of an SSP's regulatory institution – for example, the SACSSP, which incorporates several occupations as indicated in Figure 27.2 – its establishment is within the authority of the Ministry of Social Development. The Ministry, through its departmental office, the Department of Social Development (DSD), is therefore responsible for the drafting of the SSP Bill which describes the SACSSP and its regulatory sub-entities – that is, boards (Republic of South Africa 2017:33).

27.3.2 Social Service Practitioners Bill

The SSP Bill, consisting of eight chapters, is the overall umbrella legislation which prescribes the laws and rules that affect all SSPs equally. The purpose of the SSP Bill is to:

> provide for the establishment of a South African Council for Social Service Practitioners; to determine its composition, powers and functions; to provide for the establishment, composition, powers and functions of social service professional boards and social service occupational boards; to provide for the registration of social service practitioners; to promote and regulate the education, training and professional development of social service practitioners; to regulate the professional conduct of social service practitioners; and to provide for incidental matters (Republic of South Africa 2021:2).

The drafting of regulations is the next step following approval of a Bill. Regulations can be interpreted as elaborative, more operational, descriptions of the Bill's provisions to prescribe the 'workings' of the SACSSP and its respective occupational boards. At the time of writing this chapter, the process of drafting the Regulations for the SSP Bill was underway:

- Chapter 1 of the SSP Bill provides definitions and objectives for the Bill.
- Chapter 2 prescribes the establishment of the SACSSP, its overall objectives and duties as a council as well as its regulatory powers regarding the registration, education, training and development of CDPs.
- Chapter 3 presents the composition of the council and the manner in which its office bearers must be appointed. It provides extensive detail about the terms of office for council members, their fiduciary duties, the council president and deputy president, the executive and finance committees as well as the risk and audit committees.
- Chapter 4 focuses on the registrar and secretariat of the council in so far as their appointment, functions, meetings and operating procedures are concerned as well as the relevant financial regulations (Republic of South Africa 2021:7–46).
- Chapter 5 provides pertinent detail about each of the different social service practitioners. This is a very important chapter because it sets out the designation and scope for each type of practitioner, establishment of their respective social service boards and respective objectives, general

powers, appointment of board members and leadership structures (Republic of South Africa 2021:46–59). This chapter is thus very helpful for CDPs to be able to articulate their scope of practice in relation to that of the other SSPs presented in Figure 27.2.

- Chapters 6 and 7 are the subsequent most important chapters. Chapter 6 prescribes the registration of SSPs, that is, the compliance for and with registration as well as the continuing professional development (CPD) requirement for registration; Chapter 7 indicates the disciplinary powers and procedures of the respective boards regarding practitioners who did not honour their ethical code of practice (ie unprofessional or unethical conduct).
- Chapter 8 provides the general provisions for community service requirements from practitioners and how offences and penalties are to be handled (Republic of South Africa 2021:59–99).

The SSP Policy and Bill therefore contextualise, define, describe and prescribe the community development sector and its regulations of CDPs. The detailed 'operationalisation' of community development practice is further described in the Community Development Practice Policy Framework (CDPPF).

27.3.3 Community Development Practice Policy Framework (CDPPF)

Promoting social cohesion and sustainable wellbeing in an integrated and holistic manner, with collaboration and coordination by all stakeholders, is a fundamental aim of community development. The policy framework for community development practice is therefore designed to achieve this aim through its use in conjunction with the knowledge and evidence relevant to development and community development occupational practice.

The CDPPF consists of 10 chapters, all with a focus on including constructs relevant to community development practice as an emerging occupation. This is so as to provide an all-inclusive framework to which all community development stakeholders can subscribe. The aim of the CDPPF is to:

> promote an integrated, standardised and quality assured community development best practice scenario ... informs the public of what they can expect from practitioners in the community development profession in terms of: standards of service; knowledge, skills and attributes required for those providing the service; and responsibilities of CDPs (Republic of South Africa 2014:19).

Implicit within the framework is a striving toward an equitable empowerment relationship between community development practice and its view of communities as 'clients' who have a democratic right to 'human dignity, equality and freedom' (Bill of Rights – Chapter 2 of the Constitution of South Africa). This is because all people need to be able and enabled (empowered) to achieve sustainable wellbeing. The CDPPF therefore acts as a guide to all community development stakeholders regarding the following:

- Integrative and standardised implementation of community development theory and practice – by describing the values and principles of community development and its distinctive form of practice
- The legislated definition for community development in South Africa and its alignment with international definitions
- Forming the basis for regulation of community development practice in terms of: (a) the seven norms (for practice and for training curriculum development); (b) quality assurance of the seven norms against their related 25 standards; (c) the ethical code to be upheld by practitioners; and (d) the required continuing professional development (CPD) to ensure up to date skills, knowledge and attributes of practitioners.

Additionally, the CDPPF describes the skills, knowledge and attributes required of practitioners in relation to their qualifications. The seven norms and their related 25 standards were presented in Table 27.1. 'Ethically and professionally CDPs have obligations to their employers, their funders, their stakeholders – and the communities with which, and in which, they work; as well as to themselves' (Republic of South Africa 2014:19).

Chapter 1 of the CDPFF introduces the structure, followed by the rationale, vision, goals and objectives of the CDPPF in Chapter 2. Chapter 3 presents the legislative and policy framework for community development, most of which were covered in Chapter 25 of this book.

Chapters 4 to 7 deal with the conceptualisation of community development practice. More specifically: Chapter 4 presents the values and related principles for community development practice; Chapter 5 defines community development and highlights its unique and distinctive form of practice in relation to other SSPs as well as providing the professional identity and registration levels for practitioners (discussed in sections 27.2.1 and 27.2.3 above); Chapter 6 provides the norms and standards for practice (see Table 27.1 and section 27.2.4); and Chapter 7 prescribes the knowledge, skills and attributes for practitioners (discussed in section 27.2.2).

Six community development values are prescribed in the CDPPF: (1) equity and anti-discrimination, (2) social justice, (3) collective action, (4) community empowerment, (5) working and learning together, and (6) sustainable communities. These values articulate with the five ethical principles: (1) human orientation, (2) participation, (3) empowerment, (4) ownership, and (5) release (see Chapter 4). They also relate to the four practical principles discussed in Chapter 4: (1) learning, (2) adaptiveness, (3) simplicity, and (4) compassion. The community development values and principles further link with the following four overall roles of practitioners (described in Chapter 25): (1) service developer, (2) capacity builder, (3) access facilitator, and (4) change agent – as well as the six distinctive responsibilities of CDPs also described in Chapter 25.

The CDPPF chapters 8 and 9 present the institutional measures for coordination and integration of community development. The Constitution of the Republic of South Africa, 1996 in Chapter 3, Section 41, outlines the principles of cooperative government and intergovernmental relations (discussed in Chapter 25) designed to transform the South African state and government in all three spheres. This highlights the need for a community development practice that must ensure intersectoral intersectoral collaboration (ie joint and horizontal action among all stakeholders) and coordination (integrative approaches and reporting of all relevant stakeholders), where equal partnerships exist between the state and communities in order to affect community development planning and implementation.

Chapter 8 describes the institutional structures, and their roles and responsibilities from national and provincial levels to local levels. The local level should include Integrated Development Planning (IDP) forums and ward committees, because this is where communities must have a leading participating voice to champion their community development processes toward integrative and holistic, sustainable wellbeing.

Chapter 9 presents the coordination of community development and the rationale for a 'district system' linked to the role of CDPs to coordinate approaches from a district level to a provincial and national level (see also the discussion on coordination in Chapter 3). This chapter highlights that 'CDPs will be the first to go into communities and the last to leave, if at all' (Republic of South Africa 2014:62). The specific roles undertaken by CDPs in the 'district system' are listed in the CDPFF as follows (Republic of South Africa 2014:62–63):

Chapter 27: The Professionalisation of Community Development in South Africa

- '... obtain evidence for responsive, measurable and integrated service delivery;
- profile households and communities;
- capture data electronically;
- analyse data captured;
- do referrals for immediate, specific and integrated action;
- monitor referrals – visiting households and following-up with relevant Departments or agencies;
- develop and facilitate the implementation of prevention programmes in partnership with relevant DSD Units, other relevant Departments and communities;
- facilitate the development of (short, medium and long term) Integrated Community- and/or Household-based Action Plans for funding and support from the many national CommDev programmes;
- facilitate linkages with other Community Development programmes for the purpose of coordination and integration, thus preventing duplication;
- coordinate integrated service delivery by ensuring that necessary systems are in place for it;
- facilitate the development of Memoranda of Agreement (MoAs) and Service Level Agreements (SLAs) with partnering Departments and other state-owned entities, in order to ensure commitment to Action Plans and ensure management of these partnerships;
- facilitate collective monitoring of progress regarding the implementation of Integrated Community Development Action Plans against pre-agreed milestones and indicators, in partnership with communities and all stakeholders;
- provide continuous monitoring of service delivery interventions and implementation of Integrated Action Plans;
- provide development implementation support at the District level, as well as with Provinces;
- coordinate reports for presentation to Coordination Forums at different levels: for example District, Provincial and National;

- initiate local innovation – for example through a 'Bank of Ideas' to change community development problems into opportunities for the purpose of joint venture funding;
- assess social impact post intervention, review and then re-profile in order to take CommDev to the next level with the specific target group;
- revisit households and communities to update changing profiles ...'.

In Chapter 10, the CDPPF describes the different stakeholders, namely: communities, local government, provincial and national government (especially those stakeholders who are directly responsible for, and involved with, community development), as well as NGOs, FBOs, donors and other institutions (see Chapter 3 for a discussion of stakeholders). These stakeholders are described in relation to their different roles and responsibilities to present an integrative approach among all 'actors' required for community development (Republic of South Africa 2014:66–79).

27.4   CONCLUSION

Until the mid-20th century, the concept of community development was recognised, if at all, as a somewhat vague concept of social need. The idea of a professional approach to enhance and develop community – and national – welfare held little sway. Not until the 1950s did the United Nations attempt to describe and implement a global approach to community development. The result was that for those who recognised early the need for community development, practice preceded principle; 'experimental' approaches led to an ad hoc need responsive practice – which then needed formulation in a set of common principles and standards of practice. Early formalisation, both as an academic discipline and as a social practice profession, then started in Europe, the UK, Australasia and North America – the beginning of a global move towards a more standardised and quality-assured community development practice.

Implementing effective community development requires the engagement of professionals who are well placed to bridge the gap between civil society and all community stakeholders. The need for these professionals to have the necessary knowledge, skills and attributes to fulfil their role has thus given birth to community development professionalisation, with regulation of ethical conduct as well as quality of practice measured against standardised norms and standards.

South Africa is now finalising its legislated community development professional practice body which will require from community developers to register for practice at one of the three main professional levels aligned to the standardised qualifications: CDW, ACDP and CDP (community development worker, assistant community development practitioner and community development practitioner), with two further higher levels. This has set South Africa well on the road towards becoming a world leader in professional, ethical, quality-assured community development practice. In the ongoing debate on whether or not community development practices should be professionalised, the evidence to date in South Africa indicates clearly that government-legislated professionalism is the best way to ensure the application of commonly agreed, tried and tested practice standards that work to the best benefit of all concerned.

REFERENCES

Bhattacharyya, J. 2004. Theorizing community development. *Journal of the Community Development Society*, 34(2):5–34.

Chile LM. 2012. International experience of community development professionalisation. *Africanus: Journal of Development Studies*, 42(2):42–54.

Cook JB. 1994. Community development theory. Extension Division, University of Missouri. Available at: http://extension.missouri.edu/publications (accessed 31 March 2023).

Fiol CM & O'Connor EJ. 2002. When hot and cold collide in radical change processes: Lessons from community development. *Organization Science*, 13(2):532–546.

Fitzsimons C. 2010. Professionalising community development work and its implications for radical community education. *Irish Journal of Adult and Community Education*, 53–71.

Fraser H. 2005. Four different approaches to community development. *Community Development Journal*, 40(3):286–300.

Maistry M. 2012. Towards professionalisation: Journey of community development in the African and South African context. *Africanus: Journal of Development Studies*, 42(2):29–41.

Republic of South Africa. 2021. *Social Service Professions Bill*. Pretoria: Government Printers.

Republic of South Africa. 1996. *The Constitution of the Republic of South Africa, 1996*. Pretoria. Government Printer.

Republic of South Africa. Department of Social Development (DSD). 2014. *(Draft) Policy for Community Development Practice*. Pretoria: Government Printer.

Republic of South Africa. Department of Social Development (DSD). 2017. *Policy for Social Service Practitioners*. Pretoria: Government Printer.

CASE STUDIES

CASE STUDY 1
THE STORY OF SIPHO

> To illustrate how a family can be enmeshed in the deprivation trap.
> (Taken from De Beer F & Swanepoel H. 1996. *Training for development – A manual for student trainers.* Halfway House: International Thomson)

Sipho is the son of a small farmer in the deep rural area. He can remember that as a small boy he had to look after their two cows, that is until the drought came and the cows died. That drought broke his father's spirit too. It was only about a year later that his father died of TB.

After his father's death his uncle was supposed to help the family, but his uncle was so poor that he could hardly look after his own family. Sipho's mother then went to the nearest town to look for a job and he had to look after his younger sister and the baby boy.

Sipho couldn't make any progress in school. So when he was thirteen years old and in standard two he left the school to look for a job. He never got a decent job. He had to do piece jobs for small amounts of money.

His baby brother was always sick and his mother was mostly away in town with her job. Sipho remembers how the baby always cried at night until one night when the crying stopped and his aunt told him that the baby had died.

Then the big rains came. Their house was very dilapidated because there was no money to repair it. With the big rains their house just collapsed and they lost everything they had. There was no food on the land left and he and his sister really had nothing to eat. His mother would bring home a little food once a week from town, but it was not enough for them and his mother also didn't eat enough. So when she became ill she lost her job and the family then depended on him.

His sister was only twelve years old when she moved to the town to look for work, but she never got a good job and only brought a baby back that had to be fed from their meagre supplies. The father of the baby is the son of a rich trader, but he just laughed at Sipho when he went to ask for money to care for the baby. This rich man just said that he won't mix with the likes of them and that they must look for the father elsewhere.

Sipho doesn't know what is to become of them. His mother needs medical treatment, but they don't have the money. He is still trying to get their house fixed, but the job he has pays so poorly that it is difficult to afford anything but a bit of food.

CASE STUDY 2
JACOB IN THE POVERTY TRAP

To illustrate the effect of poverty on more than one generation.

Jacob is an attendant at a parking lot where he directs cars in and out of parking places. His income comes from small gratuities (tips) that he receives from the drivers. He is 23 years old. He stayed in school for about four years. He didn't go to school on a regular basis, with the result that he very quickly lost the little literacy that he had.

Jacob was a sickly child because he didn't get the type of food that would boost his health and strengthen his body. His poor health was the reason he couldn't go to school all the time. His father died early in Jacob's life and his mother had only the smallest of incomes. She could hardly afford more than maize meal, bread and tea. Jacob's mother was always susceptible to illness and other health problems with the result that she became more and more dependent on her meagre pension each month. But in spite of her absence of good health, she had six children because in her days, family planning was not a word that you mentioned in front of older people and community leaders.

In the meantime, Jacob, in spite of his poor health and small income, has got himself a girl friend who also lives in the shanty town where Jacob and his family stay. She is now pregnant with his child.

Jacob seriously thinks of leaving his job and his family to go somewhere away from all these problems. But where would he go and what would he do? He won't get a decent job because his schooling was very poor. His poor schooling is because of his poor diet he had all his life. His poor diet was the result of his parents' poverty. And in a few month his child will be born and how is he going to care for him or her and ensure that his child gets the best so that his or her ill-being will change to wellbeing?

CASE STUDY 3
A DESPERATE WOMAN

To illustrate the depths of misery for one poor household.

Her four children were all poor learners. The teacher said it was because they didn't eat properly. Things got even worse when she lost her job. She had to live off scraps. Their situation became even more difficult when the landlord told her he wanted a higher rent each month.

She was crying so desperately that her eldest son, who is 15 years of age and in Grade 5, asked her what was going on. She didn't know whether it was a good thing to tell him, but she was so desperate to share her worries, that she told him. The next day he came to her with money to pay the rent. She immediately knew that her son had stolen the money. She didn't want to accept the money, so the boy just took the money to the landlord and paid him with it.

And now her son regularly brings money for rent and food. It keeps them alive and while she knows where the money comes from, she cannot refuse it.

CASE STUDY 4
THE STORY OF THEMBALIHLE

To show that a very bad situation can be turned round.

Thembalihle with her six children was brought from the rural areas to a squatter camp by her husband. However, she wasn't there long before her husband abandoned her, leaving her with her children without any support. She lived in a single shack made out of old flattened water drums which leaked in several places on rainy days, thus soaking the muddy floor which made their sleeping most uncomfortable. The squatter settlement had very little infrastructure and Thembalihle had to walk quite a distance to fetch water. Sanitation was very poor and definitely the worse aspect of living in the squatter camp.

In an attempt to better her situation she teamed up with her neighbour who had been surviving for some time by hawking in town. This was the only avenue opened to her since she had very little basic education. She left her children in the care of her neighbour's eldest daughter while she was hawking. What she didn't know was that her children were not well looked after. One of them contracted a serious disease as a result of food poisoning from food taken from rubbish bins. To worsen the situation, the eldest child was struck by a motor car and seriously injured.

This situation forced Thembalihle to abandon her hawking effort so that she could look after her children herself. Her only way now open was to take in more children from other hawker women who paid her something if they made a little money. Obviously, there were no real facilities for these children. They played outside whether it was hot or cold and had to hide under plastic sheets if it rained.

One day a social worker noticed all the children playing around Thembalihle's shack. She enquired from Thembalihle what the situation was. Through the assistance of the social worker Thembalihle received a social grant to set up a proper day-care centre. She worked very hard at this and with further assistance enlarged the facilities. When women realised the improvement in the facilities of their children's care, more of them wanted Thembalihle to take in their children. The result was that she started to employ people to help her. At present she has five employees working in the day-care centre now named Thembalihle's Day-Care Centre. This venture was so successful that it is now used as a pilot for similar projects elsewhere in squatter and informal areas. Thembalihle herself today lives in a properly built and modern house with all the necessary facilities.

Community Development in the 21st Century   Section F

CASE STUDY 5
A DAM CAN BRING HARDSHIP

To illustrate how so-called development can work against the first principle of community development.
(Taken from De Beer F & Swanepoel H. 1996. *Training for development – A manual for student trainers*. Halfway House: International Thomson.)

Our area was completely changed when the government announced some time ago that it was going to build a dam in the river. We were very surprised because it is not such a big river. Our chief was worried about this project and wanted to know why the government was planning this dam if the people had not even asked for it. The government people explained to him, and later to all of us, that the dam was needed to provide irrigation for the farming areas some kilometres from here. They also said that we would be assured of a regular water supply for our household needs. The people thought the idea was a really good one when we were told that the government would need many labourers to build the dam and that we could all get jobs.

In the end the company that built the dam brought a lot of workers from elsewhere and only some of us could get work. Some of the labourers who were brought in from other areas had very bad ways. They taught our young people to drink and quite a few of our daughters were made pregnant. We were very glad when the work was done and the workers left again.

In the meantime, the water started to rise and a number of our small farmers were threatened by this. We were very upset about it because we were never told that such a thing could happen. However, the government people said that they had told us that some of us would have to be relocated. Eventually, about twenty families had to be moved to higher ground about five kilometres from here. It was really a sad day when they had to leave. The worst part of it, though, is that where they are living now the soil is very poor and they are so far from the dam that they can't make use of all this water.

CASE STUDY 6
THE PARSON WHO BECAME A PAINTER

To illustrate what can happen if people do not really participate in a project.

Mr Robinson was the minister of a church adjacent to a former mission hospital in a densely populated rural area. One day he decided that the church building would look much better with a garden and a new coat of paint. He asked his wife to sound out the women of the congregation about the matter at the weekly prayer meeting. She reported back that they agreed that it would make the church look better.

During the morning service the following Sunday, Mr Robinson announced that the congregation was to smarten up the church premises by laying out a garden and painting the building. He invited everyone to be at the church the following Saturday when the work would commence.

On the day a considerable crowd turned out. They were clearly disappointed when Mr Robinson announced that the garden would be tackled first. They were all obviously keen on helping to paint the church building and there was even a suggestion that the matter be put to the vote. However, Mr Robinson pressed on with his plan and the work on the garden began. Very little progress was made and less than half of the work was done by the end of the day. Mr Robinson, who had worked very hard all day, announced, grim faced, that the work on the garden would continue the next Saturday, and the next, if it was necessary and that the church would be painted only when the garden was complete. On the appointed day, only two ladies arrived. Mr Robinson decided that there were not enough people to continue work on the garden and they could start painting.

After the morning service on the Sunday, Mr Robinson was confronted by a group of dissatisfied members of the congregation. They accused him of not sticking to his original plans. They reminded him of his decision to finish the garden and to then start painting.

The result of the confrontation was that nobody turned up to work after that. The garden remained unfinished and Mr and Mrs Robinson spent several weeks painting the church building.

CASE STUDY 7
A COMMUNITY HALL WITH NO PURPOSE

To illustrate what can happen if the people are ignored in development projects.

A community hall was built in Freedom Village by a private contractor hired by the provincial government. Expectations in the community were raised when the project was launched and eventually completed. The community was under the impression that they would be in charge of the hall and that community members would be hired to do various jobs at the hall. However, the provincial government instructed community workers in its service to take charge of the hall. This upset the local community immensely. The result was that the hall operated for one day before it was damaged. The damage went on until the hall could not be used for anything.

The provincial government decided to do something about the situation by involving the local community. A community meeting was held. It was decided to renovate the hall and to put a fence around it. It was recommended that a local private contractor be used to erect the fence. This recommendation was met with loud applause. The representatives of the local government present noted this request. Yet, an outside private contractor was hired to erect the fence. This was immediately damaged and the renovations to the hall were never done. Today the dilapidated hall serves no other purpose but to remind the people that their wishes regarding the hall were not considered.

CASE STUDY 8
SMALL IS BETTER

To illustrate the principle of simplicity.

(Taken from De Beer F & Swanepoel H. 1996. *Training for development – A manual for student trainers*. Halfway House: International Thomson.)

We have a very progressive civic organisation in this town. They decided some time ago that something had to be done about the housing situation. So they called us together one day and announced that we were all going to launch a house improvement scheme. Some of us were very glad to hear this and were keen on the plan, but others had their doubts and said that they had no money for such schemes.

The civic organisation started to make big plans for this project. They brought in some experts from outside and we were told to call at the office so that we could say what improvements we wanted done to our houses. This was a big affair. We stood in queues for long hours, waiting our turn, but when the people heard that they would have to make some payments, they just walked away and some said bad things about the executive members of the civic organisation.

Eventually the civic organisation realised that this whole affair was getting out of hand. It was too big for them and most of the people didn't understand it properly, either. They changed their plans completely. They announced that those people who were interested in house improvement and who were prepared to contribute towards the costs, should meet. Only fifty people attended this meeting, but the civic people were not disheartened by the small number. They divided us into ten small groups of neighbours. Now only five of us are working together to improve our houses. This is very good because we help one another and, in the meantime, we have become good friends. We also learn from one another, so much so that when we are finished with our own houses, we are going to start a business to improve other people's houses.

CASE STUDY 9
THE DAUGHTER OF HOPE

To illustrate the right attitude, place and role of the community development worker.
(Taken from De Beer F & Swanepoel H. 1996. *Training for development – A manual for student trainers*. Halfway House: International Thomson.)

Nomsa is a daughter of this village. She was born here and she grew up here. But then she left for school in the city. When she returned, she was very concerned about many things in the village. She befriended the clinic sister and you could often see them talking with each other or with other women. Eventually, Nomsa convinced a small group of women that they should start a vegetable garden. We men told one another that only a woman could be so stupid as to work so hard for so little.

The garden project went quite well. Poor Nomsa had to find out many things so that she could guide the women in their endeavours. Then other women started to be interested in what this group of women were doing and, often, you would see one or more go to Nomsa's house for some advice about something they wanted to do. Nomsa really gained the respect of the women when she went to the chief on their behalf to ask for more land for gardening and for his support in getting the school upgraded. What the people really liked about her was that she never tried to tell them what to do. She never tried to take the place of the natural and traditional leaders in our village. She was always in the background, as if she new her place.

Nomsa's most important contribution to this village is not all the things that she has done. Rather, it is her enthusiasm. People say that when she speaks to them it makes them feel as if they are able to do things that they had thought impossible before. Even we men are becoming interested. Our wives tell us that we must start doing things for ourselves and when we don't know how to, they say we must put our pride in our pockets and ask Nomsa to help us. But we don't only hear it from our wives. We can see with our own eyes that this woman wants to and can help us without trying to make us feel that she knows more than we do.

The people like Nomsa very much. They say she knows her place and yet she gives them new things to think about. In the women's prayer meetings, they pray for the daughter of hope and, in the shebeens, this very same name is mentioned with smiles and fondness.

CASE STUDY 10
THE PROJECT THAT HAD ITS FENCES BROUGHT DOWN

> To show how a government organisation can break down initiative among grassroots people.

Mr Dube, a sports organiser in an urban area, was approached by the chairman of a soccer club about the poor condition of the local soccer field. The field was level and well grassed, but there were no other amenities. Mr Dube, who had just finished reading a book on community development, saw the potential to build a community development project around the need for better amenities. He explained to the chairman, Mr Radebe, that the town council could not upgrade the field because of a lack of money. It could contribute something, but the club had to take responsibility for the effort. They discussed the matter further. Eventually they decided to approach the other two clubs that also made use of the field to solicit their support for a project.

Mr Dube and Mr Radebe each visited the chairman of one of the other clubs. After some time a meeting was arranged between the executives of the three soccer clubs. At this meeting Mr Dube explained that it was apparent that all three soccer clubs saw there was a need to update the soccer field and its facilities. He set out the position of the town council and urged the clubs to do something for themselves.

The representatives of all three clubs seemed keen to start on a project to upgrade the facility. Mr Dube suggested that they make a list of their needs. Various needs were identified, such as new goal posts, cloakrooms, a pavilion and a fence around the grounds. They decided to take the matter to their clubs and report back at a second meeting.

At the second meeting, two clubs clearly showed their support for a fence around the grounds. That would mean, they argued, that people would have to pay to see matches which would boost the coffers of the clubs. Mr Dube explained that the town council would take a large slice of the gate money, but that the clubs would also benefit financially. The other club was not so keen on the fence. They were the smallest of the three and felt they would not be able to afford it. The matter was discussed at length and it was finally decided that they would go for a corrugated iron fence. Mr Dube was asked to get information on prices and to find out what the town council would be prepared to contribute.

Mr Dube was not very keen on a corrugated iron fence. He was afraid that it would not look so good. Nevertheless, he enquired from a senior official in the town council about the whole matter. He was informed by the official that the town council would never subsidise a corrugated iron fence. He said, however, that it might be possible that the town council would pay in full for a precast concrete wall. He undertook to submit an application and promised that Mr Dube would know the outcome within six weeks.

At the next meeting of the club representatives, Mr Dube informed the meeting of the possibility that the town council would fund the whole operation of erecting a precast wall. It was decided that the clubs would, in the meantime, get organised for the erection of the fence. It was also decided to combine the erection of the fence with a dedication ceremony and soccer matches between teams of the three clubs.

It took three months before the town council decided that the fence should be erected. When Mr Dube enquired from the senior official about the date on which he should organise the clubs to erect the fence, the official informed him that the town council had contractors doing that type of work.

Mr Dube called the representatives of the clubs together to inform them that their work would not be required. Seeing that the town council had taken over the fence issue, he suggested that they think of another need that they could address. However, the meeting felt that they should wait until after the erection of the fence. They also decided not to continue planning the dedication ceremony because, as Mr Radebe put it, 'They first want to see if the town council will ever get so far'.

In the meantime, the town council experienced a rent crisis. It had to make some cuts in expenditure. The fence around the soccer grounds was one of the first items to fall by the way. After this, all attempts by Mr Dube to organise the clubs around another need met with very little enthusiasm. At long last Mr Dube decided to concentrate on soccer and to forget about community development.

CASE STUDY 11
THE PROJECT THAT WAS TAKEN OVER

To show how an insensitive government agency can ruin a very promising venture.

Mr Kekana was a teacher in a rural village. He was born in the area and when he was posted there as a teacher, he requested from the chief a piece of land on which he erected his home. Mr Kekana decided to plant the traditional crops on his land, but to use fertiliser and modern farming methods. The result was that his crops were markedly better than those of the other small farmers. They started to talk about it, but Mr Kekana, who was expecting it, quickly forestalled any hint of sorcery or any other supernatural means of getting beautiful crops by telling the farmers simply and plainly what he did to get better crops. He also offered to help them do the same.

Over a period of two seasons, more and more farmers used Mr Kekana's advice and the crops showed a marked difference. By that stage the farmers had organised themselves into an association and they farmed co-operatively to ensure cheaper inputs and lower running costs, for example the marketing of their produce. They were so successful that the regional government got word of their work. Regional representatives visited the area so that they could see for themselves what could be done to improve agriculture. They were so impressed that they decided to help the farmers.

At the beginning of the next season, the government sent a number of tractors to the area and started to plough the farmers' lands. They then brought in the planters and started to plant. The farmers were bewildered. Everything was taken out of their hands. Mr Kekana pleaded with the government to leave the farmers to their own devices. He was told that the area had been earmarked for demonstrating agricultural methods to farmers from other areas and that the highest possible yields had to be ensured.

Suddenly, the farmers had little to do. The decisions had been taken out of their hands and even the hard work was being done by the government with its implements. The result was quite devastating. Within a season there was nothing left of the farmers' initiatives. When the government decided to hand the lands back to the farmers, they were met with disinterest.

CASE STUDY 12
THE DIVIDED COMMUNITY

To illustrate how politics can put paid to any effort at development.

Green Village is a squatter settlement now being upgraded. It had a village committee, but most of the people demanded the committee's resignation. The members of the village committee refused to oblige and, since then, there has been bitter animosity and rivalry between two groups, one supporting the incumbent leaders and the other one very much against them. Provincial government officials find themselves in the middle of this squabble. All their efforts to resolve the matter had so far failed. As a result, the whole community is prone to intimidation and lives in fear of itself.

Because of the open animosity it is impossible to establish any development action. The youth, sport and cultural day that was organised by officials of the provincial government, and was supposed to take place in the community hall, is a good example. Everything started peacefully enough. After a while, though, some people marched into the hall and told those present to disperse. They said that the village committee were going to hold a meeting. The officials of the provincial government pleaded with them, arguing that nobody had known anything about a meeting. But it was to no avail. The crowd were intimidated and forced to leave the hall or to attend the village committee's meeting. This was the end of the youth, sport and cultural day.

CASE STUDY 13
THE CLUB WITH TWO COMMITTEES

To remind us that conflict and animosity are always just below the surface.

The Hlangani women's club was asked to do the catering at a seminar that was to be held in the township. The local government paid R600 for this service and the community worker pointed out that the club could do the catering for less and then have something left to spend on themselves. The club agreed to the request and did the catering. It went very well and the club showed a profit of R185. The community worker suggested that a bank account be opened and that the money be deposited. The club agreed and chose people for the task. These people were not part of the committee, but the chairperson and the other members of the committee had no qualms about this. However, at the same meeting, it was suggested that a new committee be elected as the incumbent committee's term of office had expired. At the suggestion of one member it was decided, without discussion, that those people who were chosen to see to the banking account would be the new committee.

A few months later the community worker visited the club again. She was surprised by the small attendance. The members of the previous committee were all absent. She learnt that the bank account had still not been opened and that the money was still with the new chairperson. The reason for the delay, the community worker was told, lay with some members talking behind the backs of the new committee and this had made them cross.

CASE STUDY 14
THE CASE OF THE COMMUNITY WORKER WHO MET HIS MATCH

To illustrate how contact should not be made.

Mr Dladla was a newly appointed agricultural extension officer to a rural tribal area. He was taught at college that an extension officer should get the local people to participate and that he should identify leaders to pull the rest of the people along.

His first task as extension officer was to visit each farmer and to invite him to a public meeting the following Sunday to discuss farming matters in the area. Mr Dladla was exceptionally impressed with one young farmer, a Mr Kubheka, who farmed very progressively and was very keen to befriend Mr Dladla.

A large number of farmers attended the meeting. Mr Dladla was glad to see that Mr Kubheka had quite a following and he decided that he had already done one part of his job, that is to identify a leader.

Mr Dladla addressed the meeting. He told those present that it was clear to him as a professional that they had very low yields and that their farming methods were to be blamed for that. He emphasised how glad he was to be given the opportunity to help them to become wealthy farmers. He also stressed the fact that he could not farm for them. While he had the knowledge and contacts at the government, they had the ability to learn and to work. He sketched a picture of maize fields standing high in the cob and of broad leaved tobacco plants earning the farmers a lot of money. He implored them not to think that such progress is impossible. If they all pulled together they would reach their goal very soon.

Mr Dladla continued by suggesting that they make their first objective a doubling of their maize crop and each farmer to plant at least half a hectare with tobacco to be reached by the end of the next season. This speech drew very warm applause. The whole meeting was buzzing and it was apparent that Mr Dladla had made a great impression.

Mr Kubheka took the floor and thanked Mr Dladla profusely for his inspiring speech. He ended by asking what the next step should be. Mr Dladla ticked the various steps off on his fingers. One, they should form a farmers' association; two, they should elect a committee; three, the committee should go to the regional office of the Department of Agriculture to state their plan; four, they should hold another meeting so that the committee could report on their plans for the following season.

An elderly man then stood up and explained that they already had a farmers' association that was established some years ago. Mr Dladla interjected that he was glad to hear that an association was established, but that the committee was not doing its work and should therefore be sacked.

Mr Kubheka replied in a sneering way that the old headman was the chairman of this dormant committee. Mr Dladla immediately sensed that he was now on dangerous ground. He enquired politely where the headman was, but was told he was not present. Mr Dladla thought that he had saved the situation when he suggested that they proceed with electing a new committee and that the chairman and vice-chairman would then pay the headman a visit to discuss their further plans with him.

The meeting thought it a good idea and promptly elected Mr Dladla chairman and Mr Kubheka vice-chairman. In his acceptance speech Mr Dladla said that he would gladly lead this new effort, but that he would resign in favour of Mr Kubheka as soon as he saw that the association was well on its feet.

After the meeting Mr Dladla and Mr Kubheka talked at length about their plans for the association. When Mr Dladla said that they had better visit the headman as soon as possible, Mr Kubheka pleaded a very busy week and suggested that Mr Dladla go alone to the headman.

Mr Dladla visited the headman the following week. He was greeted by the headman saying that he heard that Dladla and Kubheka had kicked him out of the committee. Mr Dladla tried to explain that that was not the case, but that it was unfortunate that the headman was not present at the meeting. The headman replied that he was not informed of the meeting and that the meeting was therefore illegal. It took Mr Dladla more than an hour to come to an agreement with the headman that they would hold a second meeting, this time at the headman's homestead where they could iron out the differences.

The second meeting was again attended by a large group of farmers. After the headman had solemnly welcomed all present, a man stood up and proposed that they again elect a committee. Mr Dladla replied that that was not necessary. They could easily include the headman on the committee. A long debate ensued in which it was eventually decided that seeing that the previous meeting was illegal the committee was illegal too and for that reason a new committee should be chosen.

The headman immediately called for nominations for a chairman and his name was suggested by a chorus of voices. No other name came up. Then the headman asked for nominations for a vice-chairman. Mr Dladla and Mr Kubheka were nominated. Mr Dladla did not want to be in opposition to Mr Kubheka and he therefore withdrew, saying that he would rather serve on the committee ex officio as adviser.

The meeting decided that the committee should meet as soon as possible. Three weeks passed before Mr Dladla enquired from Mr Kubheka when the committee is going to meet. He said that he had not heard from the headman yet. After another three weeks Mr Dladla enquired from the headman when he planned to call a meeting. He was told by the headman that a committee meeting had been held but that there was nothing of importance to report.

CASE STUDY 15
THE INSPECTOR WHOSE HELP WAS DUMPED

To learn from the mistakes of a community development worker.

Mr Williams was a health inspector in an urban area situated close to the city centre and in a state of decline. When he visited the cafés and butcheries on his inspection rounds he was struck by the presence of large numbers of idle children.

Mr Williams noticed a boy sitting on the same café veranda every day, surrounded by followers. He made a point of regularly greeting and occasionally exchanging a friendly word with the boy. He soon realised that this boy, Gary, was regarded as a leader by many of the children.

Next to the café was a vacant lot that had originally been zoned as a park, but was now overgrown with grass and strewn with car wrecks and other scrap. Mr Williams decided that the lot could be put to good use and obtained the city council's permission to clean up the site for the children's use.

Soon after, Mr Williams asked Gary whether they would like to have a place where they could kick a ball. Gary and his friends were appreciative, but said that there was no such place. Mr Williams pointed to the adjacent lot and invited them to follow him. He explained to them that, if they could clear the site, they might use it. Gary and his friends did not look too keen, but Mr Williams suggested that they organise the children in the vicinity and then try to clean up the site over a few days. He promised that he would arrange a lorry to cart away the rubbish.

On the appointed day, a considerable number of children arrived, but most of them were rather small. Gary and his friends were the only big children. But they were not really working. They were 'supervising' the smaller children. They worked until dark and Mr Williams then realised that it would take quite a few days of hard work to get the place clean. He arranged with the children to resume work during the afternoon of the next day and encouraged them to bring more children to help them.

The next day there were quite a few new faces, but many from the previous day were absent, including Gary and his friends. Again, they worked until dark and agreed to come back the next Saturday to try to finish their work.

A few days later, Mr Williams was called by his superior who told him that parents had complained that he had used their children to remove scrap, that they had returned to their homes after dark, and that some had had their clothes torn as a result of the work.

Mr Williams visited the café adjoining the site and pleaded with the owner to tell parents who visited the café the purpose of the clean-up. He asked Gary and his friends, who were at their usual place on the veranda to gather as many children as possible for the following Saturday so that they could finish the work.

On that Saturday, only Gary and his friends were there, kicking a ball on the cleared part of the site. Mr Williams asked them where the other children were and was told that they found the work too hard and that, at any rate, the parents were not pleased with the idea.

Mr Williams decided to take a short cut. He asked the municipality to clean up the site. It took him three days to unravel all the red tape, but, ultimately, the municipality agreed and, within a week, the site was clean and the grass cut. A proud Mr Williams handed the clean site over to Gary and his friends and urged them to get the children to play ball games.

Two weeks later, Mr Williams visited the area again. He was surprised to see children idling everywhere. He arrived at the cleaned-up site and was very upset to see not a single child, but a new car wreck with several loads of rubbish next to it!

CASE STUDY 16
THE FELT NEED AND THE REAL NEED

> To illustrate that community development is a learning process through which we can also learn about our needs.

Mrs Mathebula, a social worker, had been stationed only a few months in a large, rural town when she attended a seminar on community development.

After the seminar, she was very keen to launch at least one community development project. Up to that moment, most of her cases came from a hilly area far from the main road where the people were markedly poorer than elsewhere. Nearly all the cases Mrs Mathebula had handled from this area had to do with child neglect and poverty-related problems affecting children. She identified this area as the place where people really needed help. She decided to get a community development project going among the mothers to improve their children's diet.

Mrs Mathebula first spoke to the wife of the local headman, who had a shop on the fringe of this area. From this conversation, she learnt that the mothers might be more keen to get a sewing class going so that they could make most of their children's clothes themselves.

Mrs Mathebula was disheartened by this news. She was hoping that a poor society such as this would give preference to their children's health and diet. However, she decided to talk to the women themselves. It took her the best part of two weekends to visit the women at their homes or to talk to them at the communal washing place or water pump. She was disappointed to learn that very few women were interested in improving their children's diet. Just as the headman's wife predicted, most of them were keen to start a sewing club. Mrs Mathebula had to make a decision. Either she would look for other women interested in starting a food garden, or she would start a project addressing these women's felt need. After some soul searching, she opted for the latter. From one of the women she had talked to, she had learnt that a teacher at the nearby primary school had a knowledge of sewing and could teach the women basic skills.

Mrs Mathebula went to see the teacher, Miss Makhanye. She was quite willing to give weekly sewing classes to the women. They decided to call a meeting at the school to launch the sewing club. Mrs Mathebula tried to contact as many women as she could to tell them of the meeting.

The meeting was attended by seventeen women who were very keen to start the classes. They wanted to know from Mrs Mathebula and Miss Makhanye what it would cost to buy two second-hand sewing machines and some material. The two ladies were unprepared for such questions. They had not thought of finding such information. The women expressed their disappointment because they wanted to start as soon as possible. Mrs Mathebula undertook to find out the costs and to let the women know over the weekend. She then suggested that the women elect a committee to take up leadership positions. The women thought it a good idea and promptly nominated Mrs Mathebula as chairperson.

She declined, however, explaining that she may be transferred at any time and that, as a social worker, she had many other tasks to perform. They then elected a person not known to Mrs Mathebula, with Miss Makhanye as vice-chairperson and a young woman, who had several years of schooling, as secretary. They wanted to elect Mrs Mathebula as treasurer, but she declined again in favour of someone else.

It took Mrs Mathebula a few days of hard work to find out the cost of the sewing machines and the material. Eventually she found two second-hand sewing machines in a shop in town. She calculated that the seventeen persons involved would each have to pay R10 to cover the cost of the machines and the material. Again, Mrs Mathebula spent most of the weekend conveying this information to the women. Mrs Mathebula and Miss Makhanye bought the two sewing machines and the material out of their own pockets, hoping that the women would each contribute their R10.

At the first class, twelve women were present. Mrs Mathebula explained that she and Miss Makhanye had bought the sewing machines and material and that the club would have to pay them back. Ten women had brought their money. They wanted to give their contributions directly to the two ladies, but Mrs Mathebula explained that they had to pay it to the treasurer, who would open an account in the post office before paying them from that account.

After three weeks, only five women showed a continued interest in the sewing lessons. These five enjoyed it greatly and two of them made quick progress. Mrs Mathebula and Miss Makhanye were not properly refunded. After the first ten contributions no others were made. The treasurer explained that two of the women who had dropped the classes had claimed their money back. Another had borrowed R10 from the fund but, shortly afterwards, had taken a job in town and had not been seen since. The treasurer should therefore have had R70 in the account, but it held only R50. She really could not tell what had happened to the rest. The two ladies decided to take R20 each, leaving R10 in the account.

Mrs Mathebula was unhappy that, after her initial effort, only five women were benefiting. She decided to visit the twelve women who had dropped out since the first meeting. She learnt that most of these women had found the classes too difficult. They would rather do something not requiring many lessons. Mrs Mathebula then suggested a communal vegetable garden and ten women showed interest. She arranged for them to go to the headman as a group to ask for a piece of land. On their way to the headman, they called on his wife at her shop. She told them that the clinic sister was also organising a communal garden, but that she had had trouble in getting enough women to participate.

There and then the group decided to pay the clinic sister a visit. From her they learnt that all the clinic's grounds, which were already fenced and had running water, were available for vegetable gardening. She had already obtained the help of one of the extension officers who was prepared to give the project professional advice. Her problem was that she could only get five women who were prepared to participate in the venture. That same day, Mrs Mathebula, her group and the clinic sister decided to join hands in an effort to get a garden project going.

Community Development in the 21st Century Section F

> The garden is really prospering. The garden club's membership has risen to twenty-five and it has had to obtain land adjacent to the clinic grounds to accommodate all the participants.
>
> The sewing club has disintegrated. Miss Makhanye was transferred out of the area. Two of the women who made good progress are now fulltime seamstresses. The other three will never master the art of sewing. Two of them have since joined the garden club. The other one, the treasurer, has R10 to show for her efforts, the R10 Mrs Mathebula and Miss Makhanye left in the sewing club's account.

CASE STUDY 17
MOTHERS OF THE MOUNTAIN COMMUNITY

To illustrate that community development projects can be spectacularly successful.

The superintendent of a hospital in a rural area in the foot hills of a mountainous area realised that the same women would bring their children with kwashiorkor to the hospital for treatment. The child would be hospitalised for two weeks and the mother would receive information on a balanced and healthy diet for her child. However, within a month or two she would be back with the same child needing treatment again. The superintendent decided to speak to these women about the feeding of their children. He identified the monthly clinic day when these women could collect some powdered milk for their children as an opportune time.

In his discussions with these women he soon realised that they knew what constitutes a healthy diet, but that they simply did not have the means to provide the right food to their children. This discovery of the superintendent started a discussion between him and the mothers about a food garden to supplement their children's diet. After a while a group of twenty mothers declared themselves willing to start a garden. They acquired a piece of land in the hospital grounds with ample water. Their garden was an instant success, so much so, that more mothers wanted to join them. When this one project just about reached its capacity, women started their own gardens on land acquired from the tribal chief. Some women had no feeling for gardening and they decided to start with a small poultry farm where they would raise broilers. Again their endeavour was met with instant success. The result was that a number of women's groups started raising poultry. Within a period of less than a year the market for broilers was totally sated.

In the meantime the original group of women with their garden in the hospital grounds were doing so well with selling the surplus of their produce in the area surrounding the hospital that they could afford to erect a small building in the hospital grounds with a demonstration kitchen and a lecture room. On clinic days they would invite dieticians to come and tell and show them how to prepare food to optimise its nutritional value.

The efforts of the women in food gardening and poultry farming caught the eye of the tribal authority and the service providers in the area. Through the good offices of the authorities and a few NGOs, groups were created to develop springs.

Because of the mountainous terrain there were many springs in the area. They just had to be developed and the water piped from them to tanks in the various villages. When the first efforts to develop the springs proved to be a fairly easy task, a number of groups sprang up with this in mind and a large number of villages got water in this way. As water became easier to use more food gardens appeared.

At this stage the superintendent realised that he could no longer handle the facilitating of all these projects. Through the good offices of an NGO a project manager was obtained whose salary was paid by the NGO and who got a small flat inside the hospital where she could reside.

The women not involved in food gardens or poultry farming started to talk about doing something for themselves; getting a project going that would improve their income. With the help of the new project manager they identified a possible project, namely the harvesting and selling of the thatch grass that covered a large portion of the area. They began to look for a buyer of the thatch and found one in Johannesburg. They were fortunate to have a siding of the railway line to the north in their area and they arranged with the transport services to park a railway truck at the siding which the women would then fill with thatch grass. They worked out a system whereby the women would receive a token for every bushel of grass they would bring to the truck. Later they could then exchange their tokens for a fixed amount of money. This project was a great success and really brought prosperity to the area.

The tribal authority who had representatives on a steering committee overseeing all of these projects, decided to start a few rehabilitative projects where they invited people to participate with their labour for which they were paid. These projects included rehabilitation of homesteads where huts were fixed and newly thatched and where dilapidated animal kraals were improved. It also included throwing car wrecks lying in the veld into dongas and covering them with diamond mesh wire so that soil and vegetation could take hold.

One of the serious problems at that stage was that there were too few schools and that further schools were only on the waiting list for two or three years hence. Some parents whose children were negatively affected by this came together and decided to build their own school. Through the good offices of the project manager they acquired a deal with an NGO that it would supply and fix the roof of the school if the parents would build the rest. Not one, but three schools were built in this way and every one of them were supplied with water from springs in the mountains. These schools had so much surplus water that they could make a food garden in every school yard and supply the homes adjacent to the schools with water for their everyday use.

Another educational problem of the area was that many children could not afford school books. The original project of the kwashiorkor mothers was in such a strong position financially at this stage that they decided to start a fund for poor children who could not afford their own books.

After about two years since the first project of the mothers with the kwashiorkor babies, there were about 200 projects in that area and the local people ran these projects with minimal help from the project manager and a few NGOs.

CASE STUDY 18
FOOD GARDEN IN MAPAYENI

A new dimension in human development.
Professor HJ Swanepoel (Translation of article entitled 'Mapayeni 'n nuwe dimensie in mensontwikkeling', *Lantern*, 34(2) 1985.)

A general picture of a successful community development project

Twenty women from the Gazankulu district developed a vegetable garden during one of the driest years of the century, a year when humans and animals were facing starvation. These women produced an enviable harvest, through hard work and perseverance, despite the fact that the once subtropical vegetation in the area was now reduced to red soil and Mopani trees. These women (and it is hoped those who have heard about this project) have learned valuable lessons from this community development project. Mapayeni has shown that poor and isolated people do not necessarily lack potential and energy – these characteristics are just generally hidden. This potential and energy need to be identified and channelled by enthusiastic and passionate people so that these communities are able to achieve more than they ever thought possible.

The story of Mapayeni

The small group of women who got involved in this project are members of the local Dutch Reformed Church in Africa. They are poor, but they were even more poor until a short time ago. Many of them are their family's breadwinners and some of them are already middle-aged with health problems. Caught as they were in the vicious circle of poverty, the drought and recession were like an insurmountable mountain to these women. This was, however, until something ignited their enthusiasm – something that would change their lives forever.

In 1982, when Gazankulu was reeling from a drought (the residents did not realise that the worst of the drought would hit them in 1983), the local minister from the Dutch Reformed Church in Africa planted cabbages in his garden which he later sold very cheaply to the community. And this got a group of women thinking – they realised that they could develop a garden of their own which would provide for their needs. So they laid their first garden on the premises of an outpost church, but the rains stayed away and the plants shrivelled and died in the extreme heat. Although this attempt was unsuccessful, the women did not become downhearted. They began to look for land on the banks of the Middle Letaba River – a river that runs just a few kilometres past the village – so that there would be sufficient water for the vegetables.

The women chose a piece of land measuring two hectares and obtained the necessary permission from the local tribal chief. A total of 20 women would tackle the project. They elected a committee from this group and were now ready to tackle their project.

Their first task was to clear (deforest) the land. Burning was the easiest option, but that would mean that they would destroy valuable firewood and that tree stumps under the ground would make the tilling of the land more difficult. The vegetation thus had to be cut down and carted away so that the land was bare; the women did, however, leave a few trees for shade.

The next task was to fence off the area. The women realised that they would need to erect more than a fence made of branches and twigs – the fence needed to prevent hungry goats and other animals from entering the growing area. The women were faced with two problems. Firstly, they did not have sufficient money for a wire fence and, secondly, they did not know how to put up a wire fence. But with the assistance of the local minister, they were able to get an interest-free loan from Church Aid in Need to purchase the necessary wire and poles. They were shown how to put up the fence, but thereafter undertook the work themselves.

The third milestone these women encountered was the ploughing of the land. Thanks to the loan they obtained, the women were able to get someone to do the ploughing for them. This was one of the few tasks they did not undertake themselves.

As soon as the land was cleared, ploughed and fenced off, the women were able to start gardening. The time was ripe. It was already early autumn in 1983 – the best time to plant in the Gazankulu district. The women transplanted about 20 000 cabbage, spinach, tomato, onion and pepper plants from the minister's garden which had served as a nursery while they were preparing their garden. It was a team effort. Some measured the distance between the plants, some planted the seedlings, some dug in fertilisers and sprayed for pests where necessary, while others watered the plants.

Watering a garden that is situated on the banks of a river sounds like easy work. The fact is, however, that the river is a good 20 metres lower than the garden – this makes watering an enormous task. The minister, who gave advice whenever necessary, recommended that the women should look at purchasing a pump. He believed that a pump installed on the river bed would eliminate much of the hard work associated with watering the plants. Before the women would consent to this, however, he had to demonstrate the process using a loaned pump. A further loan from Church Aid in Need enabled them to buy the necessary pump, but they had to see to the installation of the pump themselves.

By this time, the drought had become so severe that the river had dried up. The project was facing a huge crisis. The only option was to dig for water in the river bed. At first, all that was needed was a big hole, but with time, the women had to dig a long ditch and additional holes so that each precious drop of water from the supposedly dry river bed could be channelled to the vegetables.

The first vegetables were harvested in August. After months of toil, the women were able to provide their families with fresh vegetables. They were also able to provide the entire community with vegetables at about 60 per cent of the market price. So, instead of only feeding 20 women and their families, this group of women were able to assist hundreds in the community. These women also started to make a profit, which enabled them to start paying back their loans and to buy other essential items.

Within a year of the idea being conceived, this group of women who knew very little about gardening and even less about irrigation, water pumps and fencing, had turned their precarious existence around to one of resourcefulness and hope. It is important to note that this group of women did not have exceptional talents; nor were they a unique group of people. What they achieved, therefore, lies within the grasp of each person who lives in similar circumstances.

The value for the participants

This is not just a good old success story. These women live in poverty, but have turned their lives around. The most important result of this project is the physical improvement of living conditions. A balanced diet for people staring starvation in the face and a little money to buy essential items should not be scorned. These women achieved far more than just the physical improvement of their living conditions.

First, they showed themselves that they can do something about their apparently hopeless situation. They awakened their potential – something they had always underestimated. They now know that a crisis can be overcome by hard work and by working as a team.

Second, these women learned skills which they shall have for the rest of their lives. They have expanded their knowledge of gardening. They now know how to plant seeds and how to keep plants moist. They now have a good understanding of fertilisation and pest control. They have learned something about mechanics by using and maintaining a pump. They can now put up a fence and they know a lot more about marketing and selling.

Third, these women now have increasing respect for human dignity. The knowledge that 'we can' contributes to self-confidence and self-reliance. The fact that they are self-reliant makes them more acceptable to the community. Passers by mocked them when, in excruciating heat, they planted approximately 20 000 cabbage plants in dry ground. But when these selfsame women began selling their produce cheaply to the community, they quickly became 'heroes' and are now seen as pioneers by the community.

Fourth, the women learned to work as a group and they began to understand the value of co-operation. They have proved that people can achieve anything when they stand together – that many hands do, in fact, make light work. No individual would have been able to do what the group has managed to do together. The division of work was an important element of their success. As individuals, they would have been unlikely to have been loaned money, for example.

Lastly, this group has also provided their community with a long-term service. Those who initially mocked and doubted them have since seen the rewards of the project – this has resulted in some of them knuckling down to some hard work themselves. They have realised that the risk factor is not as great as initially anticipated. They have seen what these women have achieved and are attempting to emulate them. The result – a large number of gardens in Mapayeni today. The demonstration effect of this first project was thus overwhelming.

Lessons for those who wish to help

This project also has a number of lessons for those who would like to help others to help themselves.

In the first place, it is important to limit the number of people involved in a project. The work, organisation and associated costs were also limited in this case. It was thus possible for the minister to keep an eye on the entire project and each participant was able to identify with the total project. Community development projects that get too big can so easily become like a Frankenstein monster – they become unmanageable and make enormous demands on the people involved. The aims of over-large projects gradually become vague and the initial aims are soon replaced by the need to just keep the project going. The problems and work they encountered would have been far more taxing if the project had been bigger. The death-knell of a project sounds as soon as participants feel that they have lost control of the project.

This project was, in the second place, also blessed with good leadership. Leaders often need to be cultivated during a project, but this group already had a clear leader who was accepted by the group. Her strong leadership contributed enormously to the independent nature and behaviour of the group. Weak leadership or a total lack of leadership is often the Achilles heel of a project, because outsiders – such as the minister in this case – must then take on the role of leader. This encroaches on the group's initiative and independence.

In the third place, initiative must be utilised in the right place. People who want to help others often instinctively want to take the initiative. In this case, the minister's actions serve as a good example of how to help others without smothering their initiative. He never told the women what to do. He gave advice when he was asked for it, but he also allowed them to make mistakes. He gradually reduced his visits to the garden so that the women had no choice but to stand on their own two feet. He gave them detailed information about technical matters, but as soon as the women had mastered the technique, he left them to their own devices. One thing he continued to do for the women, however, was to act as their representative. He helped the women to obtain their loans and to acquire an appropriate and well-priced pump – things the women might well have struggled to do on their own. But, it is important to note that he never did anything without first being asked to do so. He never threatened their initiative; neither was he a scapegoat when the women wished to avoid their responsibilities. He was thus very valuable to the project, both as an adviser and as a moral supporter.

Fourth, organisation and self-discipline are key words for the success of any community development project. The women elected a committee right at the beginning and all the obvious leaders were included in this committee. Apart from the project leader, one of the younger women who could read and write was appointed to serve as secretary and treasurer.

Based on this information, it is clear that the committee were thoroughly organised and that they maintained discipline. The women decided early on that each woman was required to attend work each day. Any woman who failed to arrive for work would be fined 30c per day. Those women who already had other work were not excused; they had to make the necessary arrangements to ensure that someone else was available to stand in for them on a temporary basis. Once all the plants had been planted, the committee divided each group of vegetables into equal parts. Each woman was responsible for her section and was entitled to claim her portion of the harvest from her section. It was thus not possible to hide behind the hard work of another woman and then claim an equal portion of the harvest. It was necessary to spend long hours working in the garden to ensure that the plants were properly watered (the women worked long hours for many months). The committee thus divided the women into two shifts, so that there were people on duty from early in the morning until late at night. As soon as the vegetables were selling well, the committee decided that each woman should contribute R5 per month to repay their loans. One of the secrets of any project's success is that each participant is utilised optimally – and the committee was very successful in this regard. One of the older women suffered from asthma and could not keep up with the other women when they were clearing the land. She was thus given the task of collecting and burning thorns. When the pump was installed, she was also given the responsibility of ensuring that the inlet pipe was kept free of branches, leaves and other debris. A younger woman who had attended school for a few years was given the task of maintaining the pump.

The minister showed her the ropes and then left her to take full responsibility for the pump. In the fifth place, it is clear that even the simplest project needs initial capital. It is true that even the poorest communities can generate capital, but then the risk factor becomes so much greater. If they are able to borrow money on reasonable terms (ie that they do not have to pay back the money in the short term), then the risk factor is reduced and the participants can first become entrenched in the project before they are expected to produce physical results.

In the sixth place, this project shows that it is not sufficient to merely convey knowledge to those who need to learn to help themselves. There should be an emotional element to the contact between the outsider and the community. The community must be able to sense a degree of compassion and sincerity on the part of the outsider. They must be able to accept his/her intentions without question.

Once the community realises that the outsider who wishes to help them is just as dependent on them as they are on him/her for the success of the project, then progress can be made.

Conclusion

The Mapayeni project also has negative elements, because people are, by nature, fallible. This is, however, not of primary importance. What is important, though, is that these women exceeded all expectations in their attempt to do something about their hopeless situations.

The Mapayeni project is not a big and sophisticated attempt to make poor people rich. There was no blueprint that would ensure there was phenomenal growth. It was not necessary to have a group of officials to manage the project or to support the participants. The project did not require any form of advanced technology or large amounts of money. The Mapayeni women are still poor and simple people, but this project has given meaning to their existence. These women have renewed hope, as do their families and those who have followed their example. This project has enabled a group of people to turn away from being victims of their circumstances to being people of self-confidence and independence who wish to improve their lives.

CASE STUDY 19
STEALING OR TAKING OWNERSHIP

To illustrate two opposing views of community development workers.

At a troubleshooting session of an NGO conference a middle-aged gentleman stood up and said that on the whole he had few problems with running projects. The only problem he had he said was that 'every time that I have a successful project, the people steal it from me'.

A community development worker was responsible for the launching of refuse removal projects in informal settlements in and around the metropolitan area of Johannesburg. These projects did two things. First, it helped clean up the area and second, it created a small income for a group of people who would otherwise be unemployed. She came back one day from one of these areas much earlier than usual. When asked why she was not working that morning in that certain township, she reacted by saying: 'This morning when I arrived at Township X before I could drive into the area I was stopped by a group of people I know well. They are the steering committee of the refuse removal project that we have launched. They stopped me and showed me that they wanted to talk to me. They said to me that they are very thankful for what I have done and for my help to get a project going, but they added that they have decided that they can go it alone now. They don't need me anymore.' The question put to her was: 'Do you feel sad that the people have taken the project?' Her answer: 'No, heavens. This is a fantastic thing! The people have accepted the ownership of a project that was always theirs.'

CASE STUDY 20
THE STORY OF KWAMPOFU

To illustrate what usually happens in a rural area.

The rural area of KwaMpofu is an extremely poor area with very little opportunity for the population to improve their lives through gainful employment or through small one-person commercial and service enterprises. The area consists of five villages, two under one chieftainship and three under another. Many of the people found some employment in the town about 60 kilometres from the KwaMpofu area. Some of them commute daily by way of taxis, but a substantial percentage stay on in town and come home over the weekends. The town is not very big and as a result of brisk influx, it started to fall behind with services. This led directly to a stagnation of commerce and industry so that jobs were not becoming more, but rather fewer.

The provincial government is directly responsible for the wellbeing of this area. It therefore co-ordinates the various efforts by line departments such as agriculture, health, public works, water, housing and labour, on both provincial government and national government level. Apart from the government there are also a number of NGOs involved in the area. The largest and most sophisticated of these is busy with a project to create day-care centres in the three villages falling under the same chieftainship. Unfortunately because of a lack of communication the NGO is frequently at loggerheads with the chief and his council. The chief wants the NGO to discuss its projects with the citizens at public meetings, but the NGO says that will be a political act of which it does not want any part. Nevertheless the NGO is keeping on erecting these day-care centres with the blessing of the provincial government and managing them when they become operative. One of the smaller NGOs tried to create small groups of mostly women to start food gardens in the area. They were relatively successful at first until a welfare organisation heard the plight of this area regarding food shortage and decided to approach a large firm to donate fruit and vegetables to the area. The firm saw it as an advertisement for itself and dropped large quantities of fruit and vegetables on the premises of one or other public building where the people could help themselves free of charge.

The government started with the excavation for electricity. It was only when the two tribal councils enquired about the work taking place in their areas, that they were informed of the project. The government then suggested that the tribal councils could draw up lists of those houses that would like to receive electricity. The government representatives pointed out that through the involvement of the tribal councils the project could become really participatory. The reaction from both tribal councils was that all the houses wanted electricity. The government reacted by pointing out the individual costs per house for instalment and deposit. This led to a few angry public meetings and eventually electricity was only provided for street lighting. In the meantime a few of the more affluent members of the community paid their deposit and instalment fees and have electricity in their homes.

Some time ago the government really surprised the people when it started to erect a community centre. The problem was, however, that the centre was built in the most outlying village and that it was therefore difficult for most people to get to the centre. To confound the problem, the government housed a clinic in the centre. This clinic was supposed to serve the five villages of KwaMpofu. Most people from the villages other than the one where the clinic is situated, refused to pay for taxis to get to the clinic. They consequently still frequent a private clinic of many years' standing run by the Roman Catholic Church. The community hall which was part of the centre was managed by an NGO situated in the town and quite unknown among the people of the area. No one was ever informed what the function of the hall, and in fact, the whole centre would be. The NGO running the centre tried to organise an expo, but there was very little interest, firstly because the people were ignorant about the format and purpose of such a function and secondly because of the stagnated nature of the local economy. Over a period of time the centre started to fall into disuse and quite a bit of vandalism took place. The government requested the two tribal councils to arrange a public meeting to discuss the community centre. The tribal councils pointed out that each of them should arrange a meeting because that is customary. The officials of the government were however adamant that they could only come to the area on one Sunday.

The result was that members from only the tribe in whose area the meeting took place, attended. The officials tried to explain to those present what functions the centre could play. They stressed that the public should only make use of whatever is arranged by the NGO. Quite a few people, and they received general approval, said that they wanted to participate in the running of the centre. The official reaction was that the NGO was contractually the manager of the centre and that everybody should respect that. The result was that the disuse and the vandalism increased. Eventually the government informed the tribal council in whose area the centre was situated that it was going to put up a fence around the facility. The tribal council requested that local contractors be used for this task, but a firm from the town was appointed. Most of the fence was gone after one week. The NGO in charge of the place withdrew when the car of their employee working as manager of the centre got stolen.

A young youth organiser working in this area drew the attention of the two tribal councils because of the work he was doing. He got a body going calling themselves the youth network for the development of KwaMpofu. They operate under the leadership of elected people from their own ranks. They have started to contact other youth groups such as choirs, sports clubs and even the local political party youth league. Their purpose was to launch area-wide projects with the active participation of various local youth groups. They have started with a clean-up operation of the whole area. That has led to the training of a number of young people to start their own enterprise of selling bottles and tin cans for a regular income. They have also identified a number of young people to be trained as sports coaches. They made contact with a sports club in town who agreed on a mutual project where the sports club will provide or arrange for the training of people identified by the youth network for the development of KwaMpofu.

The government approached this youth group to amalgamate their activities with that of the Department of Education. The youth group welcomed any co-operation, but the government refused to accept their conditions for working together. The government is now considering the creation of an official youth co-ordinating council that could operate from the now dilapidated community centre.

In the area furthest removed from the tarred road going to the town there is quite a bit of agriculture going, mainly because a perennial river runs adjacent to this area. One of the teachers who originally came from this area requested a piece of land as the custom goes. He started to plant maize and vegetables, but he fertilised the soil with the result that his crop looked much better than that of the other farmers. He anticipated correctly that this would lead to suspicion and even animosity. He explained to the farmers what he had done and suggested that they could strengthen one another by forming a co-operative. Some of the farmers liked the idea and started such a co-operative and with the guidance of this teacher they did rather well. Because of this success more and more of the farmers joined, with the result that after two years that area is really becoming a prosperous food producing node.

In one of the villages there was a women's chicken raising co-operative. Their big problem was that the feed for broiler chickens was simply too expensive for them. Their enterprises therefore remained small with very little profit for the women. Now, however, they have approached the farmers' co-operative for a deal to buy most of their maize as chicken feed plus some of their vegetables for themselves, but also for the chickens. Now the farmers need not transport their maize to a far off silo at great expense and at the same time the women can get their chicken feed much cheaper than otherwise. Some of the women in this project are so busy that they find it very difficult to look after their children properly. After a lot of soul searching the women have decided to start a day-care centre for their children. They were lucky in negotiating a deal with a local church with a church building for the use of it during the week as a day-care centre. They started to look for young people who could fulfil the role of child minders. Naturally the youth network for the development of KwaMpofu heard about this and they approached the women with an offer to provide the women with two child minders if the women could help to pay for their training. This venture was so successful that the youth body has launched a scheme where young people are trained as child minders and then placed in day care centres in the area.

CASE STUDY 21
THE LOVING TEACHER

To illustrate how easily a community development worker can act paternalistically.

We visited the various women's groups created by the community development worker, a twenty-three-year-old unmarried woman. These women's groups were started among the wives of farm labourers on commercial farms with a view to help them gain certain skills and start small development projects. The community worker was totally devoted to her work with a lot of compassion for the women who she tried to organise into groups. We stopped at a farm and under a huge tree about 15 women were waiting for us. The community worker was very glad to see the women and there ensued hearty greetings. What I heard was a condescending overly friendly voice from the community worker: 'Oh Christina, your knitting is wonderful! I never thought you would get it right and now just look at this! And Johanna have you made this beautiful beret? I can't believe it! Oh you are so good!' I wondered where I had heard the same tone of voice and way of speaking before and then remembered it was some time ago when I had visited a day-care centre and the very kind teacher communicated with the toddlers in much the way that this community worker did. When I was introduced to the women in this group I found to my amusement (and horror) that all of them were middle aged, any one of them could have been the community worker's mother!

CASE STUDY 22
BRUTAL FORCE AMONG THE CABBAGE PLANTS

To illustrate the wrong attitude and action of a community development worker.

I was taken to a large food producing project by the agricultural extension officer who was the community development worker for the project. It was known as a participatory collective garden where the participants were responsible for the garden and had a share of the dividend produced by the garden. The agricultural extension officer had to provide technical advice only.

When we arrived at the garden a large group of people were waiting for us. As we got out of the car the officer, whose door was on the farther side of the waiting group, shouted over the roof of the car and over my head: 'Didn't I tell you to water the cabbage plants? I told you they are going to die, but you don't listen!' As he was moving away from the car towards the garden he was still going at it. The whole group of 'participants' trotted behind him with hanging heads. He was still castigating them as he reached the cabbage plants. He kept on walking and talking while you could see flying cabbage plants in all directions marking his way through them.

CASE STUDY 23
THE OLD CHIEF'S STORY

To illustrate how easily someone can be offended by a community development worker.

The other day a smart young man from the government visited me in his smart car. He stopped in front of my homestead. He got out of his car. He didn't greet me properly. He didn't give me the opportunity to greet him properly. His great hurry made him forget all manners of decency. He just came in, sat down and asked me what my weaknesses were.

CASE STUDY 24
WATER TO WASTE

To illustrate the necessity for projects to be sustainable.

A certain community living on the slopes of the foothills of a big mountain decided to develop a few of the many springs in the mountain. This was done through a project and the water was then piped from the springs down towards the valley where it was stored in three 5 000 litre tanks. The water stored in these tanks is quite enough for the community of about a thousand people. In fact, when it rains well people need this water solely for household purposes. Added to this is the problem that a number of households lower down in the valley and quite a distance from these tanks make very little use of the water because they need people to walk up the valley and then back down with full holders for their homes. Such labour is not always available with the result that these households go without or obtain their water from dubious sources.

The water from these springs in the mountain is so plentiful that the tanks are overflowing. This causes a serious problem because the waste water is carving out quite a donga that can become deep and dangerous over time. At the moment it is already forming some stagnant pools where mosquitoes are breeding. It is clear that this project has a sustainability problem.

CASE STUDY 25
THE SMART COMMUNITY DEVELOPMENT WORKER

When Mr Mphisa was appointed Community Development Worker in Shisi, he found a group of people who were at the talking phase of a project they wanted to start. He attended a meeting where the group, who were interested, were very keen to discuss the matter with him.

After a long discussion, the group decided that they would ask a possible donor for financial support for the project. They wanted to describe the situation in detail to the donor, highlighting how serious the problem was. Mr Mphisa, however, suggested that they shouldn't tire the donor, that they write down a list of needs to present to the donor. Some of the people present felt, however, that they should not leave the project in the hands of a donor, but that they should show their concern and their willingness to become part of the project.

Eventually, Mr Mphisa won the day and a list was drawn up with a number of 'needs', some of which were not part of the original discussions. One of the group, a teacher, wanted to know whether it was not advisable to compile a business plan to introduce to the donor. Mr Mphisa said, however, that it was difficult to compile a business plan and that donors always find fault with such plans. Eventually, the meeting decided on a wish list that was drawn up by the Community Development Worker and mostly contained his view of what was necessary in the area.

In the meantime, the leadership of the area decided to invite Mr Mphisa, as a new government official, to address the people at a meeting and give him an opportunity to introduce himself. Mr Mphisa was very happy and accepted the invitation.

However, he was a very busy man and he had very little time to prepare a speech. Eventually, he decided to deliver a speech off the cuff. His speech began by him saying that he had very little time to prepare for the speech, that it was his first time speaking to a group of people, and that he didn't know much about community development as the community is practising it. Mr Mphisa was really nervous when he stood before the audience for the first time. He listed a number of accomplishments he would like to achieve while he was a worker in Shisi. Eventually the speech became his own wish list among people who did not know much about development. After a while, people started to converse with one another and towards the end of the speech there was a real din among those present. By now, Mr Mphisa was so confused that he repeated things. He tried to make a few jokes but the jokes had no punch line and were not laughed at.

A few days after this meeting, Mr Mphisa was told by his boss to call a meeting in order to get the community development efforts going. Mr Mphisa wasn't sure what to do at such a meeting, so eventually he had no agenda. He called the meeting a general one.

Immediately after the meeting started, Mr Mphisa was elected as chairperson. He soon had trouble because some of the people wanted to know what was going to be discussed and what power the meeting had. When it was clear that it was only an introductory meeting, a few people left.

The rest of the meeting was very nearly chaotic. Every now and then someone wanted to know where the meeting was taking them. Some had problems with procedure and others would start to talk regardless of another speaker already addressing the meeting. This would usually lead to conflict and, by the end, Mr Mphisa had identified at least three groups who were in competition with one another. Mr Mphisa tried to ignore the conflict between them as best he could.

A few days later, Mr Mphisa was asked by his boss for the minutes of the meeting. Mr Mphisa then realised that he had forgotten to appoint or elect a secretary, with the result that he had to try to compile minutes as best he could from what he could remember of the meeting.

The original community development group never went back to Mr Mphisa for his guidance. They also never heard anything from the potential donor they had approached with Mr Mphisa's wish list. He never again received an invitation to deliver a speech. Some of his senior colleagues are still grinning about his first effort. A meeting was never again held with Mr Mphisa as chairperson. And Mr Mphisa told anyone who would listen how backward the people were that he had to work with.

CASE STUDY 26
THE TRAINERS WHO THOUGHT THEY WERE TEACHERS

Mr Nhleko and Mr Henderson became friends ten years ago while working as teachers at the prestigious St Simeon Secondary School for boys. Mr Nhleko was Deputy Principal and Mr Henderson Head of Department (Social Sciences). They both were head-hunted and joined Catch Up Capacity Building Consultancy (CUPCAC) a month ago.

Now the two friends faced their first capacity-building training in the community. When they arrived at the venue, they immediately brought order to the hall by arranging the desks in neat rows, facing the lectern. Just to be sure, they added two extra chairs in case more than the 20 invited people arrived. At 08:00 they were ready to start the training, but saw only three persons waiting outside. They found this very odd as they specifically emphasised in the letter of invitation that training will start at 08:00.

Being well-disciplined teachers, also knowing how to maintain discipline, they decided to start proceedings and invited the three trainees to take a seat. By 09:00 the 20 seats were filled and by tea time 26 persons were in the training group. Mr Nhleko and Mr Henderson did not understand what was happening.

Being well-trained and experienced teachers, Mr Nhleko and Mr Henderson had prepared their lectures a week before the start of the training and were ready to present to the class. Each had a few topics and was allocated 30 minutes per topic. Mr Henderson became irritated when, after ten minutes of his presentation, he was interrupted by a trainee who wanted to ask for clarification about something. The trainee was told to wait for question time at the end of the lecture. After the lecture was delivered, no questions were asked and Mr Henderson was satisfied that everybody understood the concepts he was explaining.

During Mr Nhleko's lecture, a trainee at the back started an annoying disturbance. He was talking softly to those around him at the back of the class, and every now and then they all giggled. Mr Nhleko asked the young man to leave the room, to which he replied that he could not, as after the training he had to report to the Civic that he represented. Mr Nhleko carried on with his lecture and the young man continued to make jokes.

Mr Henderson and Mr Nhleko did not enjoy their first day of training. One trainee kept coming and going throughout the day, disrupting the lectures. By 12:00, only 16 of the trainees remained and after lunch only 10 returned to the lecture room. The trainees did not respond to questions, nor ask any (except for the one early in the morning). The woman in the front desk fell asleep and only woke up for tea and lunch.

The worst part of the day came, however, as they were closing the last lecture; the representative of the Civic stood up and on the way out asked, 'Why don't you listen to us?'.

ADDENDUM
QUESTIONS AND ANSWERS FOR PARTICIPATORY SELF-EVALUATION

Based on the original model of N Uphoff, but extensively revised by the author. Questions and answers were changed; a number of questions were scrapped; some questions were added; process and product questions were separated; and a completely new set of questions to evaluate the work of the community worker was added.

Process questions

1. How are group decisions made?
   - 4 = Decisions are always made with the knowledge and participation of all members.
   - 3 = Decisions are usually made with the knowledge and participation of all members.
   - 2 = Decisions are sometimes made with the knowledge and participation of all members.
   - 1 = Decisions are seldom made with the knowledge and participation of all members.

2. How widely are responsibilities for group activities shared?
   - 4 = Most or all members share responsibility for group activities.
   - 3 = Many members share responsibility for group activities.
   - 2 = Some members share responsibility for group activities.
   - 1 = Only a few members share responsibility for group activities.

3. How much do members scrutinise the activities of their office bearers?
   - 4 = Members are very active in scrutinising the activities of their office bearers.
   - 3 = Members are sometimes active in scrutinising the activities of their office bearers.
   - 2 = Members are seldom active in scrutinising the activities of their office bearers.
   - 1 = Members are not active in scrutinising the activities of their office bearers.

4. How much sharing of leadership responsibilities is there?
   - 4 = There is great sharing of leadership responsibilities.
   - 3 = There is much sharing of leadership responsibilities.
   - 2 = There is some sharing of leadership responsibilities.
   - 1 = There is no sharing of leadership responsibilities.

5. How many members are ready, willing and able to assume leadership positions?
   4 = Most to all members are ready, willing and able to assume leadership positions.
   3 = About half of the members are ready, willing and able to assume leadership positions.
   2 = Less than a quarter of the members are ready, willing and able to assume leadership positions.
   1 = Only very few members are ready, willing and able to assume leadership positions.

6. How good are the chances that decisions that have been made will be implemented?
   4 = The chances that decisions that have been made will be implemented are extremely good.
   3 = The chances that decisions that have been made will be implemented are good.
   2 = The chances that decisions that have been made will be implemented are fairly good.
   1 = The chances that decisions that have been made will be implemented are small.

7. How many members participate in the meetings?
   4 = All members participate in the meetings.
   3 = Most members participate in the meetings.
   2 = Some members participate in the meetings.
   1 = Few members participate in the meetings.

8. How many members participate in other group activities?
   4 = All members participate in other group activities.
   3 = Most members participate in other group activities.
   2 = Some members participate in other group activities.
   1 = Few members participate in other group activities.

9. How productive are group meetings?
   4 = Group meetings are very productive.
   3 = Group meetings are productive.
   2 = Group meetings are fairly productive.
   1 = Group meetings are not very productive.

10. How many members usually come to group meetings?
    4 = Almost all (75%+) members usually come to group meetings.
    3 = Most (50–75%) members usually come to group meetings.
    2 = Less than half (25–49%) members usually come to group meetings.
    1 = A few (25%) members usually come to group meetings.

ADDENDUM : QUESTIONS AND ANSWERS FOR PARTICIPATORY SELF-EVALUATION

11. How good is communication within the group?
    4 = Communication within the group is extremely good.
    3 = Communication within the group is good.
    2 = Communication within the group is fairly good.
    1 = Communication within the group is poor.

12. How much information on group activities is communicated within the group?
    4 = A lot of information on group activities is communicated within the group.
    3 = Some information on group activities is communicated within the group.
    2 = Little information on group activities is communicated within the group.
    1 = No information on group activities is communicated within the group.

13. What is the quality of discussion during group meetings?
    4 = The quality of discussion during group meetings is extremely good.
    3 = The quality of discussion during group meetings is good.
    2 = The quality of discussion during group meetings is fair.
    1 = The quality of discussion during group meetings is poor.

14. How able is the group to maintain discipline in its ranks?
    4 = The group is very able to maintain discipline in its ranks.
    3 = The group is able to maintain discipline in its ranks.
    2 = The group is fairly able to maintain discipline in its ranks.
    1 = The group is not very able to maintain discipline in its ranks.

15. How able is the group to resolve internal conflict?
    4 = The group is very able to resolve internal conflict.
    3 = The group is able to resolve internal conflict.
    2 = The group is fairly able to resolve internal conflict.
    1 = The group is not very able to resolve internal conflict.

16. How clear are members about their tasks?
    4 = Members are very clear about their tasks.
    3 = Members are clear about their tasks.
    2 = Members are fairly clear about their tasks.
    1 = Members are not very clear about their tasks.

17. How satisfied are members about the fairness with which tasks are assigned?
    4 = Members are very satisfied about the fairness with which tasks are assigned.
    3 = Members are satisfied about the fairness with which tasks are assigned.
    2 = Members are fairly satisfied about the fairness with which tasks are assigned.
    1 = Members are not very satisfied about the fairness with which tasks are assigned.

18. How well are group objectives understood by the members?
    4 = Group objectives are very well understood by the members.
    3 = Group objectives are well understood by the members.
    2 = Group objectives are fairly well understood by the members.
    1 = Group objectives are not very well understood by the members.

19. How clearly is work shared among members?
    4 = Work is very clearly shared among members.
    3 = Work is fairly clearly shared among members.
    2 = Work is not very clearly shared among members.
    1 = Work is not clearly shared among members.

20. How many members contribute non-financial resources to the group?
    4 = All members contribute non-financial resources to the group.
    3 = Most members contribute non-financial resources to the group.
    2 = Some members contribute non-financial resources to the group.
    1 = Few members contribute non-financial resources to the group.

21. To what extent are members acquiring knowledge of better technology?
    4 = Members are acquiring knowledge of better technology to a great extent.
    3 = Members are acquiring knowledge of better technology to a large extent.
    2 = Members are acquiring knowledge of better technology to some extent.
    1 = Members are not acquiring knowledge of better technology.

22. To what extent does the group use local, indigenous technology?
    4 = The group fully uses local, indigenous technology.
    3 = The group generally uses local, indigenous technology.
    2 = The group uses some local, indigenous technology.
    1 = The group does not use local, indigenous technology.

23. To what extent is the group aware of the need to maintain facilities and equipment?
    4 = The group is well aware of the need to maintain facilities and equipment.
    3 = The group is aware of the need to maintain facilities and equipment.
    2 = The group is slightly aware of the need to maintain facilities and equipment.
    1 = The group is unaware of the need to maintain facilities and equipment.

24. How well does the group carry out maintenance on facilities and equipment?
    4 = The group carries out maintenance on facilities and equipment excellently.
    3 = The group carries out maintenance on facilities and equipment well.
    2 = The group carries out maintenance on facilities and equipment fairly well.
    1 = The group does not carry out maintenance on facilities and equipment.

ADDENDUM : QUESTIONS AND ANSWERS FOR PARTICIPATORY SELF-EVALUATION

25. How well does the group carry out quality control of production outputs?
    4 = The group carries out quality control of production outputs excellently.
    3 = The group carries out quality control of production outputs well.
    2 = The group carries out quality control of production outputs fairly well.
    1 = The group does not carry out quality control of production outputs.

26. How many members are involved in financial decision making?
    4 = All members are involved in financial decision making.
    3 = Most members are involved in financial decision making.
    2 = Some members are involved in financial decision making.
    1 = Only some members are involved in financial decision making.

27. How well are the financial affairs of the group run?
    4 = The financial affairs of the group are very well run.
    3 = The financial affairs of the group are well run.
    2 = The financial affairs of the group are fairly well run.
    1 = The financial affairs of the group are not very well run.

28. How well does the group progress towards self-reliance?
    4 = The group progresses towards self-reliance very well.
    3 = The group progresses towards self-reliance well.
    2 = The group progresses towards self-reliance fairly well.
    1 = The group is not progressing towards self-reliance.

29. How able is the group to operate without direction from the community worker?
    4 = The group is very able to operate without direction from the community worker.
    3 = The group is fairly able to operate without direction from the community worker.
    2 = The group is not very able to operate without direction from the community worker.
    1 = The group cannot operate without direction from the community worker.

30. To what extent is the group able to mobilise resources from within?
    4 = The group is very able to mobilise resources from within.
    3 = The group is able to mobilise resources from within.
    2 = The group is fairly able to mobilise resources from within.
    1 = The group is unable to mobilise resources from within.

31. To what extent do members show increased confidence?
    4 = Members show increased confidence to a great extent.
    3 = Members show increased confidence to a large extent.
    2 = Members show increased confidence to some extent.
    1 = Members show increased confidence to a small extent.

32. To what extent does the group monitor and evaluate its performance?
    4 = The group monitors and evaluates its performance to a great extent.
    3 = The group monitors and evaluates its performance to a large extent.
    2 = The group monitors and evaluates its performance to some extent.
    1 = The group monitors and evaluates its performance to a small extent.

33. To what extent is the group willing to try something new?
    4 = The group is more than willing to try something new.
    3 = The group is generally willing to try something new.
    2 = The group is not really willing to try something new.
    1 = The group is unwilling to try something new.

34. To what extent is the group helpful in getting similar projects among other groups off the ground?
    4 = The group is very helpful in getting similar projects among other groups off the ground.
    3 = The group is fairly helpful in getting similar projects among other groups off the ground.
    2 = The group is not really helpful in getting similar projects among other groups off the ground.
    1 = The group is not helpful at all in getting similar projects among other groups off the ground.

35. How does the group relate to government agencies?
    4 = The group relates excellently to government agencies.
    3 = The group relates well to government agencies.
    2 = The group relates fairly well to government agencies.
    1 = The group relates poorly to government agencies.

36. How does the group relate to NGOs?
    4 = The group relates excellently to NGOs.
    3 = The group relates well to NGOs.
    2 = The group relates fairly well to NGOs.
    1 = The group relates poorly to NGOs.

37. How does the group relate to CBOs?
    4 = The group relates excellently to CBOs.
    3 = The group relates well to CBOs.
    2 = The group relates fairly well to CBOs.
    1 = The group relates poorly to CBOs.

38. How well does the group co-ordinate with other role players?
    4 = The group co-ordinates very well with other role players.
    3 = The group co-ordinates well with other role players.
    2 = The group co-ordinates fairly well with other role players.
    1 = The group co-ordinates poorly with other role players.

ADDENDUM : QUESTIONS AND ANSWERS FOR PARTICIPATORY SELF-EVALUATION

39. How widely does the group co-ordinate with other role players?
    4 = The group co-ordinates very widely with other role players.
    3 = The group co-ordinates widely with other role players.
    2 = The group co-ordinates fairly widely with other role players.
    1 = The group does not co-ordinate with other role players.

40. How regularly does co-operation between the group and other role players take place?
    4 = Co-operation between the group and other role players takes place very regularly.
    3 = Co-operation between the group and other role players takes place regularly.
    2 = Co-operation between the group and other role players takes place fairly regularly.
    1 = Co-operation between the group and other role players does not take place.

41. How much community support does the group enjoy?
    4 = The group enjoys excellent community support.
    3 = The group enjoys good community support.
    2 = The group enjoys fairly good community support.
    1 = The group enjoys little community support.

42. How able is the group to resist pressure from outside?
    4 = The group is very able to resist pressure from outside.
    3 = The group is able to resist pressure from outside.
    2 = The group is fairly able to resist pressure from outside.
    1 = The group is not very able to resist pressure from outside.

Product questions

1. How well are group objectives achieved?
    4 = Group objectives are fully achieved.
    3 = Group objectives are mostly achieved.
    2 = Group objectives are partly achieved.
    1 = Group objectives are not achieved.

2. To what extent has the group been successful at generating income for its members?
    4 = The group has been very successful at generating income for its members.
    3 = The group has been successful at generating income for its members.
    2 = The group has been fairly successful at generating income for its members.
    1 = The group has not been very successful at generating income for its members.

3. How successful is the group at expanding its activities?
    4 = The group is very successful at expanding its activities.
    3 = The group is successful at expanding its activities.
    2 = The group is fairly successful at expanding its activities.
    1 = The group is not very successful at expanding its activities.

4. To what extent has production output increased?
   4 = Production output has increased dramatically.
   3 = Production output has increased substantially.
   2 = Production output has increased somewhat.
   1 = Production output has increased very little.

5. To what extent has the group increased its assets?
   4 = The group has increased its assets dramatically.
   3 = The group has increased its assets substantially.
   2 = The group has increased its assets somewhat.
   1 = The group has not increased its assets.

6. How effectively, in terms of time, was the objective attained?
   4 = In terms of time, the objective was attained in a very effective way.
   3 = In terms of time, the objective was attained in an effective way.
   2 = In terms of time, the objective was attained in a fairly effective way.
   1 = In terms of time, the objective was attained in an ineffective way.

7. How effectively, in terms of economy, was the objective attained?
   4 = In terms of economy, the objective was attained in a very effective way.
   3 = In terms of economy, the objective was attained in an effective way.
   2 = In terms of economy, the objective was attained in a fairly effective way.
   1 = In terms of economy, the objective was attained in an ineffective way.

8. How effectivel,y in terms of effort, was the objective attained?
   4 = In terms of effort, the objective was attained in a very effective way.
   3 = In terms of effort, the objective was attained in an effective way.
   2 = In terms of effort, the objective was attained in a fairly effective way.
   1 = In terms of effort, the objective was attained in an ineffective way.

9. To what extent does the attained objective serve its planned purpose?
   4 = The attained objective serves its planned purpose perfectly.
   3 = The attained objective serves its planned purpose to a large extent.
   2 = The attained objective serves its planned purpose to a lesser extent.
   1 = The attained objective does not serve its planned purpose.

10. To what extent does the attained objective serve the interests of the larger society?
    4 = The attained objective serves the interests of the larger society to a great extent.
    3 = The attained objective serves the interests of the larger society to a large extent.
    2 = The attained objective serves the interests of the larger society to a limited extent.
    1 = The attained objective does not serve the interests of the larger society.

ADDENDUM : QUESTIONS AND ANSWERS FOR PARTICIPATORY SELF-EVALUATION

11. To what extent does the group have the ability to maintain the attained objective?
    4 = The group has great ability to maintain the attained objective.
    3 = The group has some ability to maintain the attained objective.
    2 = The group has little ability to maintain the attained objective.
    1 = The group has no ability to maintain the attained objective.

12. To what extent does the group have the ability to improve the attained objective?
    4 = The group has great ability to improve the attained objective.
    3 = The group has some ability to improve the attained objective.
    2 = The group has little ability to improve the attained objective.
    1 = The group has no ability to improve the attained objective.

13. How satisfied is the group with the attained objective?
    4 = The group is extremely satisfied with the attained objective.
    3 = The group is well satisfied with the attained objective.
    2 = The group is fairly satisfied with the attained objective.
    1 = The group is not satisfied with the attained objective.

14. To what extent has the attained objective strengthened the group?
    4 = The attained objective has strengthened the group to a great extent.
    3 = The attained objective has strengthened the group somewhat.
    2 = The attained objective has strengthened the group a little.
    1 = The attained objective has not strengthened the group.

Questions evaluating the community development worker

1. What is the community development worker's reaction if something is not done on time?
    4 = The community development worker asks the group wat the reason for the delay was.
    3 = The community development worker urges the group to establish the reason for the delay.
    2 = The community development worker urges the group to stamp out delays.
    1 = The community development worker castigates the group or the person responsible for the delay.

2. What is the community worker's reaction if a mistake is made?
    4 = The community development worker helps the group to see what they can learn from the mistake.
    3 = The community development worker tells the group that they must find the reason for the mistake so that it will not be repeated.
    2 = The community development worker urges the group to stamp out mistakes.
    1 = The community development worker castigates the group or the person responsible for the mistake.

3. What is the community development worker's attitude during meetings?
   4 = The community development worker is part of the group and learns along with the group.
   3 = The community development worker is sympathetic and tells the group where they are going wrong or right.
   2 = The community development worker is bored and cannot understand why the group meetings progress so slowly.
   1 = The community development worker runs the meetings with rigid discipline.

4. What is the community development worker's role in the meetings?
   4 = The community development worker participates just like any other member of the group.
   3 = The community development worker acts as adviser and guide in the meeting.
   2 = The community development worker is the 'clearing house' for all decisions.
   1 = The community development worker is the chairperson of the meeting.

5. What role does the community development worker play in decision making?
   4 = The community development worker only helps the group so that they can make decisions.
   3 = The community development worker and the group make decisions together.
   2 = The community development worker usually suggests to the group what decisions to make.
   1 = The community development worker usually makes the decisions.

6. With whom does the community development worker associate?
   4 = The community development worker associates with all members of the group.
   3 = The community development worker associates with members who are active.
   2 = The community development worker associates with the executive committee members.
   1 = The community development worker associates only with the chairperson.

7. What is the community development worker's role in implementing decisions?
   4 = The community development worker does his/her bit just as the other members of the group do.
   3 = The community development worker does the more complicated tasks with an understudy to learn from him/her.
   2 = The community development worker does the more complicated tasks.
   1 = The community development worker does not involve him- or herself in implementing decisions.
   OR
   1 = The community development worker does most of the implementation him- or herself.

ADDENDUM: QUESTIONS AND ANSWERS FOR PARTICIPATORY SELF-EVALUATION

8. How does the community development worker facilitate the learning process?
   4 = The community development worker helps the group to identify items of learning as they arise.
   3 = The community development worker identifies items of learning and indicates them to the group.
   2 = The community development worker identifies items of learning and lectures the group on them.
   1 = The community development worker does not facilitate the learning process.

9. What is the community development worker's role in evaluation?
   4 = The community development worker helps the group to do proper evaluation.
   3 = The community development worker helps the executive committee to do proper evaluation.
   2 = The community development worker and one or two of the office bearers do the evaluation.
   1 = The community development worker does the evaluation alone.

10. How much does the community development worker know about community development?
    4 = The community development worker knows everything about community development.
    3 = The community development worker knows a lot about community development.
    2 = The community development worker knows a fair amount about community development.
    1 = The community development worker does not know much about community development.

11. To what extent does the community development worker understand the community's situation?
    4 = The community development worker understands the community's situation perfectly.
    3 = The community development worker has a fair understanding of the community's situation.
    2 = The community development worker does not understand the community's situation very well.
    1 = The community development worker does not understand the community's situation.

12. To what extent does the community development worker show respect for the people's norms, traditions and wishes?
    4 = The community development worker shows great respect.
    3 = The community development worker shows respect.
    2 = The community development worker shows some respect.
    1 = The community development worker shows little respect.

13. How much does the group appreciate the community development worker?
    4 = The group appreciates the community development worker very much.
    3 = The group appreciates the community development worker.
    2 = The group has some appreciation for the community development worker.
    1 = The group does not appreciate the community development worker.

GLOSSARY

A
abide: stick to; adhere to
accrue: increase over time
acute: serious; important
ad hoc: Latin phrase meaning 'for this'; a solution designed for a specific problem or task
adjunctive: complementary
adverse: hostile; opposing
affinity: natural feeling of liking and understanding
affluent: wealthy
aligned: associated
allay: diminish; reduce
alleged: claimed a wrongdoing
aloofness: being distant
altruistic: concerned about wellbeing of others
ambit: range; sphere
ambivalence: having mixed or contradictory ideas
amorphous: having no definite form
animosity: hostility
annexures: appendices; supplements to documents
anomaly: difference; inconsistency
antagonising: irritating
anticipate: expect; do in advance
antics: tricks
apathy: indifference; lethargy; unconcerned
apprehensive: anticipating with fear
arbitrator: judge
arduous: difficult
armoury: supply of skills (figurative); supply of weapons (literal)
ascribed: attributed; assigned
aspirations: ambitions; goals
assertive: a confident and forceful attitude
assets: useful and/or valuable things
attainment: reaching or achieving a goal
attentive: paying close attention to
augment: to make larger; increase
autonomy: self-governing; independence

B
banalities: predictable; unhelpful comments
benevolent: kind; caring
bona fides: documentary evidence showing that a person is what they claim to be; a person's honesty and sincerity of intention
bungling: unskilled; clumsy

C
calibre: standard; quality
catalysts: people who bring about change
caucusing: the practice where a portion of the membership of a

voting body agrees to vote as a political bloc
causality: the relationship between something that happens or exists and the thing that causes it
civic: public
civility: politeness
claustrophobic: confining; suffocating
cohesion: consistence
collective: doing or having things together as a group
commotion: disorder; uproar
composition: arrangement; structure
compounded: made more intense or complex
concise: brief; short
concomitant: associated
concretised: made real or particular
conducive: favourable; helpful
conduits: channels
confluence: meeting; coming together
consensus: general agreement
consequences: results
contentment: peaceful satisfaction
context: setting within which something happens
culminate: end up; climax
culmination: conclusion; result
curative: healing
cyclic: recurring; repeated

D
daunting: overwhelming
deferential: respectful; polite
delinquency: criminal behaviour by young people
demagogue: speaker who uses manipulation rather than reason
determinant: factor that determines an outcome
detriment: harm or damage
detrimental: harmful; negative
deviations: not sticking to plan or norm
dichotomy: division or contrast
discrete: separate; isolated
discretion: judgement; not attracting attention
disdain: feeling something is not worth attention; disliking something
disentangle: remove tangles; separate
disposition: attitude
disseminating: spreading widely
distortion: meaning that has changed; misleading information
docile: submissive; undemanding
dwindle: decrease; reduce
dysfunctional: impaired or abnormal functioning

E
elusive: difficult to grasp
emanating: originating from; spreading out from
empathetic: concerned; compassionate
empathy: understanding; compassion
encapsulates: captures; sums up
endogenous: internal cause or origin
engender: give rise to
enhance: improve quality
entity: unit; body
enumerate: make a list; establish number
episodic: irregular; a series of separate events
equilibrium: balance
equitable: fair
eradication: removal; destruction
erode: wear down
etcetera: and so on
evolved: changed; progressed

exhorting: urging; encouraging
existentialism: belief regarding the existence of the individual
expedient: convenient
externalise: attribute to external or outside causes
exude: radiate; display

F
flounder: stumble; struggle
foci: emphasis
foster: promote the development of
fraught: filled with danger
fruition: fulfilment

G
grandiose: grand; impressive
geotag: shows the physical location where a photo or other information was uploaded on a social platform

H
hamper: obstruct; hinder
haphazardly: randomly; unplanned
hectic: very busy; chaotic
heterogeneous: mixed; various
heuristics: a mental shortcut commonly used to simplify problems
hierarchical: ranking from top to bottom
homogeneous: of the same kind
honed: perfected; improved
hypochondriacal: having a tendency to fear or imagine that you have illnesses that you do not actually have

I
idiosyncratic: individual; peculiar to oneself
impeded: delayed or blocked
imperative: vitally important; authoritative
in toto: Latin phrase meaning totally
incentive: motivation; encouragement
inclined: likely to; wishing to
increment: cause an increase or boost growth
indigenous: naturally occurring in a certain place
induced: brought about; persuaded or convinced to do something
innate: natural; inborn
institutionalise: make fixed; have a recurring value or place
insurmountable: overwhelming; impossible to overcome
interlude: pause
intonation: pitch of voice
intrinsic: natural; essential

J
jargon: technical terminology known only to a small group
jeopardising: putting at risk; endangering

L
lateral: sideways; horizontal
lectern: stand
lethargy: weariness; laziness; lack of motivation
linear: in a straight line; without deviation
loath: unwilling; reluctant
loiter: hang around idly

M
mandates: commands; decrees; directives
mannerism: gesture

mediator: intermediary; referee; negotiator
menial: unskilled; boring
methodology: method; approach
milieu: setting; environment
minutes: written records
mitigate: making less severe or less harsh
mode: method
monologues: speeches where only one person speaks
monosyllabic: containing only one syllable
morsel: piece; scrap
muddle: disorder; confusion
multifaceted: having many facets or sides
mundane: lacking excitement
murky: cloudy; unclear

N

negated: nullified; ignored
nominal group technique: a group process involving problem identification, solution generation and decision making
nullified: cancelled out

O

obligations: moral duties
obviates: prevents
operationalise: put into use
optimal: ideal; best
optimise: make the most effective use
oracle: person of wisdom; prophet
orchestrators: organisers; co-ordinators; managers

P

paradigm: way of looking at something
parameters: boundary that defines scope
paternalistic: acting as if others are subordinate
perceived: seen or understood to
permeates: spreads
permutations: several possible variations or combinations
perpetuated: made to continue
perturbed: made anxious; worried
physiological: physical; biological
plenary: all participants meeting at the same time
plethora: a large number; excess
plight: difficult situation
pluralistic: diverse; mixed
precarious: uncertain
predetermined: decided in advance
premise: underlying assumption
preparatory: introductory; in preparation
prerogatives: choices
proffered: given; submitted
proficient: capable; skilful
profound: intense
proliferate: multiply; increase
prompted: caused; brought about
pros and cons: favourable and unfavourable conditions/factors/reasons
protracted: extended; expanded
psychological: mental; spiritual

Q

quantifiable: measurable; can be counted
quasi-: mock; self-styled
quorum: a minimum number of members that must be present at a meeting before a vote or other business can take place

R

rapport: close relationship
rationalistic: accepting reason as the highest authority
reciprocity: doing or giving something in return
reiterate: repeat
replication: repetition
retaliate: attack in return
retention: holding; keeping
revisit: come back
rhetoric: speech-making
rivalries: jealousies; competition

S

scenario: specific setting
scrutiny: inspection; inquiry
self-reliant: able to rely on own abilities and strengths
sensory: relating to the senses
sequentially: in order; chronologically
sham: pretence; falsehood
shirk: avoid; dodge
slight: insult
smouldering: slowly burning
solicit: try to obtain something
spatially: in space; three-dimensionally
specificity: quality of a fixed action or value
spin-off: benefit produced during activity
spiral: coiled like a corkscrew
strife: trouble; conflict
subsequent: following; next
subtleties: delicate qualities
synchronises: makes something happen at the same time
synergy: an effect greater than the sum of separate effects
synoptic: comprehensive; broad view
systemisation: to arrange in an order or system

T

tandem: together; as a team
tangible: touchable; concrete
tendency: trend; desire
tinged: shaded; tinted
torpedo: destroy; wreck
triangulation: to validate information through cross-checking

U

ulterior: hidden; underhanded
unbridled: uncontrolled
unorthodox: unconventional
Utopian: idealistic; perfect

V

vacuum: empty space
variable: something that changes
venture: undertaking; risk
vigorous: energetic; strong
vis-à-vis: in relation to
vistas: views; outlooks
viz: Latin abbreviation meaning 'namely'
volatile: unstable
vulnerability: weakness; exposure to harm

X

xenophobic: showing dislike or fear of people from other countries

INDEX

Note: References in *italics* are to figures or tables.

A

ABC of successful negotiation outcomes *231–233*
absolute poverty 7–8
acceptance
    barriers to 166–167
    of community development practitioners/professionals (CDPs) 326–327
access facilitators role of community development practitioners/professionals (CDPs) 489
accountability of community development practitioners/professionals (CDPs) 515
accuracy in public speaking 290–291
action at grassroots level 81
action groups 330, 355, 357, 358–359, 384–385
action training 420, *420*
active listening 174, 200, 218, 449
adaptation, responsive anticipatory 103
adaptive administration 71
    partnership action 105–106
    practical principle 105–106
adaptive incrementalist approach to planning 376–377
adaptiveness
    and community resilience to shocks 106
    difficult to attain with complex projects 107
    in monitoring and evaluation 397
adaptive orientation 48–49
ad hoc groups 119–120, 192, 564–565, 566–570
adult learners 442–445
advisory role of community development practitioners/professionals (CDPs) 133
advocacy role of community development practitioners/professionals (CDPs) 134
affect 253–254
alternatives 369–370
altruism 50
amotivated motivation 242
anonymity and confidentiality 334
Another Development 73
appropriateness, criterion in monitoring and evaluation 401–402

assessment
    and monitoring of progress 467–468
    of product in training workshops 468–469
    role in training 466–467
    of skills 467
    of training workshops 466–469
asset-based community development 16, 68, 73–74, 82, 84, 351, 512
assumptions at meetings 277
attitudes
    of community development practitioners/professionals (CDPs) 130–132, 315
    of trainees 443, 467–468
audience inhibition 249
audio clips 436
autonomy 103
awareness creation
    outcomes 83–84
    realisation of need for change 325

B

barriers
    to acceptance 166–167
    to collaboration 53–54, 54–55
    to communication 164–176
basic needs approach (BNA) 67–68
behaviour
    change models 249–250
    definition 240
    helping 247–249
    of leaders, improving 187–189
    and motivation 239, 246–247
big project trap 107

Black Consciousness Movement 501–502
blueprint approach to community development 70, 103, 105
blueprint planning 105
body language *see* non-verbal communication
bottom–up approach 4, 31, 70, 103, 105
boundary maintenance 196–197
brainstorming 369, 430–431
bureaucracies
    changing role of 71, 74
    principles to promote empowerment development 71
business plans
    format 265–268
    fundraising 268–270
    not planning document 264
    uses 265
buzz groups 428–429
buzz value of participation 93
bystander effect 249

C

capability
    approach 72–73
    behaviour change 250, *251*
capacity builders role of community development practitioners/professionals (CDPs) 489, 504–505
capacity building 70, 86, 135–136, 417 *see also* training workshops
    approach to training 441
    and leadership 188–189
    needs of stakeholders 135

case studies 549–578
    active participants in eradicating need 551, 564–565
    ad hoc groups 564–565, 566–570
    advantages 432–433, 434
    attitude and action of community development worker 574–575
    attitude, place and role of community development worker 554–555
    checklist for chairpersons 576–577
    chronic poverty 550
    clashing interests 558
    collaboration, lack of 571–574
    commitment 560–561
    communication 566–570
    conflict and animosity 558
    contact making 558–560
    deprivation trap 549, 550
    desperate woman 550
    divided communities 557–558
    empowerment, lack of 553, 571–574
    environmental problem management 575
    failure of projects 553, 555–556, 557, 558–560
    felt need vs real need 562–564
    further development 564–565, 571–574
    government imposing development 552
    government organisation breaking down initiative 555–556
    group maintenance 558
    human development 566–570
    humility, lack of 574–575
    ignoring people in development projects 553
    individual inputs 566–570
    inept community development worker 576–577
    learning opportunities 562–564
    limitations to using 433–434
    making contact 558–560
    mistakes of community development worker 560–561
    motivation 552–553
    needs, real vs felt 562–564
    non-recognition of human dignity 575
    offending people 575
    participation 552–553
    paternalism 574
    politics 557–558
    poverty trap 550
    PRAP technique 343
    problem people 577–578
    rationale for using 432–434
    real need vs felt need 562–564
    release 564–565
    relevance for training 431–432
    simplicity principle 554
    stakeholders 571–574
    status quo bias 558–560
    successful projects 564–565
    sustainability of projects, need for 575
    take-over of projects 557
    taking ownership 564–565, 571
    top–down approach to community development 552, 553, 555–556

transformation 564–565
turning situation round 551
use in training 431–432
views and feelings 554–555
causality and linkage exercise 359–360, *361*
causes of conflict 206–207
cell phones in training sessions 465–466
chairpersons of meetings
    checklists 280–281
    duties 280
    and problem people 281–285
challenges to community development practitioners/professionals (CDPs) 516–518
change agents role of community development practitioners/professionals (CDPs) 489, 500, 503–513
channels of information 154–155
chronic poverty 7, 22
citizen control 93, *94*, 118
citizen participation in democracy 515
citizen power 93, *94*
civil society stakeholders 46
clarity in public speaking 290
clashing interests or personalities 214, 218–219
climate for learning, setting 422–424
cognitive dissonance 244
collaboration *see also* co-ordination
    case study 571–574
    constraints and barriers 53–54, 54–55

discussion forums 52–53
facilitation of through legal body 57
networks 50–51
phases 58
practices 54–58
preconditions 58
six-step process 55–57
collective action 54, 78
collective participation 33
Com-B behaviour change model 250
commitment 147, 254, 437, 560–561
committee, at start of project 365–366
communication *see also* non-verbal communication; verbal communication
    barriers and causes of conflicts 216
    barriers to acceptance 166–167
    barriers to reception 164–165
    barriers to understanding 165–166
    case study 566–570
    as cause of conflict 206
    channels 154–155, 162
    coding 162
    context 163
    cyclic 163–164, 448, 450
    deliberate blocking of processes 216
    and enthusiasm 298–299
    feedback 171, 216
    immediacy behaviour 162
    during implementation process 217
    Johari window 170

INDEX

and leadership 185, 189–190
medium 162
message 162
and misunderstanding 218
models 161–164, 177
overcoming barriers on psychological level 169–171
overcoming barriers on technical level 171–172
participatory 400
reasons for barriers 168–169
receiver 162
self-disclosure 170
sender 161–162
small groups 190–191
training workshops 448–450
trust 171
communication skills *see also* operational writing; public speaking
    active listening 174, 200, 218
    development communication 176–178
    horizontal rather than traditional vertical communication 177
    learning of 85
    overcoming barriers 169–176
    training workshops 443
community
    ad hoc groups 119–120, 564–565, 566–570
    belonging 113
    definition in terms of geography 114
    definition on two levels 115–116
    elected committees 120
    groupings 113
    interest groups 118–119
    natural resource management perspective 115
    ordinary concerned people 116
    resilience 48
    as role player 116–120
    as stakeholder 116–120
    system-maintaining context 116–117
    system-transformation context 117
community activism 508–511
community advocates 507
community-based organisations (CBOs) 191, 357
community-based sector stakeholders 46
community-based social movements 509–510
community building
    outcomes 85–86
    role of community development practitioners/professionals (CDPs) 504–505
community development
    background 500–503
    British colonial policy 64, 505–506
    definitions 63, 501
    early history 63–66, 505
    identity crisis 532
    method 67, 68
    process 67, 68
    themes 66
Community Development Practice Policy Framework (CDPPF), 2014 (Draft) 483–484, 488

roles and responsibilities of community development practitioners/professionals (CDPs) 489–490, 542–546
community development practitioners/professionals (CDPs)
    acceptance of 326–327
    accountability 515
    attitude 130–132, 315
    authentic dialogue 128
    challenges to profession 516–518
    compassion 104–105, 131, 328–329
    contextual aspects guiding CDP's task 124–126
    creation of learning opportunities 104
    as 'cross-cutting' stakeholders 43–44
    diary 409
    economic challenges to 518–519
    empowerment of people 130
    enhancement of learning process 129
    ethical guidelines 126–128
    facilitation skills 200–201
    goals 129–130
    human resource practices 126
    humility 103, 131, 197
    improper acts or omissions 127
    laws affecting 493–497
    legislative and policy frameworks 481, 482, 489–490
    management with technology 308
    operational strategy 124–125, 324
    political challenges to 514–515
    position 128–129
    professionalisation of 123
    relationship with government and community 502
    as reservoirs of information 96
    roles 132–137, 198, 472, 481, 489–490, 503–513
    training 126
    transparency 515
community driven processes, external expertise and 117
community expectations 210
community initiative 67
community inputs 146
community intervention programme for change 503
community resilience to shocks, and adaptiveness 48, 106
compassion, practical principle 104–105, 131, 328–329
completeness in public speaking 291
confidence of trainees 444
confidentiality and anonymity 334
conflict
    and animosity 558
    causes 206–207, 209–215
    clashing personalities 214, 219
    community structures and institutions insufficiently recognised 214–215
    competition for resources 210–211
    cultural differences 212, 227
    definition 206, 207
    in developing countries 215
    natural social phenomenon with functional value 208

need for consensus 213, 228
perceptions of 228–229
and poor communication 206
prevention 218–220
project priorities and boundaries poorly aligned with community expectations 210
project schedules poorly planned 209
resolution through negotiation 206
role dependency 211
sources of 209–215
technical issues 213
and tension 208, 227
and tolerance 220
unintended consequences 217

conflict management
ethnic 210–211
methodology of 230–231
strategies 222–228, 229–230

conflict resolution
ABC of successful outcomes 231–233
and culture 212
mechanism to deal with unintended consequences 217
mediation 221
negotiation 220
operational (secondary) level 230
potential duality of conflict 208
steps before and during negotiations 221–222
strategic (primary) level 229–230
types 221, 222

conscientisation, ethical principle 102

consensus
need for 213, 228
on needs 358–359

Constitution of the Republic of South Africa, 1996
Bill of Rights 483, 506
and discrimination 506
ultimate law of South Africa 482–483

consultation 66, 93, 94

contact making
case studies 316–322, 558–560
different groups with different needs 358–359
entry into area 325–326
goals 326–331
objectives 315
preparation for entry 322–324
process 316

contents and relevance of training workshops 470–471

contextual aspects guiding CDP's task 124–126

control of projects
course adjustments 397
management function 146, 410–411
principle of adaptiveness 397

conviction in public speaking 291–292

co-option
to community-initiated action 66–69
for empowerment 97
as system-maintaining mechanism 117
undermining of participation 95

co-ordination 50–58 *see also* collaboration
    discussion forums 52–53
    environment in which it takes place 51–52
    strategy principles 51–52
    themes 52
cost–benefit analysis 105
cost recovery 147, 148
COVID-19 pandemic, impact 28, 29
cultural differences 212, 449–450
cultural environment 34–36
cyber attacks 309
cycle of poverty *see* deprivation trap

D

data overload at meetings 275
decentralisation
    of decision making processes 118
    of government 482
decision making
    centralised 143
    decentralisation of processes 118
    decisions register 388
    group 151–153
    meetings 274
    need for information 153–155
    participatory 143
    power 96, 97
    and problem solving 367, 370
    right to 103
defaults 252–253
delivery in public speaking 297–302
democratic features of community development 82–83

demonstration effect outcomes 84–85
Department of Social Development (DSD) 484
dependency situations 128
deprivation trap 14–16, *15*, 74, 89–90, 101, 308, 447, 549, 550
development communication 175–178
development environment
    global context of policy formulation 28–30
    local 30–37
    Millennium Development Goals (MDGs) 38
    Sustainable Development Goals (SDGs) 27, 28, 30, 38
development management
    integration of community and technical inputs 146
    vs ordinary management 146
dialogical man 418
dialogue 128
digital needs 304
dignity
    case study 575
    meaning 90
    promotion of 92, 132
direct observation 341
discipline at training workshops 451–457
discussion
    forums 52–53
    techniques 408–409
    training dialogue 420, *421*
dissemination of information 153
distraction 199

domination 199
'do no harm' principle 309, 334, 335
donor dependency 353
drainage, water and sewage 18
dynamics of groups 135, 192–193, 450–451

E

early history of community development 63–66
economic challenges to community development practitioners/professionals (CDPs) 518–519
economic environment 36
education 20
effectiveness
    criterion in monitoring and evaluation 402–403
    in objective attainment 403–404
    in terms of principles 404–405
    verbal communication 289–292
ego 254
elected committees 120
empowerment
    case studies 553, 571–574
    decision-making power 96
    end goal 95
    ethical principles 95–97
    information or knowledge 96, 133
    and learning 103–104
    milieu 336
    and participation 33, 38
    political power 95
    process 4, 53, 95
empowerment strategies, definition of development 70

enabling environment 48–49, 100
enabling role
    of bureaucracies 71
    of community development practitioners/professionals (CDPs) 135–136, 144–145
    of organisations 48–49
enthusiasm 298–299
entrepreneurial resources 357
entry into area 325–326
equilibrium of poverty 8, 21–22
    anti-equilibrium attitude 21
equitable community development 49
ethical guidelines 126–128
ethical principles
    conscientisation 102
    empowerment 95–97
    human orientation 89–92
    ownership 97–98
    participation 92–95, *94*
    release 101–102
    sustainability 98–100
ethics, and protection of personal information 309–310
ethnic conflict management 210–211
Ettawah project 65
evaluation *see* monitoring and evaluation
event cards 407–408, *408*
expectations
    climate for learning 422, 423–424
    and questions of power at meetings 276

experience
    different levels of in trainees 444
    as learning source for trainees 444
external expertise, and community driven processes 117
external motivation 242–243
external resources 353

F

Facebook 307
facilitation 57, 137
    ensuring participation 424–425
    expectations of trainees 445–446
    by group leader 427–428
    problems agenda 445–447
    of role play and games 435–436
    scarcity of facilitators 471–472
    skills required for groups 200–201
    teaching agenda 445–447
    training dialogue 418–419, 422
facilitatory role of community development practitioners/ professionals (CDPs) 33, 137, 198, 472
fear, climate for learning 422–423
feasibility
    criterion in monitoring and evaluation 402
    studies 105
features of community development
    action at grassroots level 81
    asset based 82
    collective action 78
    democratic 82–83
    integrated approach 77–78
    needs orientation 79–80
    objective orientation 80–81
feedback 145, 171, 216, 469
felt need 362–363, 366, 562–564
first project meeting
    committee 366–367
    content of 365–366
    invitations to 363
    result of contact-making phase 363
    roles of community development practitioners/professionals (CDPs) 364–365
food security 19
formulation of needs 358, 359–360
freedom, meaning 90
fundraising, pitfalls 268–270
further development outcomes 84

G

games
    advantages of using 432–433
    facilitation 435–436
    limitations to using 433–434
    rationale for using 432–434
    relevance for training 431–432
generalist professionals 499
global context of policy formulation 28–30, 480
goals of community development practitioners/professionals (CDPs) 129–130
goals of participation 142–143
governmental organisations 191
government-community partnership *see* public-private partnership

government departments 484
government spheres 481–484
Grameen Bank 48
grassroots level action 81
green war hypothesis 215
group decision making *see also* participatory management
    advantages 151
    disadvantages 152
    guidelines for success 152–153
group facilitation skills 200–201
group inequality 215
group interviews and discussions 342
group learning 445
groups
    boundary maintenance 196–197
    dynamics 135, 192–193, 450–451
    evaluation 195
    identity 194
    leadership 195
    maintenance 195, 558
    morale 193
    non-participation 199
    psychology 193
    small 115, 190
    strengthening 195–196
    success 196
    support for 198, 201
    threats to success 198–200
    wellbeing 194–197
groupthink 228
group walks 341
group work 426–428
    venue 458–459

guiding role of community development practitioners/professionals (CDPs) 132–133

H
health facilities 18–19
HIV/AIDS, education as preventive weapon 20
holism 99, 531
hot-cold empathy gap 253–254
human capabilities 12, 91
Human Development Index (HDI) 12, *12*
humanitarian engineering 384
human orientation
    compassion and 104
    as ethical principle 89–92, 128
human resource development, definition 356
human resource practices 126
human resources 355–357
Human Scale Development (HSD) approach 71–72
humility 103, 131, 197, 418, 574–575

I
identified motivation 244
identity of groups 194
impact studies 105
implementation *see also* planning
    checklist 391
    community participation 390–392
    conclusion of 391–392
    greatest test of planning 378
    immediately after planning 390

management responsibility 146
and participatory learning 378
policies 485, 487, 516
process 389
role of community development practitioners/professionals (CDPs) 392–393
incentives 252
incrementalist approach to planning 376–377
indigenous culture 35
indigenous knowledge 146
indigenous skills, vs technical skills 146–147
individual poverty 6, 27
influencers 163
informal economic sector 36, 45
informal settlements 20
information
    channels 154–155
    for decision making 96, 153–155
    deliberate blocking of flow 216
    dissemination 153
    provision by community development practitioners/professionals (CDPs) 133
    sources 133
    types 154
informed and voluntary consent 334
infrastructure 354–355
Instagram 307
Institute for Rural Reconstruction 64
institution building 86
institutions, in society 113–114
integrated approach 77–78

integrated development planning 82
integrated motivation 244–245
interactive (workshop) techniques 425–431
interconnectedness
    between community and nature 418
    between individual and community 418
interest groups 118–119, 357
inter-governmental relations 482
international financial power 73
intrinsic motivation 245, 246
introjected motivation 243–244
intrusion 216
irresponsibility 199

J
Johari window 170

K
knowledge
    for decision making 96
    determination of 467
    informal evidence of 467
    local 146
    relationship with culture and environment 99
    system 99, 100
    of and for trainees 443

L
laws affecting community development practitioners/professionals (CDPs) 125
leadership
    behaviour, improving 187–189

and communication 185, 189–190
components *183–184*
and capacity building 188–189
cyclical input–output model 190
definition of concept 182–183
of groups 195
importance 185–187
improvement 187–189
maturity 185
role expectations 186–187
skills 86
for successful community development initiatives 184–190
support for 197
threats to success 198–200

leadership development and group facilitation
    group facilitation skills 200–201
    groups 190–197
    support and enablement 197–198
    threats to success 198–200

learning
    CDPs' creation of opportunities 104
    CDPs' enhancement of process 129
    climate for 422–424
    communication skills 85
    components 105
    and evaluation 399–400
    and participation 102–103
    practical principle 102–104
    process approach 70–71, 325
    from reality 100
    reciprocal 99
    reflective 420
    of skills 85
    styles 445
    theory of autobiographical learning 418

learning outcomes of community development 85

legislation
    impact of post-apartheid democratic constitution reform 480–481
    and policy frameworks 475, 493–497
    purpose 480

linkages in society 86
livelihood security 22
local development environment 30–37
local economy
    development support 21
    stagnant 20–21
local government
    integrated development planning 82
    mandate 482, 519
    responsibilities 482
local knowledge *see* indigenous knowledge
local skills *see* indigenous skills
local survey 329
logical frameworks 147–148
    analysis 379–382
    logframe *380*

M

maintenance of groups 195
management information 154

manipulation
    by chairperson at meetings 275
    ladder of participation 93, *94*
manufactured resources 354–355
mapping 333, 436
Maslow's hierarchy of needs 10–11, *11*, 241, 304, *304*
Maslow's theory of motivation 10
maturity 185
mediation 221
meetings
    chairperson 280–285
    common problems 274–277
    criteria for good 277
    cycle 273
    environment 277
    members 286
    procedures 278–279
    role players 280–286
    secretary 285–286
    types 274
messenger 251
Millennium Development Goals (MDGs) 38
mindset 106, 108
MINDSPACE 251–254
minute taking 270–271
    decisions register 388
    planning meetings 388, 389
misunderstanding 218
mobilisation 97, 98
modernisation paradigm 3, 213
monitoring and evaluation
    central issues for evaluation 399
    control 397, 410–411
    criteria 401–406

discussion and observation as technique 408–409
do's and don'ts 409–410
evaluation as part of educational process 399–400
evaluation debate 398
event cards 407–408, *408*
motivation for evaluation 400
participatory evaluation 399–400
participatory management 146, 149
participatory self-evaluation 198
policies 485, 487
radical interpretative approach 399
record-keeping 406–408
reports 407
morale 193
motivation
    and behaviour 239, 246–247, 250, *251*
    case study 552–553
    continuum ranging from controlled to autonomous 242
    definition 241
    and group dynamics 450–451
    and maturity 185
    and mobilisation 251–255
    and participatory management 145
    private 215
    self-determination theory (SDT) 242–246, *245*
    types 242–246, *245*
motivational information 153, 154
Multidimensional Poverty Index (MPI) 12

indicators linked to specific SDG
    12, *13*
multi-direction syndrome in meetings
    274
multiple conversations at meetings
    275

N

national government 481
natural resources 353–354
needs
    analysis 329–331
    belonging 14
    concrete 129
    consensus on 358–359
    digital *304*
    esteem 14
    formulation 358, 359–360
    grassroots level 81
    identification 79–80, 326, 330–331, 358
    orientation 79–80, 425
    real vs felt 362–363, 562–564
    safety 13
    self-actualisation 14
negative energy 207
negative self-perception 80
negative state relief model 247–248
negotiation
    ABC of successful outcomes
        231–233
    as conflict resolution 220
networks 50–51
nominal group technique 429–430
non-governmental organisations
    (NGOs) 191
        commercialisation of sector
            514–515

non-government stakeholders 46
non-participation
    levels 93, *94*
    threat to group's success 199
non-verbal communication 448,
    449–450 *see also* communication;
    verbal communication
        delivery in public speaking 297
        immediacy behaviour 162
norms 252, 356–357
norms and standards for quality
    assurance of practice 537, 538

O

objective achievement 194–195
objective orientation 80–81
observation
    monitoring and assessing
        attitudinal change 468
    technique 408–409
open session discussion 425–426
operational strategy 124–125
operational writing *see also*
    communication skills; public
    speaking
        business plans 264–268
        fundraising reports 268–270
        minute taking 270–271
        reports and proposals 259–264
'Operation Dudula' 37
opportunity 250, *251*
organisational information 154
organisational resources 357
organisational skills 86
organisations as enablers 48–49
origins of community development
    Another Development 73

asset-based 73–74
capability approach 72–73
from co-option to community initiated action 66–69
early history 63–66
human scale development (HSD) approach 71–72
radicalised approach 69–74
(social) learning process approach (LPA) 70–71
outcomes of community development 83–86
ownership
　acceptance of 98
　ethical principles 97–98
　of own development 109
　of projects 128–129, 564–565, 571
　for sustainability 97

P

parliament 481
participation
　benefits 149–150
　case study 552–553
　collective 33
　community input 146
　constraints to 150–151
　democratic right 94, 141, 144, 150
　ensuring 424–425
　ethical principles 92–95
　goals 142–143
　importance 30, 95
　ladder of 93, 94
　and learning 102–103
　liberal viewpoint 4, 93
　meaning 338
　political 33
　with power 95
　real 66
　strong interpretation 117
　in training 422
　transformative agenda 69
　value 149–150
participatory communication 400
participatory decision making 143
participatory development 68
　definition 69
　schools of thought 69
participatory evaluation 399–400
participatory learning
　and action 337
　implementation 378
　planning process 378
participatory management *see also* group decision making
　concept 141–142
　control of projects 146
　cost recovery 147, 148
　goals of participation 142–143
　government policy 147, 148
　implementation 146
　monitoring and evaluation 146, 149
　of projects 144–147
　short- and long-term sustainability 147–148
participatory mapping approaches 333
participatory needs identification 79
participatory politics 510, 518
participatory rapid appraisal and planning (PRAP)
　advantages 338–339

application 344–345
direct observation 341
do's and don'ts 335–336
entitlement to withdraw 335
group interviews and discussions 342
learning through research and observation 85
principles and characteristics 337–339
problems and limitations 345–347
qualitative methodology 337
related to development approaches 336
remedies for limitations 346–347
seasonal calendars 343
secondary data review 340–341
semi-structured interviews 342
sketch mapping 342–343, 436
stories, portraits and case studies 343
techniques 339–343, *344*
time lines 343
transect and group walks 341, 436
triangulation 338, 411
uses 333
Venn diagrams 341, *341*, 436–437
participatory research
ethical principles 334–335
and evaluation 400–401
identification of community needs 335–337
participatory rural appraisal 337
participatory self-evaluation 198
partnership
action 105–106
ladder of participation 93, *94*
paternalism 131, 393, 574
people-centred approach to community development 70
perceptions of trainees 444
personal attacks at meetings 275
personal information, protection of 308, 309–310
personality clashes 214
placation, ladder of participation 93, *94*
planning *see also* implementation
adaptive incrementalist approach 376–377
blueprint 105
conclusion on approaches 377–379
logical framework analysis 379–382
management responsibility 146
and participatory learning 378
planning cycle method 382–387, *386*
process 378, 379–387
rationalistic, synoptic approach 373–375
recording of 388
role of community development practitioners/professionals (CDPs) 392–393
start of project 370–371
of training sessions 457–466
pluralistic ignorance 248–249
policies
actioning and driving for and in community development 484–487

adoption 485, 486
critical policy approval structure 486
definitions 477–479
effective policy making 479
guiding community development practice quality 487–489
impact of post-apartheid democratic constitution reform 480–481
implementation 485, 487, 516
influences on 479–480
and legislative frameworks 475, 493–497
monitoring and evaluation 485, 487
and participatory management 147, 148
policy-making cycle 484–485, 485
and programmes 181–182
purpose 480
review 487
sunset clauses 487
types and categories 476–477
policy formulation
global context 28–30
in policy-making cycle 485–486, 485
reasons for 475–476
Policy for Social Service Practitioners, 2017 488, 539–540
political challenges to community development practitioners/professionals (CDPs) 514–515
political environment 32–33
political participation 33
political power 95

political process 5
poor meeting environment 277
portraits 343
position of community development practitioners/professionals (CDPs) 128–129
positive energy 207
poverty accommodation 21
poverty eradication 68
power
    citizen 93, 94
    decision making 96, 97
    delegated 93, 94
    expectations and questions of at meetings 276
    political 95
practical principles
    adaptiveness 105–106
    compassion 104–105
    learning 102–104
    simplicity 106–108
preparation for public speaking 292–296
presentation
    in public speaking 292–296
    of reports 261
    training dialogue 421, *421*
    of training sessions 457–466
    use of PowerPoint 464–465
pre-set ideas and assumptions at meetings 277
prevention of conflict 218–220
priming 253
principles of community development *see* ethical principles; practical principles
private sector stakeholders 45

problem avoidance, at meetings 276
problem people
    case study 577–578
    at meetings 281–285
    at training workshops 451–457
problem solving 367–371
    decision making 370
    meetings 274
    planning 370–371
    problem analysis 368–369
    problem definition 368
    problem perception 368
    thinking of alternatives 369–370
procedure at meetings, confusion about 274
process
    assessment in training workshops 469
    definition 205
product assessment in training workshops 468–469
professional information 154
professionalisation of community development
    desirability of 532
    institutional formations 516–517
    lack of clear guidelines 533
    need to raise practice standards 532
    norms and standards for quality assurance of practice 537, 538
    purpose and process 534, 535
    recognition of prior learning (RPL) framework 533
    regulation of professional community development 539–549
    sector scoping and profiling 537
    in South Africa 532–538
    standardised and legislated qualification frameworks 536–537
projects
    definition 205
    memory 406
    outcomes 205
proposals, writing 259–264
provincial government 481–482
psychological barriers to communication 169–171
psychological environment 37
psychology of groups 193
public meetings
    unsuitable method of establishing contact with community 326, 328
    unsuitable method of needs identification 359
public-private partnership 143
public sector stakeholders 44–45
public speaking see also communication skills; operational writing
    effective verbal communication 289–292
    presentations 292–302
purposeful activities 194

Q

qualification frameworks 536–537

R

radical interpretative approach 399
radicalised approach 69–74

rapid rural appraisal *see* participatory rapid appraisal and planning (PRAP)
rationalistic approach to planning 373–375
reception, barriers 164–165
recognition of prior learning (RPL) framework 533
record-keeping in monitoring and evaluation 406–408
   electronic format 406, 408
   records of planning meetings 388, 406–407
redistributive justice 507
regulation of professional community development, Policy for Social Service Practitioners 539–540
relative poverty 7–8
release
   case study 564–565
   compassion and 104
   ethical principles 101–102
   vs relief 21, 79, 101
   transformation and 101–102
repetition at meetings 276
reports
   aim and purpose 259
   components 262–264
   for planning meetings 407
   preparation for 260–261
   presentation 261
   records of planning meetings 407
reprehensibility 200
resilience *see* community resilience to shocks
resources
   availability 305
   competition for 210–211
   definition 352
   external 353
   identification 352–353
   types 353–357
responsibility, diffusion of 248
role dependency 211
role incompatibility 225
role play
   advantages 432–433
   facilitation 435–436
   limitations to using 433–434
   rationale for using 432–434
   relevance for training 431–432
role players, communities 116–120
roles of community development practitioners/professionals (CDPs)
   adviser 133
   advocate 134
   enabler 135–136, 144–145
   facilitators 33, 137, 198, 472
   in first project meeting 364–365
   guide 132–133
   in policy 481, 489–490
   resource 124
   service developers 489

S

salience 253
seasonal calendars 343
seating arrangements at training workshops 458–462, *459, 460, 461, 462*
secondary data reviews 340–341
secretaries at meetings 285–286
sector scoping and profiling 537

self-determination theory (SDT) 242–246, 245
self-disclosure 170
self-esteem, lack of 37
self-evaluation 197
self-mobilisation 337
semi-structured interviews 342
sensitisation 102
service delivery
    government's imposition of 31
    protests 155
service developers role of community development practitioners/professionals (CDPs) 489
sewage, water and drainage 18
shelter 16–17
short- and long-term sustainability 147–148
simplicity
    closed agenda 364
    practical principle 106–108, 364, 554
sketch mapping 342–343
skills
    assessment 467
    meaning 443
    previously acquired by trainees 443
    training for empowerment 97
small groups 190–192
    disadvantages 426–428
smartphones in training sessions 465–466
social activism 47, 508–511
social capital 510, 511–513
social contract failure 215

social enterprise sector stakeholders 47–48
social entrepreneurship 47
social environment 33–34
social justice 27, 32, 34
    community development practitioners/professionals (CDPs) as advocates 505–507
    ethical accountability and responsibilities 506
social media 162–163
    influencers 163
    platforms 306–308
social norms 244
Social Service Practitioners Bill 541–542
social values 34, 222
socio-economic context of development 8–10
    deprivation trap 14–16, 15
    education 20
    food security 19
    health facilities 18–19
    shelter 16–17
    stagnant local economy 20–21
    unemployment 17–18
    water, drainage and sewage 18
source fields
    explanation of motivation 242–243
    of trainees 443
sources of information 133
South African Council for Social Service Professions (SACSSP) 539
    structure 540

specialist professionals 126, 499
stability 100, 105
stagnant local economy 20–21
stakeholders in community development 43–48
    capacity-building needs 135
    case study 571–574
    classification 43
    communities 116–120, 504
    community development practitioners/professionals (CDPs) 43–44
    co-ordinating 50–58
    definition 43
    identification 44–48
    organisations as enablers 48–49
start of a project
    alternatives, thinking of 369–370
    committee 366–367
    consensus on needs 358–359
    decision making 367, 370
    entrepreneurial resources 357
    first project meeting 363–366
    formulation of needs 359–360
    human resources 355–357
    manufactured resources 354–355
    natural resources 353–354
    need identification 358
    organisational resources 357
    planning 370–371
    problem solving 367–371
    resource identification 352–353
status quo bias 252–253, 558–560
stokvels 44, 352, 558–560
stories 343, 418, 420, 437
strengthening of groups 195–196
study and relaxation at training workshops 463–464
successful negotiation outcomes 231–233
support for groups and leadership 197, 198, 201
sustainability
    compassion and 104
    definition of sustainable development 99
    as ethical principle 98–100
    ownership for 97
    and participatory management 147
    short- and long-term 147–148
Sustainable Development Goals (SDGs) 27, 28, 30, 38
synoptic approach to planning 373–375
systems analysis 374–375

T

tastefulness in public speaking 292
teaching aids 431–437 *see also* visual aids
    triggering 431
teaching by discovery 417
technical barriers to communication 171–172
technical information 154
technical issues causing conflict 213
technical skills, vs indigenous skills 146–147
technology
    advantages and disadvantages 309

availability of resources 305
social media platforms 306
tension 208, 227
theory of autobiographical learning 418
therapy, ladder of participation 93, 94
threats to success of leaders and groups 198–200
time lines 343
timing and time management at training workshops 458
tokenism 66, 92, 93, 94, 96, 98
tolerance 220
top–down approach to community development 31, 70, 552, 553, 555–556
traditions 34, 35, 356–357
training dialogue *see also* teaching aids
    brainstorming 430–430
    buzz groups 428–429
    climate for learning 422–424
    concept 419–421
    group work 426–428
    interactive (workshop) techniques 425–431
    modes of training 419–421
    nominal group technique 429–430
    participation 422, 424–425
training of community development practitioners/professionals (CDPs) 126
training workshops
    adult learners 442–445
    assessment 466–469
    common features 442
    communication 448–457
    contents and relevance 470–471
    discipline 451–457
    end product 442
    establishment of teaching agenda 445–447
    feedback 469
    motivation and group dynamics 450–451
    picture of milieu 447–448
    planning and presentation 457–463
    problem people 451–457
    process 442
    raw material 442
    seating arrangements 458–462, *459, 460, 461, 462*
    setting 442
    study and relaxation 463–464
    timing and time management 458
    venue 458–462, 463
    visual aids 464–465
transformation 564–565
transect and group walks 341, 436
transparency of community development practitioners/professionals (CDPs) 515
triangulation 409, 411

U

ubuntu 11, 501
Ukraine-Russia war, impact 28, 29
unclear boundaries 219
unclear roles and responsibilities at meetings 275
understanding, barriers 165–166

unemployment 17–18
unintended consequences 217
unlearning of trainees 444
unresolved prior conflicts 209, 222

V

value of participation 149–150
Venn diagrams 341, 342, 436–437
venue and seating arrangements for training workshops 458–462, *459, 460, 461, 462, 463*
verbal communication *see also* communication; non-verbal communication
    effective 289–292
    and enthusiasm 298–299
video clips 436, 465

viral platforms 303
visual aids 295–296, 301, 464–466
    see also teaching aids
voice notes 465–466
VUCA world 518

W

water, drainage and sewage 18
wellbeing 185, 450, 490, 507, 542, 543
    of groups 192, 194–197, 367
WhatsApp 307, 466
wheel spinning at meetings 276
win/lose approach in meetings 276

X

xenophobic attacks 37

www.ingramcontent.com/pod-product-compliance
Lightning Source LLC
Chambersburg PA
CBHW061126010526
44116CB00023B/2988